THE LIFE OF A
SOUTH AFRICAN TRIBE

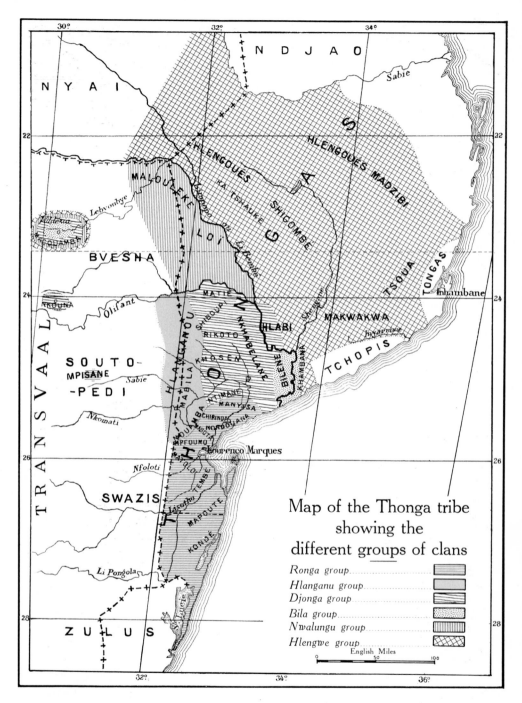

Map of the Thonga tribe
showing the
different groups of clans

Ronga group.............................
Hlanganu group.......................
Djonga group...........................
Bila group.................................
Nwalungu group......................
Hlengwe group........................

English Miles
0   50   100

This map (see page 16) shows the distribution of the Thonga population thirty years ago. Since then a considerable emigration into the Transvaal has taken place (p. 19), and the Low Country of the Leydenburg and Zoutpansberg districts, which is almost entirely white on the map, ought to show many coloured spots representing Thonga villages.

THONGA KITCHEN

ELDERLY THONGA MALE OF PORTUGUESE EAST AFRICA

NDAU *NYAMUSORO*, OR EXORCIST, OF THONGALAND

THONGA OR NDAU *NYANGA*, OR DOCTOR

OLD WARRIOR OF PORTUGUESE EAST AFRICA

THE MOTHER OF CHIEF *MADJAHANA*, SHIMBUTSU REGION

THONGA WOMAN OF PORTUGUESE EAST AFRICA, IN MOURNING

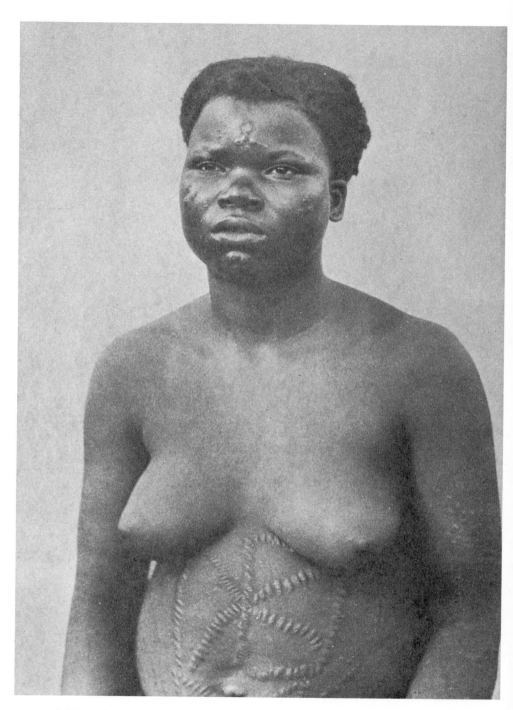

RECENTLY CICATRIZED THONGA GIRL OF PORTUGUESE EAST AFRICA

OLD THONGA FISHERMAN MAKING HIS NET

THONGA *NDJUNA* OF PORTUGUESE EAST AFRICA

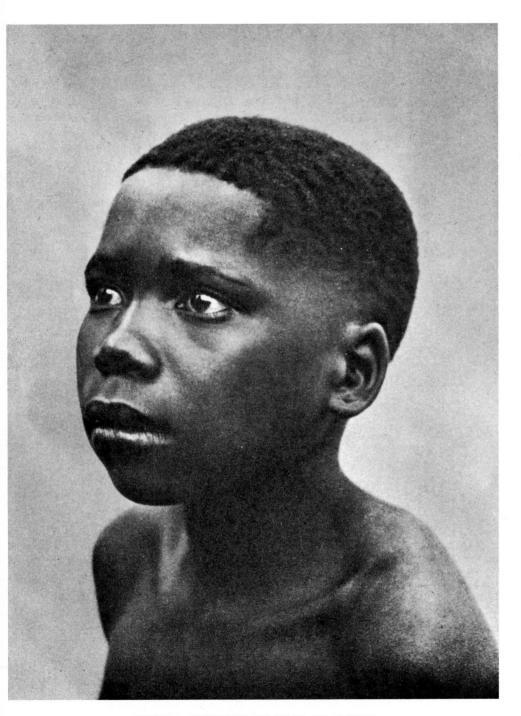

THONGA YOUTH FROM NEAR CHAI-CHAI

YOUNG THONGA MOTHER AND CHILD

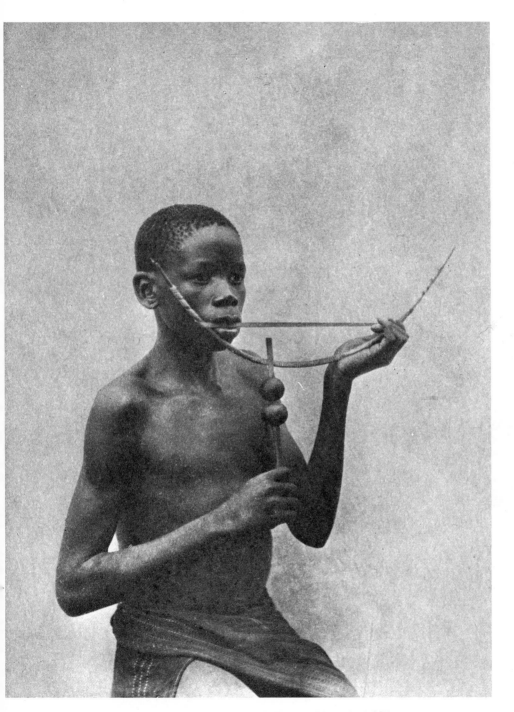

THONGA YOUTH PLAYING THE *SHIDZAMBI* BOW

THE LIFE OF
A
SOUTH
AFRICAN
TRIBE

BY HENRI A. JUNOD

I. SOCIAL LIFE

UNIVERSITY BOOKS INC. NEW HYDE PARK, NEW YORK

First Printing August 1962
Second Printing March 1966

FOREWORD

Missionary efforts in Africa are a subject for controversy. The most varied reactions have been evoked—unstinted admiration no less than derisive contempt; administrative approval no less than barely concealed suspicion. About the work of one man, however—Henri Alexandre Junod of the Swiss Romande Mission—there are scarcely two minds. Today in the 1960's, no less than at the close of the last century, his work has significance for African and for 'European' alike.

His reputation has spread widely, largely on account of his best-known work, *The Life of a South African Tribe*. It is nevertheless true that, particularly in the United States—to which he never travelled —few personal details about his life are generally known. It may, there-fore, not be inappropriate to set down a brief outline of his life.

Henri Junod was born on 17 May 1863 at Saint-Martin in the valley of Ruz in the Swiss canton of Neuchatel. Religion was pre-dominant in the life of the family into which he was born. His father, a Protestant clergyman, founded the Independent Protestant Church, and was responsible for the separation of Church and State in Switzer-land. It was hardly surprising, therefore, that the Junod children, in-cluding Henri, were steeped in religion. All the boys grew up to become ordained, and one of the two girls became a deaconess.

Henri studied at the College of Neuchatel at the Faculty of Theol-ogy of the Independent Protestant Church, later attending two semesters at Basle and at Berlin before obtaining his degree. In 1885 he was ordained, serving as a clergyman for two years in the parish of Môtiers-Boveresse. He was much interested in science and in natural history, and there appears to have been little doubt among those who knew him at that time that a brilliant career awaited him in this domain had he chosen to pursue it. After some internal struggles, of which we know little more than that they occurred, he came to the conclusion that it was the will of God that he devote his life to service in Africa. To prepare for this vocation he went to Scotland, accompanied by a close

III   25039

friend, Arthur Grandjean. In 1889 at the age of 26, the year of his departure for Africa, he married his first wife, Emilie Biolley of Couvet, like himself a Swiss. Most of the children of this marriage were destined to leave their bones in Africa.

Arriving in Mozambique, Henri Junod found the Swiss Romande Mission under the direction of the man who had established it in South East Africa—Paul Berthoud, a relative of his wife. The times were still troubled. The Zulu military power in the region had been broken barely ten years earlier, and the resulting disorders had only terminated with the British occupation of Zululand in 1887. The Swiss missionaries travelled into the interior in wagons drawn by oxen. Open warfare returned to the country with the Ronga-Portuguese war of 1894-95, at which time the mission itself, at Rikatla, was burned. The Swiss missionaries also found themselves the target of hostility from the local peoples. It was by establishing good relations with the Ba-Ronga people under these uncertain conditions that all of Junod's later work was made possible.

Junod tells us how a "chance" remark made in 1895 by Lord Bryce transferred the main focus of his attention from entomology to ethnography. (Junod's incomparable collections of South East African butterflies are preserved to this day in the Museum at Neuchatel, as well as in other Swiss and South African Museums; and a *Papillo Junodi*, together with other species bearing his name, are known to zoology). The years of preparation were over, and he was now to enter consciously upon that part of his life's work that was to establish his reputation. In 1896 his first book, a Ronga grammar and conversation manual, with vocabularies in Ronga, Portuguese, French, and English, together with an ethnographic introduction, was published under the auspices of the Portuguese Government. In 1897 he published his *Chants et Contes des Ba-Ronga*, followed by other works on language and ethnography. In 1896 he returned to Switzerland for three years, after which he undertook the direction of a school for evangelists at Shiluvane in the Transvaal. The change was not so abrupt as might be imagined, for in those far-off days administrative boundaries had not yet assumed their later significance, and—above all —he was still working among the Bathonga peoples. It was while he was at Shiluvane, however, that his first wife died, in 1901, "a victim of the climate." The loss left him desolate. Upon his return to Switzerland, in 1903-04, he re-married: Mlle. Hélène Kern of Zurich, a German-speaking Swiss whose charm is still remembered, and whose antecedents lay in Alsace-Lorraine. He returned with her to Shiluvane, but in 1907 they moved back to his original mission station at Rikatla in Mozambique. The reason for the change was that the Mission schools in the Transvaal were subsidised by the local educational authorities, and Junod feared that this arrangement would restrict the amount of time that he would be permitted to spend upon religious instruction. From 1909 to 1913 he was in Switzerland once more, serving as a pastor first at the parish of Saint-Blaise, and then at Rochefort. Nor was his pen idle. In 1909, in collaboration with Chatelain, he published a Xangane dictionary and grammar; in 1910 he published a missionary novel, *Zidji* (also translated into German) ; and in 1912 there appeared the first edition of his great work, *The Life of a South African Tribe*. While Junod was on his fourth and last visit to Africa his second wife died—at Rikatla, in March 1917. He returned to Switzerland in 1921, where he lived in Geneva. He completed the revision of the second and enlarged edition of his *Life of a South African Tribe* in 1926, and it was published the following year. He died on April 22, 1934 at the age of three-score years and ten, his span of life well spent. His ashes were sent to Africa.

Those who remember Henri Junod well speak of a handsome and distinguished-looking man with a large black beard which, in some of his later years, stood out in contrast to his snow white hair. Later still, his beard too turned white, lending him a saintly appearance. While his manner was somewhat Calvinistic—asking much of himself he also, no doubt, asked much of others—this trait was mixed with an inner kindliness of spirit. His courage was proverbial. There exists in the American branch of his family the memory of a story he told to the children in the days before 1914 of an occasion when he entered a certain thicket, after receiving a warning from friendly Africans that he must follow their instructions to the last detail, since any deviation would mean his death. It remains unclear, however, whether this episode occurred in the course of his ethnological investigations, or whether he was hunting lepidoptera in enemy-occupied territory during either the Ronga-Portuguese War or the Sikororo War. The verdict of all who knew him is, however, clear: he was a brave man, and "took many many chances."

FOREWORD

His attachment to the Bathonga peoples was deep and sincere, and manifested itself in a great number of ways. In Switzerland he sought to bring back a memory of African surroundings, going so far as to build a replica of an African hut in the grounds of his first wife's estate in Couvet, as well as to arrange for a number of African pastors to visit Switzerland, where they were frequent visitors at the Junod home. Henri Junod was held in high honour in his country, where he was made an honorary doctor of the University of Lausanne, and was also elected President of the International Bureau for the Defense of Native Interests—a name that already sounds curiously anachronistic to our ears, and that belonged to a Geneva organization that concerned itself with questions such as alcoholism, and the injustice of expropriation. It is also not without significance today that, at the League of Nations, Junod (to quote a contemporary commentator) "enjoyed a merited confidence among those men who were concerned with mandates and protectorates." Of his own conception of the motivation that led him to Africa there can be no doubt. In addition to the determination of his early years that his duty lay in the missionary service, he repeatedly expressed the view that the white man had brought so much evil to Africa—and it is understood that he had the evils of alcoholism and the previously-unknown venereal disease particularly in mind—that it was mandatory for other white men to bring to Africa also some things that were good.

*   *   *   *

What, then, is the place of Junod's study of the Bathonga in relation to African anthropoligical literature as a whole?

Now that Africa is entering into the post-independence phase (even if the tide of independence has not yet reached the Bathonga peoples themselves, subjected, as they have been, to white hegemony since the 1860's), it is becoming increasingly difficult to disentangle the three different skeins that, woven together, make up the fabric of African cultural life today, (1) those aspects that Africa has taken from the West; (2) those aspects that are traditionally African; and (3) those aspects that represent African innovations or adaptations. In this respect the contribution of Junod is of particular value for, arriving upon the scene at a relatively early stage, he was able to isolate and to define precisely those aspects that were traditional. He was undoubtedly aware that his situation was unique, and that the context in which he worked was soon to pass away. In the years that were to follow not only would some of the African customs die or fade away, but also the African peoples themselves would grow more reticent. Junod's experience in returning to Europe on a Union Castle boat in 1909, when each of three well-known Zulus "who were, I think, going to England for political reasons," proved unable or unwilling to discuss Zulu ideas of witchcraft with him, was a presage of the decades to come. This undoubtedly spurred him to greater efforts to set down the fullest possible description of one group of African peoples before it was too late.

If Junod was fortunate in his period we, for our part, have been fortunate in our author. Had he, like his brothers, been virtually entirely concentrated upon his religious vocation in the stricter sense, we—and African literature—would have been deprived of what E. W. Smith, the anthropologist, has described in the journal *Africa* as "the finest monograph written on any African tribe." Junod's earlier yearning for natural science, however, combined with his sense of vocation, provided a combination that was to produce a remarkable result. The original lustre of the Edinburgh Conference of 1910 (which "proclaimed the necessity for Missionaries of a sympathetic study of Native beliefs and social customs"—a revolutionary concept to many at that time) may have dimmed, but the significance of such studies has not, which is why Henri Junod today retains his importance for us.

Junod was not temperamentally a member of that category of eccentric and restless persons, so familiar to African history, who make their mark as innovators, striking out, if need be, in the face of the whole world to establish new ways or new concepts. That he was a personality of unusual dimensions there can be no question. One might say that he had within him the three metamorphoses of the spirit mentioned by Nietzsche—the camel spirit, which bears the heaviest burdens; the lion spirit that says "I will"; and the Child spirit that is innocence and a new beginning. Unlike Lugard, he did not come to Africa to cure a broken heart. Unlike Joseph Booth—another remarkable contemporary, working as a missionary in nearby Nyasaland—he did not come to Africa as a result of an Australian atheist's challenge: "Are there no savages in Central Africa, and if so why do you not go to them instead of casting these doubtful pearls where no one wants them." Rather Junod went for the same reason that other members of his family left their native land—because they felt a call and then were sent by the Mission. At the place to which he was sent he performed the work that he was sent to do as he saw best how to do it. Had he found himself in the same geographical field of endeavor as another famous pioneer Swiss missionary, the Rev. J. G. Christaller of the Basel Mission, who first set down the Twi and Ga languages of the Gold Coast in writing (publishing his first Twi dictionary in 1874), he would doubtless have done as well.

Junod arrived in Africa some three years after the famous Berlin Conference of 1885-86, which had provided, among other things, that religious toleration should be practised in the Portuguese-administered territories—a fact which explains the entry of a Swiss Protestant missionary into Portuguese Catholic territory. He arrived, in other words, at a watershed in African history, when the age of exploration, symbolised by Livingstone and Stanley, was over, and when the age of imperial settlement and conquest, represented by Rhodes and Johnston, was to begin. Indeed, by a historic quirk of fate, Sir Harry Johnston (three years senior to Junod, but with ten years more African experience) landed at Lourenço Marques to take up his post as British Consul there in the same year—1889—that Junod arrived to begin his work for the Swiss Romande Mission. Like Junod, Johnston included zoology, botany, and anthropology among his interests, and—in addition—was known, despite his cynical disposition and freethinking turn of mind, to favor the company of missionaries. One cannot help wondering whether, amidst the press of differing interests that held them both in those first dramatic years, they ever managed to meet.

The development of anthropological literature about Africa would seem to have begun, in a systematic fashion, with the publication of Sir James Frazer's *The Golden Bough* in 1890. Before that date a great amount of assorted data, much of which defied classification, had been accumulated by that type of explorer of which Henry Barth and Joseph Thomson are representative examples. But the major emphasis had been on geography, with astronomy, geology, botany, languages, and ethnology being treated in a more desultory fashion. The publication of *The Golden Bough*, of which the seminal influence is still at

work, provided a theoretical framework within which further ethnographic researches could be pursued. As we have mentioned we
have Junod's word for it that the "revelation" that set him to observe
the characteristics of the Bathonga with all the assiduity that he had
previously reserved for zoology came to him as a result of Lord Bryce's
"chance remark" in 1895. Although we know only that the conversation took place, it would have been surprising if Bryce—then the
British Ambassador to Washington—had been unacquainted with
Frazer's work, (particularly in view of his allusion to "our Celtic
forefathers"), or if the name of Frazer had not been mentioned. We
do know that by 1909 Junod was conducting an investigation on the
basis of questions provided him by Frazer, and that the results of this
investigation were incorporated into the first edition of his work. We
may, therefore, regard him as one of the first-generation settlers on
Frazer's newly-discovered continent. Upon landing Junod did not seek
to become a frontiersman wild but rather, like a good Swiss, marked
out a modest area of land, and dug and tilled the soil with care. He
did not, like his great contemporary, Frobenius, adventure forth, report
the marvelous, and draw poetic conclusions. Frobenius has a sweep and
style which appeal to the imagination. Junod's strength lies in the con-
centration of effort which led him scientifically to observe a people,
whom he held in the greatest affection, from every conceivable aspect,
and in the greatest detail possible. Frobenius dealt in tribes, nations,
and continents. Junod was the student of the Bathonga.

It is, incidentally, of interest that the Bathonga are by no means as
unified as certain other African tribes—one has but to think of the
Baganda or the Ashanti—and in this respect Lord Hailey's description of them as constituting a "cluster" would seem particularly apposite.
Junod was certainly conscious of this, as his statements show. The point
has, however, been taken that his concept of the clan as the funda-
mental unit of the Bathonga remains ambiguous. His statement that the
Bathonga nation "is but an enlarged family" has been criticised on the
grounds that rather than representing a patrilineal grouping, the tribe
represented a linguistic and cultural unit, not necessarily linked by ties
of blood.

In this respect it would have been interesting to have had Junod's comment on Professor Potekhin's thesis*, according to which the Bathonga would be neither on the one hand a tribe (such as the Ba-Ronga, the Tembe, or Khose), nor yet a nation (which requires "a common territory, a common language, a common culture, a common economy"), but what he calls a "narodnost," that is to say a group composed of persons of different tribal origins who, without being necessarily akin by direct family ties, live together and have evolved social classes. Potekhin cites the Zulu and Ashanti systems as examples of the "narodnost," and as the Zulu Manukosi amalgamated the Thonga clans, this would presumably have included the Bathonga also. In the process of social evolution, therefore, the "narodnost" is seen as the half-way house between the tribe and the nation.

But what of the Bathonga today? No observer of Junod's stature has emerged to tell us the sequel to his book, and—under contemporary political circumstances— it is, for the moment, virtually precluded that any qualified Bathonga commentator would be permitted to take up the torch that awaits its runner. Some general impressions may, nevertheless, be gleaned. The Bathonga people have become increasingly involved, economically, with the working of the South African and to a lesser extent the Rhodesian mines. On the basis of 1950 census figures it has been conservatively estimated that about 40 per cent of the Bathonga males work in the Union of South Africa alone. Expressed in other terms it is estimated that the average Bathonga males spends only six months of the year at home, the other six months being spent working abroad. (These estimates, incidentally, do not include those Bathonga males who have left the countryside to live in Lourenço Marques). In the mines the Bathonga workers have established a reputation for spending longer periods underground than other groups, and also for being less subject to seasonal absences in order to return home. As most of the Bathonga live in Mozambique, it will be clear that the absence of a substantial proportion of the Bathonga males abroad will have added to labor problems already experienced by the Portuguese administration. The predicament of the Portuguese is, however, one from which they can hardly extricate themselves. After the pacification of the

---

* I. Potekhin: De quelques questions methodologiques pour l'etude de la formation des nations en Afrique au Sud du Sahara: *Presence Africaine:* Dec. 1957-Jan. 1958.

FOREWORD

Bathongas in 1895, the Transvaal mining interests specified that the port of Lourenço Marques—the shortest route for shipping the gold of the Rand overseas—would only be permitted to develop in return for the right for South African interests to recruit contract labor in Portuguese territory. The Bathonga, in short, have provided a labor pool for the South African mines. Altogether over 50 per cent of the African males in Mozambique are now estimated to be wage-earners— a clear indication of the extent to which life has changed since Junod's day.

It is also reported that, under the impact of modern conditions, traditional customs have been much modified. One of the results of the impingement of the outside world upon the Bathonga peoples has, however, been a great increase in the number of accusations of witch-craft: a type of reaction which has also been observed elsewhere. Meanwhile other forces are also at work upon the context in which they live: the United Nations has become directly concerned with conditions in Mozambique, and African political parties from the territory have established themselves, albeit as yet in exile.

*   *   *   *

When the first edition of this work appeared in 1912, Africa and the world were, to all appearances, very different from what they are today. The world was still in the first flush of that liberalism and internationalism that preceded the first world war. The white man's task in Africa apeared still, despite the revelations from Leopold's Congo, as a sacred mission, and was accepted as such by African opinion—an opinion that was formed not only by the persuasive power of Lugard's Maxim guns or their equivalent, but also by contact with such men as Junod, whose motives were so patently of the best, and who showed such patient readiness to understand and to appreciate African ways. Yet, by the time that the first world war had delivered the first shock to white hegemony, that quasi-religious conviction that the little African boy whispered to himself as he watched Junod play the organ—"White people are only overcome by death"—was already beginning to fade. The second world war accelerated the process immeasurably, and in so doing revolutionized relations between black and white. By the late 1950's African states were in being and the tide of self-rule was spreading south. The vortex of change has not yet reached Delagoa Bay but it is clear that here too the change is coming.

Not only have relations between black and white been altered but so have African aspirations. The word "detribalised," associated with the creation of a South African proletariat, was not in vogue in Junod's day, although it may perhaps have already been in existence. It would, doubtless, be going too far to assert that the Thonga have become detribalised—traditions are, after all, sacred to us all, and are not lightly to be abandoned. However, a latter-day Junod might well encounter among the Bathonga the reaction that was met with by Anthony Sampson, formerly editor of the South African magazine *Drum*. When he enquired as to why the circulation of that magazine was declining he was told with uncompromising bluntness that the peoples of South Africa wanted to hear no more about lobola and the ancient ways: that was already well known. They would rather hear about contemporary life and its distractions and pleasures—cars, sports, entertainment; in a word, about modern life.

And yet, as Africans take command of their own destinies once more, as new ways are superimposed upon the old, some of the older values become blurred as the memory of former customs grows dimmer. One of the consequences of this is that written records of these customs become the more highly prized. It is reported, for example, that since the independence of Ghana the demand for the writings of M. J. Field, the English anthropologist, who wrote studies on the Ga peoples between the two world wars, has increased as the younger generation, conscious of the changes, seek to read of the traditional ways as they were set down a quarter of a century ago. The same writer in her recent *Search for Security* has also recorded the social situation which has supervened following the decline of tribal ways.

One may therefore hazard the guess that in the literature of South East Africa Junod may come to hold a place comparable to that held by, for example, R. S. Rattray in West Africa. Both African and European will surely appreciate his clarity, uncomplicated by the methodological jargon which is the bane of recent anthropolical literature. Junod himself, in writing, was clearly aware of the value that his work would have for comparative ethnology at a later date. And yet it is only now that a beginning is being made in this respect. It is only comparatively recently that Professor Joseph Greenberg of Columbia University posited the existence of a "Niger-Congo family," in place of the "long continued tradition of assigning a separate status to the Bantu." If this thesis should be upheld, the apparent importance of the so-called "Bantu Line"—the 'frontier' dividing Black Africa into two, which runs roughly between Eastern Nigeria and the Cameroons—would recede. At least linguistically we are now told that the languages of Black Africa apear to be related. A *prima facie* case to' demonstrate that many customs are also shared might also be established by comparing (for example) those pages of Junod which deal with circumcision rites among the Bathonga with pages in West African literature which deal with the same subject. Junod's description of the "sungi" or lodge bears the most striking resemblance, in its essentials, to K. L. Little's description of the Poro "bush schools" among the Mende of Sierra Leone, who live well over 4,000 miles away. Similar descriptions may also be found in the pages of the Guinean writer Camara Laye, and others.

Yet it is, perhaps, in his description of psychic life that Junod has made his greatest contribution. Here he was truly a pioneer observer, treading a literary path that was later to be travelled by such disparate personalities as Messrs. R. S. Rattray, G. Parrinder, J. B. Danquah, and le Pere Tempels. It is here that Junod has shown his greatest genius. The man of science and the man of imagination seem to have merged into one inspired seeker after truth, while the missionary of Calvinistic antecedents falls silent, suspending judgement until the fascinating process of learning shall have been completed.

We live in a political age. No doubt before long the writings of Junod, like the writings of all others who have written on Southern Africa, will be put to the test by the Africans themselves. One feels little doubt as to the outcome. Writing within the context of his times Junod showed that he already discerned the gathering storm clouds, and indicated the position that he would follow as the situation developed further. Both segregation and the proposed deportation from Southern Africa of the black man he rejected as "absolutely impracticable." From his final pages we sense that he would have been ready to say much more on the subject had the matter progressed any further at that time.

Despite contemporary strictures against tribalism as a reactionary force which lends itself to foreign intrigues, we know what Junod meant in his heart when he ended his book with the words: "May God preserve the life of the South African Tribe!" The words represented a prayer for the preservation of the soul of the people he loved. And how final, how decisive, how self-committing is that other exclamation, whose echo remains with us yet: "Africa would no longer be Africa if there were no more Africans."

KEITH IRVINE

PUBLISHER'S NOTE

Not the least remarkable aspect of this book is that its author, whose mother tongue was French, wrote it in English. As E. W. Smith, the anthropologist, noted in his review of the second revised edition, in *Africa*, Vol. 1, (1927), Junod's English had considerably improved by the time he prepared the later edition. The translation into French was not done by Junod and appeared after his death; it was published by Payot, Paris, in 1936, under the title *Mouers et Coutumes des Bantous*, and with the original title as a sub-title. The present edition is a complete reproduction of the second, revised English edition of 1927. Thanks are due to Barnard College and the Columbia University Libraries for providing a rare copy for reproduction purposes.

We have retained in the table of contents and in the text the references of the author to the Latin notes for medical men and scientists, i.e., those observations of sexual life which the author could not bring himself to set down in English. However, the Latin notes themselves have been translated into English and will be found in place of the Latin on pages 516 ff.

We have been fortunate to be able to add to Henri Junod's final version of his book the one aspect it really lacked. His version does contain some 110 illustrations but they are indifferent photography. We have now been able to add thirteen full page photographs taken by A. M. Duggan-Cronin (published in his five-volume work of photography, *The Bantu Tribes of South Africa*, edited by Junod's son, Henri Phillipe, in 1935). We have limited our selection to photographs of Bathonga still living in Portuguese East Africa. It was perhaps the last possible moment in which to photograph them in their traditional ways. Already a great many of them had gone to work in the mines of the Union of South Africa and World War II a few years later speeded up this process immeasurably.

The table of contents will be found at the back of each volume.

INTRODUCTION

In the year 1895, I had the great pleasure of receiving a visit from Lord Bryce in Lourenço Marques where I was staying at the head of the Swiss Romande Mission. This distinguished statesman, in the course of his travels through South Africa, had devoted considerable attention to the Native tribes throughout the country, endeavouring to understand them and to foresee their future. He had soon noticed however how scant is our knowledge about them, and was trying to stimulate men on the spot to undertake a scientific study of their primitive life. In the course of our conversation, I was struck by the following remark which he made to me: "How thankful should we be, we men of the XIXth century, if a Roman had taken the trouble fully to investigate the habits of our Celtic forefathers ! This work has not been done, and we shall always remain ignorant of things which would have interested us so much !"

This observation was quite a revelation to me. It was possible then, that these Natives, for whose sake we went to Africa, would themselves benefit by such a study, and that, in the course of time, they would be grateful to know what they had been, when they were still leading their savage life... This argument, in addition to so many others, had never occurred to me. Up to that date I had already collected some Ronga tales and studied some curious customs of the tribe. But the science which I was pursuing as a favourite pastime was Entomology. Delagoa Bay is a splendid place for beetles and butterflies. I had come across a wonderful forest near Morakwen where I had been fortunate enough to discover a new kind of Papilio ! Since that time Ethnography has more or less supplanted Entomology. I started on the systematic and thorough investigation which Lord Bryce recommended to me, and I very soon found out that, after all, Man is infinitely more interesting than the insect ! The material which I gathered amongst

the Ba-Ronga of Delagoa Bay was first published in my French book
Les Ba-Ronga with the kind help of the Geographical Society of
Neuchâtel in 1898.   Since then I have pursued my studies amongst the
Northern Clans of the Thongas of the Transvaal and, if I am able to
undertake this publication, in which I hope to give a more complete
description of the life of a South African tribe, I feel that I owe to my
distinguished visitor the generating idea, the decisive impulse.

*

*   *

This was the right moment to undertake this enquiry, as the following
sad experience will plainly show.   Coming home in 1909, I met, on
board the splendid U. C. Steamer on which we were travelling, three
well known Native gentlemen who were, I think, going to England for
political reasons.   I had great pleasure in speaking with them.   One
of them was the editor of a Native paper ; another was a Christian
chief, the third was at the head of a Training Institution which he
had founded himself.   One day I made up my mind to gather some
ethnographical facts from them.   They were Zulus, and I wanted to
know for purposes of comparison what were the precise ideas of their
tribe about witchcraft.   Never in my scientific career did I meet with a
more complete failure !   The editor had been born in a Wesleyan
family, and never lived amongst heathen.   The chief knew much more
on the subject but, for some obscure reason, was not inclined to
disclose his knowledge.   The Principal of the Institution was a very
clever man ; he first declared that witchcraft was met with amongst
white people just the same as amongst South African Natives, and that it
was only a form of mesmerism ; and, as he was always anxious to get
more knowledge himself, he proceeded to question me about mesmerism ; the whole interview ended therefore in a lesson which I was
obliged to give him on that mysterious subject, and I did not learn
anything new from my three friends...   I left them in quite a melancholy mood, thinking how different it was with my Thonga informants,
Mboza, Tobane and even Elias !
In fact, the circumstances in which I found myself amongst the
Thongas, were the most favourable imaginable for such an investigation.   The great bulk of the tribe is still absolutely savage.   We
have mastered its language and can understand all they tell us.   On
the other hand we have founded a Church amongst them and have

2

intimate relations with some of them. The adults in our congregations
have been heathen themselves and have practised the rites on which
I questioned them. They can describe them better than raw heathens,
as they now stand at a certain distance from their old life and can judge
of it more independently. They possess what our French historians
call *le recul nécessaire*. Enjoying their full confidence, having learned
by long practice how to put questions in order to get impartial answers,
I think that their testimony can be considered as scientifically reliable.
Of course errors are always possible. But science proceeds by successive approximations. I dare say the present monograph of the
Thonga tribe, compared with my book *Les Ba-Ronga*, will be a nearer
approach to the truth, and it is quite possible that later on a more
perfect account will be given by somebody who has had more time
to spare and more insight than myself into this delicate work.

*

*   *

When a historian publishes a monograph, he first gives a list of
his sources of information. He vindicates the truth of his results by
showing that they are based on trustworthy documents. My documents are not books. They are living witnesses, and I beg to introduce
some of them to my readers, as they have been my faithful collaborators
and I owe to them most of my knowledge.

The first man whom I questioned systematically was a Ronga of
Nondwane (North of Lourenço Marques) named *Spoon*. He had
been my butterfly catcher and I had often admired his skill and his
powers of observation. He became my instructor in the art of bone
throwing. He had been more or less a diviner, using his dice when
going to hunt ; but after the war of the Natives against the Portuguese
(1894-1895) he lost confidence in his divinatory bones as well as in
his gods, and became a Christian. He always had a great deal of
imagination. I was often obliged to verify his explanations. Spoon
certainly had the mythological sense more developed than any of my
other informants ; however he was through and through a Bantu and
whatever he said was always picturesque and striking. He died in 1924.

After him, I undertook to gather all the knowledge possessed by
Tobane. Tobane was a splendid man when I knew him in Lourenço
Marques, in the years 1895 and 1896. Tall, of a remarkably light
complexion, his eyes very clear and bright, he was a man of mark in the

3

Mpfumo clan. From his youth he had been in relation with the leading families of the tribe, being himself the son of Magugu, the Native general who brought to an end the long war of succession of the Shangaan in 1856-1862. He had been mixed up in all the political affairs of the country for a long time and had a profound knowledge of the customs of the court and of the tribunal amongst his people. He was a patriot, and when he became a Christian he did his best to

Spoon
as bone-thrower in 1894.

bring his brethren to his new faith. When he understood what I wanted, he at once did his best to satisfy me and sometimes even anticipated my questions : *"Tjika, ndi ku byela...* Keep quiet, I am going to tell you", he would say eagerly ! I owe him most of what I know about the tribal system of the Rongas.

Having then been called by the development of the Mission to leave Lourenço Marques to start a training school amongst the Thongas of the Transvaal, I met in Shiluvane near Leydsdorp with a man who was, as regards the Northern clans of the tribe, an authority as excellent as Tobane for the Southern Ronga clans. His name was *Mankhelu.* He was an elder son of Shiluvane, the late chief of the Nkuna clan, and had been for many years the prince-regent of the Ba-Nkuna, till the actual chief Muhlaba came of age. Mankhelu was the General of the army, the great doctor of the royal kraal, one of the main councillors, an entirely convinced bone-thrower, a priest in his family, a Bantu so deeply steeped in the obscure conceptions of the Bantu

4

Tobane

mind that he never could get rid of them and remained a heathen till his death in 1908. Very kind hearted, very devoted to the missionaries, he was a true friend to me and willingly disclosed to me the secrets of his medical and divinatory science. I owe to him an account of his bone-throwing system, which was much more elaborate

Phot. H.- A. Junod.

Mankhelu
standing in his village by the magic forked pole.

than the one Spoon had given me in Rikatla, though the two agree on the main points. Mankhelu had many dealings with the Suto or Pedi clans of the N. E. Transvaal. He was a celebrated rainmaker and had the greater credit amongst them as he was a foreigner. I have been on my guard carefully to differentiate what is of Sutho origin and what is purely Thonga in the information he gave me.

5

In my congregation at the station of Shiluvane was an old convert baptised, odd to relate, by the name of a professor of divinity of Lausanne, *Viguet*. He was a clever man, but not always a very good Christian, I must confess. He possessed a splendid memory. Having been headman in a village of Thonga refugees in the Spelonken, he gave me valuable information regarding the mysteries of family life as well as about the initiation ceremonies. His home was Tsungu on the Limpopo but he had moved to the Transvaal during the succession war of 1862. He was certainly a first-rate informant, possessing a clear head, always using the technical expressions and illustrating his points with great skill. He and Mankhelu have taught me most of what I know about the Northern clans. I learned however many other facts from *Mawewe*, the poet-laureate of the Nkuna court and from *Simeon Gana*, one of my pupils who belonged to an old and important family, and also from others.

In 1907 I came back to the coast to start in Rikatla (18 miles North of ·Lourenço Marques) a Training Institution for our work in Portuguese Territory. There I again found my old friend Spoon, who had been baptised Elias and was one of the elders of the little Church ; he had grown old, but was still of the same merry character and disposed to communicate anything he knew. Another man was his co-elder there, a Ronga of the Mazwaya family called *Mboza*. I found him to be a very intelligent man, quite an authority on the rites of the clan. He had been "possessed" and had gone through all the initiation ceremonies of the Ngoni possession, having become an exorciser himself. So he was able to give me new information on this mysterious subject. I undertook a systematic investigation with these two men in 1909, taking as a guide the set of questions prepared by Prof. J. Frazer for people collecting ethnographical material, and giving special attention to the question of the taboo. During this study, which took me many months, I was more than ever impressed with the immense complexity of the life of a South African tribe !

In quoting my sources of information I must also mention the pupils of my school. Every Tuesday night we had a meeting in which one of them had to relate a story, to describe a custom, to tell a Native tale... His companions then added what they knew, and as some of them were grown up men, these debates were often very instructive.

I was able to collect in all more than one hundred tales ; most of them have been published in my *Chants et Contes des Ba-Ronga* and

in the book on *Les Ba-Ronga*. I have
still a good many in manuscript, some
of which will be found in the second
volume of the present work.

*

* *

Phot. A. Borel

Spoon-Elias

as Church elder in 1907.

My aim in collecting all this
material has been twofold ; scientific and practical.

First of all scientific. The life
of a South African tribe is a collection of biological phenomena which
must be described objectively and
which are of great interest, representing, as they do, a certain stage
of human development. These
biological phenomena are sometimes at first of a repulsive character. The sexual life of the Bantus
especially shocks our moral feelings.
I did not think however that I
could entirely leave out this subject in a scientific book, and the
more I studied it, the more I saw that these strange rites have a much
deeper meaning than at first appears, and that we could not pretend
to know Natives if we remained ignorant of these facts. But while
trying to give a full account, I am convinced, on the other hand, that,
to be truly scientific, such a description must be limited to one well
defined tribe. I go even further : all the data must be localised ; in
the tribe itself there are different clans ; customs vary from one to
another. It is of the greatest importance that all the facts be classed
geographically. A similar work can be done later for other tribes, and
it is only when a sufficient number of trustworthy monographs have
been written that a comparative study on Bantu ethnography can be
undertaken. The "Essential Kafir" of Dudley Kidd is very interesting and full of useful remarks, but the essential Kafir will not be
known till a scientific and thorough study of all the tribes has been
completed. ˙My aim has been to submit the Thonga tribe to such a
study and I shall be most gratified if it leads other observers to undertake the same investigation with regard to other African tribes.

The Life of a South African Tribe

Though I do not pretend to prejudge anything about any other South African tribe, it will soon be seen that many of the customs here described are spread more or less over the whole of the Sub-Continent, and that what I write about the Thongas applies more or less to the Suthos, the Zulus, even to the Nyandjas of Lake Nyassa and to tribes in Central Africa. I think therefore that the conclusions reached by this study may be of use not only to those interested in the Thonga tribe itself but to all Africanists or Bantuists.

*

* *

There are two classes of men to whom I should like to bring some practical help in their work : the Native Commissioners and the Missionaries.

It is absolutely necessary that Native Commissioners should have a better knowledge of the tribe which they administer in the name of civilised Governments. They are apt to make the most dangerous mistakes from mere ignorance of the true nature of rites or superstitions which they do not understand. I have heard of colonial authorities receiving witchcraft accusations, believing that the pretended wizards were real murderers and anthropophagists and condemning them as such ! To govern savages, you must study them thoroughly in order both to recognise the wrong ideas against which you have to contend and to avoid hurting their feelings unnecessarily. This is imperative if you wish to win their confidence and maintain a friendly understanding between them and the alien European Government. How many Native wars might have been avoided if the Native Commissioner had had a better knowledge of Bantu ethnography, and, on the other hand, how much good has been done by those who have taken the trouble to study the Natives with sympathy in order to be just to them !

And this is equally true of Missionaries.

Missionary work is much better understood now than it was formerly. The Edinburgh Conference of 1910 proclaimed the necessity for Missionaries of a sympathetic study of Native beliefs and social customs. One of the eight Commissions which prepared that wonderful Congress devoted considerable time to this subject, and issued a remarkable report, whose conclusions are worth reading. It urges that in each field a thorough investigation be undertaken, in

8

order that the message of the Gospel may be presented in such a way as will appeal to those aspirations after the truth which reveal themselves in the religion and social rites of the Natives. How superior is this conception to that of former times, when heathenism was looked on as a creation of the devil through and through ! We see better now that, amidst darkness and sin, the heathen mind is often seeking light and righteousness, and that these rays of truth, these presentiments of a higher life, must be infinitely respected and utilised in the preaching of the Gospel of Jesus Christ. For instance, see how seriously savages keep their taboo !... This taboo—as we shall see— is inspired by strange, unscientific physiological ideas regarding defilement and contagion, which will disappear when scientific knowledge has spread amongst them. But let these ideas be somewhat amended, let the Natives understand that what is taboo is not physical uncleanness but moral evil, and their strong aversion to the act tabooed may become a powerful moral impulse for good.

*

* *

Here is the plan which I mean to adopt. After having briefly explained in a preliminary chapter what the Thonga tribe is, I shall take an individual and follow him in his career from birth to death ; the story of the evolution of a man and of a woman will constitute the first part of the book.

Then I shall pass on to the first social organism formed by these individuals, and study the life of the family and of the village, which is but an enlarged family.

The villages make up the clan and the tribe. The national life will constitute my third part, where I shall deal especially with the Chief, the Court and the Army.

Agricultural and industrial life and literary and artistic life will then be studied (as collective manifestations of the life of the tribe) and last but not least, I shall devote a considerable amount of time to the religious life and superstitions, trying to penetrate into the soul of the tribe, and to understand the manifold manifestations of its psychic life, which have always had a special interest for me.

It would have been safer for me to write this new and enlarged edition of *Les Ba-Ronga* in French, my native tongue. I decided to attempt it in English, as the public interested in South African affairs is essentially an English-speaking public and as a great portion of the Thonga tribe is settled in British Territory. I know that I can rely on the indulgence of the English public... When my readers notice that the book has been written by a foreigner—I am afraid they will often make that observation—I beg them kindly to remember that, for me, it would have been much more agreeable to write it in French...

*

* *

To work for Science is noble ; but to help our fellow men is nobler still.

In the difficult undertaking which lies before me, I shall feel immensely gratified if scientists find useful material for their studies amongst my observations. Anthropologists try to throw some light on the dark problem of the origin of the psychic life in mankind; may the picture of a South African primitive tribe bring them some valuable information. But I should feel even deeper satisfaction if my work could help my South African brethren, and contribute to the peaceful solution of our great practical problem there, the Native problem. White men soon tire of the Native when they only see the badly brought up youths who walk about the streets of our colonial towns. They despise them, find them "cheeky" and very soon come to the conclusion : "Natives are no good !" Who can deny that this attitude, adopted by so many South Africans, is as dangerous for the peace of the country as are the very defects with which they reproach the Natives, and which often come from contact with a depraved and unscupulous civilisation ? Let those who are prejudiced against the black race study more carefully its customs, its mind, such as it reveals itself in the old rites of the Bantu tribes. They will see that these Natives are much more earnest than they thought and that in them beats a true human heart. If, in their ignorance of true morality and of true religion, they have submitted themselves willingly to the sufferings of initiation, to the painful rites of purification, in order to reach what they thought to be a higher level of human righteousness, are we not entitled to hope that we shall be able to build up true character in them when we bring them under the moralising influence of Christ-ianity, and teach them to understand the religion which has saved the world ?

Should I succeed in eliciting new and more enlightened sympathy amongst the Whites for our Native brethren, should this book prevent the gulf which separates the races from becoming wider, I think it will have been worth while writing it.

May I be allowed one final comment ? Colossal changes are now taking place amongst the South African tribes. Civilisation has taken fast hold not only of the coast but of the interior. It has exercised a marvellous influence on the High Velt of Johannesburg and is spreading to the borders of the desert. Amongst those races so long stagnant, an evolution has started which is proceeding with great rapidity and a kind of fatality. What will be its ultimate result ? The ethnographer does not generally trouble himself with such questions. It is enough for him to note the facts carefully and to describe them accurately. I aim at being a faithful and impartial ethnographer in the study of customs which still exist but will soon have passed away, but I cannot forget that I am also a Missionary. I belong to that body of men who, with Native Commissioners and liberal minded Colonists, feel they have a sacred duty to perform towards the weaker race. In this most tempting basket of varied fruits which civilisation offers to the Native, we feel we must guide his inexperienced hand, pointing out to him those which conduce to his happiness and progress and those which are poisonous and might be fatal to him. This book is addressed to those who can influence this evolution, be they the Authorities puzzled by the Native problem, or be they educated Natives who are perplexed regarding the future of their race. I will endeavour to indicate the lines along which it appears to me we ought to direct the tribe in order that it may escape shame and destruction. But these suggestions will be given at the end of the volume, in special paragraphs, carefully separated from the scientific treatise. I have enough respect for science to avoid mixing the two subjects. On the other hand, I trust those of my readers who do not share my religious faith or my philanthropic hopes will not blame me for here touching upon the important problems of Native policy. Science has never opposed the betterment and ennoblement of humanity ! If this book can in the slightest degree help towards this end, such help will be its best and most precious justification.

*

*   *

Since the first edition was published, I have spent seven years more in Rikatla and gathered a considerable amount of new information, especially about the kinship system, hunting rites and ancestor worship. I intend to introduce this new material in the present second edition. I had also the opportunity of sojourning in Basutoland and amongst the Ba-Venda of the Northern Transvaal, and of collecting data which are valuable for a comparison of the customs of the various Bantu tribes of South Africa. I shall refer to these occasionally, without however abandoning my original plan, which is the description of the Thonga tribe.

Geneva, June 1926. Henri A. Junod.

PRELIMINARY CHAPTER

THE THONGA TRIBE

_____

I. *Geographical delimitation of the tribe.*

The Thonga tribe is composed of a group of Bantu peoples
settled on the eastern coast of South Africa, extending from
the neighbourhood of St Lucia Bay (28° Lat. S.) on the Natal
Coast up to the Sabie River on the north (1). Thongas are to
be found therefore in four of the present South African
states : in Natal (Amatongaland), the Transvaal (Leydenbourg,
Zoutpansberg and Waterberg districts), in Rhodesia, and chiefly
in Portuguese East Africa (Lourenço Marques, Inhambane and
Mozambique Company districts). The Thongas border on the
Zulus and the Swazis southwards ; westwards on the Ba-Mbayi,
Ba-Lauti and other Suto-Pedi clans in the Transvaal ; northwards
on the Vendas and Ba-Nyai in the Zoutpansberg and Rhodesia,
and on the Ndjaos near the Sabie ; and eastwards on the Thongas
near Inhambane and on the Ba-Chopi, north of the mouth of the
Limpopo.

The tribe comprises a certain number of clans. These clans
form six groups, which speak the various dialects of the Thonga
language.

(1) There are two rivers called Sabie in the Thonga Territory ; one is the Sabie of
the South, which flows in the Leydenburg district and joins the Nkomati not far from
Kil. 53 of the Lourenço Marques-Transvaal line, and the other, that here referred to,
which comes from Rhodesia and flows into the Indian Ocean not far from the 21° lat.
South.

II. *Tribe, Groups and Clans.*

It is necessary first of all to define clearly the precise meaning of these three terms.

We reserve the term *tribe* for the totality of the Thonga nation. This word is frequently used to designate the smaller national units, which are called after some old chief whose descendants are still reigning, like Tembe, Khosa, Nkuna, etc. We prefer for the sake of clearness to call these small units *clans*, as there is certainly a great resemblance between them and the Scottish clans. As a rule all men belonging to a clan bear the name of the old chief, who is more or less considered the ancestor of them all. In the Tembe country, most of the inhabitants will salute each other with these words : "Shawan Tembe, good morning, Tembe" ! But Tembe, the name of the clan, means not only a group of people, but a certain part of the country south of Delagoa Bay. In that country men of other clans have settled. There are also sub-clans of the Tembe clan which have already adopted special salutations, because they have formed collateral branches of the big Tembe family. However the term *clan* is the best, I think, to designate this kind of national unit, as its origin is essentially familial. Now some of these clans, those which occupy the same tract of country, form *groups* because they speak the same dialect of the Thonga language.

III. *The generic Name of the Tribe.*

As we shall see, there is no true national unity amongst the Thongas (1). They are hardly conscious that they form a definite

(1) What orthography are we to adopt when using the Bantu proper names in the plural ? Different systems are used in ethnographic books, but the following appears to me the most rational. When a Bantu proper name is used with its plural prefix, the addition of a final *s* is not justified ; but in that case the prefix ought to be separated from the root by a hyphen, in order that the uninitiated reader may understand at once that he is dealing with a plural. Thus I would write : Ama-Zulu, Ba-Ronga, etc.

nation, and therefore they possess no common name for it. The name *Thonga* (pronounce *t* + aspirated *h*, not the English *th*) was applied to them by the Zulu or Ngoni invaders, who enslaved most of their clans between 1815 and 1830. The origin of this Zulu name is probably the term *Ronga*, which means Orient (buronga = dawn) and by which the clans round Lourenço Marques used to call themselves. According to the phonetic laws of the two languages *R* in Ronga becomes *Th* when pronounced by the Zulus. (Ex. Randja, to love, in Ronga, is thanda in Zulu ; raru, three, thathu.) This word Thonga became a nickname which, in the mouth of the Zulus, was almost the equivalent of slave, and they applied it to the whole Thonga stock ; the appellation is not liked by the Thongas, but I know of no other which would be preferable to it.

Strange to say, the Thongas of the Northern Clans, especially those of the Bilen and Djonga groups, like to call themselves *Tjongas*, the Hlengwes *Tsongas*. This word is perhaps originally the same as Ronga and may have meant also people of the East, although the *R* of the Ronga dialect does not permute regularly into *Tj* and *Ts* in the Northern clans ; but this meaning is doubtful, and has at any rate been forgotten. Another name, which is much used amongst white people to designate the Thongas, is the word *Shangaan*. Shangaan or Tshangaan was one of the surnames of Manukosi, the Zulu chief who settled on the East Coast and subjugated most of the Thongas at the time of Chaka. It is possible that this name was even older, and that it belonged to a chief who lived in the valley of the Lower Limpopo before Manukosi. At any rate, this valley was called Ka Tshangaan and its inhabitants Matshangaan. But this term was never accepted by the Ba-Ronga, who consider it as an

(in the singular : Mu-Ronga, Mu-Sutho), but never Ama-Zulus, Ba-Rongas. As however ordinary readers are not acquainted with Bantu grammar, I think it is more advisable to use these Bantu proper names without their prefixes, treating them as if they were English words, and, in that case it is necessary to add the final *s*, as we generally do according to the rules of European spelling. Many writers do not adopt this system in their books ; but write the plural in exactly the same form as the singular, and it is therefore impossible to distinguish between the two. This may lead to confusion. I therefore propose to write : a Thonga, the Thongas, one Hlengwe, two Hlengwes, but it should be remembered that the final *s* must not be pronounced.

15

insult. It is applied in Johannesburg roughly to all the East
Coast "boys," even to the Ba-Chopi, who are considered by
the Ba-Ronga of Delagoa Bay as much inferior to them. Its
adoption would be objectionable on that account. I recognise
that the word Ba-Thonga does not enjoy much more favour
and is not quite satisfactory ; however considering that it means
originally "people of the East" and that the tribe is indeed
living in the eastern part of South Africa, it ought to be accepted
in the course of time without much difficulty.

Let us remark that another tribe, quite different in language
and ethnographic features, dwelling near Inhambane, quite close
to our Thonga tribe, calls itself Ba-Tonga. But there is no
aspirate after the *T* and this is enough to distinguish it from
the Ba-Thonga.

IV. *The six Groups of the Thonga Clans.*

Let us consider briefly, with the aid of the map, in the front
of the book, these six main groups.

1. All round the Bay of Delagoa, we find the *Ronga group.*
This word Ronga is a very old one and very convenient, as all
these clans consent to be called by it. The real Rongas are,
I think, the Mpfumo and the Matjolo clans, who are settled on
the west of the Bay. South of the Bay is the Tembe clan and
its two sub-clans, which have become independent : Matutwen
and Maputju. North of Lourenço Marques are the Mabota and
Mazwaya clans, the country of the latter, which extends on both
sides of the estuary of the Nkomati, being called Nondwane.
Further north are the two clans of Shirindja and Manyisa
which form the transition to the following group. The new
generation speaks a purer Ronga dialect, the old one more the
Djonga.

Continuing our survey in a northerly direction, we cross
two rivers : the Nkomati and the Olifant. From the Nkomati
to the Olifant we meet with the Djonga group, and from the
Olifant northward with the Nwalungu group. Djonga means

South, Nwalungu means North. The Ba-Djonga are the clans south of the Olifant, the Ba-Nwalungu north of it. Such designations have therefore only a relative value and have been evidently invented by people dwelling on the borders of the Olifant. But they are used in some places, and I do not find any better ones to designate the two dialects of the Thonga spoken south and north of the river.

2. *The Djonga group* includes the Khosa (in the Khosen or Cossine country) the Rikotjo, the Shiburi and the Mathiye clans, if we go directly north. To the east of the Djonga clans proper, we find a number of clans settled on both sides of the Limpopo, in the triangle formed by the Limpopo, the Shengan and the line of the 24° parallel and calling themselves the Ba-Hlabi. They speak a dialect very similar to the Djongas. Their names are as follows, from the confluence of the Olifant and the Limpopo to the south : Mapsanganyi, Tsungu, Mavundja, Nkwinika and Makamo. The Nkuna clan was settled not far from this confluence. It migrated into the Transvaal in great numbers, together with Mavundja and other Hlabis during the wars of Manukosi.

3. *The Nwalungu group* includes two different elements : first the Ba-Loyi or Ba-ka-Baloyi, in the triangle formed by the two rivers northward of their confluence, and the Maluleke further north, extending all along the Limpopo as far as its confluence with the Lebvubye River and further along the Lebvubye itself. They occupy there a part of the Low Country of the Transvaal, being more or less mixed with the Venda and Nyai population. The Malulekes, according to the Native historians, are one half of a larger clan called the Nwanatis, whose second half is settled near the mouth of the Limpopo under the name of the Makwakwas of Khambane and Ndindane.

These three groups are to be found on the central line, on the axis of the tribe. On the west we meet with the Hlanganu group and on the east with the Bila and Hlengwe groups.

4. *The Hlanganu group* is the smallest of all, including the Nwamba clan in the plain of Delagoa Bay, and the Mabila and Hlanganu clans in the Lebombo hills. The Hlangánus overflow

into the Transvaal territory and are scattered in the large desert of the Low Country of the Leydenburg district, together with clans of Sutho (Pedi) and Swazi (Mbayi) origin. The Hlanganu dialect is very much akin to the Djonga.

5. *The Bila group*, called after the name of Bila, the great and fruitful plain of the Lower Limpopo valley, includes the clans living on both banks of the river. They have suffered very much at the hands of the Zulu invaders who made their home in that fertile country, but their dialect has kept some very peculiar traits.

6. *The Hlengwe group*. In the Djonga dialect, *hlengwe* means wealth. I do not know if this be the etymology of the name Hlengwe as designating all the Thonga population of the east and north-east, from the Limpopo to Inhambane and to the Sabie of the north. The name Hlengwe applies properly only to the northern part of the eastern clans. I retain it however provisionally. It seems that this group, which forms perhaps half of the tribe, includes at least three great subdivisions : 1) The *Hlengwes proper*, facing the Malulekes and the Ba-Loyi on the west and extending as far as the Sabie to the north. Their main clans are Tshauke, Mbenzane, Mavube, Magwinyane. 2) *The Ba-Tswa* (1) of Inhambane with the Hlenbengwanes, Yingwanes, Nkumbis. 3) *The Nwanatis* with the Makwakwas, Khambanes, Ndindanes, bordering on the Chopis to the north and the west.

Outside of the proper area of the tribe, we find *colonies of emigrated* Thongas in many parts of the Transvaal. The largest is in the Spelonken district, north of the Zoutpansberg, where they form the majority of the population. There they were called

---

(1) This name Ba-Tswa, is the Hlengwe form of Ba-Tjwa, a term by which the Zulus have been commonly designated amongst the Thongas. Ba-Tjwa is probably the corresponding form for Ba-Rwa, an appellation by which the Suthos of the Zoutpansberg plains used to call the tribes of the mountains, whence comes the wind called Bu-rwa. The Ba-Rwa are properly the Bushmen, as one knows, but under that name were included Bantus of a quite different type. This shows that the Natives, in naming foreign tribes, consider the geographical relation between themselves and these tribes much more than their ethnic characteristics : so one very often meets with the word "Bakalanga" which means people of the north. The Bakalanga proper are in Rhodesia, but in Lourenço Marques the Khosa tribe is called Bakalanga.

The term Ba-Ngoni is applied to the Zulus, as well as Ba-Tjwa, but it is restricted to that clan of the Zulus which was under Manukosi.

Ma-Gwamba by the Vendas and Bveshas who possessed the country before them. These Ma-Gwamba are made up mostly of Hlengwe, Maluleke and Djonga refugees. In the Modjadji country, we find two colonies of Ba-ka-Baloyi with their own chiefs. Near Leydsdorp, a more considerable clan, numbering about 6000, is the Nkuna clan under Muhlaba. On the Sabie of the south, in the plain of the Leydenburg district, another colony has been founded more recently, since the war of the Portuguese against Gungunyane, by the Ngonis and Bilas who did not accept the new rule. They remain under Mpisane, a near relative of the late Ngoni potentate.

In the Orichstadt valley, and in many other parts of the Leydenburg mountains, little colonies of Thongas are met with, as well as in the Waterberg district (especially near Nilstrom) and in the towns of Pretoria and Johannesburg. A good many of the thousands of Shangaanes coming every year to the mines settle down definitively in the Town Locations of these great centres.

During the last twenty years the number of these emigrants has certainly increased. It was not possible to indicate on the map all their settlements between the Hlanganu domain proper, the Drakensberg Mountains and the Olifant River. On the farms of the Zoutpansberg and Pietersburg Districts they also form a notable portion of the Native population.

V. *The numerical strength of the Thonga Tribe.*

It is very difficult to ascertain the numbers of the Thongas. The census of the Transvaal taken on the 17th of April 1904 gives 82,325 as being the total Thonga population of that colony ; of these, 48,117 are located in the Zoutpansberg. This is a minimum, as it has been recognised that at least 10 % ought to be added to these figures ; there were scarcely any young men in the kraals when the census was taken. Let us estimate at 100,000 the numerical strength of that part of the tribe which is located in the Transvaal.

As regards Portuguese East Africa, we find some interesting

figures in the Mozambique Year Book. The Black population of the Lourenço Marques District is estimated at 99,698, distributed as follows :

Circumscription of Morakwen (1)	. . . . .	21,510
» » Manyisa	. . . . . .	24,183
» » Sabi	. . . .	12,960
» » Magudju (Khosen)	. . . .	18,197
» » Maputju	. . . . . .	22,848
	Total	99,698

The population of the old region of Gaza which includes Bilen, the Makwakwas, the Ba-Loi, the Hlabis and part of the Hlengwe clans, is estimated at 147,995. Gaza having now been incorporated with the Lourenço Marques district, the latter has a Native population of 257,693. However the Year Book declares that this is a minimum, and states that at least 13,000 ought to be added to this number. Let us take 270,000 for the Lourenço Marques district. As regards the Inhambane district, the Year Book estimates the total population at 750,088 ; a very small percentage ought to be deducted for the White and Asiatic population, not more than 1 to 2,000. How many of the remaining thousands belong to our tribe ? There are numerous clans of Ba-Chopi on the coast and of Ba-Tonga round Inhambane. These two tribes however occupy but a small area of this large district, the interior of which is inhabited by the various Hlengwe clans. So we may admit that at least half of these 750,000 Natives are Thongas. If we are correct in this estimate, the total numerical strength of the Thonga tribe would be about 750,000.

VI. *The History of the Thonga tribe.*

Everyone who has had to teach South African Natives has been astonished at their memory. It is so good that it sometimes prevents the reasoning faculty from developing as it ought to.

(1) I have adopted the Native pronunciation of Native names and the orthography explained in my Elementary Grammar of the Thonga-Shangaan Language. (Lausanne, Bridel.)

Some of these people are able to repeat a tale lasting five or ten minutes after having heard it twice or thrice only. It is to be wondered at therefore that they have so few traditions, or rather that these traditions do not reach further back in history. In fact, when you inquire into what they know of the past, you find first, a story about their origin which bears a strongly mythical character ; secondly, traditions more or less legendary about the migrations of the various clans ; thirdly, genealogies of the royal family containing eight to ten names, and fourthly, historical narratives which go back as far as the beginning of the 19th century, and which give the impression of true historical facts. History, amongst the Thongas, begins only one hundred years ago. What took place before that is almost entirely forgotten. This fact shows that, even amongst races possessing a good memory, before the introduction of a system of writing traditions regarding the ancient past can hardly be relied upon.

A. PREHISTORIC PERIOD.

1) *The story of man's origin* is this. The first human beings emerged from reeds. Each tribe came into this world with its present characteristics. For instance the Ba-Bvesha, who are great blacksmiths, knew how to forge their iron picks from the first day. They "came out" holding them. The Ba-Ronga group calls the first ancestors of humanity Likalahumba and Nsilambowa, viz. the one who brings a glowing cinder in a shell (the man) and the one who grinds vegetables (the woman). The Ba-Djonga call them Gwambe and Dzabana. Another story universally believed tells us how death came amongst men by the fault of the chameleon (See Part VI). All these stories are purely mythical and form part of the African Genesis which is met with in most tribes.

2) *Legends about the ancient migrations* of the various clans. Almost every clan pretends to have come from afar and, strange to say, they came from all the points of the compass. Two of their clans, without doubt, come from the north, the Ba-ka-

Baloyi and the Tembe. The Ba-ka-Baloyi, they say, came down the valley of the Limpopo in very remote times ; they came in such numbers that they opened out a wide track as wide as a wagon road : "It is the old, old road of Gwambe, the first man on earth who emerged from the reed. So well was the road trodden that to this day the grass has not grown over it." Many Thongas pretend to have seen it, white and straight, stretching from the northern bank of the Limpopo and going southwards through the desert, just like the road over which Attila passed ! At a certain place, near a rivulet where the Ba-Loyi rested, one can still see in the rock the print of the mortars of the women. "The stones at that time were not yet hardened, and they retained the marks made by the mortars in that old expedition, the marks also of the hemp pipes of the men and of their *matshuba*." (The *matshuba* are the little holes hollowed out by the Natives in four rows, as required in their favourite game called *tshuba*. See Part II, Chap. II.)

According to some of the Native historians, the Ba-Loyi came from the Ba-Nyai country along with the Ba-Nwanati, who also belonged to the Nyai or Kalanga race. They went southwards by that wonderful old road till they reached the sea coast not far from the mouth of the Limpopo. The sight of the sea, that broad unknown river, filled them with great fear. The Ba-Loyi felt they could not remain in such a dangerous neighbourhood and advised the whole party to go back to the north. In the meantime, however, their Nwanati friends had discovered a fruit not common on the African high veld, but very common on the sandy plains of the coast. In shape it was round, about the size of an orange, with a hard outer shell. When broken it was found to contain a number of stones, each wrapped in a delicate, strongly scented pulp, of which the Natives prepare an excellent dish. This fruit is called *makwakwa*. "We shall remain here to break open our *makwakwa*" said the Ba-Nwanati, and they bade farewell to the Ba-Loyi, who started back to their present abode. Hence the name Makwakwa now given to those Nwanatis.

The Nwanatis included the Makwakwas of Khambane and the Malulekes. These latter separated from their brethren and returned north, to the country of the Ba-Loyi, led by their ancestor, Mashakatsi. This man, who was a great hunter, saw that he could easily defeat the Ba-Nyai who were settled in those parts, and brought back his followers with him. He became the founder of the dynasty of Maluleke. (For further details about these legends, see Addresses and Papers of the Joint Meeting of British and South African Associations for the Advancement of Science, Johannesburg 1905.)

As regards the Tembe clan, it is said to have come down as far as Delagoa Bay from the Kalanga country by the Nkomati river on a floating island of papyrus, and to have crossed the Tembe river and settled to the south of the Bay. An old saying alludes to this arrival and to the conquest of the country :

Phandje, phandje ra nala—Tembe kulu a wela.

As the palm leaf with its numerous feelers—so did the ancestor Tembe when he crossed.

He placed his sons in all the districts of the plain to govern in his name. The Tembe people, when they greet each other, sometimes use the salutation Nkalanga, i. e. man of the north or of the Kalanga country, and there is little doubt that, notwithstanding the legendary traits in this tradition, the fact itself of the northern origin of these clans is true. In the course of time the chiefs of Matutwen and Maputju, descendants of Tembe, became independent.

Most of the other clans point to Zululand or to Swaziland as having been their first abode, which they left to invade the low country of the coast. Mpfumu and Matjolo are both sons of Nhlaruti, who is said to have been the first invader ; from him sprang their two clans which have become independent of and even hostile to each other. The Nondwane families point to the neighbourhood of Komati Port as being the place from which they came. There were successive invasions of a peaceful character. These people still turn the face of their dead to the west, because the clan came from the Lebombo hills, and this rite proves that the tradition is well founded. The Nkuna, Khosa, and Hlabi clans also claim the same western or south-western origin. Amongst the Ba-Nkuna, some old men say they know

23

the precise place in Zululand whence their forefather Nkuna started and declare that they still have relatives there.

The Hlanganus and Hlengwes seem to have no tradition of this kind. The only one I heard about the Hlengwes is this. Tshauke, their first king, took as his wife the daughter of another chief belonging to the Sono tribe. The Sonos knew how to cook their food, the Hlengwes did not : they were still ignorant of fire and used to eat their porridge raw. The son of Tshauke stole a glowing cinder from the Sonos and brought it home in a big shell. The Sonos were angry and declared war on the Hlengwes ; but these latter, having gained new strength because they had been eating cooked food, won the victory. The son of Tshauke was then named Shioki - sha - humba - he who brings fire in a shell. This tradition is connected with the name of the first man, Likala-humba, which we have just explained, and it evidently bears a legendary character.

A similar story is told about the Shiburi clan (between the Olifant and Nkomati rivers). The old inhabitants of that country were the Masilanes and Nshongos. Once, at a very remote period, a man of the Shiburi clan, who was a Pedi and dwelt in Mabulanen, at the foot of the Drakensberg Mountains, pursued an eland which he had wounded and killed it in the territory of the Masilanes. He returned home to call his countrymen to cut it in pieces and to eat it according to the custom of hunters. These people then roasted the meat and handed over some of it to the Masilanes. The Masilanes used to eat meat raw as they did not know the use of fire. They found that cooked meat was much better than raw meat and told the Shiburis : "You are more intelligent than we are ; we will serve you henceforth !" They therefore decided to get rid of their own chief. The Shiburis lighted a big fire, dug a hole and put the glowing embers into it. Then a mat was spread over the mouth of the hole and the chief was asked to sit upon it. He fell into the pit and died, and the Shiburis became the masters of the country. They abandoned their costume (the musubelo, viz. the piece of skin fastened between the legs as used by the Pedis) their language and their marriage laws, married Masilane girls and became true Thongas (Mabuyandlela).

If these stories had a historical foundation, it would prove that there was a time when the use of fire was unknown to certain Thonga clans. This, however, is hardly admissible. Fire has been used by human beings from the remotest antiquity, even in the paleolithic age, as far back as the Mousterian period, 20,000 years ago or more. It is probable that even before that time the dry velt of South Africa was often set on fire by lightning. But the recurrence of these legends, which remind one of the Greek myth of Prometheus, shows at any rate the immense value which the Thongas attach to the use of fire.

What were the races that the invaders found in the country ? Their name is still known in some places. In the Khosen Country, they were the Ntimbas and Shibambos. In the Nondwane, the Honwanas, Mahlangwanas and Nkumbas. All agree in saying that they were on a lower scale of civilisation (See Part IV) and that the new comers overcame them easily because they were more intelligent and possessed better weapons.

3) A third source of information regarding prehistoric times is to be found in the *genealogies of the royal families* which each clan has preserved more or less completely. I have gathered the following (1) :

Mpfumu : Nhlaruti, Mpfumu, Fayi, Maromana, Shilupane, Hasana (who attacked Lourenço Marques in 1868, was banished but received back his country in 1875 ; he died in 1878), Hamule, Zihlahla, Nwamantibyane (banished in 1896 to Western Africa where he died).

Tembe : Tembe, Nkupu, Nwangobe, Silambowa, Muhari (1781-1795), Mayeta (1823), Bangwana, Bukutje (1857), Mabayi (banished in 1890), Bukutje II.

Maputju : Maputju was the younger brother of Muhari and made himself independent of him. Muwayi, Makasana (1800-1850), Tlhuma, Musongi or Nozililo (1850), Ngwanazi (who fled to British Amatongaland after the Gungunyana war in 1895).

Nondwana : Libombo (probably reigning before the invasion),

---

(1) Compare E. Torre do Valle. Diccionario shironga-portuguez. Lourenço Marques. Imprensa Nacional 1906,

25

Masinga, Ngomana, Matinana, Makwakwa, Papele, Khobete (who rebelled against the Portuguese in 1859), Mapunga, Mahazule.

Mabota : Mabota, Magwenyana, Lawulana, Magumbin, Mbakana, Nwatjonga.

Nwamba : Kopo-Nwamba, Rihati, Sindjini, Malengana, Nkolele, Mangoro, Mudlayi, Nwangundjuwana.

Khosa : Khosa, Ripanga, Mabone, Molelemane, Ripindje, Magudjulane, Nshalati Pukwana, Magudju, Shongele.

Nkuna : Nkuna, Shitlhelane, Rinono, Kulalen, Nwarinyekana, Muhlari, Ribye-ra ku-tika, Shiluvane, Muhlaba.

Maluleke : Mashakatsi, Dlamana, Shitanda, Shihala, Nkuri, Mhinga, Sunduza.

These genealogies, as one can see, generally contain eight to ten names. The list of Maputju chiefs has six only, because this dynasty is not so old and did not begin before the end of the XVIIIth century. But all the others are longer. I do not pretend that they are absolutely correct ; in the same clan, there are sometimes variations according to the informants. There may have been links omitted in the chain because, to the Natives, a grandson is a son, just like a real son. On the other hand, the law of succession amongst the Thongas calls to the chieftainship the younger brothers of the deceased chief ; so some of these names may very well belong to brothers. Therefore it does not at all follow that eight names correspond to eight different generations. If that were so, estimating a generation at 30 years, we should conclude that the first chief lived some 250 years ago, viz. in 1650 ; but I have found conclusive proof that, for some of these genealogies, the first name in the list was already known in 1550. So we must consider these genealogies as being in fact too short. Many names must have been dropped out in the course of time.

The proof to which I allude has been afforded by the Portuguese reports published in the Mémoire addressed in 1873 to the President of the French Republic, who was called to act as mediator in the conflict between England and Portugal about the right of possession of the southern part of the Bay (Lisboa.

Imprensa Nacional). In this interesting publication we find the oldest documents relative to the Bay and, amongst others, we read the following account in a Report of the Portuguese chronicler Perestrello, written in 1554 : "Into the Bay flow three rivers... The first one to the south, is called Zembe. It separates the land of a king of that name from the dominion of the king Nyaka... The second is the river of the Holy Spirit or of Lourenço Marques. It separates the land of Zembe from the land of two other chiefs whose names are Rumu and Mina Lebombo. The third and last is the Manhisa, so called after a Kafir of that name who governs there." In these statements we can easily recognize the names of the actual clans of Tembe (Zembe), Mpfumu (Rumu), Lebombo and Manyisa. These names were already known at that time and the chiefs to whom they apply were settled in the same country where they now are or not far from it. The chief Nyaka has left his name to the Inyak Island. It seems that his dynasty was then reigning over a larger tract of country than now. It is possible that he was confined to the island where his descendants now live, by the military operations of Maputju. Let us remark moreover that Zembe and Manhisa were names applied not only to those two chiefs, but to *rivers*. Zembe is the actual Mi-Tembe which flows between the Tembe and Matjolo countries, and Manhisa is evidently the Nkomati which crosses the Manhisa country some fifty kilometers higher than the estuary. If the Natives already called rivers after the name of these chiefs, it is probable that the chiefs themselves were already dead, and had lived in a more or less remote past. All these arguments tend to show that four or five hundred years ago at least the chiefs Tembe, Mpfumu, Manhisa, Libombo, all of whom still have descendants, were already in the country round Delagoa Bay. I do not think any scientifically accurate statement could be made with regard to so remote a period and I propose this as a landmark in the history of South African Natives (1).

(1) For more details about the history of the Thongas and of the neighbouring tribes, see my article in the "South African Journal of Science", 1914: *The condition of the Natives of South East Africa in the XVIth Century according to the early Portuguese documents.*

B. HISTORIC PERIOD.

Having tried to fix what is historical in the prehistoric period, we now come to the XIXth century ; and here we find a great amount of detailed information in which there may be some legendary traits, but which as a whole seems to be entirely trustworthy. It does not suit our plan to narrate here all these facts. To do so would lead us much too far. Let us only say that the history of the Thonga tribe during the whole of the XIXth century was dominated by the invasion and migrations of the Zulu conquerors, who left Chaka and for their own sake enslaved the poor Ama-Thonga of the coast, just as Mosilekatsi did among the Mashonas. These Ba-Ngoni were led by Manukosi ; he found all the Thonga clans living according to the old Bantu style, each for itself, without national unity ; he easily conquered them and tried to impose on them the military system of dominion created by Dingiswayo and Chaka. Many of the Thonga clans emigrated into the Transvaal at that time (between 1835-1840) rather than submit to Manukosi ; as the Boers had settled in the country and as the Ngoni chiefs always feared a war with the Whites more than anything else, these Thongas were left undisturbed by Manukosi. They belonged to the Nkuna, Ba-Loyi and Mavundja clans, and founded numerous colonies in the Transvaal. Manukosi reigned quietly for more than twenty years in the Limpopo valley and as far as the Mosapa (Ba-Ndjao country, north of the Sabie). His death took place in 1856. Then a dreadful war of succession still known as "the war" (mubango) raged for more than six years over the whole area of the Thonga tribe. Two brothers disputed the chieftainship. According to the Thonga law of succession, Muzila was the legal heir ; but the Ngoni law was against him and in favour of his younger brother Mawewe. Mawewe was then proclaimed chief and Muzila's followers fled to the Spelonken ; the new king however behaved as a cruel despot and, with the help of the Portuguese and of the Ronga warriors, Muzila defeated him decisively on the Sabie River, August 17-20 1862. The Ba-Ronga always remained

28

independent of the Ngoni chiefs, being directly under the Portuguese authorities.

A Portuguese called Albasini, who acted during all that time as a chief of the Thongas of the Spelonken, played a considerable part in these events.

When Muzila died, his son Gungunyane succeeded him. The Ba-Ngoni had greatly diminished in number. In 1890 there were not more than a few hundred of them in the whole country. However they held it very firmly and the Thongas hated them. Therefore when the war between the Portuguese and some Ronga clans in 1894 led to difficulties between the Whites and Gungunyane, the Ngoni chief was abandoned by most of his people, even by his uncle Nkuyu : his capital Mandlakasi was burnt and he himself was captured by Musinho d'Albuquerque at the end of the year 1895 ; the despotic rule of the Zulus came to an end, and has been replaced by the Portuguese administration, much to the advantage of the Thonga tribe.

VII. *Ethnic characteristics of the Thonga tribe.*

What are the characteristic features of our tribe in relation to the other ethnic groups of South African Bantus, especially to the Zulus and Suthos ? We shall try to sketch them briefly as regards three main points : language and mental and physical character.

1) *The Language of the Thongas.* It would be useless to give here an elaborate description of the Thonga language : this has already been done for the Ronga dialect in my "Grammaire Ronga" published with the help of the Portuguese Government in 1896 (Bridel, Lausanne) and for the Djonga dialect in my Elementary Grammar of the Thonga-Shangaan language, which I published at the beginning of the Thonga-English Pocket Dictionary compiled by my colleague the Rev. Ch. Châtelain (Bridel, Lausanne 1908). I shall consider the language here only from an ethnological point of view, that is to say only to ascertain the proper place of the Thongas amongst the Bantus.

29

The Thonga idiom belongs to the *South-Eastern group of the Bantu languages* and is related both to Sutho and Zulu. All these languages have in common certain grammatical features which distinguish them from other groups. Amongst them I may mention the frequent use of the lateral sounds *hl, dl, tl*, the presence of seven or eight distinct classes of nouns, recognizable by prefixes which correspond to each other in these three languages, the formation of the locative by a suffix *ini* or *ng* and not by prefixes, the consequent absence of the three locative classes pa, ku, mu, etc. It has been asserted by people who have not studied Thonga carefully that it is merely a dialect of Zulu. This is not true (1). Thonga is altogether different from Zulu and Sutho, though it closely resembles both, especially Zulu.

Relation to Sutho. As regards Sutho, its phonetic system is characterised by the absence of a certain phenomenon common to most Bantu languages, to Thonga and Zulu especially. The Bantu phonology is dominated by a peculiar nasalisation of certain consonants when prefixed by an *n* or an *m*. This *n* or *m* is generally the prefix of the class mu-ba, mu-mi or in-tin (zin), and has the power of producing marvellous changes in this initial consonant. But, in Sutho, this prefix is dropped altogether except in a few cases, and these nasalised sounds are almost entirely lacking. As regards some other grammatical features, Sutho, especially the Pedi dialect of Sutho, is not so far from Thonga. It is not possible to quote many instances; let us only remark that Sutho possesses the roots *loya* for witchcraft and *yila* for taboo which are also present in Thonga and are lacking in Zulu.

Relation to Zulu. The great difference between Thonga and Zulu as regards phonetics is the complete absence of the three characteristic Zulu clicks (2) in Thonga. The Thongas have no

(1) Thongas and Zulus *do not understand* each other. In linguistic terminology, I think one ought never to designate as a dialect of a language an idiom which people speaking that language cannot understand at all. It is then a different language altogether, and we ought to keep the term dialect for the various forms of a single language which are of such a nature that people speaking them can understand each other more or less perfectly.

(2) The Zulu clicks are, as is generally believed, of Hottentot origin. It is not surprising therefore that they were not adopted by the Thongas, who do not seem to have had any contact with Hottentots.

clicks at all except in a few words borrowed from the Zulu like nqolo, wagon. Certain letters regularly permute from one language into the other : *Z* of the Zulu is *t* in Thonga ; *r* of the Thonga is generally replaced by *l* or *th* in Zulu.

Originality of Thonga. But though Thonga and Zulu resemble each other in many respects, Thonga possesses some peculiar features which prove its originality. As regards its sounds, it is characterised by the frequent occurrence of a labial sibilant sound, a little like *ps* pronounced with a kind of whistling, which corresponds to the Zulu *z* in the plural of the class isi-izi. It is further characterised by some special nasalisations of initial consonants. *N+k*, which remains *nk* in Zulu, becomes *h* in Thonga : for instance the Zulu *nkosi*, chief, is *hosi* in Thonga. (It is *Khushi* in Sutho-Pedi where the initial *n* has been dropped). There is a long list of words of the in-tin class which show this phenomenon (homu, ox ; huku, hen, etc.). The initial *r* when preceded by *n* becomes *nh* (*nh*ena, warrior ; ti*nh*aru, three; cf. *ra*ru, three, bu*r*ena, bravery, mo*r*ena, in Sutho, chief). This seems to be the primitive combination. In some other cases it becomes *ntjh* in Ronga and *ndj* in Djonga (*ra*ko, behind, *ntjh*ako, *ndj*ako). These two *r* have probably a different origin in the Ur-Bantu. These transformations are peculiar to Thonga.

As regards morphology, Thonga has some striking peculiarities : a great variety of demonstrative forms due to the presence of a kind of demonstrative particle *le* or *la* and also a great development of the participial forms of the verbs. In its conjugation, the verb is quite as well provided with auxiliaries as in any other South African language and we could easily discover in Thonga the one or two thousand combinations which have been counted in the Zulu conjugation.

Thonga, for all these reasons, is a language apart which has developed with its different dialects.

The six dialects. We have tried to classify them under six names, but this classification is, of course, purely formal : in fact each of them presents transition forms, and they coalesce with each other through a great number of intermediary forms (1). This is a very striking fact. I take for instance the word *ririmi*, which means tongue in Djonga, north of the Nkomati River. Here we find two *r* pronounced more or less as rolled *r*, never gutturally. If we go somewhat further South, to the Nondwane, ririmi becomes *rjirjimi*. The *r* becomes more palatal. We reach Mpfumu : there the word has changed into *lidjimi*. The first *r* has become a pure dental, the second a palato-dental (with a kind of cerebralisation). There is a regular evolution of the sound from one dialect to the other. The same process might be followed for *b* which is a true explosive *b* to the south of the Bay and becomes *v*, a fricative labial and sometimes almost *w*, a semivowel, when we go to the north. This regularity in the geographical relation of the sounds is very clear, and it shows that the language must have developed undisturbed like a tree putting forth branches, these branches separating more and more from each other till the dialects are formed, each with its peculiar sounds.

This fact is all the more marvellous when we remember that the Thonga tribe has been made up of peoples of various origin which have invaded the country, coming from different parts. The only explanation which accounts for these two apparently contradictory facts is that these invaders adopted the language of the primitive population and did not influence it enough to prevent its following its natural evolution... If this be true, the Thonga language ought to be considered as the oldest element in the life of the tribe, and we can then understand how it has given it its unity.

It is true that the course of events, from a linguistic point of view, has been totally different since the Zulu invasion of the XIXth century. The Ba-Ngoni of Manukosi did not adopt the Thonga as their language : they kept their Zulu dialect ; and most men of the Thonga clans knew and used it also together with their own national tongue. But this difference can easily be explained. The Zulu generals who followed the example of Chaka, Manukosi

1) In Appendix N⁰ 1, I give a list of the most interesting words, showing how they are pronounced in all parts of the tribe, in order to characterise the various dialects.

and Moselekatsi amalgamated clans and tribes under their military rule, and could not subsist unless they maintained a despotic domination over them ; they were an aristocratic race and considered their language as superior. Ruling by fear and by the sword, they purposely remained aliens amongst the enslaved tribes. Quite different was the spirit of the ancient invaders of 1400 or 1500 A. D. They had not such an ideal of vast domination ; they operated on a much smaller scale : they were satisfied to take the chieftainship from the aborigines, and quickly mingled with them, married their daughters (as they still do) and so became one with them.

Would the Ba-Ngoni have been able, in course of time, to establish their Zulu dialect instead of the Thonga, if the Portuguese had not broken their power ? It is impossible to say. They had succeeded in imposing all their Zulu terminology in military matters. Meanwhile the women were not learning Zulu and the women are the best safeguards of the purity of the language amongst primitive peoples. Therefore I do not think they would have been able to uproot the old language, which must have been spoken for many centuries in Thonga territory.

My conclusion is then that the Thonga language was already spoken by the primitive occupants of the country more than 500 years ago and that, together with a certain number of customs, it formed the great bond which bound the Thonga clans together in past centuries.

2) *Mental characteristics of the Thongas.* We shall only ask how the Thongas compare with the Zulus or Suthos as regards character, and especially from a military point of view.

Having had the opportunity to witness a war in which the Nkuna chief Muhlaba was allied with the Pedi chief Maaghe, in the Zoutpansberg, I can testify that the Thongas had ten times as much military spirit

Phot. G. Liengme.

A "zuluised" Thonga warrior.

as the Pedis. I saw the two armies, the same day, preparing for the same battle. The Thongas were armed to the teeth, forming a great circle, all standing, shouting their war songs, gesticulating, jumping, imploring their chief to allow them to start. The Pedi warriors were sitting under trees, taking their snuff and apparently as calm as any other day.

During the Gungunyane war, the Thongas were brave, at least those not entirely dependent on the Ngoni king, who had not allowed his warriors to kill white men. The Rongas of Mpfumu especially showed great courage and endurance, and those who served the Portuguese in their Angola war have been praised as being very steady and reliable.

On the other hand everything seems to prove that military ability is not an ancient feature of the Thonga character, and that it has been imparted to them by the Zulus, who taught them the art of fighting during the last century, pushing them to the front in their battles and calling them "Mabuyandlela," "those who open the way." Before the Ngoni invasion, the Thonga armies were ignorant of the *mukhumbi* viz. the armed circle of warriors which is the basis of the Zulu military system; (See Part IV) : they used to form themselves into a straight line and, in their battles, very few men were killed. They were normal Bantu clans, viz. people living peacefully, occasionally quarrelling with their neighbours. The idea of conquest, of vast dominion, the system of an armed nation which Chaka and his followers pursued, was something new amongst South African Natives and was probably borrowed by Dingiswayo from the Whites. This fact ought not to be ignored.

Under a just European supervision, there is no probability that the Thonga tribe will change its peaceful and mild charcter.

3) *Physical characteristics of the Thongas.* It cannot be said that the Thongas possess a very distinct and unique physical type. They are generally of a dark brown colour, sometimes purely black, much darker than the Suthos. As a whole, their external appearance bears a much closer resemblance to that of the Zulus, but, as regards face and stature, they vary very much. You may meet Thongas with typical negro faces, broad lips, flat

noses, prominent cheek bones, and the same day, at the same place, other men of the same clan with a much narrower face, thin lips and pointed noses. It seems that there are two different types amongst them, the coarse type which was perhaps more wide-spread amongst the primitive populations, and which has been kept very distinct by the Ba-Chopi of the Coast, and the finer, which belonged perhaps to the invaders, and both types have inter-crossed in all possible ways. There seems also to have been an Arabic influence in some of the clans. A Native Commissioner in the Zoutpansberg has noticed amongst some of the Thonga settlements striking Semitic features, arched noses, thin lips. Has there been any intermarriage between the Thongas and those Arabs who settled on the East Coast long before it was discovered by Vasco de Gama ? Who can say ?

FIRST PART

THE LIFE OF THE INDIVIDUAL

CHAPTER I

THE EVOLUTION OF A MAN FROM BIRTH TO DEATH

A. INFANCY

I. *The day of Birth.*

When a new member of the tribe is expected, when the mother begins to feel the pangs of childbirth (ku luñwa), the father sends word to the midwives of the neighbourhood and all of them come at once. They are called *tinsungakati* (1). Every woman having some experience in this department is a midwife, no special training being required for the qualification (2).

The *place chosen* for the delivery (phuluka) is generally the back of the hut (mahosi) where the pregnant woman lives. Some mats are brought and hung up in such a way as to form a small

---

(1) This word is interesting. Its termination *ati* is the proper feminine suffix which is found in nsati, wife, hulukati, female elephant, Nkomati, the river of that name, t he rivers being considered as female by the Thongas.

(2) Amongst certain Thonga clans, especially the Khosas of Magude, there is a person who is bound to come and assist the woman in childbirth : this is the mukoñwana lo' nkulu of her husband i. e. the woman who has been bought with her husband's oxen. The woman in labour leans her head on this woman's chest, whilst the other midwives help her in parturition. When the Rev. F. Paillard went to assist a woman during labour, the "mukoñwana lo' nkulu" told him : "You have taken my place." See Part II. Ch. I. B. 3).

enclosure. This is done to protect the woman from indiscreet onlookers. Should there be enough bush to hide her, mats are not used. A big wooden mortar is given to her to lean against during her pains. The whole place is called by a special term *fukwen* or *busaken* (the nest). Should the birth be difficult, the divinatory bones will probably be consulted and the woman will be removed to another place, inside the hut or somewhere else.

The baby may be born without any help, but as a rule the midwives consider it their duty to submit their patient to a *long and painful manipulation*, to a regular kneading, performed with the hands, sometimes even with the feet, in order, as they say, to obtain the expulsion of the child and of the after-birth all at once. They sometimes succeed in this feat ! They also often hurt the mother severely. The midwives think that they must be very rough, and have no pity at all on the poor woman. Sometimes the mother loses all her natural feelings in this painful process. I have heard of cases of her refusing to let the child come to the light, biting her helpers, running away. Hence perhaps the attitude adopted by the midwives. The mother must not *fahla ñwana*, viz. break down the child, a technical expression to designate unhappy births.

During the whole labour, it is taboo (1) for the mother to eat or to drink anything ; she would kill the child if she did so. Of course no man must attend the birth ; neither must girls come near. A newly married woman may be allowed to enter the enclosure in order to "be taught." It is also forbidden for the female relations of the woman, her sisters, even her mother to come *fukwen* ; they might be ashamed if their relative behaved badly and "broke her child." They will not come till the following day, when they hear that everything has gone smoothly ; then the father will kill a hen for them.

(1) We translate by taboo the Thonga word *yila* which means everything prohibited. I beg to give the following provisional definition of this term, which will be found from the first to the last page of this book : Any object, any act, any person that implies a danger to the individual or to the community and that must consequently be avoided, this object, act or person being under a kind of ban. As often as possible, I shall add the explanation which Natives give of these taboos.

As soon as the child has made his appearance one of the midwives ties the *umbilical cord* (likabana) near the navel and cuts it about three inches from it. The little sore is anointed with a kind of fat ; the bit of cord remaining with the baby is attended to with great care : it generally falls off at the end of the first week, and this is the signal for the end of the period of confinement.

The after-birth, the *placenta*, is also looked for with much anxiety : it is called *yindlu ya ñwana*, the "house of the child," or *hlalu*. When it is delayed too long, the midwives begin to fear "because the blood which is inside has not all come out and will kill the mother." In the Khosa clan, should the placenta not come at once, the woman is told to stand on her feet, her body half bent forward, and all the midwives begin to move their index fingers from right to left, emitting at the same time the following sound : tswi-tswi-tswi-tswi. This is said to help the placenta to come. The placenta is generally buried deep behind the hut on the spot where the birth has taken place ; but some prefer to bury it inside the house, fearing the dogs might unearth it, which is taboo.

The child is then washed with water. This water is thrown away as being polluted by the blood of the birth, which is taboo.

Naming the child. On the day of birth or on one of the following days the child receives his name (bito). There are four principal ways of choosing this.

1) Often the parents give their offspring *the name of a chief* as Musongi, Makasana, Muzila, etc. It flatters their vanity !

2) But frequently the parents like to recall a name of the old times (pfusha bito dja khale), the name of one of the ancestors, because it is a good thing to remember them. They go so far as to consult the bones. A name is proposed, and if the bones in falling do not give a favourable indication, another is tried till they feel sure that the die "has spoken" (1).

3) Or it may be that somebody asks the favour of giving his

(1) The Christian Natives like to ask their missionary to choose the name, perhaps for a similar reason.

name to the new-born child ; a friend of the family may do so, but it is also often a traveller who happens to be in the village to whom this privilege is accorded. He will *"name himself in the child"* (ku titshula ka ṅwana). This fact will establish a special relation between this person and the child, a relation which bears some resemblance to that of a godfather to his godson. Once a year he will come and give "his name" (viz. the child) presents. When the child is able to travel, the mother will go with him to pay a visit to his "friend in name" (mabitoku-lobye).

4) A fourth way of naming new-born children is to choose a name having some connection with the *circumstances of the birth.* Should a child have seen the light when his mother was travelling, he will be called *Ndlelen* viz. "on the way," "on the road ;" should the birth have taken place under a tree, the name of that tree will be chosen, put in the locative case, and you will meet many Thongas called Nkanyen (under the terebinth), Nkwakwen (under the Strychnos), Nkuwen (under the fig-tree), etc. ; or Mpfulen (in the rain), Marumbin (in the ruins), Mawewe, if the child is born during the war waged by the chief of that name, etc. When General Beyers was over-running Zoutpansberg with his commando, the Natives, admiring the swiftness of his move-ments, named many children after him (1).

The names of the Thongas are the same for the two sexes. There are only two which cannot be employed indiscriminately

---

(1) In the case of *bowumba,* viz. if a woman has lost many children (see Part. I. Ch. II. 8), should she give birth to a new one, a name will be chosen which will protect the new-born infant against the fate of his elder brothers and sisters. I know a boy who was born under such circumstances. His grandfather *Shona* named him after himself in order to bring him good luck. The Rev. H Guye, in an article entitled : "Des noms propres chez les Ba-Ronga" (*Bulletin de la Société Neuchâteloise de Géographie,* 1920) quotes an interesting instance of such a name. A boy was called *Nyamayabu,* viz. their meat. His elders had died and it was thought that they had been eaten by wizards. When this boy came into the world, his parents had abandoned all hope of keeping him alive and said : "It is their meat, the meat which the wizards will eat !" But they evidently thought that this name would be a protection to the child, perhaps because wizards would see that their evil tricks were known, and would fear to be discovered, if they killed it. Such names are called : "names of misery" (mabito ya busiwana, ya ku titjetja), as Bisana or Bisalifu, "the one who hiccoughs death :" wherever he sends his hiccoughs, he spreads death.

for girls and boys. *Nhwanin* is a girl's name, as it means "girl" and *Nwandjise* a boy's name as it means "boy" (1).

All these birth-names are abandoned later on, generally at the circumcision school, or at the age of puberty, in the clans where the custom of circumcising has disappeared ; boys and girls then choose new names. Men and women who undergo initiation adopt a new name. So do those subjected to the treatment for possession ; these take the name of their pretended possessor when he has made himself known. I refer the reader to Appendix II for further information regarding Thonga names.

Premature Birth. When a child is born prematurely and is very small and delicate, he is wrapped in the leaves of the castor-oil plant and put into a big pot, which is then exposed to the heat of the sun. This is a true incubator, and the treatment is said to be attended with success (Tobane).

Protracted Births and Illegitimate Births. There would seem to be no relation between these; but to the Thonga mind, on the contrary, a protracted and difficult birth proves that the child is not legitimate. This conviction is so strong that when a woman knows that the child which she is going to bear is not the son of her husband (nuna) but of a lover (mbuye), she will admit this secretly to the principal midwife, in order to spare herself the pains of a difficult birth, as it is taboo to bear a "child of adultery" hiding the fact : it would cause the mother untold suffering.

Therefore, if the delivery lasts too long, the midwife will begin to have doubts as to the legitimacy of the child. The first thing she will do is to send word to the husband. He knows what it means. He takes in his *shifado* (2) a little of his *semen*, mixes it with water in a shell of sala (the big round fruit of the Strychnos) and the woman drinks it. It may be that then the child will "feel his father," if the husband is really his father, and that this will bring the birth to a prompt conclusion ; but

(1) I know of an exception to this rule. The son of the Mabota chief was named Nhwanin, a girl's name, in order to deceive the malevolent powers which had killed his brothers and sisters.

(2) See Annotatio 1 at the end of the volume in the collection of Latin notes written for medical men and ethnographers

if this result is not attained, it is a proof that the child is really illegitimate and the midwife will force the woman to confess her guilt and the name of her lover. Should she have had many and hide the names of some of them "the womb will refuse" (khuri dji ta yala) and the birth will be possible only when the confession is complete.

Should an illegitimate child be born without this delay, he will come to the light with his hands closed and refuse to take the breast. This will give the midwife an opportunity of extorting a confession from the mother. These women practise a special kind of divination : they take a broken pot, put pumpkin seeds into it and place it on the fire. If the seeds, instead of burning to a cinder, explode with a noise, it is a proof that the woman is guilty. Each explosion means a lover, and all their names must be revealed. (Tobane.) This confession is strictly private. The midwives will consider it a professional duty not to divulge the secret to anyone, even the father. But the mother must confess, as it is absolutely necessary that the true father of a child be known on the day of its birth.

It is taboo for the lover of the woman to come to the door of the hut after the birth of the illegitimate child as long as the umbilical cord has not fallen off. The child would die. Even later on, should the mother be sitting on the threshold of the hut with the baby in her arms, and the man pass along the street in front of them, one of the midwives will go (has she not heard the confession ?) and take between her fingers a pinch of sand from the footprints of the lover, and, without a word, will throw it on the fontanella of the baby. If the husband happens to be present, he will know by witnessing this act that he is not the true father. I do not think he will be very angry. The child is his and, if it is a girl, nobody else will "eat the oxen !" For him this is the main consideration !

As regards the birth of twins, we shall study later on the strange customs which accompany it : in olden times one of the children was killed ; except in such a case, no child is ever put to death wilfully on the day of its birth.

II. *The first week ; Confinement Period.*

From the day of birth till the moment when the umbilical
cord falls, seven days may elapse : this forms a special period
called *busahana*, which is the period of confinement for both
mother and child. It will be concluded by the special ceremony
of the child's first outing, marked by the rite of the broken pot.
During these seven or eight days, *the mother* is restricted to a
special diet, and this is a true "marginal period" for her. She is
absolutely outside the pale of society. The diet is prescribed by
the family doctor, who knows how to treat children, and consists
of a special dish prepared with Kafir corn (1) (mabele) and called
shimhimbi, with which special medicines have been mixed. The
aim of this medication (khwebela busahana) is twofold : first to
expel the unclean blood which follows the birth, and which is a
very great taboo, and secondly to stimulate the production of the
milk. This food is cooked in a special pot (shikhwebelo sha
busahana) and is eaten not with the hands, as some particles of the
unclean blood might enter it and cause the mother to become
phthisic, but with a special spoon.

Both the pot and the spoon will be fastened over the entrance
of the hut, inside (shirangen sha nyangwa), at the end of this
period of seclusion.

A fowl is also killed during these first days, a hen if the child
is a girl, a cock if it is a boy. Some medicinal powder is poured
into the broth, and the mother drinks it and eats part of the meat,
the husband eating the remainder. This little luxury is indulged
in as it helps the mother to recover her strength sooner ; she is
attended to by her own mother, who has been summoned as soon
as the birth has been satisfactorily effected, and who helps her to
feed the child.

---

(1) This use of Kafir corn in this and other old rites proves the antiquity of this
cereal. It is probably the first which was known to the Natives. Maize is quite a
modern food amongst the Thongas, though the time of its introduction is not known.
See Part IV.

The Evolution of a Man from Birth to Death

As regards *the child*, the umbilical cord is anointed every day ; he begins to take the breast and drink the "*milombyana*," the great medicine which we shall describe later on.

During these days many taboos must be observed :

The *husband* is not allowed to enter the hut on any pretext ; this is not on account of his being unclean, quite the contrary. A birth does not contaminate the father amongst the Ba-Thonga as it does in other tribes. He is not obliged to undergo any medication. His exclusion from the conjugal hut is due entirely to the fact that his wife is polluted by the blood of the lochia, and he would run the greatest danger to himself if he came near.

All married people are also excluded (bakhili) viz. all those who have regular sexual intercourse. Should they touch the child, he would die. If however a woman wishes very much to go and see the new-born, she must abstain from relations with her husband during two days. Then she can be admitted into the hut. On the other hand young girls are welcome in the hut, but they must not kiss the baby during these first days. "It is not yet firm ; it is only water," as they say ; later on, when it begins to laugh and to play, they may kiss it. Even the father may do so then ; when he comes back from a journey, he holds it in his arms and kisses it on the temple. Supposing that the umbilical cord has now fallen off normally, the confinement period will be at an end. This termination is marked by two rites.

The mother of the delivered woman will have *to smear with clay the floor of the hut*. This is the great cleansing act which brings to an end a marginal period. It takes away all the dangerous blood, and the husband as well as all the other dwellers in the village will be allowed to enter the hut.

The second act is *the rite of the broken pot* (ku tjibelela shirengelen, viz. to make fire under the shirengele, the bit of broken pot used for the purpose). This is a medical treatment and a religious ceremony combined. It is performed by the family doctor on the threshold of the hut in the following way : he puts into this piece of broken pottery pieces of skin of all the beasts of the bush : antelopes, wild cats, elephants, hippopotami, rats, civet cats, hyenas, elands and snakes of dangerous kinds, and roasts

43

them till they burn. The smoke then rises, and he exposes the child to it for a long time : the body, face, nose and mouth. The baby begins to cry ; he sneezes, he coughs ; this is just what is wanted. Then the doctor takes what remains of the pieces of skin, grinds them, makes a powder, mixes it with *tihuhlu* (1) grease of the year before last and consequently hard enough to make an ointment. With this ointment he rubs the whole body of the child, especially the joints, which he extends gently in order to assist the baby's growth.

All this fumigation and manipulation is intended to act as a preventive. Having been thus exposed to all external dangers, dangers which are represented by the beasts of the bush, the child may go out of the hut. He is now able "to cross the foot prints of wild beasts" (tjemakanya mitila) without harm. Snakes will not bite him, at any rate their bite will not hurt him ; lions will not kill him. The remainder of the powder is put into a little bit of reed closed at both ends, which the mother has to carry with her during the whole nursing period in order to continue the treatment.

This rite of the broken pot is also the great preventive remedy against the much dreaded ailment of babies, *convulsions*. If a child suffers from this, they will say : "a tlalile shirengelen," viz. "he did not find any help in the broken pot" and the parents will go to another doctor whose drugs are more powerful, to have the child once more exposed to the smoke. It may even be that a grown-up man will undergo this treatment again, if he has been ill with convulsions, but, in this case, the broken pot with its pieces of skin is put on the head of the patient, which has been first covered with a wisp of cuscuta (hare dja yendjeyendje). The great aim of all the medication of children by the "mi-lombyana" is also to fight against convulsions, as we shall see (2).

(1) The tihuhlu are the seeds of the nkuhlu tree known under the name of mafu-reira. They are oleaginous and the fat (mafura) obtained from them is very much used for external applications amongst the Thongas.

(2) In *Savage Childhood* p. 12, Dudley Kidd describes this "baptism of smoke" amongst Zulus. Some dirt is scraped from the father's body and is mixed with other drugs in order to impart to the child his ancestral spirit. Another ingredient

The Evolution of a Man from Birth to Death

The Thonga child is always received into this world with great joy by the whole family. If it is a girl, it means oxen to buy a wife for one of the sons later on ; therefore it means increase not only in the wealth but in the number of the members of the family. If it is a boy, there is no direct material enrichment, but the clan has been strengthened and the name of the father is glorified and perpetuated. In the case of the birth of a first-born child (ñwana wa matibula), a special ceremony is performed at the end of the first week. When the grandmother has smeared the hut, she goes home, summons all the female relatives, sometimes as many as ten or fifteen ; they take with them food, ochre and fat prepared for this purpose. Two or three men accompany them. They enter the village of the child executing a special dance called *khana*, and singing the following song (which is the proper song to glorify a first-born) :

I celebrate my pot which has done *ngelebendje*...

They compare the child with a pot of clay which has gone through the firing process. It has been tried as one always tries a pot by letting it fall to the ground ; but it is not shattered, because it has not cracked in the furnace, it has kept intact ! This is what is meant by the descriptive adverb ngelebendje.

Then they smear the baby, the mother, the father, everybody in the village with ochre. It is a great feast. A goat will be killed, if possible, because the father and mother have "found a village" (kuma muti) by the child, they have "grown roots" (mila mitju). This is a law, but its omission is not taboo. When the grandparents do not perform this ceremony, it is an insult to the parents of the child, but no evil consequence will follow.

is a meteorite ground to fine powder. It is interesting to compare this use of the meteorite with the fact that, amongst the Thongas, this fumigation is intended to prevent convulsions. Convulsions, as we shall see (Part VI. Chap. II. B) are caused by the mysterious power of Heaven. The meteorite has fallen from Heaven. Thus the baptism of smoke aims at bringing the child under the influence of the two main elements of Bantu religion : the ancestor gods and Heaven.

For any subsequent children, the feast will be reduced to the presentation by the grandmother of a basket of food to *"tlangela ñwana,"* viz. to "celebrate the child."

III. *The Nursing Period.*

The little child has been taken out of the confinement hut (humesha busahanen). He is now allowed to go outside. The

nursing period then begins and will last two and a half or three years ; but before we study the rites which mark it, let us consider the manner in which the baby is carried and his diet during this period.

1) THE NTEHE.

A little child is not carried by his mother in her arms, but in a softened skin which is called *ntehe*. The preparation of the ntehe is subject to many prescribed customs.

The first of these is this : the ntehe must not be looked out before the birth of the child, or it would bring misfortune. This is a taboo which I might call a "taboo of prevision." Some other taboos of this kind are met with in our tribe.

For a first-born child, the skin must be provided by the maternal uncle. This is a rule, but the custom is not tabooed (1). The father may also prepare it, if

A South-African woman with her child in the ntehe.

necessary.

The ntehe must not be a sheep skin. That is taboo. Let them take the skin of a duiker (blue antelope), of a goat or of a mhala (impala). Sheep skins are

(1) Though the term taboo generally means a prohibition, I take the liberty of using it in a positive sense : A custom is taboo or is tabooed when its transgression is a taboo.

only employed when three or four children have died in previous years and the mother is in the state of destitution called *buwumba*. (Chap. II.)

The ntehe is arranged in such a way that the legs of the animal are used as straps, the forelegs are tied around the neck, the hindlegs around the waist and the child is in that way held well against his mother's shoulders. He can either show his head outside his ntehe or be entirely covered by it. This way of carrying babies is very convenient : mother and child get so accustomed to it that a baby, when you lift it, stretches out its legs at once at right angles with its body in order to sit on its mother's back ; and the mother can easily do all her work, even till her fields with the baby on her back in its ntehe !

2) THE DIET DURING THE NURSING PERIOD.

The child is nursed by the mother. He is allowed to take the breast at any time. There is nothing like a diet regulation amongst Natives and they would deem it cruelty to refuse the breast to a crying child.

There are some customs relating to the *milk*. When a mother has to leave her child for a short time, she squeezes a few drops of her milk on his neck in order to prevent him feeling thirsty. When she has been absent for more than one day (this can only happen when the child is able to eat some solid food) and returns home, before nursing the child again she heats a bit of broken pot in the fire and squeezes into it a little milk from each breast. The liquid evaporates. The reason of the custom is this : the mother's milk has grown cold ; it must be warmed again ; otherwise the child will be constipated. This is a taboo (1). When a baby bites the teat, it is regarded as naughtiness and the mother scratches its forehead as a punishment.

Mothers not having enough milk use a kind of shrub called

(1) Compare with the Zulu milk charms described by D. Kidd, *Savage Childhood*, page 38.

neta as a medecine. The shrub, which is an Euphorbiacea, contains milky sap. It is a treatment based on the principle : Similia similibus curantur.

The Thongas believe that milk alone would never suffice to make a child grow : *Ñwana a ḳula hi miri, the child grows by medicine,* such is the adage which is universally met with. When you see a woman carrying a child on her back, you will notice hanging to the *ntehe* the reed (lihlanga) containing the black powder which protects against the dangers of the bush, and a little calabash half filled with water. This water is not pure water, it is the medicine called *milombyana.* This word is the plural and diminutive form of *nombo,* which means baby's ailment. There is a great *ñombo,* convulsions, also called *tilo,* heaven, because this complaint is brought into a mysterious connection with the influence of Heaven (See Part VI). There is a small *nombo* ; this is the infantile diarrhea which so often troubles little children ; but both diseases are supposed to be caused by the *nyoḳa,* the intestinal parasite, the worm or snake (nyoka means both) which is in every child and must always be combated because, if unchecked, it will pass from the bowels to the stomach ; it will come and beat the fontanella (1) and will finally penetrate the chest. Then the little one will turn up his eyes, be seized by convulsions and die. Happily there are some drugs which have a wonderful effect on this dangerous guest ! One of my neighbours, who was a convert in Rikatla, gave me their names. The first is a very common Protacea (?) with large husks called the Dlanyoka, "the one which kills worms." Mixed with the roots of a Leguminacea called *Ñwamahlanga* and with two other plants found near the sea, it forces the worm to keep quiet. These drugs are boiled and the decoction is carefully poured into a special little pot called *hlembetwana ya milombyana* which will be kept in the hut. Every morning the mother will warm the pot a little, pour some of its contents into a shell of sala and give the child a

(1) Tjaba-tjaba, the fontanella, plays a great part in the diagnosis of children's doctors and they often cover it with black wax. When the child hiccoughs, his mother or somebody else will blow on the fontanella to prevent vomiting. This will " make his heart stand " (yimisa mbilu).

mouthful to drink, then dip her finger into the medecine and let two or three drops fall from it on the fontanella ; then she spits on the lower part of the shell and presses it all along the sternum of the baby as far as the navel. This is said to "nurse the child, to make him grow." Should he be sick, this treatment will be repeated many times a day. If he is well and goes about with his mother, she will pour the *milombyana* into the small calabash and give him a few sups from it from time to time.

The child must never drink ordinary water, but only the *milombyana* decoction. It is a taboo. Should the mother travel far from home and leave behind her the *milombyana* pot, she is allowed to add some water to the calabash, but she must always leave a little of the decoction in the calabash before doing so. The mother herself is not allowed to drink the water of another country. She must only drink water from home and, if she is forced to travel, she must take a little powder from the reed each time she drinks, so that the child may become familiarised with that country (1). These laws must be kept during all the nursing period.

The child begins to eat *solid food* as soon as his teeth are cut, and when he is able to take it with his own hands. But some people do not like to give it to him too soon, as they say his stools become fetid. When later on he is able to go outside and to take care of himself, then he can eat any ordinary food.

If the mother dies during the nursing period, the little one is almost sure to follow her. The baby is fed with goat's or cow's milk, but the Natives do not know that they must add water to it ; sooner or later therefore the child dies of enteritis.

I have heard of some cases in which another woman has taken charge of the child, nursed him with her own milk and weaned him successfully ; her own child being older, she weaned him earlier than the usual time and nursed the other child in his

---

(1) A similar custom is observed in the case of moving from one country to another. When a Ronga comes back from Kimberley having found a wife there, both bring with them a little of the earth of t e place they are leaving, and the woman must eat a little of it every day in her porridge in order to accustom herself to her new abode. This earth provides the transition between the two domiciles !

place. These women were wives of the same husband at Libombo near Rikatla and the foster mother claimed compensation for her deed. Another wonderful case is the following : a woman died shortly after the birth of her boy called Mayimbule ; the

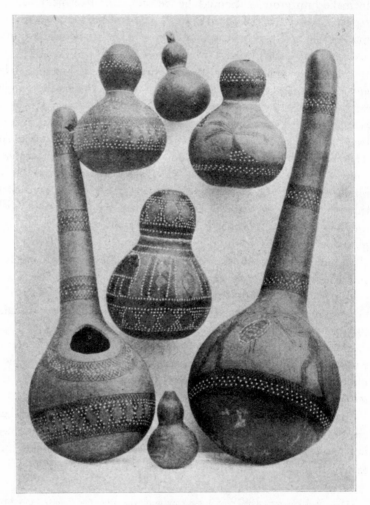

Thonga calabashes

The smallest are used for keeping medicinal powders (tinhungubane). The next in size (minkhubi) are employed for the milombyana. Those with the long handles are the mintcheko, used as bottles or for drinking.

grandmother, by name Mishidohi, who had an adult son and had had no other child since, prepared light beer and other appropriate food and succeeded in secreting milk in her own breast ; so the child was saved !

A child during these first months of its existence is regarded as a very weak creature. "I mati !" i. e. "It is nothing but water !" Hence perhaps the curious idea that a baby, just like a new born animal, is able to swim, at any rate it cannot be drowned : it floats on the water. When a woman carrying a little child on her back crosses a river and is in danger of being swept away by the stream, people shout to her from the shore : "Untie the 'ntehe' and let the baby cross. Think of yourself, the little one will follow all right." They say: "Psa yila, it is taboo that a baby should sink." Note the curious use of the word "yila" in this sentence.

3) DENTITION.

As soon as the child has cut the two lower and upper incisors, the mother takes a white bead (tjambu) and ties it to one of the child's hairs above the forehead. This white bead is said to help the other teeth to come out normally. If this precaution were not taken, the child would not become intelligent ; he would shiver instead of smiling ; he would bring forward his lips and his tongue to prevent the air from getting into his mouth ! When all the teeth are duly cut, the bead is removed and thrown away *talen*, viz. on the *tala*. The *tala* is the ash-heap, the place behind the hut on which everyone throws ashes and dirt. It plays a great part in the customs of the Thongas and other South African Bantus.

The teeth (tinyo-menyo) of the children are called figuratively *hobe*. The *hobe* (pl. *tihobe*) means the grain of pounded maize which is white and very similar to a tooth. Hence the expression : "A humi hobe," "he has got out a grain of maize," employed to indicate the cutting of the teeth.

When a child cuts his upper teeth first, it is a bad omen. In the Northern clans and especially amongst the Ba-Pedi, it is a great taboo. At his death the child must be buried in wet soil.

Amongst the Ba-Ronga the ill-omen is not considered so serious.

Later on, when the child loses his first teeth, he must not let them fall out hap-hazard anywhere. He must take the fallen tooth, go to the ash-heap, put his finger into the hole and say : "Kokwa, kokwa, ndji hwe hobe !" (Grandfather, grandfather, give me a grain of maize !) Then he throws the tooth over his shoulder on to the ashes and goes home without looking backward. Should he look backward, his grandfather (the spirit of the departed ?) would not give him a new tooth (1). This custom is no longer taboo and is disappearing.

When a younger brother cuts his teeth, they are considered as pushing away or pulling out the teeth of the elder, as the younger brother comes into the world, as a rule, three years after the elder.

As regards *hair*, the first cutting is accompanied by the following custom : the mother sprinkles some drops of her milk on the forehead and on the occiput of the child ; then she cuts his hair and throws it away in the midst of thick grass. When she cuts her own hair, she always leaves a lock on both sides of the head for the amusement of the child, till he is able to walk.

Nursing women very often anoint themselves with ochre. This is said to be in order to prevent their husbands from having relations with them.

These rites are not considered as very important. But there are three others which are most punctiliously observed, and which divide the nursing period into three subperiods : the presentation to the moon, after three months, the tying of the cotton string, after one year, and the weaning ceremonies at the close of the period.

4) The presentation to the moon (ku yandla).

The appearance of the new moon is always received with cheers by the Ba-Ronga. The first person who sees it shouts :

(1) Comparative Ethnography : I remember quite well that, when I was a boy, we were told in Neuchâtel that we must not let a broken tooth get lost, lest it should be found by a dog and a dog's tooth would grow in its stead !

THE EVOLUTION OF A MAN FROM BIRTH TO DEATH

"Kengelekezeeeee!" and this exclamation is repeated from one village to another. *Kenge* is the descriptive adverb which means the form of the crescent of the moon. Each "moon," or month, is considered as being a new one, the old one having died, and there were special names for each month of the year (See Part VI).

As soon as the mother of the child has resumed her menses (the menses are called tinwheti, months) and this happens as a rule on the third month after the delivery amongst Thonga women, she takes her garments, washes them, puts on new clothing and then proceeds to the ceremony of the *yandla*. The child must be "given his month." This is done in the following way. The day the new moon appears, the mother takes with her a torch or merely a brand from the fire and the grandmother follows her carrying the child : both go to the ash-heap behind the hut. There the mother throws the burning stick towards the moon and the grandmother flings the child into the air saying : "This is your moon!" (hweti ya ku hi yoleyo) : then she puts the child on to the ashes. The little one cries and rolls over in the dirt on the ash-heap. Then his mother snatches him up (wutla), nurses him, and they go home.

This ceremony, which is certainly a rite of passage, is said to "open the chest of the child" otherwise "his ears would die," he would remain stupid. When a child is not intelligent, it is usual to say to him : You have not been shown your moon! (1)

Therefore the *yandla* means a progress made by the child, the entrance into a new phase of his existence. The fact is emphasised by the three following changes which take place on the day of the yandla : 1) Henceforth his father is allowed to take the child in his arms. Up to that day, this was taboo, as the child being continually with his mother was perhaps polluted by the dangerous blood following the birth ; but now she has washed her clothing and has been purified by the reappearance of the menses ; so the danger no longer exists. 2) It is now

(1) However the name of the child's month is soon forgotten and is never afterwards recalled. This seems to show that the custom is dying out, as well as the knowledge of the names of the various months.

permissible to push him gently by his elbows and 3) to sing him
songs to console him (khongota) when he cries. This was taboo
before the presentation to the moon.

There is another custom which seems to be confounded sometimes with the yandla. It is also performed for small children
and is called : *kulakulisa*. When a friend of the family passes
through the village coming from afar, from Johannesburg for
instance, he takes the new-born child in his arms, throws him
up and says : "Kula-kula-kula, u ya tlhasa Johan." (Grow, grow,
grow and reach Johannesburg.) This is a minor custom (nau
nyana) ; it is more or less play and is not tabooed like the yandla.
After the yandla, a new therapeutic agent is added to the decoction
of milombyana, the *biyeketa*. *Ku biyeketa* means : "to put inside
an enclosure." Twice a month during the afternoon, when the
moon is new and when it is full, the family doctor goes to the kraal
of the baby, he lights a fire before the door of the hut and cooks
his medicines with water in a pot till they boil. Then he draws
the embers to one side of the pot and lays on them a big pill,
a *mhula*. The *mhula* is made of fat from an ox paunch or from
a goat's paunch mixed with medicinal powder. Then he places
a mat on end so as to make a small round enclosure : mother
and baby enter it, and he covers them with a piece of cotton
cloth. They expose themselves to the steam which comes from
the pot and to the smoke which emanates from the mhula. When
both have copiously perspired and the emanation has come to an
end, the mother tells the doctor to uncover them, and they emerge
from the vapour bath. Then the doctor cuts both of them with
a razor on the forehead, on the sternum, on the spine between the
shoulders, on the elbow, on the wrist, on the knees and introduces
a little of his medicinal powder into the small wounds. The pot
with the hot decoction is then taken by the doctor behind the hut,
the mother accompanying him. She pours a little of the water
into his hands : he spits into it, uttering the sound *tsu* (which is the
sacramental act in ordinary worship) and throws it on the child.
The mother rubs the whole body of the little one with it ; in the
meantime the doctor prays to his gods, viz. the spirits of his
ancestors. Begining with the formula of invocation which doctors

always use, he says : "Abusayi, akhwari ! This is the child !
May he grow ! May he become a man by means of this medicine
of mine ! May his perspiration be good ; may the impurity go
away ; may it go to Shiburi, to Nkhabelane ! (1) May the child
play well, be like his companions. This is not my first attempt !
You have given me these drugs ; may they protect him against
disease so that nobody may say there is no power in them, etc."
After this prayer the doctor takes the little child and goes back to
the central place of the village. The mother stays and washes
her own body with the decoction, praying also to her gods (but
without the *tsu*, as this has been uttered by the "master of the
drugs").

The treatment of the biyeketa is also called "hungulo dja
milombo," "the vapour bath for infantile diseases ;" it is not a
curative, but a preventive ; it aims at ascertaining if the child is
all right. If he has bad stools (a nga tlambi psinene) the mother
will perhaps remember that she has forgotten to enclose him
and she will call the doctor in at once. Should he fall sick, the
biyeketa will not be performed again but the milombyana will be
administered more frequently. However, it is of importance
for the growth of the child. To neglect it is taboo ! (2)

As for the cuts, sometimes they are followed by a second vapour
bath, as if the doctor wished to cause the medicine contained in
the smoke to penetrate through them into the body, in which case
he will only "close" them later on by introducing a healing
powder into them. Children generally cry when they see the
physician... They dread the pain of the cuts. When the mother
goes to the doctor's village, she takes with her the wood, the
mat and a pot of beer or a fowl in payment. The physician's
charge for a biyeketa is sixpence to one shilling or a hen or a pot
of beer.

(1) Viz. to the end of the world. These clans are far away to the north, outside
the Ronga country.
(2) I hear that the converts generally have not abandoned the biyeketa, but they do
not allow the doctor to perform the sacrificial act and to pray to the spirits. Sam
Ngwetsa, the children's physician of Rikatla used to pray thus : "O Father of mercy !
I pray thee ! I do not pray the dead but thee only who art in ·heaven ! Grant us
to see this child in good health, standing firm, this little lamb !"

5) The tying of the cotton string.

When the child "tiyelanyana" viz. "becomes a little firm," the mother, having to plough her fields and to cook the food, begins to seat him on the sandy soil, after having made a kind of hole of about five inches in depth. We have seen Thonga babies already sitting at the age of two months. But this "dumping" hardly meets all the requirements, and the mother looks for a girl to help her to take care of the baby (wa ku tlanga na ye, to play with him). She puts the child in the charge of an elder sister or a cousin ; a girl of five to ten is quite strong enough for the purpose. I have often admired the patience of these miniature nurses, sometimes not very much bigger than the child they carry, with their very troublesome babies.

But very soon the child begins to crawl (kasa) and this is the time when a very striking rite is performed. This rite seems to be practised all over the tribe, but it has more importance in the Northern clans than amongst the Ba-Ronga. I shall here give the description of Viguet, who belonged to the Tsungu clan and had emigrated to the Spelonken. My readers must forgive me if I cannot tell the story with all its details and if I am obliged to write some of them in Latin (1).

These are the ipsissima verba of my informant : "This is a great law amongst the Thongas. When a child begins to crawl, even before, the *puri* is tied round his waist. The *puri* is a cotton (2) string. Father and mother fix the day ; if they forget to do so, their parents, (the grandparents) will remind them of the law. They must have sexual intercourse, but in such a way that the mother will not become pregnant, s. n. i. (Annotatio 2). The mother will have to take in her hands "their filth" (thyaka ra bona) smear the string with it and tie it round the child. It will

(1) A more complete description of this rite and of some others related to the taboos of the Thongas will be found in the Revue d'Ethnographie et de Sociologie, Oct. 1910, Paris.

(2) There are plants of cotton probably subspontaneous in the Low Country of the Transvaal of Delagoa Bay.

remain there till it falls to pieces. After this operation the child is "grown up" and three things are allowed which were taboo before :

1) The child, if he dies, can be buried on the hill, in dry soil. Before the *boha puri* he would have been buried in wet soil, near the river, as is customary with twins and children who have cut their upper teeth first.

2) He can participate in the strange purification called *hlamba ndjaka* which takes place after the death of one of the inhabitants of the village (See ceremonies of death).

3) The parents can again have conjugal intercourse, though they must avoid conception till the child is weaned. Before this ceremony it was absolutely prohibited, and should they have sinned in this respect and the mother have conceived, they would be very guilty! It is a dangerous taboo! They would have "stolen" the child, stolen it from the law (yiba nawen). The child would not have "entered the law." It would be useless to tie the string round him in order to repair the evil done. Should he live long, should he even become an old man, he will have to be buried in wet soil, otherwise the rain would be prevented from falling.

Amongst the Malulekes and the Hlengwes such children are even burnt after their death. We shall speak later on about the mysterious relation established by the Thongas between these children, their burial, and the rain.

Amongst the Ba-Ronga this rite is called *boha nshale* (to tie the cotton) and can be performed in the same way or even more simply by the father (Annotatio 3). Parents, when they have duly tied the string on the little one, are said to have *fuya ñwana*, viz. taken possession of the child.

Amongst them again, another thing is then allowed which was taboo before. The child can be carried on the shoulders without ntehe by the arms alone (hi minkono).

It is clear that the tying of the cotton string means the official reception of the child into the family, even into human society. Before that, he was hardly considered as a human being, he was *shilo* (a thing), *khuna* (an incomplete being). Now he is *nkulu*, a grown up child (1).   The expression *fuya ñwana* confirms our explanation.   This custom is not a protective rite : the physician has nothing to do with it ; it is really an act by which the new-born child becomes a regular member of the community.   The strict prohibition of renewed conception before this rite has been accomplished is evidently dictated by the feeling that another child must not appear before this one has been duly received into the family.

6) THE WEANING.

A whole year, even more, will elapse after the *boha puri* before the little one can be weaned.   He will learn to speak and to walk, and it is only when his intelligence is sufficiently developed to allow him to run small errands that the date of the weaning will be fixed.   When his parents can send him to the next hut to ask for snuff and see him coming back holding the tobacco, they say : "Now the time has come !"

The rite of weaning is accomplished in the following manner in Nondwane.   (Mboza).

First of all, the father looks for a young *ntjopfa* tree which has only one root.   The ntjopfa is an anonacea bush, which colonists sometimes call the wild custard.   (Its fruit is very much like custard fruit and it is said that the true cultivated custard can be grafted on it).   The root of this tree is said to have the property of making people forget.   The mother cooks a pot of Kafir corn in which she has put the medicine.   This will help the child to forget the breast.   But the great act is the *hondlola* which takes place under the direction of the physician. The mother pounds some mealies, pours water on them and adds some leaven ; in this way she makes a little light beer (buputju).   She keeps a little of the bran of the pounded mealies. The doctor comes, kills a chicken and sprinkles this bran with the blood and *hahla*, viz. offers a regular sacrifice.   He prays to the spirits of his own family and asks those of the child's family to

(1) This word *khuna* is also employed to designate boys who have not yet gone through the circumcision school.   *Bukhuna* is the despicable state of uncircumcision. The state of a child before the ceremony of *boha puri* is another kind of bukhuna.

join with them in blessing the little one.   The beak of the sacrificed hen, one of the claws and one of the feathers (psirungulo) will be tied together round the child's neck.   A mat is spread on the ground ; the child is laid on it and greased with oil and powder brought by the physician.   Then he is smeared and rubbed with the bran.   The particles which fall on the mat are called *timhore*. They are gathered by the mother who makes a ball of them.   In the meantime the father looks for the nest of a certain kind of large ant which is common in the bush.   It lives in the earth, but the opening of its hole is tolerably large.   There the mother goes at sunset.   She introduces the ball into the hole so that the ant will be obliged to take all the *timhore* into the nest.   Then she returns home without looking behind her.   It is taboo ; should she transgress this rule, she would bring back disease to her child.

This rite is the ordinary *hondlola rite* which is performed in this or in a similar way at the close of any serious disease as the conclusion of the treatment, with the view of taking away the defilement of disease.   After having *hondlola*, the physician asks for the payment of his fees.   For a child he will ask ten shillings or five coins of five hundred reis (1).

This hondlola reveals to us the true conception of the nursing period held by the Natives.   For them these three first years of the child's life are a period of disease ; so many perils threaten the little one's well-being that he can hardly be considered healthy. He is during the whole time under the supervision of the physician, who takes leave of the little patient on the day of the weaning.

This view of infancy accounts also for some other taboos.   It is *yila* for instance to say of a child who is particularly fat : Wa tika, he is heavy : this would bring mishap to him.   One must say : A kota ribye, he is like a stone !   It is taboo also in Shiluvane to make use before a child of the word *mfene*, baboon.   There is a disease which is called by that name and it would come upon him. One must say : the thing which inhabits the hills, and so on...

---

(1) In the Mpfumu clan the rite of weaning is somewhat different.   I have published in " Les Ba-Ronga " a description of it given by Tobane.   It seems that the elements of the cotton string rite and of the broken pot rite are mixed with the proper weaning rite.   I think that the description of Mboza is more trustworthy.

The very day of his weaning, the child must leave the village of his parents and go to stay with his grandparents. A little mat and a few clothes have been prepared for him and the grandmother comes to take him. If he is the first-born, he must go to the parents of the mother ; the second child will be received by the parents of the father. Sometimes father and mother accompany their offspring themselves, during the night, to make the separation easier. It is a sad day for them as well as for the child! The following day the parents go again to see how the little one has stood their absence. They do not enter the village. They remain hidden in the little copse and look at their child through the branches! He must not see his mother, otherwise he would cry... A touching scene indeed!

Should the weaned child be obliged to stay with his parents, the mother will smear her breast with Jamaica pepper (biribiri) so that he may lose his taste for the maternal milk as quickly as possible.

The act of weaning is called *lumula*. It comes from the verb *luma* to bite, followed by the reversive suffix *ula* which means to take away, to undo (like *un* in undo). The mother as well as the child are said to have *lumuka* viz. to be in that state when weaning has been accomplished. This word is pronounced with a curious smile, because the act of weaning is in direct relation with the sexual life. As we have seen, sexual intercourse is absolutely prohibited before the tying of the cotton string, viz. for one year after the birth. Afterwards it is allowed, but the mother must not conceive another child before she has weaned the one she is nursing. The law is even more stringent : she must not conceive before her milk has entirely passed away (phya mabelen), after the weaning ceremony, because if she became pregnant, that would "cross the way of the weaned child" (tjemakanya ñwana), cut "his road" (tjemela), "go beforehand" (rangela) ; he would become thin, paralysed, with big holes below the shoulders. He must first be firm (tiyela), then a new pregnancy will not be able to cause him to suffer from dysentery or other ailments!

Often the parents do not observe this very hard law! If they see that conception has taken place before the child is weaned, they will hasten the ceremony. But they will be severely judged by the old people. Should the little one be sick, the husband will be scolded by the parents of the mother. They will say : "A djambeli ñwana," he has caused damage to the child! If a man forces his wife to transgress the law, she will run during the night to the hut of her husband's father to tell him. Actually this is a very rare occurrence. Children follow each other regularly at an interval of two and a half or three years, and seldom is the law transgressed which says : A mother must nurse her child during three "hoes," viz. three ploughing seasons.

B. CHILDHOOD

The infant, shiputja (Ro.) shihlangi (Dj.) is on the way to become a boy, mufana. During the first years of this period, which extends from the third to the fourteenth year, he stays with his grandparents. They do not give him much "education." He grows at Mother Nature's good pleasure. And as Nature is not always synonymous with morality, he sometimes commits bad actions. Sometimes also, fearing chastisement for a particularly wicked deed, he flees from the kraal of the grand-parents and goes home, where the paternal hand will hold him a little more firmly. But the father does not bother much with these little boys and they enjoy an immense amount of liberty. These years are perhaps the happiest of their whole life. They spend their time in the following occupations : herding the goats, stealing, catching game, learning the science of the velt, playing.

1) Herding the goats.

Just as the Kaffir corn is the old Thonga cereal which is used alone in the rites, so the goat is the domestic animal par excellence, no doubt the first which the tribe knew and that which is always employed in the sacrifices. Goats are very common ; everybody possesses one or two. They are kept together in one of the villages and the sons of the master of the village or of the other proprietors must tend them. They "stay with the goats" (tjhama timbutin) till their tenth or eleventh year and afterwards they are promoted to the care of the oxen, supposing there are oxen in the village.

The young goatherds, with hardly anything on—a meagre

Photo. H.-A. Junod.

Boys herding goats on the Shiluvane plain

(In the background, the Mamotswiri mountain).

belt of tails or bits of skin hanging from their loins, sometimes only in front, nothing behind,—go to the velt playing on their little trumpets, made of a bone or a reed. They pass by the gardens, and the goats look with one eye at the green mealies, the fresh leaves of the sweet potatoes which are not protected by stone walls, (there is hardly a stone all over the Thonga country) nor by barbed wire fences. But the boys are on the watch and "cut the road" from the goats (tjemetela) to keep them away from the gardens. They safely reach the little plain where nothing but hard Gramineae grow. There the boys begin to play, having handed over the charge of the goats to the youngest of the party. The little chap gets tired of watching ; little by little the whole herd goes back to the forbidden garden and eats greedily of the savoury stems of the mealies! After a while, the boys discover that the goats are gone. They run after them, and bring them back. But the mistress of the garden passes near by, coming back from the well with her pitcher on her head. She sees the harm done, inspects the traces of the goats, knows by them which herd has plundered her field, uproots some of the spoiled stems and with great clamour goes to the village of the guilty boys and throws down the mealies right before the hut of the father. No compensation is claimed in such a case, generally, but the father will thrash the boys when they come back ; or should there be a recurrence of the offence, the husband of the owner of the garden will himself administer a correction to the careless goatherds.

Boys herding the goats have certain customs. When one of them emits a certain unseemly sound from the rectum, the others say to him : "Fakisa !" He must answer : "Cita munyakanya goben." (I have let out my wind by the rectum). This formula, which is Zulu, is secret. If he does not know it, they beat him and make him look after the goats till the end of the day. Should another boy reveal the answer to the uninitiated, they will punish him in the same way.

2) STEALING.

What were they doing when the goats escaped ? They had probably themselves succeeded in stealing some sweet potatoes and were roasting them on a little fire, well hidden in the velt. Or they had discovered in the bush a broken pot, an old disused and perforated mortar, which some one had placed there to attract bees. And indeed there was honey inside. They had stolen it.. Goatherds are regular thieves and known as such.

Generally speaking the elder boys send the younger to commit these thefts, and the plunder is enjoyed by the whole company. They threaten to beat them if they return empty-handed. A sad fate for the youngsters—blows on all sides ; blows from the owners of the fields if they are caught, blows from their comrades if they bring nothing back with them!

Here are one or two tricks employed by the little thieves. In order to take a water-melon (khalabatla) out of a field without being noticed by the women who are busy pulling up their ground nuts, they cut the stalk and fasten it to a piece of string. The other end of this is attached to the leg of the thief, who moves away slowly, drawing the water-melon after him. When he is out of reach of the women, he hastily puts it under his arm and makes off at top speed.

To catch a hen without its making a sound, they dig a little hole behind the huts of the village, and put a few grains of maize in it. The fowl puts its head into the hole to eat the grains, and immediately the little rascal who was watching from behind a bush, rushes out, seizes it by the neck and carries it off before it can utter a single cry!

The penalty when a boy is caught is a good whipping without a fine. "Psa batjongwana ! It is an action of little boys !" These minor thefts are not considered serious.

3) CATCHING GAME.

Hunger is the constant companion of these boys, who do not get enough to eat at home. It is true they ate to their heart's content (shura) yesterday evening, but this morning they had only a very scanty breakfast (fihluta). They try to satisfy their never satisfied appetite by catching game : not big game of course, as they have no real weapons, but birds, field-mice, eggs in the nests (the less fresh they are, the better, because there is more meat inside!) etc. To get birds they throw their sticks at them, and are very clever at killing a partridge as it rises heavily from the grass ; or they make traps with a flexible stick to which they tie a string with a bait. They bend the stick, set the trap by means of a little bit of wood, and when the bird puts its beak into the bait, it is caught round the neck by the string. On the borders of the lake of Rikatla, boys used to catch even big birds with these traps. They set many kinds of snares. One is a cage made of sticks of palm marrows which shuts automatically when a bird enters and eats the grain by which it has been attracted. They sometimes build two walls of sticks planted in the soil and converging to the same point, where they reach a little door provided with the trap. Hares are sometimes caught in this way. They follow the wall, and when they go through the door, they tread on a hurdle which is connected with a bent rod : the rod springs back and the hare is caught.

4) LEARNING THE SCIENCE OF THE BUSH.

This life in the velt, always in the midst of Nature, develops the power of observation amongst the boys. They know everything in the bush : the big Psyche caterpillar (Eumeta cervina), which hangs from the nembe-nembe shrub (Cassia petersiana) like a little bundle of sticks, and which they call *maha-mbanindlwane*, " the one who walks with his house ;" the big Carabid beetle which appears with the first rain, the Anthia alveolata, marked with large hollows on the elytra and

Phot. G. Liengme.
A Thonga boy.

which is therefore named " the son of the smallpox ." Indeed I found in Rikatla a boy who knew that a certain white cocoon found on the branches of the nkanye tree (Sclerocarya caffra) gives birth to the splendid green Queen Moth (Argema Mimosae). Having collected beetles and butterflies extensively for years, I have had an opportunity of recognizing the power of observation of these boys, who were my best hunters! Of course they particularly appreciate things edible... especially the *shitambela*, a big Bupresta beetle which they roast and suck.

65

Learning, as they do, the native names of all these creatures and their habits, they certainly acquire a great amount of knowledge during these years.

5) Playing.

Sometimes the weather is bad ; it rains or it is dreadfully hot. Then the goatherd suffers, and his elder brother comfortably sitting in the hut trills this song :

> Far away, there where he is, he weeps, the little boy.
> The keeper of the goats and of the calves !

But the bad days are rare and the boys play more than they cry! The *games* of the Thongas are very numerous and are played either during the day or in the evening, especially when the moon shines. I shall here only consider the boys' games, and speak of the girls' later on.

Ngulube yi da mimphobo. (The pig eats mealie cobs). One child plays the part of the pig ; crawling along, covered with a mortar and a piece of cloth, he goes from one hut to another followed by a troup of his friends, who clap their hands and sing the foregoing words. People give food to the pig. It is received by its friends. When they have visited all the yards, they assemble on the central place of the village and eat the food together. Sometimes the pig suddenly turns round and attacks his followers, who flee in terror.

The game of *nsema*. This is a disk of woven grass made by boys. They pick up sides. The nsema is set rolling by one side and the opponents must run towards it and pierce it with their sticks before it falls to the ground. It is not allowable to touch it when it has fallen (yi holile). This game goes on till the disk is quite spoilt (yi bolile). Then the two sides rush upon each other and exchange a sound cudgelling, after which they all go and bathe in the nearest pool without any ill-feeling.

There is another game played with this disk, the game of the *ndlopfa-ndlopfana* (that is to say " the little elephant"). A boy makes a nsema, ties it to a string made of the fibres of certain palm-trees, and hides.   His comrades try to pierce his grass disk. But he watches.   He has the right to chase them and to beat them with his stick.   If the opponent succeeds in piercing the disk, in pulling it and tearing it from the string, ndlopfa-ndlopfana is vanquished.

The game of *homane* is very similar to English hockey.   The fruit of a palm tree, which is round and very hard, is used as a ball, and hit with a stick into the opposite camp.   If the *homane* falls between the two camps, the players rush upon it and, with their sticks, try to send it into their opponents' quarters.

In another boys' game, the *tlhuba holwane*, which is played mostly by moonlight, they also take two sides.   A stick is planted in the earth by one side and a piece of charcoal placed upon it. One of the opponents comes, hopping like a frog, takes out the stick and, still hopping, goes and plants it in his own ground.   If he reaches the goal without falling, he has won.   An opponent will take his turn, pull out (tlhuba) the stick and bring it back to his partners.   Evidently the Ronga children find this amusing!

The game of the *beetle* (shifufunu) is played as follows : one child is the beetle, and, as a distinguishing mark, he puts a hand-kerchief round his head.   A hole is dug in the sand; he enters it and nestles in it as do some insects, until he is nearly covered with earth.   He remains there perfectly still whilst his comrades sing to him the following song :

Beetle of mine...
I will marry thee...   } Say " yes " to your brother.
For the price of an ox...

There is another game of the same kind : *the honey pitcher is stirred* (mbita ya bulombe ya reka-reka).   The children face each other in two rows and clasp hands.   One of them lays himself on their arms, and all swing him, singing the same song.

The boys also play the game of *the man with the huge back who could not get out* (shikulukukwana sha ku ka buhumo).   They form a circle, one standing in the centre.   He hunches his back and rushes forward, head foremost, trying to break the circle and to get out either between their legs or otherwise. If he does not succeed they give him this long and comical name : shikulu-kukwana sha ku ka buhumo.

Quite a number of little melodies are sung by children to certain animals. When we came back in the evening to the plain of Rikatla with our ox-drawn waggon, all the goatherds used to meet us and to accompany us a long stretch of the road, shouting in honour of the oxen : " Gweymanaô, Gweymanaô (1) "! Girls joined in the demonstration, pointing out the strange machine to the babies carried on their shoulders (2).

Nkwama wa ku. (Your purse)... When they eat green mealies, one of the older goatherds gives to another some of the leaves covering the cob and tells him to go and throw them away. He refuses to do so. Then the elder one collects all these leaves, rolls them up in a ball and throws them to the boy who refused, saying to him : " Your purse ". The boy answers : " It is not mine! " They all run away. He picks up the ball and tries to throw it to another, saying the same thing. Should he miss him, they will mock him and say : " You are not a man, you are but a little boy! "

Shifufunu sha paripari. This is a kind of big Tenebrionida beetle which beats the ground with its abdomen (Psammodes Bertoloni). Groups of children, boys together or girls together, play two by two. One of the two lies down facing the ground and the other sits on his back, looking forwards, to guard the head of the one who is prone. He sings while beating the other's back : " Shifufunu sha paripari ndjuluka hi yetlele!... Beetle turn up that we may lie down! " At once all the children who were sitting throw themselves down and those who were lying down sit on their backs, and so on...

To develop their courage, boys have another more dangerous game ; this is *the war on the wasps* (mipfi). In their country there

(1) See for the tunes of these and other songs *Les Chants et les Contes des Ba-Ronga* pages 34 to 64, and also Vol. II. Part V. Ch. III.
(2) It is customary to show to babies extraordinary and fearful sights, a white man passing, for instance, in order to " open their minds. "

are big nasty yellow-brown hornets (a kind of Belonogaster) which build more or less circular nests, sometimes attaining to the size of a man's head. On a certain day the boys decide to make war on these enemies. They make shields with the leaves of the *nala* palm tree which they plait together.

They cut down branches, which they wave to protect themselves, and one of them goes and strikes a heavy blow on the wasps' nest! The irritated insects rush out on their assailants and sting them. The boys try to kill the wasps with their sticks or to crush them when they light on them. Sometimes, overcome by the pain, they run away ; sometimes, resisting to the last, they kill and exterminate their winged enemies.

Besides this there are also *big battles between the shepherds* of the different flocks. The shepherds amuse themselves by taking one another's cattle. Those who are the strongest bring the stolen herd triumphantly back to the neighbourhood of their village, but they would never let it enter the kraal. The vanquished call to their help their elder brothers, who come to recover their property and, if they can, give the thieves a sound thrashing!

Insults and fights are frequent between the clans. The boys of Mpfumu call out to those of Matjolo : " Forest gadders ! Eaters of snails and boas, of lizards and tortoises " (all of which are questionable food!) (In Ronga : Balala ! Badi ba tihumba ni tinhlaru ni makhwahle ni tinfutchu). Those of Matjolo answer them : " Crowd of women that you are, clad in cotton material! " (Babasati ! Matchimbamphela!), in reference to the fact that the inhabitants of Mpfumu, living near the town, some time ago replaced the belt of skins worn by the savages by a piece of cotton tied to the waist and hanging down to the knee (ladula).

The custom of frightening children with imaginary beasts is wide spread amongst the Thongas. The bogey man is called *Shingomu-Ngomu* or else *Shikunkununu*, and by this very expressive word they designate a huge and mighty being who walks, swaying his big body from right to left, with a sound like *ngomu-ngomu*. The ogre is *Shitukulumukumba*, a word coming originally from the Zulus, which corresponds to the Ronga *Ñwambilutimhokora*, that is to say : " the one who has scales on the heart. " He eats

69

human beings. These imaginary creatures play a large part in the native tales, especially the one who " has scales on the heart. " He feeds on vermin, lice and big white beetle larvae, which are his almonds (1).

When a child cries and cannot be comforted, someone goes and hides behind the hut and slaps his neck saying : "U-u-u," while

Boys trying to play Billiards
at Magudju's, near Antioka Station.

those remaining with the lamenting little one say to him : " Be quiet, listen! Shikunkununu is coming! "

There are also the *timbelembele*, a kind of terrible wasp which only exists in the imagination of children. When a boy does not dare to follow his companions up a tree which they have climbed, they shout to him : " Make haste! Here are the timbele-mbele coming to bite you! " And he is so frightened that he at once finds strength to climb.

(1) We shall give a complete ogre tale in Part V.

Thonga boys are so fond of games that they even try to imitate those of the Europeans. In the accompanying illustration, they are seen sitting in two rows throwing some projectiles along the ground. I wondered what game this was, and was informed that these boys, having seen Portuguese officials playing billiards at the camp, had attempted to do the same, and this was the result!

C. THE AGE OF PUBERTY

I. *Circumcision rites.*

1) SPREAD AND ORIGIN OF CIRCUMCISION AMONGST THE THONGAS.

As he grows up, the Thonga boy leaves the flock of goats and is entrusted with the care of the big cattle, oxen and cows, when his father owns any. He becomes very proud, and tyrannises over his younger brothers ; he calls himself their " hosi," their chief, and sends them to work for him; in Maputju, big boys went so far as to scorn water brought from the pool by women, and only to use water specially fetched by small boys. If they grow so important in their own eyes, the reason is that special rites are performed on them during this period, rites which are calculated to give them great self-confidence. Amongst these rites, some have a direct relation with the sexual life and some represent only the entrance upon manhood. Let us begin with a study of circumcision, then we will take the other puberty rites and the habit of *gangisa*.

In a great many Bantu tribes, the age of puberty is marked by ceremonies of initiation, often accompanied by circumcision. There is little doubt that circumcision was practised throughout the Thonga tribes in former times. It is still current with those Thongas who emigrated into the Transvaal, and this is not a custom borrowed from the Pedi clans, which have all preserved circumcision. Though the Thongas often receive initiation in Pedi schools, in the Spelonken, they possess their own schools for the Nkunas near Leydsdorp. They have a special word for the physical operation, *yimba*, (in Ronga *soka*) which is used together with *ngoma* (Sutho *goma*), the generic term for all the customs connected with it. (It must not be forgotten that the word *ngoma* is also used for other initiations, especially for the initiation of widows, as will be seen in Chap. II.)

Amongst the Ba-Ronga, circumcision was abandoned more than a hundred years ago, before the arrival of Manukosi, and they were called *Ba-butoya*, the cowards, by other Northern clans, who said they feared the sufferings of that cruel school. Mboza has seen some old Ronga men who had been circumcised probably at the begining of the XIXth Century. It is well known that somewhat later Chaka put a stop to the custom amongst the Zulus; it did not fit in with the new military system inaugurated by him. When the Ngoni general Manukosi invaded the plains of the Low Country, it is not surprising that circumcision disappeared in those clans also. The constant fighting which prevailed in those troubled times did not allow men to stay three consecutive months in a circumcision lodge. It was feared also that circumcised boys would be killed by the enemy, being unable to run away in case of an invasion. But old men in the Bilen country assert that the *Ngoma* is a very old custom amongst the Thongas, and that it has long been practised by all their clans.

Is it possible to ascertain its *true origin* ? My informants, Viguet especially, were convinced that the Ngoma was brought to the tribes of the Northern Transvaal by the *Ma-Lemba*, and it is a historical fact that, as regards the Ba-Venda of that country, the rite was adopted quite recently under the influence of the Ma-Lemba. These Ma-Lemba are a very curious people, living amongst the Thongas and the Suthos of Zoutpansberg, just like the Jews amongst the European nations, without a chief, without national unity, but with characteristic customs to which they adhere from generation to generation... They resemble the Jews in the fact that they do not eat flesh unless all the blood has been first carefully drained away. They dread eating blood above all else, and they shave at each new moon. They brought with them the metallurgic art and introduced domestic fowls into the country. All these facts tend to show that they have had intimate relations with Semitic peoples, and they themselves declare that they came from the North by sea and reached the coast after shipwreck. Now they practise circumcision with great assiduity and hold a special position in the lodges of the Spelonken. They are called there the masters of the Ngoma (1). Circumcision is wide-spread amongst Semitic nations, and one might be tempted to infer from these remarks that the custom has been taught to the Bantus by Semitic masters. This is certainly true as regards the Ba-Venda in the Spelonken (2).

In South Africa the Ngoma is much older than the arrival of the Ma-Lemba (which can be fixed some time during the XVIIIth century). What happened in Spelonken, through the agency of the Ma-Lemba, during the XIXth century, may have taken place at some earlier date in the case of other South African tribes, and the Semitic origin of the Ngoma is quite possible, though there is no proof at present extant.

2) GENERAL CHARACTERISTICS OF THE CIRCUMCISION RITES.

I am treating here of the rites as they are met with amongst the Thongas of Spelonken especially ; my informants on this point have been Viguet, who was initiated some 60 years ago, and Valdo, a much younger man, who went through the rites 30 years ago; both are from Spelonken. There Thonga and Bvesha (Sutho) candidates enter the same lodges. A boy named Pikinini revealed to me the secret formulae as they are recited amongst the Nkunas (Leydsdorp). The rites certainly vary amongst the tribes and they seem to have been simplified in late years, but there is a general resemblance between them all. Pedis have two circumcision

(1) I note in a paper by the Rev. W. A. Norton on the puberty rites of the Ba-suto (S. A. *Journal of Science* March 1910) that, if a Bushman is in a lodge, he takes precedence amongst the Suthos and that there circumcision is derived from the Bushmen just as it is from the Ma-Lemba in the Zoutpansberg.

(2) See my paper on the "Balemba of the Zoutpansberg" *Folklore*, Sept. 1908 and also, "*Zidji*," my South African novel. Chap. II. (Saint-Blaise, Foyer Solidariste).

schools during two consecutive years. The first is called *bulika*, the second *buhwira*. Thongas have only the first, and it is the one described in the following pages.

I was never fortunate enough to penetrate into a lodge, as it is a great taboo. I tried once to obtain admittance, near Shiluvane, but in vain. But the rites have been described to me with such a wealth of detail that I seemed to have lived for three months with the candidates ! (1)

A French anthropologist, Mr A. van Gennep, published some years ago a book on *Les Rites de Passage* (Paris. Nourry 1909) which throws a great deal of light on these mysterious customs. He shows that a great number of rites have been inspired by the idea of passage from one place to another, and that all the rites belonging to this category present the same general features : in the first place the separation from the old state of things is symbolised by certain rites which he calls separation rites ; then begins a period of margin, where the individual or the group concerned is secluded from society and submitted to a number of taboos or rites ; thirdly, at the close of this period, the persons who have been tabooed are again received into the community as regular members by the aggregation rites. This classification applies perfectly to the Circumcision rites, which are a Rite of Passage par excellence, and I shall now try to explain them briefly in their natural sequence. For more details see *Zidji*, a South African novel which I published in 1910 (Foyer solidariste, Saint-Blaise, Switzerland) where a more elaborate description will be found.

3) THE THREE SERIES OF RITES OF CIRCUMCISION.

a) Separation rites.

The circumcision school (Ngoma) is held every fourth or fifth year, and all the boys from ten to sixteen are sent to it by their

---

(1) A young colleague of mine, the Rev. A. Jaques was more fortunate than I and even succeeded in taking some photographs in the Masume Valley, near Shiluvane, This was a Pedi school, but, as stated above, there is no great difference between Pedi and Thonga " Sungi. " These pictures are of great interest, and I am grateful to my friend for allowing me to reproduce them here.

parents. Some may escape, but if they happen to be at hand on the next occasion, they will be included by consent or by force. Even an adult member of the tribe can be compelled to go through the initiation, if he is found in the country in an uncircumcised state. The *time of year* chosen for the opening of the school is a month during which the morning star appears, in winter. *Ngongo-mela*, Venus, is the herald of the day. She precedes the sun, so she must lead the boys to their new life, from darkness to the light! (Valdo)

One day all the candidates are gathered in the capital ; for this school is the business of the chief, and has been arranged by the council of the headmen (tinduna) over which he presides ; he has the supervision of it, and will receive the fees from the initiated later on. Boys circumcised four years ago must also attend the whole school as shepherds (barisi, psitjiba), namely as servants of the men and watchers over the candidates. They have already partly built the lodge outside the village, in a remote place, not too far away however, because the women must bring food each day for all the inmates of the " yard of mysteries ".

After having slept in the capital, early in the morning, when Ngongomela rises in the East, the band of the uncircumcised *goes out* from the inhabited world to the wilderness, to the lodge. This is the first separation rite. The second is this : they find on the road a fire made of strongly scented wood ; when they smell the smoke, they must jump over it. This rite is called : Tlula ritsa, to jump over the firebrand.

Later on, when still at some distance from the newly built lodge, they hear a great noise, a song accompanied by the beating of drums and blowing of antelope horns. They must not understand the meaning of the words which are sung by the host of shepherds and the men, as it would frighten them too much :

The little boy cries ! Bird of the winter !

Here they are halted. Eight of them are chosen and told to go forward. Each one is given an assagai, and they are pushed between the singers, who hold sticks and stand facing each other in two rows, leaving a passage between them. They thus run the gauntlet and receive a good whipping ; (the flagellation is often also a separation rite) ; having gone through this unexpected experience they are caught at the other end by four men and deprived of all their clothing. Their hair is also cut, (they must evidently sever themselves from all their past), and they are brought to eight stones and seated on them. These eight stones are not far from the entrance of the yard, in a spot called " the place of the crocodile ". Opposite them are eight other stones on which eight men are sitting. These men are called *Nyahambe*, the Lion-men. They have a fearful appearance, their heads being covered with lions' manes. As soon as the boy is seated on the stone facing the Lion-man, he receives a severe blow from behind ; he turns his head to see who struck him, and sees one of the shepherds laughing at him. The operator snatches his opportunity ; while the attention of the boy is diverted, he seizes the foreskin and cuts it in two movements, first the upper part (this is quickly done and does not cause very much pain), secondly the lower part and the string, a longer and much more painful operation. The surgeons now use an ordinary European knife ; formerly they had only native-made knives. Often the boy falls down unconscious ; they then throw a jar of cold water over him. All the circumcised receive rings of woven, very soft grass which they put on their wounds, tying them round the loins with a string (shondlo). Formerly they did not anoint the sore with medicaments : the boys used only to drink a decoction which is said to stop hemorrhage ; now they use paraffin externally.

The boy has now *crossed* (*wela*, like a boat across a river), a technical expression which shows clearly the character of this rite of passage. He is introduced into the lodge.

The removal of the foreskin, though it cannot have the high spiritual meaning of the Jewish circumcision, seems to me also distinctly a separation rite, this part of the body representing the ancient contemptible childish life from which the initiated emerges to-day.

THE EVOLUTION OF A MAN FROM BIRTH TO DEATH

b) Marginal rites.

The newly circumcised boy is now to be three months secluded from society in the " yard of mysteries " called *sungi*. Let us first describe this lodge, and we shall see what his occupations will be during this time of trial.

I. *The Sungi.*

(See the accompanying plan of the lodge).

The whole sungi is surrounded by a high fence of thorny branches. This is a sign that all that goes on inside must be

Circumcised boys near Shiluvane.   *Photo A. Jaques.*

kept secret. No one who is not initiated can be allowed to see it, especially women. This fence is extended at the entrance so as to form a long avenue by which one penetrates into the yard. Then the way of access continues between twelve poles arranged in pairs (2). The inmates alone have the right to take the road between the poles. Circumcised visitors (uncircumcised would not be admitted) go round them and cross the road five times so as to reach the men's entrance at the end (3),

and not the candidates' gate, which is on the opposite side (4).
Further on is the central court of the sungi, with the long fireplace
built with stones and called the Elephant (5) round which the boys
must sit (8), warming their right hips at the fire.   The uterine

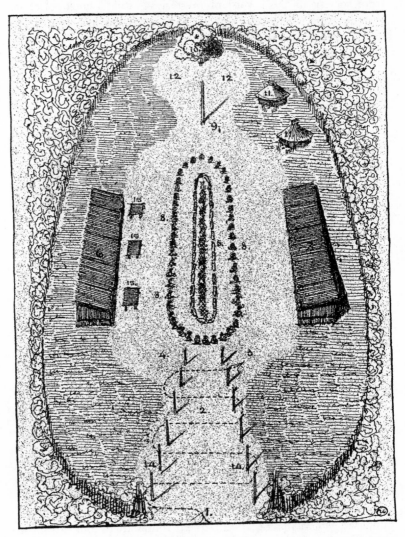

Plan of the circumcision lodge.   *Drawn by J. Wavre.*

78

nephew of the chief, the son of his sister, who takes precedence in all the rites, and who is the first to be circumcised, sits on a special stone with the others behind him. He is called the *Hwatye*. Near the fireside are the tables made of hurdles of reeds on which the porridge of the boys is served every day (15). The central court is occupied on both sides by two square sheds hastily and roughly built, the one on the right (7) being the hut of the shepherds and of the men, the one on the left (6) the hut of the circumcised. The soil is not smeared in these houses. Some of the men also sleep in separate huts behind (11). It is behind the Elephant that the big Mulagaru pole will be raised at the close of the school (9). Further at the back of the sungi is the place of the formulae where the boys are taught (12). A tree sometimes grows in the middle and the instructor climbs up it to impart his teaching (10)!

I have drawn this plan of the sungi with the help of Viguet. Having never seen it with my own eyes, I cannot guarantee that it does not omit many details... But it is correct as a whole.

The inmates of the lodge fall into three categories : 1. the " bukwera " viz. the troop of candidates who are to be initiated ; 2. the shepherds (barisi or psitjiba, the boys who light (tjibela) the fire of the Elephant) who waken the circumcised in the morning, accompany them on their hunting trips, watch them when they eat, etc. 3. The grown up men who have volunteered to come and stay in the sungi during the whole school. They eat the flesh of the animals killed by the bukwera, carve pestles, weave baskets, enjoy themselves, and form the council which looks after the well-being of the school. Amongst them are the so-called father and mother of the Ngoma, two men who are specially in charge of the school. The " father " has a difficult task ; he must keep discipline, administer punishment, etc. These two men are paid, as are also the Lion-men and the Manyabe. The Manyabe is the great doctor of the school. He has poured his charms on the fence to protect the lodge against wizards. He does not stay in the sungi, but can be called at any time to administer medicine to the boys who are unwell or whose wounds do not heal properly.

II. *The sexual and language taboos of the sungi.*

The whole sungi is taboo to every uninitiated person and especially to women. A woman who has seen the " shondlo ", viz. the leaves which the circumcised put over their wound, and which form their only clothing, must be killed. But taboos abound for everybody. The sexual taboos are most noteworthy. Sexual intercourse is strictly prohibited to all inmates, men as well as shepherds ; breaking this law would kill the circumcised. Therefore the men must not go home, or at least as seldom as possible, during these three months. Married people in the village may have sexual relations ; but there must be no noise, no quarrels between jealous co-wives ; because, if they insult each other and if this is known in the sungi, the shepherds will come one evening and plunder that village. Strange to say, in the meantime obscene language is permitted and even recommended— a contrast which we shall often meet with during the marginal periods. Some of the formulae contain expressions which are taboo at other times ; when the women bring the food to the sungi, the shepherds who receive it from their hands are allowed to address them with as many unchaste words as they like. The mothers themselves have the right of singing obscene songs when they pound the mealies for the sungi.

As regards language, there are also special expressions used during the school which are either archaic or foreign ; for instance, all orders are given in a tongue which is neither Thonga nor Sutho : Tshai goma, Go to the table ; Thari, Eat ; Khedi, Smear with white clay, etc. Often actions are not designated by the ordinary word, but by unusual terms. For instance, the daily smearing of the bodies with clay is called : " to eat sheep's fat. " To put on the leaves of the shondlo is " to eat sheep's flesh. " To be beaten with the mbuti sticks is " to drink goat's milk. " Evidently the aim of this terminology is to increase the impression of mystery which the rites must convey to the uninitiated.

As regards the rites of the marginal period, they are calculated to give the candidates the impression that they are new men,

Photo H. Gros.

Dance of the shepherds and men of the Circumcision school. (Spelonken, 1886.)

81

and that they must prove it by submitting manfully to all the trials of this hard and sometimes cruel initiation.

Every morning they smear their bodies with white clay. They are shining ; they have abandoned the darkness of childhood. When they have eaten their food they must pick up the crumbs which fall on the ground and throw them away in the pit near the fence, shouting some name in disdain, in an insulting manner, the name of one of the uncircumcised, of a *shuburu* (a term of contempt applied to boys before they pass through the school). This makes them realise their new position.

But the Ngoma " is the shield of buffalo's hide! It is the crocodile which bites !" The candidates must accept all the hardships of initiation. They are taught to suffer.

III. *The trials.*

There are six main trials : blows, cold, thirst, unsavoury food, punishment, death.

Blows. On the slightest pretext, they are severely beaten by the shepherds at the order of the men of the sungi. Every day they must sit round the Elephant and, holding a stick in their hands, lunge at it as if to pierce it, for more than an hour. They sing the following words :

Elephant keep still !

Men and shepherds dance round them singing :

The black cow kicks ! It kicks against the jug of the baboon !

They themselves represent the black cow which the boys are trying to milk, and kick the boys ! In fact during this daily exercise round the Elephant—a rite which is considered as one of the most important of the Ngoma—, they beat the naked shoulders of the initiated as much as they like, not so as to bruise them, but quite enough to cause them pain.

When the boys do not eat quickly enough, they are beaten. Sometimes they are sent to catch certain birds of the size of sparrows which they must wrap in leaves, tying them in such a clever way that the men will be unable to untie them. Should one of the men succeed in undoing the knots, the boy will get a good thrashing during the meal, and so on.

The unhappy boys who are ill and cannot take part in the hunting trips must be on their guard ; when their comrades come back, much excited, they fall upon them with sticks and are allowed to beat them for not having come to help them.

Cold. The months of June to August are the coldest of the South African winter and, during the night, the temperature falls to 41 Fah., or even lower. The boys lie naked in their shed,

Fhoto A. Jaques.

Circumcised boys sitting near the fire of "the Elephant"

heads turned towards the central court, and suffer bitterly from the cold. They are allowed to light fires in the court, but not near their feet, and it is said that one of the greatest trials of the Ngoma is that the head is warm and the feet cold. Moreover, they must always lie on their backs. Shepherds keep watch during the night and beat them if they lie on their side. No blanket is allowed, only light grass covers. The soil, not being smeared, swarms with a kind of white worm which bites severely during the night. Ashes are poured on the ground to kill them, but this is of but little use. In certain lodges, when there is a pool in the neighbourhood, the boys are led early in the morning into

the water and must remain in it a long time till the sun appears.
The shepherds prevent them from coming out. This is also said
to help the wound to heal. (Valdo).

Thirst. It is absolutely forbidden to drink a drop of water
during the whole initiation, and this taboo is said to be very
painful. Boys sometimes succeed, during their hunting trips,
in enticing their shepherds in one direction and in the meantime
some of them escape and go to the river to drink. They will be
severely punished if caught!

Unsavoury food. The law is that women, the mothers of the
circumcised, must bring plenty of porridge, twice as much as is
required for the boys. Should one of them fail to do this she will
be punished at a given time. They deposit their pots at some
distance, so that they cannot catch any glimpse of the Ngoma,
and shout : " Ha tsoo! We are burning." This means : "Our
heads are sore from having carried our pots such a long way."
Shepherds run to meet them and answer with a great many jokes
in rather dubious taste : " We know what is burning with you,
etc." Is not this the rule of the Ngoma ? The shepherds bring
back with them the empty pots of the day before which the women
take back to their homes. Should one of them have provided too
little food, her pot will be filled with long grass, and when she goes
home with her comrades, they will make fun of her. If she does
not learn to do better, the " Mother of the Ngoma " will organise a
punitive expedition to her village, and kill goats and fowls, and
thus make her obey.

All the food is placed on the reed tables, and must be eaten by
the boys without any seasoning. Should the indulgent mothers
have brought some ground nut sauce, it will be confiscated and
eaten by the men. When they hear the order : "Tshai goma,"
the candidates must rush to the tables, kneel down, and, at the
word "Thari," seize the food with both hands and swallow it as
quickly as possible. If they delay, they are beaten by the shepherds who superintend the meal. When one batch of boys has
finished, they must rush to another table where other boys are still
struggling with their heap of porridge and help them to finish
their portions. Owing to this emulation, the meal does not last

long. Sometimes, when game has been plentiful, one of the men comes and squeezes the half digested grass found in the bowels of an antelope over the porridge, saying to the boys : " You must have something of the results of your hunting too! "

This diet nauseates them at first. They sometimes vomit right on the table. No matter, every particle of the porridge must be eaten all the same. When they are accustomed to the diet, they grow fat, and it is wonderful how their physical appearance sometimes improves during these few months.

Punishments. Blows are punishments for minor offences. Should some more serious fault have been committed, the father of the circumcision condemns the boy to "drink goat's milk." There is a shrub called " mbuti ;" the same word also means goat. Three sticks of it are taken. The boy must present his hands, put them against each other and separate the fingers. The sticks are introduced between the fingers and a strong man, taking both ends of the sticks in his hands, presses them together and lifts the poor boy, squeezing and half crushing his fingers.

In former times, the boys who had tried to escape or who had revealed the secrets of the sungi to women, or to the uninitiated, were hanged on the last day of the school and burnt to ashes, together with all the contents of the lodge.

Death. The circumcised must also be prepared to die if their wound does not heal properly and if the Manyabe's medicine is not successful. Many of them have actually died. It is absolutely forbidden to mourn over them. The mother of the deceased is informed of his death by a notch cut in the edge of the pot in which she brings the food. She must not cry. The corpse is buried in a wet place, in a grave dug with sticks, as it would make people suspicious if the shepherds were to go to the village and fetch spades for this work.

IV. *The teaching of formulae.*

So the boys are taught endurance, obedience, manliness. But there is another side to the training of the Ngoma. It has sometimes been compared to a school, and it is true that there is some intellectual learning in it, though very scanty and insignificant. Every morning the candidates are brought together to the place of the formulae (nau-milau, law, prescription). There is a tree in the midst of this square. A special instructor, whose father has already exercised this function, climbs up the tree and begins to teach the boys. He says :

Little boys, do you hear me. I say...

Then come the words of the secret formulae which are a great taboo and which they must learn by heart, sentence after sentence. I have collected some of them, Thonga and Pedi. Here I will reproduce only the Thonga. They are partly incomprehensible, even to the initiated. The first is called *Manhengwana*. It is the name of a bird.

Masumanyana a nga suma...
The little bird has sung.
A nga suma tinghala ta timhingo...
It has stirred the handles of the lances which are like lions...
T'entsha ku ya tlhabana...
They pierce each other...
Manhengu. Manhengu bentshile. Bentsha tirula...
The bird... ? ?
Fula ngoma... Mukhubela wa hantana...
Forged at the lodge. Clouds come from all parts.
Milumbyana saben. Sabe khulu ra barimi.
Rivulets in the sand, forming the great Sabi.
Ntje-ntje bya ngulube... Bya shinana sha rila...
The running of the wild pig... Of the frog which cries...
Byi longolokile byi ya kamba ntjonga wa mbila.
They are walking in good order, they go to visit the mysterious hut.
Ba kuma byi ri busonga, songa bya timhiri ni timhamba...
They find it like the twisted rings of the adder.

These words, so far as they have a sense, seem to extol the Ngoma and its lodge. These assagais, which are like lions which are going to tear each other, represent the school which is starting, awakened by the bird of the winter. The clouds coming from all directions are the boys converging on the sungi from all parts of the country, like rivulets which join together to form a great river. The running of the wild pig is the life of the boy who was idling away his time till initiation made a man of him. The croaking of the frog (shinana) is his childish stupidity. The shinana is a strange animal indeed, a small Batracian which is able, when attacked, to swell considerably : then it becomes so hard that its enemies, even a cock with a sharp beak, cannot pierce it. The circumcised boy, before initiation, was a shinana before it swelled up. By the trials of the Ngoma, he will become like this frog, an invulnerable and untamable adversary. (1) In the last sentences we see the bukwera, the troup of the circumcised, penetrating into the mysterious hut, into the Ngoma, and wondering at the extra-ordinary wisdom which is found there. The laws, rites and trials are like the inextricable intermingling of many snakes.

The sungi is then celebrated again in the following sentences :

A mi ri i sungi...
Say, it is the lodge.
Hansi ka rona, i tleketleka,
On the ground, there is a disgusting smell,
Henhla ka rona i tlulawula...
On the roof, it is elevated and beautiful...
Makomole i mhandje...
Its supports are poles...
Tinga hi hala n'djibalelo...
Long rods unite the poles... etc.

Nwatjabatjabane a nga tjabatjaba...
The heavy body which goes on heavily...
Shikari ka mipungu ni mihlanga...
Through the drifts and the reeds...
Masheka ya le ndjako, marumbu a wela ndjen.
Which must be cut open from behind, because its bowels fall down inside its body.
I ngwenya.
It is the crocodile.

Shiborekeketa mahlaluku makambaku...
The beast which opens the road to the drifts for the elephants...
A ta hi ku nwa ni ku hlamba...
It goes to drink and to bathe...
A mi ri mfubu ?
Do you not say, it is the hippopotamus ?

Nwatjabatjabane makandjya ka ku oma...
The beast which marches slowly on the dry ground...
Ku sa ku baleka nhlangasi,
And a marsh is formed by its heavy footsteps,
Ndlopfu, shibangamaphesa a nga riphembe, hi yona...
It is the elephant, the one who provides clothing (by the sale of its teeth) the one who brings wealth, it is he !

(1) Another explanation : The running to and fro of the wild pig describes the coming and going of the men who bring the boys to the " place of the crocodile," like pigs searching for their prey. The " Shinana " which cries is the little circumcised boy whose voice is hardly heard amidst all the noise of that terrible day. He is a small powerless thing, like the frog.

These formulae are so characteristic that they provide the principal pass words by which the circumcised recognize each other. Should I want to know if a man is initiated, I should say to him : " *Mashindla bya ndjako*, the beast which must be opened from behind. " If he answers at once : " Ngwenya, the

Phot. A. Borel

Cutting open a crocodile near the Nkomati river.

crocodile," I know that he has been circumcised. But he must add the following words : "khekeretana wa mufagu " i. e. "the knife which circumcises."

There are also some obscene formulae which refer to certain diseases of women, of which not a word is told outside the Ngoma. Some others are so ugly that I can give them only in Latin (Annotatio quarta). Even the formulae of the crocodile and of the hippopotamus are by no means poetic descriptions of these big animals similar to those contained in the book of Job. The first alludes to the manner in which the male crocodile copulates with his female. And the second tells the story of a virgin girl whom the young boys violate in order to open the way to the grown up men who will follow them. Impure allusions are found everywhere in this teaching of the circumcision school.

When the instructor has finished, he lifts his stick with a certain gesture and all the boys shout at once : " Zithari! " Viguet told me that that exclamation meant : " They are as long as that " and that it was an obscene allusion. The old men take great delight in being flattered and, if the boys wish to add to their pleasure, they will say : " When you spit, the wind from your mouth would kill enemies at the other end of the country! "

As is plain from these quotations, the teaching of the Ngoma is quite trivial, and the formulae are rather a collection of esoteric words than a true intellectual training.

The songs of the Ngoma have no deeper meaning. We have seen already the song of the Elephant and of the Winter-bird... Every morning, just after they wake, the circumcised sing for a long time the following words, which they repeat also when coming back from hunting trips.

> Sing your song, bird of the morn
> Mafé-é-é-é !

The melody is rude, wild but very impressive. Mafé-é-é-é must mean : " We are the initiated, we are the men! "

Hunting. Hunting is the only useful thing taught in the Ngoma. Boys go almost every day to the velt and become very clever in catching game. They beat the bush, sometimes climb hills and chase all the game to the top, killing it there with their assagais, knobkerries, etc. Near Shiluvane they even attack the Mamotsuiri mountain once during their three months. All the men of the country are summoned to take part in the big expedition, which requires real strategic skill.

To sum up the rites of this marginal period of the Circumcision school, this is the programme of a day in the sungi. The shepherds awaken the boys very early. They sing for one hour the Winter-bird. Then they learn the formulae for one or two hours. Afterwards the order : "Tshayi goma" is given and they throw away the leaves of the day before and put on a new "shondlo." They go and sit round the Elephant and stab him for two hours till a shout is heard : the women bringing the food announce that they have come. The boys eat for the first time, and sing again to help digestion. At the command : "Khedi goma," they smear their bodies with white clay. The sun is already high in the sky when they start for their hunting trip. They come back at sunset, eat for the second time, stab the Elephant again for one hour and at the command "Khwerere, Mayise, Mafefo," they go to their beds on the dirty soil of their but.

c) Aggregation Rites.

I. *The Mulagaru.*

The first aggregation rite takes place many days before the conclusion of the school. One morning, very early, the men and the shepherds raise a very big pole in the yard of the formulae and fix it into a hole. At its extremity is a man, half hidden in white hair (1). The boys are awakened and led by the shepherds into the yard. They are told to lie down on their backs, all their heads turned towards the pole, which is called *mulagaru*, and to say : "Good morning, grandfather." Then a voice comes from the top of the pole and says : "I greet you, my grand-children." They must remain a long time in that position in the biting cold of the morning, talking with the "grand-father." They are allowed even to complain of their sufferings and to ask permission to return home. But they still have to stay some days in the sungi. Every morning this ceremony will be repeated. It clearly means that the boys are being put into communication with the ancestor who represents the clan, that they are beginning to be admitted to the adult life of the tribe.

(1) In some circumcision schools this man is called kokwana Masinde, a name which is applied to old women.

A few days later, the great doctor administers to the boys a purifying medicine which they drink in a mouthful of beer. This rite seems to be rather a separation than an aggregation rite. We often find, when a marginal period comes to an end, separation rites taking place. They mean separation from the *marginal period* itself; for this also involved a kind of pollution which must be removed. Such is probably the aim of the medicine given by the Manyabe. On the other hand, this is also an aggregation rite, as the boys are allowed to drink again for the first time.

II. *The Mayiwayiwane dance.*

The second true aggregation rite is called the Mayiwayiwane dance. The *Mayiwayiwane* are a sort of masks which cover the whole of the upper part of the body, a kind of armour made of woven palm leaves; on the head, they are like a very high helmet protruding in front like a beak. The boys make these masks with the help of the shepherds and of the men and, in this disguise, must perform

A Mayiwayiwane mask (1).

a special dance with high jumps before the women summoned on a certain day to attend. The boys must not be recognized. Should one of them let the mask fall, it would be a great misfortune, because women must not know who is dancing. Moreover the initiated must appear before them as a kind of supernatural beings and fill them with respect and awe. Therefore they must not fall when they dance. Should one of them totter and lose his equilibrium, the shepherds cover him

(1) This mask is that worn by Pedi boys during the second circumcision school. I cannot guarantee that the Mayiwayiwane mask is of exactly the same pattern.

with a heap of grass and the men say : " He is dead !," because a circumcised boy cannot fall and live. One of the shepherds goes in haste to a village of the neighbouring tribe and buys a fowl ; this is killed and its blood is sprinkled over the grass ; the boy who fell escapes when the women have gone home, but the next day, when they come back to the spot, they see the blood and are convinced that, in very truth, one of the circumcised dies when he falls!

Sometimes a little child is taken from the arms of its mother and brought to the place where the boys are sitting hidden during the dance. They kiss him and smile at him, because he is innocent; he may see what women are not allowed to contemplate!

III. *The last day.*

The last day is marked by the greatest and most difficult trial. During the whole preceding night, the boys are not allowed to sleep. Sleep is the last enemy they must overcome. They stab the Elephant and repeat the formulae till the morning. Then all the bits of skin remaining from the circumcising are picked up by the Manyabe ; he burns them, and makes them into a powder with which he smears the mulagaru pole. All the masks and grass mats are thrown on to the roof of the shed and, at dawn, the troop of circumcised, surrounded by the shepherds and men, is directed towards a pool and made to run to it without looking backwards ; (separation from the sungi, from the seclusion period). If they were to look at what is taking place behind them, their eyes would be pierced, and they would be blind for ever! Fire is set to the whole establishment by some of the men, and all the filth and ignorance of childhood is burnt in this great conflagration. The boys are led into the water, wash away the white clay shouting : " I am a man," cut their hair (separation rite), anoint themselves with ochre, put on new clothing and are addressed by the father of the circumcision :

" You are no longer *shuburu*! Try now to behave like men. It would be unworthy of you to steal sweet potatoes in the fields as you used to do before. Now the Ngoma is closed and it is taboo to pronounce the formulae or to sing the songs of the sungi. Don't reveal a word of them to anybody ; if a boy does so he will be strangled! " etc.

That same day the women bring porridge with sauce flavourings and the shepherds are no longer allowed to use insulting words when they receive the pots from their hands.

IV. *The Chameleon procession.*

All these are evidently aggregation rites. But the greatest of all is the procession of the initiated into the capital of the chief which takes place on the day of the closing of the sungi and on the following day. Covered with ochre, marching on mats which have been spread on the ground so that they do not touch the dust with their feet, they advance slowly, bowed to the ground, stretching out first one leg and then the other, with a sudden brisk motion, trying to imitate the gait of the chameleon, the wise, the prudent. They are men who think, and no longer boys without intelligence! Then they all sit in the central place of the capital, silent, with their heads still bent, and the sisters and mothers who have come from all the different villages must go and recognize them. Each woman brings with her a bracelet or a shilling or any small present and searches for her boy amongst the throng. When she thinks she has found him, she kisses him on the cheek and gives him the present. The boys have two sticks in their hands. One stick bears some short lateral branches on which the boys will hang the bracelets (busenga). The other is smaller and, when the mother has discovered her son and has kissed him, he strikes her, a soft blow if it is his mother or his grandmother, a much harder one if it is his sister, and utters the new name which he has chosen.

In answer to this demonstration, the mother begins to dance and to sing the praises of her son! This is the typical aggregation rite called *kunga*, the breaking of silence, which we shall meet with more than once in the passage rites of the tribe. These bracelets are all given in to the chief, who will distribute them amongst the old women. It would be taboo to give them to childbearing women. According to the same idea the fees paid by the boys to

93

the chief must not be used by him to buy a wife. This would pollute the village (makhuma). It would cause unfortunate births (timbeleko) and ruin the life of the people.

The chameleon procession is performed in the villages of the main headmen of the tribe during the few following days till, at last, the ochre of the initiated is removed and they return home definitely.

SOME REMARKS ON THE CIRCUMCISION SCHOOL

The square form of the sungi sheds, so different from the circular form adopted by the Bantus for their homes and implements, might be the trace of a Semitic influence. But, on the whole, all these rites are closely connected together and their sequence is quite easy to understand.

The Ngoma is truly a puberty rite, but not a sexual initiation. The suspension of conjugal relations, and the prevalence of licentious language might give the idea that it is in direct relation with the sexual life. But these two phenomena are met with on other occasions, as we shall see, and seem to be characteristic occurrences in most of the marginal periods. Moreover boys of ten and twelve and men of twenty-five or more can occasionally be admitted to the sungi, and this proves that the school has nothing to do with marriage, properly speaking. Neither is the Ngoma a pure act of aggregation to a definite clan. Boys of one clan often go to the sungi of another chief to be initiated ; they do not become his subjects by so doing. Even Thongas sometimes enter into Sutho lodges and Ma-Lemba have a special place in them. It is true that the Ngoma is the business of the chief. Only those who are really chiefs have the right to build a lodge. But though the initiated are exhorted to become good subjects of their chief, the intention of the circumcision school is rather to introduce the little boy *into manhood,* to cleanse him from the *bukhuna* (p. 58) to make him a thoughtful adult member of the community.

(See practical conclusion on Circumcision Rites at the end of Vol. I.)

II. *Other Puberty Rites.*

The Ngoma has disappeared in most of the Thonga clans, but there are a few other puberty rites which have been preserved all through the tribe.

The Evolution of a Man from Birth to Death

1) The custom of the erotic dream (Tilorela).

When a young man has noticed for the first time an emissio seminis, he is said to have become an adult (a kulile, a thombile) to have " drunk the nkanye." The nkanye is the tree from which the bukanye is made. It is prepared for the great feast of the new year. *To drink the nkanye* is an euphemism to designate the entrance into a new phase of life, into the age of puberty. According to Mboza, the lad must go early in the morning to wash his body, and that is all. But Tobane says that, in the Mpfumo clan, the family doctor is called ; in a broken pot, he roasts pieces of skin of all the beasts of the veldt, together with some half digested grass taken from the stomach of a goat (psanyi). The boy must eat a little of this medicine and rub all his joints with it. This will strengthen him so that, when he has relations with girls, he will not be overcome (gemiwa) by them. This rite, which is very similar to the rite of the broken pot performed for infants, is connected with the "gangisa," the sexual habits of young people which begin at the time of puberty, as we shall see later on.

At this time also, the boy begins to wear the very primitive clothing called *shifado* (sha ku siba, the thing with which one closes, see Annotatio I). In former times they wore only the *mbayi*, a small cylindrical or conical object of woven palm leaves, which was the national dress of the Thongas ; the *shifado* seems to be of Zulu origin. It is very much valued as preventing contact with the earth, as a protection against ants and an aid to continence ; the lads who do not wear it are blamed and accused of being *ba-nato*. The word *nato* means a magical medicine by means of which men of low morals throw men or women into a deep sleep during the night, enter the huts of other people and commit adultery with their wives.

2) The piercing of the ears (Ku tjunya, (Ro.), boshela. (Dj.).

This also takes place at this period. There are two ways of performing it, either by an actual piercing of the lower lobe with a thorn, or by cutting it with a knife. The first method is the old Thonga custom, and has been preserved by the women in its original form, at least amongst the Ba-Ronga ; they frequently pass a ring through the small opening thus produced. The second was practised by the Zulu-Ngonis, and was adopted by the Thonga men in order to resemble their conquerors. The result is an ugly hole. This is not a law imposed by the chief ; it is however universally observed. When a lad does not pierce his ears, his comrades mock him, saying. " U toya ! " " You are a coward ! We shall put a spoonful of porridge in this big ear of yours ! " (Viz. It will hold food because it is not pierced !)

The operation is performed in the winter by a man who knows how to do it. Before it is begun, the boy bites the *ndjao*, the root of a kind of juncus which is considered the best means of strengthening the virile force. The doctor introduces into the hole a small piece of reed ; he takes it out every day to wash the wound and puts it in again to keep the hole open. As long as the ear is not healed, the lad must eat his food without salt : he must not go about in the kraals and partake of the porridge of other people, because this food might have been prepared by women having intercourse with their husbands (ba ku khila) and this would make him very ill (1). He must also keep away from girls. When he is healed, he takes away the piece of hard reed and replaces it by a pretty white object.

Some Thongas tatoo themselves, or used to do so formerly, but this custom is disappearing and is now preserved only by women. We shall describe it in the chapter on the evolution of the woman, as well as the *hleta* custom, the pointing of the teeth.

It is probable that in former times the taboo character of these various ceremonies was more marked that now. At present they are merely a *shihita sha tiko*, a custom of the country.

(1) This alimentary taboo, as well as the interdiction of sexual relations, even of intercourse with married people, clearly shows that the piercing of the ears is a rite of passage. (p. 74).

3) THE GANGISA.

When a boy has gone through the puberty rites, he is grown up and is allowed to practise the *gangisa*. This word comes from *ganga*, which means " to choose a lover." Each girl is asked by the boys to choose one of them ; they *make them choose* (gangisa, factitive derivative). I once observed some boys—they were still very young—flirting round three or four girls just like bees round ripe plums, running after them, and saying repeatedly : " Choose me! Choose me! " There is a special blue cotton print with a large white pattern which is called " gangisa ntombi " viz. to make a girl choose, as it is offered by the lover to the damsel of his choice in order to obtain her favour. When a girl has made her choice, her boy plays with her like husband and wife, first building little huts, etc. but later on in a less platonic fashion. In fact nothing is prohibited in the relations between young people of the two sexes. A married woman is sacred amongst the Thongas, but an unmarried girl is not. However, she must not become pregnant. (1) If this happens, the parents will say to the lover : "You have spoiled our daughter, you must buy her in marriage." If he refuses, the child will belong to the family of the girl. Excesses in gangisa are condemned. A boy who commits them is said to be an adulterer (a ni bupse) ; of a girl they say : " She will lose her head (a ta ba singe). "

As the unmarried boys and girls live in special huts, the *lao* of the boys and the *nhanga* of the girls, at the entrance of the village, it is easy for them to meet during the night. During the day, they generally behave themselves becomingly. But when the lads pay visits to their girls, who sing to the accompaniment

---

(1) When a girl becomes pregnant, having had relations with her lover inside her parents' village, it is very serious; it is taboo. The boy will have to find a goat, to kill it during the night in the girl's kraal, and to rise very early; then both the boy and the girl, quite naked, must go round the village and sprinkle the fence from inside with a special decoction. None must come out of the huts to look at them. This will prevent the inhabitants from contracting the disease called mukuhlwane (cough, lung complaint) which would otherwise attack them. Moreover the guilty boy will have to pay a fine of £ 5 in excess of the sum of the lobolo.

of rattles, they sometimes stay with them till late in the night. They bring them small presents, articles of clothing or other things, and thus obtain permission to have intercourse with them. Mboza described to me a very immoral meeting which sometimes takes place in these huts in connection with the *milebe* habit, and which is connected with this gangisa. It is impossible to give the details here. (Annotatio 5.)

The gangisa custom is, from our point of view, very immoral. Amongst Natives it is not censured at all, and it would be more accurate to speak of *amorality* then of *immorality*, amongst them, on this particular point. A boy who has no such flirt, no *shigango*, is laughed at as a coward ; a girl who refuses to accept such advances is accused of being malformed. However Mboza told me he had never had a shigango himself and the abuse in this respect is not approved of by old people. In Manyisa, I heard of a young chief who was leading all the lads to gangisa and forcing the girls to accept them. The extent of this evil depends very much on the character of the boys and girls. I may add that, as regards the young people of the capital, they are not allowed to practise the gangisa because they belong to the royal family and are closely watched.

When they become Christians, Natives readily accept our standard of morality, but cases of fornication are very frequent amongst converts, so much so that this has been rightly called the African sin! I mention this fact, but I must say on the other hand that thousands of pupils in our Native Institutions lead a very moral and continent life and do not seem to find any great difficulty in doing so.

If the gangisa spoils the whole life of the young heathen, it is only just to add that they do not practise two vices which are prevalent amongst certain civilised nations, onanism and sodomy. These immoral customs were entirely unknown in the Thonga tribe before the coming of civilisation. Unhappily it is no longer so now, as we shall see in Appendix III on unnatural vice in Johannesburg.

Comparing the habits of the Pedis and the Thongas we observe this strange fact : amongst the Thongas the unmarried girl is quite free and the married woman is taboo. Amongst the Pedis it is just the reverse ; girls are absolutely prohibited from having any sexual relation before their marriage and, on the contrary, after marriage a woman who has had children can have intercourse with other men than her husband. I shall try to explain this difference when dealing with Pedi customs. (Part II. Chap. I. G.)

*

* *

In his book on Kafir Socialism, Dudley Kidd has laid great stress on the fact that the mental development of the African Native is arrested at the time of puberty, and has tried to find remedies for this inferiority. It may be said that the vivacity of mind, the rapidity of comprehension, which is sometimes wonderful amongst the younger boys, decreases when they reach the age of fifteen or sixteen. Cases can even be recorded amongst them of an arrest or slackening in the development of the psychical faculties at the period of puberty. But this is by no means the rule. In all our Institutions we have pupils who show great zeal for study and increased intellectual power between sixteen and twenty. I may say that Dr Mac Vicar of Lovedale concluded as I do, that this assertion of D. Kidd is very much exaggerated.

D. MARRIAGE

According to the old Thonga idea it was only when a boy was fully grown that he could think of marriage. In former times lads used to enjoy their youth in carelessness and pleasure, going to dance in all the villages, till they were twenty five years old. Nowadays boys marry very early. Money to lobola is obtained more readily and " gangisa " is not as easy as it used to be, two reasons which have advanced the marriage age in the present generation.

I. *Love charms.*

If a boy has not been successful in his " gangisa ", if he is despised by the girls and has no chance of being accepted, a special rite is performed to help him to find a wife. The Ba-Ronga do not know the love-philter as such, but they have a substitute for it ; the old village cock is put on the lad's head and kept there for a long time ; the cock scratches him with his claws ; he is then allowed to go. The boy will now succeed ; he will be like the cock, who never lacks spouses! (Mboza).

Other charms are used for girls, especially a certain medicine which produces an abundant lather when boiled in water. The physician washes the girl's body with it, after which she will " appear " (a ta boneka) to the eyes of would-be suitors (Tobane).

Should however a girl not find a husband in the lawful way, she has another means at her disposal—marriage by abduction, and thus no one, or hardly any one, remains unmarried amongst the Thongas. Mankhelu, who was a great doctor, treated this " complaint of singleness " with more seriousness! He used his strongest medicines to heal the boy or the girl who was unable to find a partner in life. This is the treatment followed by him. He takes a she-goat, in the case of a boy, a he-goat in that of girl, and anoints it with fat mixed with his precious medicinal powder ; he rubs the animal (hondla) from the mouth to the tail, stretches out all its limbs and kills it. No prayer is offered, but the *psanyi* (the half digested grass which is found in the stomach) is carefully collected. The boy is then called, enters his own hut, spreads a mat on the ground, sits on it quite naked and rubs his whole body with this substance. " A tihorola, a tilurulula " says Mankhelu. He rubs away from himself all his filth. When he has finished, he coughs to call the doctor, who comes and gathers into a pot all the " timhorola," the particles which have fallen on the mat ; he takes a portion of this and squeezes it into a small bag of lizard-skin so as to make a *shitjungulu* or amulet. The sister must come after sunset without any clothing into the boy's hut and tie the bag round his neck. What remains of the *timhorola* will be used to smear the hut. Then all the girls will love him ; or in the case of a girl, she will soon be asked in marriage.

This ceremony is a characteristic *hondlola*, the same which is performed on the weaning day (see page 59) and after any serious disease ; it is a rite of removal of impurity. (Notice the termination ola, ula, ulula in these verbs ; it means generally to undo, to take away).

If the love charms do not obtain the desired result, the angry boy will perhaps try to avenge himself. He will take a fowl, or perhaps only an egg, treat it with special drugs and give it to the girl in order to bewitch her. This kind of witchcraft is called *ku dambikela.* (See the Chapter on Witchcraft, Part VI). The girl will give birth not to a child, but to an animal, a pigeon, or a snake. Or her genitalia will be changed and take the appearance of the male organ. This is one of the causes why eggs and fowls are taboo for girls.

Let us now hear from Tobane the description of the marriage rites amongst the Mpfumo clan. We shall afterwards see how the customs differ in other Ronga and Thonga clans.

II. *Marriage ceremonies of the Mpfumo clan.*

1) THE BETROTHAL (Buta).

When a young man has made up his mind to get married, and when he is in possession of the necessary lobola (1) cattle, he starts, one fine day, with two or three of his friends to look for a wife in the villages. He puts on his most brilliant ornaments and his most precious skins. Here they are, arriving in the village

1) *Ku lobola* means to buy in marriage. *Ku lobota* (a factitive derivative of the verb) is said of a father who claims a sum of money from his daughter's suitor. *Lobolo* or *ndjobolo* or *bukosi* (wealth) is the sum paid, the oxen, the hoes, or the pounds sterling. We shall use these words, which are employed in Thonga as well as in Zulu and ought to be adopted as technical ethnographic terms. I use the verb for the act of paying and the noun for the sum itself.

square ; they sit down in the shade. They are asked : " What do you want ? " " We have come to see the girls ", they answer bluntly. And the reply is : " All right. Look at them. "

Of course the girls do their very best to be as pleasing as possible, as the mother has told them that these are suitors. The suitor is easily known by his special attire, a belt of skins either of leopard or tiger-cat. He goes from one yard to the other, and talks with the cooks, inquiring their names, and looking at them as, with vigourous and graceful movements of the body, they crush the mealies in their mortar. If the seekers find what they want, they return home, if not, they go to the next hamlet. (Let us say here that each village consists of not more than six to twelve huts built in a circle, leaving a central circular place, the shaded " square ", of which the oxen kraal occupies the middle.) (See Part II.)

When he is satisfied, the suitor goes home and says to his parents : "So and so pleases me. Go and woo her. (Ku buta)." Then a middle aged man of the village is sent to the parents of the young girl. He is received in the father's hut and, with all the circumlocutions required by etiquette, he discharges his errand. The girl is called and told that the visitor who came the other day has chosen her ; she is asked if she also loves him (or if she wants him... for there is only one word in Ronga to express these two kindred notions, ku randja). " Oh ! is it the one who looked thus and so and who wore this and that ? Yes, I consent to accept (to eat) the money out of his hands (ku da bukosi ku yene). " If she does not care for him, she will declare it quite as plainly : the suitor will have to seek elsewhere. It is a fact worth noting that, amongst these so-called savages, a father very seldom obliges his daughter to accept a husband whom she dislikes, except in the case of debt. If the matter is arranged to the satisfaction of all parties the buta (1) or betrothal is concluded and the messenger is feasted, while he, on his part, gives a present (shihlengwe) to the girl's parents of the value of a hoe or ten

---

(1) *Buta* may be a factitive derivative of the verb *bula*, to speak: to cause somebody to speak, to give an answer.

shillings ; this present " strengthens their bones " (ba tiya marambo) and nothing further remains to be done but to choose the day on which the betrothal visit shall take place. (1)

2) THE BETROTHAL VISITS (Tjekela and koroka).

This visit (ku ya ku tjekelen) is paid in the following manner. The fiancé chooses his best friend to be his " shang-wane " ; the fiancée does the same on her side, and these two " shangwane " must do their best to help them both during the whole of these complicated ceremonies. Then the bridegroom summons, together with his shangwane, three or four other friends of his own age, and a little lad to carry their mats. They go and bathe and put on their finest attire : rich skins, bracelets hung to their belts, horse-hair necklaces with white beads threaded here and there which swing to and fro on neck and breast. Neither do they forget their small shields of skin, which give them a martial appearance without, however, suggesting any thought of war or strife. Before starting they take a good meal cooked at home. In the evening, after sunset, they reach the village of the fiancée. They sit down outside the gate and cough to make known that they have arrived. Then the inhabitants, who were expecting them, come out to meet them and beg them to enter. The visitors make difficulties. They pretend not to wish to do so. The people of the village insist. At last, with apparent reluctance, they advance into the central square. A hut is prepared for them, and they are invited to go and rest there. They begin by refusing. But the young girls take out of their hands their sticks and their miniature shields and carry them into the hut. At last, with a

(1) Amongst the Wa-Nyika (a tribe dwelling between the Nyassa and Tanganyika lakes) the betrothal takes place as follows : A female messenger is sent by the suitor's parents to the girl's parents. She brings with her a hoe. The father calls the girl and shows her the tool saying: " This is your hoe; it comes from so and so. " If the girl looks at the hoe with a gloomy expression and leaves the hut slowly, still looking at it, it is a sign that she does not accept the proposal. Should she on the contrary cover her face with her hands and run away without looking at the hoe, she thus declarès that she consents to become the wife of the boy. (*Journal de l'Unité des Frères*. January 1926).

bored air, they enter. Mats are brought and unrolled before them ; this is the act of hospitality par excellence. They remain standing as if they had no wish whatever to sit down. The girls entreat them to rest, and finally they consent to accept the hospitality offered them with such insistence.

The parents of the fiancée then come, squat near them and ask news of their home. They answer, and inquire about the health of their hosts. This is the *djungulisana*, the exchange of greetings which always takes place when a visitor is received. Soon however large pots of well prepared food are brought. " No ", say the young men. " We have eaten at home, we are not hungry. " The same comedy is gone through again ; the masters of the place insist, the guests refuse systematically according to the Native laws of civility—or incivility! The night, however, has come ; the young men have consented after all to partake of the feast. The old people retire to their huts to sleep ; the young girls remain. The custom requires them to spend the whole night with the young men, according to the law of the *shigango* previously spoken of. The bridegroom's shangwane chooses the bride's shangwane and all the other boys choose their girl. But the fiancée hides behind her friends and takes no part in these games.

In the early morning the young men go to bathe and the girls, their amphoras on their heads, go to fetch water from the lake. On their return they perform another act of hospitality towards their visitors, namely, they throw water down their backs. The boys wash the whole of their bodies, after which the girls anoint them with fat. The day is spent in a pleasant *far niente*. The fiancé and his friends sit in the shade in the square, clad in all their ornaments. They hum songs, they amuse themselves by swaying to and fro as they sit ; the little girls keep them company. Meanwhile the elder girls prepare savoury food for them and go to the fields. Towards evening, the visitors ask to see the parents, to take leave of them ; but the old people send the following message : " No, you shall not see us. We cannot consent to your going away, we have hardly seen you. Spend another night with us. " They must make up their mind to stay a little longer.

In fact this is exactly what the young men want, and the second night is spent like the first.

The third day they go away. All the young girls accompany them along the paths, for a long distance, and, when they part, boys and girls tie together the high standing grasses on the veldt (ku ba mafundju hi byanyi), a touching symbol of their loves! Seeing these knots during the whole season at a crossroads,

Phot. A. Borel

Drawing water from the Maputju river.

passers-by will know that lovers parted there. On taking leave, the young people arrange another meeting. The girls will go after a week or two to return the visit.

In fact, to the *tjekela* of the boys corresponds the *koroka* of the girls. " They make the betrothal visit to see the husband (ba ya ku koroken, ku ya bona nuna) ". They also put on their finest attire ; red and white cloth, in their curled hair a small crown of blue and red beads, looking really pretty, on ankles and wrists bracelets of twisted iron wire.

105

On the appointed day, they go and sit outside the village of the fiancé and cough to announce their presence. The same strange proceedings begin, but this time it is the damsels who make difficulties and the young men must beg and entreat them to enter first the village, then the hut, and then to sit on the mats and to accept food. Each of the groomsmen is most attentive to the girl he chose at the preceding meeting and, to obtain her good will, he generally gives her a fowl or the equivalent in money. In the early morning the visitors rise, go and get water, warm it a little and pour it into basins before the doors of the huts, so that, on that day, the inhabitants of the village will make their ablutions with water fetched by them. Then they go and do feminine work, acting as servants of the fiancé's parents. Thus they remove the ashes from the fire-place and throw them on the ash-heap close by ; they cut the wood for the young men's mothers and light the several fires of the village. They pretend to leave when the sun sets, but no one will hear of it, and they must spend another night. At last, on the following day, they go home, accompanied by the young men and again, at parting, knot grasses together. On the day of the *koroka* definite arrangements are made for the wedding.

3) Taboos of the betrothal period.

The two families which enter into relation with each other by marriage must observe many taboos (See Part II). Here are some of those which are enforced during the visits of *tjekela* and *koroka* :

1) The visitors must not eat all the mealie corn on the spike ; they must leave a few grains on it.

2) They must not tear off the leaves which are round the spike. When they have eaten all the corn, they rearrange these leaves in such a way that the cob seems not to have been touched.

3) They must not " make a hole in the pot " (bobota hotjo), viz. they leave a portion of the liquid in the beer pot, they do not empty it entirely.

4) It is forbidden to return home in rain when one has gone

106

to *tjekela*. You must wait for fine weather, otherwise it is an insult to the future father-in-law.

5) If, during the visit, you eat monkey nuts, you must not take off the thin skin which covers the kernel.

6) The suitor—the owner of the oxen—must not eat black fish that day. Only his friends have the right to do so. These fish, a kind of barbel, are to be found in the lakes (as that of Rikatla) and in the Nkomati river. The suitor will not partake of them for fear lest the girl he wishes to marry should slip through his hands like a fish. Moreover this fish is black : it might bring darkness, unhappiness.

7) Neither must he eat honey during his visit, because honey like the black fish, is slippery... Honey flows...

8) He is also forbidden to eat fowls, because cocks and hens scratch the soil with their claws, scattering it about ; thus the marriage " might be scattered (hangalasa bukati) before it is ripe ". In the Tembe clans, formerly, any solid food was taboo until the families had killed an ox for the feasts.

These taboos are not the proper taboos of a marginal period, as if the betrothal were considered as one of these periods. They are family taboos, belonging to the category of those dictated by the mutual distrust of two allied families.

The wedding feast consists of two parts: the *lobola feast*, viz. all the ceremonies connected with the remittance of the lobolo which takes place at the bride's village, and the *tlhoma*, viz. the bringing the bride to the bridegroom's village. Should the lobolo have been entirely paid at once, these two ceremonies will follow each other without much delay. If the sum of money or the number of oxen is not complete, the *tlhoma* will very probably be postponed.

4) LOBOLA FEAST.

a) Preparations.

On both sides, the friends are informed that the feast is close at hand. The bride's family in particular must prepare in good time, as they have to provide the beer which will be consumed in great quantities. The brewing requires several days. All the relations of the young girl agree on a day to begin operations in the several villages they inhabit. First of all the grains must be taken out of all the mealie spikes which were kept in the small cellar huts (ku hula). The following day these mealie seeds are steeped in cold water, in large pots. When they have become sufficiently soft, they are pounded (kandja) in wooden mortars, the yeast of millet is added (kandela) and the preparation is then boiled (pseka). On the day of the boiling, the family of the fiancé is informed that the next day the beer will be drained off and that on the following day the wedding will begin.

That same day the bridegroom with his friends goes to his future parents-in-law. He does not find his sweetheart there ; she has wisely been hidden in the neighbourhood. He brings with him a goat which will subsequently play an important part in the proceedings. The next day the whole family of the fiancé assembles and makes sure that the provision of hoes or the number of pounds sterling for the lobolo is complete. The third day they all start.

b) The assault of the village.

Let us describe this most curious feature of the feast as it took place forty years ago, when English gold was not yet known in the country, and when the price of a wife was paid in hoes. These hoes, to the number of forty or fifty, were distributed among the relatives, who carried them on their heads. In a long row, they wind along the path. When they approach close to the bride's village, most of them sit down in the shade, whilst a few young men go on before to make the assault. The bride's brothers guard the doors of the circular thorny fence which generally surrounds the villages. Provided with their sticks, they try to prevent the aggressors from entering. In vain! The assailants leap here and there in the bush, hurl themselves over the barriers, are pursued by the sentinels, run across the square, and try to steal pitchers of beer, whilst the boys of the village hit them as hard as they can.

Taking advantage of this tumult the older men arrive, and

pointing with their fingers to the hoes they carry on their heads, they murmur the following words : " Here is our ox! It does not know how to drink! It does not know how to drink! (Homu a yi nwi! a yi nwi!)" The others rush towards them, and try to steal their burdens and to bar the way ; all this goes on amidst laughter, and until one of the old people of the bride's village says : " Let us leave them! (A hi ba tjikene!)" Then the company enters, laden with the precious hoes.

c) The counting of the lobolo.

The implements are deposited in the centre of the square and fixed into the ground by tens. The hoes used by the Thongas, whether of Native or European make, are lengthened and pointed in such a way that they can be introduced into a wooden handle, something like the tools of the lake dwellers. They have a very remote resemblance to an ace of spades with a pointed shaft.

The bride's family gathers to ascertain if the number agreed upon is there. They remark to one another that there are so and so many of them. " Look, they say, they have paid such and such a lobolo. (Labisan ba lobolile ha kukari.) " It is very important that there should be a large number of witnesses, for who knows to how many discussions and quarrels these hoes will give rise if the marriage turns out badly ? When this counting is done, all hearts being gladdened by the sight of the wealth which will eventually allow the bride's brother to get married himself, the jugs of beer, which were brought the day before by the aunts, sisters, and relations of the bride, are fetched in. They pass from one hand to another ; the old people, and the men, prefer going into a hut, where they talk over the latest news whilst they quench their thirst.

d) The wedding procession.

Whilst the old people rest, a goat is taken for the sacrifice and slaughtered at the door of the hut of the bride's mother. Whilst the goat is being cut into pieces, the bridegroom's sisters, the big girls, the stout women with strong arms, go and look for the heroine of the day, who is hidden in a hut in one of the neighbouring villages, and who has not yet been seen. At last they succeed in finding her. She refuses to come. The viragos seize her and pull her out by force. Everybody assembles. She is covered with a large cloth which hides her from the gaze of the bystanders. Surrounded on all sides, she sets forward to the village, the crowd forming a kind of procession. " Let us accompany her, then we shall return home " sing the women who bring her. (A hi mu tjekeleni, hi ta muka). This song of the *tjeka*, the only one which is peculiar to the wedding day, is the prelude to a most strange duel.

The bridegroom's family stands on one side, that of the bride on the other, and then begins the exchange of equivocal compliments.

"Ha!" cry the groomsmen to the bride, "as you are becoming the wife of our brother and coming into our village, try and leave all your vices outside. Do not steal any longer! Forsake your bad ways and become a good girl! "

To this the bride's relatives shout in return :

" You have nothing to boast about! Stop wearying the people! She is far too good for you! Does not everybody know the wild pranks of your son and the dishonour of your family! "

And they go on in this way, at first in joke, but often speaking seriously. They sometimes even go so far as to bombard each other with the half digested matter which has been extracted from the goat's stomach, but, if anyone goes too far and exceeds the recognized limit of insult, the old people will tell him to be quiet. These proceedings however are looked upon as a game and are accompanied with a particular dance called *khana* which consists in jumping first on one leg and then on the other, gesticulating at the same time.

e) The religious act.

The procession reaches the hut of the bride's mother, where the goat was killed. Mats are stretched outside. The bride and groom sit down on the finest of these. It is now that the father performs the religious rite (hahla). He takes between his first finger and thumb a small quantity of the half digested grass which has been taken from the paunch of the animal, makes a little ball of it, touches his tongue with it and emits a sound resembling " tsu "... as if he were slightly spitting. This is the customary sacramental act in most of the sacrifices. (See Part VI.) He stands behind the wedding pair and, looking straight in front of him towards them, speaks to the gods, that is to say to the spirits of his ancestors, and says : " My fathers, my grandfathers (he calls them by their names) look! To-day my child is leaving me. She enters the wedded life (bukatin). Look at her, accompany her where she will live. May she also found a village, may she have many children (mu nyikan timbeleko), may she be happy, good and just. May she be on good terms with those with whom she will be ". Here it may happen that a brother of the bridegroom will interrupt and say : " Yes, we will live peacefully with her if she does her duty well and does not worry her husband ". The old man goes on with his patriarchal prayer without taking any notice of the interruption and everybody listens quietly and attentively. This prayer which he pronounces with his eyes wide open and in a most natural manner is sometimes very long. When the people have had enough of it and wish him to stop, they send a young man to cut a piece of meat and to put it into the old man's mouth. Thus they " cut " his prayer and he keeps still. The person officiating must be the first to partake of the meat of the sacrifice.

f) The symbolical belt.

The astragalus (nhlolo) of the right leg of the sacrificed goat has been carefully kept. All along the belly they cut a strip of skin reaching as far as the neck and up to the chin, which is cut so as to form a kind of pocket at the end of the strip. The astragalus is put into this pocket and the father ties the belt around the waist of the young woman. He must not look at her face to face in doing this. On the contrary, she must turn her

111

back to him. This is doubtless done to wish her good luck and so that she may have many descendants. Natives have a special veneration for the astragalus bone which is also used in the divinatory system.

5) THE TLHOMA, DEPARTURE OF THE BRIDE FOR THE CONJUGAL DWELLING.

If the lobolo business has been duly concluded, the bride will start on the following day for the conjugal dwelling, accompanied by her friends. (1) The next day, she will be joined by the women of her village, who will help her to erect the wood pile (ku koroka shigiyane). They will all go together into the bush to cut a large quantity of branches, and will pile them up between two poles covered with ochre in the bride's village. Each of the husband's relations will take one of these logs during the following months. It is, it seems, a symbolic present from one family to the other.

As for the wood cutters, they take their leave and go home. But what a surprise! Here is the bride going with them! Her sisters are taking her home again! The husband entreats, but in vain! He pursues the woman who, two days before, became his legal wife. To no purpose! He offers her a present to induce her to stay with him. She refuses... This was foreseen; she must go to her mother to fetch her basket (shihundju), her mat, her spoon and other utensils which make up her small trousseau. A last lesson must also be given to the husband : " If we have given you our daughter, do not believe that we have had enough of her! (hi kolile). She is very precious to us and we take her back! "

Patience! To morrow she will come back accompanied by one young girl only who helps to carry her furniture. This

---

(1) It is *taboo* for the bride's parents to keep their daughter in their village when the lobolo has been entirely delivered ; because, should the bride die with them, they would have to return all the cattle, whilst if she dies in the husband's village, the consequences will not be so dreadful (See Part I. Ch. II. C.).

time it is for good! At last! "Ba mu tlhomile!" that is to say: her parents have duly settled her in her home.

In Nondwane this last surprise is spared the bridegroom. The bride comes to his home on the day of the marriage with her two mats, accompanied by a young girl only, and some days later the mother and female relations bring the rest of her trousseau and erect the wood pile. The young bride, when she has definitely accepted her fate and consented to stay, is called *ntlhoñwa* (Ro.) *nhlomi* (Dj.) (the one who has been brought to her husband). During the first week, she will fill all the pots of the people of the village so that when they awake they will find water for their ablutions and say: "We have found a bride! (He kumi ntlhoñwa!)"; she will remove all the ashes from the fire-places, and smear all the huts.

The first night when she sleeps in the hut with her husband, she may refuse to allow him his conjugal rights. The bridegroom then goes to his father and asks him what he ought to do under the circumstances. The father says: "Give her sixpence or a shilling." Then she consents! (Mboza).

III. *Marriage customs in other Ronga clans.*

The description which we have just given may be considered as typical, but there are many variations to be noticed amongst the clans.

In the *Maputju* country, South of Delagoa Bay, there are two informal visits, one of the fiancé, one of the fiancée, to each other's village (ku bona muti). This visit is very short, and they do not accept any food from their hosts. Then the *tjekela* of the boys (the betrothal visit) takes place. They behave in a very dignified manner, do not accept any food the first day and consent to eat on the following day only after having been presented with a gift of 10/ or £ 1! During this visit the girls put 500 reis or sixpence at the bottom of the pots which they fill with water for the ablutions of the boys, otherwise the visitors would say: "The water is too cold. We cannot use it." Sexual relations between boys and girls during these visits were not allowed in former times. Nowadays they are indulged in, and it may be that the fiancé will ask his fiancée to give herself to him " to test her love " (ku kamba lirandju). If she refuses, the whole affair may be compromised.

When the girls go to *tjekela* in their turn, they also observe great formality. Money must be given at least ten times to obtain their consent :

1) They refuse to enter the village.
2) To leave the square and go to the hut.
3) To cross the door of the hut.
4) To sit down on the mats. When the other girls consent, the fiancée remains standing.
5) She consents to sit down when given a shilling.
6) They refuse to answer the greetings.
7) When the others have answered, the fiancée still refuses to do so.
8) They do not consent to give news of their home.
9, 10) They still make difficulties about accepting food.

It may be that the fiancé goes to work in the mines during this period, probably in order to complete his lobolo. When he comes back, a special ceremony is performed which is called *hlomula mutwa*, to remove the thorn. The girls pay him a visit. He sits down amidst his companions, having fixed in his hair a long white thorn made of bone. The shangwane of the fiancée (chief bridesmaid) approaches him, dancing, and removes it. This is a way of saluting him on his return, it means the removal of the fatigue and the sufferings he has undergone, of the thorns which have wounded him.

The concluding ceremonies of *thloma* and of the *shigiyane* are also more developed in the Maputju country and in Nondwane.

This is the custom in *Nondwane*. Girls accompany the new bride to the conjugal home. They go to the bush to which she has fled, capture her there, and bring her to her husband with songs of mourning (hi ku djila nwana). " Where are you going ? You go to a husband whose heart is jealous! You will bring a basket full of mealies to crush : they will say it is but a handful! You will learn to steal and to bewitch (viz. they will accuse you of doing it). " The bride covers her head with a piece of clothing and weeps. So the sad procession reaches the door of the hut of the husband's mother. There the bride sits down. The husband sits near her, but she withdraws from him. Then the men of the village insult her and say : " Come near him "! The old women, the husband's aunts, come and try to remove the veil from her head : " Take it away that we may see you " they say! Two days later they will come again and give her sixpence to take away the clothing with which she has covered her breast, and then she will go about the village in the ordinary dress—or undress.

The building of the wood pile in *Maputju* is also very characteristic. The ceremony takes place on the day of the *tlhoma*. When the procession is heard coming, far away, the friends of the new husband go to meet it. But the girls who accompany the bride refuse to approach the village. They must be enticed by money ; money at each crossway, at the door, in the village square, at the entrance of the hut, etc., money to put down the logs they bring, the pots of beer they carry... And when all the women have consented to unload themselves, the chief bridesmaid still refuses to do so, and must be induced to by a larger sum of money! When they have arranged the wood pile, they dance behind it, hiding the bride in their midst. The husband and his friends are sitting on the other side of the pile. Three girls come closer to them, always dancing. One of them is the shangwane. She puts tobacco into the hand of the bride. Then the bride kneels down before her husband at a little distance and stretches out her hand to offer him snuff. He rises to receive it, but, when he has approached quite close to her and has taken a little of the tobacco between his fingers, she throws the remainder of the snuff into his eyes ; then she runs away pursued by the husband's friends. If she is swift enough, she succeeds in taking hold of a tuft of grass outside the village. Then no one dares to catch her. It will be necessary to bring more money to induce her to relinquish her hold on the grass. After this, she re-enters the village which will be her new abode, and this is really the end!

IV. *Marriage ceremonies in the Northern clans.*

I have succeeded in getting the whole description of the Nkuna marriage from a very good and clear-headed informant, Simeon Gana. It is somewhat different from that of the Rongas.

Here is the resumé (1) of the whole sequence of these rites :

The betrothal visit. (Ku buta). The suitor arrives with his shangwane and an old man who will act as his official representative or go-between (ntjumi). He has already made his choice, and the *ntjumi* at once woos the girl in his name. Her father calls her apart and asks her if she consents. If she is disposed to say yes, she begs to speak with the boy. She chooses a provisional shangwane. They are both shown into the hut of the girl's mother with their respective shangwane. Let us suppose they come to an understanding ; the suitor announces his success to his ntjumi, who goes to the girl's father and informs him that she has consented. But the father refuses to accept this notification ; he must also choose a ntjumi. This is done the same day. The following day, the two parties meet each in a different hut and the first ntjumi again comes and repeats the whole story, the second ntjumi being present.

Then a long discussion takes place (between the grown up people) as to the lobolo. This discussion is conducted by the two ntjumi, who go constantly from one hut to the other, the one conveying the questions: "How many oxen do you claim, etc", the other going in his turn to give an answer. So the two parties never see each other during this disagreeable debate about money. When they are agreed, the suitor and his friends return home and the ntjumi receives £ 1 for his assistance. There is no other *tjekela* than this. The word tjekela is unknown in Nkuna.

The fiancée's visit. As soon as they have gone, the women of the village begin to prepare pots of beer for the lobola feast. But

---

(1) I have explained these rites in detail in a novel entitled *Fazana,* published in *La Semaine Littéraire,* Geneva, Nov. & Dec. 1910.

before this feast takes place, six days later, the girl and her friends go to the young man's village to return the visit. The fiancée has been warned by her mother to be very cautious, not to accept the proposals of her suitor too readily. Boys and girls enjoy themselves thoroughly. A goat is killed for them, a goat called *the feather* because it is as it were a feather in the fiancée's hair, " a feather in her cap "!

The action of lobola follows immediately. The girls have stayed three days and gone home. Six had elapsed before they came. This makes nine days, just enough for the brewing of the beer. It is prepared in the girl's village. All the suitor's family make for it, driving the herd of cattle, fifteen head strong, which is the lobola money. The sham-fight takes place, some of the invaders, the young ones, going steadily forward, the others, the adults, hiding behind the oxen and urging them on under a shower of blows. Huts are offered to the visitors. One is especially reserved for the great *mukoñwana*, the man who has married the fiancé's sister, and whose oxen are used to buy the bride of the day. He has come to see where *his* oxen go. In the evening the girls choose their *shigango*. The next morning they will fetch water for their ablutions. This is the day when the lobolo is officially remitted by one family to the other. Long discussions take place through the intermediary of the two ntjumi, at the end of which the male relations of the bride leave their hut to inspect the cattle and criticise them, the others endeavouring to emphasise their beauty. Two oxen have been killed for the feast, one brought by the fiancé, another provided by the father of the fiancée. Dancing and singing goes on the whole afternoon ; the visitors go home at sunset ; the girls accompany them and tie knots of grass where they part.

A month after the lobola ceremony, a new feast takes place, called *the beer which washes the hoofs of the oxen*. The fiancée, together with the women of the family, (not only the girls), bring pots of beer to the husband's village. They stay outside. When the inhabitants ask them to enter, they run back some distance and only consent on being urged... and so on ! The fiancée does not put down the pot she carries until her suitor has brought a goat. Shillings must be given to induce her to enter the hut, to sit down, to accept water for washing her hands and food, to eat. Another ox is killed and the meat is divided as follows : the liver and the heart are for the bride's father, the leg for her mother, the *nyimba*, viz. the womb, which includes the ribs, sternum etc. for the maternal uncle. The women, when they return home, take all these pieces of meat to their several destinations. They put a skewer through the heart and liver and stick it into the ground before the bride's father's hut saying : " This is the notification of the husband's people. "

If the total number of the oxen has been remitted on the lobola day, *the departure of the new wife* for the husband's kraal (thloma) will not be long delayed. But should there be some oxen wanting, a wise father will not allow her to go until the whole lobolo has been paid. The husband works hard to get together the other oxen. He brings them, without ceremony, together with a sovereign, which he places before the bride's father as a present, saying : " This is my spitting for you, my father! " He does the same for the mother. He now feels the right to claim his wife. They answer : " Give us time to prepare her trousseau." The trousseau consists of two mats, two or three big spoons, some pots, a wooden platter, a pestle and a mortar, and one hoe provided by the maternal uncle, which make up all the equipment of a Nkuna bride. All her female relations meet and, after having exhorted (1) her to be obedient, to accept all the hardships she will find in her new home, they accompany her to her husband's village. This is the *hloma*. The men do not go, except the ntjumi of the bride's family. The father, on the morning before they leave, kills a fowl and *hahla*, viz. makes a sacrifice, telling his ancestors that his daughter goes to be married, and praying for her. The ntjumi,

---

(1) " Hear ! " the old women say to the bride, " you have been a good girl, so far, henceforth you will be treated as a slave ! You will be accused of adultery and of witchcraft. You will have no more happiness. But accept all that ! They will beat you, kill you and we shall not be able to deliver you, because we have eaten their oxen. " These exhortations are worth reproducing, as they show clearly the conditions under which the girl goes to her husband. She is not protected by the lobolo. On the contrary, the lobolo has made her the possession of the husband's family, from whom she must now accept any treatment. (See Part II).

immediately after his arrival, goes to the husband and to his assembled relatives and tells them roughly : " Here we are ; we bring you your dog. Here it is. With us, she was reputed to be a good girl. Now we shall hear you every day say that she is lazy, does not know how to cook, has a host of lovers... All right! Kill her! Kill your dog! Have you not bought it ? She is a witch! Let her drink the magic philter, etc. " The men keep silent... " Yes, you are right. We shall beat her. But if her husband is too hard on her, we shall try to deliver her. We shall do our best to protect her ".

In the meantime the women cut the logs of the *shigiyane*, and fill the pots with water, and the feast goes on, another ox having been killed by the husband. The married pair sit on a mat and the women of the two families begin the mutual exchange of insults which are never wanting on this day! " You dogs! " one of the aunts of the girl will say, " people of no consequence! You have not even a broken pot to remove the ashes from the fireplace. You can congratulate yourselves on getting such a good wife as this, a hard worker, a splendid cook, a nice and honest girl. " An old woman of the other party answers : " Yes! If you have exhorted her sufficiently! Perhaps she will give up her bad ways, her laziness, etc... "—" Bad ways ? You may well speak of that! Look at your son! What was he? A wild beast! We have come to cut off his tail and make a man of him! "

V. *Marriage by abduction.*

The several ceremonies which we have described belong to the legal marriage (ku teka, ku lobola). But there exists another way of getting a wife, and the poor (psisiwana), those who have no oxen, no pounds sterling for lobola, especially if they have no energy, have recourse to this method. It is called *ku tlhuba*. A young man in such a position, wishing to marry such and such a girl, will send a friend to her and propose a rendez-vous in the bush. If she agrees to become his wife in this irregular manner, she goes there and meets him. They have relations together and run to one of the relatives of the girl's mother. The family of the mother will be more lenient than the family of the father, having no right to the lobolo. The transgressors of the law will probably choose the village of the maternal uncle and settle there. The parents look everywhere for their daughter and try to get her to return home. If she is quite determined to remain with her ravisher, they let her go free, deploring their misfortune and their shame. But it is rare in the primitive state of the tribe for such a marriage not to be regularised. The thief, if he has retained any feeling of decency, will try to collect the lobolo. One morning he goes to the village of his wife's parents, and deposits a sovereign or a goat or a cock on the threshold of the hut of the girl's mother ; or he hangs a half-sovereign on the goat's neck, rubs its lips with salt to prevent it from bleating, and then shouts loudly : " We have stolen, we of such and such a clan "... People wake from their sleep, not knowing what animal has made such a noise, come out of their huts and see the culprit standing outside the fence. When he has been duly recognised, he runs away. He will perhaps bring some other presents till he has definitely " lobola " his wife. This is called the *nshonshonela*. Should he not succeed in bringing the regular payment, the first girl born of that marriage will be the lobolo. " Nwana a ta lobola mamana wa kwe " : the child will pay for her mother. In law, all the children of such a union belong to the girl's family : a man who has not lobola has no right of property in his children. (See Part III.)

Should the woman who has been stolen by *tlhuba* go at once to live with her irregular husband in his village, her parents will arrange matters in another way. They will " go as enemies " (hi bulala), make a regular descent on the village of the thief, kill a pig, threaten to take all the furniture. The men of that village will then intercede and, in the course of time, the lobolo will be paid. (See App. VIII.)

The Evolution of a Man from Birth to Death

SOME REMARKS ON THE MARRIAGE CUSTOMS
OF THE THONGAS

Though somewhat different in the various clans, the marriage customs show a strong resemblance in them all and differ only in details. There are three great "moments" to be distinguished in the sequence of the rites: 1) the *buta*, betrothal, with the two official visits of the fiancé and the fiancée. 2) The *lobola*, remittance of the purchase money on which the two families have agreed and 3) the *hloma*, the ceremony of taking the bride to her husband's home. Some of the customs accompanying these principal acts are very strange and seem at first quite incomprehensible.

1) To understand them, we must observe that marriage in primitive or semi-civilised tribes is not an individual affair as it has become with us. It is an affair of the community. It is a kind of contract between two groups, the husband's family and the wife's family. What is the respective position of the two groups or families ? One of the groups loses a member, the other gains one. To save itself from undue diminution, the first group claims compensation, and the second grants it under the form of the lobolo. This remittance of money, oxen or hoes, will allow the first group to acquire a new member in place of the one lost, and so the balance will be kept. This conception of the lobola as a compensation, a means of restoring the equilibrium between the two groups, is certainly the right one.

This need of maintaining the importance of a group, the tendency to resist a lessening of that group, accounts also for some of the other customs ; all the rites which emphasise the value of the bride find their explanation there. "A hi si kola ha yene", "we are not tired of her, we would gladly keep her", say her parents by means of these rites. The reciprocal insults which take place on the day of the hloma have the same origin. The relatives of the bride do their best to show the immense superiority of their own family over the other and of their daughter over her husband. The second group defends itself as well as it can ; hence the challenges which sometimes end in a real fight.

The sham fight is probably to be explained in the same way. The boys, the brothers of the bride, soundly thrash the brothers of the husband who dare to come and take away one of the girls of the kraal. They do not like to see their family impoverished, diminished. The old men carry the hoes and show them to the defenders of the kraal saying: "This is our ox!" Or they hide themselves amidst the cattle as claiming their protection, because this is certainly the only condition upon which the bride's clan would consent to receive the invaders. Mr. van Gennep is right, I think, in rejecting the old explanation of the sham fight as being a remnant of the marriage by capture, which would have been the primitive form of marriage amongst these tribes. The Thongas possess the marriage by abduction, but this is quite another thing, as we have seen.

2) But it is probable that some of the rites of the Thonga marriage must be explained by an older form of marriage. The Rev. W. C. Willoughby in this book on *Race Problems in the New Africa* calls the type of marriage which we have described, and which is met with in all the South African tribes, *marriage of dominion.* The system of family life which results from the marriage of dominion is patrilineal :— children will trace their descent through their father and inherit his property,— patrilocal—the mother lives in the village of the father— patripotestal—the father possesses the children and has full power over them. But in other Bantu tribes, especially in Central Africa, the system is different. There we meet with what the same author calls the *matrilineal theory of marriage.* This system is matrilocal—the wife remains in the village of her group ; matrilineal—children trace their descent through their female ancestors ; avunculipotestal—the mother's brother has power over them, not the father. They belong to the mother's group and inherit its property. Under this system, the hloma, viz. the third "moment" of the marriage of dominion, does not take place, and the lobola, the bride-price, is not so important. The husband is only a lodger or a frequent visitor in his wife's village ; he is a mere begetter of other people's children, and pays for this privilege by working for his wife's group or occasionally presenting it with gifts.

It is probable that this matrilineal theory of marriage is the older and that it has developed, under various influences, into the marriage of dominion. Mr. Willoughby supposes that men having captured women in raids and brought them to their homes found that system more convenient for them, and wished to possess their regular wives in the same manner. Change in the economic conditions must have had the same result. When, owing to a more settled way of living, property increased and cattle became plentiful, it is easy to conceive that the men of the husband's group made a kind of social contract with the men of the wife's group, offering a higher bride-price in order to obtain the transfer of the bride to her suitor's home.

Now, if this is the history of the evolution of the Bantu marriage (and we shall see later on, in studying the relation of the uterine nephew with his mother's brother, that it is quite probable that it is), we may find, in comparing these two forms of marriage, the explanation of some of the Thonga rites. The position of the wife was certainly much more satisfactory, from her point of view, under the old system. She could remain with her people and her husband had but little power over her, whilst, in the marriage of dominion, she must stay in the village of another group, work for it, and perhaps be ill-treated. Does this fact not account for her flight to the bush or to another village the day before hloma, when the female relatives of the husband go and seize her by force ? She tries to hide herself under a veil, as if she wished not to be recognised; but the husband's aunts remorselessly take it from her, and as she goes to the conjugal dwelling, her friends accompany her, singing songs of mourning. These rites are certainly more readily explained if there was, in a remote past, entirely forgotten by individuals, yet still influencing the mind of the community, another state of things, when the married woman was much freer and more happy.

3) We find the explanation of some other ceremonies when we apply to them the theory of the *Rites of passage*. For both bridegroom and bride, there is in fact passage to a new condition of life. They pass from the position of single to that of married persons. Hence the part taken by their best friends and by the bridesmaids, from whom they are separated by their marriage. For the bride there is passage from one family to another, from one village to another.

I cannot say that I have found distinct *separation* and *marginal* rites, but aggregation rites are numerous. The *aggregation rites* are first of all the common participation in the flesh of the oxen during the feasts. Nothing makes Natives more friendly towards each other than to eat meat together. Then come the building of the wood pile, the girl's acts of civility to the husband's friends during the *tjekela* and the day after the *hloma*. These rites being collective seem to represent the union of the two families. The new wife performs them herself individually during the first week of her marriage.

How is it possible to explain the calculated resistance to acts of politeness on the part of both male and female visitors during the betrothal ceremonies, and even later on ? If the girls alone made a difficulty about entering the village, the hut, and sitting down on the mats, drinking, eating, etc. we should say : This rite is also, on the part of the diminished group, a means of asserting its importance, of saving its dignity. But the boys do the same thing on their visit. They maintain the same disdainful attitude... This certainly arises from the fact that the two social groups look upon each other with some distrust, not yet being fully acquainted, and consequently observing a mutual reserve. But further information and a closer comparative study of Thonga rites enables me to give still another explanation.

The term employed to designate this rite is *kunga*. This verb is of Ngoni (Zulu) origin. Used in a general way, it means to remit a present to a chief who has sent his emissaries to claim it. The chief *"kungisa"* viz. orders to kunga. In its ritual sense, it means to give a present to a person who refuses to do something for ritual reasons. The old Thonga expression is *alula*. This word is the reversive derivative of the verb *ala*, to refuse ; it therefore means to remove the refusal, to overcome it, to cause somebody to yield. The Kunga rite is performed on at least five different occasions : 1) for the circumcised boy on the day when he is received into the community of adults (page 93) ; 2) for the girl who has passed through the khomba initiation ; 3) for the boy who has wooed a girl, when he pays his official visit to her and to her family, and for the girl, when she returns the visit with her maids, but especially when she goes to the domicile of her husband and thus enters the married state ; 4) for the first-born child ; 5) for the woman who has lost many children and consequently is in a state of bereavement (bowumba) when she again gives birth to a child. In all these cases, the person concerned passes from one condition to another ; the circumcised from the childish to the adult stage, the suitor and his bride from the unmarried to the married state, the woman who has had her first child from the state of womanhood to that of motherhood and the bereaved woman from the state of bereavement to the normal position of a mother carrying a child on her shoulders. And here we meet with the old Bantu conception of life. This passage, in the evolution of human life, is fraught with danger. The person concerned stands on the defensive. He or she refuses to speak, to look at other people, to enter their village, or, in the case of the newly married girl, to perform her conjugal duty. Those who wish them to accept their new condition must persuade them to do so by giving them presents, generally presents of little importance, a wire bracelet, a small coin, etc. This will remove the danger.

This rite, which might be called a *defensive rite*, is therefore certainly a rite of passage and this is also proved by the fact that the money or the bracelets given to the persons concerned do not remain their property. As regards the circumcised, they remit them to the chief, and the chief distributes them to the old women who are no longer able to bear children. The girl who has passed through the khomba gives them to her adopted mother, who will use them in the same way. All the money remitted to the bride will go to the master of the village, for the old women and the children. *Married people must have no share in it*, as these presents are taboo. Why ? Because they are connected with a passage, and people who have sexual relations are considered as increasing the dangers connected with these critical phases of human development, when the heart is troubled by a half-conscious fear of a new and unknown future. Amongst civilised people who have reached the era of individualism, these fears find their expression in songs and poetry. In the communistic society they express themselves by means of rites.

*

*   *

Here are some answers to the questions of Professor Frazer on marriage.

A man always brings his wife to his own home. This is the *tlhoma*, and it is a law. It is taboo for him to go and live with his parents-in- law, at any rate when he marries his first wife. In the course of time, when the children have grown up, when the *bukoñwana*, viz. the relations with parents-in-law, are of old standing, a man can go and live in his wife's village (See Part II). Another case in which this can be done is when a widow refuses to marry the man who legally inherits her, and gives herself to a stranger, a man of Inhambane, for instance. He does not pay the lobolo, and lives with her in her village ; but the children born of that union will belong to the family of the deceased husband.

There is no preparation for marriage amongst the Thongas by fasting, bleeding or keeping awake the night before. No corn or rice is thrown at the bridal pair. The bride or bridegroom is never represented at the marriage by a proxy or dummy. Conjugal relations begin immediately after marriage (see page 113), but the wife does not possess her home and her kitchen for the first year ; during that period she must cook for her mother-in-law.

There are no occasions on which men exchange their wives.

See practical conclusions on Marriage Rites at the end of Vol. I.

E. MATURE AGE

I. *The Bantu Ideal.*

The married man is called " he who has his home " (a ni le kwakwe) in opposition to the single man (nkhwenda). But let us say at once that the kind of individual called bachelor does not abound amongst the Bantus. Only the utterly wretched, invalids, and the weak-minded, are deprived of legal marriage, which for the black man is and remains the one object in life. It is through his wife and children that he becomes somebody in society. This fact does not appear during the first year of wedlock, for the newly married woman must cook at the fireplace of her mother-in-law. She is hardly more than a servant during a whole year ; she does not possess her own pot ; and this must be so because she does not yet eat the mealies of her own garden, having ploughed her fields in her former domicile the previous year. Her husband eats with her. He is not yet a lord. But if he is rich, if he is the heir of an important man, he will not be long in buying a second and third wife.

These new marriages will be contracted like the first, but with less pomp. It may even happen that the feast is held in the husband's village, if he is middle-aged and is celebrating his fifth or sixth wedding.

For each new wife, he will build a hut. He has begun his village when building the house of his first wife, the great wife, (nsati lwe nkulu) as she is called, who will remain the principal one whatever may happen. While, without compass, he was drawing on the ground, with the marvellous instinct of the South African Native, the circumference of the circle on which the patched reed walls of his dwelling were to rise, while he was covering this circular wall with a conical roof, he was saying to himself : " I establish my home ; I inaugurate my village ". During the following years, the aim of his life will be to complete little by little another wider circle... When he has bought his second wife, he will build for her also a hut of the same type. But this second hut, the third, and the fourth which may come afterwards, will not be erected in a straight row like a street. They will form an arc, which will be prolonged so as to constitute first a semi-circle and then a complete circle, if a sufficient number of buildings are added. This is the ideal of the black man, to

Fhot. H. Gross

Ndjakandjaka, a headman of Spelonken, with his men.

become the lord and master of a complete circular village. Most of the men do not realise this ideal. Three or four huts, a wretched quarter of a circle is all that they attain to! Some, better armed for the struggle of life, or more favoured by circumstances, succeed in closing their circle. Their cattle, for which they have also built a circular enclosure right in the middle of the square of the village, multiply and are not carried off by peripneumonia and hematuria, which, in this country, decimate so many herds! Every three years, theirs wives bear children. If they are boys, it is an honour ; the village will not lack heirs, neither will the father lack arms to help and to defend him! If they are girls, it means wealth ; oxen will come to the family! Their brothers will not lack wives, for the sisters will be sold to provide for the brothers. Meanwhile, the huts are erected, large and small, that of the head of the family being the largest, the *malao*, those of the boys the least well kept.

Let us consider a Ronga favoured by fate, as was Gidja, of the country of Libombo, near Rikatla. His village numbered not less than twenty-four huts, with beautiful shady trees behind ; notice the enclosure for the cattle and for the goats on the central place, that for the pigs behind the houses... There are cocks and hens pecking about everywhere, dogs wandering around in search of something to steal, for they receive hardly any food ; a crowd of youngsters leading the cattle, and everywhere the noise of the pestles crushing the daily mealies in the large mortars. He walks about proudly in his favoured enclosure, contemplating his prosperity with pleasure. Young men are ready to do the work he gives them to do. He will treat them with beer brewed by his wives. And often the people of the neighbouring villages will join his people for dances and games on the fine square, which is surrounded and enclosed on all sides by huts.

And, above all things, in the evening, each of his wives will bring him the pot which she has cooked for him. This is the essential matrimonial duty of the wife. Not one will fail in it. Gidja, the lord of six or seven pots of mealies seasoned with a sauce of monkey nuts, will feast and be satiated (shura) every day, and that means much, for the inner capacity of a Thonga is something wonderful.

He will become large and stout, and shining, which in South Africa is a sure sign of wealth and nobility. The stouter he gets the more will he be respected. But it can easily be imagined that he cannot alone empty all these pots over which he reigns supreme. He feasts his children, but others too come to pay him visits at the evening hour when they know him to be surrounded by so many good things! Sycophants are not lacking, " Good evening, son of so and so! " they say. " You are one of the great men of the country. " And in return for these and other compliments, the magnanimous Gidja shares his feast with his admirers!

Strangers are crossing the country and inquire where they can be received. " Go to Gidja " they are told. " A ni tshengwe, a fuya tshengwe " viz. " he is the possessor of a harem! He is not killed by famine! He has beer to drink every day! He can give food to poor people. Even then, some of it remains on the plate and is eaten by little boys and dogs in the square. There is always abundance there." And the travellers come and enter (khuleka) his village, after which they will tell in their homes the story of the magnificence of Gidja and extol his hospitality.

Thus the man who has succeeded in life becomes famous, his advice will carry weight in the discussions in which he takes part ; he will perhaps be even more esteemed than the chief himself, though he does not enjoy the special prestige which the royal family owes to the blood running in its veins.

Conclusion : the greatness of an African is before all else a matter of pots, and the matter of pots is closely connected with polygamy !

During these years of mature age the evolution of a man is not marked by special ceremonies. There is one custom however which is common to all, and which marks an advance in their social position. It is that of fixing the wax ring.

II. *Fixing the wax ring.*

Amongst the South Africans, the crown is not the appanage of royalty. All men having reached mature age have the right to adorn themselves with it. It is true, it is not a diadem of precious stones, but a large ring of wax. This custom seems to have a Zulu origin. The Ba-Sutho do not know it and the Ba-Thonga, who all practise it, have taken it from the conquering tribe which owes its fortune to the famous Chaka. This habit has spread all over the country from Maputju to the borders of Gaza, but only during the last hundred years. This black crown is called *ngiyana* (Ro.) or *shidlodlo* (Dj.), and the crowning ceremony is called *khehla*. From this verb has come the term *makhehla*, a name given to all those who wear this ornament.

This ceremony is accomplished in the following way. At a given time, the chief informs all the men of a certain age that they must prepare their rings. The counsellors and the sons of the royal family who belong to this " class " must go to the capital. Several oxen are killed ; the back tendons are carefully preserved and made into strings. This being done, the master hairdressers, that is to say those who know how to fix these strange appendages, are called in.

They come, supplied with small sticks (tinhlamalala, the central nervures of the leaves of the milala palm-tree) which they plait together with these strings made of tendons so as to form the skeleton, the circular frame of the crown. These strings are drawn through the curly hair, all round the head, so as to fix the frame of the crown above the temples. The remaining hair on the sides and behind has been previously shaven. The chief possesses a provision of wax ; the wax which is preferred is not that of bees, but the rosy secretion of certain grubs which is found on some bushes, and which the young boys of the capital go and collect. This wax is mixed with different ingredients to make it black. It is fixed on the frame of sticks and shaped into a large round or oval ring, as black as jet, which can be made to shine brightly. When all is finished, they eat the flesh of the oxen, enjoy themselves, dance and celebrate this great occasion!

The more humble subjects crown themselves in their own villages, where tonsorial artists come to adorn them. The poor go to the hairdresser, and do not use strings made of tendons (they have no ox to kill), but strings made of the fibres of a palm-tree, which are cheaper. It is said that nowadays palm-tree strings (bukuha) have almost entirely supplanted the others, the more so as they are not spoilt by the washing of the crown ; whilst, if the *ngiyana* is fixed with tendons, no water must fall on it, or it would soften.

Moreover the crown must be taken care of ; it can be spoilt

and knocked out of shape by a blow or if its owner goes through thorny bushes. A *khehla* who has some self-respect will frequently polish and repair this valuable ornament, for it is a sign of mature age. He who has been ordered by the chief to wear it no longer carries burdens on his head; his crown would be spoilt! He will be accompanied by a boy who carries his parcels; he himself will only carry his stick or his assagai. He will at once be known as one of the mature men of the tribe. This is not to say that the mere fact of wearing the *ngiyana* gives the right of taking part in the important affairs of the country; the counsellors alone possess this right; but from amongst the " crowned, " will be chosen the man who is sent to another chief to treat of political questions, for instance.

When the hair grows (for, though it is curly, it may become long), the crown rises with it and becomes more or less unsteady, which must be most uncomfortable! The best thing would be to cut the ornament off and then replace it. Mr. Mandjia, one of our neighbours at Rikatla, was probably too lazy to undertake this job, so he put a small red handkerchief between his skull and the crown to prevent it from wobbling.

At a certain time all the *ngiyana* disappeared from the land of Nondwane. The chief Mapunga was dead! The loss, kept secret for a year, had been made public, and the law requires all the mature men to take off their crowns when the sovereign of the country is dead. They take the wax from the frame, and make a ball of it; this they fix on a little stick, and place this stick in the roof of their hut above the door. The frame is hung up quite close by, and they leave these objects there till the new chief orders his subjects to re-make their crowns. This shows clearly that the crowning custom is in close relation with the national life of the tribe. The " makhehla " also form special battalions in the army.

Nowadays, however, this custom is not observed as religiously as in bygone times. Life is harder, one must go and earn pounds sterling in the port of Lourenço Marques, or in the gold mines, and one can no longer indulge in a lazy life! It may therefore happen that a poor man will refuse to wear the crown, and say to his chief : " What shall I eat ?   Will you feed me ?   Must I not carry burdens on my head ?   I do not know what to do with the ngiyana. " — " Tiko dji bolile, " say the old people shaking their heads, "A ke he na nao," that is to say :   " The country is falling into decay, going to the dogs.   There is no longer any law... " Oh! the good old times!

F. OLD AGE

The man however grows older, older.   His hair and his beard turn white, the wrinkles deepen on his face.   He stoops.   His skin no longer shines with health and corpulence.   His wives die and his glory fades.   His crown loses the lustre of bygone times.   If a branch scratches it, if a knock spoils it, he has not a shilling to pay the repairer!   He is forsaken.   He is less respected and often only a burden unwillingly supported.   The children laugh at him.   If the cook sends them to carry to the lonely grandfather his share of food in his leaky old hut, the young rascals are capable of eating it on the way and of depriving the old man of his meal, afterwards pretending that they have done what they were told!   And when, between two huts, under shelter of the hedge of reeds, he warms his round-shouldered back in the rays of the setting sun, huddled there, quite weighed down by his years, lost in some senile dream, they point to the decrepit form and say to each other : " He! Shikhunkununu! " — " It is the bogey-man, the ogre! "

People of mature age show scarcely more consideration for old people than do the young ones.   Lately in the district of Matjolo, an old man and an old woman, Kobole and Minyokwana, were forsaken by their children, who were moving to another part of the country.   They were left in a miserable shed, merely a roof supported by some poles without any reeds to close in the wall. Some compassionate souls took pity on this poor wretched couple, who had fallen into second childhood and did not even know what they were saying.

In time of war, old people die in great numbers. During moments of panic, they are hidden in the wood, in the palm-tree swamps, while all the able-bodied population run away. They are killed by the enemy, who spares no one (it is the law of war), or they die in their hiding-places of misery and hunger!

As may be seen, the eve of life is very sad for the poor Thonga. There are however children who, to the end, show much devotion to their parents. The most to be pitied are those who fall to the charge of remote nephews or cousins. They can only repeat in a broken voice the sad refrain : " Ba hi shanisa! " — " They treat us very badly! "

G. DEATH

I. *The last days.*

Manyibane, the headman of a big village near Rikatla, is dangerously ill. The men of his kraal, his friends, have come to inquire about the illness (kamba shinyonga) and have learned that it is serious. They issue this order to all the inhabitants : " Tlulan psilawen! " — " Keep each of you in his sleeping place, (viz. the men to the right of the hut, the women to the left) and have no more relations. It is taboo! The man would die! " Should visitors come, they are not allowed to enter the village. They must have kept " pure " for two days at least. Two sticks are planted on either side of the door of the hut, and a third is put over them so as to close the entrance. " It is the way black people have of making their proclamation, " says Mboza. " Everybody will know that a dying man is there and nobody will come in. " Should another man of the village have had relations with the same woman as the patient, he is doubly prohibited from seeing him, because the patient would break out into perspiration and die immediately. This is the great law of *matlulana*, as we shall see.

Of course the *ñanga* (doctor) has been called already. He

has tried his best. The bone-thrower also! He has perhaps discovered that the disease was due to a wizard. He has found him out by his art. The suspected one is called and solemnly ordered to heal the patient. He is shut up in the hut with him, and he must recall his deadly spells and restore the man to health. But this has not succeeded, any more than the doctor's drugs!

The dying man calls together all his relations, and utters his last wishes before them : " Somebody has not come ; go and fetch him " he says. When they are all present, he says to them : " All right, my brethren, my children. I wanted to see you before dying. I wanted you, especially so and so, who has been so good to me. The others hated me ; you always showed me love. Henceforth I entrust to you the care of my people. " He will probably designate his successor, who is to be the great one (nkulukumba), and recommend the others to obey him.

Then he reminds them of his debts, those he owes and those which are owing to him. " So and so has lobola our daughter and has not paid all the oxen... " He reveals to them also the place where he has buried some treasure. " Go to such a place, in such a hut, and you will find it. " He does not say a word about his wives and about their future, as such questions will be settled according to the laws relating to widows, which are well known.

When the breathing becomes shorter, those who watch over him begin to *bend his limbs* (ku khondla psiro (Ro.) ; ku putja (Dj.).) This is a very old custom, and is deemed so important that the operation begins before death, lest the rigidity of the body should prevent its being accomplished. When the bending of the limbs had been too long delayed, it has sometimes been necessary to break them. To avoid this disagreeable possibility, one may see those attending to the dying man take his hands gently and bring them close up to his chin, and fold his legs against his body. When asked why they do so, they will say : " It is the law. This is the way of caring for the dead (bekisa). " Or : " It is in order to have smaller graves to dig... " But I do not think this utilitarian reason to be the true one. Amongst the Ba-Ronga, where graves are dug in the soft sand, there would not be the least difficulty in making a larger hole.

THE EVOLUTION OF A MAN FROM BIRTH TO DEATH

Some ethnographers have adopted the "embryonic explanation" to account for this custom, which is found all through primitive humanity, from the Mousterian age down to the first inhabitants of Egypt, and amongst a great many uncivilised tribes all over the earth (1). They say: "Primitive man placed the corpse in the attitude of the child before birth because he believed that death is but a new birth, the beginning of a new life..." I asked Viguet if he thought this to be the true original explanation. He told me he did not know ; he would not deny it. But there is one fact which prevents its acceptance ; the Thongas have never done any dissection, and are ignorant of the position of the foetus in the womb. So probably are all primitive peoples. This kind of knowledge came much later in the evolution of mankind. The intention of this rite is more probably to place a dying man in the sitting position which a Thonga generally adopts when in his hut, as the grave is *but a hut in the earth* and he is meant to continue his life in it exactly as before. All the other burial rites confirm this explanation, as we shall see.

Manyibane is dead... In some districts they see that he does not die with *closed hands*. It is taboo, because then the children of the dead will quarrel (Viguet). They close his eyes and take away all his clothes. In the Mpfumo clan, they *wash the body*. Afterwards they cover him with an old rug. No one cries. Lamentations are absolutely prohibited before the burial is over ; it is taboo. It would " break the back " of the men who have to perform the funeral rites.

Should there be *strangers* in the village when the death takes place, they will run away quickly to avoid defilement ; otherwise they would have to take part in all the purifying ceremonies of the following days.

Without delay, the *fire* which was burning in the funeral hut is removed and carried out into the square. It must be carefully kept alight. This is a taboo. Should there be rain, it must be protected. All the inhabitants must use this fire during the next five days. It will be put out by the doctor, with sand or water, on the day of the dispersion of the mourners. He will then

(1) See my paper in *Anthropos* Sept. 1910 : " Two burials at twenty thousand years distance. "

light a new one, and everyone will take from it embers to kindle his own fire in the different huts. It is one of the conditions of the purification of the village.

The same day young people are sent to all the relatives in the neighbourhood to announce the death. Even the relations who are absent far away, in Johannesburg, must be informed; this is done in the following way. Someone takes a handful of grass, lights it and, when it is on fire, throws it in the direction of the absent one, saying : " Your brother, here, is dead. Do not fear. May your enemies (viz. your white employers) have consideration and love for you, that you may find sleep and health. "

II. *The grave.*

The men of the village then go out to dig the grave. They choose a place behind the hut of the deceased or somewhere further off in the little forest which generally surrounds the village ; or in the *ntimu*, the sacred wood, if he were one of the guardians of the forest (1), one belonging to the elder branch of the family.

First of all the diggers see that a tree is near the grave on which to hang some of the belongings of the deceased (those which will be kept but will have to be purified) ; they dig a hole of about six feet in length, four in width, and two and half or three deep. This first hole can be dug with ordinary hoes. Then, at the side of it, they excavate a second hole, more or less circular in form, using for this a light wooden board, generally the rim of an old basket. The sides of the hole are well smoothed by means of this instrument. In the Northern clans they sometimes smear it with mud taken from the river ; they also put a reed beside the corpse, and grass, which grew in water, is spread at the bottom of the grave (2). So the grave, is in a way, double. It presents

(1) In the Southern clans the grave of the husband or the wife is dug in front of the hut in which they were living (as this hut is to be abandoned) ; in the case of a child, he will be buried at the side of the hut (as, in this case, the hut will not be destroyed.) The grave is surrounded by a fence made of sticks and plastered with clay. Thus people will remember where the corpse has been buried.
(2) Compare this custom with the rite of burying little children and twins in wet soil.

two levels, the higher, the large hole, gives access to the smaller, the circular ovoid grave. The first is called *the square* (hubo) of the deceased, the second is *his hut* (yindlu or shinyatu). He will dwell in the hut, but come out from it and sit in his square underground, just as he did when living in his village (1). (Elias.)

When the grave has been duly dug, the diggers call the relatives to inspect their work, and show them that their deceased relation has been well cared for. The lower grave, being excavated in the wall of the higher, forms a kind of vault. It seems as if it were considered necessary that the earth which will protect the head should not be disturbed. When all the mourners have come at the call of the diggers, it sometimes happens that the vault of the grave falls in. This is a very bad sign. The cause of the accident is this ; either the person who has bewitched the deceased is present or, amongst the assistants, there is one who has been guilty of " matlulana " against him (2)! The grave is a *mondjo*, a magical means of divination.

III. *The burial.*

The diggers may be four in number, but they are generally only two ; the master of the mourning (nwinyi wa nkosi), who is the brother next to the deceased, and another younger near relative, for instance a son. Both must be married, because married people alone can get rid of the defilement of death by the " lahla khombo, " which we shall explain later. Should an unmarried son be asked to undertake the work of burial, he

(1) In some clans of the North there is only one hole and no excavation at the side. But what I have described here is the rule amongst the Ba-Ronga, except where civilisation has already modified the old custom.

(2) On this point Mboza and Elias did not agree. Mboza said that the falling in of the grave can only be caused by the presence of the wizard who killed the deceased. Elias asserts that the same accident happens if one of those present has *tjemakanya* the deceased, viz. crossed his way, that is to say has had sexual relations with the same woman as the deceased. (This is matlulana). As the hut of the deceased knew this man, so his new hut in the ground recognises and reveals him !

would answer : " How can you propose such a thing to me ?
Am I not immature (mbisi, properly raw) ? I am not yet ripe!
Is defilement of death not there ? With whom could I wash it
away ? " (Viguet). The first digger is also called " the one of
the head, " the second, " the one of the feet, " because one
of them will carry the corpse by the head, the other by the feet.
Women may also bury a corpse upon occasion.

So the grave-diggers go back to the hut and begin to wrap
the corpse in his rugs and in his mat (ku tjimba). They stitch
the mat twice (to prevent it from slipping ?) (Viguet). They
generally wait till sunset to perform the burial. When the time
has come, they make a hole in the wall of the hut on the right side,
as the husband dwells in the right half of the house, the wife in the
left half. The corpse must not be carried out of the hut by
the door, but by that artificial opening (1). So he leaves the
hut head foremost (2). They sometimes stop up their noses with
the leaves of a bush called ngupfana, which has a strong scent, in
order not to perceive the smell of death (moya wa lifu). They
march slowly, without a word, men and women following them
silently. The " one of the head " goes down to the first level,
the one of the feet follows him. They have already put in the
place for the head a piece of wood, a piece of a branch of nkanye,
their sacred tree, one foot long and three inches broad, to be
used as a pillow. At the bottom, on the soil, they stretch some
old rugs. They lay the corpse down (3) on its left side, the
head on the pillow. The grave has been dug in such a way
that its long axis is directed towards that cardinal point whence
the ancestors came, so that the deceased, having his head slightly

(1) In the Hlabi clans, the corpse is carried through the door, but the plaster on
both sides of the door (marimba) is beaten and falls down. It will be repaired later on.
In the Northern clans the hut of the deceased is not so strongly tabooed as amongst the
Ba-Ronga. When it has been purified it will be used again.

(2) Comparative Ethnography : In Switzerland it is a common saying that a corpse
must leave the house feet foremost.

(3) The Ba-Ngoni place their dead in the grave in the sitting position, a knife in
their hands, as they are a race of murderers! (Viguet). It may be that the reclining
position given to the corpse by the Ba-Ronga, is the result of an evolution. At any
rate, this is not the true sleeping position, as Natives generally do not bend their
limbs when sleeping.

bent backwards, is intended to look in that direction (1). Now
they take away from the deceased all those rugs in which they

Drawn by Cl. Heaton and reproduced from « Anthropos ».

A Ronga in his grave.

had wrapped him, and cut them through the middle with a knife,
making a large opening in each of them as well as in the mats, also

(1) I attended on December 17th 1908, the burial of one of my neighbours at
Rikatla, called Sokis, and described the rites which I witnessed that day in the paper
already quoted, published by *Anthropos,* September 1910.

in the pieces of clothing which have all been brought and which must be thrown into the grave. " Everything must *hefemula*, breathe its last, just the same as the deceased," said Spoon. "It is taboo." No iron must be put into the grave. Iron, black iron, is *ndjoba* ; it is dangerous to the deceased, because it does not decay as quickly as the corpse, the rugs and the mats... It must not be buried. Copper and brass still less! Because they do not even change colour. " These would call Death to the village because they remain shining ; they would shine for Death and point out other people of the kraal saying : Kill! " (Viguet) Copper and brass bracelets as well as white snuff boxes are called *nhlale*, not *ndjoba* (1).

It is interesting to notice how the different belongings of the dead are dealt with, and where they are put. There are two categories. Some must disappear with the deceased, some will be kept.

To the first category belong above all his rugs ; they are wrapped round his body. He sleeps in them ; they must not be tied, however, because it is taboo to tie a corpse ; the spirit, *shikwembu*, would become angry at being imprisoned and would cause evil (2). The mats are spread in the first hole, as well as the old jackets and trousers, because there the deceased will come and sit on them, when he goes out of his hut to rest in his square. The earthen pots, especially the old ones, are broken on the grave afterwards " to show anger against death " (Elias). The mug, which is one of them, may be occasionally put on the grave, pierced at the bottom, and offerings of beer will be poured into it later on for the dead. All these perishables are to die with him. They are called his filth (thyaka ra yena). Objects of the first category are sometimes burnt in the Northern clans.

---

(1) It is sometimes a matter of discussion to know what is *ndjoba* and what is not. I saw the digger tear off the buttons from the trousers of Sokis, when he was cutting them through, and throw them out of the grave. An old woman, thinking perhaps that they were not of such an incorruptible nature as iron, put them in again, and again he threw them out.

(2) It would even seem that no knot must enter a grave. Two bits of skin tied together and forming the clothing of Sokis round the loins were first untied and then thrown into the grave.

The second category includes the articles which are preserved as having still some value ; they will be hung on the tree, or placed at the foot of the tree near the grave, or in front of the abandoned hut, and will be duly purified during the next few days, as we shall see. Good baskets, new pots, assagais (1), knives, hoes etc.; belong to the second category. They will afterwards be distributed amongst

Drawn by Cl. Heaton from a photo of H. A. Junod and reproduced from "Anthropos".

The grave of Sokis, a man of Rikatla.

(Sokis being an exorcist, a little hut has been built on his grave).

the heirs. In the Northern clans, seeds taken from the store of the deceased are sometimes also thrown into the grave with the words : " Go with your seeds. "

But let us return to the burial. The " one of the head " officiates in the grave ; then all the relations help him to fill the hole. They

(1) The blade but not the handle, which is included in his " filth " and which is broken. " The handle is *he*, the blade is not *he*. "

push the sandy soil with their hands. With great care they remove every piece of root, as if to make the sand perfectly clean. This is a taboo dictated by respect for the deceased. To do otherwise would mean "to throw him away" (tshukumeta). The head has been covered with a towel and the earth is brought near it very gently. Now the digger takes two twigs from the branch of a male nkanye (the nkanye is a dioecious vegetable) and puts them into the right hand of the deceased, which is seen emerging from the rugs near his cheek. When the earth reaches the level of this arm, the latter is stretched out slowly so as to cause the two twigs to emerge. This stretching process goes on as long as it is possible to draw the arm outwards, the hole being gradually filled in. When the arm is fully extended, the digger clutches (wutla) one of the twigs and gives it to one of his helpers, who keeps it; the second remains in the hand of the deceased. Such is, at any rate, the regular way of performing the *rite of the twig*. But often one twig only is put in the hand and it is taken away as soon as the earth reaches it, without any stretching out of the arm; or it is made to emerge from the sand by gently pulling all the time, till the grave is filled in, so that, when the tumulus is formed, the end of the twig is still to be seen. The younger brother will then take it to perform the religious rite. The twig is called the *mhamba*, a word which we translate generally by offering, but which designates any object by means of which men enter into relation with the spirits of the ancestors. The officiating person sits at the foot of the tumulus. All the people sit round the grave silently, the men nearer, the women farther off. He holds the twig with the right hand and turns it round his head, making circular figures in the air (1). Then he pronounces the sacramental syllable *Tsu, tsu, tsu*, two or three times, prolonging the sound; he has called the spirits. He prays : " You, my ancestors, who are assembled to day... Do you not see this ? You have taken him. I am alone now. I am dead! I pray you, who are yonder (kolaho), as he has gone back to you, that

(1) This is the kind of sacrifice called *litsanwa*, explained in Part VI, Chap. II. Its aim is to secure a good reception for the deceased on the part of the psikwembu, viz. the ancestor gods.

we may remain in peace. He did not leave us in anger. Let us mourn him gently, in peace. Let us help each other to mourn him well, even our parents-in-law from amongst whom he has taken his wife. " It may be that he forgets to say something which ought to be said ; then some of his hearers remind him quietly of the omission and he adds the words to his prayer.

The wailing (ku djila nkosi). As soon as he has finished praying, those present commence crying ; the wailing begins. The women get to their feet and shout loudly, throwing themselves on the ground. The wife of the deceased cries more than any one else : "I remain alone in the lonely plain (libalen). Where have you gone? You have left me. " The wailing generally starts on a very high note and finishes a little lower, expressing the pain of the heart in a touching, penetrating manner. Here is one of these sentences, which can hardly be called a song. I heard it in 1893 at the burial of a young woman who was found drowned in the lake of Rikatla.

O my mother ! O my mother! You have left me, where have you gone? ! (1)

The parents-in-law lament over their daughter, the new widow. Everyone then begins to lament over his own relations who have recently died. The brothers weep together without shouting. They say : " You have gone first. We shall soon follow you, because there is attraction in death. "

It is during the mourning that pots, handles of assagais, etc. are broken over the grave.

Let us stop a little while at this point.

We have seen enough already to observe that, for the Thongas, death (lifu) is not only a sad event, a great cause of pain on account of the bereavement, but a dreadful contaminating power which puts all objects and people in the neighbourhood of the deceased, all his relatives, even those dwelling far away, working in Johannesburg for instance, into a state of uncleanness. This uncleanness is very dangerous indeed. It kills, if not properly treated. All are not affected in the same way. There are concentric circles round the deceased : the widows are the

(1) See for the notes of this song Part V. Ch. III. B.

inner circle and will undergo a very rigorous purification ; the grave diggers come next ; then the inhabitants of the bereaved village, the relations residing in other villages, even the relatives of the wives of the deceased. All these being unclean are placed beyond the pale of society : "Muti wu tjumile," "the village is dark," is the technical expression. This marginal period lasts longer for those who are most affected ; one year and more for the widows, one month for the village, five or six days only for the mourners from outside. But there are many taboos in connexion with this period. Sexual relations are severely prohibited amongst married people, but the *gangisa* is not so strongly objected to, at any rate in some districts. We shall also meet with the aggregation rites by which re-entry into the ordinary mode of life is secured. The funeral rites may last for one year and are very complex. There are three great moments in the sequence of these rites : 1) *The Great Mourning* which lasts a few days, just after the burial, generally only five days. Here the purification is essentially medical and aims at cleansing the persons and the objects which were directly in contact with the deceased. 2) *The sexual rites* which tend to purify the collective life of the village by the removal of its defilement. 3) *The family rites*, consisting in gatherings of all the relatives, and accompanied by religious ceremonies. These seem to aim at restoring the life of the family, viz. of the social group, which has been diminished by the death of one of its members.

This general sequence is found in all the clans. But the rites themselves differ greatly ; I shall try to depict these differences clearly. My information is more complete as regards the Ronga clans, but I owe to Viguet some entirely new and very interesting material regarding the Hlabi rites.

IV. *The Great Mourning of the first five days.*

1) THE GREAT MOURNING AMONGST THE BA-RONGA.

Just after the burial, all the inhabitants of the village go to the lake or the river to bathe. The grave-diggers nibble a *ndjao*, the root of a juncus which has magical power. Special rites will then be performed for the widows. We shall describe them in the next chapter. When they come back from the pool, one of the men climbs on the hut and removes from its top the crown of woven grass, which was its glory during the life of its master. The hut participates in the general state of uncleanness of all his belongings. This crown will be put before the door to close it, and no one will dare to enter any more till the day of the crushing of the hut.

In the Mpfumo clans, that first evening, the grave diggers have some preliminary purification rites to go through : 1) a *hondla*, viz. an ablution with leaves of the nkuhlu tree which have been crushed in a mortar with some water ; 2) in former times they used to make a pipe with the shell of a raw sala, place in it an ember and a little hen's dung, and *smoke* this disgusting mixture.

From that first day, the grave diggers and the widows, when eating, must use special spoons *(psihanti)* made from old broken calabashes. It is taboo for them to take food with their fingers from the common plate during the five days of the Great Mourning.

The night comes. All the widows sleep in the open, their huts, which belonged to the deceased, being taboo. If it rains, they sleep in the other huts of the village.

On the following day, the *doctor* comes and proceeds to the medical purification of the widows and of the grave-diggers. This will consist in three successive *vapour baths*, on the first, third and fifth day after death. These *mahungulo* are administered in the same way as the one I have already described in connection with the infantile rites (p. 55). But the drugs boiled in the pot and the pills burnt in the fire are considered very powerful, especially those of the first day, so much so that the pot in which they have been prepared must be broken on the grave. The two grave-diggers and the first widow must be exposed together to this particularly powerful disinfectant, the widow keeping on her old clothing during the operation. The second and third bath, those provided for the other widows, are not so strong, and the pot can be kept. In the case of these the widow does not enter together with the grave-diggers. These rites, as well as the obligation of using special spoons, refer only to the diggers and the widows.

Other rites must be performed by the whole community.

First the *cutting of the hair*, which must be complete for the widows and the near relations. Men sometimes cut only one strand on each side, women cut from the forehead to the nape of the neck. The operation is performed either by the doctor or by anybody who is familiar with it, and the instrument used is either an iron razor or a bit of glass. They say this shaving is an act of respect for the dead, also a sign of sadness and a means of preventing the *mayiha*, the impression of the hair standing on end from fear of death. Should mourners forget to cut their hair, they might lose their senses, and become delirious (hahama).

Then they put on *malopa*, viz, pieces of dark blue cotton cloth which have been used for a long time amongst the Ba-Ronga. The first widow must have them before she enters the enclosure of the second vapour bath.

A third general rite is the *luma milomo*, the purification of the food of the deceased. This is not a medicinal operation, but it seems that, by this act, every relative removes from himself the danger which is in the contaminated food. The word *luma*, which we shall often find in the Thonga ritual, means originally to bite (like a dog) or to cause violent, internal pain (colic or pains of labour). But in the ritual terminology it means to accomplish certain rites in relation to some given food in order to remove the danger which is attached to it. The *milomo* are seeds of each kind of cereal which the deceased had in his storehouses. Some beans, grains of maize, kaffir corn, kaffir peas, etc., are cooked and poured into one of the baskets (lihlelo) of the deceased. The *ntukulu*, viz. the uterine nephew, the son of the sister of the deceased, is first called. It is he who must begin the rite and this is so important that, when people go to pay their mourning visit, they always take with them a girl or a boy who is a " ntukulu " of the one they mourn. The child stands before the pot, his feet together. The master of the mourning, (in this case, the first widow) kneels before him, takes a few drops from the pot, and some of the cooked food which remains at the bottom, and pours this between his great toes. He bends his body and rubs the two great toes against one another. Then he turns his back to the place and goes away. He must not look behind : it is taboo. Then the other relatives say : " Let us all go and *luma milomo.* " He has given them the right to do so.

A little of the *milomo* is carefully kept in a pot for months. When relatives who were absent on the day of the death come back from Johannesburg or from elsewhere, they must perform this ceremony before entering the village and eating any food in it. " Ba yila muti " — " they are taboo to the village." The rule applies only to relatives. Other people may very well eat from the deceased's store of food without any harm, as its contamination is dangerous only to his family. Another variety of this rite consists in preparing light beer with the mealies of the dead and taking first one mouthful which must be spat out on the right side, then a second one on the left side, after which one is allowed to drink.

The *gardens* of the deceased must also be purified, and this is done by the rite called *baninga mabele,* to give light to the mealies. The widows and all the female relatives go to his fields holding an old and empty *shikutja.* The shikutja is the hard shell of a sala fruit, the size of an orange, in which has been kept the provision of vegetable *tihuhlu* fat (see Part IV) and which is still impregnated with it. The women set fire to it and walk through the gardens holding it up and illuminating the fields. This is perhaps in relation to the idea that death means darkness, and that its contamination is " black " (ntima) so long as the cleansing has not taken place.

During the five days of the Great Mourning, relatives and friends come to pay the *official mourning visit* (1). They enter the village, the women shouting their lamentations (mikulungwana). Some one leads them to the grave and they walk round it uttering cries of mourning, taking leave of the deceased. At the burial of Sokis, I heard a woman saying with a trembling voice : " Good-bye ! You have gone ! Do not forget us. Remember Mulalen."

(1) This visit can be paid one, two, or three months later on, because, as they say, " nkosi a psi boli, " — " the mourning does not get rotten." But it is only during the five days that dances take place.

Mulalen was Sokis' little daughter. They bring with them presents, five hundred reis, a hen, a goat, some light beer, perhaps a mat for the widow because hers has been thrown away or a piece of mourning cloth. The inhabitants receive them politely, and spread mats on the ground for them. They tell each other the news (djungulisana). Then after having *luma*, they eat and drink. The Ba-Ronga have their drink already prepared: it is the red wine which Banyan merchants sell to them all over the country. The visitors get drunk. They dance, and the mourning ceremony turns into an orgy with dances and songs of all kinds. The singing during this Great Mourning consists either of war songs executed by the men, which are very impressive, or of ordinary dancing songs, the licentious ones being particularly appropriate and being performed by women. (Annotatio 9). In fact they are the proper mourning songs, those which are specially chosen when it is wished duly to lament a great man. I have witnessed these performances at a mourning ceremony of the " breaking of the hut " and shall refer to this subject again. In Vol. II. Part V Ch. II. B. I shall quote some of the mourning songs which have a peculiar stoic character. Here are two others from a collection made by Mrs Audéoud, the wife of one of our missionaries. They were sung at the death of the chief Tshutsha, near Makulane in the Maputju country. One of these was a war song accompanied with drums. It sounded as follows :

THE EVOLUTION OF A MAN FROM BIRTH TO DEATH

The other is a curious apostrophe to the wizards who were believed to have bewitched the deceased, and means : " Good bye, wizard! Good bye, wizard! You will kill people. You come to kill people, you come during the night. "

But the *closing day* arrives at last, the *day of the sprinkling* (shuba). When the grave-diggers have well perspired in their vapour bath, the doctor takes the pot in which the medicine is still boiling. All the women sit down with their children on their backs, the men stand in a line, holding their assagais and sticks in their hands. The doctor sprinkles his decoction over them all with a branch covered with leaves. The children cry because the burning drops hurt them. The women try to hide behind each other. The men gesticulate as if striking enemies with their assagais ; this is to show that their arms are strong and that they can now go to the war, as it would have been taboo for them to join the army before this purification had taken place. Should a man be absent from home, his sticks are also brought to the sprinkling to be purified (1). Then the doctor goes with his pot, sprinkling all the village, the huts, the doors, the backs of the roofs, the fence, the belongings of the deceased which are kept to be distributed amongst the heirs. After this operation, the village is pure as far as material things are concerned. The contamination which had fallen on all of them by reason of their owner's death is removed. Before the sprinkling it would have been dangerous to remove anything. Now if any one should have left anything in the kraal before the death, he can come and recover it. This is the act by which " the mourning is scattered " (hangalasa nkosi).

Visitors go home, having put on their *malopa*, if they are Ba-Ronga ; strings of milala palm leaves round their heads, their necks, arms, and legs, if they belong to Northern clans. The custom of wearing a white handkerchief round the head is spreading. If a goat is killed, every one wears a bracelet made of its skin round the wrist, and the widow and the principal grave-digger

---

(1) In the Northern clans, says Viguet, a little of this mixture is kept to sprinkle, visitors during the following days, because " they are taboo for the things of the village, not having been cleansed ; " (ba yila psa le mutin, hikuba a ba basisiwanga.)

put strings, made from the same skin, over their breasts. The widow adds new strings when other goats are killed during the mourning visits which will take place later on, and until the adjudication of the inheritance. It is a sign that her husband is dead (a feliwile).

2) THE GREAT MOURNING IN THE NORTHERN CLANS.

The foregoing is the sequence of the rites of the Great Mourning in the Ronga clans. In the Northern clans, according to Viguet, the same elements are found, but in another form.

As soon as the mourning lamentations begin, the grave-diggers send some men to fetch the *tinyele*, which are bits of skin taken from the soles of elephants' feet. These are burnt on charcoal, together with cocks' dung, and the mourners come and inhale the smoke with reeds, when they are tired of wailing. The *tinyele* are considered to be a powerful medicine. It is taboo to eat or even to snuff before having inhaled this smoke.

That first night, everyone sleeps in the open, and the grave-diggers are not allowed to use their mats. They must cut grass to cover them for fear that their impurity might contaminate the mats. As usual, sexual relations are suspended between married people, but the *bugango* is not taboo in the Northern clans, as girls (psigango) are not wives (basati). When, on the following days, visitors come to the mourning, they go straight to the grave with a small basket of mealies and spread them over it saying. "Go! Die! You have left us." This spreading of mealies is a *mhamba*, an offering. Then the doctor comes. It seems that his operations last only three days. There are no vapour baths properly speaking, but the doctor burns his powders together with bits of bark in broken pots, and all the mourners come and inhale the smoke through reeds, as they did on the first day.

The *purification of the food* is performed by a rite which corresponds with the *lumisa milomo* of the Rongas. The doctor cooks the mealie pap together with a certain drug. He prepares "bupsa bya muri," the medicinal porridge. The grave-diggers make a ball of this food, while it is still hot, and act as if they were throwing some of it into their mouths, but in reality they throw it over their shoulders. Then they put some more porridge into their mouths and eat it. The master of the mourning then takes the food and goes all over the village to perform this ceremony for all present. This is done also for the visitors arriving during the following days. Under no other condition would they be allowed to eat food in the village!

As regards the purification of the food for relatives who may come for a visit later on, after the Great Mourning, it is obtained by the rite called *mafularela*. "Fularela" means to turn one's back to another person. The day the absent one comes back to the mortuary village, the master of the mourning, the woman who has begun the *hlamba ndjaka* (see later on), takes one of the big wooden spoons which are used to distribute the porridge ; she pours water into it and puts salt into the water. Then she puts into it a glowing cinder. The water partly evaporates. She then kneels down in front of the new comer, turning her back to him, passes the spoon round her waist from left to right and afterwards gives it to him to drink; this ceremony removes the *yila* of the food. Should it not be performed the food would cause disease or even death to the returning relative.

The master of the mourning, or of the death (ñwinyi wa rifu), the wife of the deceased or the grave-digger who held the head in the burial, accomplishes a second act of purification or of strengthening for all the mourners ; it is called the *nganganya*. The doctor takes a bulb of a big Lilliacea called *gonwa* (Crinum Forbesii), crushes it, adds to it some medecine and warms it on a stone which has been heated in the fire. The operation then begins with the infants. The grave-digger covers his fingers with this substance and, standing behind the child, puts the fingers of both hands into its umbilicus and brings them round its waist, pressing them firmly against the skin until they meet again on the spine. Should a child not yet have had the string tied round his loins (boha puri, see page 56), the strap of its ntehe alone will be anointed with the medicine. As regards adults, the operation of *maganyo* is performed as follows ; the master of the mourning passes his hand down from the knee to the toes. This rite is evidently in connexion with the act of walking, which is thus purified, and with standing upright (yima), which means health and strength.

Cutting the hair is also a medicinal act amongst the Hlabis. The physician takes a broken pot, pours into it water and a purifying powder, washes the head of the deceased's wife with this preparation and cuts her hair with a razor. Everyone takes a little of the mixture and washes his own head, and they then shave each other. The hair is thrown away into the bush, not on the grave.

The Great Mourning is concluded by the *phunga*, the sprinkling, corresponding to the Ronga *shuba*, which is performed exactly in the same way while the water is still boiling. The doctor sprinkles a whole potful on the people ; then he pours fresh water into the pot and sprinkles the doors, the back part of the kraals of the oxen and of the goats. —"How about the pigs ?" I asked Viguet. He laughed heartily ! —"The pigs? They are nothing ! They have come from the White people They are so new to the country that lately the Pedis killed them outside the villages and the men only ate their flesh !" The pig has no part in the Bantu ritual !

V. *Sexual rites of purification.*

This is a most curious and mysterious subject and, to understand it thoroughly, it is necessary to penetrate deeply into the Bantu mind and to forget our own conceptions of conjugal life I hope none of my readers will be shocked by ceremonies which are evidently performed with the greatest earnestness and are a real aspiration toward purity, purity as it is conceived by a tribe still plunged in the dim notions of collective morality.

The Evolution of a Man from Birth to Death

These rites are somewhat different in the Hlabi and Ronga clans. They are called in the Northern clans *hlamba ndjaka*, in the Southern *lahla khombo*. I will begin with the description of the first, as being the most characteristic. Viguet, who has seen them practised, and who took part in them himself, gave me a graphic description of them.

Ndjaka means two things. Firstly, the objects left by the deceased, which will pass to his heirs in the course of time. The heirs are called *badyi ba ndjaka*, the eaters of the ndjaka. But *ndjaka* also signifies the frightful malediction accompanying death : "it is something which kills a great many men." Therefore the *ndjaka* must be washed away ; *hlamba* means precisely to wash away.

This malediction or dangerous impurity contaminates objects, which must be cleansed by the sprinkling (phunga) as we have seen ; but it affects still more deeply the village as a whole, the *muti*, the organism which is at the base of all Thonga society, and which has a life of its own, a collective life. That life must be purified. During the whole mourning, and even during the last days of the deceased, when death was threatening, all sexual relations have been forbidden. Why ? Because the village was in a state of contamination... "Muti wu tjumile." It cannot return to the ordinary course of life without a special collective purification.

Let us see how this is managed on a particularly serious occasion, when the headman or other great personage dies. Some weeks after the burial, all the married people of the village assemble, the men apart, the women apart. They discuss in what order the different couples must proceed to the purifying act. They question each other to know if each one has duly observed the law of continence. Should one of them confess that he has sinned (dyoha), he will have to take the lead. Should he have sinned and not confess it, he will be very guilty. But he himself will suffer for his bad action ; he has stolen the inheritance (a yibe ndjaka), and it will not be wonderful if he begins to cough, grows thin and dies of consumption ! If there has been no transgression of the law, then the master of the mourning will have to begin. He goes out of the village with his wife

153

to the bush. There they have sexual relations in the ritual fashion, viz. s. n. i. (See Annotatio 2). They come back by separate ways. The woman has taken with her a pot full of water ; she goes straight with it to a certain spot, which has been decided upon during the discussion, either in front of the main entrance of the village or at the door of the hut. There she washes her hands which contain "their impurity" (thyaka ra bona). All the other couples do the same, each woman coming in her turn to cleanse her impurity at the same place. When this is over, the men also come to this spot and stamp on the ground. Sticks belonging to absent young men, or a piece of clothing of a girl who happens to be away from home, are also brought to this spot and are purified. The same is done to the straps of the ntehe of the infant, as we have seen, but he is not allowed to be present, as it might cause his death. When the purifying act is finished in all its phases, men and women go to the river and bathe; the men higher up, the women lower down. (Annotatio 6).

Such is the *hlamba ndjaka* amongst the Thongas of the North, when the life of the village has been deeply affected by the death of an important member of the community. The rite is performed with less publicity when a child dies. Then the act takes place, not outside, in the bush, but inside the hut, as it is a private mourning. Should the husband have had regular intercourse with his wife before this purification has been carried out, it is a very great sin. His wife will go and confess their fault to one of the women of the village. This woman will tell it to her husband's mother, who will have to find the remedy. The guilty husband must not eat at all... If he eats, he will have eaten the contamination of death (u mitile rifu). The *hlamba ndjaka* of the whole village will have to take place. (Annotatio 7).

The hlamba ndjaka concerns first of all the inhabitants of the mortuary village, but it sometimes extends to the parents of the women of that village, who dwell, of course, in other places. If the first wife of a man dies, his second wife, the one with whom the widower has begun the purifying operation at home, will have to go to her own parents *to give them water* (ku ha mati), as they say, viz, to cleanse them. She takes with her in a pot a portion of the water used for the purification, arriving early in the morning in the neighbourhood of the paternal kraal, and calls her mother. Then she washes her hands on the spot and all her relatives will come and stamp on the ground. This is considered a great duty which a married daughter ought never to forget, otherwise she is said to have turned her back on her parents (a ba fularelile). They will be angry with her and not visit her for at least a year (Annotatio 8). The woman who has done this is called "the one who has cleansed the inheritance" (muhlantsi wa ndjaka). She has taken upon her the contamination, but she will not suffer from it, because she belongs to another family, and the contamination of death is dangerous more especially to the people who are of the same blood as the deceased. This woman will assuredly be praised and even rewarded with two hoes. When she goes to her relatives "to give them water," she will make a present of these two hoes to her father, who will say: "All right! You have cleansed those people." Then she will have the right of adorning herself with the bracelets of her deceased co-wife! Old women no longer having sexual intercourse are allowed to appropriate the old clothing of a deceased woman.

The Ba-Ronga do not know the expression hlamba ndjaka. They have a corresponding rite, performed in the same manner, which they call *lahla khombo. Khombo* means misfortune, *lahla,* to throw away. It is the medicine of death (muri wa lifu), said Magingi, an old heathen of Rikatla. It is also said "to heal the mourning" (daha nkosi). This rite more especially concerns the grave-diggers. The one who carried the legs of the deceased begins. The sexual relations take place very early in the morning. When his wife comes back, she washes her hands at the door of her hut, and all the inhabitants of the village come and stamp on the wet place ; then they enter the hut. The doctor comes and prepares a steam bath for the man. Then the second grave-digger performs his *lahla khombo,* and the same gathering of all the members of the community takes place before his hut. Afterwards the village is pure. But if the grave-diggers are cleansed, the widows are not yet purified, and we shall see that, for them, the *lahla hkombo* will last much longer.

155

A man who transgresses the law of continence before the lahla khombo is said in Ronga to have "crossed the village" (a tjemakanya muti). He has taken the mourning (nkosi), the misfortune (khombo) upon himself. He will have sores all over his body and will begin to cough (consumption).

Amongst the Rongas, it seems also that the *bugango* is prohibited in mortuary villages during the marginal period. The men even prevent boys going to the villages to see their girls, says Mbekwa, an old inhabitant of Nondwane.

VI. *Family rites.*

After two or three months, a first gathering of the whole family of the deceased takes place. Amongst the Ba-Ronga its function is to close or break down the mortuary hut. Amongst the Northern clans, no relation is established between this family gathering and the fate of the hut. But everywhere its principal aim seems to be to restore the family whose head has been removed by death, and which must be reorganised.

1) AMONGST THE BA-RONGA.

For the Ba-Ronga the habitation of the deceased is tabooed. It is a *shira* (grave), as well as the place in which he has been buried and, for this reason, it must be destroyed. But this destruction is not accomplished at once. Some time must elapse (1), two, three, nine months, before the family gathering takes place. I witnessed it near Rikatla on December 15th 1907 and can therefore describe this rite in detail.

Manyibane had died five or six months previously. He was

---

(1) At any rate, such is the old law. But nowadays the Rongas sometimes crush the hut at once during the five days to save trouble. This was done in the case of Sokis.

the headman of a large village in the Shifimbatlelo district (18 miles North of Lourenço Marques). His son Mugwanu had been chosen to take his place, but Manyibane had a younger brother, called Fenis, who had taken care of the village in the meantime. All the relatives were assembled. Groups were formed under all the trees. At 4. 30 p. m. the men began to gather near the old black-roofed hut ; one of them, an elderly man, took between his teeth a piece of a root of a special juncus, called *sungi*, bit off a little of it and, after having chewed this substance, rubbed both his legs with it (evidently to find courage and strength for the work he was undertaking) and penetrated into the old hut. He came back bringing with him a dozen beautiful white eggs!.. The hen did not know that the habitation of the deceased was a tabooed grave, and had laid her eggs in this convenient refuge! Then all the men approached and began to pull out the poles of the wall, digging on both sides of each pole ; some of them lifted the roof so as to make room enough for the poles to be pulled out. This work was accomplished with great care ; the earth was carefully placed in a pot and slowly poured out some distance away ; the poles were gently laid down in front of the entrance, on the top of the door, which had been previously placed there, thus forming a regular heap. These precautions are taken out of respect for the deceased. It would be an insult to him to do otherwise, and a relation guilty of such an offence "would at once be seized by colic, the disease of the wolves (masule)." Some boys, clad in European dress, threw the poles violently on the ground. Spoon laughed : "They know the *shilungo*, the ways of the White men," he said. "They have lost their respect!"

When all the poles were removed and there remained only the reeds of the wall, the men jumped on the roof. The roof is a big conical basket made of sticks tied together and covered with grass. It at once sank down under their weight. But they wished to flatten the cone, to crush it down to the level of the soil. Therefore some of the men pulled the sticks out of the roof to lessen the resistance ; some kicked it in order to break the sticks. They could not succeed ; the cone was still there more or

157

less out of shape. In the end they brought axes and chopped all round, about half way up the cone, and with loud shouts brought the destroyed hut level with the ground. Everything belonging to it will be left there to rot. No one dares to remove or to burn this ruin. It is a taboo (1).

The men were satisfied. They had succeeded : "The mourning had not overcome them," (nkosi a wu ba hlulanga), as would have been the case had one of them met with an accident during the operation. Some pots full of water were brought and they washed their hands and their faces conscientiously. They retired a while and all the members of the family, the women included, came and settled themselves as shown on the accompanying illustration of the scene. In front of the crushed hut *(1)*, in the space bet-ween it and the small hut of the first widow *(3)*, the old men sat down *(4)*, near them the *batukulu*, viz. the uterine nephews of the deceased *(5)*, their wives, and a few old women *(6)*. The other men *(10)* and women of mature age *(9)* took their places between the neighbouring huts, leaving a wide place for the dance. The brother of the deceased, Fenis, brought on his shoulders a young goat. Two hens and a cock were provided, in all two male and two female offerings. Some branches covered with leaves were spread before the heaps of poles *(2)*, and the *batukulu* began to kill the victims. One of them took the cock by the legs, his brother held the head and cut the neck half through. At each cut of the knife, all the women uttered their *mikulungwana* (piercing cries). He threw the fowl down, still alive and panting. They did the same with the three fowls, everybody laughing and amused at seeing them jump before they died. Then one of the *batukulu* seized the goat by one of the forelegs, lifted it up as high as he could, and planted an assagai under its shoulders, trying to reach the heart. The face of the goat was turned towards the North (2). At once more mikulugwane! The animal was crying

(1) In a neighbouring district, one of our evangelists built a chapel near the ruin of the chief Gwaba. For months it was impossible to remove that ugly decaying roof ; those on the spot were opposed to it and the chieftainess of the Mabota district gave permission only because the evangelist was connected with White people.

(2) I suppose the Manyibane family came from the North, and they wanted the goat to cry in this direction to call the spirits of the ancestors to the sacrifice.

pitifully ; its agony lasted five minutes at least and the whole time the women were shouting with pleasure, because it is necessary that a victim should cry! In the groups, men and women were discussing where and how the sacrificer ought to introduce the blade in order to kill the goat more quickly. His wife came and

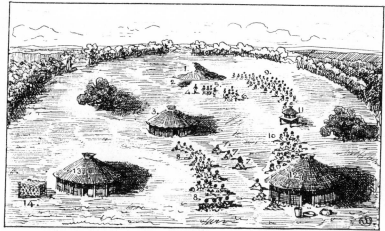

Drawn by J. Wavre.

The ceremony of crushing down the hut.

1. Deceased's hut, crushed down. 2. Heap of poles. 3. Provisional hut of the widow. 4. Sacrificer. 5. Uterine nephews. 6. Wives of the uterine nephews. 7. Dancers. 8. Women clapping their hands. 9. Other women. 10. Men. 11. Henhouse. 12. Hut of the younger brother. 13. Hut of the tall woman who danced. 14. A "shigiyane", wood pile built by her daughter-in-law's relatives.

helped him, and not until after ten minutes, at least, did they succeed.

Then, while the batukulu and the old men were busy with the victims, cutting them up and squeezing the psanyi (half digested grass) out of the bowels, the other mourners began to sing and to dance. First an elderly woman, of a very clear complexion and a mephistophelean face, very tall, with a curiously licentious smile, came into the middle of the place, opened her arms wide and *suma*, began to sing. Together with her song she performed a strange mimicry with her thighs. This mimicry took on a more and more lascivious character ; it became a regular womb dance, so immoral (Annotatio 9) that the men dropped their eyes, as if they feared that she would take off all her clothing. But the other women seemed thoroughly to enjoy this horrible performance, and encouraged her by clapping their hands and beating their drums. The words of her songs were also of a very questionable character. She described an adulterous woman going during the night from one hut to another, seeking for lovers, knocking on the walls (to attract the notice of the men ?).

> The walls of the huts have deceived her fellow-women when she goes knocking on them...

Another old woman, of at least seventy years of age, followed her, and running with a mincing gait through the place, uttered words of the same kind.

This seems very immoral indeed. Let us remember however that, in the opinion of the Thongas, these songs, which are taboo in ordinary life, are specially appropriate to the mourning period "These women have been uncovered by the death of their husband," said Mboza. "There is no longer any restraint on them. They are full of bitterness when they perform these lascivious dances." The reason is perhaps deeper, as it is not only the widows who sing these words ; we are still in a marginal period, the period of mourning, and these phases of life are marked for the Bantus by this strange contrast : prohibition of sexual intercourse and a shameless outpouring of impure words and gesticulations (Annotatio 10).

But in the meantime the *batukulu* had finished their work. They had already distributed the various parts of the victim according to rule, to the visitors, who would eat them on their way home, not in the village ; it is taboo. They had put aside one shoulder, the lungs and one of the hoofs for the sacrifice. Relatives had made a provision of *psanyi*. An old man then took a pill made of the *psanyi*, that found in the smallest stomach, called shihlakahla. He pressed it against his lips, took into his mouth a little of the liquid squeezed from it and spit it out again with the sacramental *tsu*. He then proceeded to pray : "You, Manyiban, you have left us. People used to say you were a wizard (a clever man who could overcome death). In what has your witchcraft resulted ? Are you not dead! You have left us in peace. Go to Tlotlomane ; let Tlotlomane go to X ; let X go to Y, etc. (He utters the names of the ancestors.) Call each other to come here and look. Are we not gathered together ? Here is so and so. The batukulu also are here. Accept this offering and may we live peacefully together ; visit each other (Annotatio 11). Even if they do not come to pay me visits, let them come to Fenis ; he is their father now. And you, Mugwanu, you remain at the head of the village. You are their headman now. Do not scatter your people. Cultivate good relations with each other."

But a woman suddenly stands up and interrupts him : "Bring everything to the light," she says! The old priest stops. She goes on : "They say I am a Muchopi" (a woman of dissolute manners). The mikulungwane are heard on all sides. It is a family drama which we are attending! This woman is the daughter of the deceased ; Manyibane has sold her to pay off his debts ; he has not kept the lobola money to buy a wife for one of her brothers ; that is the reason why they hate her. They do not receive her in the village. She pours out her grievances before them in this family gathering, when they are praying to their ancestors. It is the favourable time! She goes on : "Is it my fault ? Did I not obey our father ? I have not fled away. Now what am I to do ? He alone received me here! You despise me. Say everything! Do not hide it!"

Her interruption has lasted five minutes at least and she goes back to her place very angry. Sometimes relatives who have serious complaints to make against their kinsfolk choose this precise moment to vent their anger and leave the gathering with violent words. In such a case, it is said : "The mourning has overcome this family."

The old priest is a little disconcerted. He speaks at random, always calling his Tlotlomane. The whole scene is perfectly natural, but the participants do not show the slightest religious awe. Suddenly one of the batukulu rises, takes a bottle of wine which has been also brought there as an offering, pours a little of it into a glass and raises it to the lips of the old man. "He cuts his prayer" and while all the attention of the public is concentrated upon this act (which belongs also to the ritual, as the priest must be.the first to partake of the offering), the wives of the batukulu rush towards the shoulders, lungs and hoofs of the goats and the bottle of wine, seize them and run away towards the west. They have stolen the meat of the sacrifice! At once all stand up and follow them laughing, shouting and pelting them with the *psanyi*, which they had kept for this purpose. The thieves hide themselves behind some bush and eat the meat. Uterine nephews are representatives of the gods, as we shall see later on, and they assert their right by stealing the offering and eating it up.

This ceremony is highly characteristic as it embodies some of the principal ideas of the Thongas in the domain of religion, social life and taboo. It was worth while describing it, and we shall refer to it later on, when dealing with sacrifices and the position of the uterine nephews in the family.

The crushing down of the hut is not performed in exactly the same manner amongst the Ba-Ronga. In the clans *South of the Bay*, they only *close* it (pfala yindlu). They dig holes in front of the door, into which they insert poles of the bush called *nhleha*, tying thorny branches horizontally to them. The shield of the deceased is placed against the door. The religious rite then takes place and from the skins of the sacrificed goats strips are cut, which the widows will have to wear *en bandoulière* during the following months of their widowhood. The astragalus bones are kept and hung round the neck. The gall-bladder is also preserved and fixed in the hair of the new master of the village as a sign of his new position.

In the *district of Makaneta*, on the estuary of the Nkomati, the ceremony comprises two successive acts. First there is also a *provisory closing* of the hut, which can take place one month after the death and is accompanied by the family gathering and the religious ceremony. One year later, when the inheritance is adjudicated, the hut is crushed down, but only if it belonged to a headman of the village and if the kraal is obliged to move in consequence of the death.   If it be the hut of one of the subordinates, the roof is simply lifted off and thrown away into the bush.

Another very significant rite in connexion with the closing of the hut is accomplished on the death of the master of the village. A branch is cut from the tree of the village, the tree which was revealed by the divinatory bones as the one near which the headman had to build (See Part II Ch. II) ; half of the branch is placed across the great gate of the village, which is then closed and another gate opened, at some distance, in the fence ; the other half is put over the door of the crushed hut.

There seem to be great variations in the performance of these ceremonies everywhere.   I believe, without being able to vouch for it, that when two family gatherings take place during this last period of the mourning, the first is held to proclaim the new master of the village and the second to distribute the inheritance amongst the heirs-at-law.   At any rate these two important acts take place at the gatherings.   As the inheritance consists mainly of live stock — human stock, the wives of the deceased, I shall describe the adjudication when treating of the fate of widows.

2)   FAMILY RITES IN THE NORTHERN CLANS.

A month after the burial, there is a first gathering of the grave-diggers.   They are invited by the widows to a beer-feast.   This beer is called : "the beer of the hyenas," as the hyenas also dig graves ! No equivocal compliment is intended, the widows merely meaning to thank these men for their services.

In the northern clans, *yindlu a yi yili*, the hut is not taboo. It can be slept in again after the five days of the Great Mourning. The plaster of the doorposts is repaired, and a new crown is put on the top when the hut again finds an owner (1).   The feast of the

(1) The hut of a leper alone is considered irremediably tabooed as the sufferer is buried in it.   They dig a hole into which he is pushed by means of sticks.   The roof is crushed down over him.

closing of the hut is therefore replaced by what is called the *beer of the mourning* (byala bya nkosi). All the relatives, brothers, brothers-in-law, nephews, etc., bring a goat, or half a sovereign, or a sovereign, to the master of the mourning, the heir of the village. That individual must give them back as much as he receives from them, a goat for a goat, (timbuti ti labana), a sovereign for a sovereign, and all the animals are killed according to rule. There were fourteen of them at a certain gathering held in the Nkuna capital to mourn one of the wives of the chief Shiluvane in 1905. A sacrifice is offered ; the men sit on one side, the women on the other ; the *kokwane*, viz. the maternal uncle of the deceased, takes the *psanyi* and squeezes it on them all while praying, or rather insulting the gods who have afflicted them with such a bereavement. All rub their chests with this green liquid and add their insults to those of the priest.

According to Viguet, this is the first occasion on which the deceased is treated as a god and prayed to : "Look! You have left the village without a head to lead it! Keep them! Bless them and increase them." The *batukulu* then come to take that portion of the victim which has been put aside for the gods. It does not appear that they steal it, as is the case amongst the Ba-Ronga.

*

*   *

Such is the story of the mourning. Here are some technical expressions in connexion with it : Hamba nkosi, to conduct the mourning. Djila nkosi, to utter mourning lamentations. Daha nkosi, to treat it by purification ceremonies. Kota nkosi, to cope with it. Nkosi wu wupfa, it ripens. Nkosi wu hela, it comes to an end. A wu boli, it does not get rotten, viz. it is always possible to pay a mourning visit.

The name of the deceased when quoted is often preceded by the word "Matjuwa," exactly as with *feu* in French and *late* in English. In the Northern clans the expression employed is "Sira" which means grave : Grave so and so.

VII. *Various cases of death.*

So far I have treated specially of the death of a headman, who had reached adult age, and died at home. There are a few other cases to describe.

Should the man *have died far away from home*, in Johannesburg for instance, no ceremony will take place before the news is entirely confirmed. Then all the relatives assemble. A grave is dug and all his mats and his clothing are buried in it. These objects which he was in the habit of using every day, and which have been soiled by the exudations from his body, are *himself*. A sacrifice will be made over the grave, not by means of the nkanye twig but with a fowl which is thrown on the grave. Formerly the fowl was left on the ground, but nowadays the uterine nephews steal it. The widow will eat with her hands till the burial, though death took place long before and was already publicly known ; she will begin to use a spoon only after the burial has taken place. This fact illustrates strangely the ritualistic notion which is at the base of all these mourning customs! The steam baths, the sprinkling on the fifth day, the singing, dancing and condolence visits take place just the same as in ordinary mourning.

In the Northern clans, the belongings of a man who dies far away (matikwen, in the lands) are burnt. The purifying sprinklings are performed. The same is done for relatives who die accidentally and whose corpses have not been buried ; for instance, if they were killed by a wild beast or in battle.

When a *stranger* dies in a Thonga village, and no one knows him, "*a nga na ntshumu*"—"he does not matter," says Viguet. The grown-up men will bury him. They dig a hole and drag the corpse into it with a rope. They do not touch it. There is no contagion, therefore no ceremony of purification. Amongst the Malulekes and Hlengwes, such a corpse is burnt. They attend to the cremation and do not leave the spot till they hear an explosion (boom!), which shows that all danger (khombo) has departed.

When an *infant* dies, it must be buried in a broken pot. The

165

pot is placed in the earth, the opening being half covered with a layer of ashes, in such a way that there remains a passage for the air. It is taboo to bury it otherwise, until it has passed through the rite of presentation to the moon (page 53). *An older child* is buried in the ordinary way, but with very few ceremonies. There is no religious act. The mother alone attends the funeral. The father digs the grave, but he does nothing else. He says : "We, holders of the assagai, do not bury such little ones. They are but water, they are but a womb, (nyimba) they are but a *ntehe*." A father pays very little attention to little children. It is only when they begin to smile that he will show them some affection. Then it may be that he will press his little one against his breast and kiss its temple, especially when he returns home from a journey.

In the case of suicide, the corpse is buried according to ordinary rules. But the tree on which the man hanged himself is cut down. It is taboo : other people might commit suicide at the same place. Its wood is not used for fuel.

If a woman dies during pregnancy, she must be cut open to see what the sex of her child is. This must be done inside the grave, before the earth is covered in. As Mboza said : "The air (moya) must come out." He told me the story of a husband in the Mabota country who nearly fainted when obliged to perform this painful operation. But it is a great taboo, as the woman might become a god of bitterness (shikwembo sha shibiti), if buried without this precaution (See Part VI). In the Maluleke clan women who die pregnant, or in confinement, are cremated.

Lepers alone are buried in the hut. In Maputju the father and the mother are buried in front of the hut whilst the regular place in other parts of the Ronga territory is behind the hut, *mahosi*. The members of the reigning family are buried in the *n'imu*, the sacred wood which belongs to them. Every big fami.y may have its *ntimu* and the men are buried there according to tł eir villages ; each village has its place and the place is called after the name of the headman of the village. So in the Lebombo sacred wood, there was "the village of Nkolele, to the south, the village of Shihubane, to the north, etc."

166

The Evolution of a Man from Birth to Death

The bones of the dead are never disinterred. It is a taboo ; a grave is respected and women do not dare to till the ground over it. Often one comes across a small thick bush in the midst of mealie gardens, and one sees broken pots under the branches. It is an old grave. Later on, when no one remembers who has been buried there, agriculture regains its sway. If a bush fire has reached the sacred wood and damaged it, the person who lit it must atone by sacrificing a fowl in order to "quench" (timula) it.

REMARKS ABOUT DEATH AND BURIAL

These very complicated funeral rites of the Thongas clearly show the existence of three great intuitions in their minds :

1) Man is immortal and becomes a god through death.

2) There is extreme danger attached to the defilement which accompanies death. This uncleanness contaminates the community and can only be removed by collective purification.

3) The social group, being diminished by death, must be reinforced by special means (family gatherings, choice of a successor, etc.). Hence three categories of rites : *religious*, *purificatory* and *social*.

On the other hand some of the rites we have described present unmistakably the character of *passage rites*, because death also means a passage : for the deceased, passage from the world of the living to the world of the dead ; for his relations, passage from one phase of life to another.

Separation from terrestrial life is symbolised for the deceased by the rite of piercing the wall of the hut in order to solemnise, as it were, his official departure from his former dwelling. I should consider also as a separation rite the custom of cutting through all his garments and mats, in order to make them "draw the last breath." To effect aggregation to the new world, the grave-diggers prepare for him an underground hut and square place, they place him in his new dwelling in a sitting position (if such is the true explanation of the folding of the limbs), they direct his eyes towards the cardinal point whence his ancestors have come. I have sometimes had the impression that even in these rites, the idea of a marginal period, or of a period of transition, was not lacking ; the deceased is not prayed to prior to the great family gatherings, which take place three, six, or twelve months after the death. Then his hut is crushed or closed. It would seem that he has gone

167

through an evolution towards deity, as his corpse was decaying in the grave, and the closing of his hut, with the placing of his shield before the door, might well mean his definite incorporation into the world of the dead, and also a means of preventing him from returning to this world and bringing misfortune to his relatives.

As regards the relatives, they separate from the former phase by the cutting of the hair, putting out the old fire, leaving off their clothing and wearing mourning attire. A very distinct period of margin then begins, marked by the sexual taboos accompanying it, and they are aggregated again to the ordinary world and to the new phase of their life by all the ceremonies which I have explained at length. Here, however, as the seclusion was caused by a certain most dreaded defilement, the aggregation rites all bear the character of removal of uncleanness : uncleanness of the food, of the gardens, of the bereaved, chiefly grave-diggers and widows, of the whole community, which is cleansed by the sexual rite of hlamba ndjaka, etc.

If classification were equivalent to understanding, we might say that we have fairly well understood the complicated Thonga rites which accompany death... But who can boast of having fully understood so profound and mysterious a subject ? Death is the great shadow which hovers over life and chills the human heart. Outside of an enlightened faith, it is, and remains, the King of Terrors. Never more than at the graveside did I pity my poor black brethren, wondering how they tried to calm their hearts and overcome their sorrow. There is something profoundly touching in their most absurd rites, because, after all, they are all imposed by a craving for life and purity. Will my readers allow me to conclude this subject by a personal reminiscence ? The day I attended the burial of Sokis, when his relatives had finished filling in the grave, they asked me to lead them in worship. Bantu heathenism is so poor, it feels itself so weak that it readily accepts the help of a higher religion. So I tried to turn the eyes of my hearers away from the underground hut, and to fix them on the eternal dwellings of the Father's house. Then Sokis's youngest brother took the nkanye twig and performed the heathen religious ceremony, calling his ancestors to come and bless them and entreating the deceased to leave them in peace. The contrast between these two prayers made at the same grave was indeed striking. And, whatever we may think, even if we had no religious convictions at all, should we not earnestly desire that, for these people, the bright comforting Christian hope may dispel the darkness of their thoughts and the sufferings involved in their rites ?

CHAPTER II

THE EVOLUTION OF A WOMAN FROM BIRTH TO DEATH

Essay of a Ronga girl on the subject.

In July 1897, the School Inspector gave to the big girls of the
Swiss Mission school at Lourenço Marques the following subject
for an examination in composition : "The life of a Ronga woman."
This is the translation of one of the pupils' essays on the life of
their country women :

"When a girl is born amongst the Ba-Ronga, people come and
congratulate the mother and say : "A ma buyeni mati," that is
to say : "Let the water come !" When the time is at hand when
she will come out of the hut, ochre is crushed for her and a calabash
full of the fat of *nkuhlu* almond is prepared, and the two ingredients
are mixed and smeared over her.

"Her curly hair is stretched out in corkscrew fashion, and
ochre is put on it to transform it into a kind of rats' tails.
(This is the operation called *hora ngoya*.) The mother also smears
herself with ochre, and puts on her head a crown of small strings
(shikupu) (1). Then, when the child lets her head fall on account
of the weakness of her neck, a plaited string, which is just the right
size for a necklace, is tied round her throat. 'Thus,' they say,
'her nape will be strengthened.'

"A small calabash with medicine is given her to drink ; they
also prepare for her a small pot of the medicine, and they say it

(1) I have heard this custom explained as follows : the mothers amuse the children
by shaking their heads ; the small strings dance about and make the babies laugh. This
can only be true of infants already two or three months old.

169

is to lessen the dangers of growth (pumba nombo), so that the sickness should not be too bad. (These are the milombyana,

Phot. A. Borel

Girls with babies at Makulane

(Maputju country.)

170

see page 48.) After her birth she is carried in the skin of a gazelle (mhunti) which her mother ties round her neck and loins. When that skin has become too small, they get one of an antelope (mhala). She begins to walk ; when her mother sends her on an errand she is able to do it. She also begins to talk, and to know her father and mother. Then, when she has grown, they prepare for her a small pot of pounded and cooked mealies so that she may eat of it. After three years she is weaned and goes to stay for a time with her grandmother. After that she returns home.

"When she has learnt to walk, she is very fond of playing with the shells of the sala. She cooks in them. Then, when she has done with them, she takes small pots and cooks little dinners. She also gets a small calabash, she goes to the lake to draw water and, on coming back, she gives it to her father so that he may wash his face. Here she is now gathering small bits of wood ; she makes small bundles of them and brings them home. Later on she will make heavier bundles.

"When she has grown up more, she will take charge of the work of her mother. She will do the work. But if the mother sees that she cannot do it all, she will help her. It may however be said that the mother needs no longer to crush her mealies, neither to go to the well nor to the fireplace. When she is quite a grown up girl, the suitors come. If they are accepted, they bring the purchase money. They buy her (lobola) and do all they like. If she is prolific, she will bear many children. Now and then she returns to her parents' village, then she comes back to her husband. Her children grow. They go to get water, to cut her wood, to plough her fields. She goes with them. When they are grown up, they get married. If amongst them there is a son, he goes to buy his wife. Thus she looks for a mother-in-law for her son. He will then be truly a man because he has got a mother-in-law! When her children are married, the mother again begins to do all her work. She steeps her mealies, crushes them to make flour, she cuts her wood, cooks her beer ; she prepares the light beer ; she smears the floor of her hut ; this is what she does till she is quite old.

"When she is quite old, they feed her. Her grandchildren are

171

sent to bring her food. When they are hungry, they stop on the way and eat it themselves. On their return they say : 'We have indeed given it to her.' In the morning they put a stick in her hand and help her to get out of her hut, so that she can warm herself in the sun.

"Then when the Ronga woman is quite old she begins to see no more and to hear no more. She falls into second childhood. All she does is to complain and to say, crying, that she is ill treated. And this is the end!"

The girl who wrote this essay was but emerging from childhood, and has consequently enlarged more especially upon the first phase of the life. The life of a woman is not very different from that of a man at that stage. Differences however come in later on, and we shall have to add some important facts relating to the fate of women before marriage, during the conjugal life, and in widowhood.

A. BEFORE MARRIAGE

I. *The Girls' games.*

As we have seen from the essay of the schoolgirl, Ronga girls imitate the doings of their mothers, their cooking, their gathering of fuel, etc., just as the boys imitate the fighting and hunting of the men. They also play with *dolls*, nursing them as they see the women nursing babies. These dolls are called *vule*. The origin of the game is as follows. A little girl asks her mother who is carrying a younger child on her shoulders : Mother, where did you find your baby ? — Oh! I found it in the bush (ntlhaben). — Please bring me one also, mother. — All right!— Next day the mother plucks a sala in the bush, removes all the stones inside it, lets it dry and fixes it to the end of a stick. She pierces the upper part of the sphere, passes bits of string through the holes to imitate hair, smears them with ochre, ties a little clothing round the stick and gives it to the girl! Or if the mother says : "I found the baby in the banana grove," the father will cut a banana stem, take the heart of the bulb and beat it so as to separate the fibres, which will then represent the hair of the baby ; the girl will then play with it for a time.

Girls, like boys, have also special games.

First the *ntshengu -ntshengu*. A big girl takes the part of the mother and all the little ones hide behind her. She stretches out her arms to protect them against another girl, who is the thief and tries to take the children away. Notwithstanding the mother's efforts, all are taken one by one, and the stealing is done whilst they sing :

> Alack ! Mother ! Protect us, protect us !

The mother answers :

> All my children are taken, all will soon be taken,
> All will soon be taken, there, behind me.

> (Yo ! Mamana ! ntshengu-ntshengu ! ba hela hi shiruba).

The capture being effected, all the children sit down in a row and cross their legs. To their right and left they dig small holes which represent wells or pots. The mother passes. She stretches out their legs and they allow her do this. Then she pretends to drink water from their pitchers and says: "My child, where did you find this water ?" The child says : "Oh! I have drawn it over there, at the spring, under the banana trees, in the cool shade." Then comes the girl who plays the part of the thief. She tries to stretch out their legs. But the children refuse ; they stiffen themselves. She tastes their water and enquires where they brought it from. "I drew it in a nasty hole full of frogs, mud and dirt." They add all the different remarks they can think of.

As the boys sing to the transport oxen when a wagon comes along the road, so the girls address a kind of *incantation to a big grey lizard* called *galagala*, which can turn its head blue at will. The lizard is found lying on a branch, warming itself in the rays

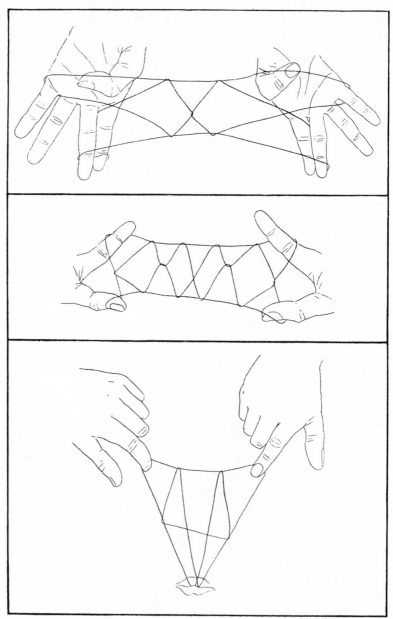

Drawn by J. Wavre

Various forms of buhlolo (string game.)

174

of the sun. One girl approaches it, and claps her hands under
its nose, singing in a monotonous tone :

> Gala-gala, hana-hana nhloko !
> Big lizard, lift up, lift up your head !

It seems that the lizard is so fascinated by the song that he
stretches his neck and swings his head to and fro during the
whole time that the girl claps her hands.

To the *crabs*, which are very numerous in the slime on the
sea-shore, and have only one claw, coloured green, violet or enamel
blue, they sing :

> Ba ka mphembemuñwe, tlakula silawuto !
> Come along, you animals with only one claw !   Lift it up and bring it down again.

The little girls who go hunting crabs as a condiment for their
food assured me that, on hearing this song, the crustaceans do
come out of their holes, and that the harvest is then a large one.

When an *owl*, mistaking the time, comes out of her hiding
place at noon, she is received with applause, and they sing to her :

> Shikotana, gaulela fole !
> Owl ! flap your wings !   You will find tobacco !

Another girls' game, which is wide-spread, and in which the
young Thongas acquire great proficiency is called : *ku tha buhlolo*.
They take a string tied at both ends so as to form a large ring, and
make all kinds of complicated figures by twisting it with their
fingers and even with their lips.   I have made a drawing of some of
them.   Girls compete together and try to surpass each other in
inventing new figures.   They teach each other this *buhlolo*.

Another old game, which is found under various forms in a
great number of countries, is the *mathakisana*, knuckle bones.
Girls gather stones of the nkanye fruit (tinfula), dig a hole, and
put them into it.   One of them takes a kind of ball (shigungu),
perhaps a small sala fruit or any other fruit.   She throws it in the
air and, in the meantime, takes out of the hole four or five stones
and puts them back, leaving only one outside.   This stone is then

put aside. She must be very clever and very quick in removing and replacing all the stones except one, because the ball will soon fall down and she must catch it in her hands. Should she take only one stone out of the hole, she has failed (a tjongolile) ; should she leave more than one stone outside of it, she has again failed (a hoshile). Should the ball fall to the ground, it is taboo. (psa yila)! She has lost her turn. If the ball falls on her body, it is not so bad. Her companions will say to her : "Gangasheta." Then she must throw the ball and catch it two or three times on the upper part of her hand, then again in her hand, and if she succeeds in this, she is allowed to go on. When she has been able to take all the stones from the hole without making any mistake, she has beaten her co-players (a ba mphyinshile).

Natives do not play for stakes as a rule, but, if two of them challenge each other, each claiming to be the best at the game, they may arrange that the one who loses must give a fowl to the winner.

The ordinary word for *play* is *ku tlanga*. But there is another word *ku tha*, which is used for the more refined games, the buhlolo, the mathakusana, the tshuba, the reciting of tales, riddles or proverbs (psitekatekisa) and guessing games (mhumhana). We shall describe these four last games when treating of the life of the village and literary life.

II. *Nubility customs.*

1) THE KHOMBA RITE.

When a girl comes of age, no special ceremony is performed amongst the Ba-Ronga. She is said, just like the boy, to have "drunk the nkanye" (page 95). She confesses to her mother that her menses *(tinwheti, viz. months)* have appeared for the first time, and the mother simply answers : "Hi ku kula"— "this means growth."

But in the Northern clans a characteristic rite has been preserved, or borrowed from the Sutho-Pedis, who attach great importance to it. It is called *khomba*, or *yisa matin*, to lead to the water, and is performed in the following manner. The girl, when she thinks that the time of nubility is near, chooses an adoptive mother, possibly in a neighbouring village. She works for her, and helps her in gathering her fuel. When the day has come, she runs away from her village and goes to this adoptive mother "to weep near her" (a rilela ka yena). These are distinct separation rites. She says : "Ndji khombile" — "I am of age." Then will begin a *seclusion period* of one month. Three or four girls receive the initiation together. They are shut up in a hut, and when they come out, must always wear over their face a veil consisting of a very dirty and greasy cloth. Every morning they are led to the pool, and their whole body is immersed in the water as far as the neck. Other initiated girls or women accompany them singing obscene songs, and drive away with sticks any man who happens to be on the road, as no man is allowed to see a girl during this period. If a man happens to come near the group, the women ask him the secret formulae of the circumcision school, not the long ones but the short ones, probably those which contain licentious words. Should he be unable to answer, they beat him. It is said that a man who sees a girl during this month becomes blind! When the cortege of women accompanying the initiated has returned home, the nubile girls are imprisoned in the hut. They are teased, pinched, scratched by the adoptive mothers or by other women ; they must also listen to the licentious songs which are sung to them. Though they are trembling from cold, being still wet, they are not allowed to come near the fire. They are also instructed in sexual matters, and told that they must never reveal anything about the blood of the menses to a man. They are also exhorted to be very polite to every grown up person, and must salute everybody entering the hut, even those passing before the door, by clapping their hands. Sometimes the wind moves some dead leaves ; they mistake this noise for the sound of steps and salute reverently!

At the end of the month the adoptive mother brings the girl

home to her true mother. She also presents her with a pot of beer. A feast takes place on this occasion and the kunga rite is performed, just as for the circumcised boy on the day of his aggregation (page 93). Little presents will be brought by the girl to her adoptive mother who will distribute them to old women. If the initiated girl has been already bought by lobola, the mother goes with her to her future husband and says to him : "She is grown up." He will give her a present of £. 1., and the veil will be taken away. These last rites distinctly mean the aggregation of the girl to adult society, and all this khomba custom is a very good example of a passage rite, the passage being from the asexual to the sexual group.

The Pedi-Sutho clans of the Transvaal also practise this rite, which they call khoba. In addition they have the bale, the initiation school for girls, corresponding to the circumcision school of the boys. The Nkuna clan of the Thongas is said to have practised it also in former times, but the bale has entirely disappeared all through the Thonga tribe.

There are three other customs more or less related to nubility : tattooing, the pointing of the teeth and the milebe custom.

2) TATTOOING (Tlhabela tinhlanga).

There have been different methods of tattooing amongst the Thongas. In former times, in the Northern clans, the Ba-Thonga used to disfigure themselves by making very big black pimples on the forehead, the nose, and the cheeks. Hence the name of *Knobneusen* which they received from the Boers in Spelonken. Even the men were tattooed, but they shewed only one line of pimples down the middle of the face, from the forehead to the chin. Women had, in addition, two horizontal lines on the forehead and three on each cheek. It was a custom of the primitive population and is still observed by the Ba-Chopi. The invaders of the XVth or XVIth century adopted it because they were mocked by their subjects, who said : "Flat noses are not right!" When the Ba-Ngoni of the XIXth century came, they submitted themselves to the custom, not from fear of mockery, but to hide their Zulu nationality. Chaka had sent his impis to kill them and, as they were recognised by the absence of pimples, they began to tattoo themselves. When the danger was passed,

Phot. H.-A. Junod.
Tattooed women of the Nkuna clan.

they ceased to perform the operation. They began in their turn to mock the Thongas who had followed their example.

Amongst the Ba-Ronga it is not certain that the big black pimples ever existed. In former times men used to make two lines of small pimples on both sides of the body, extending from the nipple and from the shoulders downwards. Now the custom is dying out ; it is practised only by women, undoubtedly in connection with nubility or with marriage. But the tattooing of the face has disappeared almost entirely. What remains is the tattooing of the shoulders and of the epigastric and hypogastric regions.

The operation is painful ; girls sometimes cry and must be forced to submit to it. The patterns are triangular. Four triangles are first drawn on the shoulders on both sides ; the upper triangles meeting with the lower ones at their apex, so as to leave a square place, not tattooed, in the middle of the back. This drawing is made with ochre ; the skin is caught up and lifted with a little iron hook all along the line and slightly cut with a razor All the incisions must be of the same size. The blood oozes out and is stopped by the ochre, which is profusely spread over the small wounds. Tattooing of the back is not very painful. It is more so on the anterior part of the body. These four triangles are also drawn under the breasts, leaving a square place of which the navel occupies the exact centre. But between the two upper triangles two others are introduced, forming a conical shaped pyramid whose point comes between the breasts.

Such is the ordinary arrangement of the tattoo pimples in Nondwane, but it varies considerably according to the clans, as the two adjoining plates clearly show. The two Nkuna women whom I photographed at Shiluvane in 1900, have only two lines of pimples, forming a right angle under their right breast. The Rev. Alex. Jaques has kindly sent me two other photographs of tatooed Tembe girls taken in August 1926 and Mrs. Jaques has drawn an enlarged figure of the marks which shows plainly the patterns adopted in that part of the country. I reproduce them in a second illustration. Here the four triangles are distinctly seen.

The freshly tattooed girl hides herself for a week, after which she shows herself to her boy (shigango), who will kill a fowl for her to congratulate her. He says : "It is pretty to tattoo yourself. Otherwise your belly would be like the belly of a fish, or of a white person!" The time of healing is considered as a disease (perhaps as a marginal period). It is taboo to put salt in the food during

180

these days, or to go to the village to eat the food of other people (just as it is for boys who pierce their ears). Girls prepare themselves for the operation by eating a special food which softens

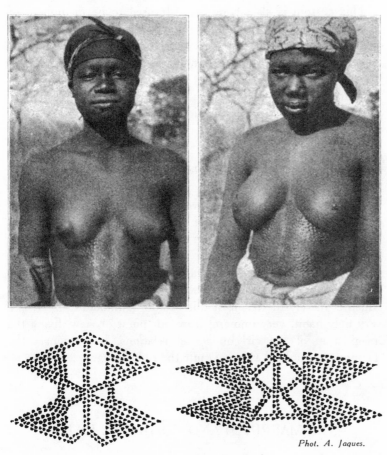

Phot. A. Jaques.

Tattooed women of the Tembe clan.

the skin of the belly (nabyala khuri). All these rules tend to show that, in former times, tattooing had a deep meaning, a ritual value which has more or less disappeared. Mboza told me : "It is not a regular taboo (yila), but only a custom (shihila) of the country."

3) Pointing of the teeth (Ku hleta).

This custom is also dying out. It used to be incumbent on all the girls. Now many do not observe it. They have seen that teeth deformed in this way decay more quickly. The operation is performed on the incisors, and girls must keep their mouths closed for two or three days, not showing their teeth to anybody.

Near Rikatla, the hleta custom was still in force in the heathen villages in 1910. It gives the girls a kind of canine aspect.

4) The milebe custom.

This is very wide-spread all over South Africa. Though it has disappeared now amongst most of the Ronga clans, it is still practised in the Manyisa country, over the whole of Bilen and in the Northern clans, amongst the Zulus, the Pedi-Suthos, etc. It is probably the origin of the famous "Hottentot apron," which some ethnographers thought to be a congenital malformation, and which is merely the result of this custom (Annotatio 5). It is a very ugly habit, very immoral from our point of view, fixing the imagination of the girl on sexual relations, but amongst the Thongas it is upheld as being quite the right thing.

B. MARRIAGE AND CONJUGAL LIFE

1) Conditions of Marriage.

In the primitive Bantu tribe every girl gets married, some, however, sooner than others. Suitors prefer pretty girls to ugly ones! But what is their standard of beauty? The ideal is tall stature, strong limbs and well developed breasts. A proverb

says : "Nsati wa mabele u nga nabele loko u nge na bukosi."
— "Do not covet a woman with large breasts if you have no
money..." This does not mean that she will cost more, but her
father, knowing that she will not want for suitors, will not consent
to let her go unless the full lobolo is paid at once. On the other
hand a girl with an elongated face is admired more than one
who is too broad-faced. Of the first they say : "She is pretty, she
resembles an antelope" (a kota mhala) ; of the second : "She is
chubby-cheeked, she is like a sow." A light complexion is preferred
to a very dark one, because the white or yellow races are regarded
as superior, and a Native laying claim to any European or Asiatic
blood is proud of it. Parents, who also have their say in the
question of marriage, insist on two other points ; the working
capacity of the girl, and the absence of any witchcraft blot in the
family. Should her mother have been convicted of being a witch,
the girl will be feared. However, every girl finds a husband in the
land where polygamy flourishes. If he be slow in coming, she
will apply to her doctor, who will prepare the *love charms*, which
will make her "appear," so that she will be noticed by the boys
(See page 100). If even that does not succeed, she has other
means at her disposal and may go herself to make proposals to a
man (wopsana). He is seduced by her, and constitutes himself a
thief who has *tlhuba*, viz. "taken in marriage by abduction" (See
page 119). The parents will claim the lobolo and he must pay it.
Marriage and childbearing remain the only carreer to which a
Thonga woman can look forward. Hence a number of special
feminine taboos which are very curious.

2) SPECIAL FEMININE TABOOS.

Some of them concern girls *before childbearing* and cease after
parturition. In the Tembe and Maputju clans, girls must not eat
pork, because pigs root nervously with their noses ; the future child
would also move its head from one side to the other, when on the
verge of birth, and this would make delivery difficult. Other

animals are taboo for girls : the *hare* because it is too cunning ; and the antelope *nhlengane*. This antelope raises the foot when it hears a noise ; hence the idea that its leg is hollow and that it perceives the sound through it. The child would do the same, if its mother were to eat the meat of the nhlengane. It would be unable to hear with its ears, only with its hands!

The *legs* of fowls (tibias) are also taboo for all women, because the hen scatters the sand... So are the *hoofs of oxen*, and *pigs'feet*. A woman eating them would walk too much... She would go everywhere to look for husbands!

It is taboo for a girl to *walk amongst pumpkin plants* (maranga), to pluck the fruits. She is only allowed to pluck those which can be reached from outside. Were she to transgress this law, she would emit a bad odour, and no boy would court her. Her mother, having no fear of being despised, can walk amongst the pumpkins. A second taboo relative to pumpkins is this : unmarried women must cut a "pumpkin nose" (nhompfu) viz. the end of the stem, and fix it at their waist when plucking the pumpkins, lest they get abcesses in certain regions of their body.

It is taboo for them to eat cooked *oxen blood* (bubendje).

The following taboos apply also to *married women*. They are not allowed to eat what is called *nkopfu*, viz. some parts of the bowels which are cooked together with the stomach of the ox. "It would spoil the child inside." The *testicles*, which are generally given to the uterine nephew when the meat is distributed according to the laws, and the *underlip* of any animal are also forbidden to them. So is also the *tongue*... because it is reserved for old people as a mark of respect! The *rectum* (gobana) is taboo for women and children. Children might make unseemly noises from the rectum! Women must abstain from *porcupine* and *monkeys' flesh* ; all their offspring would resemble these animals. Such cases have happened, it is said! Women must not eat *eggs* ; they would run a double danger : their child might be born bald and remain so ; or they might be like a hen, which runs in all directions when laying an egg. They would have no peace in child bearing! (See also page 101.)

Nubile girls, during their "tiwheti," must not *approach the oxen kraal* and look at them. The cattle might suffer, be attacked by a bad cough (mukhulwane), get thin! This taboo is instituted to protect the oxen, not the human inhabitants of the village, as D. Kidd says is the case amongst the Zulus. (Part IV. Ch. I. E.)

When women have passed the time of child-bearing, most of the taboos cease, and they can eat monkeys and porcupine if they wish!

3) THE FIRST YEAR OF MARRIED LIFE.

I shall not return to the subject of marriage rites, which have been fully explained in the preceding chapter. Let me say that, though a Thonga woman cannot imagine life without marriage (ku kandja bukati), she does not enter on the new state with any enthusiasm. Her parents have warned her that she will be illtreated, accused of witchcraft and adultery, etc. Her sisters bewail her fate on her wedding day in song. The fact that she has been paid for, though it does not constitute an actual sale, puts her in an inferior position (See Part II).

During the first year, she has no *ndangu*, viz. no fire-place of her own. She cooks for her mother-in-law. During the three first weeks the husband eats with her and with the girl who accompanied her to her new home. Afterwards, he goes back to eat with the men. In some places it would seem that the husband eats with her the whole year, until she has her own pot (hlembeto).

4) HUSBAND AND WIFE.

What are the relations between husband and wife after the honey-moon ? Of course they vary very much according to the character of both. As a rule however, the married people have very little intimacy with each other ; the man remains with his companions on the "bandla," the village square where they meet, and only occasionally comes into the "ndangu," the reed enclosure of the fire-place, which is the true domain of the lady of the hut. The first wife is certainly the most respected ; she is called the "great one" (nsati lwe' nkulu) ; those who are taken in marriage afterwards being the "little wives." She is the true wife and acts as such in some old rites, those which accompany widowhood and the foundation of the village, as we shall see.

When speaking of divorce, we shall notice the principal causes of quarrel between married people and how they are dealt with.

As regards conjugal relations, I have explained them as fully as was possible to me in the paper already quoted (Revue d'ethnologie et de sociologie, Paris. Ernest Leroux, 1910, p. 143-151). This paper however being now very difficult to obtain, I am obliged to treat this subject here also, as it is of paramount importance. No one could pretend to know the life of an African tribe if he were ignorant of these facts. I do not give them to satisfy mere curiosity, but because they play an immense part in the social life of the Bantus and reveal to us some of their most characteristic physiological ideas.

It is generally asserted that Bantus, especially the men, have the sexual instinct very strongly developed. This is true to a certain extent. Polygamy has increased it enormously. In a royal kraal like that of Gungunyana, the excesses were awful. (See Annotatio 14). But even amongst monogamists the indulgence in sexual relations is sometimes very great. We often heard women pounding their mealies in the middle of the night in order to escape from the assiduities of their husbands. However this statement must not be exaggerated. Amongst Bantus as amongst other races there are great differences between individuals in this domain and I have already pointed to the fact that hundreds, and even thousands of young and grown up men can remain continent for months and years in the Institutions and the Compounds of South Africa.

The fact that heathens also submit themselves readily to the prohibition of sexual intercourse during more or less protracted periods for the welfare of the community shows that even in the primitive state Bantus are capable of exercising control over themselves in that domain.

The Evolution of a Woman from Birth to Death

*

*   *

Let us consider first how conjugal relations are regulated in normal circumstances.

Every month during her "tihweti" the woman is taboo and no intercourse is allowed. This is one of the severest taboos, Should a husband infringe this law, his health would fail, and, should he be called to go to war, "his knees would shake," he would tremble and be unable to fight (1). As regards the woman, these days constitute a real marginal period during which she is absolutely secluded from her husband. She must keep to the left half of the hut and not trepass across the centre line. If she wants snuff, she is not allowed to go to her husband in the part in which he lies ; she must send a child to fetch the tobacco she wants! During these days she sleeps on a special mat and puts on special clothes, the old ones which she brought with her for this purpose on the day she first came to the conjugal dwelling. When cooking, she must not touch the mealie meal with her hands, but with a spoon. A rich man who has plenty of spouses, and therefore plenty of food, will not touch the pot of the tabooed wife! At the end of the period, she smears the floor of the hut and puts on her ordinary clothing. (Annotatio 12). This is evidently the aggregation rite by which the woman returns to everyday life.

Normal relations continue during the first year of married life. Should the wife become pregnant, they are not suspended. It would even seem that they are rather recommended, as is shown by the following story : A young man once complained to me that he had been bewitched by his maternal aunt. The result of the spell she had cast over him was that he was no longer able to have sexual intercourse with his wife ; and he was very angry, as he asserted that the aim of his aunt, in doing this, had been to prevent the successful issue of the pregnancy. She wanted

---

(1) The woman during her tihweti is also taboo for other persons. I heard of the case of a child who suffered from a hernia in the scrotum five days after birth. People said that it was the fault of certain women who had taken it in their arms during menstruation.

to hinder the child from growing and to put in its place, by means of her enchantments, a snake, a hare, a quail or an antelope!

After the birth, owing to possible contamination by the lochia, sexual intercourse is prohibited till the rite of tying the cotton string (p. 56) has taken place. It is then allowed, but conception must be avoided till weaning, when relations are resumed in the normal way, and this goes on till the time when the woman is no longer able to bring forth children. I know of no special rules in connection with the menopause.

*

*   *

But, amongst Bantus, sexual relations are not an individual affair, as amongst nations more advanced in evolution. There is a mysterious relation between them and the collective life of the community. Hence the fact that, on certain given occasions, they are recommended, even ordered, or prohibited.

1) Cases of recommendation.

Sexual relations must take place on two principal occasions : when the inmates of a village abandon it and go elsewhere to found a new one, and when the widows perform the painful rite of "lahla khombo" (to cast away misfortune). We shall see, when studying these customs, that sexual relations have here a twofold signification : 1) they "consolidate" the little community in its new abode, viz. they strengthen its structure by confirming the authority of its chief ; 2) they provide the principal means of getting rid of all contamination, especially of the defilement connected with death. (Annotatio 13.)

2) Cases of prohibition.

Married people are not considered as being in a state of defilement, as mourners are, for example. Yet this class of persons, called "ba-ku-khila," constitute a danger for those members of the community who are in a weak state of health. They must not come in contact with the circumcised, because in that case their wounds would not heal properly.

188

They must not enter the hut of a person dangerously ill ; this would hasten his death. People who are just recovering from a disease, when they walk about on the paths, must tie around their ankles the root called sungi, which will protect them against the perspiration or emanation left by married people in their footprints, because, as one of my informants said, "ba-ku-khila ba hisa," viz. married people are hot.

Moreover not only individuals but the whole social life would be endangered if sexual relations took place when the community itself is in a critical position. They are prohibited therefore in wartime, during the whole duration of hunting parties, and also during the marginal periods. Strange to say, this law does not apply so severely to unmarried boys and girls amusing themselves according to the "shigango" custom (p. 97). It seems that it is not the act in itself which is tabooed, but the act in as much as it is accomplished by regularly married people ; in this case only has it a bearing on the life of the community.

What is the reason of these prohibitions ? "Married people are hot." What does this aphorism mean ? The following rite may help us to understand it.

In the Maluleke country, when the whole population enters a lake to kill fish according to the tjeba custom (Part IV. Chap. I), a little boy and a little girl are chosen and laid down under a lion's skin, as if they were husband and wife, and told to remain very quiet during all the time the grown up people are fishing. Not knowing anything about sexual intercourse, they will obey ; then the fish also will keep quiet and will be killed easily. Why ? Because there is in the sexual act something wild, fierce, passionate which, according to the law of correspondance which is at the base of all Bantu magic, has an influence on the hostile forces ; these will be excited and more difficult to overcome : enemies in battle, the animals of the bush during hunting and fishing parties, disease, danger of contamination at death and during the marginal periods. Life is, so to speak accelerated by the sexual act, and this acceleration is communicated to the whole of Nature. Therefore : Keep quiet, be continent!

This profound conception of life also explains why so often certain actions must be accomplished by children, not yet able to have sexual relations, or by old women who no longer practise them.

Let us remark that all these rites do not belong to Animism, properly speaking, but to Dynamism (Part VI. Chap. I), which plays a part almost as important as Animism in Bantu primitive philosophy.

5) Sterility.

In the Northern clans, when a woman does not conceive, a special sacrifice is offered, very similar to the one made by the Rongas on the day of the conclusion of the marriage. A goat is killed; a long piece, one foot in width, is cut from the skin of the animal in the ventral region, and three openings are made, one for the head and the two others for the arms. The three openings converge to a point where the astragalus bone of the goat is fixed to a strap. The sterile woman puts on this skin; the astragalus will be seen on her breast. She will also fix the gall-bladder in her hair and wear these ornaments for a time. To the mind of the Thongas, it seems evident that children are given by the gods; hence the idea of a sacrifice in case of sterility. But in addition to the religious rite, native doctors have many drugs to militate against this misfortune (1). The special porridge cooked for a sterile woman (mhika, shimhiko) is called *shiboleko* amongst the Ba-Ronga. The poor woman is despised.

Sterility can be a cause of divorce; the husband has the right of sending his wife home. But generally the parents of the woman find a *nhlampsa*, viz. a younger girl, and give her to the husband as a second wife.

6) Pregnancy and Miscarriage.

A special treatment is followed for the first pregnancy when the breasts begin to swell, a condition which is called *munyama* (darkness). The physician makes small incisions near the breast and on the legs, and draws out a little blood. The pregnant woman also drinks a decoction for the same purpose, i. e. to

---

(1) A Pedi man told me that in his tribe the first thing to do was to ascertain if sterility were due to the husband or to the wife. For this purpose a little bit of the clothing of the husband and of the wife was cut off and placed near a spider's nest. This spider is a kind of mygala of enormous size. If the spider took the piece of the husband's clothing down to its nest, it meant that he was in fault, and vice versa.

remove the blood. The Thongas think that, as the menses are suspended, the blood accumulates in the body and must be taken away.

Pregnancy is not considered as a tabooed period. As we have just seen, sexual relations are allowed during that time, even recommended as favourable to the growth of the child. However, in view of the impending birth, some special taboos have been added to those which apply to all women.

A pregnant woman *must not drink water when standing up*. She must kneel down, otherwise the water would fall violently on the head of the child and hurt it!

It is taboo for her to *wrap her body* in too much clothing. She must keep her belly bare and never throw her dress (kapulane) over her shoulders, lest the baby come to the light with its head covered with membranes, a complication which is very much dreaded by Thonga women.

She must not take *the sauce* of her porridge *too hot*. The child might be scalded inside and have black spots when born.

It is also taboo to *prepare the ntehe before the birth*, as no one knows what will happen. The child might die!

The future mother must not eat *pigeon's meat*, because pigeons have no blood in the muscles of their breast. She would have no milk herself wherewith to nurse the baby. Nor must she even *look at a monkey*, lest she "take to herself" (tekela) the form of the animal and the child be like it!

A woman, in the beginning of pregnancy, must not visit a sick person. The latter might die.

As regards women dying during pregnancy, see page 166.

Miscarriages are very much feared amongst South Africans, not for themselves, but because they are accompanied by an uncontrolled effusion of a blood which is a terrible taboo. The discharged foetus must be buried in wet soil, otherwise the rain will not fall ; the country having been polluted will be dried up by hot winds. A strange rite called *mbelele* is performed in times of drought, when all the graves of children born prematurely and buried on the hill are searched, and their contents thrown into the mud, near the river. We shall discuss in Part VI the origin of this extraordinary idea. A woman who has had a miscarriage is impure for three months at least. Menstruation must have taken place two or three times and have cleansed her before her husband can have any sexual relation with her. (Compare Annotatio 7, which applies to the transgression of this rule.)

7) Parturition.

We have described, when treating of birth, the many taboos which accompany parturition. The *busahana* period, from the moment of delivery till the fall of the umbilical cord, is very much dreaded. When a woman is suffering from *shilumi* (a disease which sometimes follows delivery, probably owing to a displacement of the organs) she must not enter the hut of a woman who has been confined. The ailment would "jump over to her" (tlulela). There is however a way of preventing contagion. The visitor must take the piece of clothing which she uses as a girdle and throw it to the patient, and the patient throws back her own girdle to the visitor. Then she can enter : "They have acted according to the law, there is no more *yila*."

A mother must not drink any milk from the birth of the child until its presentation to the moon. Afterwards she is allowed to drink only milk from cows which have calved many times.

The rite of *kunga* is performed in the case of a first-born child. This child is called *ñwana wa matibula*, the child by which the woman has *tibula*, viz. has become a mother. The etymology of this word *tibula* (Zulu zibula) is not known. When people come to greet the baby, its parents will not allow them to take it in their arms. They must pay something for permission to do so, even a brother, a sister, or a grandmother. The father is not subject to this rule ; "the child is his, belongs to him." Nowadays this ceremony means only that these people are happy to receive the new born child amongst them. There is no taboo in it. But it is certainly related to the fact that in giving birth to a child for the first time, the woman has passed from womanhood to motherhood.

A demonstration of joy takes place at the birth of any subsequent child, but the kunga is only performed for the first-born. It does not seem that in the case of the first-born child, as in the case of bowumba (see p. 125) the gifts of kunga are subject to any taboo.

8) Loss of children.

A woman who loses an infant (wa ku felwa) is deeply contaminated with the defilement of death. She must bury it herself without aid from her husband. Next day, she goes behind the hut, kneels down and draws off her own milk on to the ground. She does this until the secretion has ceased. This is taboo ; her milk is polluted ; no drop of it must fall in the gardens. She must avoid crossing the fields and going to the storehouses to fetch food. Until she has been "put right again (busetela)," she eats with a spoon. To use a spoon is a bad omen for a woman, because it reminds her of death. That is the reason why men adopt this civilized custom more readily than women. During her mourning, no sexual relations are allowed. When menstruation begins again, she first keeps silent, and does not tell her husband. Only on the second or third occasion does she inform him of the fact. He can then purify her ; this is done in the same way as in the case of widows. (See p. 154.) Then he buys new clothing for her and she resumes her ordinary mode of life. Everybody seeing her with this new attire will know that "she has been repaired." Should any one else than the husband give her this clothing, the latter will be greatly offended and accuse her of having relations with a lover.

A man does not put on *malopa*, mourning clothing, for a child who was not yet of age. The woman alone does so. However a husband is always grieved at the death of his child and a sad event like this often leads to dreadful results. He will begin to think that his wife is a witch and has eaten her own child by her magical powers. Such an accusation is almost sure to end in a divorce.

A woman who has *lost many children*, three or four, is considered

193

as being in a special position, called *bowumba*, and there are many rules to be observed in order to deal with this "state of bereavement." Should a child be born after the death of many elder brothers, he must be carried in a *ntehe* made of a sheep's skin instead of an antelope or goat skin. (See p. 46.) To carry him in an ordinary ntehe is taboo. Should it be a boy, the mother will put girl's clothing on it, and vice-versa. The mother's breast will be smeared with a special medicine, because they are "breasts of the dead (mabele ya bafi)." The child, if it lives, will be weaned as early as possible and be taken to its grandmother. Two curious rites are also practised to protect it against bad luck. The first is the *kunga* ; the second, *rangela bovumba*, seems to belong rather to the Northern clans.

The *kunga* rite which we have already met many times (see p. 124) is also performed in the case of a mother who has given birth to a new child whilst in the state of bowumba. To neglect it is a taboo. The bereaved mother keeps silent before her visitors until they have deposited their gifts at her feet and have thus "opened her mouth." Old women having no means to buy a present take a bit of grass and fix it in her hair. Then she consents to speak. She gathers all the bracelets thus obtained and puts them on the ntehe, carrying them everywhere with her.

Another rite is observed in the Northern clans. The child whose elder brothers and sisters have died is taken by the mother to the village of her own parents. There it is buried in the ash-heap up to its neck. Then somebody runs to the village, takes a handful of grains of maize and throws them on the child. Afterwards it is dug up, washed, smeared with ochre and brought home. This rite is called *rangela bowumba*, viz. to *precede* bowumba, to cut it, to treat it : the bowumba will not now come as it has been "preceded". It will be deceived, it will no longer desire the baby, as the baby has been thrown away together with all the refuse of the village on to the ash-heap. It is no longer able to eat mealies, even if it is given grains of mealies ; it is dead! Let the bowumba take no notice of it! (This description of the "rangela bowumba" was given to me by an old Thonga from Spelonken. Mankhelu, my Nkuna informant, called this rite

Phot. from Pretoria

Thonga women of the Transvaal.

195

"*ringela bowumba*," from the verb ringa, to try ; it is the attempt to bring some influence to bear on the misfortune of the bereaved mother.)

9) ADULTERY.

Amongst the Thongas *true* adultery for a *man*, married or unmarried (bumbuye), consists in committing sin with a married woman. Should he have relations with a girl, it leads to no consequences at all. Nobody will blame him, if the girl does not conceive. Should she have a child, he will only be forced to marry her ; she will become his second wife. His first wife will not at all resent his bad conduct. Sometimes she will herself get him the girl he wants. There is nothing in her heart like the jealous dignity of a European spouse! She will keep all her capacity for jealousy (bukwele) for the time when the second wife comes to the village, and shares with her the affection of their common husband! Adultery with an unmarried woman is nothing more than "gangisa."

But should a man have abducted a *married woman*, a woman who has a master (ñwinyi), who has been paid for, then the matter becomes very serious. The husband is very skilful at discovering her misdoing. As soon as he begins to have doubts about the fidelity of his wife, he chooses a friend and asks him to watch her. She is very cunning, her lover also ; but the friend is on the watch and some time perhaps, catches them in the bush, when she goes to gather fuel, or near the pool, where she draws her water. He comes back to the husband and informs him that he has caught them in the very act. Then the husband tells his wife that proof has been obtained and that she had better go at once to her lover and take something from his hut ; she obeys, and comes back with his blanket or any other object. This is "la pièce à conviction." The husband goes with it to the counsellor who is in charge of his village ; together they apply to the chief. The chief sends the counsellor who is responsible for the village of the lover to summon him. The confrontation takes place and the story of the case is investigated.

The woman is questioned, and confesses when, where, and how many times he has sinned with her. If he denies this, the object taken from the hut is exhibited. The adulterer is condemned by the chief to pay a *whole lobolo*, £ 15 to £ 20, as much as is necessary to buy a wife. He is rebuked before the whole assembly. "If you had taken a girl, it would not have mattered at all. Why did you abduct a married woman ? Do you not know that it breeds endless trouble at court (tindaba) ?"

The counsellor of the deceived husband goes to the counsellor of the lover to claim the money. The latter must go to the guilty man. The parents of the adulterer insult their son : "You see! All this money lost now! If only you had lobola a wife with it!" They must help him to find it at once, because this is a law universally recognised : the price of adultery must be forthcoming. (Nandju wa bumbuye a wu pfumali). The poor man will have to pay ; he will even have to add a hoe to "drive away" (hlongola) the counsellor, who keeps it for his reward!

Why is adultery so strongly prohibited and punished ? Not at all from any moral consideration of purity or chastity, but for two other reasons. First a social one. Adultery with a married woman is a theft, because she is owned by a master. She is not punished herself, except when the watcher finds her out and gives himself the pleasure of thrashing her to his heart's content. The whole punishment falls on the man ; he is the thief. But there is also a physical reason for it : the *matlulana*! We have already met with this word. *Tlulana* means to jump over each other, to compete with each other. In the sexual domain it is said of two men who have relations with the same woman. "They have met together in one life through the blood of that woman ; they have drunk from the same pool" (Viguet). This establishes between them a most curious mutual dependence : should one of them be ill, the other must not visit him ; the patient might die. If he runs a thorn into his foot, the other must not help him to extract it ; it is taboo ; the wound would not heal. If he dies, his rival must not be present at his mourning or he would himself die (See page 137). Should he even be the actual son (sometimes it happens that a son commits adultery with one of the younger wives of his father, which is considered as *biha*, very bad), he must not take any part in the burial, though he might be the regular "master of the mourning." Relatives will drive him away because they have pity on him, they know what misfortune threatens him. It is a terrible taboo! There are medicines to remove this contamination ; the *yila* is removed by them, but the *biha* (bad action) remains! However in the case of the disease called *mpondjo*, (which I believe to be the lupus), medicines are of no avail ; should a man visit his rival, who is suffering from it, he will die. We have also seen the terrible complications which are believed to take place at the birth of children, when there has been a question of adultery. (P. 40.)

These great taboos show that there is a deep feeling amongst the Thongas that promiscuity of any kind is a bad and a dangerous thing. Even in the case of *gangisa*, boys are censured when two of them court the same girl.

10) DIVORCE.

Adultery is one of the causes of divorce. The guilty woman, instead of obeying her legitimate husband and helping him to get his compensation, may choose to go to her lover and live with him. This leads to an immediate divorce. The husband goes to the parents of the unfaithful wife and claims his lobolo. They have perhaps no money to give. However they will try to get it as soon as possible, even if it is by the dissolution of the marriage of their own son ; they will perhaps send back his young wife to her parents and claim the lobolo paid for her, in order to meet the claim of the angry husband (See Part II). It would seem easier to go to the thief and claim from him the lobola for the adulteress whom he has stolen (tlhuba). But a thief is not a reliable man! If he has stolen, it proves that he had nothing (1). (See Appendix VIII.)

Divorce frequently takes place for more trivial reasons, for

(1) Women of low morals are called in Ronga gwababana, prostitute. There are plenty of them all round Lourenço Marques, where morality has sunk to a very low level ; but this is the result of degeneration.

mere incompatibility of temper. Heathen men are often hard to their wives. They refuse to give them money to buy clothing. "They are stones," said one of these men to me. "Though you scratch a stone with your nail, the nail will break and the stone will remain!" On the other hand, the women are by no means sweet, obedient creatures ; therefore quarrelling often takes place. When she thinks she is persecuted (shanisa), the wife *runs home*. This is her great weapon. The husband heaves a sigh of relief... But very soon he becomes aware of his misfortune. No food, no cooked meal in the evening! His companions share their own food with him for some days, but they will not consent to feed him long. He will have to go modestly, humbly to his parents-in-law and ask his wife to return. Then they enquire into the matter, and he perhaps receives a good scolding. It may be that the domestic life will improve, both fearing the renewal of the conflict. It may however be that the situation will grow worse and worse, and then it will lead to divorce, viz. the husband will claim his money and, when he gets it back, the marriage is dissolved (ku dlawa ka bukati).

An accusation of witchcraft may also cause divorce, especially after the death of a child ; so also can sterility, as we have seen, p. 190. Gross selfishness on the part of the husband may lead to it ; many tales tell the story of a man who in time of famine succeeded in killing an antelope, kept the meat for himself and did not give any to his wife and children. The wife noticed it and, when the famine came to an end, she invited all her relatives to a beer feast. Then she shewed them the bones of the antelope, telling them how badly her husband had treated her ; her parents took her home together with the children. Sometimes the conclusion of the tale is that the man even lost his lobolo money, as a punishment for his evil deed! (See *Grammaire Ronga*, page 202. *Chants et Contes des Ba-Ronga*, page 260.)

11) WIDOWHOOD.

When a man dies all his relatives are contaminated by the defilement of death, as we have seen (Page 143). There are concentric circles around him, some people being more affected than others. The wives form the first circle, especially the first wife. They have therefore to perform peculiar purifying ceremonies which throw great light on the profound feelings of the Thongas regarding life and nature. On the other hand they are the property of the husband's family and they are part of his belongings. How are they to be distributed amongst his heirs ? This is a very delicate matter. It is more or less regulated by the tribal law. Hence there are two series of rites to consider, in the customs relating to widows : 1) The rites of purification, 2) the laws of distribution.

Let us describe first the fate of the great wife amongst the Rongas (See for supplementary details : The fate of widows amongst the Ba-Ronga. S.A.A.A.S. 1909).

a) *The first day*. Manyibane is dead! — a sad event for his wife. She is called to inspect his grave. She assists silently at his funeral. But as soon as the younger brother of the deceased has finished praying, she bursts into tears and cries aloud! Her parents cry also : "Our child has fallen into misfortune! Now the cold has come for her! She will learn to know the cold water!" This is an allusion to the kind of life which the new widow will have to lead. Every morning she must go to the lake or the pool, with her companions, to have her whole body washed till the days of purification are completed.

The first of these purifying rites is performed just after the burial. The widow, surrounded by other women, goes to the pool and there all must wash their bodies. Most of them return home at once. But the widow remains there with *other widows* who have lost their husbands in former years. They form a *secret society* which assembles only to receive new members into its ranks. Nobody must see the strange rites performed by them. It is a *Ngoma* (the same word as for the circumcision school). However, the mysterious company takes possession of the great road (gondjwen), and every one must take care not to pass along it at that time, for great misfortune might overtake the imprudent one who should approach too near and catch a glimpse of the proceedings. A wise man, on seeing the suspicious group of mourning women sitting on the main road, prudently stops and makes a long detour to avoid the place... What is done at this meeting ? One of the widows makes an incision with a knife or a bit of glass in the skin of the new member of the society, in the inguinal region on the left side, "where the husband was resting." If the blood flows freely, it is a good sign. The women are satisfied ; they say there was a good understanding between husband and wife ; if the blood does not flow it is a bad omen. Then one of them lights a little fire with a handful of dry grass ; this grass has been torn from the roof of the deceased's hut. A little excrement from a cock (not a hen!) is then thrown into the fire, and the widow must expose both hands to the smoke. Afterwards she must extinguish the fire with her own water. Should she be unable to do this, it is a further proof that she has not been faithful to her husband and that she has killed him by her adulteries. These rites are very similar to the first circumcision rites, the incision performed recalling the ablation of the foreskin, and the exposure to the smoke, the jumping over the fire. These are great taboos. Evidently they are initiation rites, accompanying the passage from one condition to another. Why does the ceremony take place on the main road ? Because later on the contamination of death will attach itself to travellers passing that spot, and the mourners themselves will get rid of it in this way.

After that, the company returns home. The other widows take every bit of clothing from their companion, and tie a reed or a palm thread around her waist with some broad leaves attached to it. With this scanty garment, they bring her home. She walks surrounded by them. Someone warns the men to leave the road as they are not allowed to see the procession. They hide themselves in their huts. The widow is led to her hut, the hut of the great wife which has now been uncrowned. She must accomplish *the last crossing of the hut*. Entering through the door, she shouts loudly : "My husband! My husband! You have left me alone! What am I to do ?" Then she goes out, not by the door but by the hole which has been made in the wall to carry the corpse to the grave. Behind the hut her friends are waiting for her and give her back her old clothing, which has been washed in the pool and which she will wear again for two days (1).

b) *The following days of the Great Mourning*. Without delay a new hut, a small provisional hut, is built in front of the mortuary one. Here the great wife will stay during the whole of her widowhood ; the space between this and, the old hut is more or less taboo and most of the possessions of the deceased are placed there, under the roof near the door on the outside. (See illustration p. 159.)

The other widows do not leave their huts, but they participate in the other purifying acts, the vapour baths and the general sprinkling of the fifth day. As regards the vapour baths, however, the first wife is associated with the grave-diggers, viz. she must be exposed to the strongest medicinal smoke, while the inferior wives are cleansed with weaker drugs. They all put on the *malopa* and eat with spoons during the whole year of widowhood.

c) *Provisional decision regarding the fate of the widows*. A few days after the Great Mourning, a fresh gathering takes place, not in connection with the defilement of death, which is now provision-ally cleansed, but *to settle provisionally the fate of the widows*. The sisters of the deceased have to play a special part in this gathering. They will lead the discussion with the widows about their new husbands. It is indeed a happy custom to let women decide on the subject. Not that they have unrestricted power in the matter. The law has provided a certain rule for the distribution and this is seldom departed from. However, some liberty is allowed in its application, and modifications can better be made if proposed by female intermediaries. Should the husband possess a harem (tshengwe), that is at least five wives, they will most likely be given to the following heirs. The great wife, being "the pole of the

(1) *Widowers* also form a similar society and undergo the same rites ; but just as it was only the great wife who was subject to these laws, to the exclusion of the little wives, so it is only when he has lost his first wife that a man is initiated into the widowers' society. After having buried her (he holds her head) he goes to the pool, washes himself, and another widower comes and makes the incision in him in the inguinal region. Then he throws aways his *shifado* (Annotatio 1.) and also carries out the same crossing of the hut in tears. These three acts constitute the actual widower's mourning : the vapour baths and *lahla khombo* are part of his purification as being the principal grave-digger.

village," must remain in it and belongs to the younger brother (1) who becomes the master of the kraal. The second goes to the second brother, the third to the third, the fourth to the *ntukulu*, viz. to the son of the sister of the deceased. The fifth will then become the wife of one of the sons of the deceased. This may appear shocking, and is really shocking even to the ideas of the Natives ; but let it be remembered that she is the youngest of all ; she was taken when the father was already old, and the first son is perhaps older than she. As regards the elder wives, the first and second especially, no one would think of keeping them for the son ! Incestuous relations are very rare amongst the Ba-Ronga. Even in this case, the feelings of both parties are more or less respected. The men advise the son to begin to play with the young widow, to ask her jocularly for tobacco, and he gradually accustoms himself to consider her no longer as a mother (mamana) but as a wife (nsati).

Of course the general rule is apt to be very much altered according to circumstances. Should the deceased be the youngest of the family, his elder brother may inherit the first wife. But this is not the regular procedure.

The distribution having thus been decided on, the sisters of the deceased call the widows and say to them : "You so and so, you shall give food to so and so (phamela manyana)." But then the struggle begins. One of the widows, being old, may altogether refuse to have anything to do with any of her brothers-in-law. She may say : "I am taking my young son as a husband" which means : I do not want to be the wife of anybody. Or she will say : "I choose the big tree of the village where my late husband has built his hut." This answer may mean two things. Either : I do not leave this kraal and I will stay here without a husband ; or, on the contrary : I consent to be the wife of the man who becomes the headman of the village, viz. the eldest of the younger brothers. Another will say : "I love my *ntukulu* so and so." Should, however, the first wife desire to go to a man who does not

(1) Amongst the Ba-Ronga, an elder brother of the deceased cannot inherit a widow. It is taboo. He is a father to her, not a husband. He sometimes takes the lead in the discussion, having no personal interest in the matter. (See Part II).

live in the village, the family council will certainly object strongly to her wish, as her departure would mean that the village would cease to exist. But in the case of the younger widows it is quite possible that an exception to the ordinary law would be allowed if they insisted upon choosing another husband (1).

After all, this is but a preliminary consultation, and the men who are rejoicing at the idea of getting new wives will perhaps be badly deceived later on, as we shall see. However the man provisionally chosen as the future husband of a widow, will at once pay visits to her, "march to her" (ku mu fambela), according to the technical expression.

d) *The casting away of misfortune.* But before any new and happy life can begin for the widows, they have still to go through a very hard trial. They must perform the *lahla khombo*, the throwing away of the malediction of death, and this is much more difficult for them than for the grave-diggers or the other members of the village. The main point in this strange act of purification is this ; before a widow can become the wife of her new husband, she must have sexual intercourse with another man whom she deceives. Should she succeed in freeing herself from him so that the act keeps its ritual character, s. n. i. (see Annotatio 2), this man will take on himself the malediction of death, and she will be purified. On the contrary, should the man accomplish the whole act, the widow has failed and will return home with shame and in despair! Here is a description of this sad expedition of the widows. It takes place a few days after the gathering just described. The men of the village send the widows away, telling them : "Go and scatter (hangalasa) the malediction through the country and get rid of it before some other misfortune happens to us."

(1) What would happen should the widow choose a husband outside her husband's family ? To the mind of a heathen woman the idea would never occur. But suppose a Christian widow, having only married suitors, refuses to become their wife, her conscience forbidding her to contract a polygamic union. Her case would be very hard indeed, as I do not think her wish would be taken into consideration by heathen relatives. It would have to be brought before the White magistrate, who would probably try to help the widow. I think that, even if the woman consented to submit such family matters to the European court, she would have to give the *lobola* or her children back to her brothers-in-law, and that might be an impossibility for her. It would be interesting to know how Native Commissioners proceed in such cases.

With their conical baskets on their heads they all go, each accompanied by a friend who will act as witness. They pay a visit to some distant relative and try to flirt with the men of the village. Their aim is clearly understood ; morals are so dissolute that it is not difficult for them to attain their desire. (But the purifying act is useless unless interrupted abruptly before its completion). If the widow succeeds, she is full of joy, and comes back saying : "I have coped with the mourning, I have overcome it." Should she not succeed, she has then been "overcome by the mourning." This is a serious condition, which can only be dealt with by special medicines. The man who has unconsciously purified a widow and who becomes aware of it, will also have recourse to the ñanga to get rid of the pollution of death (1). The widows endeavour to come back all together ; they stand by the main entrance of the village and announce their success with the mikulungwana shouts, which mean at the same time joy and sorrow. Everyone meets them there, and they form a procession to the grave to tell the deceased what has happened : "You have left us in the open field ; we have had to go through a painful trial ; it would not have been so if you had not left us !" But, after all, this is a day of rejoicing, and the men, the heirs to the widows, are particularly pleased. The same day the widows put on a new undergarment and complete their purification by another steam bath.

At this time the mourning is said *to have ripened* (wupfile). The widow's hair has grown again. What remains is to *kill the mourning* (dlaya nkosi). This is done by the man who "marches to" or visits the widow. In the evening, he is allowed into her hut : they make a fire in it, put into the fire two pills of a purifying medicine, and expose their limbs to the smoke. Then they put it out with their own water, after which they can have sexual relations without harm. A certain time must, however, elapse before the adjudication of the inheritance takes place.

(1) He may also avoid the danger of being killed by the contamination of death in the following manner : Supposing that the woman who tries to seduce him is a widow, he tears off a little piece of her most intimate undergarment before the act. Later on he asks a ñanga to prepare a medicine into which this bit of clothing will be introduced. Then he covers himself with a blanket, burns the medicinal pill on a live charcoal and inhales the smoke. He is safe, and the woman also has been cleansed.

The description I have given of the *lahla khombo*, translating exactly the narratives of Mboza, Elias, and an old widower called Magingi, refers to the rite as it was performed in the normal fashion some twenty years ago amongst the Ba-Ronga. Now customs are changing. There is, all around the town of Lourenço Marques, an agglomeration of Natives coming from many tribes. Immorality there has become terrible owing especially to alcoholic excesses, a free and enormous sale of adulterated wine taking place in this region. The widows are sure to find there a hundred men for each of them, when they wish to cast away their defilement. But in this promiscuity the poison of syphilis makes terrible ravages. According to our medical missionary, 90 % of the Natives are contaminated by this disease. When the men up country saw that their wives came back ritually purified but physically contaminated, they began themselves to accomplish the necessary act. This has become the general custom to such an extent that, when a widow goes to Majlangalen, (such is the name of that hell of drunkenness and immorality), it is now said of her : "She will refuse to stay with her legal heirs!" However the law of the *lahla khombo nhoben*, to cast away the male-diction in the bush, remains inexorable in the three cases where the defilement is considered as being of the worst kind : if the husband died of phthisis or of leprosy, or if the woman has had twins.

Old widows who can find no lovers may be purified by means of drugs.

e) *The year of widowhood.* Though the widows have found new husbands, they still remain in the old kraal. They must accomplish there "a full hoe," viz. a whole year of ploughing. In their new fields they leave the dry sticks of the mealies of the year before, in such a way that everybody passing by will know at once that this is the field of a widow. But what they harvest this year will belong to the new husband. They have now the right to *fambelana*, viz. to go to each other. The suitor brings clothing to the woman, and the woman pays him visits with jars of beer. They belong more or less to each other. But the marriage of the inherited woman is not absolutely settled. Her final fate will not be known before the last and most important act : the adjudication of the inheritance.

f) *The day of the adjudication of the inheritance.* This is a most typical ceremony prepared for with great care, because the day is full of surprises and dangers. Every precaution is taken to avoid misunderstanding, and to bring the mourning to a peaceful and satisfactory conclusion. It is winter time ; the mealies have been collected from the fields of the widows, the small cobs called *makunula* have been set carefully apart, as they have to be used especially to prepare the beer for the feast. The council of the family is again assembled and decides that the time has come. The divinatory bones are consulted. Should they be favourable, the ceremony can take place. The bones are again asked a number of questions :. Who must take the mealies from the granary and put them in the pot to soften them in water ? (first operation of native beer making). A newly married woman who has had only one child is chosen by preference. Then it is asked how long this softening must continue ; who is to shout her *mikulungwane* to accompany the work ; who will have to get the mealies out ; which woman must give the first blow in the mortar to pound the softened mealies, etc.

All the relatives assemble in the mortuary village. One year has elapsed since the death, and the bitter feelings of mourning have passed. Nobody will miss the feast, certainly not the *batukulu*, viz., the nephews, sons of the sisters of the deceased. Some may be disappointed this day, but one of these nephews may return home richer than when he left ! Most of the relatives arrive before the great day, to help in the preparation of the beer. When the woman designated by the bones has given the first blow, all her companions start at once pounding with vigour : "Ghe-ghe-ghe-ghe," and they sing songs of mourning. This is one of these songs, and a very significant one :

> Hi rilo, hi rilo ! Hi ta ku yini ku we, Hosi ndjina ?
> We are weeping, we are weeping ! What shall we say to thee, King !

This king is without doubt Heaven, the more or less personal being who kills or gives life, and whom we shall often meet with in these pages.

207

The first of the ceremonies of this day is the sacrifice on the grave. The master of the mourning takes a pot of beer, and followed by the crowd, especially by the *batukulu*, goes to the place where the deceased has been buried. He stops there and prays : "See this jar of beer! We bring it to thee ; we have gathered to tear to pieces the mourning. We beseech thee that this ceremony may be performed in peace and good understanding." Then he pours a little of the drink into the cup which is on the grave, the same which the deceased used when alive. One *ntukulu* then takes the jar, which is still almost full, and drinks the contents with the other *batukulu*. This has been done calmly. But this act has made the *batukulu* bolder. They become troublesome. As soon as the crowd has come back from the grave, they steal another pot of beer. They insult the masters of the village. They say : "Why! You have never sent us any notice about the decisions concerning the mourning! We are tired! We will go and take our wives with us!" But some of the old men go to them and say : "Be good! Do not spoil the feast!"

By the end of the afternoon all the relatives assemble near the door of the mortuary hut, and bring the goats which they have given for the feast. Here the true sacrifice, the living offering, is made, very much in the same style as that described when treating of the crushing down of the hut (p. 158). The old man who prays, says : "See us here! We have come together to conclude our mourning. May there be no noise, no misunderstanding, no anger amongst the *batukulu*! This is our ox (the goat). It has been provided by so and so. Many others have been brought. See! You have died as a great chief!" At this very moment a *ntukulu* rises and begins to insult the old man who is praying : "You have no concern for us! Why do you leave us out ? You do not give us our wives! You are killing us!" And the other *batukulu* join in chorus. The end of the sacrifice and of the prayer is always the same in these big, religious, family gatherings of the Ba-Ronga : the *batukulu* steal the part of the victim set apart for the gods. The throng pursues them laughing, and pelts them with balls of *psanyi*.

THE EVOLUTION OF A WOMAN FROM BIRTH TO DEATH

The sun is now setting. All the men go to the central place of the village and sit round the fire. The widows remain on the spot, between the deceased's hut and the new hut of the great wife, where all the belongings of the late husband have been kept during the whole year. The other widows of the family surround them once more ; no other woman is allowed to approach. The present ceremony is another secret rite of the company of widows. They sing the following mourning song to recall all the sufferings of the year of widowhood :

> Angoma nkulukumba ! Tatana a nga fa, a ba siya
> Na ngoma a nga si ba byela !
> Our secret law is a great law! Our father has gone, he has left them,
> And he had not told them about that law !

During this song the old women take away all the clothing of the widows, and wash their bodies. Then they lead them into the hut of the great wife and put on them new clothing, the clothes which their suitors and other relatives have brought for them. When they are all seated, the sisters of the deceased proceed to the last distribution. They first ask the great wife : "You, to whom do you belong ?" She answers : "Do you not know him ? It is the man who has taken care of me, who has been visiting me! I choose so and so!" She may also say : "I kill so and so!" *(Ndji dlaya man)*. That means : "As I have killed my first husband, I might do the same for the second," a very promising declaration! As soon as the widow has given her answer, the women in the hut begin shouting loudly, and one of them goes out to the men, and cries : "So and so says she kills so and so !" They proceed to ask another : "You, whom do you choose ?" The woman remains silent. "What do you mean?" — "I do not choose anybody." — "How is that? Be sensible!" — "No! I do not want anybody!" — "Why ?" They begin to press her : "You know well who has taken care of you, who has visited *(fambela)* you the whole year." — "I do not want him!" — "How is that possible ?" — "No, I do not want him. I want the *ntukulu* so and so." A frightful noise is heard in the hut ; they are all shouting together. What has happened ?

Probably this widow was not pleased with the man to whom they had destined her. Seeing more of him during the year, her affection had not increased. On the other hand, she had some liking for one of the *batukulu*, and she arranged secretly with him, and perhaps also with his mother, that she would keep silent till this day and then choose her nephew. It is quite possible that the mother of the *ntukulu* will say in that case : "Has this widow not been bought with the money which I secured for the family by my marriage ?" Of course the official suitor objects strongly to this spoliation. He becomes angry. During a whole year he has given clothing to the ungrateful one. Things may grow so bad that the *ntukulu* carries off the fractious widow at once, saying : "Good-bye! I go with my wife!" The old men will then follow him and implore him to come back. If they see that the woman is quite decided, they will allow her to go to the husband of her choice. They had better consent to it at once, because it not infrequently happens that the *ntukulu*, if repulsed that day, will go to the family of the woman and claim the money *(lobola)* paid for her by her late husband, saying : "That *lobola* comes from my mother. If you do not give us our wife, if you allow her to stay with another man, then give us back the money." Or it may happen also that the widow, brought perforce to the house of a younger brother-in-law, will run away to the *ntukulu*, and the rightful husband will be helpless. There is a saying to this effect : "A woman inherited cannot be forced." Of course such cases of conflicting interests cause a great deal of friction between members of the family, and the Natives are much distressed about it ; they try to avoid it as much as possible. But the desire of getting one more wife is so strong in the heart of a Ronga that such disputes are by no means rare, and the day of the adjudication of the inheritance is universally dreaded. However, they never go as far as fighting, and ,if an uncle and a nephew have parted from each other on bad terms, they will very likely try to mend matters by the sacrifice of reconciliation *(hahlelana madjieta)*, which is one of the admirable features of the Ronga religion (See Part VI).

The widows are truly the most important part of the property left by a man. When they have been distributed, the minor possessions of the deceased are adjudicated. As regards *oxen, money*, these have been already remitted to the younger brother or, in his absence, to the sons. The younger brother will use them as family property to buy a wife for his son or for the son of the deceased, when he comes of age. In the distribution of the implements which have been cleansed, but left lying on the ground in front of the hut up to this day, the *ntukulu*, viz. the principal uterine nephew again plays an important part. He has the right of *tjhumba*, viz. of picking out for himself one of the assagais of his uncle, just as the maternal uncle takes (tjhumba) one pound from the lobola money (See Part II). Every warrior possesses at least two assagais ; the big one belongs in principle to the chief, and must be inherited by the eldest son. The nephew takes the smaller one, but he must precede his cousin in choosing ; in appropriating this weapon, he *surrenders* or transmits (nyiketa) the inheritance to the true heirs. This is a very characteristic expression. It seems as if he wished to assert his right ; but he takes the less valuable weapon and leaves the better one to the son. The explanation of this custom is probably to be found in the evolution of the family system which must have taken place amongst the Thongas (See Part II). In fact all the *batukulu* stand in a line and receive a portion of the property of the deceased, a knife, an axe, a small punch, etc. Women.never inherit (a ba di pfindla). When no heir exists except females, they may receive something, but the valuable property must be kept by them for their sons, the uterine nephews of the deceased. Why ? Because, in the mind of the Thongas, a woman is not capable of possessing ; she is not able to build an oxen kraal and repair it ; how could she possess oxen ?. The only thing she can do is to arrange a pig's kraal. Therefore she can own pigs, but nothing else !

The end of the feast of the adjudication of the inheritance is the distribution of the flesh of the victims. The company breaks up, each party having received one of the limbs. They must eat it on their way home, somewhere under a tree, on the road ; neither in the mortuary village, nor in their own kraal. It is

taboo. Those who have received a wife go home rejoicing.
When he has reached home, the fortunate husband kills a fowl
or even a goat to make a fitting reception for his new wife. This
is the end of the long period of widowhood, in which it is easy to
discover the whole sequence of the passage rites.

Such is the old normal way of reinstating a widow in society.
But there are special cases where the rites are slightly different.
If a widow is old and cannot expect to deceive a man, she simply
buys medicines which are supposed to cleanse her.

The case of the wife of Sokis (see page 139, footnote) was
more difficult. She had a baby, and sexual relations were
consequently prohibited. Moreover the man who legally inherited her was in Johannesburg and could not provide for her
purification. One of the grave-diggers took his place and "ran
for her" (tjutjumela). This is a different expression for *fambela*.
As far as I could understand, this man had ritual relations with his
own wife in order to *lahla khombo*, to be purified himself. Then
he tied the cotton string (boha nshale) round the waist of the
widow. A sick widow will also be treated by *tjutjumela*. The
grave-digger possesses the means of cleansing them, having gone
through the mourning together with them.

These attenuated processes of purification seem the rule amongst
the *Northern clans*. According to Viguet, the widows must also
go to the bush (hula ni nhoba) to meet with a man who will free
them of the defilement of death. The man who performs this act
is called the *shikomho* of the widows. There are certain individuals
who make a real business of this. Knowing drugs with which to
cleanse themselves (ku tirulula), they claim a reward for their
help... The widows remove their mourning attire (bracelets of
strings on that occasion), and return home adorned with beads.
In the Djonga dialect the adjudication of the inheritance is called
pandja ndjaka. It is not accompanied by a sacrifice. There
seem to be some differences in the ideas of the Rongas and of the
Northern clans. For the former the defilement of death contaminates the hut to a greater extent. This must be destroyed, and the
widow has to undergo the very hard casting away of misfortune
(lahla khombo). For the latter the impurity rests more on the

village itself, which must carry out the collective purification of *hlamba ndjaka*.

I must further mention a new custom which is spreading amongst the Ba-Ronga in the neighbourhood of Lourenço Marques. When a widow objects to becoming the wife of the legal inheritor, she goes home and adopts another husband. There are plenty of men of other tribes, coming from Inhambane, Quelimane, Mozambique, who have no wife. They accept the proposal of the widow and go to live in her village. They are generally despised and called by the insulting name of *mugomo*, a Zulu word meaning an empty iron oil-tin. They are as hard and unfeeling as such a tin! If children are born, they belong to the family of the deceased husband, who paid the lobolo.

Sometimes also a widow chooses a nephew who is still a child. She gives him food as if she were his wife, but she lives with another man whom she loves. It even happens that she may choose a girl, the daughter of another wife of the deceased. (Annotatio 13.)

C. OLD AGE AND DEATH

An old woman, having in some sort gone out from the sexual community, enjoys some privileges which are taboo for her sisters who are still capable of childbearing. She is allowed to put on the clothing of the widows ; contamination of death is not so dangerous for her. She can proceed to the purification of the village, in certain cases of epidemic, and of the weapons of the warriors in war time (Part III). After the sacrifice of the black ram for rain, old women and small girls alone are allowed to eat the flesh of the victim.

But old and decrepit women are despised. As long as they can still till their land, they are treated with consideration, but when they have lost all their strength and must be fed by their children, they are looked upon as troublesome burdens. I must say that, as long as she still has an atom of vigour, a Thonga woman goes to her field and tills it. During all her life time

she has contracted such an intimate union with Mother Earth
that she cannot conceive existence away from her gardens, and
she crawls to them with her hoe, by a kind of instinct, till she
dies.

The death of the woman is accompanied by the same rites as
the death of a man. I must mention, however, the custom of
mahloko, which takes place when a woman dies while still in her
prime. Mahloko comes from nhloko, head. The explanation of
this technical word is this : the parents of the woman say : "Our
head (viz. a person belonging to us) has died ; let us go to mourn
her."

Let us first see how this mourning takes place in the Ronga clans.

If the two families were very friendly, the parents of the deceased
will probably bring with them a little girl, saying : "This is our
little green meat (mbuti), our little orange (rather sala, fruit of the
nsala tree)." They offer her to the husband to take the place of
the deceased wife, and a new contract will be made. The widower
will then at once pay a first part of the lobolo, £ 5 for instance, and,
in the course of time, he will marry his sister-in-law. But
generally the visitors are angry, and the mahloko ceremony is very
unpleasant. It may be that the deceased wife had not been
entirely paid for. In that case her parents will come at the end of
the mourning to "claim the herd" (ramela ntlhambi).

But though there may be no difficult lobola question in the
way, uneasiness is felt, because the brothers of the deceased
cannot help thinking that their sister has been killed by witchcraft.
It was not yet time for her to die ; so she must have been bewitched
by the husband's family, probably by her co-wives, who were
jealous of her. When the Great Mourning took place, they
hardly came to the mortuary village. One or two went to see
their "head," and mourned her in their own kraal. To day, the
day of mahloko, they assemble, and throw bones in order to
know who will have to speak, who will receive the mahloko money,
whether the money has been bewitched ? The whole company
starts for the mortuary village, driving a goat before them. They
sit down outside in the bush with dark looks ; there is no longer
any hut to receive them... They have been noticed by the

214

inhabitants of the kraal. One of them, the saluter (mulosi), goes to meet them and offers them a shilling. They keep silence. He tells them the news of the village. They do not answer. He leaves them and comes a second time with a fresh present. Then they consent to tell the news of their home, but they do not enter the village. The same man returns to them a third time with £ 1 ; they refuse to accept it. He adds 10/. (£ 1.10 is considered the normal sum to be paid as a kind of fine by the widower to the parents of the deceased.) They refuse again : this is an insult! Happily the *ntukulu* is there ; he will act as mediator between the two families. The visitors summoned him on their arrival and he has been sitting with them the whole time ; is he not the son of their sister ? But before he went to them, his father has given him his instructions : "Tell them that I have not eaten your mother." The *ntukulu,* as we shall see, is very free with his maternal uncles. He has the right of teasing them, even insulting them. Seeing that they do not accept the money, he stands and gives vent to his grief, throws sand at them, tries to drive them away, weeps. "No! Father has not killed mother! He is not a wizard! She died a natural death!" They see his tears, and then consent to enter the village.

In front of the mortuary hut, all the belongings of the deceased wife have been piled up, together with the straw crown of the hut : her pots, plates, baskets, spoons, mortars, etc. The brothers break everything. Should there be any new implements amongst them, they will perhaps give them to their nieces. Then they lift up the roof of the hut and throw it into the bush. They pick all the plaster from the walls and throw it away where they threw the roof. The sacrifice is then accomplished amidst the ruins of the destroyed hut. Whilst it is being prepared, the women of both families insult each other. The female relatives of the deceased say to the women of the village : "You have killed her because she was a splinter in your eyes" (shilabi). The others answer : "Have you seen us kill her ? Perhaps people do not die with you ?" The *bukwele,* the special jealousy which almost always exists between co-wives, explains how it is possible for them to address such amenities to each other. But the victim is prepared, all the limbs cut off, the portion of the gods set apart. The elder brother of the deceased woman prays in these words : "My sister, go in peace, be not angry ; because we love you, we have come to mourn you to-day. Do not say we have not mourned you. Go to so and so (father, grandfather, etc.), call them here, give us good sleep and good health, etc." The batukulu appropriate the offering and the mourning ends in laughter, dancing and drinking. The neighbours come and take part in the rejoicings.

When they return home, the mourners spend all the mahloko money in buying wine. They sometimes become quite intoxicated. Afterwards both families begin to visit each other again.

This custom of the mahloko fine is so strong that converts still adhere to it. But they usually send the money to the wife's family when informing them of the death, and no other ceremony is performed.

In the Northern clans the mahloko are also paid, but it seems that the family of the widower considers that it has the right to claim the repayment of the whole lobolo, when the deceased wife has left no child to compensate for the loss. In Nondwane, though we are still in Ronga territory, when the woman dies shortly after marriage the lobolo must be repaid. Further north the procedure is as follows : the deceased woman is buried by her husband according to the ordinary rules ; one year elapses and a special feast is celebrated, similar to the "beer of mourning" (page 164), in the village of the wife's parents, where both families gather together and provide the necessary victims. It commences with a sacrifice in which the father of the deceased wife squeezes the *psanyi* of the goat on to those present, all the time insulting the gods who have killed his child and made trouble between the two families. He ends with words addressed to the widower's relations : "I cleanse you from your misfortune." The widower's father does the same thing, insulting also his own gods, and every one rubs his body with the green liquid squeezed from the *psanyi*. Then prayer for new blessings is offered and the sacrifice is made, as customary, and the actual discussion as to claims takes place. Each family takes possession of a hut, the widower's family assembling as usual in the house of the deceased wife's mother, and the parley takes place through the go-between (tintjumi), as in the discussions which precede marriage. Let us call the husband's family A and that of the wife B. A sends two hoes to B as a notification :"Your child died with us last year." B answers "All right! Then pay the fine for her head (nhloko). Because you had only bought her legs. Her brain, her head, her name was still ours." A sends five hoes to B, to pay for the brains of the deceased. B takes two of the five and sends them back to A, saying : "One of them is to cleanse you from the misfortune, and we shave your head with the second." A accepts the two hoes and returns home. Should the wife have died childless, there will be a second act to the procedure: A has "opened the door of the claim" (a pfurile nyangwa wa nandju). He will come back shortly to lodge it with B.

Here he comes. Using his go-between (ntjumi) as a mouth piece, he says to B : "Look at us! We gather our ashes with our own hands and we dig water in small shells of sala,— viz. we have no wife to do this feminine work for us!" It means : "Please give us another wife or repay the money to buy one." If B happens to have a girl of marriageable age, he will say : "Do not kill us ; we put a log of wood across the road" (hi hingakanya ntjandja). This means : "We have put something to prevent you from coming to us as enemies. Here is a new wife for you." A understands quite well and goes home satisfied. He comes back without delay and brings twenty or thirty hoes, which is a beginning of lobola payment. He says : "We thank you for the wife." The girl then follows him at once, if she is of marriageable age ; if not, she stays at home until she is grown up, and during all this time her new husband provides her with clothing. When, having gone to live with him, she gives birth to a child, B comes to A and says : "Nwombekazi a yi ambi nandju," viz. "A cow which has calved is not used to pay a debt," that is to say : she must be paid for herself. This technical expression means therefore : As our daughter has given you posterity, pay the full lobolo for her! A will certainly do it "hi bushaka," on account of the friendly relation existing between B and himself. But if B has no girl to give in compensation, if he has no money, what will happen ? A will

217

follow his oxen where they have gone, namely into the family of the girl who has been bought by B for one of his sons. This woman is for the widower his great *mukoñwana*, the woman he fears the most in all the tribe. We shall see what will then happen when treating of the extraordinary relations existing between these two individuals. This wonderful story of the consequences of the death of a wife, so characteristically told by Viguet, provides us with an excellent opportunity for transition to Part II of this work, which will explain the relations between all the members of the Thonga family.

SECOND PART

THE LIFE OF THE FAMILY AND OF THE VILLAGE

Having followed a man and a woman from the beginning to the end of their existence, I now come to the Life of the Family and of the Village. Both subjects are in close connexion. As a rule, a village is but a family composed of the headman, the father, his wives, his children and the old folk who depend upon him ; but in many cases his younger brothers live with him, sometimes a son-in-law, or even a stranger, and all these inmates compose the village, *muti* (1). In the first chapter we shall consider the family itself, its constitution, the system of relationship, and in the second, the village, the concrete embodiment of the family, its foundation, its main laws and the respective occupations of its members.

CHAPTER I

THE LIFE OF THE FAMILY

The kinship system of the Thongas and, I suppose, of all the Bantus is widely different from ours, and greatly surprises the

---

(1) Native villages are generally called *kraals* by South African colonists. This expression comes from the Portuguese word *curral* which means properly stable. I shall employ it to designate the enclosure where oxen are kept, the cattle-kraal, but it does not seem right to apply it to the *muti* which is a *village*, however small and poor it may be. The Portuguese call native villages *povoaçâo*.

uninitiated student who tries to understand it. It is a very complicated matter indeed. In *Les Ba-Ronga* I have given the genealogy of Tobane and tried to sketch the system, and even to explain it. I cannot say that I was altogether satisfied with this first attempt. When later on I had an opportunity of studying the subject in the Northern clans, I found that a comparison between the customs of the different parts of the tribe helped greatly to an understanding of the whole matter. This led me to extend my investigation to neighbouring tribes, and, after the publication of the first edition of this book, I made inquiries amongst the Vendas, Pedi-Khahas, Suthos, Chopis, Ndjaos and Tongas. I then conceived the ambitious plan of drawing up a table of the terms of relationship in all these tribes or sub-tribes, being convinced that it would be of great interest, both from the linguistic and from the ethnographic point of view. I publish it in Appendix IV, at the end of this Volume. My chief concern remains with the Thonga tribe, but after having described in detail the kinship system amongst the Thongas, I intend to sketch some of the most characteristic customs met with amongst their fellow Bantus in South Africa.

May I add that though it is comparatively easy to discover the main ideas in relation to the family in the Thonga tribe, yet the whole tangle is extraordinarily difficult to unravel. I had believed that it was composed of two threads only, twisted together and knotted a hundred times : the lobola and polygamy customs. But I saw that many other threads were entwined with these : remnants of an ancient state of society where the mother-right prevailed, and perhaps traces of the old group-marriage system which is still extant amongst Australian natives. My aim is more modest to-day. I do not claim to explain everything, but to present a wider, more complete statement of facts, which I offer to professional anthropologists in order that they may fix the place of the present Thonga system of relationship in the evolution of the human family.

THE LIFE OF THE FAMILY

A. REMARKS ON THE TABLE OF TERMS OF RELATIONSHIP IN TEN SOUTH AFRICAN TRIBES OR SUB-TRIBES (APP. IV)

Some particulars as to the way I obtained the lists contained in this Table may interest my readers.

First of all I would express my gratitude towards the late and much regretted Rev. F. Bridgeman, who compiled the *Zulu list*, and to the Rev. R. Godfrey, to whom I owe the *Xosa list*. I could hardly have found more competent collaborators for the Zulu-Xosa group.

The *Chopi tribe* is settled on the border of the Indian Ocean, from the mouth of the Limpopo up to Inhambane. A considerable number of its members have emigrated into the Lourenço Marques district. One of them, belonging to the Zandamelan clan, gave me his genealogy and explained to me the Chopi system of relationship.

As regards the *Suthos of Basutoland*, my informant was Neftali Motswenen, the assistant of Dr. Hertig, in Morija, in 1915, and the list was kindly revised by my friend the late Rev. E. Jacottet and by the Rev. P. Ramseyer.

The *Khaha* tribe is a portion of the Pedi population of the Northern Transvaal. I spent some years in the neighbourhood of its chief, Maaghe, who was staying near the Mission Station of Shiluvane, and owe my information chiefly to a young Khaha named Malupi, who was one of my pupils (in 1906).

During a prolonged visit to the *Venda country* in 1920 I met an intelligent Native called Shifaladzi who did his best to disclose to me all the mysteries of the customs of this interesting tribe, especially its kinship system.

As regards the *Tongas* in the neighbourhood of Inhambane, I got my first information from one of them living near Rikatla ; the list was later on submitted to Mrs. Keys, the wife of an American missionary, who kindly completed it as far as possible.

The *Ndjaos*, also called Ba-Nyai, live further north, between the Sabie River and Beira. One of my neighbours in Rikatla belonged to that tribe and gave me an intelligent account of their family life.

I cannot guarantee the absolute completeness of all these lists. There are blanks in some of them, either because my informants failed to find the proper term or because that term does not exist or has been

221

forgotten (especially in Basutoland). It may also be that some mistakes have been made, and I must apologize if such is the case. However I give this table as it is, after having done the best I could, knowing, as I said in my introduction, that Science proceeds by successive approximations and hoping that it will be a useful stone in the building up of African ethnological Science.

*

* *

As regards the spelling of all these words, I have followed as well as I could the system used in the books of the different languages. As, however, there is a deplorable multiplicity in the orthographic systems of South Africa, certain signs have not exactly the same value in all the columns. It is impossible to avoid this drawback, but it is of minor importance, my first aim being ethnographic and not linguistic. In Thonga I render by *ps* the sibilant *s* which is represented by *s* with a circumflex in the Thonga-Ronga books, and by *tj* and *dj* the cerebral *t* and *d*. I employ undiscriminately *b* for the strong *b* which is more common in Ronga and for the soft *b*, represented by *ṽ* in Thonga-Djonga books.

The Rev. P. Schwellnus has kindly transcribed most of the Khaha terms collected by me in the orthography recently adopted for Pedi books. Thus the letter *g*, when found alone or after *ḳ*, represents the greek *ɣ*, a hard fricative guttural, whilst *g* associated with *n* corresponds to the nasal guttural *ng* in the English "singing" (*ñ* in Thonga). The cerebral *t* (*tj* in Thonga) is represented by *c*. In this form the kinship terms do not entirely agree with the Khaha pronunciation. The Khahas have a tendancy to soften many sounds (*dz* instead of *ts*, a kind of *d* instead of *tl*). I have adopted, however, the official Pedi orthography, as it is inadvisable, from a practical point of view, to preserve all the peculiarities of less important dialects or semi-dialects.

In the Sutho orthography *ḳh* corresponds to the Pedi *ḳg* ; *l* before *i* and *u* represents a sound intermediary between *l* and *d*, also present in Chopi, a soft cerebral *d* ; in Pedi it is written *d*. This sound occurs in the feminine suffix *ali* (Sutho), *adi* (Pedi) often met with in kinship terms (*ati* in Thonga, *azi* in Zulu, *adzi* in Venda). *O* and *u* are used both in Sutho and Pedi for the semi-vowels *w* and *y*. *Ch* in Sutho is pronounced like *tsh* in Thonga and Zulu.

222

THE LIFE OF THE FAMILY

*

*   *

Grammatically speaking, most of the Thonga terms of kinship belong to the class mu-ba, the personal class. They form their plural in *ba* (batatana, bana, bamakwabu, batukulu). Some however are of the class yin-tin which comprises mostly animals, but also names of trades and of family relations : Ndjisana, nhondjwa, namu, nhombe, nhlantsa forming their plural in *ti*. The five following terms, Tatana, Mamana, Rarana, Malume, Kokwana, are treated as proper nouns when they are used as such. For instance when I say Tatana, it means *my* father, the one to whom this term applies par excellence. In this case Tatana is not preceeded by the initial vowel *a* or *e*, which is always prefixed to the common nouns (See Elementary Grammar ot the Thonga-Shangaan Language, page 26 § 65). If I wish to say "his father," I should say : Atatana wa kwe (Ro.), or Etata wa yena (Dj.) etc.

B. EXPLANATION OF THONGA TERMS OF RELATIONSHIP

Let us go deeper into the study of each of these terms, trying to ascertain their principal and derivative meanings. We shall consult the three genealogies here given, those of Tobane (A), of Mboza (B) and of his wife Nsabula (C), endeavouring to ascertain not only the social but also the moral relation existing between these several people. There are two kinds of relationship : blood relationship or consanguinity and marriage relationship, relationship on the wife's side or affinity. Amongst blood relatives, there are two categories which differ more from each other amongst the Bantus than amongst us, relatives on the father's side and on the mother's side. On the father's side, the relatives are called bakweru (Ro.), barikweru (Dj.), those of our home ; and on the mother's side, bakokwana, the ancestors.

We shall consider each of these three relationships separately, though it will be found impossible to isolate them entirely from each other. In each of them, we shall find two sets of terms : terms of correspondence and of reciprocity. We shall see also

A. Genealogy of Tobane

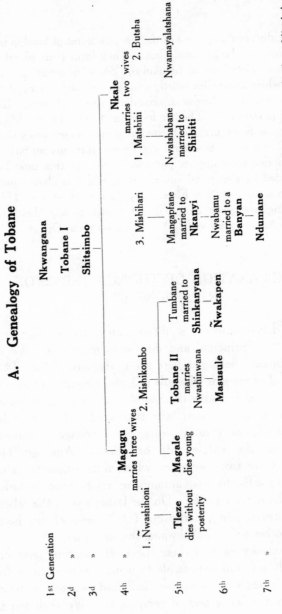

Mishikombo has two brothers, **Shigwalati** and **Mahwayi** and one sister Budiulu, **Shigwalati** has one daughter, Mintshale.
Ñwashihoni has a brother, **Madyondjo** and a sister, Ntungwen.

B. Near Relatives of Mboza

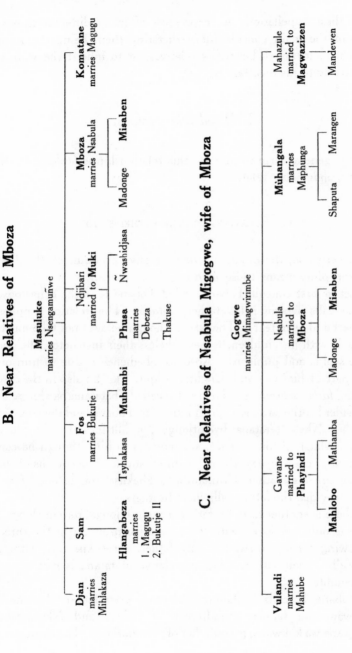

C. Near Relatives of Nsabula Migogwe, wife of Mboza

N. B. The names of the male members of the family are printed in dark type.

that these appellations are expressive of many different things, one of the main considerations dictating them being the right of a man to marry his wife's relatives, or to inherit the women belonging to his own family.

I. *Blood relationships.*

The general term to indicate this relationship is *bushaka* (from *shaka, mashaka*), relatives.

1) RELATIVES ON THE FATHER'S SIDE.

(Bakweru : *ba*, those, *ku*, at, *eru* possessive pronoun of the first person plur. means those *with us*, in our home.)

Let us first consult Tobane, called Tobane II in the genealogy.

He calls Magugu his father, *tatana*. The relation implies respect and even fear. The father, though he does not take much trouble with his children, is nevertheless their instructor, the one who scolds and punishes. Absolute obedience is due to him on the part of his sons and daughters (App. V). So also in the case of the *father's brothers*, who are also called "batatana ba shirare :" the elder brother who is a "great father" to Tobane, and the younger brother Nkale, "tatana lwe'ntjongo", a "little father." Their wives, Matshini for instance, are mothers to him, though he can in certain cases marry them by inheritance. The cousins of the father are also fathers (Muhambi to Thakusa, for instance, Gen. B.), provided the father calls them brothers.

There is another term for father, *rara* in Djonga, *roro* in Ronga ; *roro* is only employed with the possessive pronoun in the three following forms : rorwa'nga, my father, rorwa'ku, your father, rorwa'bu, their father. The correlative of tatana is *ñwana*, son or daughter.

Tobane II calls Shitsimbo *kokwana*, grandfather, Tobane I kokwane wa tatana, grandfather of father, and Nkwangana kokwana wa kokwana, grandfather of grandfather. The expression tatana wa kokwana, father of grandfather, is never employed. The great-grandfather and the great-great-grandfather are sometimes designated as follows : he who does not see his grandson when he has been sent by the women to bring him food ; the boy eats it on the way and the old man does not notice it ! (Page 132). These progenitors call Tobane *ntukulu*, grandson. He is the true ntukulu of Shitsimbo ; to Tobane I, he is the *ntukulu wa shikandjatjolo*, "the one who sits on the knees ;" to Nkwangwana, the *ntukulu wo shikandjamirombo*, a word which seems to mean "the one who sits on the toes." In Djonga there is one more of these curious expressions applied to batukulu, *ntukulu wa shinguhe*. "When he pronounces that name," says Gana, "my great-grandfather points near by ; when he says *ntukulu wa shikandjatjolo*, he points further down." To understand this properly, we must imagine the following patriarchal scene : a very, very old man is sitting on the ground, holding his son (ñwana) in his arms, and with his grandson (ntukulu) on his thigh, his great-grandson (wa shikandjatjolo) on his knees and his great-great-grandson on his toes (1). The fact that these terms have become almost obsolete shows that the system of counting descent from the father is at any rate very old in our tribe. There must even have been a time when the ancestors in the paternal line were better known than now. The wives of these bakokwana are also bakokwana, in the same way as their husbands.

The father's sister is *rarana* (Ro.) *hahane* (Dj.). The two words are the same, as *r* often changes into *h* in Thonga phonetics ; the prefix of the first class, *mu* or *n*, now dropped, may have caused this change. Rarana approaches very closely to rara, father. It is employed in this form when it means *my* aunt. When we wish to say your aunt, his aunt, rarana becomes rarakati wa ku, rarakati

(1) There is another interpretation of these terms as applied to the grandparents : *kokwana wa shinguhe :* he is poor, miserable ! When an ox is killed in the village, they do not even send him his share ; he is far away. *Kokwana wa shikandjatjolo :* he is almost blind. When he wants to see his great-grandson he calls him and tells him : " Sit down on my knees." *Kokwana wa shikandja-mirombo :* mirombo or mitjombo means the small ears of mealies used to prepare the beer of the offerings. This kokwana, the great-great-grandfather, is already almost like one of the ancestor-gods to whom sacrifices are made !

wa kwe. This word means exactly female father. (See the meaning of this suffix *ati*, page 36, foot note.) Tumbane is rarana of Masusule. Masusule, to her, is also ñwana. He shows her great respect. However, she is in no way a mother (mamana). Yet, amongst the paternal relatives, she is the one to whom a boy or a girl will tell their secrets; her nephew or niece will go to her in order to get advice and help in their difficulties. Occasionally she will intercede for them with their father and her influence may be decisive. The rarana may be called on to officiate in a sacrifice offered on behalf of her nephews, the children of her brothers, if the latter are all dead.

Any female who is a near relation of my father or of my paternal ancestors, is also by extension a rarana : the daughters of my paternal grand-uncle, for instance, who are like sisters to my father, etc.

The husband of my paternal aunt is neither a father nor an uncle, but a *mukoñwana* or *namu*, brother-in-law, because, as we shall see, he has a kind of prior right to marry my sister (1). (Shinkanyana versus Masusule, Gen. A ; or Muki versus Muhambi, Gen. B.) To Madonge, Muki is *nkata*, husband, on account of this possibility. He is a potential husband for her. Consequently Madonge is a potential co-wife of her paternal aunt, a co-wife of a particular kind, and the term used to indicate that relation is *nhlampsa*. We shall explain this term more fully by and by.

Tobane II calls Tumbane *makwabu* ; this term, which is

(1) Though the husband of the paternal aunt is a mukonwana, a term which implies respect, the respect shown to him is not great. Gana says: "When he passes through our village, I shall say to him: Good morning, namu! We tell each other freely the news of the day (djungulisana). He eats with us. We buy for him a little rice, a fowl. If I go to his village, I open the door of his hut and put my stick inside without asking permission... a thing which I would never do in the village of my wife's parents, who are my true bakoñwana. I sit down and say to him : ' Give me this or that..., for instance your hat.' He may refuse, but if he possesses two hats of the same shape, I insist and say: ' Give me one! We shall be like each other.' Thus we make fun together, we jest together (mpfhabelana)." — Would the uterine nephew behave in the same way towards his maternal uncle ? — Not at all ! The behaviour of the uterine nephew is called nyenyela. He shows no restraint at all; he comes and catches a fowl, a goat; he steals a pot of beer. When they see him coming, they say : "Here is the wizard, etc." (See later on. p. 232).

reciprocal, means brothers as well as sisters. If he wishes to specify, he adds to makwabu : "of the assagai," or "of the basket." It is never employed except when united with the possessive pronoun : *makweru* means my brother, *makwenu* your brother, *makwabu*, his brother or sister. The elder brother is called *nhondjwa* (plur. tinhondjwa). The nhondjwa is also called *hosi* (plur. tihosi) chief. The hierarchy of age is very strictly observed amongst the Thongas. The elder brother is treated with great respect and gives orders to his younger brothers with almost the same authority as the father. It must be noticed also that the position of elder brother is not only a matter of age, but, in the polygamic family, all the children of a first wife, or of the first house, are *tihosi* to the children of secondary or posterior wives or houses, though they may have been born after them. They take precedence of them. Amongst girls, an elder sister is often called *mamana*, mother, whilst an elder brother is never a tatana (father) but a hosi (chief).

The term *makwabu* is applied to all my first and second cousins who have the same paternal grandfather, or great-grandfather, as I have. Cousins on my mother's side are also bamakwabu, some of them at least, those who are my maternal aunt's children. But cousins on the father's side are more fully bamakwabu than those on the mother's side : Muhambi is more so to Hlangabeza than to Mahlobo, because the two former belong to the same shibongo, family name ; they are men of the Makaneta clan and Muhambi could therefore inherit Hlangabeza's wives ; Muhambi and Mahlobo are not of the same clan, and could not inherit from each other. From this fact we begin to see that the laws of inheritance, and especially the laws of the distribution of the widows amongst the family which has bought them, are closely connected with the system of relationship.

The man who has married my wife's sister is also a makwabu to me, a nhondjwa if he has married her elder sister (Phayindi to Mboza), a ndjisana if the younger (Magwazizen to Mboza). The brothers of Phayindi and Magwazizen are also called brothers by Mboza.

There is a special term in the Northern clans to indicate the relationship of two men who have married two sisters born of the same mother. They are called : bamakwabu ba shinauma, an expression which is the simplification of the following sentence : shi na wuñwe mamana, i. e. there is only one mother. This term seems to have been borrowed from the Pedis.

2) RELATIVES ON THE MOTHER'S SIDE.

Tobane II calls Mishikombo *mamana*, mother. She is his true mamana and this relation is very deep and tender, combining respect and love. Love however generally exceeds respect. The proper word for tenderness is *timpsalu*, which comes from *psala*, to beget, and the mother is often called *mpsele* (a term which is applied also to the female of all animals). It is the word which answers best to the feelings of a mother for her children. She is generally weak with them and is often accused by the father of spoiling them.

The mother's sisters are *bamamana* in the second degree, because, if the true mother dies, one of them will probably take care of the children. Their husbands are *batatana* : Phayindi is tatana to Madonge and Muhambi. He calls them *bana*, children. Mboza is also a tatana to Mahlobo and Mathamba, being a makwabu, brother of their father, owing to the fact that he and Phayindi have married sisters.

All the co-wives are also *bamamana*, mothers by polygamy, (Ñwashihoni and Mishihari to Tobane). They are *bamamana ba shitshengwe*, harem mothers. I respect them but they are further from me than my mother's sisters. A more familiar term for mother, corresponding to roro, father, is *ñwa*, a word always used with the possessive pronoun and only in the second and third person : ñwaku, your mother, ñwakwe, his mother. Ñwaku is employed in certain insults and oaths, and is to be avoided as being vituperative.

Many other women are mamana : the wife of my paternal uncle (Magugu for Muhambi), though I can inherit her in certain cases ; the daughter of my maternal uncle, because she is the potential wife of my father (Shaputa to Misaben), not to mention those women of my wife's family who can be so called. An elder sister is also mamana to her younger sister, and sometimes a husband calls his wife mamana (1).

If the mother's sister is a mother, the mother's brother is by no means a father. He is called *malume* or *kokwana*, and here we meet with one of the most characteristic features of the Thonga, and even Bantu, system of relationship. The term kokwana means first the paternal grandfather and all the ancestors on the father's side, and this is its proper essential meaning. The bakokwana are also all my mother's male relatives : her brothers, fathers, uncles, etc. They form a group which I call "ka bakokwana" which means "my mother's home," just as *kweru* means my father's home, my official home. Kweru comes first ; ka bakokwana next. "The bushaka on the father's side is the head ; on the mother's side, only the legs" (Mboza). Let us remember that a child lives at his father's home and only goes on a visit to his mother's village. He may stay there for years after the weaning, but if he chose to settle there, he would be made fun of and severely censured by his father and his paternal uncles. "You are stupid," they would say, "you leave your own village, you go to the village of your bakokwana to increase it ! This is true folly. Has not your mother been bought with money? The children she bore belong to your father, just like the calves of his cows." (Mboza.) But if the home of the mother cannot become the home of the children, the relations they maintain with

---

(1) The term mamana is frequently used by an interlocutor, without any idea of relationship, when speaking to married women of a more advanced age than himself. Such an extented meaning is also frequent with tatana, kokwana, ñwana. Any man older than I am can be addressed by me as tatana and will answer by calling me ñwana. If the difference of age is greater, we shall treat each other as kokwana and ntukulu, Speaking in the third person a child will always put tatana before the name of any grown up man, though he belong to a totally different clan. Women round Lourenco Marques often call a White man nkata, husband. This shows that kinship terms are employed as expressing moral relations as well as blood or family relations, and we must not draw hasty conclusions from the way in which these terms are applied, or necessarily see in them the traces of a previous social state in which every grown up man or woman was looked on as a true father or mother. The Thongas may give to these terms an extended meaning. Nevertheless they differentiate perfectly between their technical and their derived sense.

their bakokwana are of a much freer, more agreeable and kindlier nature than those with their father's relatives.

Amongst the Thongas of the North the maternal grandfather and the maternal uncles are called indiscriminately kokwana. The Ronga dialect makes a distinction between kokwana, maternal grandfather, and malume, mother's brother; but the malume is often called kokwana. In the Northern clans the *uterine nephews*, viz. the sons of my sister, are always called *ntukulu*, which is the term corresponding to kokwana, as we have seen ; amongst the Ba-Ronga, they bear a special name, *mupsyana*, which seems to be becoming obsolete, being often replaced by ntukulu (1).

Let us consider these various relatives on the mother's side.

The maternal grandfather is the great, the true kokwana. He is respected for his age. He is however more lenient to his grandson by his daughter than to his grandson by his son. If the first damages anything, he will say : "That is no business of mine. Let the father of the child scold him, as he does harm to his property. I have nothing to do with their affairs. It is not my village." But if it were his grandson by his son, it would be a totally different matter, and he would be hard on him. However, should a child take too great a liberty with his kokwana, the old man will say to him : "Go and play with your malume." The malume, indeed, for his uterine nephew, is quite different from any other relative. No respect at all is necessary towards him ! "You go to *bombela* in his village ; you do what you please. You take all the food you want without asking permission. If you are ill, he will take special care of you and will sacrifice for you" (Viguet). In the Ronga dialect this bombela is called *nyenyela*. When the mupsyana goes to his maternal uncle, accompanied by his comrades who scent a good meal, the wives of the malume call to him : "Come along, husband (nkata)! Look here, your malume has hidden some food in the back part of the hut (mfungwe), behind the large basket (ngula). Go and take it." The boy steals the food, runs away with it and eats it up to the last morsel

(1) This is one of many proofs that the Ronga clans have preserved some old customs better than their Northern compatriots. Their language also possesses certain archaic features which are wanting in the Northern dialects.

with his friends. The malume comes back and is angry. But when he hears that the trick has been played by his mupsyana, he shrugs his shoulders and says : "Oh it is all right if it is the ntukulu who has done it ! A shi biwi ntukulu! The nephew must never be beaten!" When another day the nephew comes again, the malume says : "You starved us to death the other day!" — "Is there any more food handy that I may do it again ?" answers the boy. The sons of the malume seem to have less patience with their cousin than their father has. When the cousin goes definitely beyond the limits of their endurance, they will chase him out of the village saying : "Go away, you dog!" The niece is sometimes as troublesome as the nephew. If she is married and pays a visit to her malume with her husband, she will leave the latter comfortably settled in the malume's hut and search the whole village to discover pots of beer, which she will bring to him as if she were the mistress of the home. She may even catch a fowl and give it to him.

Sometimes the malume himself points to one of his wives and says to the ntukulu : "This is your wife. Let her feast you well!" The woman much enjoys the situation, which she finds quite entertaining. She makes a feast for the ntukulu and calls him *nkata*, husband. It will sometimes go so far that the nephew will say to the uncle : "Please make haste and die that I may have your wife!" — "Do you intend to kill me with a gun ?" says the malume... But all this talking is a mere joke. The nephew can take many liberties with this aunt, especially in the Ronga clans. He will never however have relations with her during the life of her husband. Should he do so, he will have to pay the high fine due for a true adultery. Possibly he will inherit her when the malume dies, but she will not be his full property : she will only be given (nyika) to him, and the children will eventually belong to the malume's male relatives. All over the tribe this right of inheriting a malume's wife is recognized. In the Northern clans she is called *kokwana* ; in Ronga territory she is called kokwana by her nieces only, but her nephews call her *nsati* (wife), and this term seems also to be an old feature of the relationship system. This relation of malume and mupsyana is so important that I intend to treat it more fully later on in a special paragraph, when considering the traces of older forms of family life amongst the Thongas.

The true malume is the mother's full brother. But all her half brothers are also bamalume in the second degree ; so are also the brothers of the true malume.

What about the *children of the malume*, my cousins, or rather my cross-cousins, sons and daughters of my mother's brothers, viz. Shaputa and Marangen as opposed to Madonge and Misaben ? In Zulu, Sutho, Pedi there is a special term to indicate this relation, (mzala, motsoala, mudzwala, muzwala). And the main feature of the family system in those tribes is that a cousin has a prior right to marry the daughter of his maternal uncle, his mzala. Amongst the Thongas there is nothing of the kind. The special term does not exist except in the Maputju clan, at the Southern extremity of Thonga territory, where it is met with in the form of *ntale* (corresponding to mzala, according to the law of phonetic permutation) (1) or *shitale* (when preceded by the prefix shi). But the right of marrying this cousin is not recognized in the Thonga tribe. One can play with her, steal some object from her in fun, but never take her as a wife. Such a breach of the custom would be punished by the chief. Later on, when the special relation of cross-cousins has been more or less forgotten, marriage could take place between them, but, at any rate, the ceremony of dlaya shilongo (see p. 256) would be performed, in order to "kill" the previous relationship and to replace it by the new relation of husband and wife.

This being so, how do cross-cousins behave towards each other in the Thonga system ? As regards the daughter of their maternal uncle, the relationship is somewhat different for Misaben, a boy, and for Madonge, a girl. To Misaben the boy, Shaputa, his cousin, is mamana and she will call him son, ñwana, because, as we have seen, Shaputa is a potential wife for Mboza, father of Misaben, and Mboza calls her nkata, nsati, namu. To Madonge,

(1) They also employ the cognate form *muzali,* which is more akin to the Zulu regular term, and this tends to show that the Maputjus have borrowed this expression from their Zulu neighbours of Northern Amatongaland.

the girl, Shaputa is also a mamana ; but the term makweru, my sister, is more frequently used. So we find this strange fact : Maphunga, the mother of Shaputa is a wife to Misaben, while her daughter, Shaputa, is a mother to him!

As regards the son of my malume, he is also a malume or a kokwana, though he may be of the same age or even younger than I, because he belongs to the family from which we take wives and also because he has a kind of right to offer sacrifices for his ntukulu, as we shall see. Totally different is the relationship between Misaben and Mahlobo and Mathamba, *children of his mother's sister.* They are *bamakwabu* as truly as the children of rarana, the paternal aunt, because they have sucked from the same breast (ba yañwele bele djinwe).

At this point of my treatise I must stop for a moment to consider more closely the use of these two terms, *kokwana and ntukulu,* which are so widely employed in the Thonga kinship system. They are applied first to the relation between a grandson and his grandparents on the father's side, i. e. his paternal grandfather and his paternal grand-mother; secondly to the relation between that same grandson and his maternal grandfather and grandmother and to the relation of a nephew to his maternal uncle and to all the male members of his mother's family. Now my informants point out very decidedly that these two relations are very different from each other, and they call the bakokwana on the father's side *bakokwana ba shinene* (the true bakokwana), whilst the bakokwana on the mother's side are *bakokwana ba shisati* (the bakokwana on the female side) ; one also speaks of *batukulu ba shinene,* the real batukulu and of *batukulu ba shisati,* the batukulu by females. How is it possible for them to make such an identification, an identification which we find in almost all the South African tribes (See Table. App. IV) ? They recognize that the two relations are not the same, and the description which we have just given clearly shows the difference.

It would be useful to know the etymology of these two terms. Unhappily my informants could not ascertain it. Kokwana is the diminutive of koko, which has been preserved in its original form in the Zulu word gogo and in the Khosa koko. This root, associated with prefixes which are not those of the personal class, means either the dried carcase of a dead animal, or a person with stiff limbs, who cannot stretch them out. I must leave Zulu linguists to decide if it is really the same root. If so, the etymological idea would be that of a person worn out and paralyzed by old age.

The only explanation that I can give of the common use of the terms kokwana-ntukulu for both relations is this. Both the paternal grandparents and the mother's relatives are similar in their dealings with a child in the fact that they are more lenient towards him than his father. The two grandmothers are equally kind to him. The maternal grandfather is more lenient than the paternal grandfather ; but, according to the explanation given above, it is because the latter belongs to the same family (shibongo) as his grandchild and may be called on to scold him if his conduct is prejudicial to the interests of their common village, whilst the maternal grandfather does not worry himself if the child damages the property or the good reputation of his parents. It is not his business.

The malume is the most indulgent of all. We shall see how this fact can be explained by the matriarchy hypothesis.

Another connotation of these two terms, when applied to social groups, i. e. to two different families, is this. The bakokwana are those from whose family the batukulu have the right of taking their wives. As we shall see, this meaning is much more marked in the category of tribes which belong to the Pedi-Venda group than amongst the Thongas and other tribes of the same category.

II. *Relations with parents-in-law.*

1) RELATIONSHIP ON THE WIFE'S SIDE.

a) General characteristics.

Once, when speaking on this subject, old Viguet told me solemnly : "By your betrothal, as soon as you have been accepted, you enter into a new kind of respect and must remain in it till your death." This relationship is called *bukoñwana*, a word that is generally pronounced with a peculiar feeling of uneasiness. Why is this? On account of the relations of husband and wife. Mboza calls

Nsabula *nsati* (a term corresponding to *nuna*, husband) or *nkata*, a reciprocal term, or *nkosikazi*, a Zulu word which means queen, or *ntjibeli*, cook, even *mamana*. I have already described the moral relation which the word nsati implies : no very great tenderness, not much intimacy, but a certain amount of love mingled with respect, and even fear, because a wife can get her husband into endless trouble if she begins to quarrel and runs home ; then all the bukoñwana relations will be spoilt by interminable discussions.

The word bukoñwana is composed of three elements : the root *ko*, which is an ancient Bantu root, found also in Zulu-Xosa (kwe), in Sutho (hoe) and Pedi (χwe). Its meaning is etymologically unknown. To it is added a suffix, *ñwana*, and a prefix *bu*. The prefix bu has a double meaning ; the meaning of abstraction (and then bukoñwana indicates the relationship between a man and his relatives-in-law) and the meaning of place (when bukoñwana indicates the village where relatives-in-law dwell). They say, employing this word in the locative case : To go bukoñwanen, or in an abbreviated form : bukwen.

I have been fortunate enough to obtain from Mboza the full nomenclature of his wife's relatives. It so happens that the Gogwe family is extraordinarily complete. Nsabula has both an elder brother and elder sister, a younger brother and a younger sister. Owing to this, I have been able to study all the possible kinds of relationship of Mboza with his wife's relatives.

The terms used to express these kinds of relationship fall into two categories, which present a striking contrast. On the one hand a man, when he goes to his wife's village, meets with the persons he fears most in the world : these are his *bakoñwana*, properly speaking ; on the other hand he finds there the women towards whom he behaves with the greatest liberty ; these are the *tinamu*. Describing these two sets of relatives-in-law, one of my informants said : "Bakoñwana are those persons who produce wives for you ; tinamu are those persons who produce children for you, because they are your presumptive wives. Even if you do not marry them, their children will call you father."

Let us study these two categories in detail.

b) The bakoñwana.

First of all, *the wife's father*. There is a great respect in the heart of his son-in-law towards him, even a certain amount of fear, because, should a quarrel arise between a man and his wife, the father-in-law will preside over the painful discussions which will take place, he being the natural protector of his daughter. However, in normal cases, the two men live on good terms with each other, and very soon the son-in-law calls his father-in-law tatana, father ; of course the word tatana is not used here in its technical sense, but only by extension.

Secondly the bakoñwana are *the wife's brothers*. When their father dies, they take his place as protectors of their sister. Hence the uneasiness and fear with regard to them, which is, however, less marked in their case. The wife's brothers will never be called bamakweru (as they will never be ba-kweru, those of my house) but they are frequently designated by the term *soar*, or *sibar*, which is merely a corruption of the Dutch word zwager. This curious adoption of a foreign term is modern ; it is spreading more and more amongst the Zulus, Xosas and Suthos of Basutoland. Amongst the Thongas I only once heard the word soar used. The tendency to assimilate that kind of relationship to the European conception is a proof that the old fear of brothers-in-law is disappearing in the new generation.

But it is in the relation with two women of the wife's family that the respect of bukoñwana is pushed to the greatest extent : the wife's mother and the wife of the brother-in-law. In these cases there is not only respect but *avoidance*

The wife's mother.

Let us listen to Viguet telling the story of a man meeting his mother-in-law in the bush. "If one of the two sees the other coming a long way off, soon enough to escape without being noticed, he will speedily hide himself and reach his destination by making a long circuit, half a mile if necessary. But if they have come too near to have recourse to flight, this is what will happen. You leave the road ; you enter the bush on your right

238

side. She does the same. Then you sit down according to men's fashion, crossing your legs. She also sits down bending her legs, and putting one knee over the other as women do ; then both parties salute each other, you, as a man, clapping your hands against each other, holding them parallel, and the woman holding hers at right angles. Then you begin to talk..."

Suppose the son-in-law has had the good luck to reach the village of his wife's relatives without having met his mother-in-law, but sees her sitting somewhere near a hut. This is dreadful. She looks at him and at once covers her breasts with her cloth. He himself turns his eyes aside. I saw in Natal a curious photograph representing the scene. Amongst the Zulus the avoidance of the mother-in-law is perhaps more marked than in any other tribe ; the man is shown in the picture hiding his face with his shield. Should the mother-in-law be taking her meal when her son-in-law arrives unexpectedly, she throws away the mouthful she was eating, and he does the same.— Suppose then that he has entered the village without seeing her ; then the tinamu, his wife's sisters, come hastily to meet him. They take his sticks, joking with him meanwhile and put them in his mother-in-law's hut. This hut is his ; he has the right of staying in it during his whole visit. They spread a mat on the ground, and bring him food. They chat with him. Then the mother-in-law comes in her turn, but she dares not enter the hut. She sits down outside and, without seeing him, salutes him, saying : "Good morning, son of so and so." She must not pronounce his name. He answers in the same style, and must also say : "Daughter of so and so." Should he call her by her name it would be a breach of etiquette and his wife would be angry and say : "How dare you ? Did she not bring me forth ? Rather say : Mother!" During the first years of his married life, the son-in-law never eats with his wife's mother.

This peculiar behaviour is the rule, not only towards the wife's mother, but also towards her sisters.

In the course of years there is a *lessening* of this terrible taboo. In the Maputju clan, the son-in-law will provide an ox as soon as possible and he will "communicate" (tlhangana) with her, partaking

239

of its meat with all his relatives-in-law. Then both will be allowed to eat together. Until that present was made, it would have been impossible. In this clan, a future son-in-law does not eat at all with his bakoṅwana until the marriage is concluded, and this rule is sometimes observed till he has given "the ox for communicating together." Amongst the Zulus it is said that a mother-in-law will never eat with her daughter's husband. In the Khosa clan the custom of lessening the avoidance taboo by offering a present to the mother-in-law also exists. The son-in-law will one day bring a plate of food to her with his gift put on top of it. She will accept it and eat together with him. Then it will be possible for these two persons to "djungulisana" i. e. to tell each other the news of the day when visiting each other's village. But when this monotonous recital is finished and concluded, as is customary, by clapping both hands, this must be done with care, and not in a hurried fashion, as when speaking to an ordinary person, but slowly and respectfully.

What is the reason of this extraordinary conduct of the son-in-law towards his wife's mother ? The Khosa Native who gave me this last information said : "A wise man will carefully observe the bukoṅwana rules, because, if he hurts his parents-in-law by infringing them, they will not give him his tinamu as wives." This is true, but the same may be said of all the taboos of the bukoṅwana, and the mother-in-law is not the principal person to be consulted on the question. Another more profound reason was once alluded to by an old Thonga, of Spelonken, Abraham Mabanyisi, who said to me : "I fear my mother-in-law because I shall never marry her : Such a thing has never been seen." This statement has been confirmed since by information gathered in the Maputju clan. Notice the almost reflex action of the mother-in-law in covering her breasts when she sees her son-in-law coming unexpectedly. It shows that there is a sexual element in the behaviour of the woman and also in that of the man, who hides his face in order not to see her in her half nakedness. Dr. Rivers, who has met exactly the same rites of avoidance amongst the Melanesians, supposes that they are dictated by a more or less unconscious desire on the part of both these persons to fight against the temptation to have sexual relations with each other. Bantus also, in the course of the evolution of the family, have come to the deep conviction that such intercourse is bad and must be banished from their thoughts. They obey that conviction when practising the avoidance rites.

The wife of the brother-in-law, the Great Mukoñwana.

This particular respect is even more marked in the relations of a man with the wife of his wife's brother. Indeed the avoidance is pushed further than with the mother-in-law. A Native of the Ndjao tribe (which has the same customs as the Thonga tribe in this respect) described to me vividly the extraordinary marks of fear that these two persons show each other when they meet on the road. The story will be told when speaking of the Ba-Ndjao. Here are some other marks of this extraordinary respect.

The wife's brother's wife must always keep her breasts covered in the village of her husband's sister's husband. Only when she has had a child is she permitted to "open her clothing ;" but then she must fix a leaf in her hair (as if to show that she does not forget the special reserve which she is bound to maintain). (Khosen region.)

When a man travels with his great mukoñwana and they have to cross a river, they will avoid entering the same boat. It may happen to anyone to emit an unseemly sound from the rectum ; but if the great mukoñwana is present, she looks on this as a grave offence. A fine must be paid to her, a hoe, for instance. If the guilty man has nothing to give her, he at once breaks a twig from a tree and presents it to her as a token that the proper fine will be forthcoming in due time ! He must never use words of insult in her presence, even if he addresses them to another person. If he loses his temper before her she will go to the old people of her husband's village and tell them : "He has insulted me." On the other hand the great mukoñwana is bound to go and assist the wife of this man when she gives birth to a child. At least this is the rule in the Khosa clan and also in Maputju. The two women live on very good terms with each other ; they are *tinhombe*. The man himself, when he visits his relatives-in-law, has the right of sleeping in the hut of the great mukoñwana. We have seen that, during the first months after his marriage, he is received in the hut of his mother-in-law. Why is this ? Because the oxen of the lobolo are still in the hands of the father-in-law. But later on these oxen are used to provide a wife for one of the sons, and the woman thus obtained is the great mukoñwana; therefore her hut belongs in a certain sense to the man with whose oxen she was bought. When he arrives, he may first be "shown" (komba) the mother-in-law's hut and rest there for a while, but at once the hut of the great mukoñwana will be prepared and he will move into it for the night; of course the mistress of the house has gone elsewhere, and it is the tinamu who will sleep in her hut to keep him company. (However should the visitor have not yet paid the lobolo, he will not be received in this hut. It may happen that his bakoñwana will say to him : "Where is your hut ? Sleep outside!")

Why do the relations of a man with the wife of his brother-in-law resemble so greatly his relations with his wife's mother ? Let us remember that this man is the potential husband of the daughter of the first, just as he is the actual husband of the daughter of the second. It is probable that the great principle that "a man must not marry a woman and her mother" dictates this extraordinary fear and avoidance in both cases. But, in the case of the wife of the brother-in-law, there is still another element : "The oxen!" This woman has been acquired by the oxen paid by the man to obtain his wife, and this explains the uneasiness which characterises their relation.

This second reason is perhaps more readily recognised by the Thongas than the first ; they sometimes tell you that it is the only reason. But I think they are wrong, and that the same deep feeling that to marry a woman and her mother is incestuous is certainly at the base of these taboos. I may mention two facts in proof of this :

a) Once when I asked a woman of the Maputju country if her husband would be allowed to marry the wife of his brother-in-law, she seemed extremely shocked by the idea and exclaimed : "What are you thinking of ? Marry his mother!" To her it would be incest, as much so as if the man had sexual relations with his own mother.

b) The wife of the brother-in-law is not the only great mukoñwana. The wives of his brothers, and of his sons and grandsons are all classed under that term. Why is this ? Because a man has a prior right to marry not only the daughter of this special woman but all the daughters of his bakoñwana, and all these women, who are their mothers, are consequently his potential mothers. He avoids them all, not on account of the lobolo oxen, which he did not actually pay for their daughters, but because it is intolerable to think that he might have relations with a woman and her mother.

But no doubt the fact that oxen have been paid by the man, oxen by means of which his great mukoñwana was bought, is the principal cause of the fear which they both feel towards each other. These oxen have created a sort of interdependence between them. Mboza says : "Should my home be disturbed by quarrels, should my wife Nsabula leave me and run away to her parents, or should she die without children, I shall go and claim my oxen... But the oxen have been employed to buy a wife for my brother-in-law, (Maphunga for Mahangale). If Gogwe has no other means at his disposal he must separate the pair Maphunga-Mahangale, cancel their marriage, send Maphunga home and claim the money from her parents. Or I might myself take Maphunga as my wife, and in either of these cases the marriage Maphunga-Mahangale would be annulled."

Thus it may happen that Mboza may marry his great mukoñwana, though such a union is really incestuous, according to the deep moral feeling of the tribe. This is truly terrible!

But does this ever really happen ? I have put this question to many Thongas, in the various clans of the tribe, and remarked that there are differences amongst them.

Amongst the Nkunas of Shiluvane it is an absolute impossibility. Another woman is offered to meet the claim of the son-in-law who has lost his wife. This is called : "Ku hingakanya ntjandja", i. e. "to put a log across the road." The woman offered may be a little girl, still at the breast of her mother, or even a little boy. This is your wife, his parents will say to the son-in-law, and he must be content to know that, as this male baby will no doubt have a sister in the course of the two following years, the girl to be born will replace his wife. "Ntjandja a ba tluli" i. e. "One does not jump over the log." The man will not persist in his claim, and will not insist on taking the great mukoñwana to replace his wife.

Amongst the Khosas and Bilas, such a marriage can take place if there is really no means of avoiding it. In the Maputju clan, it is also prohibited ; but "owing to the Whites," owing to civilisation, which alters the old, sound laws of the tribe, it sometimes occurs. Everywhere such an occurence is looked on as a great misfortune.

It is in the neighbourhood of Lourenço Marques, ka Mpfumo, that the reluctance is least pronounced. I have from Mboza the description of what will happen in that part of the tribe when a woman dies without children. Viguet has told us the first half of the story (p. 217). The husband has paid the *mahloko* ; the mourning is over ; but the parents of the deceased wife have no money, no young girl to give as compensation. Here is the second part of this family drama. The father of the deceased wife having no other resource "opens the way of bukoñwana to his son-in-law, the widower." Let us suppose it is Nsabula who has died. Gogwe goes, together with Mboza and his official go-between, to the father of Maphunga. Let us call him Mbekwa. He gives him two hoes and says : "We have brought your mukoñwana (Mboza) because we have had a sad affair (hi humele)." Mbekwa asks Mboza : "How many hoes did you pay for your deceased wife" ? — "Fifty," says Mboza. — "Well, we have received from Gogwe as yet only thirty for Maphunga !" Gogwe acknowledges that it is so. He must at once find the missing twenty hoes and give them back to Mboza, who returns to Mbekwa taking them with him, so as to complete the lobola. All this was only preparatory. Now Gogwe has no further interest in the matter, and returns home. It concerns Mboza alone. Mbekwa calls Maphunga and says : "Look ! this is your great mukoñwana ! Now he is your husband." She may say : "Yes, very well." Then Mboza fetches a goat, and a most curious ceremony takes place, which we shall describe later on, the rite of *killing bukoñwana* or *shikoñwana*, the aim being to kill a certain kind of relationship which must be replaced by another, after which Mboza can marry Maphunga. But most probably Maphunga will say : "No ! I fear him too much ! It is taboo !" Her feelings cannot accept such a change in their relations. Viguet does not say : "She loves her own husband too much to go willingly to another !" This seems to be a minor consideration. If she definitely refuses, Mbekwa will try to find another woman. Maphunga may perhaps have a daughter who will do. Or Mbekwa may have a married son whose daughter can also be offered. If the great mukoñwana is only pregnant, the child about to be born is quite enough *ku hingakanya ntjandja*, to put a log across the road and an end to the claim. But the child will perhaps be a boy... not a girl. Never mind! Mboza will wait patiently for a girl ; Shaputa will be born ; he will wait again until she is of age, then he will marry her and she will *pfusha yindlu ya rarana*, viz. raise up the house of her aunt Nsabula (1). Naturally if matters take this course, Gogwe will have to pay the lobola of the girl who has taken the place of the deceased. Nowadays it is not very difficult : he will work, or send one of his sons to work, for the money.

c) The tinamu.

When a man goes bukoñwanen, his heart is full of mixed feelings. He trembles lest he may meet the two terrible bakoñwana whom he wishes to avoid ; but, on the other hand, he is greatly rejoiced at the idea that his *tinamu* will welcome him with hearty laughter and jokes and make much of him. Who are these tinamu ? They belong to three categories, which correspond to three kinds of *bulamu*. First of all *the younger sisters of the wife.*

Namu, plur. *tinamu*, in Ronga, *balamo* in Djonga, comes from the archaic verb *yalama*, which means to *follow*, to come after. My tinamu are those who follow my wife, who have been born after her, her younger sisters in particular. They are my *presumptive wives*, therefore I can play with them with the greatest freedom ; I eat together with them from the same plate. They go so far as to smear my face with ashes (tota hi nkuma) and afterwards wash it with water. I have the right to pat their shoulders gently, to snatch something from their hands, to force them to give me something to eat ; and, if they refuse, I will say to them : "How dare you stint me, you, my wives!" They go

(1) One more fact. If Muhangala has taken another wife besides Maphunga, his daughter born of this second wife cannot be used to meet the claim of the widower.

so far as to sleep in the hut of my great mukoñwana together with me (p. 242). Nevertheless sexual relations are not allowed. Should a man commit this sin, and should his sister-in-law become pregnant, he will have to pay a fine, or rather he will go to his father-in-law and say : (Viguet) "Ndi dlele ku dya"-"I have killed in order to eat" which means : I have committed a bad action but with the intention of repairing my wrong by marrying the girl. He brings five hoes when he makes the announcement and will remit the remainder of the lobolo later on. A younger sister when married to the same husband as the elder, is called *nhlampsa* of the latter. This term comes probably from hlampsa, to wash, because she washes the dishes of her sister and works more or less as her servant.

The right of marrying one's wife's sisters is by no means an obligation. I am not in any way forced to do so, if I do not like them. Most probably, even if I wished to marry them all, I should not have enough oxen to "lobola" them all. On the other hand, the bakoñwana are not obliged to give them to me. If I am not a good husband to my wife, if she complains that I illtreat her, her parents will not consent to receive my oxen for her sisters. Should my tinamu marry other men, of course the peculiar bulamu relations will cease. I can no longer allow myself the intimacy I previously had with them. But if they have children by these men, they will call me tatana and I shall call them bana, because I might have been their father, having a prior right of marrying their mothers.

My wife's elder sisters are not tinamu to me ; they are bakoñwana. Why so ? Because when I married my wife, her elder sisters were already married, according to the law that an elder sister must always marry before the younger. A father would never consent to give away the younger before the elder. Therefore I have never had the opportunity of playing with my wife's elder sisters and considering them as possible wives.

By extension the term namu is also applied to my wife's younger brothers. They are bakoñwana, in fact (p. 238). Their daughters are my potential wives. However, the relations I have with them are easier than with the elder brothers and with the father of my wife, as these are her natural protectors.

In this first category is included the daughter of my wife's brother (Shaputa versus Mboza). With her the relations are perhaps even more free than with my wife's younger sisters. I call her *nsati*. The intimacy is so great that I can hold her breasts (tamele mabele). I can do so even in the presence of my wife, who is her paternal aunt. She will be pleased to see that I am disposed to avail myself of my right to marry her, because her niece will thus become her nhlampsa, she will hlampsela rarana, i. e. become a second wife by the side of her father's sister. But I dare not take such a liberty with the girl if her father is on the spot and sees me. I probably do not possess the oxen to pay for her, and the father looks chiefly to the oxen.

As already pointed out, all the girls belonging to my bakoñwana are in the same position towards me. I can marry them all... if I am rich enough to "lobola" them. The grand-daughter of my wife's brother is a namu, a nsati. She will probably be a baby whilst I am a grown-up man. Never mind! If I meet her, a little girl on her mother's back, I go and take her in my arms, and say to her : "Good morning, my wife!" As regards my wife's cousins, those whose father is a brother of my wife's father and who bear the same family name as my wife, they are also tinamu, but here a distinction must be made. Should the father of one of these girls be younger than my wife's father, I can marry her ; but should he be older I must not do so. Why is this? Because the girl, belonging to an elder branch of my wife's family, takes precedence of my wife ; she is her "hosi", her chief. On the other hand my wife, being my first wife, is the mistress of the house ; this cousin of hers ought therefore to obey her. But she is her chief! That would not be right. The natural family relations would be disturbed.. Such a union is not taboo (a psi yili) but it must be avoided.

The *second category of tinamu* includes those women whom I might marry, not on account of the prior right of a group to the women of another group, but because I might *inherit them*. They are the wives of my elder brothers. If their husbands die, I am their legal heir. Relations with them are easy. We joke together, but there is more reserve towards these tinamu than towards those of the first category. Sexual intercourse with them is a great taboo, and a man daring to commit such a sin would be likened to a wizard : he has killed his brother. This is the sin called matlulana (App. VI). My younger brother's wives are not tinamu ; we call each other ñwingi. I do not inherit them except in extraordinary cases when the deceased has no brother younger than himself.

There is still a *third kind of bulamu.* I also call tinamu the cousins of my wife who are the daughters of my wife's mother's sisters. These girls do not belong to my wife's clan ; they bear the family name of their father. Therefore I have no right to inherit them : "A hi delani ndjaka," i. e. "we do not inherit from each other." The relations with these tinamu are agreeable, but there is no hope of marriage between us.

2) RELATIONS ON THE HUSBAND'S SIDE.

So far we have considered the relation of Mboza with his wife's family. But what about Nsabula and her position towards her husband's relatives ? Nsabula calls Masuluke and Nsenga-muñwe ñwingi, and the term is reciprocal. It implies great respect. As we saw, the young bride must work a whole year for her mother-in-law. The same respect is shown by Nsabula to Djan, Sam, Fos, her husband's elder brothers. They are also ñwingi to each other. "Should I send her to call Djan," says Mboza, "she will kneel down before him and say : 'My father! Mboza calls you!' or : 'Ñwamasuluke (Masuluke's son), you are wanted with us." She will not dare to address him by name. This extraordinary respect is reciprocal. Djan will consider Nsabula as his inferior, but he will never play with her. On the other hand, Komatane, Mboza's younger brother, is only a *namu* to Nsabula. Both will joke together and even occasionally smear each other with ashes. So will Sam, Fos, Mboza and Komatane with Mihlakaza, the wife of their elder brother. Thus we note this law : a woman will generally respect the elder brothers of her husband (bengi), and hold very free intercourse with his younger brothers (tinamu), and vice-versa. A man will keep away from his younger brother's wives (bengi) and play with those of his elder brothers (tinamu). Why is there this difference ? Because, as we saw, the wife of an elder brother is a possible wife for all his younger brothers, as they have the right of inheriting her, should this man die. On the contrary, an elder brother inherits his younger brother's wife only under quite exceptional circumstances. One does not marry a ñwingi! This would be an insult to one's wife. Nsabula would leave Mboza if Mboza were to marry Magugu, Komatane's wife, because they have been accustomed to call each other ñwingi.

To a wife, her husband's elder sister is also a ñwingi (Ndjibari to Nsabula). The husband's younger sister is a namu or *nhombe*, and two tinhombe have very free relations, just as in the case of the tinamu. This freedom exists between female tinamu as well as between tinamu of different sexes.

There is a final term to be mentioned : *bakhoti* or *bakhoti-kulobye*, in Ronga, *basevele* in Djonga, a reciprocal term by which the parents of a husband and wife call each other.

How far is a woman incorporated in her husband's family ? She belongs to it till her death, provided the lobolo oxen have been paid, but she does not accept the ancestor-gods of her parents-in-law as being her gods. She keeps her own gods, and prayers are frequently addressed to them by her father or by her brothers in favour of her children. In this respect Thongas differ widely from the old Aryan peoples, where a woman had to adopt the religion of her husband's clan when she married.

*

*   *

Before leaving the subject of relations with parents-in-law, and in order to show to what extent the uneasiness and fear which characterises them are carried, I will briefly mention the taboos of the bukoñwana, which play such a great part in Bantu family life. Let me say that most of these taboos (psiyilayilana, small prohibitions), are not so severe as those connected with sexual relations, disease and death. It is not believed that a breach of these bukoñwana rules would cause death. Yet they are religiously kept as necessary to ensure normal relations between the two families.

We have already seen the taboos which must be observed during the betrothal period (p. 106). Later on, during the gatherings which take place *before marriage*, other taboos are imposed.

1. In the discussion concerning the lobola, when oxen are counted, the bridegroom's parents must never offer eight head of cattle, because one of them will be killed for the feast, and so eight means only seven. *Seven* is counted by raising, one after the other, the five fingers of the left hand and the thumb and index-finger of the right. In raising the index-finger, they might point it at the bakoñwana, and this would be a mortal offence. To point at anyone with the index-finger is as bad as bewitching him. It is done only in anger, and all the preceding discussions might be nullified if such an imprudence were committed.

2. Should one of the oxen be frightened by the shouts of joy with which the arrival of the herd is greeted and by the sham-fight of the lobola day, and run away home, it is taboo. The ox has seen that something is wrong and has consequently fled. Even should they succeed in bringing it back, "timpfalo ti tjukile," the conscience (or the diaphragm) has been stirred!

3. If one of the oxen has no horns (homu ya mhulu), or only abortive horns, psa yila : *bukoñwana byi ta pfumala timpsalu,* viz., the relations with relatives-in-law will have no tenderness, because such an ox moves its head to and fro as it wanders in the night ; it is abnormal. The bride's family will not accept it.

4. Should the lobolo consist of hoes, and should the rain fall on them while they are being carried to the bakoñwana, it is taboo. The lobolo must not be brought in a wet condition, otherwise the new relations will be spoilt (bukoñwana byi ta tshipa) ; the young people will not be able to marry.

5. Do not bring with you tobacco in the leaf when going *bukwen* as a fiancé, bring only ground tobacco, or misfortune will happen. Later on, when you have married your wife, it is allowable.

6. Never eat zebra or reedbuck's meat when staying with your parents-in-law. Should they kill one of these animals while

you are there, or on the road, have nothing to do with it. The zebra is *mbalamberi*, an animal of two colours; moreover it has no horns. The same holds good for the giraffe. It has two colours, it has too long bowels. Psa yila! The reedbuck cries: "Dzoo." It is a witch: a mukoñwana must not eat it. For the same reason a sheep without horns is never given to bakoñwana.

7. When you go with women to the parents of your fiancée for a *shirwalo*, viz., to bring them beer, should one of the jugs fall to the ground, psa yila! Return home!

8. From a Thonga of the Maputju country I once heard that it was a great taboo in that district for a man to drink milk with his parents-in-law; let us say rather to *eat* milk, as Natives always take it in its solid form, i. e. curdled. This man was a Christian; he had given up many heathen customs and had gone so far as to partake of milk with his mother-in-law, but, the people all round were very much shocked at his conduct. Pushing my inquiry further, I heard that the milk taboo was observed not only with bakoñwana, but with all the inhabitants of the country who did not belong to one's clan; curdled milk was to be eaten only with people bearing the same family name. In other words, it is forbidden to eat milk *in any village where one can take a wife*. In a very interesting paper published in the *South African Journal of Science*, 1925, p. 481, Mrs A. W. Hoernlé says that this custom is wide-spread amongst many Bantu tribes of Central and South Africa, and explains it by the very intimate relationship which is thought to exist between human beings and cattle. The oxen are one with the clan to which they belong, and only members of that clan can partake of the milk of their cows. I never met with this idea in the other parts of the Thonga tribe, and I may remark that, as the Maputju clan is settled very near to the Zulus and has been more or less "zuluised", this custom might very well have been borrowed from its neighbours. Further researches will show whether the other Thonga clans have preserved what seems to be a very old Bantu idea, or at any rate traces of it. This is quite possible.

9. Do not build a hut for your wife before you have married her. Mankhelu says: "Even if you have plenty of money to lobola, if you make such a blunder your wife will be taken

251

from you... In the same manner, do not prepare the skin for the child before it is born. Your wife would not bring forth a human being. Should you transgress this rule, you would bring misfortune on yourself (wa tihlolela, wa singita), and on your family. If you go to Moneri (the missionary) and ask him for a skin for this purpose before the birth of your child, he will tell you it is so." Note the deep-rooted conviction of the old heathen, who appeals to the authority of the missionary to strengthen the taboo!

10. Later on, when you are married, you must avoid eating honey with your wife for a whole year, till she has had a child. The bride is allowed to eat honey at her parent's home, but not in her new domicile and with her husband. The husband can eat it in the bush, but he must wash his hands when he comes back, lest his wife should notice it. She would run home if she knew of it. We have already met with this prohibition in the tjekela visit, and heard the reason for it : honey flows ; the bride would go! The explanation now given is this : honey is too sweet, and your bride is too sweet also. (Is it not your honey-moon or honey-year ?) The two things do not go together. (Psa yalana, they hate each other.) A third reason is this : Bees, when they have eaten their honey, fly away from the hive. So would your wife do... After a year this misfortune is no longer to be feared.

This last idea is very curious. It shows that the bukoñwana taboos *decrease in severity as time passes.* The strained relations between the son-in-law and his wife's mother also become easier. He begins to call her mamana, and she calls him ñwana. This transformation even goes so far that in some cases a mukoñwana can go and dwell in his parents-in-law's village, especially if he has children and if the children are grown up. And this fact gives us the natural explanation of these curious rules.

Marriage, as we have seen, is not an individual affair in the collective stage of family life. It is a contract made between two groups, which enter by it into a special relation towards each other. This relation is fraught with danger, because the interests of both groups are involved ; a bride and bridegroom are inspired with a mutual feeling of fear, knowing that an

252

eventual misunderstanding between them will have its "contre coup" throughout the two groups. The two families regard each other with mistrust, especially the two married couples who depend so closely upon each other, owing to the lobola ; but when they have become acquainted, when they are assured that common life is possible and even agreeable, when the first alliance has been strengthened by others amongst the tinamu, then the bukoñwana taboos more or less *fall off*. This is an explanation of these strange relations between relatives-in-law ; I do not pretend that it is absolutely adequate. There may also be in this domain some remains of previous customs which have now disappeared, and Comparative Ethnography will probably throw more light on this problem in the course of time.

C. MARRIAGE RULES

The study of the terms of relationship has shown us the constitution of the Thonga family. We have seen that they are often dictated by the possibility or non-possibility for a man of marrying certain women. There exist distinct marriage rules, and I propose to recapitulate them here, at the risk of some repetition, in order to throw as much light as possible on this difficult but very important subject.

Generally speaking it may be said that the Thongas are *endogamic* as regards the tribe and the clan, and *exogamic* as regards the family. They are *endogamic* as regards the tribe, that is to say they marry within it. Members of clans very remote from each other may find it difficult to contract unions, (see later on), but they do so, especially in Spelonken, where representatives of many different parts of the tribe have met by force of historical circumstances. In the neighbourhood of Lourenço Marques you may find Thonga women married to men of other tribes and even to white people. But this is the result of a new state of things, which the old Thongas did not foresee ; nor would they have approved of it, I am sure. In Shiluvane, I was in a very favourable position to judge of the real feelings of the Thongas. There were two tribes there, which had been living side by side for more than seventy years, tribes united by old friendship and military alliance, viz., the Nkuna clan of the Thongas and the Khaha clan of the Pedis. I did not see a single case of inter-marriage between them. The difference of language could not account for the fact, because generally speaking, all the men could speak both Thonga and Pedi. When asked why they did not contract unions with the Pedis, the Nkunas answered : "Their customs are too disgusting for us." They meant more especially the freedom with which Khaha women commit adultery. Pedis would probably have made the same objection to the immorality of Thonga boys and girls. Whatever may be the cause, they have not intermarried up to this day.

On the other hand the Thongas are *exogamic* as regards the family. To understand properly these exogamic rules, let us classify the cases in the four following categories : Cases of absolute prohibition of marriage ; of conditional permission ; of unconditional permission, and cases in which marriage is recommended.

I. *Cases of absolute prohibition.*

As a rule marriage is prohibited between a tatana, mamana, rarana and a ñwana, and between bamakwabu.

On the father's side the prohibition is particularly severe. Amongst the Ba-Ronga, it is taboo for a boy to marry a girl when both can lay claim to a common ancestor in the paternal line. It seems that the rule is not so stringent in the Northern clans. According to Mankhelu, marriage is absolutely prohibited between all the descendants of a grandfather, viz., between first cousins. Between second cousins it is permitted conditionally, "by killing the family tie," and between third cousins it is allowed. "Third cousins" as Mankhelu says, "are *batlandlamani ba tolo* ; they belong to families which were relatives yesterday. We are no longer taboo for them, we can go and take a wife amongst them."

On the mother's side, this absolute prohibition extends to first cousins when the mothers are sisters. They are true bama-kwabu ; they have been nursed at the same breast. But more remote cousins marry more easily when their relationship is on the mother's side. The bakokwana do not marry their batukulu, owing to their duty of sacrificing for them, but the batukulu have a kind of preferential right to women related to their mother : "Where father has married, I may also go to find my wife," said Gana. However the rule remains that bamakwabu must not intermarry.

When asked : "Why?" the Thongas generally say : "Because it is so. Psa yila. It is our law." It is however possible to find some more satisfactory reasons ; for these prohibitions are dictated to a certain extent *by fear of consanguinity*. Natives have probably noticed that the offspring of such unions are sometimes weak in intellect or altogether wanting. Therefore, in this polygamic family system, they make a careful distinction between relatives who are of the same mother and of the same father, and those whose mothers are different. When a cousin is by another grandmother, though I call her makwabu just as I do my true sister or first cousin, I may contemplate marrying her. She is my half first cousin only. However the fear of consanguinity is not the only nor perhaps the strongest reason for these exogamic rules. If it were so, why should relatives on the father's side be more taboo than those on the mother's side ? Moreover it is strange to see that in the royal families the same prohibitions are not maintained. Ñwamanti-byana, chief of Mpfumo, married Mimalengane, his rarana, his first cousin once removed on the father's side. If the physical dangers alone arising from consanguinous unions were thought of, such marriages ought to be doubly feared in the royal family!

It seems to me that there are two other reasons :

In the Thonga mind there is *a natural repulsion to confounding and intermingling bushaka and bukoñwana*, relationship by blood and by marriage. Bushaka is a kind of relation which they do not deem compatible with bukoñwana, as we shall presently see.

To the Northern clans this is not so repugnant : with them, it is a current saying that bukoñwana revives bushaka when bushaka has become weaker in the course of generations (1).

A third reason for these strong taboos, a reason which explains also why the prohibition is stronger on the father's side than on the mother's, is found in *the lobola custom*. Should a woman who is a relative on my father's side become my wife and should our union be put an end to by quarrels, I should go to her father to claim the lobolo. If her father happens to possess no oxen to return to me, he will have to go to his relatives to get them... He may have to come to my own father, who is his brother and belongs to the same family, a consequence which would be indeed absurd, because then I should myself pay the debt due to me!

On his wife's side, a man cannot marry the elder sister of his wife, who is mukoñwana to him, nor the daughters of his wife's sisters, who are *bana* to him, as we have seen.

II. *Marriages conditionally permitted.*

In some cases a marriage which ought not to take place may be allowed on condition that the whole family will perform the rite called *dlaya shilongo*. This is a most curious custom, and is found all through the tribe. I know of two cases in which it has been resorted to: a certain Mkili, of the Makaneta sub-clan (Nondwane) wished to marry Minsabula, his makwabu. Both had a common ancestor Muwayi. Muwayi had by a first wife a son called Basana, and by a second wife another son called Nsabula. Basana was the father of Mungobo, father of Mkili, and Nsabula

---

(1) It is also very much against the feeling of the tribe to confound *bukoñwana* and *bulamo*. A man named Filemon had married the daughter of a woman of dissolute habits, and the woman had given herself to a man who was the brother of Filemon's maternal grandmother. This man was therefore a malume for Filemon, and his wives were balamo, even basati, possible wives for him, as he had the right to inherit them (p. 233). For this reason he said : "My wife's mother cannot marry that man, not only because of the Christian law which we have accepted, but also because of our own old customs. Why ? Because she is my mother in-law, my mukoñwana, and by her marriage she would become my namu and I might inherit her. That is impossible."

was the father of Minsabula. Mungobo and Nsabula were first cousins or half first cousins (as their grandmothers, wives of Muwayi, were different). Therefore Mkili was the first cousin once removed of Minsabula. Both were ba ka Makaneta. Another case was that of Michel, son of Gana and Nwashiluvane, who married Djamela, daughter of Mankhelu, who was Nwashiluvane's brother. Mankhelu was the malume of Michel and Djamela was his mamana, being the possible wife of Gana (See page 233). For a Thonga to marry her malume's daughter, *psa yila*, (See p. 234) whilst for a Pedi it is the proper thing. This is one of the great differences between the law of the two tribes. A Pedi has a real right of pre-emption on his *mudzwala*, whilst amongst the Thongas it is the father who possesses that right. (See later on G.) Possibly this Pedi custom encouraged Michel to entertain an idea which is repulsive to the Thonga mind. But the official *dlaya shilongo* took place in his case also.

I tried to discover in what other cases such a prohibited marriage was rendered possible by the performance of the rite, and found the following.

Conditional marriage is permissible with the daughter of my great-uncle, the younger brother of my grandfather ; and with the daughter of my grandfather by a wife other than my grandmother. Both are rarana. According to Mankhelu, it might also take place between himself and Shiluvane. This Shiluvane (who is not the chief Shiluvane, of course, but an entirely different person), is the daughter of the maternal great-uncle of Mankhelu, brother of Shidyele, who is his true grandfather, the father of his mother. Shiluvane is therefore the first cousin once removed of Mankhelu on his mother's side. She is a mamana.

But what is this rite of *dlaya shilongo* which has such power that it removes the taboo character of such marriages ? *Shilongo or mulongo* is an archaic word retained only in this expression and which corresponds to bushaka, blood relationship. This root exists also with that meaning in the Sutho word *seloko*. The relation by blood must be killed in order that the relation by marriage may be substituted for it.

Let us first see how this is done *in the Northern clans*.

A young man who has the courage to think of marrying a near relation is regarded as a wizard. *A lowa*, he bewitches! This term, which is applied only to actual witches, is not too strong to designate his action. He was not allowed to *gangisa* her, and now he wants to take her as his wife! But this word lowa, or loya, is used here in another sense: "Bushaka byi lowa hi tihomu" (the blood relationship is bewitched by the oxen). "Bumamana byi lowa" (the mother relationship is bewitched). (Viguet.) Those who consent to such an act must be prayed for publicly and anointed with psanyi (the grass found in the bowels of a sacrificed goat.)

So the young man goes to his uncle, the father of the girl, to announce his intention of marrying her; he must *be homu*, beat an ox, viz. bring an ox with him as a first step to appease his uncle. This ox is said to "open the hut." The ox may be only a goat, the goat which will be used for the sacrifice, — because a religious ceremony is necessary. All the relatives assemble on a certain day in the girl's village. The wedding pair are inside the hut, the goat is killed, the offering prepared, the psanyi put aside. Then the bridegroom and the bride are called outside and made to sit on the same mat; the man's leg is passed over the girl's leg; (this is done to "kill the shame" *ku dlaya tingana*); they are both anointed with the green liquid of the psanyi; the skin of the goat is then taken, a hole is cut in its middle and it is put on the heads of the two cousins. Through the opening the liver of the animal is handed down to them, quite raw. They must tear it with their teeth. It must not be cut with a knife; this is taboo. They have to bite it, to pull vigourously on both sides so as really to tear it, and then they must eat it. Shibindji, liver, means also patience, determination. "You have acted with strong determination! Now eat the liver! Eat it in the full light of day, not in the dark! It will be a mhamba, an offering to the gods (Gana)." The priest of the family will then say: "You, our gods, so and so, look! We have done it in the daylight. It has not been done by stealth. Bless them, give them children." Should this sacrifice not be made, misfortune would indeed come upon them and the woman would remain childless. When the prayer is ended, those present take all the solid psanyi, put it on the wife's head and say to her : "Go and bear children."

In the Ronga clans the *dlaya shilongo* is somewhat different. The bridegroom must first give £ 1 to the father ; this is over and above the lobolo, of course. Both families provide a goat. These goats are killed without the assistance of the uterine nephews, in front of the hut of the girl's mother. The grandfather prays to the gods of the girl's father : "So be it ! They have decided to marry each other ; you, gods of the boy and the girl, unite them together so that they do not hate each other ; let them not remind each other that they are brother and sister ; let their union not be spoilt by such remembrances, nor by other people saying to them : "You have been guilty of witchcraft ! You have married your relative !" By this prayer a general notification is given to everybody, and the feeling of shame is removed. Afterwards the officiating relative continues, exhorting the new wife, telling her all that she must do for her husband, mentioning all the details of her conjugal duties with such realism that she begins to cry. The bridegroom bows his head in shame. The preacher goes on till somebody puts a piece of meat into his mouth to stop the exhortation !

The whole country has gathered to see the proceedings and to eat the meat. The wedding pair do not partake of it, because *the goats have been sacrificed for them* (ba hahlela bone). The relatives go home, roasting on the way the joint of meat they have received so as to eat it before reaching their village.

The aim of the *dlaya shilongo* is lawfully to kill one kind of relationship and to replace it by another, because the two are not compatible. However, in the case of inheritance of a rarana, for instance, when a blood relative has to change his relationship and to become a relative by marriage, he can inherit without any rite being performed, if there is no nearer legal heir ; in this case it is said : "Bushaka byi ta pfuka — the blood relationship will be revived." It will be strengthened by the new marriage relationship.

In the case of marriage with the great mukoñwana, this rite is also performed, as previously mentioned (p. 244). The wedding pair are also covered with the goat's skin. This goat is called *the cat*, because it is like a cat which is put on their shoulders and scratches them. It scratches away the bukoñwana which prevented their marriage. (Viguet.) In this case it is the *shikoñwana* which is killed. So the taboo is removed and they can marry.

III. *Marriages permitted.*

Relatives from the eighth degree of relationship can marry unconditionally (Mankhelu). The choice of a boy is unlimited within the clan and even within the tribe. However, marriages into a *too far distant clan* are not recommended, according to Viguet, for the following reasons : 1) If the marriage were unsuccessful, the parents-in-law against whom the claim would be brought might run away with wife and oxen, and we should lose our herd. 2) If our oxen multiplied in the other clan, we might be tempted to go and make war on our parents-in-law in order to appropriate the cattle. So blood would be shed on account of our own oxen! This would bring shame upon us! Whilst if we marry amongst friends, even amongst remote relatives, should a quarrel occur, we shall try to settle it peacefully These people are amongst those with whom we discuss in the hut. With strangers we discuss outside, on the square, and we occasionally fight with them and drive them away. So a difficulty can better be dealt with when our bukoñwana are people living close by.

IV. *Marriages recommended.*

Here we must take into account two different cases : some marriages are contracted on account of a kind of right of pre-emption, others on account of a right of inheritance.

1) RIGHT OF PRE-EMPTION.

There are amongst the relatives of a man certain women on whom he has a kind of preferential claim, or a right of pre-emption, and whom he calls spouses, because he would be welcomed if he were able to lobola them. They are his *tinamu* or *tinhlampsa*, viz., his wife's younger sisters or the daughters of his wife's brother. These marriages are considered as peculiarly appropriate. This does not however constitute an absolute right for the man. Should he not prove a good husband, his parents-in-law will not let him have their other daughters (p. 240).

As regards marriage with the wife's brother's daughter, who is the nhlampsa proper, there are different possibilities to be considered. It may very well happen that a man's wife, wishing to have a young girl to help her in her domestic work, approaches her brother and asks him to lend her his daughter, the woman's niece, to stay in her village for this purpose. He consents, and she grows up there. Later on however the girl's parents say to their sister : If your husband has oxen, he may take her as a wife. She returns home and discusses the matter with her husband. Should the latter be agreed, he will send his wife with £ 1.10.—to make a proposal to the girl's parents, and he will take the girl at once without much ceremony. The remainder of the lobolo will perhaps be paid afterwards. If a son wants to marry and has no means of buying his wife, then the girl's parents will say to their sister : "Please remind your husband that he has not yet given the oxen." But they will not urge this too strongly as it is their sister who arranged the marriage in order to secure help for herself. On the contrary should the husband have taken the initiative, and sent his wife to ask her parents to give him the girl because he wanted her, then the lobolo oxen will be claimed at once, or at any rate the bakoñwana will be in a position to insist on a speedy remittance of the bride-price. But as my informant says : "Psi ya hi bhanu," i. e. "it goes according to the people." It depends on their character.

However there is a reason which militates against such marriages. If I quarrel with my first wife, who may have a particularly difficult character, and she goes home, her younger sisters or nieces, who are her tinhlampsa, will certainly follow her, and I shall remain quite alone without a single dish to eat in the evening. Should the quarrel end in a divorce, I shall lose all my wives at once. The custom of marrying a wife's tinhlampsa is approved of; it is however not very frequently observed in Thonga families at the present time.

Other women to whom a man has a special right are his relatives on the mother's side, as we have seen; to take a wife from the family in which the father found the mother is recommended and approved of as long as she is not too near a relative.

2) THE RIGHT OF INHERITANCE.

The second class of cases does not concern unmarried women whom I mean to lobola, but widows whom I may inherit after the death of their husband. Those whom I may eventually inherit are generally called by me *namu* or *nsati,* and I have very free relations with them, but as already pointed out this liberty never goes so far as to allow of sexual intercourse (p. 247). "Ndi nga da," viz. "I can eat, inherit by prior right" *my elder brother's widow*: she is my regular legacy. As regards my younger brother's widow, I can only marry her if she is old and no longer able to bear children. But if she is still a childbearing woman, to take her is very much against the feelings of the tribe. The reason of the prohibition is this, says Viguet : suppose that this widow of my younger brother already has children. I take her, and have a child by her. The child takes precedence of the first children of its mother : he is their *hosi,* because I, myself, the father, am the elder brother of the deceased. On the other hand, he is *ndjisana* of his other brothers, because he was born after them by the same mother. This is impossible ; it runs counter to the most elementary notions of the family. In exceptional cases, however, when no one else can claim my younger brother's widow, I may take her.

Next to my true tinamu comes *the widow of my maternal uncle.* If he had many, one might be alloted to me in the distribution. But of course, in this as in all other cases of inherited women, the children born of our union would belong to the family who paid the lobolo, and not to me. I have, in a sense, only the usufruct of the property. She will till the fields for me and serve me with my daily plate of porridge, but she is not really mine. She is given (nyika) to me by favour, and only under specified conditions. I can also inherit *bakokwana*, the widow of my malume's father (not my true grandmother, of course, but her co-wife), the widow of my father's brothers.

Muhambi can inherit Magugu, *the widow of his cousin* Hlangabeza. This cousin is a brother (makwabu) and the two fathers are brothers. But he could not inherit Debeza, wife of Phusa. Why so? Because Phusa, being a cousin by the father's sister, belongs to another *shibongo*, the shibongo of his own father Muki and not to that of his mother. Should Muhambi lay claim to Debeza, the men of Mashabane (the name of Phusa's clan) would say : "We are opposed to it, because your doing so would in fact mean that you *eat two herds*. You have eaten one herd when we bought Ndjibari from your people. Ndjibari has had two children ; we have sold her daughter Nwashidjasa to lobola Debeza for Phusa. The oxen were ours. If Phusa dies, Debeza belongs to us and not to you." So Muhambi can inherit the widow of his cousin, the son of his paternal uncle, but not the widow of his cousin, the son of his paternal aunt.

A man can inherit also *one of his father's wives*, as we have seen (page 203), but only under certain circumstances. The dlaya shilongo is never performed in the case of inherited women.

A rule on which Viguet insisted, but which is disappearing, is this : women, when their husband had no younger brothers, must be inherited by *batukulu* and not by *bana* ; batukulu, i. e. either true grandsons, sons of the son, or uterine nephews, sons of the sister of the deceased. The reasons for this law are : 1) Bana, sons, would take liberties with their father's wives and make balamo of them, if they could inherit them regularly. This would spoil the life of the village. 2) If I, being ñwana, a son, inherit my father's wife and have a child by her, this child is ñwana, a son, to me. On the other hand, this inherited woman may have had children by my father, and they are my brothers. So, one of this woman's children is my son, the other my brother ! "A beleki tinshaka timbiri." — "She has had children of two generations !" This must not be.

263

These marriage regulations show us plainly how the family is constituted amongst the Thongas. A glimpse at the system of relationship of the primitive tribes will help us to understand something more of the strange features of this family law.

D.   REMNANTS OF PREVIOUS SYSTEMS OF RELATIONSHIP.

Modern ethnographers have tried to ascertain how the human family has evolved through the ages, and this is, roughly speaking, the theory adopted by some of them. The first stage was marked by universal promiscuity ; there was no family. Then, in a second period, restriction began to be enforced as regards marriage. Definite groups formed ; all the women of one group were the regular wives of all the men of another group. This system still prevails in some Australian tribes. It is called *group marriage*. In a third phase, the family constituted itself round the mother. She was the owner of the children, who traced their descent through her and her female ancestors. In this form, which is called the *uterine family*, or matriarchy, the mother's brothers bore a special relation to the children : the father being hardly known or without authority, these male relatives of the mother had to defend the offspring of their sisters. In the end, the uterine family passed into the *patriarchal or agnatic family*. The father became the head, and descent was traced through the males. The development of property seems to have favoured this last evolution. The husband, who owned the property, became the master of the family, and he therefore took his wife to himself and made a home. (Compare p. 122.)

Whatever may be the truth of this theory, we must recognise the fact that the Thongas have now reached this fourth stage. The family is definitely agnatic. The father's right is paramount. However, there are in this family system some features which appear to be a relic of former periods.

THE LIFE OF THE FAMILY

I. *Original promiscuity.*

As regards the idea that promiscuity prevailed originally—a supposition which is combated by some scientists (see W. H. R. Rivers, "On the origin of the classificatory system of relationship," Anthropological Essays), I see no trace of it amongst the Thongas. Amongst the Pedis, there is one day when free intercourse is allowed all through the clans ; it is the closing day of the second circumcision school. But this custom can be explained on a totally different basis.

II. *Group marriage.*

As regards *group marriage*, we may see a remnant of the system in the fact that a man has a special preferential right to certain women of his wife's family, the tinamu. His son will also consider it peculiarly appropriate to take a wife from his mother's clan, the one into which his father married.

The tinamu custom might be explained in that way. There is however a very marked difference between the group-marriage system and the Thonga family law. Amongst Australian aborigines, whilst a man of a group has the right of marrying all the women of the other group, a woman of the other group has the same right to marry all the men of the first. Amongst the Thongas it is absolutely taboo for a married woman to have relations with anybody except her own husband. Polygamy exists and is approved of, but polyandry is strongly censured and considered a disgusting custom. The main reason for this is no doubt the *matlulana* superstition, which bears all the character of a very ancient idea in the Thonga system. The story of P. K. which I relate in Appendix VI, will show how deeply the sin of polyandry is felt (1).

(1) It is true that the Ba-Pedi who are neighbours of the Thongas, have a kind of polyandry (See page 99). But this has nothing to do with group marriage, and the wives of a rich man whom he allows to have intercourse with other men, choose their lovers as they like and not according to a law of preferential right binding two groups.

Though laying much stress on this very important difference we must notice, nevertheless, that there is a certain correspondence between the rights of men and women in this respect. A man has a preferential right to his wife's younger sisters, and to the daughters of his wife's brothers, be these men younger or older than his wife. He is a potential husband for all these tinamu. It results from this fact, that, as regards a woman, she is also a potential wife for all her husband's younger brothers, who can inherit her and are also called tinamu by her, and for the sons of her husband's sisters, be they older or younger than her husband.

Another feature of these early Australian forms of society is that all the persons belonging to a given generation call each other brothers (or sisters), and call the preceding generation fathers and mothers and the following generation sons indiscriminately. We may compare with this classificatory system the Thonga custom of calling all the father's wives and all the mother's sisters mothers ; and all the father's brothers fathers. But this is not necessarily a trace of group marriage. As we have seen before, the meaning of kinship terms is very often extended to other people as a sign of respect or of love ; the Thongas, nevertheless, know perfectly well the difference existing between the technical use of these terms and their wider connotation. There is something natural in these appellations. When we call such and such a person Father Morton, Mother Fuller, Brother James or Sister Agnes, no one would take this to be a relic of the group marriage phase! On this point my conclusion would therefore be : certain customs may be considered as traces of this old system, but it is not absolutely necessary to explain them by this hypothesis. The preference accorded to a wife's sisters, or nieces, may very well owe its origin to the following cause : when a group has ascertained that its women are well treated in another group, it welcomes new alliances with that group, thinking that, in this dreadful lottery of marriage, the guarantee given by a previous happy union is not to be despised!

THE LIFE OF THE FAMILY

III. *Matriarchy*.

But as regards *mother-right* and the *uterine family*, I must confess
that I have altered my views since writing Les Ba-Ronga, and
would testify my gratitude to Mr. S. Hartland, who encouraged
me to study this subject more attentively. I had not then gathered
all the facts, and the identity of the *ntukulu* and the *mupsyana* only
became clearly apparent to me when studying the Northern clans.
Now, having inquired with special care into this most curious
feature of the Thonga system, I have come to the conclusion that
the most probable explanation is that, in former and very remote
times, our tribe passed through the matriarchal stage. Let us
carefully consider the relation of a malume with his uterine
nephews, recapitulating all the facts.

1) DUTIES AND RIGHTS OF THE MATERNAL UNCLE.

As we have seen, the uterine nephew all through his career
is the object of special care on the part of his uncle : if he is a
first-born child, the malume prepares his ntehe. (See page 46.)
When weaned, he goes to stay in the village of his mother's
relatives for many years, a girl sometimes till she is grown up.
Later on, when she marries, the maternal uncle claims a right
called *tjhumba*, £ 1, on the total amount of the lobolo. It is
taboo to refuse it ; should a father dare to keep that £ 1, his
brothers will say to him : "Do you not fear the gods ? The
mother's gods will kill you ! Your daughter will have no children.
Did you alone bring her into the world ? Did not these people
help you in bringing her forth ? And has not your wife
grown with the assistance of those gods ? Her brother must be
allowed to have his *tjhumba*" (Mboza).
On the day of the remittance of the lobolo, the maternal uncle
and all the mother's relatives are invited to the feast, and for them
a special part of the festal ox is reserved, called *nyimba*, viz. the

womb, the uterus ; this consists not only of that organ, but of the whole belly, from the sternum to the hind legs ; the bride's mother eats the *mbata* and *khondjo*, viz. the extremity of the spine (Mboza).

On the day of hlomisa, when the bride is led to her husband's village, her maternal relatives receive a special gift, a young cow called *mubya wa mana wa yena*, i. e. the skin in which her mother carried her on her shoulders when she was a baby. This cow will be sent to the family when the first and the third daughter marry. In the case of a second and fourth girl, the nyimba alone is sent.

In the *equipment of the bride*, the mother's relatives provide her with a hoe, with fat to anoint her body, with a mat and clothing and sometimes with bracelets. The paternal aunt (hahana) does not give anything, neither does the paternal uncle, the latter only helping the father occasionally. Should the mother's relatives not fulfil this duty of providing part of the trousseau, next time they will not be given the *nyimba* to which they were entitled (Viguet).

But the most characteristic prerogative of the bamalume or bakokwana, is *their special right of intercession* on behalf of the uterine nephews. In fact, as Mankhelu said in his picturesque language, "as regards sacrifices (timhamba), the mother's relatives mostly perform them. They are the stem. My father is the stem as regards the oxen, but my mother is the true stem ; she is the god ; she makes me grow. Should she die when I am an infant, I shall not live. The village of my mother is as the home of the gods (ka mamana hi ko psikwembyen)." Simeon Gana added : "We have the special charge of sacrificing for our batukulu ; our sons also are priests to them, and can officiate in our place, even should they be younger than our batukulu. That is the reason why we do not marry them. We are their elders (bakulu)." Of course the bones will always be consulted and they will tell if a sacrifice must be offered to the gods of the mother or to those of the father, but a kokwane will preferably be called upon to sacrifice for a sick child. (See Part VI. Chap. II, II.)

In the ceremonies following death, especially in the feast of the mourning beer (page 164), the malume will be the officiating person and squeeze the *psanyi* over his batukulu to cleanse them.

A last right possessed by the malume is that *of raising his village*

268

(pfusha muti) by means of a ntukulu. Should he see that he has no children, that his village is in danger of "dying," he will take his unmarried sister to his village and refuse to accept the lobolo for her. He will say to her : "Do not fear! If you die, I will bury you!" This duty falls in the first place to the husband ; but the brother is ready to fulfil it. She will have lovers, and perhaps give birth to a son. As she has not been lobola, this child belongs to the mother's family, according to the great rule of Native law. The uncle will appropriate this male offspring of his family, who will bear the *shibongo* of his kokwana. A uterine nephew, adopted under these circumstances, can save the family of his mother from extinction.

2) RIGHTS OF THE UTERINE NEPHEW.

The attitude of the ntukulu wa shisati (the uterine nephew) to his malume is quite peculiar. "Ntukulu i hosi, a nyenyela hikwapsu ku malume." — "The uterine nephew is a chief! He takes any liberty he likes with his maternal uncle" (Mboza). These prerogatives of uterine nephews with regard to relatives on their mother's side, their bamalume and bakokwana, appear clearly in the religious ceremonies. We have seen the prominent part which batukulu take in these rites. "Ba yima mahlwen ka psikwembu" — "they stand before the gods, in their stead" (Viguet). They must be the servants of the altar, and the consumers of the offering. In the great sacrifice for rain, as accomplished in the Northern clans, an offering of beer is made, together with the sacrifice of the black victim. (See Part VI.) It is the uterine niece of the chief who must fetch the mealies from the granary, pour them into the pot, take the first handful to crush it in the mortar, give the first blow with the pestle, and begin each of the complicated acts of the brewing. When the black victim is brought, some one puts an assagay into her hand and helps her to stab the animal. She it is who "gives over to the gods" (nyiketa psikwembu). The same thing happens in the great family gatherings : one ntukulu holds the leg, another the

269

assagay. The batukulu dispose of the portion of the limbs offered to the gods. They *cut* the prayer and, at that moment they steal the meat or the beer of the sacrifice and run away with them. Why is this? "Because a ntukulu does not fear the saliva of his malume" (Mboza). They live in such intimacy with them that they can eat that which was reserved for the gods (1) (See p. 162).

The ntukulu *also takes precedence* in some other rites ; in the circumcision school the uterine nephew of the chief is at the head of the circumcised. In the *luma milomo* (page 146) he starts the purifying ceremony, and "gives to the others" (nyiketa) the use of the food of the deceased.

But it is especially in the question of the inheritance that he shows himself in his characteristic aspect. Father-right has set in and is strongly supported by the lobola custom. Therefore the sons of the deceased have the sole right to the property of their father, wives as well as implements. The batukulu, however, the uterine nephews, refuse to be left out! You will find them everywhere, trying to get something for themselves. They were already planning with the malume's wives to take them as spouses after the death of their husband. Remember how they teased the whole family, on the day of the distribution of the widows (page 208). When the implements were distributed, they came and claimed their *tjhumba* (a technical expression, it would seem, which means precisely this kind of claim lodged by a malume or a ntukulu). They were given the small assagay, the big one remaining for the son. In this way *ba nyiketa pfindla, they give over the inheritance to the legal heirs*. This is a most vivid representation of a right which no longer exists, having in fact become

----

(1) Some ethnographers have supposed that ancestral worship only began when the father took command of the family and consequently did not exist in the period of mother-right. This seems to me absolutely false. The spirits of the mother's family are invoked as well as the father's ancestors, and the special place of the uterine nephews in worship down to this day is best explained in this way : before the gods of the father were known and prayed to, those of the mother were worshipped, and consequently the batukulu held a special position in the ritual. When the ancestors on the father's side made their appearance in the Bantu Pantheon, beside those on the mother's side, or after the institution of father right, the batukulu preserved that special position.

obsolete, but which asserts itself in virtue of the survival of an old custom. I have often been struck by the unconscious way in which they act on all these occasions! They give the impression of people who have been hypnotised and ordered to do something next day, when no longer in the mesmeric sleep. You see them carrying out the act, constrained by a mysterious necessity and without knowing why they do so. The hypnotising factor here is the weight of heredity, of all this hoary antiquity, which belongs indeed to the past, but still influences the subliminal life of the tribe...

As regards the chiefs, I may add that the uterine nephew may be given the chieftainship over a certain part of the country. He is well received at the Court, better than the nephews on the brother's side, because, with these, there is always the risk that they may become usurpers. This also explains why a chief, when in danger, will ask help from his bakokwana rather than from the relatives of his own family. The latter may seize the opportunity for "bangana buhosi", i. e. to dispute the chieftainship with him.

Mother-right most probably existed amongst the ancestors of the Thongas, whatever may be the country in which they then lived and the name by which they were called. But everything seems to prove that this phase has long ago passed away. No one remembers anything of the kind. Genealogies, which are the oldest records of the tribe, mention only the ancestors of the father. They are recalled much better than those of the mother. The lobola custom, which is the strongest support of the paternal right at the present time, has been practised since time immemorial (1). See also the special names of the great-grand-fathers in the paternal line (p. 227).

---

(1) Lobola is however not incompatible with the uterine form of the family. I have been informed by the Rev. E. Allégret, working in the French Congo, that the Mpongwe and Galoa of the Lower Ogowe have still partly preserved the mother-right. But lobola exists. The first lobolo is payed indifferently to the father or the mother of the bride, and the choice is made according to the personal relations existing between the husband's family and the families of the bride's parents. When a second daughter marries, half the lobolo is given to the maternal uncle. The children stay in the father's village, but they are under the guidance of the mother and of her family. They belong to the mother's clan. This system evidently denotes a less advanced stage of evolution. However matriarchy is passing into patriarchy, and the lobola custom will probably hasten the process.

THE LIFE OF A SOUTH AFRICAN TRIBE

In a paper published in the *South African Journal of Science*, 1925, under the title "The Mother's Brother in South Africa," Professor R. Brown deals at length with the facts related above and strongly opposes the matriarchy hypothesis. In his opinion the peculiar relation of a nephew with his maternal uncle is the result of the natural tenderness and indulgence which characterises the relation of a mother and her child. The feelings of the child towards its mother are extended to all the relatives of the mother, and a certain pattern of behaviour is thus created, the behaviour of a ntukulu towards all his bakokwana.

I cannot here enter upon a full discussion of Mr. Brown's theory, but I must confess that it does not seem to me entirely satisfactory. I will mention only three reasons why I find myself unable to accept it :

1) If the peculiar relation existing between a child and his bakokwana really originated from the feelings of that child towards his mother, feelings which are extended to all her relatives, why should the *paternal* grandfather and grandmother be classified amongst the bakokwana as well as the maternal relatives ? (See p. 227, 235.)

2) There is a term which Mr. Brown's theory does not explain the word *nyiketa*, which is the technical expression used by the Thongas to describe the part played by the uterine nephew in the ceremonies connected with the adjudication of the inheritance. My distinguished opponent, summing up what I wrote on the subject, says : "The nephew claims some of the property of his mother's brother when the latter dies, and may sometimes claim one of the widows." There is much more than that in the Thonga custom. The nephew *nyiketa* the inheritance to the sons of his mother's brother, who are the actual legal heirs. Nyiketa comes from nyika, to give. It is a derivative which reinforces the meaning of the simple form nyika, and may be translated by the English word *surrender* or *transmit*. What does it mean in this connection ? It means that, consciously or unconnsciously, the nephew considers himself as the legitimate heir ; but on account of a change which has taken place in the laws of the tribe, as the recognised heirs are now the sons, he gives up his right and transmits it to the sons. The fact that he does so is best explained by the supposition that he possessed that right in a previous phase of family relations. I do not see how this "nyiketa" could be accounted for if these customs were dictated only by the natural feelings of a child towards his mother, feelings which had been extended to the mother's brother.

3) In the Rev. Ed. W. Smith's book on the Ba-Ila speaking people (Vol. I, p. 317) we see that amongst the Ba-Ila the mother's brother "is

very highly respected, that he has the right of life and death over his nephews." The relation between a maternal uncle and his nephews is totally different in that Central African tribe from what it is amongst our South African tribes. There, at any rate, the pattern of behaviour inspired by the mother does not apply to her brother, and Mr. Brown's theory is at fault. On the matriarchy hypothesis, on the contrary, it is not impossible to explain this fact. There has been an evolution (whilst there has probably been no change in the feelings of a mother towards her child from the beginning of the human race up to the present day). If, in the course of this evolution, there was a time when the family system was matrilocal, a time when a child dwelt in its mother's village, close to its mother's brother, one can understand that the latter, at that time, took upon himself the duty of educating the child, of reproving him. His attitude, in such circumstances, was more severe, more dominating than now. As the Ba-Ila have preserved a kind of matriarchy, possessing, as they do, totemic clans in which matriarchal customs prevail, we ought not to be astonished if the relations of uncle and nephew are so different amongst them. In the South African tribes the authority has completely passed to the father. Hence the great respect shown to him by the children ; hence also the want of respect and the great ease in the relations with the maternal uncle.

At the end of this argument, may I allow a Native to give his opinion ? Natives often refuse if asked to explain these mysterious customs of theirs. Yet when we have the chance of hearing an intelligent Bantu formulate a reason for one of them, we are bound to consider such testimony as very valuable. Natives feel what we, Europeans, can only guess, and they have actual experience of the Bantu kraal life... Speaking on this very subject of the mode of behaviour of a Thonga toward his father's and mother's family my informant said : "If the paternal grandfather is less lenient with his grandson than the maternal grandfather, it is on account of property" (p. 232). The paternal grandfather and his grandson belong to the same clan, or sib, or family. They bear the same name (shibongo). They possess in common certain property, oxen, implements, etc, which all of them have the duty of preserving, increasing, defending. If a child spoils or destroys this property, he commits a wrong which is resented by all the other members of the clan. His paternal grandfather will reprove him. He will do so also if the honour, the good reputation of the clan is at stake. But the maternal grandfather has nothing to do with such matters. The spoiled property does not belong to him, and, whatever the child may do in this respect, the ease and indulgence which characterises his relations with his nephew will not be altered. Thus whatever influence the natural feelings of tenderness of the mother towards her children may have had on the special mode of behaviour of the batukulu towards their bako-kwana, they are not the only factor, nor perhaps the most important factor to be considered. Property plays a greater part in the determi-nation of that kind of relationship in the present circumstances, and as regards its first origin, the matriarchy hypothesis goes a long way to explain its characteristics.

But let me frankly recognise that the matriarchy theory is but a hypothesis. As Mr. Brown rightly shows, there is not a tribe amongst the Bantus, as far as we know, where that family system exists in its integrity, i. e. matrilineal, matrilocal, matripotestal. Everywhere there seems to prevail a mixture of the two systems. However if there has been an evolution (and an evolution has certainly taken place) and if one system preceded the other, it must certainly have been matriarchy, as its traces, in the present patriarchal system, bear all the character of relics of a former period.

I have tried to look far back into the past of the Thonga family system. Now I would ask : What about its future ? The question must be asked, because we are not considering the South African tribe only as a subject of scientific study. We are deeply interest-ed in its welfare and in its destiny. New forces have appeared which act in a new way on primitive society.

What will be, what must be the nature of the evolution ? How must it be directed by those who have a responsibility for the shaping of the future Bantu society ?

We shall answer this question in our Practical Conclusions, at the end of this Volume. For the present we shall be satisfied with a scientific collection of the facts in relation to the two great customs which lie at the base of the whole family system of the Bantus : Lobola and Polygamy.

THE LIFE OF THE FAMILY

E. THE LOBOLA CUSTOM.

I. *The History of the Custom. How it is practised.*

As far back as Natives can remember, lobola has always been practised. First it consisted of *mats* and *baskets*, in those remote times when white people had not yet made their appearance. *Large iron rings* were procured by barter from sailors who anchored off the shore (see Part IV), and were employed for the purpose. Later on white traders settled in the country. *Beads* were bought from them (nkarara), especially large ones (mubatlwana). A chief used to lobola with ten handfuls of these, a subject with only five. Large *brass rings* were also used in old times. Two of them have been found lately in the Maputju country, and one came into my possession. It weighs more than two pounds. They were called *litlatla* and were very much sought after. One was enough to buy a wife.

Oxen have also been used for a very long time for lobola. Some say that they were the regular means of getting a wife in the 18th century. When Manukosi came, in 1820, he appropriated all the cattle, and the Thongas were obliged to use beads and hoes for that reason. At any rate the Nkunas, when they emigrated into the Transvaal in 1835, were paying lobolo in oxen. A father claimed ten for his daughter. The Pedis of the country claimed only two or three, and this was one of the reasons why the two tribes did not intermarry. Strange to say, I never heard goats mentioned as having served for this purpose, though the goat is certainly the oldest domestic animal of the South African Bantus! Whatever may have been the objects first used, sooner or later oxen, live stock, became the usual means of lobola. This appears plainly in the technical expressions : to go out with a herd (ntlhambi), viz., to go to lobola,—to eat the oxen, viz., to accept a lobolo,—the woman of my oxen, viz., the one bought with the oxen given by me for my wife, etc.

275

The scarcity of oxen, probably caused by the wars with the Zulus, was no doubt the reason why they were replaced by hoes. *Hoes* were universally employed from 1840-1870, together with oxen, when available. Ten was the regular price for lǫbola. Later on fathers asked twenty, thirty, fifty. They were first of native make ; the Vendas of Spelonken, near the Iron Mountain, provided the whole tribe for a time with that heavy currency, until the Europeans saw that there was good business to be done by supplying them. (See Part IV). Portuguese traders of Delagoa Bay began to send Natives to Gaza with guns and powder to hunt elephants, and paid them in hoes : twenty, fifty, one hundred hoes for a tusk, according to its size.

But hoes have also been superseded by the universal power of the *pound sterling*. After the death of Manukosi (1858), early in the sixties of the last century, some Zulus came to Delagoa Bay from Natal, sent by Englishmen to hunt elephants in Gaza. They told the people of the country that money could be obtained in Pietermaritzburg (Umgundhlovo) by working, and the first Ba-Ronga went *ku berengen*, viz., to serve white people there. In 1870, in the year still called Daiman by the chroniclers of the tribe, many more went to Kimberley, especially from the Transvaal colonies of Thongas, and gold coin began to spread amongst the tribe with all its usefulness and all its dangers. It is now becoming more and more current, as from 50,000 to 70,000 Natives of the Thonga tribe are working in the Johannesburg mines. First of all £ 1 was worth ten hoes, and the lobolo money was fixed at £ 8 by the chiefs. But this price was soon considered insufficient by the parents. They wanted £ 10.10.0, ten guineas! They had already learned that, amongst cultivated people and in refined transactions, we talk of guineas and not of pounds! Later on it rose as high as £ 20 for an ordinary girl, £ 30 for a chief's daughter. The average round Lourenço Marques was £ 18 at the beginning of this century and in the Transvaal £ 25 (1). When a

(1) There is a tendancy constantly to increase the amount of the lobolo. Nowadays it is nearer £ 30 than £ 20. In this connection I may mention the following fact. A man named Mpunzi had payed £ 28 for his wife, and the matter was looked on as concluded ; but later on his parents-in-law came to claim £ 2 more. Why? They had purchased a wife for their son and had obtained her for £ 28 ; it was all right so

Banyan takes a native wife (or rather a concubine), he can get her for £ 10, and the father consents to this lower price, first because a "white man's" wife is better treated and fed than ordinary native women, and secondly because the Banyan will soon go home, to India, and this kind of marriage is tacitly looked upon as temporary. The influx of money had also the following unexpect-

Cattle in the Nkomati River near Antioka.

ed effect on the native custom. There are two kinds of lobolo : 1) the lobolo which a boy obtains from his sister's marriage, and which he employs with the consent of the family to buy a wife for himself ; this is the true old-fashioned way for him to contract a marriage ; 2) the acquired lobolo won by a boy who has worked for it, and who has *started a herd for himself* (tisungulela ntlhambi). This second kind of lobolo became much easier to procure under

far. But the people who had given their daughter for that sum wanted to lobola a girl and were asked £ 30. Therefore they claimed £ 2 from the bakoṅwana of Mpunzi and these, in their turn. came to him asking for £ 2 more. And it was so arranged. This story fittingly illustrates the explanation of the lobolo which I set forth below : it is a compensation.

the new conditions, especially when a stay of a year or two in Johannesburg was long enough to save the necessary sum. Boys who had no sister, and who would have been destitute in former times, could then dream of a *tshenwge* viz., of marrying three or four wives! And they had this advantage that, their wives not having been bought with family property (their sister's oxen), no bakoñwana could disturb them in their domestic happiness, as may happen to those who marry by means of the first-mentioned lobolo.

This leads us to consider :

II. *The original meaning and the consequences of the lobola.*

As we have said previously, the only way of understanding the lobola, as well as other similar payments in kind which we meet with amongst a great number of uncivilized or half civilized nations, (1) is to consider it as *a compensation given by one group to another group,* in order to restore the equilibrium between the various collective units composing the clan. The first group acquires a new member : the second feels itself diminished, and claims something which permits it to reconstitute itself, in its turn, by the acquisition of another woman. This collectivist conception alone explains all the facts.

In this way, the acquired wife, though she keeps her shibongo (clan name), becomes the property of the first group. She is aggregated to it by complicated marriage ceremonies, representing the passage from one family to another. She is owned by the new family, herself and the children who will be born of her. She is not in any way a slave, but she is nevertheless owned. She is not the individual property of one man, but the collective property of a group. Hence the following facts :

1) Her whole family take part in the marriage ceremonies, especially on the day when the lobola is brought by the bridegroom

(1) See A. van Gennep, *Les Rites de passage*, p. 170. The *Kalym* of the Turko-Mongolians, the *Nyen* of Southern Thibet, etc., correspond to the Bantu lobola.

(See page 109). Every male member of the group has his say in the matter.

2) Brothers will always be ready to help a poor relative to lobola : they work for their group.

3) The acquired wife is their presumptive spouse, though they cannot have sexual relations with her (matlulana). They will inherit her if the husband dies, according to the laws which I have explained in the preceding paragraphs.

4) Children will belong to the father, live with him, bear his shibongo (family name), and owe him obedience : boys will strengthen this group, girls will be lobota (factitive of lobola— sold in marriage) for his profit. Father-right rests on the lobola. This is so plain that any child born of a woman who has not been paid for belongs to the mother's family, bears her shibongo name and will live in the malume's village. In Appendix VII, I relate the story of Spoon Libombo as an instance of this primordial law. This is the reason why, when the question is discussed, men insist so much on the preservation of the lobola. They say : "Who will guarantee us the possession of our children if lobola is suppressed ?"

So the lobola is by no means a purchase made by the husband, and still less a present given to the wife's parents.

1) ADVANTAGES OF THE LOBOLA CUSTOM.

In the primitive collective stage of society the custom has certainly *great advantages* : 1) It strengthens the family, I mean the patriarchal family, the right of the father. 2) It marks the difference between a legitimate and an illegitimate marriage and, in this sense, takes the place of an official marriage register. 3) It puts hindrances in the way of dissolving the matrimonial union, as a wife cannot definitely leave her husband without her group returning the lobola. Therefore it obliges the married pair to have a certain regard one for the other.

However, these advantages must not be exaggerated. Marriages

concluded on the lobola basis, are frequently dissolved (1). The
tie being purely material, it is easy to sever it. When the husband
"bitana tihomu," claims his oxen, who could refuse to return
them ? It is certainly erroneous to say that the lobola is a contract
made between two families in order to guarantee the good
treatment of the wife by her husband and vice versa, to prevent
the husband beating his wife or the wife deserting the conjugal
home from mere caprice. It has even been asserted that this sum
of money was a pledge, a security, claimed by the wife's parents
for the protection of their daughter! There is nothing of the kind
in this institution. The exhortations addressed to the bride on
the day of her *hloma* (page 118) prove clearly enough that, on the
contrary, owing to the lobola, the husband has every right over
her, and that she has no right to protest if he uses or abuses this
right.

2) BAD CONSEQUENCES OF THE LOBOLA CUSTOM.

1) And this is the first *regrettable consequence of the lobolo* : the
woman is undoubtedly reduced to an *inferior position* by the fact
that she has been lobola. *a)* This appears clearly in the fact
that, though she is not looked upon exactly as a head of cattle,
a marriageable girl is in principle entirely at the mercy of her family
as regards the choice of her husband. In the same way a widow
to be inherited is in the hands of her deceased husband's family.

(1) I will give only one example which I witnessed amongst my neighbours and
which shows that, with women of loose character, at any rate, the payment of
lobolo helps very little to strengthen the matrimonial tie. A girl named Hlapfuta,
daughter of Bandi, married a first husband. The " bukosi " (name commonly given
to the lobolo money) was used to procure a wife for her brother. But she left her
husband and was married by Ñwamusi. This second husband paid the lobolo, which
was then returned to the first. But Hlapfuta ran away a second time and joined
a man called Matshubele. She did the same thing five consecutive times, and finally
she moved to Majlangalen, to the suburbs of Lourenzo Marques, the favourite quarter
of the prostitutes. There she was lost, and the "bukosi" also. Her paternal uncle,
who had been put to any amount of trouble to recover the "bukosi" in order to
give it back to the five abandoned husbands, seeing that it would be impossible to
satisfy the last, could no longer bear the strain and committed suicide by hanging
himself from a tree not far from my house in Rikatla. The debt remained with the
girl's brother who "had eaten the bukosi."

Men are often better than their principles, and we have seen in the study of marriage and inheritance customs that the consent of a girl, and of a widow, is generally asked before any decision takes place. This is done as long as the male masters of the woman have no special interest in the choice. But should they have reason to impose a certain husband upon her, they will not hesitate to force her to accept him ; a young girl will be given up to a dirty old man, for whom she has no liking, on account of a lobola debt of twenty years standing! The lobola hardens the heart and the woman is unable to defend herself. She can always run away. But where will she hide, if all her relatives agree on her being sacrificed to the interest of the family ? Or she can threaten to commit suicide, and she occasionally does so. *b)* She must work for her husband, who gives her very little in return. It is true that she is not a *slave*. She is however *owned*. *c)* This is partly the cause of the shocking difference established between a husband and his wife. The married woman is henceforth absolutely prohibited from adulterous relations — which is a very admirable provision — but her husband is quite free in this respect : he has not been bought. *d)* As regards her children, whatever may be her love for them, she does not in fact possess them. They belong to the father. If divorce takes place and the lobolo is not returned to the husband, he keeps them and the mother will be separated from them for ever (1).

2) A second series of consequences arising from this custom are the *strained relations* between the two contracting groups. We have sufficiently insisted on this subject. What makes dealings with parents-in-law so difficult ? It is the lobolo, the sum of money which has perhaps not been Fully paid, and

(1) The Rev. H. Dieterlen, of Basutoland, in a paper on the lobola, wrote the following words, which apply to the Thongas as well as to the Ba-Sutho : "A woman married under lobola bears children but possesses none. The children belong to those who gave the cattle. Whatever may be her own merits, she can see her children pass into the hands of the rawest heathen and be given over to the cupidity of rapacious and rascally relatives. She can be illtreated, driven away, abandoned, repudiated : she will have to live without children ; she will resemble a woman who has never had any. She is not supposed to have the heart and the feelings of a mother. And her children are treated as if they had no filial affection."

the debt remains as a permanent cause of irritation. If there is no reason for friction on that point, the threat of quarrels ending in divorce is always impending like the sword of Damocles. If this takes place, the sad event will be made ten times more painful by the terrible dispute which will arise by reason of the lobola being claimed back. And the contending couple will not suffer alone. It may be that another marriage, that of the great mukoṅwana, which was perhaps a happy one, will be destroyed in consequence of the divorce. (p. 243) "A ba ruli timbilwin," remarked Mboza. "They don't find peace in their hearts."

These complicated relations due to the lobola poison the whole of native life. Life should be easy for South African Natives. Their wants are few and they have enough to satisfy them under their invariably blue sky. They are generally speaking mild and good-natured. But the lobola question fills the African village with hatred and bitterness. *The milandju*, the debts! Milandju comes from landja, to follow, and this etymology is very instructive. A husband whose wife has gone away must *landja* his wife or rather his money. His whole family will help him in following this property until it has been recovered. Natives will go from one end of the country to the other to follow a few pounds, and at least three quarters of the cases which are brought before the Courts are lobola cases.

As regards the attitude to be adopted towards the Lobola custom, see Practical Conclusions. III.

F. POLYGAMY.

I. *Origin and spread of Polygamy amongst the Thongas.*

Polygamy is uniformly practised all through the tribe. This is not to say that every man has many wives ; the automatic rule, by which the number of males is always about equivalent to that of females and which has been recognised by physiology, has its effect also amongst Natives, and, in ordinary circumstances, women are not more numerous than men in Bantu tribes. Many men are monogamists, not from choice, but by force of circumstances. Others are wandering about in Johannesburg, or Kimberley, and marry later in life, whilst girls marry much earlier. In the villages round Lourenço Marques the headman often has two or three wives. Three is however an unusual number. The chiefs, of course, take more, and Mubvesha, for instance, the chief of Nondwane, had as many as thirty. In the Gaza country chiefs go even further, at least they used to do so in the good old times, under Gungunyane. Bingwane, the chief of the Ba-Tswa, had so many wives that he hardly knew them and at any rate did not know all his children.

What is the origin of the custom ? It might be assumed to be a remnant of the old system of group marriage, supposing the Bantus to have also passed through that stage of family evolution. At one time all the men of a group would have considered as their wives all the women of another group, and vice versa. It was a state of polygamy and polyandry at the same time. The fear of the matlulana (page 265) put a stop to polyandry, and polygamy alone survived. Or it might be supposed that monogamy existed first and that polygamy appeared later, owing to the following reasons : 1) *Wars* diminished the number of men. As women were not anxious to remain "old maids," and as the tribe wanted to make the most of them, in order to increase and strengthen itself, the unmarried ones were taken by married men and so the polygamic family arose. In fact polygamy was very much fostered by the Gungunyane wars, during the historic period. Every year the Ngoni chief planned expeditions against his Ba-Chopi enemies on the coast, north of the mouth of the Limpopo. Men were killed and women enslaved, and each of these became the wife of her capturer. The position of these slaves was not very bad : however they were called *tinhloko*, heads, (a word which has the same meaning as heads of cattle), and could be sold by their owner. A great many of these Chopi women were bought in and round Lourenço Marques, before the suppression of slavery. Hundreds of them still live there and are recognisable by their very broad, coarse features. 2) The *laws of succession* which regulate the present agnatic Thonga family also lead to polygamy as a necessary consequence. A young brother inherits the widow of his elder brother, be he married or not. If polygamy began in this second way, its increase in later times is not to be wondered at. It answers admirably to the Bantu ideal of life. As we saw, a man who has a harem, tshengwe (page 126), is a man who has succeeded in his career! This is the regular method of becoming a rich man, an ideal which is by no means confined to the black race! On the other hand sensuality develops very quickly in the polygamic family and its very development reacts on the custom and tends to foster it.

I do not think the origin of polygamy can be traced with certitude. However, there are amongst the Thongas some striking customs, giving to the "first" or "great wife" a special position, which seem to confirm the hypothesis of a primitive monogamy. The first of these is the ritual incision made by the first wife in the inguinal region after the death of the husband ; it is not performed by the other widows (p. 200). In the same way the widower carries out this rite only after the death of the first wife and not when "little wives" die. The second is to be found in the rites of the foundation of the village ; as we shall see in the next chapter, the first wife has a special part to play in these significant ceremonies. When I asked Magingi, an old Rikatla heathen, why such a difference was made between the first wife and her co-wives, he told me : "The first is the true wife and the others are but thieves. That is why it is said at the death of the first wife : the house of the husband has been crushed (a tjhobekelwi hi yindlu ya kwe). When another dies, it is only said : he has lost a wife (a felwi hi nsati)"...

The species of sacredness which surrounds the first wife appears even more plainly in the case of the marriages of chiefs. The principal wife of the chief is in one sense not the actual first wife, but the woman who has been bought with the money collected by his subjects and whose son will be the heir to the chieftainship (See Part III). Generally the "wife of the country" is not the first

in date. At her death the chief does not perform the incision : the
first in date remains the first from the ritual point of view. All
these facts show that, for the Thongas, there is a deeper, more
mystical conception of matrimony than at first appears, when we
consider their present polygamic family. For them, true,
complete matrimony is the union of two persons, not of three or
ten, and little wives are not much more than concubines. This
feeling may very well be explained by the supposition that the
race has passed through a previous monogamic phase.

II. *Consequences of polygamy.*

A happy consequence of the custom is that, in the primitive
Bantu tribe, no disconsolate old maid is to be found. This is no
doubt an advantage. I fear, however, that when monogamy sets
in, this unblessed singleness will follow in its train.

But the evils of polygamy by far exceed its few advantages!
1) The first is the dreadful development of sexual passion which
occurs amongst polygamists. White people who have lived in
close touch with Natives in a head kraal where men have many
wives, can bear testimony to the frightful excesses in which they
indulge. See Annotatio 14, the observations of Dr. Liengme at
Gungunyana's residence.
2) A second evil resulting from the custom is the domestic
quarrelling which prevails in the villages of polygamists. There
is a special term which indicates the peculiar jealousy of a wife
towards her co-wives, *bukwele*. The prefix *bu*, in Bantu languages,
designates abstract things, ideas, feelings. It is also an indication
of place. *Bukwele* therefore also means the special spot between
the court yards, where the wives of one man go to insult each other
(rukutelana). The story of Leah and Rachel, in the book of
Genesis, may give some idea of the reason of such quarrels!
Sometimes the husband amuses himself by fostering these by no
means edifying feelings amongst his spouses. Tobane says :
"He will say bad things (psitokoro) to one of his wives, his

favourite, about another who is perhaps superior to her. He says to her : 'You are much nicer than so and so! She is not like a woman (A nga twali lepsaku i wansati).' The favourite will make haste to report to her superior what she has heard. She will draw her attention to the fact that the husband calls at her hut more frequently than at the others... The superior becomes angry, and people say of the husband : 'A ni gudjulisana, a ni bandjisana,' 'he makes his wives hit each other.' He himself, after a time, will try to regain the goodwill of the despised one (a ta mu batela). She will violently repel him. He may even kill a chicken to bring about a reconciliation!" One can easily imagine the jealous scenes which occur in the village of a polygamist (1)!

3) Polygamy, when practised on a large scale, even brings about *the ruin of the family*. Two examples show this clearly. First the case of Bingwana, to which I have already alluded. He had a great number of wives and used to place them in his various villages, viz., in the capital itself and in all the districts of his kingdom, going round from place to place to visit them. But they were so numerous that he could not visit them Frequently enough and they committed adultery wholesale with the men of these villages. The result was that Bingwana had hundreds of children and that, in the end, he married his own daughters without knowing it. He died tragically. The Gungunyana's yimpis surrounded his fortress (hkokholo). His son, Sipenenyana, fled during the night and he remained alone. He then shut himself up in a hut where he had gathered together his treasures and his gunpowder, set fire to it and died amidst the flames.

The second example is that of Mubvesha who died on Nov. 5 th 1910, a man of weak character, whose intrigues caused the war of 1894-1896 and who was installed by the Portuguese as Chief of the Nondwana country at the close of that war. (See

(1) Here is a pretty little Nkuna song about bukwele. A despised wife sings :
   Rirakara ra mina ri khele hi wanuna,
   Wanuna a nyika dokori ya kwe !
   My nice little pumpkin has been plucked by my husband !
   My husband has given it to his favourite !

She sings this song to excite a quarrrel... after which she hopes that she will obtain her rights.

Appendix **X**.) He used to lobola the younger sisters of his wives (tinhlampsa) when they were still little girls, and had between thirty and fifty spouses. But he was terribly jealous, keeping them in their villages, away from all the world, under the supervision of a trustworthy induna. All the men were forbidden to cross the large road which separated this

Phot. A. Borel

Chief Mubvesha with some of his wives (Nondwane 1908).

district from the rest of the country. The result is to be seen in the photograph taken in 1908, when I paid him a visit in his kraal. He was a man of sixty-five or seventy. His younger wives were over thirty ; I saw *one* child only, called Nwadambu, after the surname of the Nondwane Portuguese Administrator. One child and thirty wives! This shows the result of polygamy when practised under such conditions. It ruins the family.

What is the opinion of Christianised and civilised Natives about Polygamy ? I made an inquiry amongst the pupils of the Rikatla

287

Training Institution, asking them to set forth their views frankly on the subject. Most of them were full grown men, some were married, some had been polygamists themselves. I obtained about twenty written answers, and this is the summary of these little essays :

Reasons for :

1) A Native proverb says : Wansati muñwe a nga yaki muti, i. e. One woman does not build (constitute) a village. This proverb is confirmed by two others : Litiho liñwe a li nusi hobe, i. e. One finger does not bring the cooked grains of maize to the mouth ; and : One single arrow is not able to kill a snake (Ntumbana muñwe a wu psi koti ku dlaya nyoka).

2) To have many wives is the glory of the headman of a village. He is honoured in proportion to the number of his wives.

3) The polygamist can thus practise a generous hospitality, each wife bringing her plate of food for the evening meal.

4) If the first wife dies, he is not left alone.

5) If she is ill, he does not want for food.

6) There are many hands to perform the village duties : his many wives help each other.

7) The polygamist has many children.

8) No woman is left unmarried, which is a good thing, because how could the unmarried ones find money to buy their clothing ?

Reasons against :

1) Tshengwe dja kajata, i. e. Polygamy is troublesome... on account of bukwele, jealousy.

What is the source of this feeling ? A husband shows his preference for one of his wives, either by giving her a more valuable present than he gives the others, by visiting her on two consecutive nights in her hut, or, when he returns from a hunting trip, by giving her a better piece of meat, the leg, for instance. This arouses bukwele in the heart of the others, and, when this has once been the case, a trifle will suffice to kindle the fire anew. And how does this feeling manifest itself ? By mutual insults of these women to each other, going as far as accusations of witchcraft. (One of them will exclaim : "O! May my rival die and I remain alone in possession of everything!" This is almost equivalent to an act of witchcraft) ; by insults and menaces to the husband ; by the refusal on the part of the despised one to cook his food and to get in his harvest ; by deeds of violence against his person : (One of the wives of one of the witnesses went so far as to drag him out of the hut of her rival, and they made life so intolerable to him that he fled from his village and went to Johannesburg to find rest) ; by criminal attempts on his life ; by hatred manifested to the children of the co-wives. (These children are called *mabokonyo*, which is a term of contempt. They are taught to hate each other and to hate their father, as the angry mothers give vent to their grievances before them without shame.) Finally bukwele sometimes ends in the suicide of the despised wife.

2) Polygamy encourages drunkenness on account of the great abundance of corn harvested and of beer brewed by so many hands.

3) It develops pride in the heart of the polygamist.

4) It is expensive, as the husband must pay £ 1, the hut tax, for each wife.

5) It destroys the man's strength owing to sexual excesses. (However this reason put forward by one of the witnesses seemed to have little weight in the eyes of the others. It rather made them laugh.)

On the attitude to be adopted towards Polygamy see Practical Conclusions IV. I shall there add some remarks about this interesting inquiry.

G. SOME FEATURES OF THE RELATIONSHIP SYSTEM AMONGST OTHER SOUTH AFRICAN TRIBES.

The tribes that I have studied can be classified into two categories as regards their relationship system : those in which a man has the right of marrying the daughter of his wife's brother, and those in which it is his son who marries the girl, who is his cross-cousin, the daughter of his maternal uncle. This difference is absolute as regards marriage between cross-cousins. In the first category such a marriage is taboo and never happens unless the rite of *dlaya shilongo* is performed, an exception which confirms the rule. As regards marriage of the uncle with his wife's niece, it is prohibited in the second category, but may eventually take place, at least amongst the Pedis and Vendas, if the man has no son to marry the girl. This difference is deep enough to provide a principle of classification, as it has important consequences in the respective life of the two allied groups. However both customs are manifestations of the same general law existing in all the South African tribes, i. e. the right of a family which has taken a wife in another family to marry more wives belonging to the allied family.

289

THE LIFE OF A SOUTH AFRICAN TRIBE

1) Tribes in which a man has the right of marrying the daughter of his wife's brother.

The Thonga tribe comes first. I have explained its customs at length. The other tribes belonging to this category are the Chopis, the Tongas of Inhambane and the Ndjaos. Notice that all these tribes are contiguous, geographically speaking, being settled in the same area.

The Chopi tribe.

Its system of relationship is very similar to the Thonga system, though some of its other customs are different. (For instance the Chopis build square houses; they arrange them in a straight line; they are specially gifted for music; they believe that their ancestor-gods dwell in the rivers, etc.) I have noted however the following peculiarities in their family relations.

A Chopi boy does not call by the same term his brother *(Nkoma)* and his sister *(Ndi ya ngu)* and vice-versa. We notice here for the first time that opposition of the sexes which is one of the features of the Sutho system.

Both the son and the daughter of a woman's brother are called *Tsandzana* by this woman, who is their paternal aunt *(hahani)*. This term corresponds to the Thonga *nhlampsa*, but, in Thonga, *nhlampsa* is only the niece and not the nephew, the girl who can become the co-wife of her aunt, in order to "wash her dishes (ku hlampsa)." My Chopi informant denied that the word tsandzana had this etymology, though he could not furnish another. He said : "It is a term transmitted from the beginning." At any rate the fact that the nephew is also called by this term inspires in me some doubts as to the etymology given by my Thonga informants, as a boy will never go to the village of his aunt to wash her dishes. It is quite possible that these words tsandzana, nhlampsa, come from another source, expressing, as they do, such a striking and peculiar family relation.

Amongst the Chopis, the wife's father is treated with more familiarity than amongst the Thongas. He is more a father *(tate)* than a mukoñwana *(musade)*. The same may be said of her mother. The son-in-law can ask her for food. But the avoidance and fear is more marked towards the wife of the brother-in-law, called *nkokati*. It is perhaps not so great as amongst the Thongas ; on the other hand she will never be taken in marriage by the man who "follows his oxen." A substitute will always be found.

The wife's brothers are the true bakoñwana.

The Tonga Tribe.

This tribe, which is settled in the neighbourhood of Inhambane, has a language totally different from the Thonga. It evidently belongs to another linguistic group. But, as regards its system of relationship, it seems to observe very similar rules. The women with whom a man can "joke" (hesa) are the same. These Tongas have a peculiar way of swearing : a man swears by pronouncing the name of his sister and a woman by pronouncing the name of her brother. In both cases they add the syllable le to the name. Thus my informant, Mahandise, says : Nyakhudile, ndi ya ngu, by Nyakhudi, my sister, and she says : Mahandisele, by Mahandise.

The Ndjao Tribe.

Here again we find a tribe whose language is very remote from the Thonga, possessing some features which belong to the Central African linguistic group, but whose habits, as regards marriage rights, are exactly the same. My informant has described to me in a graphic manner the extraordinary behaviour of a man and his wife's brother's wife when they have the great misfortune to meet unexpectedly on the road :

"When I see my great mukonwana coming along the road (she is designated by the term ba-mbiya), I at once kneel down, bend my head to the ground, extend my hands in front of me and clap them against each other to salute her. She also prostrates herself and extends her hands in front of her but keeps them closed. She salutes me, but we do not look at each other; then we rise to our feet and depart each in his own direction. When visiting her village, I do not enter by the main door, but follow a little path behind the huts in order to avoid her. Should she see me coming, she will hide herself at once. The tinamu will come and salute me, take my assagais and put them in the hut. They are my wives. If I find my great mukoñwana eating, she will abandon her meal and leave the spot. Such will be our relations until I have provided an ox to buy her. On account of this ox it will henceforth be possible to both of us to see each other. She will also give me a small present, a bracelet, and then she can enter my hut. But the peculiar way of saluting each other will never be abandoned."

Notice the fact that this man must *buy* her *ba-mbiya* in order to be allowed to be on an easier footing with her. We found a similar custom in the Maputju clan in regard to the mother-in-law, and, in that case there was even no question of *buying* her, but only of making an alliance (tlhangana) with her. The prohibition against marrying this woman is however not so strict as in most of the Thonga clans, if no proper substitute is procurable.

The wife's brother's daughter is here also a potential wife, but it seems that she only becomes actually the wife of her paternal aunt's husband in the case of the aunt's death. Then she comes to "reopen the house" which had been closed by the death of the first wife. There does not exist a term corresponding to nhlampsa.

Amongst the Ba-Ndjao the nephew can inherit his maternal uncle's wife just the same as amongst the Thongas.

The reader will notice many blanks in the Tonga and Ndjao lists. In fact I give these lists only provisionally, hoping that those who live in contact with these two tribes will be able to complete and if necessary to correct them.

2) Tribes amongst which a man has a prior right to marry the daughter of his maternal uncle.

The Khaha-Pedi Tribe.

I am not sufficiently aware of the marriage customs of all the Pedi clans of the North-Eastern Transvaal to affirm that everywhere the marriage with the maternal uncle's daughter is the rule. It is highly probable that such is the case, but I will confine my remarks to the Khaha tribe, in whose territory I have been living for many years.

This small tribe is settled in a remote valley at the foot of the Drakensberg Mountains, a valley dominated by the beautiful cupola of the Mamotswiri (Kranzkop). When I obtained my information, in the year 1906, these people were still living their old, tribal life and had been very little touched by civilisation. They venerated the duiker as totem and kept carefully apart from their Nkuna-Thonga neighbours. I believe that their customs were of a very archaic type.

THE LIFE OF THE FAMILY

Let me sum up the information given by Malupi, son of Madowu :
"My father Madowu has given our oxen to Malaban, and Malaban has bought a wife, Magugu, for his son Masigowana. Masigowana and Magugu have had a daughter. This girl, Mohale, has been begotten by our oxen and I must go, myself, Malupi, and follow our oxen by taking her as my wife. It is a law, a very firmly-established law. I have the right to take her ; if I want her her father cannot refuse. If I am a poor man and possess no herd, he must be contented with one ox only. Mohale, my *motsoala*, must accept me. My father has paid the oxen for her when I was still a baby ; she was my wife from her birth. She has a sister Musibuli ; I can also take her ; she is a motsoala ; however I shall most likely leave her for others ; but if any one wants to marry her, her father will inform me first and ask me if I agree to abandon my right over her. Thus this custom of marrying my maternal uncle's daughter will be observed for generations and generations; we shall always marry in the same family, the family of our mother, and even if one of us transgressed the law in one generation, his son would resume the tradition and follow the oxen of his grandfather."

To show how strong this custom is amongst the Khahas, another informant added the following particulars. Amongst the cattle which a Khaha pays for his wife, there is a cow called "the cow used to nurse the child." This cow is meant to provide milk for the girl "begotten by the oxen" who is to become the wife of that man's son. When this son is grown up, he will have the right of claiming from his maternal uncle this special cow with all its offspring, even if they are dead, and these cattle will form the nucleus of the herd which he must pay to obtain his cousin. Should the girl refuse her cousin, her parents will force her to consent. He is perhaps lame ; no other girl would take him for her husband. Never mind! The motsoala is his wife! If her parents cannot overcome her resistance and she definitely refuses, the father of this boy will go to the Court and claim not only the cow to nurse the child, but all the cattle which he paid years ago to obtain her mother, and the chief will admit his claim.

Let us examine this term *motsoala* with closer attention. The lists compiled in our general table show that this term is extensively used in all the tribes of this second category, which might well be called the *Motsoala category*. It is employed in exactly the same sense as our expression cross-cousins, that is to say it means both the cousins of a man who are the children of his mother's brother, and those who are the children of his father's sister. As regards the ortho-cousins,

293

children of the mother's sister or of the father's brother, they are all brothers and sisters and called and treated as such. What is the etymology of the word motsoala ? According to Malupi it comes from the root tsoala (psala in Thonga, zala in Zulu) which means to give birth. My motsoala is the one with whom I give birth to children, says he. This perfectly applies to the official motsoala, the daughter of the mother's brother, as we have just explained, but not at all to the daughter of the father's sister. When I asked Malupi if he could not marry that motsoala as well as the other, he emphatically denied it and even laughed at the possibility of such an idea. Why then do the Khahas call the father's sister's daughter motsoala as well as the mother's brother's daughter ? I cannot explain it ; but the fact remains that the daughter of the maternal uncle alone is a *potential* wife. We can go further and say that she is the *regular eventual* wife of her cousin, and the reason for this is that she is, in a way, the product of the oxen which were given by her cousin's father to buy her mother; this is not at all the case with the daughter of the paternal aunt.

This very characteristic custom has consequences which determine the nature of many of the family relations.

A cousin has very free relations with his batsoala, *the malome's children*. He jokes with them as if they were brothers and sisters, even more freely, as the girls of the village are his future wives. One of them has probably already been bought for him at her birth, perhaps before her birth, and he gave her a present when she passed through the initiation (p. 178).

On the other hand this nephew will have an immense respect for his *maternal uncle's wife*. Is she not the mother of his future wife ? He calls her makgolo (kokwane), but there is "bukoñwana" in this relation, declares Malupi. Notice the enormous difference from the Thonga system, where the malume's wife is a nsati, a wife, with whom all liberties can be taken because it is quite possible that the nephew will inherit her.

What will be the relations of the father of this boy with this woman, who is *the wife of his wife's brother* ? In the Thonga system she is the great mukoñwana. Amongst the Pedis, this woman is also very much feared and even avoided, for two reasons ; on account of the oxen (the same great difficulties may occur which I have described on p. 243, and in that case, a marriage with her may be resorted to, though very reluctantly) and also because this woman's daughter will become the wife of the man's son ; it seems as if it were also a moral impossibility amongst the Pedis, for a man to marry a woman, and his son to marry this woman's daughter. Remember moreover that, as we have already pointed out, it is not absolutely impossible for the man to marry the girl who is destined for his son, if he should have no son. In this case the fear and avoidance of the wife's brother's wife would be explained by the same reasons as amongst the Thongas. Another consequence of the motsoala marriage is that the two kinds of relationship which we have met with amongst the Thongas, *the bukokwana*, relation with the mother's relatives, and the *bukoñwana*, relation with the parents-in-law, become strangely intermingled in the Pedi system, whilst they are carefully distinguished in the tribes of the other category. If a boy marries his maternal uncle's daughter, his mother's relatives at once become his parents-in-law. It is thus obvious that the great Bantu principle that it is the proper thing to marry amongst the mother's relatives is carried out by the Pedis much more fully than by the Thongas. It may happen therefore that a man can have *two kinds of sons-in-law*. This was the case of Madowu. His elder daughter had been married by Siligane—a man belonging to a totally different family, whilst his younger daughter had become the wife of her motsoala, Bazile. Madowu called Siligane *mokgonyana*, which is the proper term for relatives by affinity ; but he called Bazile *motlogolo*, nephew, thus preserving the old term of consanguinity. Malupi did the same : Bazile was the son of his paternal aunt, his motsoala ; by marrying his sister, Bazile became his brother-in-law, his *mogoê* ; yet Malupi preserved the term motsoala in his relations with his cousin-brother-in-law, whilst he called Siligane mogoê. The Ba-Pedi do not feel the need, as the Thongas .do, to kill one kind of relationship in order to adopt a new one. This confusion of bukokwana and bukoñwana no doubt explains two curious terms in the Pedi and Venda lists. The son-in-law who belongs to another family calls his father-in-law *makgolo* (kokwana) and not mokgonyana because, by his marriage with his daughter, he has assumed towards their family the position in which a man stands towards his bakokwana, viz. towards those amongst whom he himself and his children find wives. On the other hand, the man who has married Madowu's sister will be called by him and by his whole family motlogolo, ntukulu, because he has taken a wife in that family ; Madowu and all his people have become his bakokwana.

Thus we arrive at this extraordinary result : a grown up man, whom we should call an uncle by marriage, is denominated, even by the small boys of a Pedi family, by the same term which originally means grandson!

Two more remarks about the motsoala marriage. It is obvious that, as the betrothal sometimes takes place as early as the birth of the boy and girl, there are many chances that the marriage will never take place. This happened in the case of Malupi. He became a Christian ; his cousin-bride refused to follow him in his new faith ; he therefore renounced her. What was to be done ? It would have been a want of respect to claim the oxen already paid to the malome. Moreover a part of the sum had not yet been remitted. Malupi gave his father £ 1 and his brother Faster added four goats ; these Madowu brought to the father of the girl, and took the girl for himself! We have seen that amongst the Khahas, when there is no son to marry the cousin, the father performs the office in his place!

A question which one cannot help putting is this : do Pedis really see no physical danger for the race in these consanguineous marriages repeated generation after generation ? It would seem that a fear of this kind was not entirely absent from the Thonga mind (p. 255). Further has not this custom caused the degeneration of these peoples ? I do not think so. It does not seem that there is more disease amongst them than amongst the Thongas, who carefully avoid these unions. The Pedis themselves have not the slightest idea that marriage with a cousin may have bad consequences for the offspring of the pair. These facts certainly do not agree with opinions current on the subject. A thorough medical enquiry ought to be undertaken amongst these tribes and would probably produce very interesting results.

Some other terms of the Pedi list are worth mentioning. *Kgaecadi*, which corresponds with *khaitseli* in Sutho proper and with *khaladzi* in Venda, is the term employed by a boy in speaking of his sister and by a sister in speaking of her brother. This phenomenon of the opposition of the sexes in the terminology is remarkable and one would like to know what the etymology of this word is. Seeing that the Tongas of Inhambane swear by their sister by adding the suffix *le* to her name and vice-versa (p. 291), I wonder if the term kgaecedi may not have a similar origin and signify : the one by whom I swear. The fact that the Vendas really swear by their khaladzi gives much weight to this supposition.

Mogadibo is the reciprocal term by which a woman and her husband's sisters call each other. The particular husband's sister whose sale procured the oxen which were used to acquire the wife calls her "mmam-muea," i. e. "the one who has been brought." The mmammuea must show much respect to her husband's sister who stands in that peculiar relation with her on account of the oxen. She knows that her own marriage is dependant on the marriage of this sister of her husband ; if the latter is dissolved, the marriage of the mmammuea may also come to grief and the abandoned husband may claim her as a substitute for his departed wife—a case which sometimes arises, as we have seen. Hence the uneasiness experienced by these two women in their relations. In the Thonga system these two women, who are tinhombe, are very free with each other.

The rules governing the *distribution of widows are* the same as amongst the Thongas ; but, in the case of the malome having died, his widow will never been inherited by the nephew, as I have already said. She will become the wife of the younger brother of the deceased, or, if there is none, of his sister. We here meet with this curious custom, very rare amongst the Thongas, but frequent and entirely approved of amongst the Pedis, according to which a woman can inherit another, for the benefit of the family. She is said to "hold" the widow. A husband will soon be forthcoming who will live with her without paying any cattle, but the children will of course belong to the former husband's family.

Thongas often say that Pedi customs are disgusting to them. When asked why, they answer : "Because these people do not respect the co-wives of their mother." On the other hand they must recognize that the Pedis are much more anxious than they themselves are about preserving the purity of their daughters. There is no "gangisa" amongst them (p. 99); and this is deemed so important that, on the marriage day, the bride is submitted to a physical examination conducted by the old women of both families. This examination takes place in a hut, the whole throng remaining outside, waiting for the result. If cries of triumph are heard in the hut (mihululi, the Thonga mikulungwana), a sigh of relief escapes from every breast ; if the old women remain silent, it is terrible. The girl has sinned. Even if the marriage is not cancelled, the parents of the bridegroom will retain one of the oxen of the bride-price as a fine.

I somewhat doubt whether the precautions taken to preserve the virginity of the girls really owe their origin to any great elevation of moral standards amongst the Pedis. I am afraid that this morality imposed on the girls, as well as the immorality reproached against those who do not respect the co-wives of their mother, may well both have their source in a certain physiological idea found amongst all these tribes but specially marked amongst the Pedis. They think that the lochia, the secretion which flows after the birth of a child, and even more after a miscarriage, is highly poisonous and greatly injures the man who has relations with a woman during the days following on it. My Thonga informant tells me that there are Pedi women who employ this means to kill the men they hate. If one of them happens to be pregnant she will secretly cause an abortion; she will then call the man of whom she wants to rid herself and ask him to help her to brew beer; then she will give him drink; when he is intoxicated, she will seduce him and in this way kill him. These women sometimes perform a certain danse called musebetju in which they place themselves in a line, having one cheek painted black with charcoal, the other red with ochre, and dance and boast of their high deeds before those who are more innocent. Such a degree of wickedness is hardly credible. But it is understandable that a young husband who believes in such superstitions, should be particularly anxious to be sure that his young wife is physically pure, and that an examination is therefore "de rigueur."

This idea, which I call a physiological conception, also accounts for a curious feature of Pedi married life, at least as regards the chiefs. The Khaha chief used to buy a wife, live with her only till she had a child, and then buy another, and so on. The abandoned wives were left to his counsellors or other men of his village, who had relations with them, the children naturally belonging to the chief. Thus was created a kind of polyandry, not the typical polyandry when a woman has many husbands at the same time, but a handing over of regularly married wives to other men, a custom which the Thongas greatly blamed, and which is in reality highly prejudicial to a healthy village life. In this way the chief escaped the dangers of contamination, and, as regards his substitutes, well, their life was probably not so precious... or rather, they knew of medicines to protect themselves!

These facts explain why, amongst Thongas, the unmarried girl is free and the married woman is taboo (yila), whilst amongst Pedis it is just the contrary.

The Sutho Tribe (in Basutoland).

It would perhaps be more correct to say : the Sutho Nation, when speaking of the 500,000 Natives of Sutho origin who dwell in Basutoland. It is well known that, in the course of last century, the great chief Moshesh succeeded in grouping a number of widely different clans under his suzerainty and that he created amongst them a political unity which has been preserved by his descendants down to this day. This unification undoubtedly brought with it many changes in the customs of these people, and there is a long distance between the small Khaha-Pedi clan, with its population of hardly 2000 souls, buried in the mountains in which it led its primitive and uneventful life, and the large progressive nation which has passed through so many political crises and which, moreover, is rapidly becoming christianised. No wonder if we can detect the traces of that evolution also in the domain of family relations.

I have no intention of publishing here all the information which I gathered on this subject when sojourning in Basutoland in 1915. Many missionaries or colonists know much more than I do of Sutho customs. I wish only to mention a certain number of facts, chiefly for the purpose of comparison and in order to give the Sutho system its due place amongst the others.

First of all : is the characteristic custom of the *marriage with the maternal uncle's daughter* observed ? Undoubtedly. In that tribe it is the law that the father chooses the first wife for his son. Later on the son may follow his own inclination, but not for the first. The father will often have a preference for the *motsoala*, and if he goes to woo her, her father must not refuse the proposal, especially if his sister, the mother of the boy, presents the demand. There is a peculiar relation between this boy and his motsoala, to such an extent that, should he, later on, commit adultery with her, after she has been married to another, he cannot be brought to court : "She is his wife." These facts are quite in keeping with the Pedi laws.

However, the Suthos marry not only their cross-cousin on the mother's side but also their cross-cousin on the father's side, the daughter of their paternal aunt, and, what is more serious, the daughters of their paternal uncles, an action which would be contrary to all the ideas of their Pedi brethren, and of most South African Bantus. As regards the paternal *aunt's* daughter, such a marriage may perhaps be understood ; she is a motsoala ; her father belongs to another family and can receive a bride-price for his group ; but in the case of the daughter of the paternal *uncle* it is very difficult to conceive how it can be possible. Is not this cousin classified as a khaitseli, on exactly the same level as a sister, and what about the oxen ? Are they remitted by the boy's father to his own brother ? And if the wife abandons her husband, does the father go to his brother to lodge his claim ? Amongst Thongas this would be absurd (p. 256). It would be interesting if those who have witnessed such cases would tell us how they are dealt with.

Is this liberty of marrying all the various kinds of cousins a new departure amongst the Suthos ? Feko, an old Christian dwelling in the neighbourhood of Morija, an intelligent Native who was said to be about 100 years of age, declared that, when he was young, this was already a feature of the Sutho family system. However, the special importance of the maternal uncle's daughter, if we compare it with the part she plays amongst the Pedis, induces me to suppose that, in very remote times, marriage rules were the same amongst all the Suthos.

The term *Khaitseli* has the same meaning as in Pedi. A boy calls by that name his sisters and his ortho-cousins, the daughters of his paternal uncles and of his maternal aunts, and vice-versa, according to the law of opposition of the sexes. But this term has a wider connotation in Sutho than in Pedi. It is applied by extension to the husbands and wives of the regular khaitseli. Thus khaitseli will also indicate the husband of my sisters and of my ortho-cousins ; it will be applied by a further extension to my wife's brother. In all these cases khaitseli will no longer imply an opposition of the sexes. Finally khaitseli is also used for the *wife's brother's wife*. This terrible person, for whom Thongas and Pedis had nothing but fear, before whom they kneel down, is a simple khaitseli for the Suthos, a sister, a person of no consequence! Why this difference ? It is a mystery! I must add that nowadays the sister's husband and the wife's brother are both called *Soar* or *tsware*, a corrupt form of the Dutch schwager,—a characteristic fact which shows plainly that some of the old family notions are gradually disappearing and are being replaced by the simpler European conceptions.

The custom of applying the term used for a woman to her husband and vice-versa is observed also in two other cases. The husband of the paternal aunt is called *rakhali* like her (notwithstanding the feminine suffix ali) and the wife of the paternal uncle is called *rangoane*, like himself (exceptionally *mangoane*).

The tendency of the Sutho system seems to be to lessen the difference existing in other tribes between the father's family and the mother's family. Cousins of both families can be married. *However the peculiar relations of the nephew and his maternal uncle* exist amongst the Suthos as well as amongst the Thongas and I will mention the duties and priviledges of both these persons, as far as they have been explained to me, and without further commentary.

First of all we must note that the Sutho system does not confound the nephew and the grandson as happens in the Thonga term ntukulu (p. 227, 232). The word corresponding to ntukulu is *setlohŏlŏ* and applies to the grandson only, whilst the uterine nephew and niece are called *mochana* (mupsyana in Ronga).

300

Nor does there exist in Sutho a generic term for all the relatives on the mother's side comparable to the Thonga bakokwana.

The uterine nephew does not enjoy amongst the Suthos the great freedom he possesses in regard to his maternal uncle amongst the Thongas. The only special duty which he must perform for him is to hand over to him his first earnings in the form of a cow. On the contrary, the uncle often intervenes in his nephew's carreer. When the boy leaves the circumcision school, it is his uncle who gives him his new blanket. When later on the boy marries, his malume provides one or two oxen for the lenyalo (lobolo) and another for the feast at which he is specially bound to be present, as he must be amongst those who count the heads of cattle. On the death of the nephew, his maternal uncle inherits "his filth" i. e. all the property which he has constantly touched and which is covered with the exudation of his body : his blankets, his trousers, his gun, his horse, his assegais ; these objects are not cleansed with drugs ; it is the malume who removes the filth of his nephew. On a given day he will come and take the inheritance and they will give him an ox (it may be only a calf) to carry it home.

The uterine niece is also the object of his care. When she marries he claims for himself an important part of the price paid for her (litsoa). Suppose the lenyalo to consist of 20 oxen, 10 or 20 sheep, one horse (it is never paid in cash in Basutoland) ; he may take 3, 4, or as many as 7, or 10 head of cattle, even all the oxen, leaving to the father only the sheep and the horse. When I asked my informant why the malome appropriated such a big part of the bride-price, he said : "Because he has given oxen to help the brother of his niece to buy his wife, and he is now reimbursing himself." — "But", I said, "the paternal uncles have also helped their nephew for the lenyalo. Do they also claim something when the niece is paid for ?" "No!" — "Why is that ?" — "Because it is so!"

The malome keeps a watch on his nieces, when they are married, in order that they shall be well treated ; at least such is the law ; he also takes care that the bride-price obtained by the marriage of one of them shall be used to buy a wife for her own brother and not for a boy born of another mother.

If there is no fear nor avoidance of the wife's brother's wife, these are very marked in the case of the *mother-in-law*, and there is also a special avoidance by the father-in-law of his *daughter-in-law*, especially before the marriage has taken place. Later on, the son's wife will always avoid pronouncing the name of her husband's father. The day she comes to dwell in the village of her parents-in-law, her friends take food along with them to give her, because she must not eat the food of her new family on that first day. The second day her father-in-law gives a sheep to those who accompany her ; they kill it, cook the meat and feed her with it. This provides for the transition period. For the first year she has no hut of her own, no reed enclosure, no independant fire-place. She works for her mother-in-law and is treated like one of the girls of the village. Both the bride and the bridegroom are looked on as children during this first year of their married life. The husband does not even call the medicine man for his young wife when she is ill : it is the father who does this. When she has done her first harvesting, then the parents will build a hut for the young couple and they will begin to have their own cooking-pot. But they will become really independent and important when their first child is born. They adopt his name, preceded by the masculine prefix Ra, for the father or the feminine Ma for the mother and they will always keep that name, even if they have other children later on, or even if the first child dies.

In conclusion, here are some interesting expressions, communicated by the Rev. P. Ramseyer, by which polygamists call their different wives. *Mosali, mofumahali* is the great wife, the first, the one chosen by the father. *Moqekoa* is the common name of those chosen later on by the husband ; *serèthè*, the generic term for the little or minor wives ; *lepelo*, the prefered one ; *toali*, the beloved one ; *sethepu*, the one bought as a slave ; *nyatsi*, the concubine ; *mahetla-a-thebe*, the shield's shoulders, the wife's sister who has become her co-wife. We can see that the polygamist vocabulary is sufficiently rich!

The Venda Tribe.

This very interesting tribe is settled in the extreme East corner of the Transvaal, in the Zoutpansberg Mountains. It had not yet been much transformed by external influences when I visited it in 1920, and I had the good fortune to find there a very clear-headed man, one of the best informants I ever met, who gave me a very complete account of the religious ideas and of the kinship system of the tribe. I have published the first part of this information in the *South African Journal of Science* (Vol. XVII, No. 2, p. 207-220. *Some features of the Religion of the Ba-Venda*) I will now sum up the second part, insisting only on what is essential. As a whole the Venda system is not very different from the Pedi ; but it contains elements of another origin. I think that the

THE LIFE OF THE FAMILY

Ba-Venda possess these elements in common with the Makalangas dwelling on the other side of the Limpopo river. The peculiar totemistic ideas of the Vendas, strangely connected with their ancestor-worship, are the same as those of the people of Ruanda in Central Africa. (See article quoted.)

The law of *cross-cousin marriage* dominates the whole Venda system. The initiative is generally taken by the maternal uncle. He comes to his sister's husband and says to him : "I have a daughter of age to be married... Do you want her for your son ?" The father may refuse, if he has no oxen or if the age of the girl does not correspond to the age of the boy (She must be somewhat younger than her cousin). In this case the father will "untie" his wife's brother saying : "Never mind! Later on if you have a daughter and I have a son, we will discuss the matter again." But should the maternal uncle offer his daughter to others, before having given his nephew a chance of having her, the parents of the latter would be angry and his mother would say to her brother : "If it is so, return to me the oxen which I provided for your marriage and which have begot the girl." And in reality the maternal uncle would be obliged to hand over these oxen to his sister .

But the initiative is more often taken by the father of the boy. If he happens to possess oxen, he goes to his brother-in-law and offers them to him for his daughter. Both this man's son and the malume's daughter are perhaps still little children ; they are perhaps not yet born. No matter ; these two men have acted in conformity with the law, and the marriage will take place years later, if possible. Or it may be that the father of the boy has no oxen to offer to the maternal uncle ; this is not an insuperable difficulty : he will show him the little toe of his right foot ; we shall see presently what that means. The maternal uncle must not refuse. Why ? No doubt on account of the oxen : they give a man the right of claiming for his son the girl whom they have begotten, just as they do amongst the Pedis. But my informant gives other reasons which seem to have more weight. A father prefers to go to his wife's brother because he is a friend, being the nearest relative of his wife : *he will have patience.* If no oxen are at hand, he will accept the argument of the little toe. Moreover the marriage with the cross-cousin *strengthens the family* tie and is therefore particularly approved of.

This last reason throws a welcome light on a question which we put in relation with the Pedi system and which remained unanswered : Why is the *cross-cousin on the father's side,* i. e. the daughter of the paternal aunt, also called mudzwala (the one with whom her

303

cousin gives birth to children), whilst he never marries her ? Amongst the Vendas, this marriage is allowed and practised, but only very seldom and under the following conditions. When there is no nephew to marry the daughter of his maternal uncle, the son of that uncle can marry the daughter of his paternal aunt. This will be done in order to keep relatives strongly united and to prevent the dispersion of the family. It is not a common occurence, and there are people who condemn such marriages. Yet they may take place and it is interesting to note that they are dictated by moral considerations only and not by a legal right based on the remittance of oxen.

Let me add that, as might well be expected from such a primitive tribe, marriage with ortho-cousins, daughters of paternal uncles and maternal aunts, is strictly forbidden amongst the Vendas. They swear by their khaladzi. Shifaladzi says : Nga Nyamofe, by Nyamofe (my sister). This no doubt means : "As surely as I could not have sexual relations with Nyamofe, so certain it is that I speak the truth."

There are very special rules in Vendaland, as regards *the payment of the bride-price* which is called *mumalo*. Let us take for instance the family of Shifaladzi : his father is Mabidja and his mother Nyadenga ; he has an elder sister, Nyamofe and an elder brother, Kari ; he is the third child and has still a younger brother, Khabatondwe. It is the duty of the father, Mabidja, to provide the bride-price for his elder son, Kari. He has therefore sold his daughter Nyamofe in marriage to a certain Mikosi and with his oxen has acquired a wife for Kari. Now he has accomplished all his duty towards his sons and it is Kari who must obtain the wife of Shifaladzi, his younger brother. Should there be many brothers after Shifaladzi, the second ought to provide for the third, the third for the fourth, and so on ; but the last forms an exception : it is his mother who must acquire a wife for him. Nyandenga must find the wife of Khabatondwe, and not Shifaladzi. How is she to do so ? The Venda tribe is the most advanced I know as regards feminist principles. A woman, amongst the Vendas, can own property, oxen, goats etc. She can kill them and eat them without asking permission of her husband. The latter may go to her and humbly borrow from.her what he needs. She may obtain this property by her labour, or in payment of debts (as in the case when her brother has refused to give his daughter to her son and she claims the return of the oxen to herself. See above). The mother will use her possessions to pay the brideprice of her last born. She may even buy many girls, and give one to Kari, and one to Shifaladzi, but these who are her two elder sons will only "hold" the women for the lucky Khabatondwe, who has no other merit than that of being born last!

Let us return to Kari who has the duty of providing Shifaladzi with a wife. If he possesses oxen, he pays at once and all is over ; if he has none, the matter is more difficult ; he would have no chance of being well received by ordinary people ; *so he goes to his malume*, especially if there is in the maternal uncle's village a mudzwala of about the same age as Shifaladzi. Kari explains his intentions to his uncle, and when the latter inquires about the oxen that his nephew intends to remit to him, Kari shows him the little toe of his right foot, and says : "She is still growing." "She" is Kari's daughter, who is a baby, or who is perhaps not yet born. He means to sell her in marriage when she is marriageable, and the oxen thus obtained will then be remitted to the malume for Shifaladzi's wife. The maternal uncle will at once consent. The argument of the little toe is all powerful, and he will wait ten, fifteen years without grumbling. People who are "comme il faut", gentlemen of breeding, always take that attitude amongst the Vendas ; it is only a malume of an inferior quality who will unduly press his nephew to hasten payment! However it may be that, after having waited for a long time, the malume loses patience and claims the oxen. Kari will then try to find a friend who will consent to advance him the herd (which generally consists of eight oxen). He will show him the little toe of his right foot again and the good man will agree. Let us suppose that the girl was so far from being adult that she was really not yet in this world ; her mother was pregnant and Kari was only expecting to become a father. The child is born,—but alas ! it is a boy ! No matter—a big feast is prepared with plenty of beer, and the friend who has given the oxen is invited to attend. Kari shows him the baby and says to him : "This is your wife". The creditor keeps silent ; he well sees that this wife is not of the required sex. However, when he speaks, he utters only words of gratitude, and adds : "Power is with Mudzimo (God)." He firmly trusts that a girl will come in due time, three years later. Only it happens that the next child is also a boy. Kari will not inform his friend of this birth. They will both tacitly wait till the next child is born. And if Kari's wife gives birth only to males ? Then it will be necessary to wait till Kari's elder son has himself a child, a daughter, and she will pay the debt when she is grown up enough to be sold in marriage! Thirty years will have elapsed and more since Shifaladzi married his mudzwala!

There are still other possibilities. It may be that Shifaladzi himself, seeing that Kari is in great difficulties, will provide the oxen due to the malume by selling his own daughter in marriage and remitting the herd to his wife's father. In that case the daughter will *mala*, i. e. lobola the mother. Or, nowadays, he will go to Johannesburg and earn money to pay off the debt.

In this connection I may mention the following curious fact which shows how important these lobola laws are to the Vendas. If a boy first obtains his wife by earning money, as is now so easy, and if later on his elder brother provides him with the wife whom it is his duty to find for him, this second wife will be regarded as the first, legally speaking, as she is the one acquired according to law.

The frequent occurence of the cross-cousins marriage—a man marrying the daughter of his maternal uncle—has the same consequence amongst the Vendas as amongst the Pedis ; but the result is even more marked : viz. the two kinds of relationship so carefully distinguished in the Thonga system, the bukokwana and the bukoṅwana, are almost entirely confounded ; at least as far as the terms of relationship are concerned. The maternal uncle becomes the father-in-law ; he was malume, he becomes makhulu, which means kokwana, and kokwana is almost the same as malume. There is no special term for father-in-law. I would observe also that the term *malume* is used much more extensively than in any other South African tribe known to me. Naturally it means first and foremost the *maternal uncle*, provided he has not become the father-in-law. His relations with his sister's children are kindly, but not by any means so easy as amongst the Thongas. He can punish them, if he sees fit to do so. However, a nephew has more liberty in his maternal uncle's village than in the village of his paternal uncle. If the sauce of the porridge is not well made, he may refuse to eat it and tell his malume : "Give me fresh meat instead", a sentence which he would never dare to pronounce in the village of his father's brother. On the death of his sister, the malume does not adopt an attitude of anger and criticism as amongst the Thongas : he pays his mourning visit quietly and says : "It is so because Mudzimo (God) willed it so." A curious obligation which rests upon him is the following. Should his sister have had only male children, and no daughters to provide these boys with oxen to buy their wives, the malume is bound to find the lobolo for the elder of his nephews. Why ? Because the oxen which my father remitted to my malume for his sister ought to have provided our family with a woman capable of giving birth to girls as well as to boys. It is the fault of my malume's family if we have no sister to give us the possibility of getting wives. Therefore the malume must help us!

But the word *malume* does not merely indicate the maternal uncle. Under that term are included also my wife's brothers and the sons of my wife's brothers, i. e. the men of the family from which we take our wives and who would be regular bakoñwana in Thonga. And correspondingly the term *muduhulu* will indicate all those who have come or can come to marry our sisters or daughters : first my sister's son, who has the right of marrying my daughter, and my daughter's husband, who will probably be one and same person ; then the husband of my paternal aunt, the husband of my paternal uncle's daughter, and also my sister's husband ; all these men are our baduhulu. The relationship on the mother's side has almost completely blotted out the relationship by affinity. However the relation by affinity, the bukoñwana, is not entirely lacking ; it is called *bukwasha*, and these men who have taken their wives from our family are called not only baduhulu but also *bakwasha*. But the taboos are no longer so severe, as some of these bakwasha are our near relatives on our mother's side. The only taboo I heard of is that a future son-in-law must not eat with his parents-in-law on the village square, nor play the noisy game called in Thonga tshuba ; he might have to pay a goat as a fine. He is allowed however to eat with his parents-in-law inside the hut. The avoidance of the mother-in-law exists also amongst the Vendas, and also the characteristic fear of the wife's brother's wife, called makhulu. It does not however seem so impossible for a Venda to marry that relative when his wife abandons him. Only after having claimed her and obtained her as compensation, he will probably give her to some man who is just in want of a wife. This man will "hold" her according to the custom already mentioned and the children born of her will naturally belong to her proper master. Shifaladzi assured me that it might very well happen that the man would marry one of the daughters of this woman, though they are bana, children to him!

The possibility of a man's marrying the daughter of his wife's brother's wife under ordinary circumstances (i. e. when she lives normally with her husband) exists amongst the Vendas. But such a union is not frequent. Shifaladzi strongly asserted that the true candidate for the hand of this girl is the man's son, her muzwala, and the Vendas definitely belong to the category of tribes where it is the son who marries his cousin and not the father his niece.

Two unusval terms deserve an explanation : *Mubuye*, corresponding to the Pedi mmammuea : the one who has been brought. A woman gives this name to the woman who has been acquired for her brother by the oxen provided by her marriage. *Muhadzinga* is used by a woman to designate her co-wives and the wives of her husband's brothers; *Mazwale* (with a sibilant *z*) means not only the father and mother-in-law of a woman, but all their brothers and sisters.

The Zulu-Xosa Group.

I possess no adequate information to describe the Zulu-Xosa system in detail. The two full lists contained in the table are interesting to consult, and many reflections may be made and many questions put in connection with all these terms. What is certain is that these numerous tribes belong to the Muzala category : the term *um-za* or *um-zala* is employed to designate all the cross-cousins. Does this mean that the marriage of a man with his maternal uncle's daughter is the rule ? It would not seem so. The Rev. R. Godfrey writes to me : "Native law seems to be totally against the marriage of cousins, but I gather that such marriages do occasionally take place." A strange fact is that the uterine nephew is a *ndodana* for his maternal uncle, i. e. a son (ñwana) and not a ntukulu as in all the other tribes ; he is sometimes called motshana as in Sutho. It is probable that the amalgamation of 300 clans by the sanguinary conquests of Chaka had a profound influence on their old customs and the ancient family status, even more so than the peaceful unification of the Sutho clans under Moshesh. The ultimate result of these modern influences is a great simplification in the terms of relationship. The relations themselves lose their special character, and the ancient term is soon forgotten. This process is now continuing at an accelerated rate as the South African tribes are becoming more and more educated. The Rev. R. Godfrey tells me that when he inquired about the old terms amongst the students of the Blythswood Institution, he found great difficulty in obtaining satisfactory answers : "*Ompi* was universal, with its diminutive *ompana* for uncle ; *anti* is also used commonly for aunt with its diminutive *antana* ; *usibari* (or usibali or uswar) has almost completely replaced the Kafir term for brother-in-law."

There is another little tribe situated between the Thonga, Zulu and Sutho domains which seems to occupy an intermediate position as regards customs, as well as in geographical situation. This is *the Swazi tribe*. From a conversation in a railway carriage with some Swazis, I gathered the following facts.

The wife's brother's wife (mukoñwana lwe'nkulu) is called malukatana. She cannot be taken by the husband of her husband's sister if the latter runs away. The daughter of this woman is the *nhlanzi* of her paternal aunt, which means that she is the potential wife of the paternal aunt's husband, exactly as in the case of the Ronga nhlampsa. Thus the Swazi tribe belongs to the first category. But the son of this man may also marry this girl, who is called his muzala, as in the tribes of the second category ; he is allowed to marry her however only *when his father has died* without using his right! Consequently, it may rightly be said that the Swazi tribe occupies an exactly intermediate position between the tribes of the two categories.

*

* *

This rapid study of the kinship systems of all these South African tribes leaves me with a double impression.

Although there is a common stock of ideas regarding the constitution of the family, what an extraordinary variety of views and customs is met with amongst these people, so much alike from other points of view! How greatly they differ in this respect from European nations, where the resemblance is so much closer!

But these old Bantu systems of family life are in process of rapid transformation, and it is imperative, from the point of view of science, that a thorough investigation of this important subject should be made as quickly as possible. I have devoted a great deal of time to this study, which I found fascinating, but I am well aware of all the deficiencies of my treatise, and that it requires completion and perhaps amendation on some points. It may however be useful as a basis for further inquiries, and when all the necessary data have been collected and carefully classified, a very precious light will be thrown on the great and enthralling problem of the evolution of the human family.

CHAPTER II

The life of the village.

The Thonga village (muti) is not a hap-hazard agglomeration of people. It is a social organism with a well-defined construction and is regulated by strict laws. After all, it is merely an enlarged family : the headman and the old people who have fallen to his charge, his wives, his younger brothers and their wives, his married sons, his unmarried sons and daughters. All these people form a community whose life it is most interesting to study.

Let us describe its outward appearance, the laws of its "foundation" and "moving", its organisation under the headman, the doings of its different members and the rules of etiquette which are observed. While our first chapter gave us an insight into the internal constitution of the Thonga family, this will show us how the social organism, which is at the base of all the tribal life, manifests itself outwardly in the village.

A. THE THONGA VILLAGE.

We have already caught a glimpse of it, from the inside, through the eyes of the headman Gidja (p. 128). Now we enter it from outside, as foreigners, with the curiosity of the ethnographer and the philosophical interests of the sociologist.

The Thonga villages present a remarquable uniformity all through the tribe. The same laws regulate their construction in the Ronga as in the Northern clans. Let us suppose that we have left Lourenço Marques and reached the Mabota and Nondwane

310

district, fifteen miles to the north, far enough from the town, where the ugly galvanised iron sheds have not yet supplanted the old typical hut. We see, in the bush, on the slope of the sandy dune, a little forest of mimosa, *minkanye*, *mikawakwa* (Strychnos). In its midst nestles a village. Thongas like to build amongst trees, to protect themselves against the terrible south winds which frequently blow across the plain, and perhaps also to shield themselves from the inquisitive eyes of people passing along the road. The little community prefers to live by itself, as it is entirely self-sufficing. This small wood is also used for other purposes. Thongas have not yet learned to build the kind of outhouse which is described in English by two letters (W. C.), and they "go outside" (*humela handle*) into the little copse. The air is not very pure when we cross it, so we hasten to reach the village. The accompanying plan (p. 312) represents a combination of features observed in many Thonga kraals; it is rare to find a "muti" as complete as this.

We first note the external circular fence *(lihlampfu)*. It is made of branches, thorny or otherwise, one and a half to two feet high, more or less rotten. It is not built as a protection against enemies. In this tribe, villages are not fortified, and, in case of war, the only resource is flight. The fence protects against spiritual enemies, witches, as we shall see later on. The path leads us straight to the main entrance (16) the *mharana*, which is three or four feet wide. But the fence is open in some other places for narrower passages called *psiruba* (17), one for about every three huts; these smaller openings lead to the wood and are used only by the inhabitants to "humela handle." Passers by, as a rule, do not enter by such back gates. They are private. On either side of the large gate is often seen a growing tree and some poles, which clearly show the entrance. This is never closed during the day. On our right, a little court with some broken pots which denote a fire-place, is the *bandla* (21), the place where the men congregate. In front of us, at the other extremity of the circle, is the headman's hut (1) or rather the hut of his principal wife. On the way to it, we cross the *hubo* (22) the central square and pass round the *ranga*, (Ro.), *shibaya* or *shibala* (Dj.) (18), the oxen kraal, when the village possesses oxen. They are rare now, plague and Texas-fever having more than decimated the herds. Small enclosures at the sides

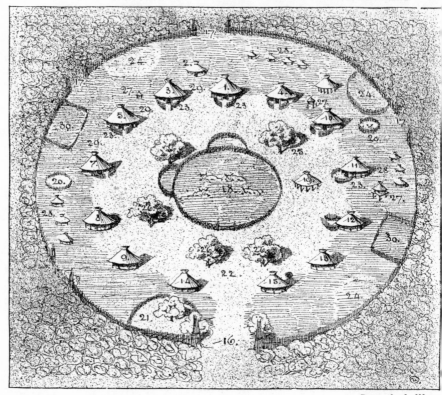

Drawn by J. Wavre.

Plan of the Thonga village.

1. Hut of the headman's first wife. 2. Headman's private hut. 3. Hut of the headman's second wife. 4. Of the third ; 5. Of the fourth. 7 and 8. Huts of the two wives of the headman's younger brother. 9. Wife of third brother. 10. Wife of fourth brother. 11. Headman's son. 12. Headman's nephew. 13. Hut of a stranger. 14. Lao of the boys. 15. Nhangu of the girls. 16. Main entrance. 17. Back gates. 18. Oxen kraal. 19. Goats' kraal. 20. Pigs' kraal. 21. Square of the men (bandla). 22. Square of the village (hubo). 23. Fire-places. 24. Ash-heaps. 25. Tree of the village. 26. Shade-trees of the hubo. 27. Henhouse. 28. Storehouses. 29. Place of jealousy. 30. Tobacco-gardens.

are reserved for the calves, which are kept there when the cows go to feed during the afternoon. On the right a small hut, a conical roof supported by poles without a wall so as to let the

312

air circulate, is the goats' kraal (19). It may be placed somewhere else, behind the huts, for instance ; or sometimes goats are tethered every night by the leg to sticks round the hubo. The pigs are never kept on the hubo, but always behind the hut : they are newcomers in the Thonga village and have hardly yet won their "droit de cité." Let us salute, as we pass by, the tree (25) which is, as we shall see, the mystical stem of the village. We may perhaps see, hanging upon it, a piece of clothing offered to the gods, or at its base a broken pot which is the *gandjelo*, the altar of the village. The gandjelo is often placed, by preference, among the poles of the main entrance on the right. The village tree, which has a ritual significance, is not to be confounded with the trees of the hubo (26), which are but *mindjuti*, shade-trees, under which the inhabitants are fond of sitting.

So we reach the main hut which faces the gate. This is the dwelling of the headman. In hut 3 lives his second wife, in 4, his third and in 5 his fourth. 2 is called *shilubelo*. Great personages, men owning a large kraal, like to build such a hut, which is smaller than the ordinary ones and where no woman sleeps. It is the headman's own hut, where people *luba*, viz., pay their homage to him ; a kind of office of the master of the village! He may sleep in it and summon his wives to come to him there. But he generally prefers to sleep in his wives' huts, one month in each, according to the polygamic custom.

Behind 4 and 10 is a *mhala*, a shed for the implements. It is built, like the goats' kraal, without plaster walls, and is smaller than a hut. There may be three or four of these in the village.

The headman and his wives occupy the back of the village. At the sides live his younger brothers, one, who has two wives, in 7 and 8, two others, those who have but one wife each, in 9 and in 10 respectively. In 11 lives a married son ; in 12 it may be a nephew, son of the headman's sister, or a son-in-law ; (see page 252). 13 might be the hut of a stranger (mulubeti), who has asked permission to stay with the headman of the village, as he wished to be under his protection. The case is not frequent, but may occur, and in order to be received into the mystic unity of the community, this man will have to "hlamba ndjaka" (See page 153), together with all the inhabitants of the kraal. The two huts near the entrance are, on the left, the *lao*, where unmarried boys sleep (14) and on the right (15) the *nhangu* where the girls live. Often the nhangu is built behind the huts of the mothers, near the mhala ; in this way the girls are kept under more effective watch. The boys of the *lao* have to guard the door, which they close at night where it is the custom to do so. The *hubo* and the *bandla*, the squares, are generally kept quite clean.

In front of each hut is a *yard* (*ndangu* pl. *mindangu*, 23) which is also generally well swept. In the centre of each of these are some broken pots (mapseko), or pieces of hard clay taken from ant-hills (psirubu) ; this is the *fireplace (shitiko)*, where the mistress of the hut cooks her food. The fence round the yard used, as a rule, to be made of poles or even trunks of trees planted near each other and forming a circular wall. Nowadays, especially amongst the Rongas, these yards are enclosed with reeds and may be built square, a single wall fencing off as many as three or four huts. The top of this wall is sometimes crenelated. I rather think this arrangement is modern ; the circular wall of the ndangu is an old custom, as is proved by the following fact. On the day of *hloma*, when the bride's-maids and female relatives bring the bride to her husband, they not only build up the woodpile (shigiyane, see page 112), but, in the northern clans, they must also erect a new ndangu which will be called *tsandana*, and so people will know that in the yard there is a *nhlomi*, a bride, working for her mother-in-law! The ndangu is the place where women tell folk-tales of the tribe to the children and to each other, whilst they attend to their cooking, or after the evening meal.

If cleanliness prevails on the square and in the yards, the same cannot be said of the region between the huts and the fence. This is called *mahosi* or *makotini*. It is the place where old baskets and broken pots are kept. The chicken houses (*shihahlu*, 27) are built there ; these are generally little huts, with reed walls, placed on a floor of palmtree boards, supported by four poles forked at their upper extremities. The *ash-heaps* are somewhat further on (24). They are called *tala*, and play a part in certain rites, representing, as it would seem, the place

314

of desolation and of sorrow. (Remember Job and compare the rite of rangela bowumba, page 194.) The *store houses, psitlanta* (Ro.), *psitlati* (Dj.), 28) are close by and are built in various forms ; little huts with reed walls, when intended for the mealies, with plastered walls, when built to contain ground nuts or sorgho (*madulu* (Dj.). They are sometimes placed on a palm-tree floor resting on short poles, or they are suspended to the boughs of a

Phot. A. Borel.

The interior of a Ronga village. (Nondwane).

tree. *Pigs' kraals* (*hoko* 20) are to be found in the same region ; sometimes they are placed even further in the forest on account of their offensive smell.

Mealie leaves, heaps of makanye stones, broken mortars and discarded pestles lie about behind the huts. If anyone wants to keep the place tidy, he can plant pine apples there (30), or tobacco, or Chili-pepper (biribiri). Pumpkin plants often creep over all this disorder. Flowers of European origin are sometimes seen on the hubo in the neighbourhood of Lourenço Marques, especially "everlastings", or the tropical periwinkle, Vinca rosea

315

(L.), with its white or pink blossoms, which have spread all over the coast.

Having now finished our first general inspection, let us add some details about the huts and the open places in the village.

The hut, the construction of which we shall describe later on, (Part IV) has an opening (nyangwa) of variable dimensions closed by a door. In some parts of the Gaza country it is so small that one must positively crawl to enter it. Everywhere one must at any rate stoop low (korama). As regards the *threshhold* (ntjandja wa shipfalo), it is not taboo to step over it. The headman's threshhold however is dreaded because it was treated with medicines when the hut was built, so it is taboo to sit on it ; these powerful medicines might do harm and even cause death. In the middle of the black clay floor is a kind of raised circle, in the centre of which fire is occasionally lighted in winter on account of the cold. It is the interior *shitiko*. Cooking may be done here if it rains ; glowing embers sometimes remain on it during the night and numberless babies have been burnt to death by falling into the fire while their mothers were sleeping. On the left, on entering, is the sleeping place (shilawo) of the wife, on the right that of the husband. They both however generally spread their mats on the right and sleep beside each other. It is only during the tabooed periods (menses, nursing), that the husband must keep to his own particular side (p. 188).

The back of the hut is generally occupied by the big basket (ngula) in which clothing and seeds are kept. This spot is called *mfungwe*. In the roof *(lwangu)* are fixed or suspended various articles : ears of sorghum or millet, cobs to be used as seed at the next sowing, assagais, sticks and knobkerries etc., and against the walls one frequently observes rough drawings made with white clay, or, in the vicinity of towns, chromos of Queen Victoria, Edward VII, or Don Carlos, as the case may be!

The hubo and the bandla differ from each other. *Bandla* is a Zulu word which has supplanted the Ronga term *shisiso*, viz., "the place where one finds shelter from the wind." Men light a small fire there to warm themselves. They also eat together in the bandla, and it is strictly reserved for them. Women are allowed to penetrate into it only when they bring food. Boys must remove the ashes from the fireplace, not women. The *hubo*, on the contrary, is open to all. A shed is sometimes built on it to afford shelter during the rainy days. There are special acts always performed on the hubo : the cutting up (shindla), the slaughtering and butchery of animals and the feast of "eating the head." The head of any slaughtered ox belongs to the men, and they eat it together on the hubo (See letter C.). It is the business of the young men to keep the hubo clean, and they sometimes assemble to pull up the grass which may have grown on it. In former times it was taboo to come to the hubo with sandals. Sandals are used for hunting and must be taken off before entering the village.

Another place to which I have already alluded is the *bukwele*, the "place of jealousy," where angry co-wives insult each other! On our diagram it would be located between 5 and 4, for the wives of the headman.

The Thonga village, this closed circle of huts, is a living organism. All its members form a whole whose unity is remarkable. This common life never appears in a more striking form than at the evening meal. Let us look at our diagram. In every yard the mistress of the hut has cooked her mealies and her sauce in different pots, and, when the sun sets, she distributes the contents (phamela) in wooden or earthen plates. The largest is for the husband. He sits on the bandla with his companions, the other men of the village, and the youths waiting for the meal. All these plates, generally carried by small girls or boys, are brought from all sides to the men's gathering. All do not necessarily contain the ordinary mealies pap ; some are filled with manioc, some with sweet potatoes, etc. The men attack the first plate, all of them taking the food with their fingers. They pass on to the second and so on to the last. Meanwhile each mother has filled other smaller plates, one for the girls, one for the boys, one for herself. She has even sent to each of the other women of the village a little of her cooking, and the others have done the same to her ; so each member of the community, when

317

he or she has finished the meal, will have eaten a little of all that has been cooked on all the fires. It is impossible to imagine a more perfect communism than this as regards food! I myself witnessed this custom of the evening meal in Spoon Libombo's village in Rikatla. Amongst the inhabitants of the kraal there were two blind male adults, the wife of one of them being half blind herself ; the wife of the other was an old woman who could hardly till a few square yards of mealies and ground-nuts, and keep the birds and the hens away from them. Spoon's wife and the wife of another man of the village alone were healthy and able to work normally. So the whole burden rested on their shoulders, as the share the other women could take in the feeding of the men was necessarily small. However I never heard Spoon grumble ; being the headman, he made it a point of honour that all the people dwelling with him should have enough to eat. Everybody who has lived with South African Natives has admired their wonderful readiness to share any food they may have with those present. Even children are much superior in this respect to White children. I attribute this virtue to the community of food which reigns in the Bantu village, and which is certainly one of the most attractive features of Kafir socialism. Village life has not taught the Thongas merely bad habits.

B. MOVING A VILLAGE AND FOUNDING A NEW ONE.

Large kraals similar to the one shown in our illustration were more numerous in former times than now. It is rare to meet with such a number of huts and so many people under one headman. Why ? Because, say my informants, the superstition of witchcraft has considerably increased in later times. Suppose the wife of one of the younger brothers should die ; the divinatory bones reveal that this death is due to a witch ; they go so far as to designate one of the wives of the headman as guilty. No common life is any longer possible. The widower will move elsewhere and build a fence around his own huts to protect them against would-be-witches. In this way many villages are broken up by fear of witchcraft. Generally speaking the Thonga village cannot long remain of any considerable size ; it tends to fall to pieces.

But there are other causes which may destroy the village and the idyllic life of the small community. The death of the headman, and lightning striking the village, are the two main causes which may bring about this event.

Death of the headman. There is a mystic tie between this man and the social organism which is under him. Should he die, the village dies also... It is not abandoned at once. The whole year of mourning will elapse before the moving. But as soon as the widows and property have been distributed, the successor of the deceased will go and found his own village and the old one will remain a ruin (rumbi). Should any one else die, his hut will merely be thrown into the bush and the village will not be abandoned. But should these deaths increase, then the divinatory bones may order the place to be deserted, as it is defiled and dangerous.

If *lightning* strikes the hubo, it is a very bad omen. The medicine man who has the power to "treat the place struck by lightning" is called in. Should he be able to exhume from the ground the mysterious bird which causes lightning, or at least the coagulated urine which it has deposited, and which is called Heaven (See Part VI), the people are allowed to stay. But if he does not discover it deep down in the soil, the village must move, as the presence of the mysterious power of Heaven inside the circle of huts would bring disaster. This is a taboo.

Another cause of moving is the *exhaustion of the gardens.* When the fields are "tired" (karala) and do not produce sufficient food for the inhabitants, they leave the place and look for pastures new. In that case the bones will be consulted. Sometimes, even, the village may be transported elsewhere for the sole reason that the people are tired of the place and want to change. If the bones confirm their wishes, they will move.

The founding of a new village is the occasion of most interesting and characteristic rites, which afford us a new insight into the nature of that social unit, the Thonga *muti*. I shall give the sequence of these rites first in the Northern clans, according to the description of Viguet, and secondly amongst the Ba-Ronga, according to Mboza.

I. *In the Northern clans.*

1) The headman goes first to examine some spots where he would like to build. He *breaks small twigs* from various trees and brings them home.

2) The bones are consulted and help in *making a choice*. The twigs are placed on a mat one after the other. When the stone of the *kanye* (see Part VI) falls in a certain way in front of one of the twigs, this shows that the tree from which it has been broken is the one near which the hut of the headman must be built.

3) Building material is collected. When everything is ready to proceed to the construction of the huts, the headman goes with his principal wife to the spot chosen. They leave the old village for ever ; they must not return to it any more. In the evening they have *sexual relations* in the new place and in the morning they tie together some tufts of living grass. Next day all the people of the old village must come and step upon this grass. This rite is called to *tie the village* (boha muti).

4) Then begins the period, of about one month, called *buhlapfa*, time of moving, which has its laws. Two great taboos dominate it : 1) Sexual relations are absolutely prohibited. Should any one transgress this law, he has sinned gravely against the headman ; he has stolen the village (yiba muti). The headman will be ill, perhaps paralysed. The guilty woman will also be punished : she will not be able to bear children again ; she will be "tied by the village" (bohiwa hi muti). The culprits have "crossed the way of the master of the village" (tjemakanya). Strange to say, the headman himself is bound by this law. He must have no relations *with his younger wives*, because the village belongs to the principal spouse. Should such a transgression be discovered, the work

320

of building will be stopped at once and the little community will find another place to which to move! Moreover the guilty woman will have to ask the principal wife for forgiveness. 2) A second great taboo is this : — No one must wash his body during the whole "buhlapfa", as this might cause the rain to fall and it would interfere with the building operations.

5) The building of the huts begins immediately, each man making the circular wall first. When all the walls are ready,

Carrying a roof.

the *roofs are carried* from the old village to the new by all the men together. They lift each roof on to their shoulders, after having removed the old grass, and go out of the village, not by the main entrance, but by one of the back gates which has been widened for the purpose. A broad road has been prepared through the bush. They follow it, marching as fast as they can, and singing the obscene songs which are reserved for special occasions (see Part VI). In these they insult the women who accompany them, carrying the baskets, the mortars, the pestles. "The village is broken in pieces, so are the ordinary laws. The insults which are taboo are now allowed" (Mboza). This suspension of morality in speech is only allowed on the day when roofs are carried to the new village. Some days later, again, the women will take their revenge when they smear the floor of the huts ; then they too will sing their songs, insulting the men. But all this is done in fun. It is a great day of rejoicing for the "tinamu", who tease each other as much as they like. A man may be wanting in respect even to his great mukoñwana on these days!

6) When the huts are ready, the *fence* is built. The family doctor is summoned. The medicine man throws leaves or stones treated with his drugs along the circular line, where the headman intends to place the branches which will form the future fence of the village. This being done, the men erect the fence.

7) Special precautions are taken for *the main entrance*. Poles are erected on both sides, but before they are put in place, the doctor pours medicine into the holes in the ground and also smears the poles with it at the bottom and at the top. Mankhelu used to bury a black stone, taken out of the river, at the gate. This stone had also been smeared with drugs. "In this way, I prevent enemies from entering. Those who come to try their charms against us (ku hi ringa hi maringo) will be attacked by disease and go and die in their houses."

8) The building is finished. Nothing remains to be done but to *ripen the village* (wupfisa muti). Men and women assemble in two separate groups and ask each other if they have been continent during the whole "buhlapfa". If one of them confesses to having sinned, he has stolen the village from the headman ; the whole work is spoiled and must be recommenced elsewhere. If all the members of the community have behaved well, they proceed to a purifying ceremony exactly similar to the *hlamba ndjaka* which takes place during the mourning ceremonies. Each couple has sexual relations according to a fixed order of precedence, one every night, and they all go to trample on the spot where the women wash their hands. The principal wife is the last to perform these rites.

9) Then comes the *drawing to himself of the village by the headman* (kokotela muti). At dawn, after the night when she has had her ritual sexual relations with the headman, his principal wife takes his shield and his assagais and stands at the main entrance, everyone being present. Outside is a thorny branch prepared for the occasion. In her martial attire, she drags this branch to the entrance and closes it.

322

10) Having closed the village in this way, she *performs a sacrifice.* She sips a mouthful of water from a tumbler, spitting out a portion of it (phahla) towards the people ; then she washes her hands, and throws a little of the water towards them in order *to give them* the village. This act is accompanied by the following words : "Be not tied by the village! Bring forth children ; live and be happy and get everything. You gods, see! I have no bitterness in my heart. It is pure. I was angry because my husband abandoned me, he said I was not his wife; he loved his younger wives. Now, this is finished in my heart.We shall have friendly relations together..." The prayer being concluded, the headman goes to the main entrance, pushes the thorny branch aside, and opens the village.

11) The last act is the *khangula,* the *inauguration ceremony.* Beer is prepared, neighbours are invited and they all drink together, the neighbours coming *to see the new village* (ku bona muti).

As regards the old one, when the moving has been accomplished through the back door widened for the purpose, one of the inhabitants closes the main entrance with a branch. Hence comes the expression which is applied to a village all of whose inmates have died, and which has, on that account, disappeared : "Those people have all died and there was not even one left to close the gate."

II. *In the Ba-Ronga Clans.*

The sequence of rites for the removal of a village is very much the same as in the Northern clans.

1) The headman examines some spots and consults the bones : "Must I built at such and such a tree ?"

2) When the tree has been designated, he goes to it and places at its foot his furniture (nyundju) and his instrument of worship, his altar, (a pot, a jar, see Part VI). The altar may be placed at the main entrance later on, if the bones so order it. As already mentioned, there will be a mystic relation between him and that tree. He must never cut it down. If any of the branches should be

troublesome and he should wish to remove them, he must ask some one else to do it. On the day of his death, or rather when his hut is crushed down, a branch of that tree will be put on the place where the threshhold was, and another used to close the main entrance of the village, a new entrance being then made through the fence and used as the gate during the rest of the mourning period.

3) He has sexual relations on the new spot on the first night with his principal wife ; in this way he will *fuya muri*, viz. "possess this tree," and also *fuya muti*, "possess the village." The Ronga *fuya* corresponds here also to the *boha* of the Northern clans (Compare boha puri and fuya ñwana, page 57). If someone precedes him in sexual intercourse, he is guilty ; he has "preceded the village" (rangela muti). By this act the headman has definitely left the old village. The others can go back to it to fetch what remains ; for him it is taboo.

4) The same day, all the inhabitants come and move all the roofs, if it is possible to do this in one day. One hut is rapidly built to afford shelter to the inhabitants, in case of rain. The first roof to be transported is that of the hut of the principal wife. This is also done to the accompaniment of obscene songs. These songs are not allowed when only one hut is transported, which may happen when some one goes to live in another village.

It is definitely a custom which goes with the moving of a whole village.

5) The following day two huts are erected, one for the men, the other for the women, because they must not sleep together. "They are still in the bush ; it is buhlapfa ; the village is not yet firm." Those who break this law cause injury to the headman. The bones will soon reveal that "he has been preceded as regards the village ; (a rangeliwile muti)." All the huts are smeared twice ; the women begin to sleep in them, but not the men. The fence and the main entrance must first be prepared.

6) The *main entrance* (mharana). The men pull up the grass all the way from the back hut to the place where the main entrance must be, so as to make a road all through the village. All the dried plants weeded out during this operation are carefully

gathered in a heap. The headman, on the advice of the medicine man, cuts from certain very vigorous trees such as the nkanye and the ntjondjo, two branches which can live when transplanted. He digs holes on both sides of the entrance and puts the branches into them. Across the gateway, he buries a third branch of the ntjopfa tree, "which causes oblivion" (p. 58): this will be smeared with special drugs in order to increase its efficacy ; it is intended to prevent the baloyi, witches and people speaking bad words. (lit "with bad lips"), from thinking about the village and spoiling it.

7) On the evening of that day, the headman and his principal wife have intercourse in their hut and, at dawn, while it is still dark, they go and wash their hands at the main entrance. Mboza does not say that all the other couples must do the same, or trample on the spot. In Nondwane this is sufficient and the rite does not apply to the other couples. But at Manyisa, midway between Lourenço Marques and Khosen, where the Djonga customs are sometimes met with, all the couples must have relations, one after the other, according to order of precedence. It is deemed so important to keep the due order in this "giving to each other the right of resuming sexual life" that, should an elder brother have been absent when the village moved, on his return he must undergo a special treatment in a neighbouring village, during a few days, to avoid any bad consequences resulting from having been unlawfully "preceded" (rangeliwa).

8) After the night during which this sexual rite has taken place, at daybreak, all the dried grass is piled in front of the main hut and burnt ritually. The headman throws into the fire a special medicinal pill in order to *give the village over* to his people (nyiketa muti). They all warm their bodies at the blaze, and go and set fire to all the other heaps of dried grass which they made when clearing the soil.

9) The medicine man comes on that same day, and sprinkles the fence with his drugs, in order to protect the village against bush fires, wizards and disease. He walks all round the fence saying : "Happy village! May misfortune not enter here! These are my drugs!" — He starts from one of the poles of the main

entrance and finishes his walk at the other, hanging upon it the branch with which he has been sprinkling.

10) Then he sacrifices a hen. A young man accompanying him cuts its throat ; the doctor plucks some feathers from the neck, sacrifices in the ordinary way and invokes his gods : "You used to treat villages (daha miti) with these drugs and I do the same. I do not act of my own wisdom ; you have given it to me. Bless this place, etc." Then he plucks a feather from the hen's right wing, and suspends it at the main entrance or in the main hut, inside, over the door, according to the directions given by the bones. This is the *shirungulo* (see Part VI) and the act is called : "to tie the village" (tjimba muti).

Amongst the Rongas, there are some other *buhlapfa taboos*. It is not allowable to light any fire in a village until it is completely built. During the whole building period, cooking is done outside the fence ; crushing mealies in the mortars and dancing are also prohibited. Whistling (ku ba noti) is forbidden, as it might call the wizards inside the village before it has been protected by the charms.

If a man has many wives, he may build a second village for himself and establish one of them there. A grown-up son, the son of the woman, will represent the headman in that village, but the law of "tying the village" will also be observed in this case. The headman will perform the act with this woman, and preside at the burning of the dried grass and of the medicinal pill, by which he *gives* the village to the inhabitants.

When a younger brother, or a son, leaves the headman and founds a village for himself (tihambela muti), he does it according to the same laws as those observed at the regular moving of a village.

III. *Some remarks on the rules of moving.*

Let us now analyse the two parallel sequences of rites which we have just described, and which complete each other. It is easy to discover amongst them three series of rites, social, protective and passage rites.

THE LIFE OF THE VILLAGE

1) *Social rites.* The muti, as we have seen, is a little organised community having its own laws, amongst which the most important seems to be the law of hierarchy. The elder brother is the undisputed master and no one can supersede him. He is the owner of the village. No one must "steal it" from him. Should any one do so, the whole community would suffer and no children would be born ; the life of the organism would be deeply affected. That is the reason why the headman must go first with his principal wife to have relations with her in the new village, and thus *take possession* of it or *tie* it. For this same reason, when the headman dies, the village *must* move. It is taboo to remain in it. Until the inheritance has been distributed, it is still *his home* (kwa kwe) ; but as soon as this ceremony has taken place, the villagers must go away, and close the door with a thorny branch. The part played by the principal wife in all these ceremonies is most remarkable. It is absolutely imperative that the headman should "tie the village" with her, and not with another of his spouses. Should she be very old, the law must be observed all the same ; should she be ill, and unable to have sexual relations, the village simply cannot be moved. In the Northern clans we see her taking the shield and the assagai, closing the village and "giving it" to the inmates, even performing a sacrifice and praying to the gods. It is very rare to see a woman presiding at a public religious ceremony ; but she is the owner of the village as well as the headman. Moving is imperative when she dies as well as after the death of the headman. The main gate must also be closed and a new entrance made in the fence to be used during the year of mourning ; in the case of her death, this opening must be made on the left of the regular *mharana*, whilst, when the husband dies, it is made on the right side ; just as in the hut, when the corpse is removed for burial. (See page 138.)

2) *Protective rites.* These are those which concern the fence. This fence does not afford material protection. The branches dry up very soon and, in the case of a bush-fire, for instance, they would do more harm than good. It is a spiritual protection, a barrier of charms, of magic influences, to prevent the entrance of wizards and of all the hostile powers of the bush. We shall understand this better when treating of witchcraft superstitions. (Part VI.)

3) *Passage rites.* The reader will have been surprised to observe amongst the ceremonies of the moving of villages, many features which we have already met with in the circumcision school, or in the mourning customs. At first sight there seems to be no relation what-ever between the moving of a village, the initiation of boys and the

mourning over the dead. The inner connexion existing between these three events is that, in all of them, there is a passage. Hence the resemblance of the rites. This striking similarity is, to my mind, the best proof that the passage rites constitute a peculiar category. When a headman has decided to move, he leaves his old kraal, he *separates* from it, not by the ordinary gate, but by a special opening made at the back of the village. He is not allowed to return to it again. Then, for him and for all his people, begins a *marginal period* of one month or more, the buhlapfa (notice the prefix *bu* which indicates a period here, as in busahana page 42). We see the village, during these few weeks, put beyond the pale of society. The ordinary laws are suspended, (licencious songs), and many special taboos are enforced (prohibition of sexual relations, fire taboo, water taboo, etc.), just as in the period of mourning ; at last the village returns to the ordinary course of life by a final act of purification, the mysterious *hlamba ndjaka*, which seems to be the most powerful means of cleansing the collective life. This last ceremony shows that, here, the marginal period has been instituted on account of the uncleaness, the impurity of the old village. Let us remember that in most cases the village has been moved on account of death! All the adult members of the social organism take part in the cleansing (at least in the Northern clans) and so the village begins a new and purified life. No one can deny the deep significance of all these rites and the mystic conception of the Thonga village.

C. THE HEADMAN AND THE ORGANISATION OF THE VILLAGE.

Each village thus possesses its superior (hosi), its master. He is called *munumzane* or *numzane*, a curious expression which is also employed in Zulu ; it means owner of a kraal, gentleman, and is often used in saluting grown up men. We have seen the mystic relation between the headman and his *muti*. The village, the muti, is the primitive social organism. The clan (tiko), which is the gathering of all the *miti*, reproduces all the features of the village life on a large scale. So the *numzane* corresponds to the *hosi*, chief of the tribe. Both certainly possess great authority, but it must not become tyrannical. They must govern for the benefit of their subordinates.

This peculiar position of the numzane amongst his people is illustrated, in a striking way, by the laws of distribution of the joints of meat on the day when the headman kills an ox to feast them. The various portions must be distributed to the relatives according to the place which they occupy in the family. The headman, nominal proprietor of the ox, will keep the breast (shifuba). This is not only the sternum and the ribs, but most of the viscera which are contained in them. The tripe, the heart, the kidneys will be put all together inside the stomach, and constitute what is called nkopfu wa homu. The headman will probably send the heart and the kidneys to his wives (tinkosikazi, his queens!). The brother who comes next will receive one of the hindlegs ; the third in rank one of the forelegs. The elder son will eat the second hindleg, and the younger son the second foreleg. They will eat this meat with their families, or houses (tiyindlu). This custom is very old (1).

Let us continue with the distribution. To the brothers-in-law, or to the relatives-in-law generally, the tail is sent. It is the portion of the sister. But it does not consist only of the tail properly so-called ; it comprises all the hind parts of the animal, especially the rump (kondjo). The malume (maternal uncle) receives part of the loins (muhlubula). The liver is put aside for the grandfather and the old people generally, because it is soft and they have no teeth to gnaw the bones. The head belongs to all the men of the village, who must eat it on the hubo, as we have seen. They may give the tongue (ndjaka) to the old men. It

(1) This custom is illustrated in a very interesting manner by the relative position of the three clans occupying the South of the Bay. They are all descended from Tembe (See page 23). *Tembe*, the ancestor, representing the elder branch of the royal family, ate the chest. He was the superior (hosi), and this rank is still held by his descendants in the direct line. *Sabi* or Mpanyele, the second brother, or son of the second brother, ate the hindleg ; he was established later on in the Mathuthweni district, between Tembe and Maputju. *Maputju*, the younger brother, head of the third branch, ate the foreleg. But he revolted against his elder brother and carved out for himself a kingdom which very soon became stronger than those of Tembe and Mathuthweni. Mathuthweni became more or less independent. But when people wish to remind the Maputju people of their inferior origin they say to them : " Tembe ate the breast, Sabi the hindleg and Maputju the foreleg !"

is taboo for the women to eat it, or the under lip (See p. 184). From each limb a small piece is taken (tshumbuta) and placed on a skewer ; it is the portion of the shepherds and of the butchers, (makotjo ya babyisi). (See the tale of Piti, *Chants et Contes des Ba-Ronga*, page 152). Sometimes the shepherds also receive the lungs and the spleen.

This way of distributing ox meat is called "ku tlhaba homu ba hamba milao," viz., "to kill an ox according to rule." Should a younger brother or a son kill an ox, he will send the breast to the master of the village, but he keeps all the limbs and does not observe the rules because, as he says : "It is enough to pay taxes to the chief of the country." Often one of the legs is sent to the chief of the clan.

Strange to say when a goat is killed none of these prescribed rules are followed, as they only concern the oxen.

These customs show clearly the position of the headman ; he is the master but also the father of his subordinates, and their provider.

1) He must *watch* over the village (basopa, Dutch word passop, universally adopted by the Natives). During the night, if his son is away working in Johannesburg, he takes care that no lovers come into the huts of his daughters-in-law, (a langusa bumbuye), and if he happens to catch one, he will make him pay the fine.

2) He is a true *justice of peace* amongst the inmates of the village, doing his best to maintain good relations amongst them. Suppose for instance that the pigs belonging to one of the inhabitants come out of their enclosure and over-run the gardens of another man. This man will go and say to the owner of the pigs : "Such and such a thing has happened, please close the pigs' kraal more carefully." Should the same thing happen a second time, he will complain to the *numzane*. The headman will then go to the culprit and say : "You have not heeded the warning ; you must pay compensation (djiha)." If the culprit listens to the "voice of the blood" (bushaka), he will obey and the matter will end smoothly ; if not, the headman can only keep silent : he has no soldiers, no means of enforcing his judgment ; the plaintiff will then go to the chief of the tribe to complain. The case will be

judged before the Court, in the capital, because the offender has refused to follow the way of persuasion, he has "mocked the family love" (a yalile bushaka). Such misdemeanours are very frequent in the life of the village. Most of the Natives bear philosophically with these annoyances. Should some one, however, be really ill-natured, and wear out their patience (wa ku karata), he will be forced to build a hut for himself, alone, outside the village. If the damage is done by *children*, if they have stolen sweet potatoes, as we have seen, the wronged proprietor gives them a good thrashing but does not claim a fine. Occasionally the headman himself thrashes them in presence of their father, and the father will say to them: "You see the numzane will beat you if you are not good." Children who mock at cripples are also severely beaten by him, all the more so as, in this case, the offended party has the right of claiming a fine.

3) The headman also possesses *authority over his younger brothers and his children*. He can even confiscate their money if one of them is addicted to drinking and ruins his property. However his authority in this respect must not be overstepped, and the headman must take care how he exercises it, as it is based more or less on sufferance. The younger brothers, for instance, maintain the right of making contracts, especially lobola contracts. Should the numzane restrict their liberty too much, they will leave him and found their own villages. A successful headman is he who knows how to keep the whole family together to the general satisfaction.

4) The headman has also the right of imposing *statute labour*, especially when the oxen kraal must be rebuilt, or when the weeds must be removed from the hubo ; he sends his young men to do the work. But he must not exact too much from his people or forget to feast them with beer or with meat when the work is finished.

5) Lastly the headman *presides over all the discussions* which take place in the village. He is the master of the hubo. The discussion can be conducted in three different places ; when it deals with a secret matter, the men go *inside the hut* : they debate the matter indoors (ba bulabula ndlwen). Private questions

affecting the life of the village are generally settled there. Questions discussed with strangers and those regarding which there is no secrecy, and in which every one can take part, are discussed *on the central square*, on the "hubo". *Hubo* means the square, and also the council of the men of the village which the headman summons there to settle matters (ku khanela timhaka). Should they be able to come to an agreement together or with their visitors who have come to bring a claim, the matter is "cut" (ba tjema mhaka), viz., "ended". In the opposite case, when they disagree altogether, the question will be carried to a third place, before the *hubo of the chief*, in the capital. (See Part III).

Every one is welcome to take part in the discussions except women. As a rule men speak as little as possible with women on these matters. If a husband has a sensible, discreet wife, he may ask her advice. But if he has agreed with his companions on a point and changes his mind after having spoken with his wife, he will be severely blamed and accused of "spoiling the village" (hona muti).

The headman is more or less *responsible for all the claims* lodged against his subordinates. Should one of his younger brothers be prosecuted for a debt, the creditors will go to the numzane, and he cannot say : "This matter does not concern me." He will say to his brother : "Pay your debt," and, if the brother has no funds, he will help him, if possible, but it is only a loan, and the younger brother will pay back the money. As a rule members of the same family help each other in these matters. This is so much the custom that children are expected to pay the debts of their deceased parents, even if they have not inherited anything from them. This does not however procede from a moral sense of family dignity. They do it because the native authorities hold them responsible. They might be "arrested". In the case of a father who has died still owing some lobola money, the children will try to pay, but they will do it in order to obtain possession of the woman. Should a father have committed adultery with a married woman, and die without having paid the fine, his heirs are not considered responsible. On the other hand, if the father has been condemned as a wizard

332

by the chief, and dies, his heirs must pay the compensation claimed. All these rules clearly illustrate the communism of family life and family property, under the supervision of the headman.

Should a numzane be absolutely unable to govern his village, *the family council can depose him* and put another man in his place. This council will be formed of old relatives, especially the paternal uncles to whom the younger brothers will go and complain of the misbehaviour of their headman. A younger brother will then be proclaimed and the elder will be despised. They will say : "Hi singe! A fahla muti, a hluli hi muti!" "He is a fool! He breaks the village ; he is overcome by the village," viz., not able to keep up his position.

As regards the *law of succession* to the headmanship, the second brother takes the place of the elder, and so on. The son of the elder cannot become headman until all his paternal uncles are dead. We shall find this principle also observed in the succession of the chiefs. (Part III.)

D. DAILY LIFE IN THE VILLAGE.

From the oxen kraal to the huts, from the square to the little wood, through the doors and in the reed yards, black forms are moving to and fro. Everybody seems busy. There is talking, laughing, playing and working. The expression "working like a nigger" is hardly applicable, for they do not kill themselves with work. It would, however, be quite as great a mistake to believe that the Natives spend all their time in loafing about. Far from it!

I. *Women's occupations.*

Women, especially, are very busy. When the sun rises, they emerge from their huts, wash their faces, and light a little fire to warm the mealie pap which was left from the evening meal.

In a small pot they prepare a fresh sauce of monkey nuts to season
it. The family takes its *morning meal* (fihlula) ; then, if it is the
season of tillage, *they go to the fields*, with hoes on their shoulders,
the shihundju (conic baskets) on their heads, and sometimes
their babies on their backs. The whole morning they will dig up
sweet potatoes, grub up their future plantation, or weed their

Phot. H. Gros.

Spelonken women preparing the evening meal after their return
from the fields.

mealies. In the heat of the day they come back in order to prepare
the evening meal. Sometimes, if the gardens are far away,
or when they are employed in scaring the birds from their sorghum
plantation, they remain the whole day in their fields, and cook
their evening food there, bringing it back to the village at sunset
quite hot (1).

(1) I saw a Rikatla woman coming home under such conditions, carrying her child
on her shoulders and the burning monkey-nut sauce in the shihundju on her head. Her
foot caught in a root ; she tottered ; the pot fell on the baby, which was scalded
to death.

Many other home duties may oblige the woman to leave the fields at noon ; her head still laden with her basket, she may go to the swamps, near by, and dig out a store of black clay (bompfi). She comes back, mixes the clay with the fresh dung which she has taken from the oxen kraal, and, spreading this mixture with her hands, smears the floor of the hut. This work is called *sindja* (Ro) or *kopola* (Dj.). Dust and vermin will at once disappear under this plaster of black earth, which will dry in a few hours time. Woe to the woman who has not put enough dung in this novel kind of cement! The floor will crack. The clay will shrivel and, when people walk on it, it will crumble into dust! The work will have to be done all over again two or three days later. But if the clay is of good quality, it will harden and last at least a week, the more so as neither wooden shoes nor nailed boots will spoil it.

Another woman will go with her primitive axe in search of dead ,wood. She makes a bundle which she ties with grasses, strengthening these grasses by entwining them with small twigs (1). On returning to the village, she throws her burden on to the ground, before the door of her hut, with the exclamation : "Hu!"

Others go to their storehouses, the small huts on poles, where mealies, monkey nuts in their husks, millet and sorghum are kept. They take what they need from these stores (tshaha) by lifting up the roof of the little hut, come back and empty the mealies into the mortar, whilst a friend rubs off the grains from the ears of millet or shells the monkey nuts. Two or three women seize their pestles and begin to pound, in measured time, the bottom of their mortars : Gu-gu-gu-gu. Quite a long way off, on the other side of the copse, this pestle song can be heard, resembling the noise of the flails when corn is threshed in the barn. And the busy women stream with perspiration! This method of crushing the mealies in an erect position, by a vigorous up and down movement of the pestle in

---

(1) Men, when they fasten a bundle with a string, make a knot (ba fundju) whilst women twist it with a little stick (sulela hi linhi) ; when a woman ties a knot, the two ends of the string will be at right angles to the string, whilst when a man makes it, the ends will be parallel with it. (Mboza).

335

the mortar, is a very healthy one and gives the Thonga women a straight and slender figure. In the tribes where the millet is mostly ground between stones, the women who do this work kneeling are shorter and stouter.

Before putting the mealies on the fire, the women go down to the village well, their round pitchers on their heads, to fetch the water they need. In the Ronga country these wells are simple holes dug in the sand, in the centre of the hollows (1). Wells are generally surrounded by thorny branches so as to prevent the cattle from coming to drink and fouling the water. It must be observed that it is not a spring which feeds the well ; it is the underground layer of water which has been reached, and which always maintains the same level except in times of drought.

Phot. A. de Meuron.

Shiluvane girls returning from the well.

The sun goes down on the horizon. The long shadows of the trees round the village lengthen on the square. Through the leaves, a few rays still reach the fireplaces and traverse the smoke which rises peacefully from the various kitchens. Between broken pots, or between the pieces of termitine clay which constitute the hearth on which the pots rest, the women place some pieces of dead wood ; when these burn away in the centre, they push them further under the pot where the flour is cooking (ba hlanganyeta ndjilo). Evening has come. The men have arrived. With a large spoon (nkombe) the lady of the house

(1) In the Transvaal, where there are rivers, water is taken from them, or from wells dug near the spruit into which the water leaks through the soil, being more or less filtered by this process.

places the food (phamela) on plates of the size of small basins or dishes (mbenga). We have seen how she distributes it amongst the inhabitants of the village. When all have finished eating, the women wash the plates, put aside the pots which contain the food left for the next morning, and tidy up the yards.

Whatever we may say, the day has been a well-filled one for the women. They are very rarely seen playing in the day time. We shall see how they recuperate themselves in the evening.

II. Men's occupations.

As for the men, their life is far from being as active as that of the women. They have not, like their diligent wives, the regular continuous work of preparing the food, not to mention the care of the children. The duties which fall on them, and which they are willing to perform, only require of them isolated efforts from time to time.

As regards *agricultural work*, it is generally believed that men leave this entirely to the women. This is exaggerated. Amongst the Rongas each man possesses his own field which he himself tills, and this is an old custom, a special term even being applied to the field thus tilled : it is called *mpashu*. He may sow seeds in it, but he does not weed it, leaving his wife to do this troublesome work for him and also to reap it. He makes only one exception in the case of the sorghum, of which he consents to go and cut the ears. But he helps his wife in other ways, for instance in the storing of the food; he builds the little huts used as storehouses, prepares the *tjala*, viz., the mat stretched on four poles on which ground nuts are dried in the field, digs holes for the *buhiri*, the shelf at the back of the hut where the basket containing the seeds is placed. His wife does not think him a lazy fellow at all. When the harvest is finished, she takes the smaller cobs of mealies (makunhula), those which will not be kept, or the grains of millet and sorghum which are found on the threshing floor after the threshing, and with them she prepares a special beer to

337

thank (tlangela) her husband for his kind help! This is her method of notifying him that all the grain has been harvested, as, whatever the man's share of the work may have been, the mealies belong to him.

The main work of the man is the *building and repairing of the huts*. This is truly an arduous job, but it is not of yearly recurrence. Every third or fourth year they are obliged to re-thatch the roof. The huts are built and repaired during the winter, from May to September.

A second domain, which is exclusively man's, is the *care of the cattle* ; the boys milk the cows, construct and repair the kraal : the little boys herd the goats, and the young men the oxen, as has already been mentioned.

·It is also the men who *make all the utensils and tools* used in the village, pots and other crockery excepted ; mortars, pestles, handles for axes or hoes (mimphinyi), wooden platters, carved or forged articles, all this work pertains to them. They must also make the *ntehe* for their wives, or sisters, after the birth of the babies. This is probably the explanation of the curious fact noticed amongst Native Christians, namely that they are much more clever at needlework than their wives. Big fellows are often seen forsaking the hoe to work with the needle, and there are fathers who make their own clothing as well as the dresses for their wives and children!

Hunting and fishing are, of course, also men's work... or pastime. For some of them hunting is an actual trade, at least such was the case in former times, before the White Governments imposed strict regulations and levied heavy licences on that sport. We shall study, in Part IV, the curious customs relating to these two favourite occupations of the Natives.

A great part of their time is devoted by the men to *paying visits*. They are very fond of calling on each other, and sometimes they go great distances to see relatives or friends. They do not travel to pay visits only, but they frequently journey to claim payment of their debts (milandju). To regain the possession of a miserable head of cattle they willingly lose whole weeks! And what endless discussions in the *hubo*, when an unfortunate visitor comes to ask for his property! What cunning displayed in confusing the real issue and evading payment! (1)

Travelling consequently plays a great part in the life of these tribes, and it is no wonder that it is subject to many rules and that many taboos must be observed on the road in order to succeed in these expeditions.

I may mention first the four following taboos.

A traveller must not *take salt* with him when he goes either to pay a visit, or to hunt, or on a business trip, or else he will not succeed in his object ; he must avoid *sharpening assagais* on the road ; this would rouse his enemies and "awaken thorns" on the path ; he must take care *not to pluck milala leaves,* those used for weaving baskets : it would be an insult to the people on whom he is calling. Let him cut these leaves when returning, or else he will find trouble in the village to which he goes, lamentations, shoutings, disgusting sights. When he finds on the road people occupied in *digging a grave,* he must go at once and help them for a while. If he neglects this duty, he will take upon himself the misfortune (titekela khombo). He will not succeed in his purpose. Should he be in the village when some person dies, he must take part in the purification of the inmates.

There are some kinds of animals which bring bad luck to the traveller. In order to "keep the road clean" (basisa ndlela), he must beware of the *mampfana bird,* a kind of crane called "the preventer of the journey" (sibaliyendjo (Ro) shitsinyariendjo (Dj). Should this bird fly across the road, with wide-spread wings, it would be enough to make the party return home : there is danger of death before them and the "mampfana" comes to warn them

---

(1) One day one of my neighbours, named Mandjia, was arranging to start for Bilene to "follow his goods" (landja bukosi) ; he came and requested me to give him a letter. "What for ? Your debtors do not know how to read and I do not know anything about your affairs." — "It does not matter," said he. "The important point is that I should have a paper in my hand. They will be afraid. They will think that I come from the White people with their authority." I did not like to refuse a small favour to a neighbour ; on the other hand I was somwhat reluctant to help him in a none too moral plan, so I gave him a letter addressed to the Portuguese Intendant of these countries in which I stated that I knew him. It was a kind of pass... What use did he make of it ? The fact remains that he came back with his oxen, and I believe the sight of the mysterious paper was not without influence in the transactions which ended in the recovery of his property !

that the road is not "clean" (Viguet). The flesh of this bird is used in the preparation of the charms carried by travellers. There are also two mammals which give the same warning : the duyker antelope (mhunti) and the polecat (mangobo). Should a boy going to Johannesburg meet with any of these three animals, he will go to his kokwana (grandfather) and ask him for help ; the old man will then take a mouthful of beer or water and project it towards the traveller (to make "phaa") with the following prayer addressed to the ancestor-gods : "You, so and so, look to this child who wants to travel! Bless him in his journey! May the Spirit of the bush (Shikwembo sha nhoba) remain asleep."

The *discussion of affairs* (ku khanela timhaka) on the square of the village also fills many an hour in a man's life.

On the whole, men have but little to do. We can fairly estimate at three months the time required for the work which they have to do for the village and for the community. The remaining months are devoted to pastimes and pleasure (1).

III. *Games of adults.*

Having already described boys' and girls' games (p. 66 and 172), I now proceed to those of the adults, as forming an important part of the Life of the Village.

(1) Much has been said and written about the division of village work between men and women in the Bantu kraal. I shall try to show in the Practical Conclusions, No. V that civilisation is bound to produce great changes in this region. But, as already pointed out, it is certain that to the Natives themselves their system appears perfectly natural and that the women do not at all complain of their fate. The following charming story which is told by a Moravian missionary, The Rev. Th. Bachmann, who lived for a long time amongst the Wa-Nyika, between Lake Tanganyika and Nyassa gives fresh proof of this assertion :

One day, as the rain was pouring down, I saw Walusangano returning from his garden with his wife, Leya. The wife was walking in front with a big bundle of wood on her head. On the wood was a basket containing maize, cucumbers and beans, as well as the hoe. On her back Leya was carrying her youngest child. The other children followed and the father brought up the rear-guard, carrying only an open umbrella. We were greatly shocked at this sight, and I thought it my duty to intervene on behalf of the women. On Sunday night, at public worship, I spoke of what I had seen in the most expressive terms possible. But my speech did not make the impression I expected. The men looked very much embarrassed ; the women indignant.

The following week, at sunset, I was under my veranda, watching the lightning and

The Life of the Village

1) Men's favourite pastime in South Africa is *drinking beer*. There are no bars on the velt... But every village is from time to time a brewery and a drinking place. Beer is prepared in large quantities. As we shall see, the brewing lasts about nine days. Near Lourenço Marques, Natives fill not only pots but big casks with it! One of the jugs is put aside for the headman to try it. He must pour a little of it into the *gandjelo* ; this religious act is obligatory. Next day the men of the village assemble in the morning to sample it also, and, at noon, all the friends from the neighbouring villages arrive. Everybody is welcome. Even a leper can take part in the beer-drinking ; but he will come with his own calabash and they will fill it with a special ladle. As a rule near neighbours also bring their calabashes, but people coming from afar are not expected to do so. The beer is drunk with great haste. Before it is all finished, the headman puts aside a pot for his father-in-law, his uterine nephew, and the friend who invited him on a previous occasion... Of course after having filled their stomachs, men and women dance on the hubo in the afternoon, and especially in the evening, when the moon shines ; the shouting sometimes becomes dreadful when drunkenness has overcome all

the rain which was pouring down. Suddenly I noticed the Walusangano family returning from the garden in the same order as the week before : in front Leya with the bundle of wood, the basket of vegetables, the hoe and the baby on her back, followed by the children, and behind, the father with the protective umbrella. "Such are the fruits of my efforts." I thought! But I refused to consider myself beaten. I said to myself : "I will speak to them once more ! The women will certainly be on my side, these poor overworked women !"

On the following Sunday Nesheye (one of the best Christian women of the congregation) came to see me after the sermon. She had something to tell me... She said : "You observe us, and you wonder at certain things. We also, on our side are observing you, and we see things which we also do not understand. When your wife does the washing, you remain standing by and do not help her. With us it is the men who do the washing. Again, we have seen your wife sewing and mending your clothes and the clothes of the children, and you beside her, not thinking of helping her. With us it is the men who mend the clothes."

Having spoken thus, Nsesheye put her two hands joined together on the mat, then separated them as if she were cutting something in two, and said to me : "That is the way your forefathers distributed the work, a little heap here and another little heap there ; and they said : This is the work of men and that the work of women. Our forefathers proceeded in the same way, and said : This is men's work and that is women's work... We must leave it so. The Gospel has not to concern itself with these matters. We do not wish to have the reputation of being lazy and you do not wish it either."

(From the *Journal de l'Unité des Frères*, January 1926.)

musical instinct. Some days later, another headman invites his neighbours to another beer-drinking, and so they eat and drink together (ba delana, ba nwelana) as long as there is plenty in the storehouses. When provisions become scarce, they begin to spare the mealies. But the advantage of the polygamist becomes apparent here ; his storehouses are many and he can feast his friends for many months.

These beer-drinking customs are essentially demoralising ; they

Phot. A. Borel.

Beer-drinking party in Maputju country.

are one of the curses of primitive Native life. But let me remark that, as the making of the beer takes nine days, these excesses cannot be very frequent, and the habit of drinking wine at the White man's store is ten times more harmful, as in this case alcohol is never lacking. We shall speak later on of alcoholism amongst Natives. (See Part IV.)

Another pastime, very much appreciated by some, but not so general, is *hemp smoking* and the accompanying *saliva contest*. Hemp (mbange) has been cultivated for a considerable time amongst the Thongas, especially on the coast, not to make ropes, but for smoking. The date of its introduction and its origin are unknown. The pipe used for smoking is made of a reed (lihlanga) with a small pierced wooden or stone ball (mbiza) fixed at its upper extremity. In the ball the hemp is placed and lit. The lower

Phot. A. Borel.

Hemp-smoker.

extremity of the reed is introduced into a horn half filled with water. The reed soaks in this water. With one hand, the smoker closes the horn, leaving only a narrow opening through which he sucks vigorously so as to form a vacuum. The smoke is thus drawn through the reed and the water into the mouth of the smoker. Its passage through the water cools it. Without this precaution the smoke would be too strong, stop the saliva, and

343

make the man drunk at once. It is called *shingwandja*, when pure, and is not liked, whilst they say that when it has gone through water, it has an agreeable taste. It makes the smokers cough terribly, but they thoroughly enjoy this exercise. Moreover it excites an abundant flow of saliva which is the chief requisite for their favourite game. They take a hollow grass, called *shenga*, and begin the fight by blowing their saliva through it on to the ground. The simplest form of the game consists in squirting as

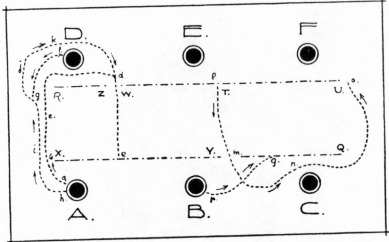

Drawn by J. Wavre.

Illustration of the saliva contest of hemp-smokers.

long streams of saliva as possible. He who squirts the furthest wins. But it is sometimes much more complicated. In the accompanying diagram the reader can follow the wonderful combinations of this game, called *ku tjhuma* or *hlazelana*. There are two sides, each with its pipe. Three men, A. B. C. oppose three others, D. E. F. First of all, each side protects itself by making a saliva fence, line X. Q. for the first side, R. U. for the second. Unhappily for D. E. F. the saliva dries up on the point Z. W. and so their fence is broken. A takes his advantage. He begins to squirt out his saliva on the line *a, b, c, d...*, passes through the opening Z. W., and, having come back victoriously to *e*, he has destroyed all the fortifications R. Z. Suppose D. wants to protect himself. He tries to close the access to his position by drawing the line *f, g*. But, arrived at *g*, he comes to the end of his saliva (a helela), and A. who started at *h*, having arrived at *i*, turns round the point *g*, where his enemy has stopped miserably, and, going on, *j*, *k*, reaches the opening *d* and triumphantly ends his campaign in *e*!

But E. of the opposite camp has noticed a gate in the barrier X. Q. The saliva has dried there. He quickly carries his blow-pipe across the battle field, squirting all the time, and passes through the opening Y. He draws the line *l*, *m*, *n*, *o* and so destroys the part Q. Y. of the fortification X. Q. Should B. be quick enough, he might prevent him accomplishing his plan by drawing the line *p. q*... And so on! Young men, even men of ripe age, take an immense delight in these saliva battles. But the saliva must be blackish... It must be *ntjutju* saliva, viz., saliva produced by hemp, and not the ordinary white saliva, called *matjafula*. Should one of the players try to supplement the blackish by the white, he would be disqualified... His enemy would seize him by the forehead, and force him to lift his head and stop his attack. Should he go on, however, the other would say : "What ? You come to me with matjafula!" This may lead to quarrels, even to blows... The hemp-pipe falls down and it all ends in cordial laughter.

This hemp-smoking custom becomes a passion with many young men. To cure them their parents break the pipe, take a little of the soot which is found inside, and mix it with their food without their being aware of it. When this has been done three times, it is said to fill them with disgust for hemp... Similia similibus curantur... We shall often meet with this medical principle in the Thonga superstitions.

The most interesting game played by men, a game which fascinates them and which is certainly more refined than hemp-smoking, is the *tshuba*. It is at the same time one of the most widespread games of mankind. Mr. Stewart Culin says, in the Report of the Smithsonian Institute for 1893 and 1894, that it is played under the same name by the American Negroes, and that it is but a variety of the *mancala*, the national game of Africa, which is found in many other countries, Ceylon, Indo-China, Bombay, Java, Jerusalem, Liberia, Abyssinia, Cairo, Gabon, Angola and amongst the Central African tribes. From the ethnographic point of view and for purposes of comparison it is, therefore, very interesting to note its rules all over the world. I tried (and I think successfully), to discover those of the Thongas, which at first seemed to me incomprehensible. The accompany-

Phot. A. Borel.

Men playing tshuba naer Rikatla.

ing illustration will help to explain them. The apparatus required is most simple. Let us imagine it played in its most elementary form, when two men only are engaged in it. Each of them digs two rows of four little holes, behind which he squats. They face each other. So there will be sixteen holes, eight belonging to A and eight to B. In each hole they put two stones, either real stones or fruit stones. Those of the kanye fruit are mostly used, but, by preference, Natives play with the pretty shining grey seeds of a shrub found near the sea, which resemble the marbles used by European boys.

No. I shows two players ready to commence, with the sixteen

holes filled. *A* must always follow the course 4, 3, 2, 1, 5, 6, 7, 8 and *B* 1, 2, 3, 4, 8, 7, 6, 5.

II. *B* starts. He takes the two stones out of hole 6 and puts one in 5, one in 1.

III. He goes on taking the stones out of one hole and putting them, always one at a time, into the following holes, till his last stone reaches an empty hole So he chooses three which are in 1 and puts them, one in 2, one in 3, one in 4.

IV. He chooses the three which are in hole 4 and distributes them in 8, 7, 6. The last one having reached an empty hole, he has succeeded ; he wins and takes the stones of *A* in holes 6 and 2, which are opposite the hole he has reached. This taking is called *ku tha*. Moreover he has the right to *kill* (dlaya) another hole by taking its contents. He chooses hole 1 I represent the regular taking (winning) by a black dot, and the supplementary killing by a cross in the hole. Having *beaten* (ku ba, such is the technical word employed when a player has succeeded in taking his enemy's stones), he stops and *A* starts.

V. *A* starts from hole 5, takes the two stones, and puts one in 6, one in 7.

VI. He takes the three stones in 7 and distributes them in 8, 4 & 3.

VII. He takes the three stones of 3 and puts them in 2, 1, 5 : "A bile !"—"He has beaten." He wins the three stones of hole 5 of *B*, opposite hole 5 which he has reached. Moreover he takes and "kills" the three which are in hole 8.

VIII. *B* takes his turn. He starts from 2 and reaches with his last stone 8 : "A bile" : 8 was empty. So he picks up the three stones in his enemy's hole 8 and the three in hole 4. He kills moreover the single stone in 2.

IX. *A* who has now only three stones left, one in 1, one in 5 and one in 6, starts from 6, puts his single stone in 7 and picks up those of holes 7 and 3 of *B*. He moreover "kills" 6.

X. *B* moves his stone from 8 to 7 ; he picks up 7 and in addition he "kills" 1 !

XI. *A* starts with his last stone from 5 to 6. But there is nothing opposite to him, nothing to pick up, nothing to kill!

XII. *B* moves from 7 to 6. He picks up the last stone of *A*

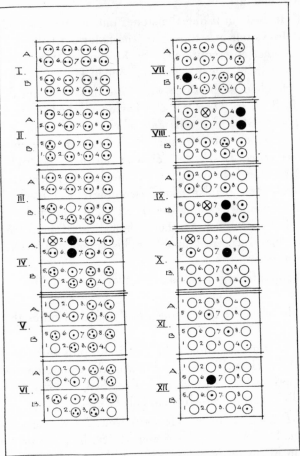

Drawn by J. Wavre.

The tshuba game and its laws.

who is thus beaten (a mphile). He has vanquished him! (A mu mphyinshile!)

The rules are clear enough and this game does not seem to be very difficult. It is, however, most complicated, and I do not

348

wonder that men sometimes spend half the day, bending down over the ground, talking with animation and sometimes fighting when they think that one of them has transgressed the rules.

When the tshuba has only four holes in a row, it is called *shimunana* (from *mune*, four) and is not very exciting. But it can also be played with 8, 10, 16, or even 22 holes, and then it becomes very complicated. Six holes will not do (a psi thi), because successful combinations are impossible. I have also learned the tshuba of 16 holes. Let us suppose our two players to be *A & B*; we number their 16 holes from left to right, the outer and inner rows bearing the same numbers. *A* will start from hole 12 outer row, and will follow the prescribed course all round his holes, going from left to right, until he comes back successfully to the same hole. He will shout : "tsheun !", imitating the noise of a gun, and pick up his enemy's stone in holes 12 of the outer and inner row, and "kill" in *B*'s outer row holes 15 & 13. *B* will start from hole 14 of the inner row and reach 12 of the same row. He picks up the stones in the two holes 12 of *A* and "kills" hole 3 in the outer row, etc. etc... Hours will sometimes elapse before one player has beaten the other.

A single stone in a hole is called *tshonga*. Two stones are called *mbiri*. If the following holes are empty, and if these stones cannot lead the players further, *mbiri* takes the name of *mpalati*. It is bad luck! (Compare No. IX, on the drawing.) When you arrive with your last stone opposite two full holes, and consequently pick up 4, 5, 6 stones at a time, it is luck! It is *malu*. When only one hole is occupied and you win only one or two stones, it is *muhaha*. You have beaten in a "muhaha". (U bile muhahen.) When you do not reach the place you aimed at, not having had enough stones, you are said "to sleep on the road." When you start, full of courage, hoping to succeed, you say ; "I go to kill meat" (ndji ya dlaya nyama), and this expression shows that the game represents two hunting parties. But it evidently also represents a fight, as do most of the games ; hence the cries of triumph which accompany it. When one of the players happens to empty two holes with three stones in each, he says : "The fight is hot! (sha lwa). I have captured warriors!" If they contain

349

but one stone, a poor *tshonga*, he says : "I have only caught women!"

Fighting and hunting are great sports for Natives ; hence the popularity of the tshuba game. It has become such a passion with the men that they neglect all their duties to indulge in it, and it has been necessary, in certain Christian villages, to prohibit the tshuba altogether, as the whole male population was abandoning its work for the game!

The *evening games* are happily not so dangerous for the moral well-being of the village. Women who have worked the whole day now have their innings. This is the *tha* par excellence, the most refined amusement, the story telling. It takes place at eventide. It is taboo to *tha* in the middle of the day. Those who should transgress the law would become bald (!), and persons affected with loss of hair are commonly and jocosely accused of having told tales at midday. So, when the moon shines, when all the work of the day is ended, all the inhabitants assemble at one of the firesides to amuse themselves. They rarely gather together on the hubo for that purpose, as the square is reserved for the discussion of matters of importance or for dances. The diversions at first consist of a parlour game, which is also known amongst Europeans, *guessing the charcoal piece (mhumhana)*. Two sides are formed opposite each other, women on one side, men on the other. One of the women, holding a piece of charcoal, puts it into the hands of one of the other partners, saying : "Dana, u shura ṅwanaaaa'nga," (eat and be satisfied, my child). Then both present their closed hands to the other side saying : "Mhumha!" The man opposite must guess in which hand the charcoal is hidden. He flips one of the four hands with his finger saying : "Give me! Here it is!" If he has guessed rightly, he has won, and then proceeds in his turn to hide the charcoal in the hand of one of his own side. When they have had enough of this game and wish to finish it in the proper manner, *they pull their fingers* and make them crack *(ku ba tindjwati)*. Each of them pulls a finger in turn. The first who is unable to produce a sound is expelled from his side. Then those who have been beaten make faces, as ugly or funny as they can, at their victors ; these must

350

keep serious and not laugh. Should they be unable to keep their countenances, their victory is lost!

But these games are only a preliminary. The farther we go, the nearer we get to true literature! Now they ask each other riddles *(psitekatekisa)*, simple and antiphonic. We shall study this form of folklore later on... If the second side is unable to give the right answer to the riddle, it asks permission to propose one in its turn and so the intellectual combat goes on until they have exhausted the series of riddles they know. Those who have had the worst of the duel must pay the forfeit by *telling tales (tha psihetana)*. A woman may be present who is a renowned story-teller and she holds the whole company under the charm of her tale for half an hour, perhaps longer... Children shudder when they hear the terrible story of the bogey man! They burst into laughter when she describes the funny tricks of the Hare, or of the frog *Shinana*. They heartily approve when the younger brother, despised by his elders, becomes their saviour and teaches them a good lesson... Thonga folk-lore is very rich; it is one of the most interesting manifestations of the psychic life of the tribe. We shall study it with the attention it deserves in Part V of this work. Here it is sufficient to show what a great and happy part it plays in the life of the village.

E. RULES OF POLITENESS AND HOSPITALITY.

The village life is dominated by the *respect for hierarchy*. I do not think this term is exaggerated. Etymologically hierarchy conveys not only a moral but a religious idea. This religious feeling is not absent in the fear felt by a younger brother for his elder, because the elder member of the family is its priest, the only possible intermediary between the family and its gods (See Part VI). So no wonder if, in their relations with each other, though these are extremely free and natural, Natives follow strict rules of etiquette.

351

In *addressing* an elder person, it is not becoming to call him by his name. You will say to him : "Tatana," father, or "mamana," mother, as the case may be. Or you address him by the name of his father preceded by Ñwa, if it is a man, Mi, if it is a woman. So Mboza was called Ñwamasuluke, and Nsabula Migogwe. You may also say to a counsellor : "Ndjuna," to the chief : "Hosi," to the headman : "Numzana," to any grown-up man : "Wa-ka-Manyana," viz., man of such a clan, or descendant of such a man. Even speaking of an adult in the third person, you will not use his name but employ similar respectful expressions. After the birth of her first child, the mother is generally called after it, not so universally, however, as amongst the Ba-Sutho. So Magugu, the wife of Spoon, became Mamana wa Modjadju, especially when spoken of in the third person. The names which are the most taboo are those of the mother-in-law, and of the "woman bought with my oxen." Speaking of a deceased person, one puts before his name the expression *"Matjuwa,"* which corresponds to our : "late." In the Northern clans, the word *shira*, grave, is employed for "late".

The principle *salutations* are : *Shawan* : Be saluted, said by the arriving guest, to which you reply also : *Shawan*. *Hamban* : Good-bye or *Salan* : Remain, is said on leaving, and you answer : *Famban* : Go, or *Famban kahle* (Zulu) : Go happily. Other greetings are employed only at certain times of the day : *Avushen* ! a kind of locative, "at the dawn," equivalent to "Good morning." (Vusha means dawn). *Hi nhlekanhi* : It is midday ! *A dji pelen* : or *a dji hlwen* : At sunset, properly : time when the sun sets. When retiring to sleep : *Yetlelan* (Ro.) : Sleep ! or *sibaman* (Dj.) : lie on your belly ; or *hi ta pfushana* : we shall say to each other good morning to-morrow ! A curious salutation addressed to people working is : *A psi fen* (Ro.) : Let it die. Its origin is as follows. When a man had killed a large animal, a hippopotamus or an antelope, his companions are in the habit of saluting him thus, hoping to share the meat with him. Now it is said to anybody working in the fields ; it then means : "Let your work die." The word "Nkosi," with which Natives salute white men, means Chief in Zulu. They lift up their hand when pronouncing it. It is not as if they were trying to raise their hats, as they do not wear any. The explanation of the gesture is this, according to a Transvaal Native : the Boers taught black people to point to heaven, when saluting a white man, with this meaning : I compare you with the One who is above!

In the Northern clans, salutations are generally accompanied by a clapping of hands (omba mandla). Men beat their hands against each other, placing them parallel to each other ; women do the same, placing them crosswise or at right angles. Amongst the Ba-Pedi this salutation with the hands is performed in a somewhat different manner ; when a Pedi enters the hubo, and wishes to greet a gathering of men, he claps his hands before his breast ; but when he salutes only one person, he bows down and claps his hands at the height of his knees, either on the right side or on the left. Amongst the Ba-Ronga, clapping the hands is a sign of thankfulness ; they say as they do so : *I khani mambo,* which probably means : "I dance before you, Sir." ("Mambo" means chief in the Ndjao language.) In Djonga the proper word for thanking is *nkomo.* The etymology of this word seems to be : "I homu," "it is an ox." If anyone gives me a hen, he presents it to me saying : "Take my chick." When he brings a goat he says : "This is my hen." In both cases I answer : "Nkomo," "it is an ox!" The Thonga etiquette requires that the giver depreciate his gift and that the receiver magnify it! Another less polite way of thanking is this : *Yengetan!,* — "do it again," or *ni mundjuku,* — "and also to-morrow!"

Thongas used not to *shake hands* in former times. Now-a-days the civilised Natives have adopted the European fashion, but this kind of familiarity is not approved of by the old folks, especially by the chiefs. Natives, when they shake hands, often do it in two movements : first they catch the four fingers and then slide on to the thumb. I do not know where they have learnt to do this! *Kissing* was formerly entirely unknown. A good mother would occasionally wipe her baby's nose, but this can hardly be called a kiss. When they saw the custom adopted by the Europeans, they said laughingly : "Look at these people! They suck each other! They eat each other's saliva and dirt!"

Even a husband never kissed his wife. On coming back from a journey, a man would hardly greet his wife ; she would see him passing through the village, prepare food for him, and when it was cooked, she would come and salute him by presenting it to him. But if he has a good friend in the village, and if this friend sees him coming back after a long absence, their meeting will be much more touching. The friend will go to the main entrance of the village, exclaim : "Ha-Ha," take his parcel from his hands, put his arms round his shoulders (a ku mu buso hi mandla), remove the perspiration from his face, and pat him gently, saying : "Your ancestor-gods have their eyes open! They have worked well! They have brought you back."

Hospitality. When strangers enter a village, men sit on the *bandla*, and women go further on and sit on the *hubo* ; they remain quietly there till the people of the village come and salute them (losa). Should the inhabitants delay too long, the visitors move on, saying : "These people are not good." But this is very rare. Generally the master of the village comes to them, inquiring who they are, whence they come, where they are going, and asks them : "Do you wish to spend the night here ?" If they say : "Yes," the headman will empty one of his huts by putting two of his wives together, and will himself sleep with the visitors. Should there still be food, he will give them some. If not, he says : "*Ndlala!*" "Starvation!" After a little while, a mat is unrolled and the official ceremony of "djungulisana" takes place. This is a very amusing custom. The headman sits together with his hosts and enquires about the news of their home. One of the visitors begins in a monotonous tone and pours forth volubly a flow of words with a peculiar cadence and almost without taking breath. His interlocutor interrupts him after each sentence, with "Ahina, hina," that is to say "Indeed, indeed!" till the whole skein is unwound ; the two men finish with a longer "*Hina,*" the inhabitants of the hut adding an emphatic "*khani,*" a heartfelt "thank you ;" then the master of the village begins to relate his own news in the same tone. It is impossible to imagine anything more curious than this "mélopée" in two parts.

This law of hospitality is general all over the tribe. Should travellers be refused the customary hospitality in a village and incur misfortune later on, the chief will make the people of that village responsible and they will have to pay a fine. In Gungunyana's country, warriors were sent to plunder such a village. Lack of hospitality, however, is not considered as a taboo (yila), because "it does not kill ;" it is a bad action (biha).

Now-a-days, customs are beginning to change ; hundreds of young men (magaisa) coming from the towns after working there, pass through the country, and it would be impossible to put them up and feed them all. They sleep on the *bandla* and cook food for themselves, occasionally buying some mealies or a hen from the inhabitants. Moreover they have plenty of money and they can pay !

It must also be added that, if they dispense hospitality liberally, the Thongas can be very hard on people who do not belong to their special clan. Feelings of humanity are sometimes strangely deficient. I heard of a boy of the Manyisa district who had fallen down near the lake of Rikatla, unable to proceed further on account of a bad wound received while working on the railway at Lourenço Marques. Nobody took pity on him because he was of another clan, and he would have died there if a Christian woman, named Lois, had not received him in her village and nursed him. Fear of death and its contamination may partly explain this want of compassion for strangers.

As already mentioned, it was formerly taboo to enter the village square wearing boots. These boots consist of sandals made by the hunters for their long trips through the thorny bush. They were not allowed on the hubo. A subject was not permitted to sit on a mortar or on anything else ; the chief alone could do so, and it was considered a sign of pride to sit on anything but the bare ground!

The habit of offering a concubine to passers-by is never met with amongst the Rongas as it is in other tribes. Now-a-days dissolute women may offer themselves. But they have learnt from white men this new kind of immorality.

On the fate of the Thonga Village, see Practical Conclusions. V.

355

THIRD PART

NATIONAL LIFE.

Having sketched the Individual and Communal life of the Thongas, we will now consider the National life. We have seen what the *muti*, the Village, means to a Thonga. What does the Nation, *tiko* mean to him ? As we have already pointed out, what we call the nation, tiko, is not the big tribe, numbering many hundred thousand people, but the special clan to which this Thonga belongs. There is no feeling of national unity in the tribe as a whole ; its unity consists only in a language and in certain customs which are common to all the clans. So the true national unit is the clan.

CHAPTER I

THE CLAN.

A. THE ACTUAL ORGANISATION OF THE CLAN.

Whatever may have been the social system of the Bantus in past ages, the existing clan can be directly traced from the patriarchal family. I have particularly studied the composition of two of the Thonga clans, the Nkunas of Zoutpansberg and the Mazwayas of the estuary of the Nkomati. Let us see how the clan is composed in both these instances.

THE CLAN

The *Nkuna clan*, which migrated from the confluence of the Oliphant and the Limpopo to the country round Leydsdorp, in or about 1835, is certainly of purer descent than most of the other Thonga clans, owing to its disturbed history, and its numerous migrations, which prevented other people from joining it, and strengthened the national tie. The common ancestor is Nkuna who, some centuries ago, left Zululand to settle in the plain of the Lower Limpopo. His son was Shitlhelana, his grandson Rinono. All the sons of Rinono are still known. One of them was the founder of the present royal family, and the present *hosi*, or chief, Muhlaba, is descended from him. The descendants of the others, who call themselves by their names, are the Mhuntanyanas, the Mashonganas, the Mbhalatis, the Kulalas, the Mushwanás, etc ; they form what is called the *doors* (tinyangwa) of the clan, each of these districts being under a petty chief, who is *hosana* (diminutive of hosi). So the nation is but an enlarged family, and everyone depends on his *hosana* and his *hosi*, the members of the royal family alone having only a *hosi*.

In the *Nondwane country,* on either side of the estuary of the Nkomati river, the situation is somewhat different. The whole land was first occupied in the XIIth and XIIIth centuries by three independant clans, the Mahlangwan, Hoñwana and Nkumba, which were on a lower scale of civilisation, having no iron weapons nor oxhide shields. They were scattered as far as the Mabota country and their numbers must have been very small. The first invasion took place before 1500, when a chief of the Lebombo hills, called Libombo, settled almost without fighting on the Western part of the estuary. This is the chief whom the old Portuguese chronicler Perestrello met in 1554, and who said to him : "Mena Libombo," — "I am Libombo." The original clans submitted to the invaders who mixed with them, being of a race not very different from them. Then, later on, came the clan now reigning, the Mazwaya, which conquered the whole country. According to the custom generally observed, the Mazwaya chief placed his relatives and his sons in the various parts of the land as petty chiefs (tihosana), retaining the old Libombo chiefs as counsellors (tindjuna) to watch over them and assist them.

357

This is a wise method of procedure ; the old deposed chief becomes responsible for the welfare of the new one ! Thus many *doors*, or provinces, were formed, and each of the petty chiefs founded a house and had his *shibongo*, his laudatory name. There were the Mazwayas Masinga, the main branch, near Morakwen ; the Mazwayas Tjakame, not far from them ; the Mazwayas Hlewane, Mazwayas Matinana, Mazwayas Makaneta, etc. As the complicated law of succession frequently leads to disorders, as we shall see, the main branch lost its paramount power and became secondary. The kingship passed to the Matinana branch. However the Masingas retained their authority in their own jurisdiction, and it would be taboo to place a member of a younger branch over them. The religious regard for hierarchical order prevents such an offence from being committed. Lately, as a consequence of the war of 1904, the Hlewane branch has in its turn -supplanted the Matinana. Thus, from all these facts, it appears that two hundred years ago the population of Nondwane was already composed of three different and successive strata. Since then, the situation has become even more complex. A great number of immigrants has settled in the country during the last century, coming in groups and asking the Mazwaya chiefs and headmen to receive them. This is a very frequent occurrence amongst Thongas. They leave their clan, either because they want change, or because an accusation of witchcraft has induced them to flee, and they settle in another country. When I was living in Rikatla, one of the outside districts of the Mazwaya country, before the war of 1894, the hosana was Muzila, a young man of the reigning family ; but there were very few Mazwayas under him. He had as induna a Tembe man, called Mandjia, whose father, Mankhere, had come long ago to Rikatla and was so well known that people used to call the district : "Ka Mankhere," "at Mankhere's." Another village belonged to Hamunde, a Djonga from the Shiburi country. A third had been built by people from the Manyisa clan, Ñwamangele being their headman. So the population of the estuary of the Nkomati, which, at that time, had reached the number of six to eight thousand, became very mixed. However the country continued to be called

"At Mazwaya's." It belongs to the Mazwaya clan. Such is the composition of most of the Thonga clans. Though their origin is certainly the patriarchal family, they are far from being of pure descent.

I am under the impression that this is the old, normal political state of the Bantus ; small tribes of some thousand persons with a tendency to break up when they become too numerous, as happened in the cases of the Tembe-Mapute and also with the Mpfumo-Matjolo, who were first united under Nhlaruti. (See p. 23.) During the first half of the XIXth century, South Africa witnessed the birth of many great Native kingdoms, in which a large number of tribes were amalgamated, thus forming much larger political units. This process began in the country now called Zululand, in 1800. There were then ninety-four different small tribes comparable with our Thonga clans, that of the Zulus numbering only 2000. They were amalgamated from 1818 to 1820, by the well-known military raids of Chaka, to such an extent that, in 1820, this terrible despot had more than 100,000 warriors, and had added half a million people to his tribe, having deprived three hundred clans of their independance. Two Zulu generals followed the exemple of Chaka ; Moselekatsi amalgamated the tribes of Mashonaland, and Manukosi the Thonga clans, not to mention Songandaba and the Angoni of Nyassa. The same process was accomplished more or less peacefully for the Bantus of Basutoland by Moshesh, and for the Ba-Pedi by Sekukuni, so that the original state of autonomy of the South African clans was generally replaced by large kingdoms in the greater part of South Africa.

Was this development a natural evolution of the Bantu clan ? I do not think so. We must not forget that the first idea of transforming the clan into a conquering army, the idea which inspired Chaka, was brought to Zululand by the Umtetwa chief Dingiswayo, and that he conceived it on seeing an English regiment in Cape Town. The military spirit of the Bantus, which might have remained quiescent for a few .more centuries, was awakened or stirred up by this sight. The seed found a wonderfully well-prepared soil, I confess. But without that seed, this terrible movement of amalgamation would probably not have taken place, and I think we may consider the clan life, as it is still met with amongst the Rongas, (who were never subject to the Ngoni chief), as the typical Bantu political state (1).

B. THE LAUDATORY NAME OF THE CLANS
AND TOTEMISM.

Each clan is known by the name of the old chief who is believed to have been its original ancestor. So the Nkuna clan comes from Nkuna, who lived four or five hundred years ago, and left Zululand for the Bilen country. The Mazwaya clan descends from Mazwaya, grandfather of Masinga and ancestor of all the heads of the sub-clans, Makaneta, Hlewane, etc. This name is a kind of *family name* for all the members of the clan. In the course of time, when sub-clans begin to aspire to independence, the first ancestor tends to fall into oblivion and is supplanted by the ancestor of the sub-clan. This process is easily noticeable at the present moment in Nondwane, where Mboza, for instance, calls himself a Makaneta. He says : "I am wa ka Makaneta," — "a man of the Makaneta house ;" but if he wants to be more precise, he will say : "I am a Mazwaya Makaneta." — "Shibongo a shi diwi," "the family name is never eaten, it is eternal!" (Mboza.)

This old name is called *shibongo* from *ku bonga*, to laud, to praise. It is a *laudatory name*. It is used as such on two different occasions : 1) *When people salute each other*. A friend who meets Mboza on the road will say to him : "Shawan, Makaneta," "Good morning Makaneta!" But also : "Shawan Makhetshe!" (Makhetshe is the grandfather of Makaneta) ; or : "Shawan Mazwaya" or "Shawan Ñwamasuluke." (Masuluke is the true father of Mboza.)

---

(1) The objection might be raised that, in former centuries, the celebrated Monomotapa founded a great kingdom. But what this exactly was, nobody knows. The descriptions of the chroniclers of those times are not very trustworthy, as we shall see from a quotation which will be made later on.

2) To soothe babies. Should Mboza's son cry, his nurse will say : "Miyela, Makaneta ñwa yindlu ya ntima," "Keep quiet Makaneta, of the black hut." It may also happen that some one wishing to console himself in affliction will do the same. Notice these last words : "of the black hut." They mean : "You who belong to a village where the huts have had time to become black ; they have never been destroyed by enemies, as no enemy dares to attack your clan! So the roofs have blackened inside from the effects of the smoke and outside from those of the rain!" It is customary to add to the name of the ancestor words such as these, in order to flatter more highly the man you salute, or the baby you console.

Thus each clan has a *laudatory phrase* which is sometimes much longer than the Makaneta one. Masinga is called "wa le hondjo-sin," "the one who reigns over the red earth," (more fertile than the sand). The Matinanas or Ngomanes are lauded thus : "Nkandjetele wa ku woma, ku baleka minambyana" — "the one who tramples on a dry place, and rivers begin to flow," because he is so heavy, so powerful! (Compare p. 87.) A Ngomane man will address his paternal aunt with the same words, when offering her a present.

Here are some of the best known shibongo. Their meaning is sometimes unknown, as they often contain ancient and obsolete expressions :

Hoñwana : Nwahomu ya ntima ñwa mu-Nondjwana, — The black ox of Nondjwana (or Nondwane).

Shirindja : Mudzunga ntima wa le dzungen, — Black South of the South ?

Mpfumo : Ba hlela misaba ba khabuta, — They winnow the sand ; they eat it. (The sand is so white in their country that it resembles mealies flour : they never lack food.)

Libombo : Libombo la Ndlopfu, — Elephant's face.

Nkuna : Ba homu! Ba nyari! ya makhwiri, Nwashitjimba buraka, ba mahlwen ka ntima. — Those of the ox! Those of the buffalo, the buffalo with the large belly which rolls in the mud, the one with a black spot on the forehead!

Rikotjo : Ba Nyamasi, — Those of the nyamari tree.

Khosa : Ba ripanga ro sheka ba ntsindja, — Those of the keen edged sword which "cuts" disputes brought to the capital. (The, Khosa chiefs were reputed for their wisdom in deciding judicial or political matters.)

Hlabi : Ba Nhlabi ba ku bengwa, Nhlabi ya Makamu ya Mavuse ya nkoñwana, — The Hlabi who are hated, sons of Makamu, of Mavuse, of the calf (?)

Hlengwe : Shikobela sha Matsheme, Tshauke wa Matsheme (names of old chiefs).

Tembe : Mulao Ngolanyama madlaya a nga di, makhama a nga di, a dlayele bahloti : — Mulao (son of Tembe ?), the lion which kills and does not eat, the hawk which kills, it kills for the hunters, viz., it is so well fed itself, so rich that it can leave the meat for others. Such a sentence was pronounced in former times by subjects entering the royal kraal, crawling on their knees, when they wished to receive food from the chief.

Nhlanganu : Ba ku hlomula fumo, ba renga ndlela : — Those who unsheath the sword in order to buy the road, (the right of passing through a foreign country) (1).

In addition to these laudatory phrases of clans, each individual has his own sentence or sentences by which he praises himself or by which others praise his qualities. They are specially common in the case of boys, but even girls possess them. In the case of chiefs, such praises are much longer. See for instance the praise of the Nkuna chief Muhlaba (Part III, Ch. III, III).

*

* *

If we cross the plain of the Sabi and reach the Drakensberg, we find that all the Pedi tribes dwelling together with the Thongas in the Leydenburg and Zoutpansberg district, possess laudatory

---

(1) This custom of praising the various tribes in such terms is so familiar to the Thongas that they have invented similar expressions for the white people. The Portuguese are : Ba ka nâofazmalo, — the Sons of Never mind, because they seem to the Natives to be somewhat careless or indifferent. The English are : Bana ba Nhluleki, a hluleka ku hleka, a tiba ku lwa, — the sons of the one who cannot, he cannot laugh, he knows how to fight! Perhaps Natives consider them, on the contrary, somewhat too earnest, too keen !

names which they also call *seboko*, the same word as shibongo ;
but most of these names are names of animals, and are called by
the technical term *muthupu*, totem ; the animal is the emblem
or totem of the group.   The Pedi clans are totemic.   This
means that, not only do they glorify themselves by comparing
themselves with an animal and taking its name, but they think
that there is a mysterious vital connection between it and their social
group.   I cannot give here all the facts I collected amongst them
on the subject.   They were published in *Le Globe*, the organ of
the Geneva Geographical Society, Volume LXIII, under the
following title : *Le Totemisme chez les Thongas, les Pédis et les
Vendas*.   Let me merely mention the following details.   The
Khahas of the Shiluvane valley have the small grey antelope, called
duyker, as totem.   They salute each other in these words : "Goni!
Phudi!"   *Goni* is probably the name of an old ancestor, the same
as Nkuna for the Ba-Nkuna ; but *phudi* means duyker.   They
consider it taboo to make a *ntehe* of its skin for their children.
Some of them do not eat the flesh of that antelope, fearing that their
children would become idiotic, or be covered with boils.   They will
not sit near a man of another clan who is handling the skin of a
duyker.   The Mashilas (Sekukuni's people), who have the porcupine as totem, say : "It is taboo even to tread on its dung; the soles
of the feet would become sore."   Many clans are afraid to kill the
animal which is their totem ; this is not a law enforced by the chiefs;
the totem itself punishes them if they trangress it.   However,
nowhere did I find the idea that they are descended from the totem.
They say: "The old people noticed that the flesh of such and such
an animal made the people of their clan ill ; so they proclaimed
it taboo." Amongst the Vendas, or at any rate amongst certain
Venda clans (Ba-Laudzi, Ba-Ngwe, Ba-Shidzibe) the totem is
connected with the ancestor-gods.   At his death, each member
of the clan is transformed into the animal venerated by his clan
and joins his congeners in the sacred wood where they live.
   Nothing of this kind is met with amongst the Thongas.   The
Thonga clans are *atotemic*.   Many men bear the name of animals,
but this is merely a means of glorifying themselves ; there is no
taboo with regard to the flesh, skin, or dung of that animal.   I have

come to this conclusion after a careful investigation. Here are
the only facts that I have discovered which may be said to
be connected with totemic customs.

The first is that the shibongo sometimes gives an opportunity
for *more or less witty jokes.* There is, near Rikatla, a clan called
Shibindji. Shibindji means liver. When a man of this group
meets with others who eat liver, they say to him : "Come along,
we are going to run this skewer through you and roast you!"
Another clan is the *Ntcheko*; this word means a tumbler or a
small calabash with an elongated handle used for drinking purposes
(p. 50). At the bukanye time, when everyone is getting these
calabashes ready for the feast, they say : "Alas! poor creatures that
we are! People are going to carry us from one end of the country
to the other, to dip us into their pots and drink out of us!.." And
so on. This is not totemism. I have however met with four more
facts which must be mentioned, and which are very interesting.

1) In the neighbourhood of Pietersburg a Thonga who belongs
to the Rikotcho clan, but whose shibongo is Ñwangwenya, the son
of the crocodile, is said to "dance the crocodile" (tshina ngwenya).
These Thonga words are the expression used by the Pedis to
indicate their totemic customs, (ho bina kwena), not that there is
any special dance or song performed in honour of the sacred
animal ; this may have been the case formerly, but is not so now.

2) The laudatory name of the Nkuna clan is also said to be a
ntshupu, though it does not imply any taboo. This word, which is
unknown in other parts of Thongaland, corresponds to the Pedi
muthupu, which indicates totemic animals. The Nkuna men like
to be saluted by these words : "Nkuna! Homu (ox)! Nyari
(buffalo)!" There are a number of Pedi tribes who "dance to the
buffalo." Mankhelu assured me that, as the Nkunas have the
same totem as these tribes, they have a common origin, and have
come from the same place in Zululand. This assertion is so
evidently erroneous that he could not maintain it. The old man
had not the slightest idea of historical accuracy: he had only
unconsciously drawn the conclusion of a common origin from a
similarity of totem. Moreover, in his set of divinatory bones, he
used to represent his own tribe by a small piece of ox bone, just in

the same way as Pedi diviners do for their various tribes, representing them by the astragalus of their totems.

As regards these two incidents, they are easily explained by the influence of the Sutho tribes amongst which these Thongas have been living for a long time. Nothing of the kind is met with amongst the Thongas who have remained in their own country, and Maaghe, the Pedi-Khaha chief, assured me that this appellation of the Nkunas, Nyari, buffalo, is modern and borrowed from the Pedis. The Nkunas do not observe any taboo in connexion with the ox, and this shows that their totemic custom is a mere external imitation of that of the Suthos. These two instances might be called cases of *secondary* or *adopted totemism.* Considering only the Thongas as compared with the Pedis, we might be tempted to conclude that the Thongas had preserved the old Bantu custom of naming themselves after their ancestor ; just as the Thongas used to add to that name other laudatory expressions, we might suppose that the Pedi tribes had adopted names of animals to glorify themselves ; in the course of time, the essentially totemic fears and taboos may have been introduced into the customs, owing to the importance given to the shibongo. This would be a rationalistic explanation of totemism. *A priori* it could not be said to be impossible. Though totemism appears to be a very old custom of humanity, it is not necessary, *per se*, that the Bantu tribes should have all passed through that phase of primitive belief.

3) I must, however, mention a third instance which shows that this notion of a community of life between an animal and a human group must have existed also amongst the ancient Thongas. There are, *in their folklore*, tales which seem to have been inspired by such old ideas now lost, especially the tale of Titishan, which I have published in "Les chants et contes des Ba-Ronga," page 253. A girl named Titishan marries a man. When she goes to her husband's home, she asks her parents to give her their cat. They refuse, saying : "You know that our life is attached to it." She insists, and they at last consent. She shuts the animal up in a place where nobody sees it. Her husband even ignores its existence. One day,

when she goes to the fields, the cat escapes from its kraal, enters the hut, puts on the war ornaments of the husband, dances and sings. Children, attracted by the noise, discover it and inform the master of the village of the strange dancer they have seen... He goes and kills it. At that very moment Titishan falls to the ground, in her garden. She says : "I have been killed at home." She asks her husband to accompany her, with the corpse of the cat wrapped in a mat, to her parents' village. All her relatives attend. They severely reproach their daughter for having insisted on taking the animal. The mat is unrolled and, as soon as they see the dead cat, they all fall lifeless to the ground, one after the other. The Clan-of-the-Cat is destroyed and the husband returns home after having closed the gate of the village with a branch (See Page 323) : "Their life was in the cat."

Folk-tales are very ancient, and this one is by no means unique of its kind. (Compare Jacottet's "Treasury of the Ba-Sutho Lore," Morija 1908, Masilo punished for having eaten zebra's meat.) It shows that the totemic idea existed in former times, in those primitive periods of evolution which some Bantu tribes have now outgrown.

4) A fourth fact tends to show that a mystic relation between an animal and a clan existed in former times. There is, in the north of the Transvaal, a kind of antelope called by the Natives *Shidyanaman*. It is taboo to kill it : "If a Nkuna does so, his family will die during the year, his wife, his children, his own head. Should he kill one by mistake, he must cry with a loud voice and shout : — Yoo! Shana n'ta da na mane! Alack! with whom shall I eat it ?" Mankhelu says it is taboo to eat its flesh, but the taboo is removed by this formula. The Ba-Nkuna do not know how to explain this custom. It may be a relic of former totemic ideas. However Mankhelu does not call the shidyanaman a ntshupu, a totem, and these customs may perhaps be connected with the *nuru* superstition (Comp. Ch. IV and Part IV, hunting customs). But even supposing that the Thongas have gone through the totemic phase, the present clans have entirely forgotten these ancient beliefs.

THE CLAN

*

*   *

My aim in the following chapter is to describe the typical Bantu clan, that small community of some hundreds or thousands of souls, with its hereditary chief, and not the larger tribe, formed by the amalgamation of many clans by a military despot (Chaka), or a cunning diplomat (Moshesh). Some of us have seen the court of Gungunyana at Mandlakazi, before this last South African military Empire was destroyed by the Portuguese in 1895 and 1896. Dr. Liengme, one of my colleagues, has described some of the striking customs of this court in the Report of the S. A. A. A. S. of 1904 and in the *Bulletin de la Société Neuchâteloise de Géographie*, of 1901. I refer the reader to these publications and shall be satisfied with the more modest, but not less interesting life, of the old Thonga clan.

In this small community the *Chief* forms the centre of national life. It is in him that the clan becomes conscious of its unity. Without him it loses its bearings ; it has lost its head. The republican conception is as far removed as possible from the ideas and instincts of these people! So it will be necessary to study first the customs relating to the chief. Then we shall see the part played by the *Counsellors*, a second institution which strengthens and limits the first. The political system of these tiny kingdoms having been sketched, we shall consider the *Court* and the *Army*, these being the two domains in which national life chiefly manifests itself.

CHAPTER II

The Life History of the chief.

A. BIRTH AND YOUTH.

(Information received from Tobane, and applying specially to
Ronga clans).

When the principal wife of a reigning chief, she who is called
"the wife of the country" (nsati wa tiko), perceives that she will
in due course present her lord with an heir, she is sent away from
the capital into one of the provinces, under pretext of illness. It
must not be whispered abroad that she is pregnant, for, from this
moment, every precaution must be taken to hide the future chief.
Thus, should the event occur in the country of Mpfumo, the
expectant mother might be sent into the province of Phulane.

The infant comes into the world ; should it prove to be a
boy, the fact is kept a secret. Only the most renowned doctors
of the country, those attached to the royal family, those who
are "the strength of the land" (le' ti yimisaka tiko), are assembled
to watch the birth ; they prepare, with special care, the *milombyana*
(p. 48). When the queen goes out carrying her child on her
back, she covers it with a piece of cloth to prevent anyone seeing
whether it is a boy or a girl! She even dresses it in girl's clothing,
because it is dangerous (psa henyanya), it is taboo to say in a loud
voice : "This child will be a chief." Such an imprudent declaration would bring him bad luck (singita), just in the same way as
would male clothing. (Mankhelu.)

The royal offspring grows, unrecognised, and is weaned in the
same way as other children. The mother returns to the capital,
the child remaining in the village where it was born.

However, specially appointed persons watch over him and report of his well being to his father. His youthful playmates are taught to respect him ; he is surrounded in his games by a miniature court, from which he chooses his favourites (tinxekwa) ; some of his companions act as counsellors and reprimand those who do not treat him with due respect. They play at court... also at soldiers ; the juvenile troop wage war with the wasps, and also with the boys of the adjoining villages.

When the child reaches boyhood, the bones are consulted, and sacrifices offered in order to ascertain from the gods whether it be well to take him to the capital. Should the answer be in the negative, there is nothing to do but wait. When the dice declare the propitious moment to have arrived, the transfer is effected and the boy taken to his father. This is a great occasion for the counsellors who have watched over the boy and who thenceforward supervise his education. They feast themselves well (ba fumisana), kill goats, perhaps even an ox, and offer a sacrifice to proclaim to the gods the return to the capital of the heir to the throne ; to his ankle is tied the astragalus of a slaughtered goat, as a protective amulet.

At puberty the boy undergoes, in the same manner as his companions, all the ceremonial rites usual at that period. The principal doctors of the country treat him, in order that henceforth he may be a man (ba mu yimisa a ba wanuna), having full right to enter into the sexual relations of gangisa (p. 97). Care is taken, however, to attach to his person comrades of riper age, who will prevent him giving way to excesses, (suka banhwanyana la' bakulu ba ta mu gema, ba mu sibela ku kula), which would arrest his growth and render him small and feeble. He thus lives in relative continence, participating in the play and in the work of boys of his own age, and looking after the herds. At times he gives a feast, when his father happens to have presented him with an ox with which to make merry.

Now we see him arrived at manhood, at the age when the Blacks take a wife. If his father is still living, the young man is not allowed to marry officially. He may certainly lobola, viz., contract regular marriage in the usual way, and possibly

369

some woman may come and live with him (titlhuba), as in cases of elopement — in which case he must go, according to the law, early in the morning to the parents of the girl and denounce himself as the abductor (p. 119) ; but none of these women can be his official wife ; they may bear him children, but these will be *makohlwa*, those who have no right to royalty ; the young chief may not wed his official wife, she who is to become the mother of the heir to the throne, until after the death of his father.

There is a saying, a precept of the royal code as follows : "Hosi a yi faneli ku bona ntukulu," a chief must never see his grandson, i. e. the one who will eventually succeed his son in the royal line. The Ba-Ngoni of Gungunyana (in Gaza) have the same custom ; but with them things are arranged differently. The eldest son of the chief's principal wife, when at the requisite age for marriage, takes a wife and loses the right of succession ; it is the youngest son, still young at the time of his father's death, who inherits the throne, because he has no children of his own. This leads to jealousy and civil war between brothers ; it has brought numberless misfortunes to the royal family of Gaza, and it was one of the causes of the downfall of Gungunyana. The Thonga custom is much more simple and less dangerous to the maintenance of peace ; the chief must not see his grandson, therefore his son will not be officially married until after his father's death. Any wives he may previously have taken will be morganatic and their children are not entitled to inherit.

I have been told by Mankhelu that when a chief lives to be very old and does not wish to delay the marriage of his son and heir, he can himself pay the lobolo and acquire, for his son, the official wife who will be considered as being "the wife of the country." But this seems to be an exceptional occurrence.

B. CORONATION OF THE CHIEF.

In all Thonga clans the death of a chief is kept secret for one year or more, as we shall see. Amongst the Nkunas the official mourning for the deceased takes place the same day as the coronation of his successor. All the regiments of the army are summoned, together with groups of warriors delegated by foreign clans. The mourning ceremonies are first performed. (See later on). Then, at the end of the afternoon, says Mankhelu, the great counsellors send a herald to the circle of warriors. He shouts : "Khaula!" viz., "keep silent!" The new chief comes out of the hut and stands alone in the midst of the circle. "Do you see him," says the herald... "It is the chief!" — "Who is he ?" ask the warriors, who wish to know his new name. — "It is Muhlaba Dabuka," he answered, when the present Nkuna chief was proclaimed. Formerly his name was Shikuna. Now he adopted this new name, borrowed from one of the Ngoni chiefs of Bilen. "He who wants to fight, can fight," he adds. This is an invitation to those who wish to protest against the coronation to state the fact plainly. When Muhlaba was proclaimed, the Masakomo family left the capital in anger, as they thought they were deprived of their right. (See later on.) Such an occurrence is not rare owing to the irregularities which so frequently take place in the succession.

If the chief is still a child he is carried on a shield, or put on the roof of a hut, so that everybody may see him.

In the Ronga clans the ceremony is conducted as follows. Let me describe it with all the details supplied by Tobane.

First of all sacrifices are made to the gods to ask that this ceremony may pass off quietly, happily, without quarrelling, and then the date is fixed. Invitations are sent to the surrounding little kingdoms, or at least to all those who are on friendly relations with the tribe. For instance, supposing the installation to be that of the chief of Mpfumo, invitations would be sent to Maputju, Tembe, Matjolo, Nondwane, Ñwamba and Shirinda. Manyisa and Ntimane are regarded as "being of a different mind" (moya muñwana), and "good will only reaches as far as the river Nkomati," to give a literal translation of the expression used by my informant ; this means that relations with the more distant countries are hardly those of even ordinary civility. The warriors of the invited tribes assemble, in greater or smaller numbers ; sometimes only a few delegates attend, but they do not proceed at once to the capital. Etiquette requires that each one should

first go to the Mρfumo Counsellor, who now acts as an Agent
General for his own tribe ; they are well received by him and fed
while waiting for the day of the coronation.

When it is known that all the foreign military contingents
have arrived, then the Mpfumo army is also assembled and all
together march to the capital.   The royal family council,
composed of uncles and the older relatives of the new chief, meets
in a separate hut.   The presiding member opens the proceedings
as follows : "Si hi humeliliki : si hi humililiki, hi fanela ku beka
hosi kutani!   (See what has happened!   This having happened
to us we must install a new chief!)"   The rest approve and reply
according to etiquette.   On an immense open space, all the
warriors form a circle (biya mukhumbi).   Battalion after battalion
takes up its position within this living enclosure.   An opening is
left in this otherwise perfect circle, and through it enters the
bodyguard, composed of young men of the same age as the new
chief, with the chief himself hidden in their midst, wearing his
full military uniform and accoutrements : ostrich feathers on his
head, strands of hair from cow's tails on his biceps and the calves
of his legs, etc.

A specially appointed functionary, the bearer of the chiefs
(mutlakuli wa tihosi), penetrates into the middle of the bodyguard
and raises the young chief on his shoulders in the presence of the
assembled armies.   The great counsellors, the secondary chiefs,
and all the young men of the royal family, then accompany the
bearer of the king and with him march round the inner side of the
circle of warriors, shouting as they go :

> Hosi hi leyi ! Dlayan ! Dlayan !
> Behold the chief ! Kill him ! Kill him !
> A ku na yimbeni !
> There is no other than he !
> Hi tiba yoleyi.
> We recognise none other.
> Dlayan ! Lwa nga ni yimpi !
> Kill him ! if there be any here who can raise an army (to oppose him).

To these shouts of defiance the several battalions reply consecu-
tively as the procession passes them : "Bayete!   Bayete! Ndjao!"
These words form the royal salute, to which all the independent

chiefs are entitled (1). The *elevation and the presentation* ended, the next proceeding is the *gila* or war dance. The heroes of the army (batlhabani ba fumo), and the young men of blood royal rush one after the other into the enclosure brandishing their weapons, jumping as high as they possibly can, imitating acts of prowess on the battle field and simulating the transfixion of their enemies. The *gila* continues until the cry is heard : "Ye-yi, yé-yi, ye-yi." This murmuring sound uttered by the whole army marks the end of the jumping, and all re-form into line. All the shields must now touch one another, forming an immense unbroken circle, and then comes the *guba*, the intonation of the solemn chant which is at once the principal patriotic song of the tribe, the coronation hymn, the dirge of mourning, the war-song, and the sacred melody par excellence :

> Sabela ! Sabela nkosi ! Ji ! Ji !
> Answer us ! Answer us, O chief ! Ji ! Ji !
> Si ya ku wela mulambu mkulu wa ka nkosi.
> Yes, we will cross the great river, the river of the chief.

This chant, which is in the Zulu language, is difficult to understand. The soloist commences with : "Sabela nkosi" which may be translated "Obey the chief ;" but the meaning would rather seem to be : "Reply to us, chief!" and, if taken in this sense, these words would be a request made by the army

---

(1) The word *Bayete* is said to be of Zulu origin and to convey the following meaning : bring thine enemies hither and destroy them ! *Ndjao* means lion. The warriors employ these terms to extol the power of their chief and, at the same time, to express their allegiance to him. There is a modern tendency to use this solemn salutation in a more general manner : for instance it is addressed to the Whites and not only to those in authority, but more or less to every one, even, in certain cases, to missionaries ! I always remember my arrival at the village of Shirinda, when I went to call on the chief Mahatlane, then unknown to me. I arrived at the gate of the kraal mounted on a most unpretentious little donkey and enquired of two young men who were there, where I could find the chief. " Bayete ! " was the salutation I received and there was certainly nothing very regal either in my appearance or my " mount." One of these young men proved to be Mahatlane himself ! *Bayete* is also frequently used in acknowledging a gift from a superior and would then be merely the equivalent of " thank you." In Gaza, Gungunyana would not allow Bayete to be said to any one but himself. All the petty chiefs of the Ba-Ronga insisted on their royal salutation and the Ngoni king could not put a stop to it, as they were direct dependencies of the Whites and did not derive their authority from him.

to the chief, to which he will reply by executing the dance which follows. To this exclamation of the soloist the warriors respond by striking their shields with their assagais, producing a hard sharp sound, which the chant tries to render by the syllable "Ji! Ji!" Then they stamp their feet, saying: "Vu! Vu!" and this enigmatic sentence follows: "Yes, we will cross the great river, the river of the chief." What is this river? Can it be that which separates the Mpfumo country from Khosen, namely the Nkomati? Or the Mitembe, marking the frontier between the Northern and the Southern Ba-Ronga? Or do not these mysterious words rather refer to the river of death, which the entire host should cross without hesitation if called to do so by their chief? Whatever the exact meaning may be, this chant must be an assurance of loyalty on the part of the warriors to their king and probably also an appeal to his valour.

The chant ended, no one is allowed to leave the ranks. The chief alone rushes into the enclosure; every warrior holds his shield in his hand and strikes it with hard sharp blows (ku ba ngomana); on hearing these, the chief begins to *gila* in his turn. He executes the war-dance brandishing his assagai, as if killing invisible enemies. The crowd encourages him, inciting him to still further efforts, crying: "Silo! Silo! Silo! Beast of the fields! Lion!" Volleys are fired. The chief redoubles his exertions, gesticulating furiously, perspires profusely, is well nigh exhausted and finally stops! The whole army sits on the ground and the young king is supplied with a jug of beer to quench his thirst.

When the ceremony has lasted long enough, and the warriors have enjoyed at their ease the spectacle of their chief's prowess, the Commander-in-chief dismisses the battalions, one after the other. The circle (mukhumbi) breaks up and all rush to the residence of their respective counsellors, singing as they go the praises of the particular army-corps to which they belong. The members of the royal family return to the capital, where they remain. A counsellor presents each group or regiment with the ox which has been allotted to it; this is accepted with shouts of "bayete." The men cut up the animal, divide the meat and eat it in their respective quarters.

It is worthy of notice that no sacrifice is offered on this day, neither is any religious ceremony whatsoever performed. The coronation appears to be a purely military affair, a sort of oath of loyalty taken by the people to their chief and by the chief to his people.

C. THE OFFICIAL MARRIAGE OF THE CHIEF.

The chief being duly installed, the next thing to do is to provide him with his officially recognised wife, *the wife of the country*, she who is to become the mother of the future king. This wife must be bought with the pennies of the people : a characteristic custom demonstrating forcibly to how great an extent the royal family is at once the property and the pride of the nation.

One fine day, says Tobane, when the counsellors go to visit the new chief, they meet with a very cold reception : "Who do you suppose is going to feed you ? Who will cook the meat ? Who is going to brew the beer ?" They return quite crestfallen, but having perfectly understood the allusion. The chief wishes to remind them that the time has arrived for them to find him a wife. This roundabout way of coming to the point is much in vogue with the Blacks. The matter is at first discussed in secret by the brothers and sisters of the deceased ruler, a family council which holds its conclave "in the hut," i. e. privately. After due consultation, a messenger is dispatched to the principal men of the country, to the heads of the younger branches of the royal family (to Khobo, Pulane, Kupane, if Mpfumo be the clan in question) with the following message : "Has not the moment arrived to set up the chief, to cause him to grow, to increase properly ? For the country is sustained by its cock! (1)" The great ones discuss the affair, each in his own village, and a

(1) *Dji yima ni nkuku*, a proverbial expression meaning : as the poultry-yard cannot flourish without a cock, so must care be taken of the chief of the country, in order that he may be able to perpetuate the race and secure the succession.

day is fixed for a visit to the capital where it will be concluded.

Let us consider the procedure in the case of the marriage of Ñwamantibyane, the youthful chief of Mpfumo, who has since been exiled. The following account of the discussion preparatory to the marriage is given on the authority of Tobane, a witness of the proceedings, and will aptly illustrate the etiquette observed on such occasions.

The dignitaries are assembled, and one of them, the brother of the deceased chief, commences thus : "Well, you the chiefs of Mpfumo! In truth! If we are assembled here to-day, is it not that we have truly seen that we must, in fact, increase the chief, and give him the wife of the country ? This is all the business, you, the chiefs." One of those addressed replies : "In putting the matter before us, hast thou been unequal to the task ? (No! understood.) And we, what further words could we add ? Nothing remains to be said... You then tell us what we shall have to give you, dwellers in the capital!" Then the secondary chiefs say : "For our part, we will give each one pound sterling or an ox, as you may prefer." The headmen of the villages will each contribute ten shillings and each village one shilling besides. In former times, before the circulation of money in the country, each one gave a hoe.

The secondary chiefs go back to their own districts and get together the money or the oxen as the case may be. This done, the fact is duly notified to the capital and all the contributions are conveyed to the chief. An account is kept of all monies or cattle contributed. When Ñwamantibyane was married the special subscription amounted to thirty pounds sterling and twenty oxen.

The future queen was chosen from the royal family of Matjolo ; her name was Mimalengane. The young chief had only seen her on one occasion, when she was returning from Gaza. Nevertheless she was his first cousin once removed ; Hamule, father of Zihlala and grandfather of Ñwamantibyane, married the sister of Malengane, chief of Matjolo, and his daughter was Mimalengane (the prefix *mi* signifies daughter of), who was now to become Ñwamantibyane's wife. We have already mentioned the fact that marriages between relatives are sanctioned in the royal families. The chiefs of Mpfumo generally marry into the reigning families of Mabota and Matjolo, and these latter seek their wives at the court of Maputju.

All the preliminaries being settled, the purchase money collected, the young girl chosen, Matshibi, the Mpfumo counsellor acting as Agent General for Matjolo, sent Ñwamatshabane, the boy who was his messenger, to Sigaolé, chief of Matjolo, to make the actual proposals for the marriage. The messenger did not address himself directly to the chief, but made his approach through the Matjolo Counsellor in charge of Mpfumo's affairs, whose name was Mambene. The request was made thus : "We have come to ask our *kokwana*, (that is to say our relative on the mother's side, p. 231) in marriage." — "It is well," replied Sigaole, when Mambene had transmitted to him the honourable proposal. — "Go home again, thou shalt come for our reply." A meeting of the members of the Matjolo royal family was then convened, matters discussed, the demand agreed to and the same envoy, attended by a companion, came, as arranged, to receive the reply. The hut was carefully swept and the enquirers renewed their message : "Our chief is still celibate... He sleeps in his bachelor's quarters" (This was not true, as he had already several wives, but they did not count!) "He is anxious to get married. Make haste to give him Mimalengane." — "It is well," said the others, "on one of these days we will go and discuss the affair at your place. When will you expect us ?"

A day is fixed and the great ones of Matjolo go to see Ñwamantibyane. A gorgeous reception has been prepared for them : an ox has been killed in their honour, but they are at first treated in a niggardly manner, and are given very short commons for breakfast ; for, before anything else can be done, the tiresome money question must be settled.

In the large hut all these important personages take their places with some constraint... The suitor is not present. The real business of the purchase money is not immediately referred to ; endless compliments, all sorts of circumlocutions are indulged in, of which the following is a resumé. One of the chief men of Matjolo commences by saying :

"It is quite right that you of Mpfumu have desired to renew to-day the old ties of relationship... Hamule your grandfather took his wife from Matjolo. Well! we are obliged to you. Nevertheless Sigaole has sent us to enquire how you intend to make payment for her ?"

— "We have thirty pounds sterling" reply the representatives of Mpfumo.

— "Ah! Thirty pounds ? That means that Mimalengane will have to chop her own wood and draw her own water ?" (That is to say : Thirty pounds suffice for the princess... but payment must also be made for two girls, the younger sisters (tinhlampsa), who must accompany her, to help her in the household duties, as is customary.)

— "We will ask Nwamantibyane what he has to say to this" continues the headman of Mpfumo.

— "How about those twenty oxen ?" says the chief to his representatives, when the matter is put before him. The envoy returns to the hut and announces : "There are also twenty oxen!"

— "It is well," say the men of Matjolo, "that will do for two girls to help in the work of the household."

Thus this delicate business is transacted without any great difficulty. The feasting then begins in earnest. All eat until they *shura*, that is until satiated, the stomach protruding in a gentle curve beneath the sternum, which is the black man's idea of a thoroughly satisfactory meal!

The betrothal being duly arranged, there still remain the betrothal visits to be paid and the wedding to be celebrated. Strange to say the chief, in these ceremonies, is conspicuous by his absence! His male friends alone go to see the betrothed, mainly with a view to reporting on her appearance, etc., to their royal master. Moreover when a chief is concerned, the betrothal visit of the suitor's friends is not returned by the girls, as in the case of ordinary mortals.

The marriage feast takes place, of course, at the bride's home. In Matjolo quantities of beer have been prepared, and the people of Mpfumo are notified when it is sufficiently fermented ; the latter then mobilise their military contingent, consisting of a picked battalion of youths and men wearing the wax-crown. They are magnificently attired in skins of civet-cat and other warlike apparel, but carry sticks only and small toy shields (mahahu), as the object of the expedition is eminently peaceful and entirely actuated by friendship. They go first to the house of their Agent General, Mambene, where they are met and conducted to the capital, taking with them the money and oxen which must be handed over to the parents of the princess. The curious sham-fight, details of which we have already given when describing ordinary marriages, also takes place on this occasion, the Matjolos trying to carry off the oxen and the Mpfumos defending themselves and endeavouring to appropriate the jugs of beer which are in the capital. This mock engagement is fairly lively, sticks are wielded with some force and the blows fall heavily until a few wounds are apparent and a little blood is let, when hostilities are at once stopped and friendship reigns supreme.

The money and oxen are given to Sigaole, chief of Matjolo, in the presence of witnesses. Mpfumo kills a bull for Matjolo and Matjolo slaughters a cow for Mpfumo, without any kind of religious ceremony : a sacrifice has previously been offered in Matjolo to propitiate their gods in favour of Mimalengane. On the other hand the young folks of the two countries execute the dances peculiar to each clan, trying to outrival one another, for the honour of their country. The guests pass one night at the capital of Matjolo and return to their homes the following day.

The relatives of the bride prepare her trousseau, which is not much richer than in the case of ordinary people ; a *ngula*, large basket, in which are placed some maize and other cereals which she will plant in her new home, sundry cooking utensils, saucepans, winnowing baskets, a hoe, an axe ; on the subsequent day, all the women accompany her to her husband's dwelling and then go to perform the ceremony of building the wood pile (p. 112). They are regaled with a couple of oxen and return to their home.

The chief's wife is not compelled, as are young married women generally, to live with the mother-in-law and to wait upon her

379

during the whole of the first year of married life. The chief, immediately on the home-coming of his bride, calls together his young men, who rapidly build for him a new village, his village, which will henceforth become the capital of the country and will be given a distinctive name.

Ñwamantibyane's royal kraal was known as Hlanzini, and he had chosen a site for it on the confines of the Ñwamba country in order to avoid a too close proximity to the Portuguese Commandant living at Hangwana.

Crowned, married, installed in his new residence, the chief has now nothing to do but reign.

*

* *

Mankhelu relates the proceedings of the official marriage amongst the Ba-Nkuna in the following manner : — All the principal headmen send an ox to the capital, assemble there, kill one of the oxen, eat it and discuss who shall be the "wife of the country (1)." They ask the chief : "Whom do you love ?" He answers : "The daughter of such and such a chief." They go to the father of this girl and say : "Eat the lobolo and give your daughter to the chief." The man may refuse. Should he consent, the girl will become the wife of the country : "the earth has bought her ;" she will give birth to the future chief.

Should a great number of oxen be provided by the country, those which are in excess of the lobola price will go with the chief and princess to their new village "in order to provide milk for them."

(1) In the case of Muhlaba, Mankhelu himself received the fifteen oxen of the lobolo of the village and kept them for a time. Other subjects had given £ 1, a hoe, a goat, or nothing, if they could not afford to contribute. Nobody refused, but some had nothing to give ! No matter ! In the meantime one of the oxen broke its leg. The mother of Muhlaba said to Mankhelu : " See ! the oxen of the lobolo die. Take a wife for the chief." Muhlaba was consulted and chose a girl from the Makaringe clan. Mankhelu had already taken a wife amongst these people, who were consequently his bakokwana. He went to them with the proposal ; they consented. Then Muhlaba accompanied Mankhelu on a second visit to the Makaringe people, who killed an ox for him and helped him to eat it !

The reason why it is not taboo for a chief to marry a near relative is this, according to Mankhelu : "Nothing is taboo for him because he is the earth (hosi i misaba, a yi yili ntshumu). He may even take a girl from the houses of his younger brothers because everything is allowable for him. He has no sin. He is the one who makes the laws. Even if they are bad, people must accept them..." This identification of the chief with the earth is most curious and we shall speak of it again when treating of the sacred character of the chief.

The wife paid for by the money of the country, though on the one hand she is the official wife, is on the other hand inferior to the first wife married by the chief. He does not perform the rites of widowhood when she dies (See page 202).

A chief, when he travels, always takes his wives with him.

D. THE REIGN.

I. *The sacred character of the Chief.*

Let me say at once that, amongst the Ba-Ronga, the paraphernalia of royalty are reduced to a minimum. The chief is as scantily attired as are his subjects ; possibly his belt of tails may be more plentifully garnished with these appendages. His huts are built on the same lines as the others ; his village may be larger, but is sometimes smaller (1).

(1) One day when taking a walk on the hill of Rikatla, I came to a field where, in the shade of a magnificent tree, I found three individuals — the three most powerful personages of the country — modestly squatting on their haunches and scaring the sparrows from their plantation of sorghum. The trio consisted of Muzila, the young chief, his brother and Makhani, his chief counsellor, who were devoting themselves to this tiresome occupation in the same way as the meanest of their subjects !

This same Muzila had several younger brothers, one of whom was engaged to look after our oxen, at a salary of ten shillings a month. One day the boy was ill. It happened to pour in torrents on that particular day, and whom should I see about ten o'clock in the morning, coming along absolutely drenched through and through, but the chief Muzila ! "I am looking after your oxen to day" said he "in place of my brother... Here I am, and I have just come to let you know that I am going to water them !"

In the old Portuguese documents, and in particular in an account written by a military commandant to the prelate of Mozambique, at the end of the XVIIIth century, the chiefs of the countries in the vicinity of the Bay were described in grandiloquent terms : "They are very powerful, very rich, most honourable, generous and respected." The Chief of Khosen is called the Grand Cacha, and is described as "a kind of Emperor." Though it is probable that, in former times, the regal paraphernalia of the Thonga chiefs were more brillant than now, these are manifest exaggerations, such as are often met with in the tales of the old explorers ; nevertheless there is a good deal of truth in these accounts. "Royalty," in the mind of the Native, is a venerable and sacred institution ; respect for the Chief, and obedience to his commands are universal ; his prestige is maintained, not by a great display of riches and of power, but by the mystical idea that, as the body lives by nourishment taken through its head, so the life of the nation is sustained through its chief.

The Thongas do not explain this in abstract words, but by images which are very striking. The chief is the Earth, as we have seen. He is the cock by which the country is sustained. (Tobane.) Mankhelu adds : "He is the bull ; without him the cows cannot bring forth. He is the husband ; the country without him is like a woman without a husband. He is the man of the village. Should a dog bark, if there is no man, nobody will dare to go out of the hut and ascertain the danger that threatens, nobody will have the courage to chase away the hyena. A clan without a chief has lost its reason (hungukile). It is dead. Because who will call the army together ? There is no longer any army! The chief is our great warrior (nhena), he is our forest where we hide ourselves and from whom we ask for laws. The counsellors (tinduna) cannot proclaim laws."

Conscious of this position, the chief does his best to maintain and to increase his prestige. He must not be too familiar. He does not eat with his subjects, except with certain favourites. Sometimes he eats alone in his hut. Or, when he has slaughtered an ox, he chooses amongst the various joints those he prefers, and feasts before his subjects, who look on respectfully, "swallowing their own saliva," (viz., their mouths watering the while). He sometimes throws a piece of meat to one of his favourites, who accepts it with both hands, shouting : "Bayete!" In the Tembe capital, men crawled on their knees before the chief, shouting: "Ngolanyama" "Lion!". Ñwangundjuwana, the chief of Ñwamba, was known for his more democratic ways. He used to eat with his men.

To shake hands with a chief was also considered as taboo before the days of Christianity. Now Muhlaba somewhat reluctantly accepts the hand which is extended to him by the most modest of his subjects, even by children on Christmas Day. The idea which is at the bottom of the fear is that the chief is a magical being. He possesses special medicines with which he rubs himself or which he swallows, so that his body is taboo (ntjumbu wa hosi wa yila). He is dangerous. "When he points at you with his finger, you are a dead man" (Mboza). Owing to the charms with which he had smeared his body, Maphunga, the chief of Nondwane, made those who discussed State affairs with him, even White people, "unable to answer him or to resist his will" (Mboza). In order to increase this salutary fear, some chiefs had the curious custom of *disappearing for a time* (tumba) "just like a big caterpillar when it enters the ground and becomes a chrysalis." The same Maphunga used to remain invisible during one week each year before the great bukanye feast (1). We shall see the same rite practised by the great magicians, who also aspire to create a deep impression on the imagination of the people. (See Part VI.) As already mentioned, the chief alone must be addressed by the royal salutation "Bayete" or "Baheti." The hosana has no right to it legally, and must be addressed by the term "Baba," "Father." As regards subjects, they are called *malandja*, from the verb ku landja,

---

(1) This custom is met with amongst the Pedis, where old chiefs abandon their kraals and go to live in the desert for years, leaving a prince regent in their stead. This kind of hermit life gives them great prestige. The Pedi chief Sikororo, near Shiluvane, is the best-known case of such a disappearance. Sexual continence, even repugnance to women, was one of his reasons for this seclusion, which lasted until his death. (1903 or 1904).

to follow, the followers. The Chief is the one who walks in front, whom the malandja, the ordinary folk, follow from motives of submission and fidelity, much as a dog follows his master from attachment, but is ready to fight for him should occasion arise.

The *name of the chief* must not be pronounced on any and every occasion. Should it contain a word which designates another object, the name of this object must be changed. So the Mpfumu chief *Ñwamantibyane* felt that his name was too similar to *ntibu* (diminutive *ntibyane*),a certain antelope. It was henceforth taboo to call this animal ntibu in his territory. It had to be called nguya. Zihlahla, the father of Ñwamantibyane, had gone even further than his son ; his counsellors complained that he gave them no meat to eat, keeping all for himself. "He is a dog," they said. The chief overheard the remark and took action in the following decree:"Let it be known all over the country that *mbyana*, the dog, is I. When you pronounce this word, you will be referring to your chief. I therefore command you hereafter to call real dogs *kalawana*." And this was done for some time. So, in Nondwane, people proclaimed as taboo the verb *ku phunga*, to sprinkle, and replaced it by *ku kweba*, which means to drink, in order not to offend *Maphunga*. This custom of showing respect by avoiding the use of the name of a chief in connexion with ordinary objects, is even extended to other men, if they are of particular note. So a great personage of the Maputju clan having been named Mahlahla, which means small branches, these had to be called mavinda. The prohibition to pronounce the name of the chief can go so far that even names of deceased chiefs are taboo, at least in the Bilen region. So the petty chief of Rikatla had been called *Muzila* after the great Ngoni chief, son of Manukosi and father of Gungunyana. But people used to call him *Mbozin*, fearing lest the warriors of Bilen might say : "What is this ? Where have you hidden him ? Show us Muzila. We assert that he died long ago!"

These are traces of the *hlonipha* custom, which is, however, not so much developed amongst Thongas as amongst Zulus.

The name of the chief is sacred in so far as it is generally used in oaths. When asked to swear, a Nondwane man will say : "Maphunga!" (1)

II. *The Regalia.*

Kings everywhere like to adorn themselves with specially imposing objects, insignia of their office, which differentiate them from their subjects. The Thonga chiefs have no peculiar crown — the shidlodlo belonging to all adults (p. 129)—, no special garment, no sceptre and no throne. We sometimes translate by the word throne *shilubelo* viz., the place where one *luba*, pays the tax ; but this is only a hut smaller than the others and subjects can also possess it. (See page 313). However there are, in some of these small kingdoms, royal objects which may be called regalia (bukosi bya hosi).

Amongst the Nkunas, the chief possesses a large copper bracelet called *ritlatla*, which was bought a very long time ago, in Lourenço Marques, by the Nkuna clan in exchange for tusks of elephants, says Mankhelu. According to others, the ritlatla was made in old times by Natives from the copper, or perhaps from the gold dug by them. The ritlatla was in the hands of the elder branch of the Nkuna clan ; Hoshana was its headman, but he had fled into the Ñwamba country during the troubled period of 1855 to 1860. When he died, his people brought the ritlatla to the chief Shiluvane who belonged to a younger branch, thinking that, at his death, the ritlatla together with the chieftainship would be given back to

(1) Kidd, in his *Kafir Socialism,* has asserted that Bantu chiefs are very jealous and kill their subjects when they become too rich and thus overshadow them. This may be the case in other tribes or when a military government has taken the place of the old patriarchal system. Amongst the Thongas it is not true. My informants could not quote a single instance of a murder committed by a chief for that reason alone. I heard of Shiluvane killing a subject called Muhluhluni who had acquired too much power ; but Muhluhluni had declared that he wanted to usurp the chieftainship ; so it was a case of high treason ! A rich nduna, in the territory of Nhandja (Nondwane), was also killed and his oxen taken by the chief because he had tried to abduct one of the chief's wives. But many headmen had as many oxen as Maphunga and were not troubled by him on that account : " Why should he hate them ? They could not harm him, as he was protected by the supernatural powers, and they brought him all the more beer as they had plenty of wives and consequently of mealies !"

them. But they were disappointed in their hope : Shiluvane kept both the ritlatla and the power and bequeathed them to his son, Muhlaba, as we shall see. Legends are current about the ritlatla. It is said to be able to move of its own will. "This piece of metal is indeed a wonderful thing," wrote a young Nkuna, to me "because when it is buried in the soil, as black people are in the habit of doing with their treasures, a piece of iron must be put inside it to prevent it from going away; if this precaution is not taken, the ritlatla may leave the place where it was and go somewhere else. In the space of one year, it may go as far as the Masetana spruit (about one mile)."

Another royal property of the Nkuna family was an *elephant's tusk*, which vanquished enemies had brought as a token of their submission.

In Nondwana, the old chief Papele who preceded Maphunga and lived in the middle of the last century, wore a *kind of chignon* or bun made by plaiting his hair, which was a sign of royalty (shifoko). But this custom has passed away. There was also *a long stick* which was kept exposed to the smoke of the royal fire in the sacred hut of *nyokwekulu*, which I shall describe presently, and which was called *ntjobo* and also *mhamba*, viz., offering ; this was evidently of religious value to the clan, and was taken outside when the army assembled. It possessed the power of becoming invisible to enemies. Moreover this magical stick was very useful because it warned the clan when some danger was threatening. The ntjobo was then put into a fire ; if it did not burn, this showed that the clan had nothing to fear from its enemies ; if it burned, it meant that the clan would be attacked and defeated. Then another stick would be prepared and put into the fire with the hope that it would resist it.

We shall speak in Part VI of another sacred *mhamba* which most of the Thonga clans possessed, made of the nails and hair of the deceased chiefs in the Tembe clan, and of the dried skin of their faces in the Shirindja clan. It was used as a means of propitiation in national calamities. In the Khosen country, the chief also possessed the *mhamba*. This was a mysterious object which the clan had always possessed, from time immemorial, from the beginning

"when the Ba-Khosa had emerged from the reed" (See Vol. II,
Part VI, III). Nobody might see it except the chief, who kept it
hidden somewhere in a hole amongst the rocks. His uterine
nephew alone (ntukulu) knew the place, and when it was necessary
to use it in order to pray to the deceased chiefs, the chief and his
nephew alone were permitted to approach the hiding place ; those
who accompanied them had to stop at a distance. This mhamba
is lost. Even the chief Ntshongi, who was the paramount chief of
the Ba-Khosa at the beginning of this century, had never seen it.
It had been taken by his predecessor Mavabaze and had disappeared
during the political troubles of the Gungunyana's war. Thus it is
impossible to say of what it consisted, and this will probably never
be known. There is no doubt however, that it was used for the
same purpose as the mhamba of the Tembe and Shirindja. Its
magical and religious power came from the fact that it was anointed
with the "nsila" of the deceased chiefs. On the death of a chief,
his "nsila" i. e. the layer of filth resting on his body, was taken
away and the mhamba was rubbed with it. This gave the reigning
chief the power to influence his ancestor-gods, in accordance with
the magic principle : the part influences the whole. It is said that
in former times the Khosa chief Shihanyisane having ill-treated his
two younger brothers, Malashwane and Shalati, these two men
succeeded in taking the chieftainship away from him with the aid
of the Ñwamba clan. Eventually Shihanyisane made peace with
his brothers and gave over the mhamba to Malashwane : a proof
that this mysterious object was in truth considered as the most
important attribute of chieftainship.

These regalia are not indeed very imposing to the eye. Thonga
royalty had no brilliant insignia... But it had more than that!
Each clan possessed a special medicine whose magical virtues were
greatly esteemed ; its possession made the chief invincible, the
warriors invulnerable, the country unconquerable. This powerful
charm is called *mbhulo* (Dj.), *mphulo* (Ro.).

Amongst the Nkunas, the mbhulo is called *Ñwantikalala*. It
is kept by those belonging to the Mushwane house, and a man
called Papalati is responsible for it. It consists of four calabashes,
two male and two female (medicines are considered as having sex,

see Part VI) called Madyakakulu, N̄wahondyane, Mbengatamilomu, Masemane. The bones are always consulted to ascertain which calabash (nhungubane) must be employed. The uses of this medicine are as follows. Every year it is mixed with the first fruits in the ceremony of *luma*, which will be described later on. In war time the mbhulo is employed to "fence the country." Envoys go to all the drifts on the boundary, take stones out of the river, smear them with the magical powder and place them on the roads, at the crossways ; should enemies invade the country, they will be deprived of their strength. The weapons also are sprinkled with a decoction made of this royal medicine, as we shall see, and it is given to the chief to prevent disease. The father of Papalati was accused of having sold some of this powerful national drug to the Pedi chief Sikororo, an act which amounted to high treason.

I have been fortunate enough to be informed of all the rites connected with the royal medicine in the Mazwaya clan. There, it is called *nyokwekulu*, a word which is probably derived from the verb ku nyuka, to melt. Let Mboza tell us, with awe and profound conviction, of the marvels of this wonderful drug. He was present at its preparation in the year 1893, before the war scattered the clan and destroyed its military power.

Each year the nyokwekulu is renewed. Its exact composition is known only to one man, Godlela, the royal magician and priest, to whom the care of preparing it is entrusted. This man belongs to the house, or sub-clan, of Tlhatlha. He is very much feared. Nobody dares to dispute with him, and he has the right of cursing even the chief. His function is *hereditary*. His father Malubatilo was in charge of the nyokwekulu before him. The law of succession is this ; when the elder brother dies, the position is held by his younger brother. The headmen of the tribe box his ears and say to him : "You will be the master of the medicine! Take great care of it." When all the brothers are dead, it passes to the sons.

So, when the right time of the year has come, the chief consults the bones. The first thing to do is to send messengers all over the country to find a *forked branch*, a "shiphandje," to which the calabash containing the medicines will be hung.

The Life History of the Chief

When they have chosen it—it must be the stem of a nkonono tree—they cut it and bring it back to the capital. In front walks the master of the ceremonies, Godlela, and behind him four men carrying the shiphandje. Those who accompany them have the right of entering the villages and stealing fowls. Woe to those who meet with this troop! They will be relieved of all they carry, "because the forked branch of the great medicine of the chief is taboo."

The sacred branch having duly reached the capital, Godlela proceeds to the second operation, the *burning of the drugs*. Mboza saw the magician take pieces of skin cut from buffaloes, lions, hyenas, elans, panthers, snakes of various kinds and, last but not least, from the bodies of men, enemies killed in the wars : part of the skin of the forehead, the heart, the diaphragm, the nails, a finger, some ears... All these are roasted in a large pot. On some mats are spread various magical roots cut into small pieces; these are also thrown into the pot. The chief and all the sub-chiefs approach and, with hollow reeds, inhale and swallow the vapour and the smoke which emanates from it (1).

The preparation of the great medicine having been sucessfully accomplished, the great drum (nhumburi) of the capital is brought on to the square, and everybody dances, even women, who take assagais in their hands and sing : "We are thankful if we die (hi tlangela ku fa)" viz., "The country is in security, our invincible medicine is ready! We shall not be killed by enemies but will die a natural death." Before extinguishing the fire which was used to roast the medicines, Godlela takes a little water, pours it on the glowing embers and, when it vaporises with the customary sound, he emits the sacramental *tsu* and prays to his gods, the departed spirits of the Tlhaltha family, as doctors always do, in order to obtain their blessing on the nyokwekulu.

(1) The Hlewane sub-clan, which revolted many times against the legal chief and succeeded by its intrigues in provoking the war of 1894, after which it became the reigning family of Nondwane, used to abstain from participating in this "swallowing of the smoke," because, in former years, it had been defeated by Maphunga's people and some of its men killed ; their flesh had been used in the concoction of the nyokwekulu. So they feared to go and inhale the odour of their fellow clansmen.

The royal drug, having been burnt, is reduced to powder and this powder is poured into the calabashes. The forked branch is planted in the sacred hut, which I shall shortly describe, and the calabashes hung upon it. Each sub-chief receives a calabash and takes it to his kraal, where it will help the district in which he reigns to perform the *luma* ceremony. But the greater part of the powder remains at the capital. There it will be used not only for the luma, and for the sprinkling of the warriors (see Chapter IV), but also for two other purposes : 1) for the protection of the country by means of the wooden pegs ; 2) for the filling up of the magical horn.

1) *The wooden pegs* (timhiko). A certain day is fixed for planting the forked branch in the house where the great medicine is kept. Then the doctor, accompanied by some members of the royal family, steals out secretly during the night and goes to the cross-ways, to the strategic points on the borders of the Mazwaya territory. It is taboo for anyone to meet with the party. He plants wooden pegs, and smears them with the powder. As soon as they have been smeared, they become invisible. No one can see them nor tear them out except Godlela. They do not rot. White ants do not attack them. The country is fenced by them.

Should there be any dispute as regards the boundaries of the country, Godhlela will be called. At once the pegs which were invisible appear ; they come out as much as a foot above the ground. If a hostile army was approaching, it will turn back at once, seized with fear at the sight of these pegs.

2) *The magical horn.* The remainder of the powder is mixed with a special kind of honey, the honey made by the small black bee called *mbonga.* This bee makes a large spherical nest deep in the ground. Natives have a number of superstitions regarding it. They say the mbonga honey may be eaten by anybody, but it is only members of certain families who can see the nest and dig for it. For other people it is invisible. (See Part VI.) The Ngwetsa family, in Rikatla, was one of the favoured ones! It must be said that the hole through which the mbonga bees penetrate into the soil is in truth very small and escapes the notice

of most people! This honey comes from below. It is a hidden, a mysterious thing. A little of it is added to the drug and the mixture is poured into a double horn, viz., two horns whose large ends are firmly fixed to each other, the point where they meet being carefully covered with dung, which acts as glue. A hole has been made in the upper horn and the drug is introduced through this. It is a great means of divination. When war is imminent, the nyokwekulu begins to ferment, and exudes through the hole : "It knows all about war." So the country can prepare for it. No wonder that this powerful medicine is preserved with superstitious awe and the greatest care.

A place of honour is reserved for the magical horn in the hut of the first wife of the chief. In the middle of the hearth a perpetual fire burns ; it must never be allowed to go out ; it is taboo. The wood used for it must be that of a tree found on the sea shore, and called ntjobori. The Makaneta sub-clan must furnish it regularly. It is taboo to take embers from this fireplace, which is called the royal fire, the medicinal fire (ndjilo wa buhosi, wa muri). Should the principal wife let the fire go out, then Godlela must be called on to light it again, rubbing together two sticks of a shrub called ntjopfa. The fire produced by burning this shrub is considered dangerous. It is taboo to cut its branches or to use them for the purpose of warming oneself ; the genitalia are said to swell when this law is transgressed (See Part IV). But Godlela does not fear ; has he not his drugs to protect himself ? He can and must use ntjopfa to re-light the nyokwekulu fire, and he will be given a good reward for his work! The ntjobori, in burning, produces an abundant smoke which leaves a deposit on the horn, on the forked branch and on all the calabashes containing the provision of powder.

The queen Mimpanyanhoba who was in charge of the nyokwekulu had no sexual relations with the chief on that account. I do not know if absolute continence is always enforced on the keeper of the sacred fire, as was the case for the Roman Vestal Virgins. But I have been told by Mboza that this woman prevented her co-wives from coming near her hut ; it was taboo.

The grass of the roof of this hut must never be removed, though it may rot owing to the rains. It is taboo. One simply puts a layer of new grass over the old one, a thing which is rarely done in the case of ordinary roofs.

In case of war, should the clan be obliged to leave the country, a special little hut is hastily built in the bush and the precious medicine is deposited therein. There is no fear that the enemy will take it, either Whites or Natives, because this hut also has the attribute of invisibility. This happened during the war of 1894 (1). In the case of the *mhamba* of the Tembe and Zihlahla clans it is different; the man who keeps it must run away with it and with the chief.

Such are the laws of the mphulo. This great medicine may certainly be regarded as a part of the regalia, and the most important part. It is, for the chief and sub-chiefs, a means of strengthening their authority, as will be seen in the description of the luma rite. On the other hand the mphulo is a collective possession, the powerful magic means by which the clan resists its enemies or conquers them. It occupies the very centre of the national life.

In the Manyisa clan the war-medicine is called *mabophe*, and is kept by a man called Chikiza, who belongs to the Ntjeko clan, not to the royal family. He is said to have inherited it from his forefathers. The medicine however belongs to the chief. It is administered as follows. The *ñanga* prepares small heaps of wood on the road, pours a little of the drug over them, sets fire to them and the warriors tread on the embers and extinguish the fire with their feet. This makes them invulnerable or at least protects them against fatal wounds. When they are ready to start for battle, the bones are thrown, and give the following intimation : "Do not kill the first enemy you meet with, but catch him alive, be it a man or a woman, and bring him to the chief." The chief, accompanied by some indumas, must stab him outside the royal kraal ; the body of the deceased enemy will then be cut open, and

(1) In the Nondwane the nyokwekulu is still kept by the heir of Maphunga, Magomanyana. The new chief, the usurper, tried to find it, but Godlela refused to give it to him. Thus Mubvesha has no *mphulo*.

the fat collected in order to mix it with the war medicine, the flesh being left to the dogs to eat and destroy.

In some clans, chiefs possess *other personal charms* which are very much dreaded and called *psitjemba*. So, in the Maluleke clan, each of the children of the ancient chief Mashakadzi received from him one of these psitjemba. It consists of a part of the skull of a child, the top of the head, where the pulse is seen beating at the fontanella. This has been smeared with the vitreous humour taken from the eyes of lions or elephants, and powders made from the skins of wild beasts. The possession of this charm gives the chief a supernatural power. If, being irritated with you, he invokes his gods by sucking it and emits the sacramental tsu, he can call on any wild beast he likes to kill you... He has sacrified with the psitjemba ; you will die!

Some chiefs of the Northern clans used to *swallow one of the stones* found in the stomach of a crocodile. It is said that crocodiles, when cut open, are found to contain a certain number of stones, as they are supposed to eat one each year, when the rainy season comes on. One of them is chosen and smeared with special medicines and swallowed by the chief. Natives firmly believe that this stone remains in the body of the chief, and that it is "his head, his life" (Viguet). When it is passed in his stools the first time, this is a premonitory warning. When it occurs a second time, it is a clear announcement that the chief is about to die. So chiefs can always know when their time is near. In other clans the crocodile stone is replaced by what is called *ndjalama*. Amongst Nkunas this word designates a kind of bright copper button, which the Pedis of the Palaora mine used to make and sell. But ndjalama also means large sized beads. Whatever it is, some chiefs swallowed the ndjalama and were warned by it of their death. This object, as well as the crocodile stone, is taboo for subjects to swallow. They would die. It is "buloyi bya hosi" — "the magical power of the chief."

On account of these powerful and dangerous charms possessed by them, chiefs of different clans regarded it as a taboo to stay in each other's company ; they were afraid lest they might be killed by the magical power of their colleagues. Maphunga seems to have been particularly feared. He had even bought poison from white people and is said to have killed his rival, Musongi, chief of the Maputju clan, with whom he fought the battle of Malangotiba in 1870. He sent a woman of bad life to Maputju. The woman succeeded in winning the confidence of the king and poured this poison into his glass. Nowadays the Ronga chiefs have been taught by the Authorities to sit in council when discussing matters.

The two principal prerogatives of the chief are the right of *luma* and taxation.

III. *The right of luma, and the first fruits rites.*

We come to a set of rites which might be dealt with when considering the Agricultural life, but I prefer to describe them here, as they provide us with a typical illustration of the constitution of the clan ; they are highly characteristic of the Bantu community, a community which is essentially agricultural in its pursuits, animistic in its beliefs, and hierarchic as regards its social and national life.

We have already met with the word *luma* and noticed that its ordinary meaning is *to bite* ; its ritual sense is to *remove the injurious character of a given food by a certain ceremony*. The luma is a necessity before eating the flesh of certain wild beasts, as we shall see when studying the laws of hunting (See Part IV). But it is of still more importance, and one of the great laws of the clan, that the official luma shall take place before the subjects eat the products of the new year. There seem to be two ideas at the root of this strange taboo :

1) To eat certain kinds of food is dangerous for one's health, and the first mouthful taken must be seasoned with the royal drug.

2) The gods, the chief, and elder brothers, have a prior right to enjoy the products of the soil. To precede them in doing this is a sin which would bring them misfortune. The hierarchy must be absolutely respected.

The Life History of the Chief

The law of luma seems to have applied to all kinds of food in former times. Nowadays it is not observed for the following products : maize, Kafir beans and peas, rice, sorghum, water melons (makalabatla) and monkey nuts. It is partly observed for mafureira almonds (tihuhlu), strychnos paste (fuma) and pumpkin leaves (magawane). It is strongly enforced for black Kafir corn and bukanye. Such is at any rate the case in the four clans of Nondwane, Mabota, Ñwamba and Tembe. Amongst the Zulus and Swazis on the contrary, I have been told people luma maize and do not luma kafir corn. Kafir corn is probably the most ancient cereal amongst the Ba-Thonga, and bukanye has always existed in the country. This is perhaps the reason why these luma rites, which bear a very old character, are still applied to these products to the exclusion of other more modern cereals.

I. *The luma without a religious ceremony.*

Let us first study the less ritualistic kind of luma, the luma of the *mafureira almond*, for instance. It is practised in each sub-chief's village, and, though it is tending to become obsolete, it is still enforced by some "tihosana." Thus my neighbour in Rikatla, Habele, the hosana placed by Mobvesha over this part of the territory, met some time ago a boy who was eating these almonds, the description of which I shall give later on.— "Who gave them to you ?" asked Habele... The child kept silent.—"Come with me to your parents !" Having found their home, the sub-chief scolded them severely : "You have started sucking (munya) the almonds before us. You wanted to kill my head ? Pay a fine !" They answered : "The birds made them fall from the tree... The children were not guilty !" However they had to pay 500 reis.

The luma of almonds, which takes place in December, when they are ripe, is performed in the following way. The almonds are dipped into a small calabash full of water to soften them. Some of the powder of the nyokwekulu is added to them. The headman first takes some for himself and then distributes them to his people. They suck the almonds, take in their hands the part which is not eaten, and rub their faces with it. But *no religious ceremony is performed*. It is the same for the *fuma*, a paste made with the contents of the kwakwa fruit, a kind of Strychnos very similar to the nsala, but of a different taste. The ceremony was even more simple than with the almonds ; the chief used to send a little of this paste to each village saying : "Let this be the first bite you swallow : the new year has come !" (Luman, ku tlhese nguba.) No powder was used in connexion with it. The magical drug was used, on the other hand, when the luma of pumpkin leaves took place.

II. *The luma of the Kafir corn.*

The great, the official luma, amongst the Ronga clans, is that performed for the Kafir corn (mabele). The great wife of the chief grinds the first grains of Kafir corn reaped in the fields. She cooks the flour in a pot and pours into it some of the royal powder kept in the calabash, so as to make a *shimhimbi* (See page 42). The chief takes a little of the food and offers it to the spirits of his ancestors, at the main entrance of the royal kraal. He prays to them in the following terms : "Here has the new year come ! Precede us, you gods, and luma, so that, for us also, Kafir corn shall help our body, that we may become fat, not thin, that the witches may increase the corn, make it to be plentiful, so that, even if there is only a small field, big baskets may be filled! (Nguba hi yoleyi! Rangan ñwine, mi luma, ñwi Psikwembu! Na hine, mabele ma tjhama amirin yeru psinene, hi kuluka hi nga wondji. Abaloyi ba yandjisa, psi tala ngopfu, nambi shi shisi-ñwanyana shi shiñwe, a ku tale tingula!)"

After this religious ceremony everyone luma in turn, the chief first, then the sub-chiefs, then the counsellors, then the warriors who have killed enemies in battle, then the headmen of the kraals who have all been summoned to the capital. Should one of the headmen be prevented from coming by illness, his younger brother will not precede him. He will bring him the *shimhimbi* in a leaf ; the elder will take it, and, after him, the other brothers. Women do not eat the magic powder. Neither do strangers, even those who are settled in the clan. They have their own medicine and luma for themselves, though they must not do it before the chief of the country.

III.   *The luma of bukanye and the great national feast.*

The most characteristic of all these ceremonies connected with the first fruits is the luma of bukanyi. Tobane has given me a circumstantial description of this feast and it deserves to be reproduced in all its details, as being a typical manifestation of Bantu national life.

The *nkanye* (1) is a large tree, one of the finest in the country. Its botanical name is Sclerocarya caffra (Sond); it is generally known amongst the English of Natal as the Kafir plum.

It bears fruit of the size of a greengage, which when ripe is a beautiful golden yellow and has a strong flavour of turpentine and a penetrating odour. It is a dioecian tree, the male bearing bunches of flowers while the female has single flowers. The Natives are quite aware of this ; they cut down the male plants but take care to keep a few in each district to fecundate the female. The fruit — the kanye — begins to ripen in the month of January and falls to the ground. The odour is perceptible everywhere, and it is then that the principal men of the country approach the chief and say to him : "The time has come to luma."

In the luma of the bukanye it is easy to discover four consecutive ceremonies :

a) The luma of the gods and of the chief.

The first ripe makanye are gathered and pressed at the capital, and the sour liquor thus obtained is poured out on the tomb of the deceased chiefs in the sacred wood ; they are invoked to bless this new year and the feast which is about to be celebrated.

---

(1) Nkanye, plural minkanye, is the tree in question. Kanye, plural makanye, is the fruit of this tree ; bukanye is the drink made from this fruit. In the same way the wild apricot tree is called mphimbi, plural mimphimbi. The fruit himbi, plural mahimbi ; the drink made from the fruit, buhimbi.

Nkolele, the sub-chief of Libombo, used on this occasion to pronounce the following prayer : "This is the new year. Let us

The "Nkanye" of Rikatla (16 miles North of Lourenço-Marques).

not kill each other! Let us eat peacefully! (Hi yo nguba! Hi nga dlayane! A hi nwenen ha hombe!)" Here is another formula : "May this bukanyi do no harm! May we not slay each other under its influence. May it cause no serious quarrels." They are afraid that, during the general intoxication which will shortly prevail, quarrels will arise, some of which may terminate fatally. During the whole month of bukanye drinking, all business is at a standstill, just as with us all bankruptcy proceedings and all prosecutions for debt are held in abeyance for two weeks during the New Year holidays!

The gods having luma first, the bones are consulted. Should the throw be propitious, the chief will luma next ; thus the opening ceremony of the feast is concluded.

b) The luma of the army.

The young people are now assembled to clean up the public square and all the roads ; the ball room must be prepared! The women of the capital start out early in the morning, beating the psibubutwana, that is to say sounding the call that is produced by striking the lips (bu-bu-bu-bu), and they go all over the country gathering the golden fruit ; this is piled up in an enormous heap on the public square and the brew is proceeded with in the following manner. The makanye are pierced (tshunya) with a pointed wooden splinter ; the stone falls covered with a transparent white pulp into the jar ; into this jar is also squeezed out with the fingers all the juice which remains in the pulp adhering to the skin ; this is continued until the jar is half full, when the stones are taken out, and on the following day the pressing is resumed until the jar is full. On the third day the beer has sufficiently fermented to be pungent and agreeable to the taste and is ready for consumption. Empty barrels are easily procurable in the environs of Lourenço Marques. The women of the capital brew ten or fifteen huge casks of the precious liquor! This accomplished, the second ceremony begins.

A convocation of the entire male portion of the tribe is held in the capital, but the first to respond to the call must be the men, the warriors of the army, who come in full array, with all their ornaments, and carrying their small play shields. One cask of beer is selected, into which is thrown the black powder, the great medicine of the land, called in this case *buhlungu bya miluru*, the powder of the miluru. The nuru, plur. miluru, is the mysterious spiritual influence which a man or a beast killed by the assagais can exert on the slayer, making him lose his head and commit acts of folly, or, at least, have red eyes (shenga mahlo). We shall again meet with this curious conception when

Bukanye drinking near Antioka. (Portuguese East Africa.) *Phot. A. Borel.*

studying the rites of the army and of hunting. All those who are proudly conscious of having killed a man in war must first drink the new beer which has been medicated to keep them from killing any of their compatriots during the ensuing weeks of the bukanye. They approach one after the other, the chief also, if he be a man-slayer. Each of them receives a small calabash, (ntcheko, p. 50) full of the fermented liquid. He jumps and runs in the direction of the entrance, drinks a mouthful, spits it out with *tsu* and says : "Father and mother! May I live! May I hold the calabash! Even to morrow! For ever!" People laugh. He is very happy! Others sing and dance the war dance :

"We drink the bukanye anew! Who would have thought that we should drink again from this cup", viz., "that we should have escaped all the dangers of war" (Hi nwa nkanyi lomu'mpsa! Afa hi nga hlayi epsaku hi ta nwa ntcheko lo kambe).

After this, the casks are distributed to the other warriors, who drink to their hearts' content. The addition of the black powder is not absolutely necessary in their case. They can luma without it. Then the war circle is formed and the principal counsellors harangue the assembled warriors, giving them the following advice : "Drink in peace (ha hombe). Let no one spoil this bukanye by transfixing his brother with his assagai. Go and drink in your villages. Do not pick quarrels with strangers passing through the country, etc." The gathering then disperses.

c) The luma in the village.

The preparatory luma is accomplished. The *yila* has been removed. Now comes the third act : the drinking in the villages.

The women who remained at home while the men-slayers went to luma at the bidding of the chief, have gathered large quantities of makanye. The tree is to be found extensively all over the country, as no female plant is ever cut down ; there is one or more in every field, and every one possesses such a tree, as every one owns a field ; when all the trees in the gardens have been stripped of fruit, the women pass to the trees growing in the bush far from the villages.

But here also everything must be done in right order of precedence ; the petty chief of such a district must commence to luma in the presence of his subjects, and not until after he has done so can the people drink freely in the villages. From this moment, however, there is no further restriction. Drinking continues day and night, night and day! When the supply is finished in one village, they go to the next. These feasts are the saturnalia, the bacchanalia, the carnival of the tribe! During these weeks some individuals are in a continuous state of semi-intoxication. Orgies on all sides, songs and dances! The younger men run along the paths, with a more or less unsteady gait, brandishing sticks with pieces of red cloth attached as pennants. They are in search of full barrels! It must be said that the inebriety produced by the bukanye is of a rather mild type, as this Native beer contains very little alcohol ; but the quantity absorbed is so enormous that it ends by going to their heads : this is more especially so with the bukanye brewed from a species of nkanye called *nunge*, which appears to be stronger and more intoxicating.

How far does sexual licence go during the bukanye ? Not to the point of general promiscuity, as amongst the Ba-Pedi after the circumcision school. However many cases of adultery occur. Men and women forget the elementary rules of condvet. They attend to the wants of nature in the same places, which is taboo under ordinary circumstances : "Nau a wa ha tiyi,"—"the law is no longer in force."

Still, in the midst of all this carnival, the payment of the tax must not be forgotten... This is the time to carry to the chief the liquor which is flowing so freely on all sides, but of which he claims the lion's share. Each petty chief sends his people to the capital with brimming jars. This is termed "lumisa hosi," supplying the chief with new wine. The women do not enter the capital at once, but go to one of the counsellors, who promptly abstracts a couple of jars for his own use. The chief returns one or two jars to the carriers, as they have come a long way and are doubtless thirsty ; the remainder will be kept to refresh the very numerous guests at the Court ; any coming from afar will spend the night and not return until the next day. I have seen a company of these women carrying baskets full of makanye to Muzila. How graceful was the Indian file winding its way along the path and singing, amongst others, the following chorus : (See for further particulars *Chants et Contes des Ba-Ronga*, page 46.)

Chwe ! Chwe ! Hi laba shimungu — Leshi ka — Le tilwen !
Chwe ! Chwe ! Shimungu hi mani ? — Hi Mzila ! — Hi Mzila !
Hi ! Hi ! We seek the hawk ! — Who soars — In the sky !
Hi ! Hi ! Who is the hawk ? — It is Mzila ! — It is Mzila !

THE LIFE HISTORY OF THE CHIEF

There is quite a collection of these carriers' songs praising the chiefs. Mzila (or Muzila), whom we saw a short time back scaring sparrows, is here compared to the mythical lightning bird, to the hawk that swoops down from the clouds. (See Part VI.) Why does he not once for all annihilate the sparrows which pillage his fields of sorghum ? But this is poetry! and there is often a wide gap between poetry and reality!

d) The feasting of the chief in the villages.

The fourth and final act of the bukanye feasting in which, as we have seen, the chief plays a prominent part, is the *nsungi* which may be called the "fin de saison" orgy. The chief now returns the visits of his subjects and casks of beer are prepared for him in every village. Dancing and singing are in full swing. He is fêted and acclaimed! But the makanye are getting over-ripe ; a new month, a new moon is at hand, which is called *sibandlela* "she who closes the roads ;" the paths leading to the foot of the trees become almost impassable, owing to the grass which grows to an incredible height during the rains prevailing at this season. The fine weather is over. Winter is knocking at the door.

Amongst the Nkunas the luma ceremony called "to eat the new year" (dyaka ñwaka) is performed with a special pumpkin (kwembe) cooked at the capital together with the medicine used for rain-making. The chief first eats of it in the evening and makes the sign of a cross on the big drum, which is then beaten to call the people in his village. Then all the men come, bringing the little horns in which they keep the rain medicine (See Part VI). They eat a little and smear the rim of these horns with the medicine ; the horns also must "eat the new year." Then everybody can enjoy the products of the harvest. Should anyone precede the chief, this would be fatal to the latter or make him ill... Such is the testimony of Mankhelu. I suspect these rites to have been influenced by the proximity of the Ba-Pedi. "Now we have no longer any first fruits' feast (mulumo)," says Mankhelu with some melancholy. "White people have killed it. Everybody

403

eats freely in his house according to his good pleasure. Formerly we used to take the oxen of the man who had dared to steal the new year."

Conclusion on the luma rite.

All these luma rites of first fruits seem to have primarily a *religious origin*. The Bantus do not feel that they dare enjoy the products of the soil unless they have first given a portion of them to their gods. Is it not these gods who make the cereals grow ? Have they not the power even of controlling the wizards who bewitch the fields ? These rites are also evidently dictated by the *sense of hierarchy*. A subject must not precede his chief nor a younger brother the elder in the use of the new harvest, else they would kill those in authority. Such an act is against order. We shall see that, even when the seeds are sown, the elders must take precedence. But the custom seems also to have been actuated by the idea of *passage*. There is a passage from one year to another. For the Thongas, I think the new year begins twice every year : it begins when tilling recommences, in July, August, when the heat returns. This is the hlobo. It begins a second time at harvest, and then there is passage from the food of the last year to the food of this year. This is the nguba (Ro.) or ñwaka (Dj.). Though the luma rites do not bear all the characteristics of a true passage rite, like those of circumcision or moving, we may observe in the luma of bukanye a kind of marginal period of general licence, when the ordinary laws are more or less suspended. The taking of a first mouthful probably signifies the aggregation to the new period, the magical powder used on this occasion being a protective measure to shield them from the calamities of this unknown year... And after all, is it not that feeling of fear which so easily takes possession of the heart of man when entering on a new state and starting something fresh, which has led the savage to surround the use of the first fruit with so many ritual precautions ?

IV. *Taxation.*

The chief governs (fuma). *Fuma* means to command, but also to live in plenty, to be rich. The subject (nandja, follower) obeys ; he follows the chief who marches before him just as the wife in the path follows her husband who walks at his ease, with his stick in his hand, whilst she carries his belongings in her basket on her head... If the prerogative of the chief is to live in abundance, the duty of the subject is to pay taxes! This duty is expressed by the word *luba* (Dj.), *hlenga* (Ro.). It is so true that this is the principal function of the subject that, when a man leaves his clan and goes to live in another clan, he comes to the chief and says : "I want to *luba* or *nkonza* (a word borrowed by the Rongas from the Zulus), to pay the tax..." This is the proper way of making his submission.

The explanation of the rites of the first fruits throws much light on the Bantu conception of the chief's position in respect to his subjects. For them he is certainly endowed with the divine right more fully than the King or the Kaiser in any European country ; he is the *son* of the gods, not only their protégé... The gods are the lords of everything... He shares this lordship with them. Hence his right of taxing his subjects. On the other hand we saw that he is the *soil*! He is more than Lewis XIV, who could say: "L'État c'est moi!" The Bantu chief can say : "I am the earth! — Le sol c'est moi!" Hence, on the part of the subjects, the duty of sharing with him the products of the soil and also of their hunting.

The Thonga chief taxes his subjects in four different ways : he takes a regular portion of the harvest ; he claims a part of most of the wild beasts killed ; he makes his people work for him ; he also taxes the revenue of those who go away to work for the Whites. A fifth source of his revenue is found in the fines imposed in judicial cases.

1. As regards *taxation of the products of the soil*, it consists in a basket (shihundju) of mealies contributed by each village at harvest time. This is the regular taxation. Moreover those who brew a great quantity of beer for a feast always send some jars to the chief, especially when the season of tilling the fields or threshing the grain has come. This is not a regular tax, at least amongst the Ba-Ronga, and is considered as *mashobo*, an act of civility, and not as *hlenga* proper. Bukanye must be brought to the capital in great quantities during the great national feast.

405

In the Northern clans it seems that these payments in kind called *shirwalo* (carrying of beer, from ku rwaɫa, to carry), are expected from all those who are not hunters and bring no meat to the capital.

2. The right of the chief *over wild beasts killed in hunting* is not the same for all game. Rhinoceros is not taxed ; it is even taboo to bring its meat to the chief. On the contrary when a man has killed a wild buffalo, an elan, a giraffe or an antelope, he must first cut some joints for the chief. If it is a panther or a lion, he must give up the skin ; if an elephant, the tusk which scratched the soil when it fell belongs to the chief ; it is "the tusk of the soil," and the chief is "the soil." The other tusk is for the hunter (ndlayi). In the Maputju country, it was even forbidden to kill elephants. Ngwanazi, the chief who was deported in 1896, had reserved the monopoly of elephant hunting for himself and his warriors. The hippopotamus is taxed more heavily than any other beast. The hunter who has succeeded in killing one has not the right of cutting it open. Should he do so, it would be considered a serious offence. He might be put to death. (Mankhelu.) He must at once send word to the capital, and the men of the Court will come immediately and cut up the animal, taking half the joints to the chief. As for the crocodile, it must also be opened by the men of the Court, because it contains many things such as marvellous stones used in magic, and bracelets of the women whom it has devoured. The chief appropriates what he pleases amongst these objects.

3. *Statute labour* is one of the main revenues of the royal kraal. In some cases, subjects must come to the capital, led by their sub-chiefs, and till a field for the chief or rather for the queen who has been bought with the nation's money. In Nondwane, which is a large country, each of the sub-clans must till a field for the wives of the chief in its own territory. For instance, in each of the districts of Mapulangu, Bandi, Manuel, Maghebeza, Malwan, Hlangunyingin, the chief Mubvesha possessed a royal field which his subjects weeded and harvested every year, and the sub-chief Habele, who was in charge of those districts, had to gather the mealies and carry them to the capital. This official tilling is done

in the form of a *djimo*. (See Part IV.) Moreover the young men are always at the disposal of the chief to clean his public square, build his huts, repair the thatched roofs of the royal kraal and organise hunting expeditions for him.

4. But the greater part of the royal revenue consists now in *money* which the chief receives from his subjects. Mubvesha taxes each village a sum of 500 reis besides the regular basket of mealies. At the end of the bukanye feast, each village must send him another 500 reis to notify him that the feast is ended. When a young man returns from Johannesburg having made enough money to lobola a wife, he must leave £ 1.10.0 in the hands of the chief. The latter also recruits boys whom he sends to the recruiting agents, getting as much as £ 1 or £ 1.10.0 per head. When a sub-chief dies, his people inform the paramount chief of his death, bringing a sum of money (1500 reis). The chief, however, does not receive any portion of the inheritance in the case of a death. There is no taxation on the succession.

5. A great deal of money comes into the hands of the chief *owing to fines which he imposes* when acting as supreme judge. When a plaintiff brings a case and the culprit is condemned to pay him £ 25, Mubvesha keeps £ 10 for himself ; he retains £ 5 if the fine is £ 10.

Sub-chiefs do not tax their subjects as a rule. They must bring to their superior all the products of taxation. They do not "eat" anything. But in some cases the chief gives them a part of it. Thus Habele, sub-chief of Rikatla, used to "eat" half of the taxes brought to him by young men coming back from Johannesburg.

V. *Dangers and difficulties of the Chieftainship.*

Endowed with supernatural power which he owes to his magical medicines, feared and sometimes loved by his subjects, with plenty to eat and richer than any of his people, who readily consent to be taxed, the chief occupies an enviable position. The chieftainship (buhosi), therefore, is very much sought after and no one refuses to be a chief. Thonga tales recounting the story of some one who succeeded wonderfully in life often conclude by saying that this person was given a territory and became a chief... which seems to be the highest reward of virtue or wisdom. Nowadays, however, one may meet with cases where the heir to the chieftainship, having become a Christian, renounces that high position because he feels that there is an incompatibility between the Bantu way of ruling and his new faith.

But it would be a great error to think that a Thonga chief is, or can be, an autocratic despot. This may have been the case with Chaka, Lobengula or Gungunyana, when the tribe became an amalgamation of clans held together by military power ; in order to maintain their usurped authority, these chiefs had to be cruel despots. But this is a late development in the Bantu political system. I am now only taking into consideration the primitive form of tribal life, which is the clan life.

For a chief dangers may arise from three sources : from his own character, from the Thonga system of government itself, and from the law of succession.

1) THE CHARACTER OF THE CHIEF.

A chief who wishes to succeed in his government *must have a good character*. If he imposes taxation, he must not use his wealth in a selfish way. For instance, when women bring him a *shirwalo* of a dozen pots of beer, he must give them back one or two to quench their thirst. Moreover he must distribute most of the remaining pots to his men, who are on the *bandla*, always ready to share with him the advantages of his position.

Should he buy oxen with the product of the fines, he will be wise to slaughter one from time to time for his counsellors and for the whole clan. A chief who is good (a ni timpsalu) is said to *maintain* or to *save the country* (bekisa tiko). If he does not do that, he is severely criticised. Mubvesha, who used all his money to buy wives, and prevented all the men from seeing them, whilst he himself was too old to content them, was considered

408

a bad chief. He did not even allow "bandla," viz, the gathering of men in the capital, because he was full of jealousy (mona). If he had not been placed in the chieftainship and supported by the White Government, he might have been deposed. Cases in which a chief has been deprived of his right and replaced by another man are not wanting (1). I have even heard of a chief in the Shiridja clan who was put to death. Deposal is generally proclaimed by a council of the royal family.

To reign over a Bantu clan requires much tact, ability and patience. The chief must be a father to his people and not a tyrant (2).

2) THE SYSTEM OF GOVERNMENT.

In order to keep in touch with his subjects, a chief generally places his wives in the various provinces of his little kingdom

(1) The annals of the Nkuna tribe provide an instance of the deposal not only of a certain chief but of the elder branch of the royal family, owing to an act which hurt the human feelings of the clan. We have already met with the name of Shithlelana, son of Nkuna, who lived at least 300 years ago. His principal wife was Ñwahubyana. In his old age he was very ill and the woman, fearing lest he should die in her hut, drove him away ; he was obliged to take refuge in the hut of another of his wives, Ñwantimba, mother of Rinono, and died there. Then the headmen assembled and said : "As Ñwahubyana has driven away her husband from her hut, she has also driven away the chieftainship from her son. He shall not reign. Rinono shall reign because he is the son of the woman who took care of the sick chief." This story, in which we see the sacred law of succession transgressed for a moral reason, is most interesting because it provides a good illustration of the conception of the clan regarding chieftainship, and proves that, even in ancient times, feelings of humanity could have more weight with the tribe than an article of the royal code.

(2) Two interesting Thonga riddles illustrate this disposition to criticise chiefs. The first riddle enigmatically describes the characteristics of an unworthy chief ; it comes from the banks of the Limpopo :

Bupsa ga shisule. — Hosi leyi i ni mona...
Some cyclamen flour. — This chief is full of hatred...

The shisule — a word which I translate by cyclamen — is a plant which grows on the ant-hills, bearing large tubercles; these can be cooked and ground into flour; but it is only good in appearance. the taste is unpleasant and nauseating. This chief is bad ! He is like that flour ! Corruptio optimi pessima !

Here is another riddle which holds the chiefs up to ridicule rather wittily :

Tinsindji tibiri ti rendjeleka tchuka. — Tihosi tibiri ti hleba nandja.

Two mice chase one another round an ant-hill (They will never meet) — Two chiefs malign a subject. (They also will never meet, i. e. agree.)

Each wants to have the last word and will therefore depreciate the arguments of his opponent. He will seek to disprove the statements of the other chief, making fresh ones which the latter will seek to refute in his turn !

and pays them regular visits, staying some days in these secondary capitals.

But a more effective way of holding the country is to place his son or his near relatives as sub-chiefs in all these districts. If the son is still young, the chief will send along with him a trustworthy counsellor to watch over him. Thus, when he dies, and when the elder son is called to the succession, the new chief will have his brothers as co-chiefs or sub-chiefs. Should they be ambitious, should they have acquired some power during the last years of their father's government, they may refuse to obey and proclaim themselves independent. This has happened many times amongst the Rongas. Let me shortly recapitulate the three instances already mentioned. In the Tembe kingdom Maputju, who "ate the foreleg," made himself king of the greater part of the territory. The separated brothers became fierce enemies and often fought against each other, all the more as Tembe greatly resented the revolt of Maputju, and Maputju knew he had not been fair to his elder brother (p. 329). The same thing happened when Matjolo became independent of Mpfumo, his elder brother ; both were sons of Nhlaruti. The origin of the war of 1894-1896 was the same ; Mubvesha, belonging to the Hlewana branch of the Mazwaya family, wished to become independent... even to take the chieftainship from the elder branch to which Maphunga and his successor Mahazule belonged.

So the Thonga clan has a tendency to fall to pieces, just like the Thonga village, and it requires a good deal of firmness and diplomacy on the part of a chief to keep his kingdom intact.

3) THE LAW OF SUCCESSION.

Its main provision is this ; when a chief dies, his elder son is the regular heir, but all his younger brothers must reign before the son, the true heir, is crowned. This system attempts to reconcile two principles which we have already met with as governing the family life : 1) the absolute preeminent right of the elder branch, 2) the community of property amongst brothers.

But whilst they may be reconciled in ordinary life, these two principles become antagonistic when carried into politics, and this law of succession has been the source of endless disturbances amongst the Thonga clans. It is true that the younger brothers of the chief, when taking his place, are looked on more or less as princes regent, holding office on behalf of their nephew, who is the lawful heir to the throne. They are said to "make him grow" (kurisa) to "keep his tumbler" (hlayisa ndyelo).

But if the former chief died in youth, and if his younger brother has lived and reigned for a long time, and has become very popular, he is very much tempted to appropriate the chieftainship for his own family and to order the tribe to crown his son, to the exclusion of the son of the first chief, who belonged to the elder branch, but who has been more or less forgotten during all these years. This leads to conflicts and fighting. The lawful heir will contest (*banga*, a Zulu word) and a *mubango* (civil war) will follow. Or, if he is not able to fight, he will keep to himself, full of bitterness, and ready to seize the first opportunity of asserting his rights.

Such a usurpation has twice taken place in the Nkuna tribe. It is not easy to know exactly what happened, because there are conflicting statements. Those who hold the chieftainship do not tell the story in the same way as those who consider that they were robbed of their right. This is the testimony of one of the latter, Mbokota, son of Madjubane. There were three brothers, Hoshana, Mbangwa and Ribye (1). During

(1) *Genealogy of the Nkuna family showing why and how contests arose for the succession.*

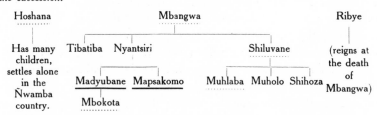

The names of the chiefs who reigned are thus underlined ··············
The names of those who were deprived of the chieftainship, thus ————

411

the disturbances caused by the Ngoni invasion, Hoshana fled to the Ñwamba country and lost touch with the main body of the clan which settled in the Transvaal. He however possessed the *ritlatla* (p. 385). On his death the royal appanage was brought to Shiluvane, but it never went back to Hoshana's children, who lost their right for ever. Mbangwa had three children, a daughter, Tibatiba, and two sons, Nyantsiri and Shiluvane. On his death, his younger brother Ribye reigned. He died, and then the chieftainship came back to Mbangwa's children. In the meantime Nyantsiri had died, but he had left two children, Madyubane and Mapsakomo. Madyubane, the elder, was still a child. So Tibatiba, the elder sister, said to Shiluvane : "Take the elephant tusk belonging to the Nkuna royal family and reign in the place of Nyantsiri ; but you have only to 'keep the tumbler' of Madyubane." Shiluvane sold the tusk and bought wives, beads and clothing for himself. Madyubane died some years later ; but he had a younger brother, Mapsakomo, and also a son called Mbokota. The chieftainship ought certainly to have returned to the elder branch. Mbokota told me himself that Shiluvane, before he died, ordered his counsellors to proclaim him as chief. So, on Shiluvane's death, a great contest arose. The headmen came to the capital and asked which son of Shiluvane had been designated by the late chief as his successor. No one dared reply, because there were four men who claimed the chieftainship : Mapsakomo, a younger brother of the legal heir Madyubane, Mbokota the son of Madyubane, Muhlaba and Muholo, both sons of Shiluvane. The great counsellor Shikhibane then said : "I heard Shiluvane say he wished Muhlaba to reign." The headmen accepted this statement, but the other pretenders greatly resented it. Seeing that many Ba-Nkuna were opposed to Muhlaba, Shikhibane assembled the whole tribe in arms to proclaim his protégé. He wanted the army itself to manifest its will. Mbokota, Mapsakomo and Muholo protested. But the warriors took Muhlaba, who was still a young man, and brought him to his new residence in an epic march all through the country during which they sang the war songs. The contest was finally settled by the Boer Authorities ; Captain Dahl, then Native Commissioner for Zoutpansberg, confirmed the choice of Muhlaba. The Pedi queen Magayibia, of the Nyarin clan, also asserted that she had heard Shiluvane designate this young man as his successor, and the other pretenders were obliged to keep quiet. But they remained very discontented (1).

I have seen another similar case of the elder branch losing its right on account of a younger brother placing his son on the throne, to the exclusion of the legal heir. It happened amongst the Ba-ka-Baloyi who took refuge in the Mudjadji country. The sons of Nkami, younger brother of Shitshabe, tried to seize the chieftainship to the detriment of Munyamana, son of Shitshabe, and this gave rise to a war in consequence of which, however, Munyamana regained his right. (See S. A. A. A. S. Report of the Meeting of 1905. Vol. III, page 251.)

All these facts tend to show that the position of the chief is attended with many dangers and difficulties, not to mention those which arise from the presence of the White Government, with which I shall deal later on.

So it must be recognised that the Thongas have not been able to discover a political system guaranteeing the peace of the country in a satisfactory way. The habit of dividing the power between brothers who soon become rivals, and of allowing the younger brothers to reign before the legal heir, both tend to destroy the unity of the clan and give rise to quarrels and unrest. Another bad consequence of these features of the royal right is this ; a chief, when he ascends the throne, will do his best to *get rid of troublesome brothers* in order to reign alone and to ensure the chieftainship to his son. This has often happened, especially in the case of Maphunga, chief of Nondwane, who killed as many as four brothers or near relations : Sitjobela, Ñwanambalana, Zulu and

(1) I remember one day paying a visit to Mbokota, and hearing him complain bitterly about his fate. He had tried to show his independence by establishing a separate circumcision school for his people so that they should not go to the "sungi" of Muhlaba. The chief did not prevent him from doing this, but he had just sent a messenger to claim the fees paid by the boys. Mbokota was much grieved at being obliged to remit them, and, if he had had enough men, he would certainly have revolted. But he had but a handful of warriors. He was not popular amongst the tribe, so he did not think it wise to "banga" and eventually submitted to Muhlaba.

Gigiseka. The last named was very courageous, and the cunning Maphunga succeeded in poisoning him treacherously, through the agency of a dissolute woman.

E. DEATH.

When a chief has grown very old, he no longer goes out of the royal hut. His counsellors take his place in the management of affairs and he dies surrounded by mystery. It must be so, as his death must remain unknown during a whole year. "We reap and we bow down (korama)" viz. "we till the ground and reap again before the event is made public (palusha)" says Mankhelu. So the chief is buried during the night ; no lamentations are heard ; his wives and his grave-diggers undergo the purification ceremonies and take the vapour baths in secret. It may be that the wives who dwell in remote places will not hear a word of their husband's death. The fire of the royal hut will not be kindled in the usual and ritual way, but it will be kept burning the whole year. The decease is formally announced to some few individuals, to the White Government officials, to the heir (who views the corpse), and to the counsellors, but the rest of the country is supposed to be in ignorance of the occurrence. Of course the secret will not be kept absolutely. The truth will leak out... But no one will dare to speak openly on the subject (1). A special hut is set apart into which the counsellors enter under pretext of discussing matters of state with the chief, who is said to be very ill and unable to show himself. As a matter of fact, he has been buried for some time.

(1) I was staying at Nondwane when Mapunga, the chief who preceded Mahazule, died, and I heard on several occasions, in June and July 1891, the warriors practising on their antelope horns the airs to be played when the mourning should be made public. The death must have occurred during 1890, but nothing was said about it. After the news had been published, Manganyele, a young heathen of the district of Libombo, remarked to me one day : " When last season (about Xmas 1890) we saw the miphimbi (trees bearing fruit similar to an apricot) so heavily laden with fruit, (there had been an exceptionally heavy crop), we felt sure the chief must have died and that he had sent us this plentiful supply. ." A typical remark, aptly illustrating the semi-ignorance in which the tribe is kept of the death of the chief.

What is the reason for this silence ? According to the old men I consulted, it is to prevent enemies taking advantage of the confusion consequent on the death of the chief to attack the country. Undoubtedly this custom is also intended to give the principal counsellors time to prepare for the installation of the new chief and to prevent bloody contests.

The grave of the chief does not differ from those of his subjects. As it has been dug secretly in the sacred wood (ntimu), its whereabouts are not known to most of the people. In some clans or sub-clans the earth of the tumulus is levelled, so that no sign whatever remains to show where the body has been buried. This is said to be done in order to prevent enemies from exhuming the corpse and cutting off the ears, the diaphragm and other parts of the body to make powerful war-charms (See Chapter IV). The graves of the chiefs of Nondwane are said to be invisible, just like the hut of the nyokwekulu. They are known by Magomanyana alone (Mboza). (Magomanyana is the nearest relative of the late Maphunga, the only brother whom he spared).

When the year of secrecy is over, the official proclamation of the mourning is made. (Ba palusha nkosi.) The people come to the capital, clan after clan, sounding their fanfares on trumpets of antelope horns (bunanga, see Chapter III), and bringing with them an ox or a goat. These animals are slaughtered and their bladders are presented to the heir, who pins them into his hair, so that, without any official proclamation having been made, every warrior at once recognises the future chief. All heads are shaven in sign of mourning, the adult men remove their wax crown (p. 129) and the people are clothed in *malopa* (a blue cloth) ; but as the death is not of recent date and has been known more or less for some time, the outward manifestations of grief are reduced to a minimum and dances follow in their train. The delegates from the adjoining countries also come to express their condolences. When all have paid their respects, the mourning is really ended (nkosi wu yu !). The King is dead, long live the King !

As we saw, amongst the Nkunas the proclamation of the death of a chief is made on the same day as the installation of his successor.

415

As regards the *queens* (tinkosikazi, a Zulu word), the chief's wives, there is not much to say about them. We have seen that one of them occupies a particularly honourable position, having been bought with the people's money and being "the wife of the country," she whose son will be the heir to the chieftainship. However, she is not necessarily the great wife. This name is applied to the first married who remains the real spouse, she at whose death the chief will perform the ceremony of widowhood. Should the wife of the

Phot. G. Liengme.

Ngoni Queens.

country die and should she not be the first married, he will not go through that rite on her account.

Princesses are lobola with more money than ordinary girls. Except in this, they do not differ from them. It is not common for a woman to be called to the dignity of chieftainship amongst the Thongas; in this respect they differ from the Ba-Pedi, or Transvaal Ba-Sutho, who have had many illustrious reigning queens : Modjadji, Male etc. I only know one such case amongst the Rongas, and the queen was still living in 1912. Her name was Midambuze, daughter of Dambuze. Dambuze was the chief of a part of the Mabota country, northward of Lourenço Marques.

On his death, his son Gwaba was put in his place. But he was deported by the Portuguese and his sister, Midambuze, filled the position. Consequently she was not lobola, but chose a husband for herself, a man of common origin (a titlhuba nuna). Her son may succeed her ; in this case only can a uterine nephew of a chief take his place.

At Gungunyana's court queens played a great part. This seems to be in accordance with the Zulu custom. After the death of Chaka's mother, sexual relations were taboo for the whole tribe during one year, and children conceived during that time were put to death by order of the chief! (See Colenso : Ten weeks in Natal.)

I know of no case in which a foreigner became chief of a clan through having married one of its princesses. He can become hosana, but the true hosana will be his wife and he himself will be but a prince consort. I have heard of two instances in which this happened.

CHAPTER III

THE COURT AND TRIBUNAL.

Although Royalty makes but little display amongst the Ba-
Ronga, still each chief is the centre of a court of more or less
brilliancy.

A. THE VILLAGE OF THE CHIEF.

The village in which he resides is not called *muti* (as is the
case with the ordinary hamlets of his subjects), but *ntsindja*, that
is "the capital." It is generally larger than the ordinary villages,
is built by the young men of the tribe, after the marriage of the
chief, and is also kept in repair by them, one of their principal
duties being to keep the public square in a state of constant
cleanliness and to weed it at certain seasons of the year.

One of my countrymen, Dr. J. de Montmollin, visited the
capital of the Tembe clan in July 1900 and took some interesting
photographs of it. The whole village was surrounded by a high
and thorny circular fence, much stronger than is the case with
ordinary kraals. The inside of the fence was divided into two
parts ; the front part, to which the main entrance gave access, and
the back part with the huts of the queens. The front part was the
square (hubo and bandla) with shady trees, under which visitors
were sitting ; there was only one hut on it, on the left side near the
fence ; the back part comprised the huts of the queens, which were
separated from the square by a high wall of reeds, carefully built,
and in which only a few narrow entrances were left. The traveller
was told that access to this kind of gynecium was taboo for all

Phot. Dr J. de Montmollin.

Main gate of the Tembe capital.

Phot. Dr J. de Montmollin.

The "hubo," square of the Tembe capital.
(The huts of the queens in the background, behind the reed wall).

the men. However he was allowed to visit it. Behind these huts were two passages between poles carefully arranged, one leading to the pig-sties, another to the bush. The photographer was told that this was intended to secure an exit for the queens in case of war... I suppose it had a more common and practical use in every day life! They are the *psiruba* of the queens (p. 311). In the royal kraal these back entrances are taboo.

It is on the square that the men of the neighbourhood love

Phot. Dr J. de Montmollin.

Back gate with hen-house.

to meet in the morning, when they come to pay their respects to the chief ; they sit down in groups and discuss the news of the day ; this is called, as we have seen, "ku ya bandla," "to go to the men's square." Everyone is welcome there, not only members of the reigning family, but also those of the clans conquered by the present chiefs, (as the Hoñwana, Mahlangwane etc., in Nondwane. Page 357). There is no lack of beer, made from maize or millet, when crops have been good, the women frequently bringing brimming jars to the capital ; the daily visits of the men are not therefore altogether disinterested.

420

B. COURT PERSONAGES.

Amongst those most frequently seen at the Court, must be mentioned the Counsellors, the Favourites, the Herald and the Official Vituperator.

Phot. Dr J. de Montmollin.

Back gate.

I. *The Counsellors.*

The Counsellors, tindjuna (1), constitute a Cabinet which assists the chief in carrying on the functions of Royalty. There are several grades of these functionaries ; first the Principal Counsellors (letikulu) whose province it is to discuss and decide

(1) The Zulu word *induna* is well known and has been more or less adopted in current speech in South Africa. The Thonga form is ndjuna, pl. tindjuna. I employ both these forms indiscriminately.

the more serious questions which affect the country. These are generally the uncles of the chief, or men of riper age from the collateral branches of his family. In Nondwane, during the war of 1894, it was Magomanyana and Mundulukele, brothers of the late Maphunga, uncles of the then reigning chief Mahazule, and later on Nwakubyele, who had charge of the interests of the eastern portion of the country, together with Nwambalane.

Sunduza, Chief of the Maluleke clan, with his Counsellors (N. E. Transvaal).

These tindjuna watch over the chief, and have the right of finding fault with him if they are not satisfied with his conduct.

In the second place come the Military Counsellors, the Generals of the army (tindjuna ta yimpi) who direct fighting operations, (Shitleñwana in Nondwane, Mpompi and Mahagane in Zihlahla).

Then there are Counsellors who are especially entrusted with the business of the adjoining countries, whom we might call Agents General, one being appointed to represent each country. We have already seen that these officials form an indispensable link in the diplomatic, and even in the matrimonial relations, between one kingdom and another.

If these men are intelligent, they acquire great influence with the chief and may even be able to impose their will upon him. This was the case in September 1894, when the young king Ñwamantibyane was prevented by his counsellors from obeying the summons of the Portuguese Government, who claimed his assistance in fighting Mahazule (See App. XI). They often act as a useful counterpoise to the autocratic power of the chief.

Lastly we find another category of Counsellors, those appointed by the chief in the various districts to act as overseers or magistrates, to adjudicate the petty differences of the people ; they must refer to the capital all important affairs (timhaka), the quarrels which the head of the village is unable to settle, and all matters which can only be judged by the chief, to whom they are of the greatest assistance in his decisions, being past masters in the art of Bantu reasoning.

The tindjuna are thus a complete organisation, as necessary to the chief as they are to the orderly development of tribal life.

II. *The Favourites, or Messengers.*

When the chief is crowned while still young, he gathers around him a circle of personal friends of his own age who are called *tinxekwa*. This is a Zulu word, and it would seem that this custom has been borrowed from the Zulu court procedure. In Ronga they are called *tinyumi*, which means messengers, and they generally build a *lao*, viz., a bachelor's house, near the capital, to be ready to answer any call. They partake in the games of their royal comrade and also in his feasts, but they have no official authority.

III. *The Herald.*

On one occasion I happened to be the guest, together with one of my colleagues, of the chief Ñwamantibyane, long before there was any question of the war of Lourenço Marques. Stretched in our hammocks, which we had fixed to the roof inside a hut placed at our disposal for the night, we were trying to sleep when, about 4 a. m., we were awakened by an extraordinary sound ; it was in a very high key, words sung, shouted, volubly and monotonously, in fact a most peculiar and never-to-be-forgotten musical production ! Further sleep was impossible, and for more than half an hour we were obliged to submit to this ear-splitting performance :

"Yethi (Bayete), we hosi, wene shitlangu sho ringana tilo, mathathala i tinyeleti, nkungu wa shone i hweti! We! nkandji wa ku wona, ku baleka minambyana!" — "Bahete! O chief! You shield us as heaven! The marks of this shield are like the stars! You who trample dry ground so that rivers at once spring forth!"

It was the *mbongi wa ku pfusha*, the herald sounding the reveille ; an individual who has "the chest well developed," as they say in Ronga, which does not mean that he is sound in the wind and possesses healthy lungs, but that he is a man of great eloquence. In our tribe the chest (pectus) is held to be the seat of knowledge and of the gift of oratory! Every morning, before sunrise, this royal flatterer comes to the door of the chief's hut and sings the glorious deeds of his ancestors, recalling their names and acts of prowess ; to these praises, he adds a general disparagement (sandja) of the chief himself, referring to him as a coward, a child in comparison with his father, his grandfather and all his noble deceased progeniters. "Lead us to battle! Show us what you can do!" And the chief must be awakened every day by this strange concert, which sometimes lasts for hours!

The flatterer likes to accompany his chief when he goes to visit the Whites. In front of the offices of the Municipal Council of Lourenço Marques, I once witnessed the arrival of Sigaole, chief of Matjolo, who came thither to look at Gungunyana, taken prisoner by the Portuguese in January 1896; his *mbongi* was among his following. This was an old man, named Ma-bobo. Dressed up in a jacket, by no means too clean, and with a cap on his head, he yelled the praises of the royal family of Matjolo ; this was in Zulu and doubtless in a special terminology.

He shouted like a madman and no one took the slightest notice of him!

When the chief kills an ox and possibly some little delay occurs in distributing the meat, the *mbongi* is the duly qualified beggar who goes to claim the soldiers' share. He addresses the chief much as follows : "Don't you see all those men in your village ? Are they not dogs ? Why do you starve us ? You only give meat to the women... Is it women who will defend you when the enemies attack you ? etc. etc." At the coronation of the chiefs it is this herald who sings their praises in the procession I have already described. Strange to say, the *mbongi* is allowed great licence and may even insult the chief without provoking his anger ; on the contrary, the herald is respected and a special portion of meat is reserved for him. Any one can aspire to the office provided he be sufficiently garrulous.

The most eloquent of the Thonga heralds whom I ever met is Mawewe, the mbongi of the Nkuna clan. He was an elderly man in 1900 and had a long career behind him, having been the mbongi of Manukosi. "I used to praise him from morn to night (ndji peta dambu) and he gave me a heifer as a reward." As the French writer Buffon used to put on his cuffs before writing, so Mawewe, when he intended to praise his chief Muhlaba, adorned himself with the tail of the nsimango antelope, with the feathers of the nkulunkulu (the bird of the chiefs) and of the eagle, with the skins of snakes, of the reed buck, and of the leopard, and with the nails, teeth, or hair of elephants, rhinoceros and hippopotamus ; then he began :

Muhlaba Shiluvane, (1) you are like the rhinoceros who seizes a man, bites him through and through, rolls him over and cuts him in two! You are like the crocodile which lives in water ; it bites a man! You are like its claws ; it seizes a man by his arms and legs, it drags him into the deep pool to eat him at sunset ; it watches over the entrance to prevent other crocodiles from taking its prey... Muhlaba! You are like the ram ; when it butts with its head, it knocks a man down ; like a goat, like the son of the goat, which is herded by the boys,

(1) Father of Muhlaba.

which is very cunning : it pricks up its ears, it prepares itself for defence, when attacked!

Tail of nsimango, you are like Muhlaba, you are of a great beauty, you are shining inside the forest, the black forest, you are sparkling, kati-kati-kati, (1) a man may truly fear when he sees you!

Give them meat, that they may all eat! Give your men the foreleg,

Muhlaba, the Chief of the Nkuna clan.   *Phot. A. Borel.*

give them the hindleg, that they may all eat to their hearts' content... Pull their legs forward (ba koke milenge), so that they fall back in terror of you!

Why do you govern them so mildly! Look at them with terrible

(1) Descriptive adverb.

eyes! You are a coward! The Bveshas want to kill you! Act with bravery and defend yourself!

Muhlaba Dabuka! Men are coming, oxen are coming. You are on the top of the hills, you are like heaven which roars... The lightning is like you, it is full of strength, it is terrible! Your saliva is white, your eyes are beaming, your face is elongated, your body is like the stone of gold (auriferous quartz) ; your fingers are long. You are known in every country. At Gungunyana, they know you. At Ngwana (Swaziland), they know you. The Zulus know you! At Mosilakatse, they know you. You are like the grass on the road ; when people trample on it, they crush it to the ground, but when the rain comes, it grows again and covers the earth. You are like the water of the river, how beautiful! The water is clear and pure, though impurities may float upon it, they pass away and the water is pure again!

The Bveshas weep at Sikokoro's kraal! (1) They weep at Sikhukhunu's! You have taken their charms! You have sprinkled your warriors with them. Muhlaba, you have beaten them with the shaft of the assagay, your men crossed the river, they went to kill the enemies in their own kraal!

You are like the ostrich feather, the white one, very white, or the red one of the bird which cries tswe-tswe, the bird called rivi, which adorns the chiefs!

At Nyarin, (2) they dispute chieftainship (banga buhosi) ; they are going to kill each other. Mapsakomo says : "It is mine!" Muholo says : "It is mine!" Shirundju (3) took him (Muhlaba) in his arms... Mankhelu is like the duiker antelope! They catch him by the ear and he escapes from their hands! He is like the water of the well : they draw it off... it springs up again and fills up the well. (Viz., Mankhelu is never tired when defending the cause of Muhlaba.)

Run, go and tell Mandlamakulu, Shiluvane's brother : "The

(1) In 1901, there was a Native war in which Muhlaba and the Pedi chief Maaghe fought against their neighbour Sikororo and his ally Sikhukhukhu, heir of Sekukuni. On the 7th of November a fierce battle took place in Shiluvane where the assailants were repulsed and more than forty of them were killed. (See App. X)

(2) Here Mawewe makes an allusion to the circumstances in which Muhlaba took over the chieftainship and which have been explained when dealing with the law of succession. The capital of the tribe was still at Nyarin, at that time, viz., in the hills near New Agatha. (See page 413.)

(3) One of the great counsellors who took the part of Muhlaba as did also Mankhelu and Shikhibane.

power belongs to me." Run, go and tell Mpapalati : "The power is mine." Run, go and tell Mulondjo : "The power is mine!" (1)

Such is the laudatory song of Mawewe, one of the great men at the Nkuna court. Undoubtedly this is one of the best examples of Thonga poetry and a characteristic piece of primitive literature. In the savage tribe the mbongi is the prototype of the poet laureate of civilised Courts. But there is yet another functionary to be considered, whose duties are still more strange than those of the herald.

IV. *The Public Vituperator.*

(Shitale sha tiko.)

This is a kind of Court Jester who has the right of casting the vilest insults, the most disgraceful accusations in the teeth of any and all the Natives of the country. He never abuses strangers, but as long as he confines his vituperations to his own countrymen, he enjoys perfect immunity.

Even the chief is not safe from his attacks ; he dares to say anything! "Just see him arriving in your village," said Tobane to me, in his picturesque language. "He begins shouting out the most frightful things. He accuses you of incest, of taking your own sisters as wives! Even if he sees you talking to your 'great sister-in-law,' whom your wife's brother married with your oxen, whom you treat with the greatest respect, he will not hesitate to pass remarks which will make you blush with shame! He will go and take the food you are cooking, will even snatch from the chief's hands the meat he is eating... So, when you see him coming to your village, you hasten to meet him and take him a present to try and avoid having to listen to his horrible insults. Sometimes the *shitale* of the country behaves

(1) Quotation of the words of Muhlaba himself, who sent messengers to all his uncles, to all the petty chiefs under him, to announce officially that he had assumed the chieftainship.

himself quite nicely, stays in his own village and attends the national assemblies as quietly as any other person, but, once he begins to rattle off his vituperations, beware! Nothing will stop him! He respects nothing, human or divine!" The Court Jester is of undoubted Thonga origin, as old as the tribe itself, according to Tobane. The position is official and even hereditary. At Zihlahla it was Nwachapane who held the extraordinary post of Public Vituperator. In Nondwane it was Mutjunkwa of the Shibindji family. He insulted the chief with the word : "Musathanyoko." There was also a woman who dared to do the same to Maphunga.

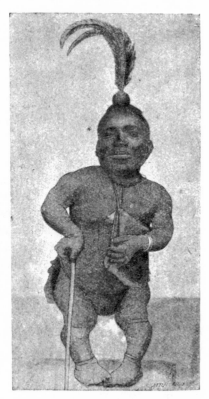

Phot. P. Berthoud.
Molwele, the dwarf.

It is difficult to understand the raison d'être of this strange institution. Is the *shitale* a public censor, to whom the tribe entrusts the privilege of calling attention to facts which others would not dare to bring to light ? Is there some analogy between this "fool" of an African Court and Triboulet ? (1) I cannot say.

(1) In this connection I reproduce from a photograph, taken at Shiluvane in 1885, the portrait of a remarkable personage who was not a Thonga but a Pedi, a subject of the chief Maaghe. Although this extraordinary dwarf did not act officially as the Vituperator, he was widely famed for his witty sayings and his incomparable mimicry, The Native Commissioner took him to Pretoria and Johannesburg some years ago as a curiosity, and it seems that he was exhibited for money ! The name of this little man is Molwele, a veritable ethnographic phenomenon, although he is not exactly the Public Vituperator of the country.

C. SUNDRY COURT CUSTOMS.

The paraphernalia of royalty are very modest in the Thonga courts. However there are some to be mentioned in addition to the regalia which I have described.

I. *The Big Drum* (Muntshintshi).

This is found in every capital, even sometimes in the sub-chief's villages. It is made of a hollowed stem, somewhat like an ordinary mortar; or it may be rounded, and even provided with three legs, as in Nondwane; a piece of skin is stretched over the opening. This may be the skin of an elephant's ear, of a buffalo, of an ox or of an antelope *mangulwe*. This instrument is subject to some taboos; when the skin cracks, it is forbidden to look inside. There is something mysterious about it and nobody must disclose that mystery. People say that a bullet is introduced into it when it is made. In Shiluvane they asserted that the skull of the hostile chief, Sikororo, killed in the battle of Nov. 1901, had been put into the big drum! At any rate, there is a special individual who is summoned to repair it and he receives a fowl as reward.

The big drum is beaten on various occasions :

a) To announce a great fatality, especially the death of a chief, or the day of the publication of the mourning ; also the approach of the inundation, when the Nkomati river rises, in January or February, and threatens to cover the whole land ; again when the bush fire threatens to destroy the capital.

b) To summon warriors to the capital in case of imminent war.

c) To execute various musical performances. The big drum leads a special dance (nkino), which takes place at the capital during the winter, when the harvest is ended, and the country happy and prosperous. It is accompanied by a smaller drum (shikolombane) which is called the "son" of the big one. The *shikolombane* is more elongated and has no legs. Its sound is high and piercing, while the tone of the *muntshintshi* is deep and low. The music proper of this dance is provided by the *bunanga.*

II. *The Bunanga.*

This is the regular *band*, which is met with in every royal clan. The word comes from *nanga*, trumpet (pl. tinanga). But the trumpets composing the bunanga are not the common pierced tibias of goats used by the herdboys. They are larger horns of the mhalamhala (Hippotragus Niger), or of the mhala (Zulu impala), pierced at their base in such a way that they produce different tones. These instruments are made by specialists, (it was Nwamatshomane in Nondwane), so as to form a kind of orchestra (simo) composed of ten instruments. To play them is a veritable art. The players stand round the two drumbeaters. The big drum gives the time : when it beats slowly, "tu-tu-tu," the ten musicians must dance in a ring, viz., they must march after each other, playing, making certain grimaces and gesticulations. When the drum beats more slowly and more softly, they must retire in a line and march slowly. The drum quickens the time : then they come to the centre once more and dance in a ring, quicker and quicker. The executants follow each other in a given order, the largest and deepest horn being in front, the smallest and highest toned one at the end of the group. Sometimes three or four orchestras perform at the same time (1).

The bunanga is an old Ronga custom and is very picturesque indeed. As for its musical importance, I shall refer to it again in Part V.

(1) I remember having heard the bunanga practising in the various sub-clans of Nondwane in 1891, as each sub-chief had his own. They were preparing to go to the capital to mourn Maphunga whose death had just been announced. I saw the bunanga performing its best melodies before Lord Selborne, when he came to pay a visit to the Portuguese settlement of Morakwen in 1908. The Administrator had organised a "batuque" for him (the name given by the Portuguese to these native dances), and the warriors of Nondwane did their best to interest the White Chiefs !

III. *The shipalapala.*

Speaking of the musical instruments of the Court, I must also mention *the trumpet of assembly, shipalapala,* which is the reco-gnised means of summoning the subjects to the capital. The sound of the big drum, though heard at a great distance, cannot reach to the confines of the country. So, when the chief wants his men to assemble at once, he uses the *shipalapala.* This is a horn of mhalamhala, or of nyala or of phifa antelope, the sound of which is like mpu-ù-u (with an accent on the second syllable). The envoy of the chief runs to the capital of a sub-chief, blowing all the time. When he has reached that village, he transmits his mes-sage and a young man starts at once with the shipalapala of the sub-chief to another district. So, in a short time, notice is given to the whole tribe to assemble.

IV. *Visitors.*

When a stranger passes through the capital, he must sit down outside the central square and at some little distance from it. Some one will come and inquire what he wants ; he replies : "I come from such and such a country, and I wish to pay my respects to the chief." Then the counsellor or "Agent General" charged with the affairs of the traveller's country will come and converse with him and announce him (bika) to the chief, who will receive him affably and possibly assign him a hut to sleep in, in case he wishes to stay the night, at the same time providing him with food. Should the chief be particularly well disposed towards his guest, he will kill a calf or even an ox for him ; and he, on his return, will speak in praise of the hospitality he has received, saying : "The chief made me share his reign," literally : "He made me reign, (a ndji fumisile)." Such is the procedure when the respective countries of guest and host are adjoining and the tribes on good and friendly terms. Should relations between them be at all strained, or should war be imminent, all the roads would be closed and no one allowed to enter the capital.

V. *The Kondza custom.*

The chief is also approached by those who may wish to become subject to him, to be naturalized ; this is called *kondza*, from a Zulu word conveying this meaning. The chief will assign to the new *nandja* a dwelling place, and he will be incorporated in the nation without further ceremony. By this kondza, he binds himself to. pay the taxes (See the story of Mutipi. *Les chants et les contes des Ba-Ronga*, page 164).

Naturalised strangers, however, do not eat the first fruits (luma) with the same drug as the people of the country. They have their own medicine and take it according to their own rules. They are however forbidden to luma before the chief of their adopted land (p. 397).

VI. *Diplomatic relations.*

We have seen that these are very carefully conducted, each of the neighbouring clans having one counsellor entrusted with the care of its affairs. In case of war, friendly clans frequently make alliances (shinakulobye). They send messages to each other, or they have special means of communicating news in case of war. Supposing, for instance, Nwamba and Nondwane should fight against Matjolo. They put two traps at their common boundary, on the side of the road, one on the territory of Nwamba and one on that of Nondwane. These traps consist of a rod bent by a string fastened to the ground. Should the army of Matjolo have made an invasion during the. night into Nwamba territory and put the people to flight, the men of Nwamba

433

will at once go and undo the trap which is on their side ; in the morning, the people of Nondwane will know that they must also fly.

D. THE TRIBUNAL OF THE CHIEF.

In the Thonga Court there is no separation of powers. The legislative, executive, and judicial powers are all in the hands of the chief, aided by his counsellors. The chief is the supreme authority and his decisions are without appeal.

I. *Legislative affairs.*

The *chief* makes the laws (p. 382) and presides at discussions which end in a resolution. But his counsellors assist him.

Here is an example of such a decision taken at Maphunga's court. There was no uniformity as to the money to be paid for a lobolo, and some fathers claimed as much as £ 20 or £ 30 for their daughters. The great counsellors of the capital decided (tjimba mhaka, viz., to tie the matter) that a lobolo should be £ 15.10 as the maximum. They "tied the matter" with the assent of the chief. Then all the sub-chiefs and counsellors were summoned to the capital. The chief called the roll to ascertain if they were all present. The great counsellor then said to the assembly : "The herds which people claim are too large. Have you gold mines and do you know how to make coins ? Henceforth do not lobola with too much money. £ 15.10 is quite enough!" Every sub-chief, on his return home, called his men and informed them of the decision : "Hi to timhaka! Such are the matters!" said they. The subjects were disappointed. They wept! But they had to accept the decision. To oppose it is taboo! "Psa yila!"

A *native debate* or discussion is conducted on very different lines from those to which we are generally accustomed, nothing ever being put to the vote. The chief presides. A proposition is put forward in short sentences, generally interrogative, by one of the counsellors. The assembly listens in silence until the mover concludes with an energetic "Ahina," being the equivalent of "That's all right." (See p. 354.) Another individual elaborates the matter further, saying : "Did you not hear what he said ? He said so and so." This is the way of seconding the motion. The debate proceeds, and, little by little, objections are brought forward and the assembly comes to a decision.

It often happens that the chief does not say a word ; when he see that the counsellors are agreed and if he has no objection, he merely shows his assent by nodding his head. So the decision is arrived at without his intervention and without any vote being taken. The voice of the majority has not been ascertained by any show of hands, but it is generally perceived by intuition in a very remarkable way, and grave counsellors, who have been squatting in a circle all through the discussion, jump to their feet and disperse, knowing perfectly well what has been decided. If however the counsellors do not agree, they put the matter into the hands of the chief, and the chief,

Phot. A. Borel.

An habitué of the Nkuna Court.

after having listened to the arguments pro and con, "cuts the matter" (tjema mhaka) by some short sentences, after which everybody must shout the royal salutation : "Bayete!"

When there are two parties present, the debate is conducted according to other rules. For instance, if a stranger wishes to have speech with a chief or to proffer some request, he is generally accompanied by a counsellor. The chief, together with some of his men, receives him either in the hut, if the affair must

435

be secret, or on the square, if there is no objection to making it public. The chief and his men sit on one side, the visitor on the other ; if he wishes to conform strictly to all the laws of etiquette, he will first explain the matter to his own Agent General, who will communicate with the chief's special counsellor, repeating the words of the visitor, sentence by sentence ; the counsellor will, in his turn, communicate with the chief, again telling him the whole story, as if he had not heard a word of it before. The affair will thus have passed through three hands and the answer should, in due formality, be given through the same channels. These precautions, which seem eminently superfluous, even somewhat ridiculous, to a person unacquainted with Bantu etiquette, evidently proceed from the fact that there are no stenographers or secretaries to furnish any written record of the proceedings, so that it is necessary to have as many witnesses as possible and that these should thoroughly understand the matter under consideration.

II. *Judicial Cases.*

1) SENSE OF JUSTICE.

As has often been remarked, the Bantus possess a strong sense of justice. They believe in social order and in the observance of the laws and, though these laws are not written, they are universal and perfectly well known. The law is the custom, that which has always been done. The old men, the counsellors and more particularly the counsellors of the capital, are those who can speak authoritatively. But everybody is welcome in the *hubo*, where matters are discussed ; even a stranger can take part in the discussion. "No one is excluded, if he speaks rightly ; only fools, those who do not know anything" (Mankhelu).

This participation in the discussions of the hubo has developed the sense of law to a wonderful extent amongst the Bantus. They are all born advocates and judges, and take a great interest in this business! No wonder therefore that the Thonga vocabulary

436

possesses a rich store of *judicial expressions*. Here are the most common : *Nau* (pl. milau) means law, custom. *Ku tlula nau*, to jump over the law, means transgression. *Nandju* (pl. *milandju*) means the fault resulting from transgression. This interesting word comes from *ku landja*, to follow. It applies in the first instance to cases which lead to a prosecution, but secondly to any fault. *Ku doha*, is to be wrong and *ku dohela mhunu*, the applicative derivative, to wrong another. *Ku da*, to eat somebody, or *dela*, is also a picturesque expression employed for injury to property. *Ku ramba* (Dj.), *ku rjamela hosin* (Ro.) is the technical expression to designate a complaint lodged before the chief. *Ku riha* (Dj.), *djiha* (Ro.) means to pay a fine, and *rihisa, djihisa* (the factitive derivative), to impose a fine.

This strong sense of justice however differs from the European on certain points. Owing to their collectivist notions, the Bantus consider relatives as responsible for the debts of their own kin, as we have already seen (p. 332). Another case in which they entertain ideas which seem very strange to us is this ; when anyone has lent you an implement and you make a bad use of it, the fault is as much the lender's as the borrower's. I remember a queer case which took place in my school in Rikatla. Some boys had to go in the afternoon to work in the vegetable garden under the supervision of their overseer. On the way one of them happened to hurt his foot by treading on a thorn. So, when he arrived in the garden, he borrowed a knife from the overseer and began to make sandals of palm-leaf pith. The elder boy entreated him to work. He refused to obey, so the overseer denounced him publicly, when the weekly inquiry into the conduct of the boys was made, on the following Friday. But the temporary shoemaker did not admit to being guilty of anything at all, and his final argument was this : "I cannot understand how Mr. Overseer can accuse me when he himself lent me the knife which I used to carve my sandals!" D. Kidd tells similar stories about Pondos in his "Essential Kafir."

So there are differences between Native and European conceptions of justice, and Bantus do not always draw the same conclusions as we do from given premises. Native Commissioners

437

must remember this and, in order to enlighten the Native mind, they must try to find where these differences lie. But these are minor points, and the sense of justice is nevertheless one of the most striking and promising characteristics of the Bantu.

Before enumerating the various cases which can be brought before the Native Court, let me remark that, generally speaking, Bantus are very peaceful, law-abiding people, under normal circumstances; when protected against alcoholic excesses they are little addicted to crime. In the Blue Book for Native Affairs of Cape Colony, 1908, the Chief Magistrate of the Transkeian Territory comments on "the general docility of the Natives, the perfect immunity from crimes of violence, which the European population, male and female, enjoys amongst them, and the cheapness of police administration." He adds : "The policing of the Territories, including the Detective Force, costs only 7d. per head of the territorial population, or, counting Chiefs and Headmen whose functions are mainly administrative, 10d., against 6s. 3d. per head for policing the Colony proper. Reports from twenty districts comment on the paucity or absence of crime. Kentani, with a population of 34,000 did not furnish a single case for the Circuit Court. The Magistrates of four districts remark on 'the peaceable and law-abiding character of the Native,' the Magistrate of Kentani adding : 'when kept away from the drink curse'." (*Christ. Express*, Aug. 1908.)

I think the same report might be made in most of the districts of South Africa where Natives still live by themselves.

The state of affairs would be very different in the Town locations, where we meet with a great number of men and women of dissolute morals. They are often backsliders who have left the Mission Stations because they did not like to submit to the Christian rule of morality. So they have freed themselves from all restraints, tribal as well as Christian, and, if they have not entirely lost all sense of justice, they, at any rate, do not walk "in the paths of righteousness." I am here only concerned with clan Natives.

The Court and Tribunal

2) Civil cases.

I will not assert that Thongas know the exact difference between civil and criminal cases, the same tribunal judging them both and all being called by the same name, milandju.

If any distinction is made, it would be between private and official cases, *private cases* being those which are settled by the two parties concerned alone, without the intervention of the chief ; whilst *official cases* are those in which the matter (mhaka) has been brought to the capital. As already explained, the headmen of the village try to settle the difficulties themselves ; if they succeed, all the better, as the fine will be reduced to its minimum, whilst, before the Court, the fine would be doubled and the chief would keep half of it !

Ninety per cent of the civil cases are in connection with *lobola*. These are sometimes most intricate and I would refer to the description already given of some of them (p. 282 and Appendix VIII).

Divorce cases are also common. When a woman has definitely left her husband, her relatives must return the lobolo money. "You must give up to them £ 5 or an ox," says Mankhelu. The chief Mubvesha who was known for his avarice used to arrest the husband and make him pay £ 25 ; he returned £ 15 to the wife's relatives and kept £ 10 for himself.

When money is returned, the children belong to the mother (See page 279).

Many cases may occur in connection with *cattle*. The case of *redhibition* is foreseen : when I buy an ox and it dies on my hands from a disease which was not known at the date of my purchase but which already existed, I have the right to go and ask for another in its place. But I bring the skin of the dead ox with me and one hoe inside it for the meat which I have eaten. If the seller refuses to accept my claim, I go to the chief and complain. He will summon the recalcitrant person and say to him : "Did not this man act well when he put a hoe inside the skin ? Give him another ox !" (Mankhelu.)

When goats have damaged somebody's garden, there is no fine to pay. The shepherds are whipped and the matter is thus concluded. Should the father of the boys, however, take their part and protect them with his weapons, he will be summoned to the tribunal of the chief and have to pay a fine of £ 5 or two or three goats.

Thonga Natives who have but a few head of cattle, are accustomed to entrust them to the care of neighbours possessing a large herd, in order to spare themselves the trouble of finding herding boys. There are some laws regulating this matter. If the owner of the cow, or the pig, or the goat, gives money in advance to the master of the large herd, all the calves, pigs, and kids, which may be born revert to him. But if he has not paid anything, the master of the herd is entitled to choose one pig out of the first litter ; or he can keep the third or fourth calf or kid. If it be a hen, one of its chickens will belong to the man who took care of it. Should the owner forget to remit the due reward, there will be trouble (pongwe). When he goes to take his cattle back, the master of the herd will keep one head for himself, and, if a dispute arises, both will go to the chief, at least if the matter is important, if the animal in question, for instance, is an ox.

If an ox incorporated with another man's herd dies, the master of the herd will inform the owner in order that he may go and dispose of the meat. Should he be living too far off, the ox will be eaten on the spot and the skin will be sent to the owner. Suppose the master of the herd pretends that the ox is dead, but has only put it with another herd, and sent a skin to the owner to deceive him, it is a case of theft, which will be judged as such.

3) CRIMINAL CASES.

Adultery. Our tribe punishes adultery very severely indeed, at least when the woman is married. The fine is a full lobolo. (See page 197.) Amongst the Nkunas if the accused man denies his guilt when questioned indoors, the bones are consulted, or even the magicians who practise the "vumisa" divination. (Part

VI.) If found guilty, he will have to pay an extra fine of two oxen (1).

When the abducted woman is an unmarried girl, the matter is not serious. No trouble is entailed, provided she does not become pregnant. In the latter case, the seducer can say : "Ndji dlele ku dya: I have killed to eat," viz. "I am ready to lobola the girl" (p. 97). If the girl does not consent, the man is free. But if the man does not wish to marry the girl by paying a full lobolo, whilst the girl and her relatives want him to do so, he will have to pay as much as £ 30 and an ox. "He has spoilt his cause!" His own relatives will be arrested and forced to pay. They are responsible for him and will scold him severely. (Mankhelu).

Fighting ending in blows. The wounded man runs to the square of the capital and shows himself. The assailants will have to pay a fine of £ 8, three for the chief and five for the victim, or of two oxen, one for the chief and one for the plaintiff. (Mankhelu).

Murder. A distinction is made between involuntary murder, which is an accident (mhango, Dj.), and a deliberate assassination.

In the case of *involuntary murder*, Mankhelu describes the proceedings as follows : — Should you have killed a man by accident in a hunting trip, for instance, you will try to arrange matters directly with his relatives, if you were good friends ; your relatives will give them a girl. You dare not offer your own daughter, because they may refuse her, on account of their bad feelings! The same objection will not be made if your people provide the girl. They will accompany her with ten hoes and an ox, saying : "This is fat to smear our daughter." The notion which is at the base of this custom is not that a human person is the natural compensation for another human person, but that you give the diminished family a means of making good its loss. In fact as soon as the girl has born a child to the relatives of the deceased, she is free. If these men wish to keep her as their wife, they must

---

(1) The neighbouring Chopi tribe, on the contrary, leaves the husband to arrange matters as he likes. Formerly he used to kill the adulterer. But cases of adultery are never brought before the chief.

lobola. Viguet explains that this is done according to the old saying of Native law : "Ñwombekazi a yi ambi nandju" viz. "a cow which has calved is not used to pay a fine ; the calf pays it." (See page 217.) He adds that the ten hoes sent with the girl pay for the ribs of the murdered man. (The Ba-Thonga believe that the human body has only ten ribs !) A case of involuntary homicide is generally not brought before the chief, as the law is well known and no one would try to evade his duty. Should however the murderer not have been on good terms with the deceased, the matter will be discussed before the Court.

If the murder was *deliberate*, it is punished by death. At least such was the law in former times, when Natives still possessed the power of condemning to death. Now the fine is also the remittance of a woman. But owing to the existing hatred, and from fear of being obliged to lobola the relative of the murderer, the family of the deceased does not take the girl. She is sold by her parents and only the money is remitted to the plaintiff. (Mankhelu.)

Amongst the Ba-Ronga, when a near relative of the murdered man wishes to avenge himself by killing the assassin, his people prevent him from doing so, in order to bring the matter before the chief. When a man called Mashabe was killed by the son of Gigiseka, Maphunga's brother, the murderer, had to pay £ 20. The fine may be as much as £ 25, but the idea is also to help the bereaved family to acquire a new spouse and, through her, new members. As for the murderer, he is regarded with scorn, and despised by the whole community. For a whole week, he must eat apart. He is unclean. So, at the time of luma bukanye, (page 400), he must also take miluru medicine together with the warriors who have killed enemies ; but he does not drink it boastfully, extolling his deed ! People say of him : "Look at the murderer !" (Mboza.)

The vendetta, the savage custom which makes it incumbent on the relations of a murdered man to avenge his death themselves at all costs and by any means, is absolutely absent from Thonga custom. It may be said that, as regards punishment of murder, they have reached quite a civilised stage in their judicial

442

procedure. They are in advance of many tribes. The same cannot be asserted when dealing with witchcraft!

Witchcraft (Buloyi). To the Thonga mind this is one of the greatest crimes which a man can commit. It is equivalent to assassination, even worse than murder, as a dim idea of anthropophagy is added to the simple charge of killing. A wizard kills human beings to eat their flesh. We shall study the conceptions of *buloyi* later on (Part VI) from a psychological point of view. Here it is mentioned only in as far as it gives rise to judicial cases. This particular crime being committed in great secrecy during the night, and in most instances even unconsciously, the Bantu tribunal uses two or three magical methods for discovering it. These *methods of inquiry*, which civilised nations have long ago abandoned, are :

1) *Divination by casting lots.* The objects used in our tribe for this purpose are the magic bones, the astragalus of goats, antelopes, etc, and shells, which I intend to study in a special chapter. When they have designated (ku ba, to beat) the wizard or witch (noyi) who has killed such and such a person, they are consulted a second time. If they confirm their verdict, the relatives of the deceased go to the chief and lodge their complaint. The accusation becomes official and is now in the hands of the tribunal.

2) The chief sends the plaintiff and accused to the magician who proceeds to the *divination by questioning* them and working himself up into an ecstatic condition (vumisa).

3) Should the accused be again designated and should he deny his crime, he may request to be submitted to the *ordeal*, viz, the trial by the solaneous plant called mondjo. If the drug intoxicates him, his guilt is confirmed for the third time and the tribunal will condemn him. The punishment for *buloyi* is death, either by hanging, or by empaling, or by drowning in the river, if the wizard was in the habit of perpetrating his murders by sending crocodiles to kill his victims.

Nowadays Native chiefs dare not put to death suspected witches. Since the Ba-Ronga have been under the jurisdiction of the Whites, the *death penalty* has been abolished. On the other hand, under

Gungunyana, executions were of frequent occurrence. When the chief had condemned a man to death, he merely made a sign to one of his executioners, who followed the unfortunate individual, as he went away into the bush, possibly quite unconscious of the fate awaiting him, and dealt him a heavy blow from behind with either club or assagay, killing him on the spot. Chiefs now only expel wizards or witches from the country, accompanying them to the boundary, or impose a high fine on them, keeping half of the amount. However there are still individuals who avenge themselves for the death of a relative on the suspected murderer by killing him. Such cases are not infrequently brought before the Courts of Pretoria and Johannesburg.

What is the duty of the civilised tribunal in such instances ? White judges generally condemn to death a man who has killed a "noyi". I know of cases in which even an induna who had hanged a "noyi," duly condemned by the Native Court, was himself considered a criminal and condemned as such. This happened to our friend Mankhelu, one of the pillars of the Nkuna tribe, the General of the army... He only escaped death owing to petitions sent to the Boer Authorities by both Blacks and Whites. This happened, I think, in 1888. Are European judges right in pronouncing the capital punishment in such cases ? This is questionable. It is certainly erroneous to assimilate Mankhelu's act which, in his own eyes, is an act of justice, to an ordinary murder, and to punish him as an assassin. He did what he thought to be right according to his knowledge. The husband of a bewitched woman who kills the murderer of his wife is more blamable, because his act is not sanctioned by the authority of a regular Court. However neither one nor the other deserves death.

I fully recognise that such acts of the Native tribunals must be stopped. A chief who accepts accusations of witchcraft ought to be punished, especially if it has been duly explained to him that a White Government does not allow any such case to be judged in the country. In the course of time Natives will understand this and the witchcraft superstition will dwindle away. But let us be patient with them, remembering that our forefathers of 300 years ago did exactly the same thing and burnt hundreds of suspected witches after having subjected them to horrible tortures.

In an essay on the subject published in the S.A.A.A.S Report of

1906, I ventured to suggest certain means of checking the *buloyi* superstition. The Department of Native Affairs might give the following directions to its subordinates, the Native chiefs :

1) The crime of buloyi is not recognised under penal law.

2) The Native chiefs are prohibited from trying any buloyi case.

3) The plaintiff must be reprimanded as disturbing the peace of the country.

4) The witch doctor or mungoma (magician), who pretends to have smelt out a wizard, must be fined as using his authority to deceive people and foster hatred amongst them.

5) No evidence based on the use of divinatory bones must be accepted.

These rules, if strictly enforced and combined with Christian teaching and the progress of civilisation, will in the course of time put an end to the scourge of witchcraft.

Insults. Ku rukana or ruketela, to hurl insults at each other's head, is very frequent amongst Thongas and does not lead to any judicial case, if not accompanied by assault and bruises (1). There are however insulting deeds which are considered as crimes. To take human blood, or spittle, or excrement with a stick and to push it into the mouth of a child, for instance, is considered a very serious insult which must be judged before the Court. A man who committed such an offence would have to pay a fine amounting to a whole lobola. I heard of a woman who gave a child a butterfly to eat. The parents of the little one were very angry. She denied having done such a thing. They said to her: "Confess your sin and pay a fine of 5/—." She refused and offered to undergo the ordeal, viz., to drink the mondjo philtre. "If you insist" said they, "you will have to pay £ 10." However she persisted and became intoxicated ; this was a proof of her guilt. She was fined to the amount of £ 40, £ 20 for the child and £ 20 for the chief!

To point at any one with the index finger is also a grave insult which may have judicial consequences, because this action is brought into close relation with *buloyi*.

---

(1) The most common insult which women can cast in each other's teeth is ntlhañhwaku (Ro) or nyañhwaku (Nkuna) which means: the genitals of your mother. A scuffle with blows is sure to arise when that word has been pronounced. It is also used when taking an oath. Men swear by the name of their chief.

Theft (ku yiba) is universally condemned, not so much for its immoral character as for the fact that it renders a normal social life impossible. The notion of *individual property*, though it is not developed as in more civilised nations, is nevertheless at the base of the whole Bantu system. The Bantus are agriculturists. They believe that the products of their labour belong to them and that no one else is entitled to appropriate them. The notion of property is in direct relation to work accomplished. (Compare Part IV.)

To steal growing mealies is not usual. A thief breaks off the cob, whilst the master of the field first uproots the stalk and then takes the cobs. If a friend of his who happens to be travelling passes through his gardens and wants to eat a cob, he is quite welcome to do so. He also uproots the stalk, puts it on one side of the road or leans it against a tree and draws a line on the ground from the place where the stalk grew to the spot where he has put it. Perhaps the owner of the field will discover the uprooted stalk after a whole month. If he inquires who has helped himself to his mealies, his friend will say to him : "Did you not see the line ?" And they will laugh over it (hlekelelana). A thief acting hastily would not have had time to draw the line!

There are certain magical drugs with which people smear mealie stalks (see Part IV) and they assert that, if any one tries to penetrate into their garden to steal, he will have his hand caught and will not be able to get rid of the plant! For some reason or another, these magical methods do not always work. So the injured person has recourse to the tribunal.

Should the thief be caught in the very act, there is no difficulty! His own field will be taken by the owner of the stolen mealies and he will have to pay a fine of one ox, otherwise the matter will be brought before the Court, and the only difference will be that the fine will be of two or three oxen, one of which will remain in the hands of the chief. (Mankhelu.) If the thief has been clever enough to avoid being caught, if he has stolen from a store hut, Natives are clever detectives and he will probably be discovered. These store huts are generally built in the middle of the field, or in the little bush which surrounds the village ; the grass all around

446

has been pulled up and the sand nicely smoothed down, so that any traces of a thief would easily be seen. He will possibly be recognised at once by the trackers, owing to some peculiarity in the marks on the sand, the foot-print of each individual being more or less known ; clever detectives can even ascertain the height and gait of a man from the length of his stride! If there are no peculiar marks in the foot-prints, the trackers will follow them and reach the village where the thief lives. They will perhaps take him by surprise in his hut. If the matter cannot be settled by the headman of the village and has to be brought before the chief, the guilty party will be fined as much as two, three or even five pounds sterling (Tobane) (1).

When detectives have been unable to trace a thief, they assume a philosophical attitude and say : "Only wait. A man who has stolen will steal again, and you will catch him another time!"

Revolt against the decisions of the chief's hubo is very rare. Should any person take the part of a condemned man and encourage him to oppose the decision of the Court, he will be beaten with a shambock on the square of the capital. "U onhi hubo," "he has spoilt the Court!" Moreover he may have to pay a fine of £ 2. (Mankhelu.)

Answer to some of Professor Frazer's questions on Government. There are no separate chiefs for war and peace. But in time of war the great induna, who is the Commander-in-chief of the army, directs all military operations. — The chief is never required to marry his own sister or daughter. The only similar case of which I have heard, is that of a hunter who must have sexual relations with his daughter before going on a hunting trip (Part IV). — The king's mother does not hold any special office.—

The chief does not keep any portion of his deceased predecessor excepting the nails and hair used for the mhamba (See page 386

---

(1) The following interesting couplet in two sentences aptly describes the thief :
Shishlungwa rendjeletane ? — The crown on the hut nicely rounded ?
Mangatlu a psha ritiho... — The hawk burns his claws...
The thief is like a crown on the top of a hut. He is a lazy person, he attitudinises and will not work. Evil will befall him, as with a hawk who tries to snatch the meat that is roasting and burns his claws !

and Part VI). — To protect and to prolong his life, diviners sometimes call together the whole clan in order to discover and eventually arrest those who might bewitch and kill the chief. This gathering is called *nyiwa* (See Part VI). — As for rain making, it is in the hands of the proper rain doctors (Nkuna) or is done by the ceremonies of *mbelele* (Part VI). — He is not held responsible for public calamities. — If his bodily or mental powers fail, the tinduna discuss matters in his stead and he is not deposed.

Chiefs are never worshipped during life time. After death, they are deified for their own family, who worship them, but not for their subjects. — They are not supposed to turn into wild beasts after their death. — The custom of appointing mock kings does not exist. Only on the death of a chief can one of his relatives be nominated to take his place, and watch over his property until the adjudication of the inheritance.

CHAPTER IV

The Army.

A. WAR-LIKE PROCLIVITIES OF THE THONGAS.

As mentioned in the preliminary chapter (p. 34), in former times the war-like spirit seems to have been but little developed amongst the Thongas. The primitive population possessed no iron weapons, and the invasions which took place from the XVth to the XVIIIth century seem to have been peaceful. Conquerors and subjects soon intermarried and no recollection of bloody contests remained. When clans fought against each other, in those remote times, namely before the arrival of the Zulus (1820), they thought they had done doughty deeds when two or three warriors had been killed, and the vanquishers returned home saying : "None of the enemy is left!!" The army used to form in a straight line, not in a circle, as was the case later on under Zulu influence.

When the cruel hordes of Manukosi subjugated the plain of Delagoa, all that was changed. Of course the Thonga yimpis were defeated very easily. First of all, those of Maputju and Tembe ; in the country of Matjolo, which was afterwards invaded, the chief Mashekane was so stout that he had been surnamed "Mitahomu ni timhondjo" — "the one who swallows an ox, horns and all..." He fought bravely but was also defeated. In Khosen, says Hendrick, an old man who stayed for years in Rikatla and who was then a child, the aborigines were deceived by the perpendicular sticks which the Ba-Ngoni invaders had fixed to their ox-hide shields ; they mistook them for reeds and thought they could break them easily ; but their three united yimpis, that of Khosen under Mbanyele, of Rikotsho under Makwakwa, and of Shiburi under Shitlhama, were repulsed, broken through by the Zulu phalanx.

These Zulus or Ngonis taught the tribes of the plain a system of war much more cruel than the old one : "kill everything," — such is the rule. No exception is made except in the case of women, who are taken prisoners. The Thonga clans readily accepted this new mode of fighting. They adopted the Zulu system wholesale, the proof of which is that all their military terminology is pure Zulu. Their apprenticeship began during the invasion ; the Ba-Ngoni seeing that the Thongas had a certain aptness for war, incorporated them into their own regiments and used to send them forward to the attack, as previously mentioned. They praised them by calling them the *Mabuyandlela* — those who prepare the way, — a kind of nickname which the Thongas have kept to this day and of which they were very proud.

However I do not think it would be unfair to the Thongas to assert that the old peaceful basis of their character is still preserved, notwithstanding this influence. We have had an opportunity of judging of their warlike capabilities during the war of 1894-1896 with the Portuguese. (See Appendix X, Short account of two South African wars.) The Natives did not fight from choice. While some of them gave proof of great endurance, and the army fought in some cases with a certain tenacity, Thongas and especially Ba-Ronga did not show themselves very able warriors. Want of discipline, mutual distrust, timidity resulting in frequent retreats, inability to follow up their successes, such were the main causes of their defeat. The wild soldiers of Maputju, who considered themselves the equals of the genuine Zulus, showed their courage only when there was no danger !

B. WAR COSTUME AND WEAPONS.

One day when we were comfortably seated under the beautiful tree at our station of Rikatla, a strange looking monster suddenly appeared on the scene, running towards us ! The children fled and the women hid themselves... It was Charley, our milk-man, who, with some other warriors, was going to a military review, to be held by his chief Mahazule. He approached us, a giant of 6 ft. in height, decked out in a costume which was certainly grotesque, but of which I at once caught the general idea ; he had evidently tried to resemble a wild animal and had succeeded admirably in the attempt. Such is most likely the origin of the war costume in mankind! As for Charley, he was thoroughly delighted to note the terrorising effect produced by his appearance on the youngsters and folk of weak nerves.

He was, admittedly, the handsomest warrior in our locality, and condescended on one occasion to allow us to photograph him, when he explained in detail the several component parts of his costume, which, as a whole, was certainly formidable! The photograph was a failure, but the get-up has remained imprinted on my memory.

To begin with the top ; the head was decorated with three plumes of long slender feathers, taken from a bird called *sakabonyi*, the widow bird, which is only to be found in the mountains ; sometimes the feathers of other birds are added (magalu, mafu-kwana); one of these plumes is worn in the centre, the others one on each side, and all three are fixed on to a conical helmet (shintlontlo) trimmed with ostrich feathers. This helmet is set on a kind of toque of another skin, which is held in place by a chin-strap. This style of head gear makes the head look about twice the natural size, and, to give it a still more ferocious appearance, it is adorned here and there with porcupine quills.

Round his neck Charley wore a necklace of plaited thongs of black calf skin (tinkocho). Armlets of long white ox hairs, carefully selected from the tail, ornamented his biceps, and garters of a similar make were on the calves of his legs.

The belt around his loins was very rich, the beautiful skin of a civet cat (nsimba), with its fine yellow stripes, hanging down in front to the middle of his thighs, and small antelopes' skins behind (madjobo ya nhlengane). Finally, to complete the wild animal appearance, calves and ankles were covered with bracelets of large black seeds, which come from the North (timbavu), each seed being as large as a cherry. The size of the legs is thus considerably increased and conveys the idea of a pachyderm ; when he jumped heavily or stamped his feet on the ground, it sounded like the tread of an elephant.

This costume is a warm one, and the warrior carries a sort of bone curry-comb, made of the rib of an ox, shaped and sharpened, which he uses to scrape the perspiration from his face and body, when taking violent exercice or indulging in the dances descriptive of his prowess. Such is the native pocket-handkerchief!

The several component parts of the war-dress are kept in a little hut raised on poles, near the owner's dwelling, and are carefully looked after, being frequently dusted and exposed to the sun to preserve them from moths and weevils. A complete uniform is worth several pounds sterling!

Arms among the Ba-Ronga are of a very primitive kind, those of most ancient date being doubtless the *club* (nhonga) and the *knobkerrie* (gungwe) (1) of which two specimens are given in the accompanying illustration (No. 4). The Native never journeys without his stick, using it to kill snakes, should any cross his path, and should fortune smile on him, to knock over any quail that may rise at his feet. In quarrels or in war time this *nhonga* can be a dangerous weapon. The stick with the fluted head comes, I am told, from Bilen, and it seems that this style is in great favour in Gaza. It may have a phallic significance.

But the most formidable weapon of the South African Black is the *assagai* (tlhari, fumo (No. 2), of which there are two kinds ; the larger (likhalo) consisting of a sharp, pointed, double edged steel blade, fixed on to a stick with iron or brass wire, and the smaller (tindjombi) with a blade of the size of our arrow-head, fastened to the handle with strips of bark or of palm leaves. The former is for hand-to-hand combat, and the warrior never releases his hold of it, while the latter—of which three or four may be held in the hand when entering the fight—are thrown at the enemy from a distance (2). The length of the large assagai on the right of the illustration is as follows : Blade 14 inches ; binding of iron

(1) These sticks were given to me as dentistry fees for the extraction of decayed teeth !

(2) I once had an opportunity to observe the effects of the assagai. A young evangelist of our Mission was surprised on the railway line by some Zihlahla warriors

wire, 4 ½ inches and handle 34 ½ inches. The small one, on the left, measures : blade 7 in., iron stem adjoining blade 7 in., binding

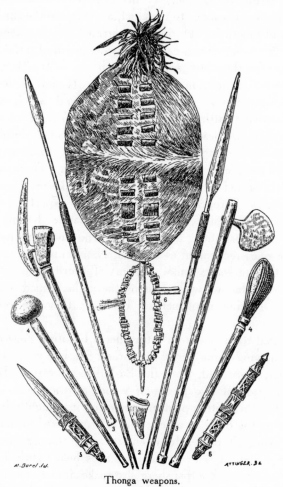

Thonga weapons.

1. Shield ; 2. Assagais ; 3. Battle axes ;
4. Knobkerries ; 5. Dagger ; 6 and 7. Necklace
and little horn worn by men slayers.

in ambush during the 1894 war, and was transfixed at one blow. (7 th January 1895). He had fallen on his knees and the wretches struck him in the back ; the assagai was only prevented from going right through his body by a note book which he was carrying in the breast pocket of his coat.

of palm leaves 5 in. and handle 35 ½ inches. As previously mentioned, the handle of the large sized assagai is broken at the warriors' death, being "he," or his defilement ; but the blade "never dies." It belongs to the chief, as does also the shield, and the son will inherit it. During the warrior's life, it is kept in the hut of his *first wife*. She is called the owner (ñwinyi) of the assagai. It is taboo for the other wives to touch it ; another fact which shows the special position of the first wife. (Comp. p. 284.)

Another weapon in more restricted use and which can also be employed for cutting wood, is the *axe* or *hatchet*, of which I have met with two descriptions (No. 3) ; the blade (mbimbi) may be narrow and elongated—it is then called shingwatane,—or broad and rounded,—when it is the shiyema. These hatchets are firmly inserted in their wooden handles like the axes of the lake-dwellers. European manufacturers now export a considerable number of semicircular hatchets, similar to the one on the right in my illustration, to Delagoa. The one here portrayed will be at once recognised as being of Native make. I may also mention the big *knives* (mikwa), a sort of sword ; one sometimes meets brawny fellows walking along the paths, armed with these dangerous looking implements! However they are quite inoffensive.

I managed to obtain from a traveller a beautiful *dagger* which he was carrying slung across his breast ; it is a rare specimen and comes, I am told, from the Ba-Ndjao tribe (No. 5). The sheath is made of two pieces of wood, artistically carved and fastened together with a plait of iron wire ; it is slightly hollowed out to allow the blade to enter ; this is firmly fixed in the handle through which it passes from end to end, coming out at the extremity, where it is bent back and thus held tightly in place. The Ba-Pedi in the Zoutpansberg also make similar knives.

Finally, when the warrior holds in one hand his large assagai, in the other will be found his *shield* (shitlhangu) (No. 1), which he grasps by the stick around which this piece of defensive armour pivots. The Thonga shield is made like that of the Zulus, of a piece of ox-hide, oval in shape and of varying size, sometimes all of one colour and sometimes variegated. (The several battalions in the Chaka army were distinguished by differently coloured shields.) On either side of the central line, from top to bottom, two parallel rows of small square incisions are made (magabela) through which are run strips of hide of a different colour, the effect being a series of oblongs. By an ingenious device the ends of these strips are so tied at the back of the shield as to form several sheath-like nooses into which is inserted the stick by which it is held. The space between the two lines of oblongs is called the back (nhlana) of the shield. The nooses or sheaths are four or six in number : two or three at the top, and two or three at the bottom, a space being left in the middle, where the warrior grasps the stick. This stick tends to strengthen the shield, but, being merely passed through the nooses, it acts also as a pivot around which it can turn ; it is this pivoting action which gives to the shield its chief value as a protection. An assagai (usually thrown with considerable strength) would easily penetrate the ox-hide, but when it strikes the shield, the force of the impact causes it to pivot and the weapon is deflected to one side : should it strike exactly in the middle, it would hit the stick, break it and lose all further impetus. It is hardly necessary to add that the *shitlhangu* of the South African Black is absolutely useless when opposed to bullets ; it was invented to protect the warrior against the dreaded assagai, at a time when firearms were not yet thought of!

During the last century the Ba-Ronga have begun to use guns for hunting and also for war. Although the sale of firearms to the Natives has often been prohibited, the Ba-Ronga were reported to possess several hundreds of rifles at the commencement of the 1894 war, and also to be fairly proficient in their use... very different from the Madagascans, who removed the sights from their rifles on the score that they were in the way when taking aim!

C. THE MOBILISATION OF THE ARMY.

In the Zihlahla country, when the chief wished to muster his forces, he did so by means of the *shipalapala*, the rudimentary trumpet which I described in the preceding chapter. A swift messenger (shigidjimi) ran from village to village, blowing this instrument ; when he was tired he passed it on to some other good runner, who carried the summons further afield ; he ran and ran until he was exhausted, when he handed the trumpet to a third, and so on until the whole country had been covered.

At the sound of the well-known call of the shipalapala, the warriors shout : "A hi hlomen !" — "to arms !" They at once put on their war costumes and repair to the capital.

In Nondwane all the sub-chiefs possessed their shipalapala, and each of them summoned his own people. There the shipalapala mostly sounded to call for dances and for feasts. When the army was mobilised merely to discuss matters quietly, messengers ran through the country shouting : "Mayivonule !" — "take the shields !"..., to which the warriors answered : "A hi hlomen !" — "to arms !" The messenger had to go quickly. "He did not lose time in grinding tobacco ;" he only indicated the time when the army was expected in the capital.

Should matters be more serious, should a hostile yimpi have invaded the territory, every one can give the alarm (tlhabela mukhosi), shouting : "Yi ngeeneeeeeee !" "It has entered !" (viz., the hostile army has invaded our territory). All the women flee away and the men run to the capital.

D.   THE MUKHUMBI, THE CIRCLE OF WARRIORS.

Decked out like wild animals, the warriors hasten with all speed to the chief's village, where the regiments muster. The army (1) is divided into a certain number of *battalions, mabotshu,* or *meboko,* all men of about the same age forming a *botshu.* The *botshu* itself is made up of several *companies, mitlawa* or *mabandla,* and may therefore vary very much in numbers.

(1) Yimpi (pl. tiyimpi) in Thonga corresponds to impi in Zulu.

THE ARMY

In the army of Matjolo there were nine battalions, commencing with that composed of youths from sixteen to twenty years old, up to that of "crown men" (makehla) and the grey beards who where still capable of handling an assagai ; for every able-bodied man is a soldier and makes it a point of honour to join the army when it is mobilised.   In the Zihlahla clan, the battalions of young men were called *Megajlela* and also *Ndumakazulu*, "the one who is celebrated as far as Zululand," surname of the chief Ñwamantibyane.   After them came the *Nyonibovu*, *Giva*, *Malwabo*, *Djanungwana*.

Mankhelu, the Commander of the Nkuna yimpi, gave me the names of his battalions and the explanation of them.   The old men formed the regiment called *Mamphondo*, those of the horns. Some of them used to tie a horn on their foreheads ; they imitated the rhinoceros or the buffalo.   The following regiment was the *Mamphisi* (timhisi), the hyenas ; then the *Machoni*, the sea birds, a kind of duck, very swift ; then the *Timbulwane*, a sort of lynx, the *Mafakubi*, representing the ndakazi antelope and, lastly, the most numerous regiment, the *Dhlanazo*, "those who eat with others (dya na bu)."   Each regiment has, as we shall see, its own war-cry, in which it imitates the animal whose name it bears.

When all have reached the capital the first procedure is the "formation of the circle," in Thonga *biya mukhumbi*, to fence the circle or *aka mukhumbi*, to build the circle.   This is accomplished in the Zihlahla army by a special summons which I might call "the order to fall in."   Heralds scatter in all directions, enter the huts, approach the groups encamped around the capital, and shout in a high and monotonous key the following Zulu words.   It will be noticed that the formula given is that which was made use of by the heralds in the Mpfumo clan during the war of 1894.

> Izwana !   Otyo ndjalo, Muvelu, (1)
> Be nga m'thandi ba ka Nkupane,
> Umta'ka Sihlahla, esikulu si ka Hamule,
> Malobola ge dyose e bulandin ka Mbukwana.

(1) Muvelu, the Zulu surname for Ñwamantibyane.

Listen ! This is what Ñwamantibyane says,
He whom the people of Nkupane do not love, (1)
The son of the Great Forest (Sihlahla) of Hamule, (2)
He who took a wife and used the sword in the country of
    his parents-in-law, in Mbukwane's country.

Gwalagwala a libuvu,
Ilihlengo ngo kubekeka,
Umpathi we sibamo,
U za ku debula Mangole ni Maputukizi.

The royal bird with red plumage (3),
Magnificent to contemplate,
He who holds in his hand a gun
With which he will fire on the Angolese and the Portuguese.

Nduma kuti, lo wa khiti,
Mo nga ngesilwana,
U ti ka : a yi funule !

He whose fame spreads afar, our chief,
Who is as a wild beast,
It is he who says : "To arms !".

This final exclamation, prolonged and finishing abruptly on the last syllable, carries a long distance ; all the warriors jump to their feet and, brandishing their assagais and shields, run to the chief's village, where the circle is to be formed. Each

(1) The people of Nkupane are one of the younger branches of the royal family of Mpfumo. They lived close to Lourenço Marques, on the other slope of the hill, to the West of the town. They would have liked undoubtedly, in common with many others, to assert their independence by throwing off the yoke of the elder branch, and even attempted to do so when Mahombole tried, in 1867 or in 1869, to overthrow Zihlahla. But the elder branch, whose chiefs were energetic men, succeeded in maintaining its authority over the whole clan. The fact that the people of Nkupane "do not love" Ñwamantibyane redounds rather to the credit of the latter.

(2) Ñwamantibyane's father was Zihlahla, his grandfather was Hamule. Sihlahla, or Zihlahla, in Zulu means forest, hence the herald's play on the word. The reign of Zihlahla, which we may place at from 1867 to 1883, was very troubled, at least during its first few years. The young chief, on his return from Natal, after the death of his father Hamule, married Mbilwana, a princess of the royal family of Mabota. During the bloody wars then raging, Zihlahla was angry with Mabota (whose chief was Mbukwana), for playing him false, and, one fine day, he made a raid into the country of his parents-in-law, killing many people. To have thus treated his "bakoñwana," who are ordinarily held in such great respect, (see Part II) was a proof of valour which is remembered to this day, more than fifty years after the event. It must be said that, after this exploit, Zihlahla left his residence near the town and took refuge in the Nwamba territory ; the Whites with whom he was fighting put in his place a certain Ñwayeye whose name we shall find in a war song to which we shall have occasion to refer later on.

(3) The nkulunkulu is a bird which is shot in the forest on the borders of the Nkomati ; its feathers are red, and only chiefs are allowed to wear them.

458

regiment, with its counsellors at its head, is called in turn by
the organisers of the army ; (at Zihlahla they were Mahagane,
the chief's uncle, and Mpompi), and the several companies of
the regiments form ranks one behind the other. I have already
described this imposing circle, when treating of the coronation
of the chief. Every warrior can take in at a glance the entire
assemblage. Seen from the interior, it is an unbroken circle
of shields, resting perpendicularly on the ground, and all touching ;
behind, a crowd of men, the greater the number, the deeper the
ranks, a forest of feathers waving above their heads.

The mukhumbi is not however a perfect circle. It is rather
like a *horse shoe*, as there remains an *opening* (nyangwa or sangwa),
which gives access into it.   On either side of this *door* the regiment
of the young men takes up its position ; the Dhlanazo in the
Nkuna mukhumbi and the Ndumakazulu in that of Zihlahla.   At
the opposite end, facing the entrance, is the *chest of the army*
(shifuba sha yimpi), where the chief stands surrounded by the
men of riper age, the strongest of whom act as a body guard.
Between the chest and the opening, on both sides, the middle-aged
warriors occupy the wings, the elder ones nearer the chest,
the younger nearer the entrance. This disposition is highly
significant ; notice that it is exactly the same as that of the village
itself, a large door (mharana) ; on both sides of the entrance, the
huts of the unmarried inhabitants (lao and nhanga) ; at the back
the huts of the headman, and, at the sides, those of his younger
brothers. The idea of age and of hierarchy entirely dominates
both these social manifestations!

As regards the numerical strength of the mukhumbi, one
of my informants who belonged to the Ndumakazulu regiment
—young men from 19 to 25 years old—told me that he estimated
the war strength of his regiment at about 500 men : the entire
Zihlahla circle might be put at 2000 strong.

I have often seen the Nkuna mukhumbi assembled. I had
even the opportunity of addressing its warriors during the Sikororo
war of 1901. They were between five and six hundred in all.
But this clan is very much scattered and many warriors were not
present.

459

Before going into battle, certain rites have to be accomplished. In order to stimulate a war-like courage and to imbue the warrior's minds with a certainty of victory, it is necessary to proceed to the performance of the war-songs (guba), of the war dances (gila), and to administer the medicine which will render the soldiers invulnerable.

E. WAR SONGS.

The performance of war songs is called *guba*. I have already fully described the Mpfumo national song, (p. 373) which would seem to be more adapted to celebrate a coronation than to serve as an incentive to battle ; it is however used indiscriminately for both purposes.

Another war-song which is very popular in the Mpfumo clan is the following :

> Zulu : U ngwa si mu thini,   Mayeye ?
> U banga muhlaba, u bulala bantu !
> Ronga : U ta ku mu yini,   Ñwayeye?
> U banga ntlhaba, u dlaya bhanu !
> What will you succeed in doing to him, Ñwayeye ?
> You take the country and slay the people !

This is a question addressed to Ñwayeye, the rival of the chief Zihlahla ; Ñwayeye was placed in authority near Lourenço Marques by the Portuguese between 1860 and 1870. He accepted the position, but was unable to retain it any length of time, and the recollection of his failure is perpetuated in this song which is intended to extol the royal family of Mpfumo.

A third song, also in vogue with the Mpfumo warriors, runs thus :

> Zulu : Zi m' thini ? A ba ze zi ba bona, abantu bezizwe !
> Ronga : Hi ta ku yini? A ba te hi ba bona, bhanu ba matiko !
> What shall we say ? Let them come and let us see them, the people of the enemy's country !

This is a defiance hurled at the adversaries.

The Army

In Nondwane, they also sing this last song ; another runs as follows :

> Zulu : Ngambala !   ngi file...O..o..o.. Zinkomo zito !
> Ronga : Ñwamboten, ndji file !   O..o..o.. Tihomu teru !
> My friend !   I am killed.   Oh!   oh!   oh!   Our oxen !

The warriors doubtless refer to the ruin which would be entailed were the enemy to carry off their cattle, and thus they encourage one another to fight stubbornly!

Another Ronga song performed in the guba ceremony is this :

> Zia yi khalelo muhlu ya se mananga
> We are weeping for the giraffe of the desert.

The giraffe may be the chief of the clan whom the warriors are determined to protect, or perhaps the enemy's chief whom they will go and kill.

This song is also one of the great guba songs of the Nkuna clan, but the words are slightly different.   I have collected two others :

> Hi yi kwa makhosi !
> Si phuma ka makhosi, Si gambuza !
> U mkhonto use sandhleni, Eji !   Eji !
> U mkhonto usao gobee...
>
> War comes from the chiefs !
> It is ordered by the chiefs !   We go and kill !
> The spear is in our hands !   Eji !   Eji !
> The spear kills and bends in the wound !

The oldest of the Nkuna guba songs, which was already in use before the arrival of Manukosi, at the begining of the XIXth century, when the army still formed in line and not in circle, runs as follows :

> Hi bo yima hi bo yima !
> Mi teka burena mi nyika tinuba (?) ta bambe.
> Let us stand fast, let us stand fast !
> Do not let your strength go, it would help the enemy to conquer.

The words of this song are Thonga, as the Zulus had not yet imposed their terminology on the Thonga yimpi.

One of the finest war songs is that sung in the armies of Maputju

and Tembe, an antiphon seemingly very ancient, which changes
from the minor to the major, producing a truly grandiose effect :
(For the music of most of these songs, see Vol. II. Part V.)

"At break of day," sings the solist,....
"Who was it that crowned thee, Muwai, king of Maputju?" reply
the warriors.

Muwai is the great-great-grandfather of the chief Mabai, deposed
in 1896. He reigned at the close of the XVIIIth century, his son
Makasana having been chief from 1800 to 1850. Muwai is
compared to the rising sun, or at least the song recalls his coronation, which must have taken place very early in the morning, at
daybreak. It is evidently in praise of the royal family that the
entire army chants this glorious souvenir.

Loko ku ti qa, loko ku ti qa
U bekwe ngubane Muwai ?
Muwai, ka Mabudu ! Muwai ka Mabudu !
U bekwe ngubane ?

At day break — At day break
Who was it that crowned thee, Muwai ?
Muwai, king of Maputju ! Muwai, king of Maputju
Who was it that crowned thee ?

As we see, the war songs are tolerably short ; a declamation
of three or four words by a soloist (musimi) who dances in the
middle of the circle, and a chorus sung by all the warriors, stamping
their feet on the ground and striking their shields with their
assagais. (Hence the exclamation "Eji" found at the close of some
sentences.) Or sometimes the whole throng brandish the assagai
in a rythmical fashion, raising it first to the right, then to the left,
afterwards inclining it to the side, and lastly downwards as if to
pierce...

When the great war-induna wants the song to stop, he gives
a signal. At once all the shields are elevated and a sibilant
murmur runs through the ranks : shi-shi-shi-shi, or a special
click : nqu-nqu-nqu. Hence the verb nqunquzela, to stop a
war song.

And then the war dance will take place.

THE ARMY

F. THE WAR DANCE.

The *guba* is itself a kind of war dance, as dancing does not mean a change in the dancer's position. Nodding with the head, gesticulation of the hands and slow motions of the feet constitute a dance (kina). In some guba songs, there may be a backward and forward movement of all the warriors to widen or narrow their circle. I have even seen men crossing the mukhumbi, two by two, or three by three, during the guba.

But the true war-dance is the *gila* (Ro.) or *giya* (Dj.) the representation of deeds of valour by warriors who have killed an enemy in battle. The massed chorus of the guba is most imposing, but still more deeply does the *gila* impress one by its wildness. Look at this elderly man who suddenly detaches himself from the circle, stamping with all his might on the ground. His feet beat the earth in cadence, one blow being long, the three following ones short : -ꞷ ꞷ ꞷ. He goes on, making the ground shake, brandishing his weapons with all his might, perspiring from his efforts and pronouncing Zulu words which the throng inter-rupts by wild shoutings, as if to encourage him... Then he returns to his place, and the whole army concludes the performance by a kind of whistling : zu... iiiiii. ..... prolonged on a high and piercing note, which suddenly descends to a deep and guttural tone : i. aaaaa...... He has hardly resumed his place in the ranks when a young man springs into the circle, jumping like an antelope, holding his assagai and gesticulating all the while, as if transfixing an invisible enemy. His eyes glare like those of a wild beast, and immediately the army entones a song, his song, the one which has been composed to glorify his deed. Possibly his return to the ranks will be greeted by another shout : I..a...Nda-u! — Lion! comparing him to a lion returning to his forest which nobody will dare to attack. The encouragement given by the warriors to the *bagili* and their great final cry are called *khuza* or *khunzela*.

"At that very moment," says Mankhelu, "the hearts of the young men tremble in their breasts! Their hair stands on end...

463

An extraordinary war spirit comes over them all..." And every one having witnessed these performances in the Thonga or Zulu mukhumbi will confess that they are wonderfully impressive. It is a mixture of dramatic, epic and lyric poetry, three literary *genres* which are still confounded, the whole being enhanced by a deep, wild music and subject to the laws of a certain artistic style.

The fighting instincts are excited to the highest pitch by these patriotic choruses and dramatic representations. Thus should the troops be slow in making a start, the young men go dancing to the chief and beg him to "grant them permission" to go forth and slay, or rather to "give them men" to slaughter (ku nyika). The Native idea appears to be that the chief holds the lives of the enemies in his hands ; without his permission they cannot go forward, but this once given, they rush enthusiastically to the fray. They even go so far as to taunt him with being an old woman, a coward, because he will not let them go at once (1).

When the excitement has reached the culminating point, and it has been definitely decided to fight, the time has arrived for the magic treatment by which the warriors will be rendered invulnerable.

G. ADMINISTERING THE WAR-MEDICINE.

This custom is probably of ancient origin, but I have reason to believe that, amongst the Ba-Ronga, it was practised without any great formality until the advent of the Zulu influence, when it was brought into much greater prominence and invested with more solemnity. "Drinking the war-medicine" took place on several occasions during the revolt of 1894 to 1895. At *Zihlahla* this potion was administered to all warriors before the rebel attack

(1) Gungunyana, on one occasion, when his warriors were importuning him with similar requests, sent the more ardent spirits to wage war unarmed against the wild beasts, and I was told they actually succeeded in capturing a leopard alive and brought it back to the chief !

THE ARMY

on the town of the 14th October 1894 ; also prior to the ambuscade
in the outskirts of Lourenço Marques, on the 7th January 1895,
and before the battle of Morakwen, the 2nd February following.
According to my informant, the chief doctor of the army prepared
the medicine in a huge dish with leaves and roots cut into slices.
These ingredients possessed an effervescent quality ; the medicine-
man stirred up the decoction and with it sprinkled the whole army
formed in a circle.   After this every warrior was fully persuaded
that he was invulnerable, that the bullets would be deflected on
either side of him, or, even should they hit him, they would be
flattened against his body and fall harmless to the ground.   The
charm could only be broken by the warrior turning his back to the
foe.   Then the bullets might pass through him.   I have met with
very intelligent Natives who were perfectly convinced of this fact,
although open to reasonable argument on all other points.   They
told me that certain Natives who were bowled over by grapeshot,
picked themselves up after the fight, came to life again, or rather
regained consciousness and then, with their fingers, extracted the
bullets, which had all remained imbedded in the skin!

A *Nondwane* warrior described to me, in the following terms,
the administering of the magic potion, as it was done on the
7th January 1895 before the battle of Morakwen.   The whole
army was assembled at Nkanyen, on the bank of the Nkomati.
It was there that the magician prepared the medicine, with two
young girls as assistants.   While he was brewing the mixture
and making it froth, the soldiers, formed in a semi-circle, looked
on, standing erect, poising their assagais on a level with their
heads.   Then a *ntjhopfa* was cut down (the shrub of oblivion,
often employed by Native doctors and of which we have already
noted the use in other ceremonials) and a branch laid across the
road.   The several battalions were called up, one after the other,
and every man had to jump over the branch and take a mouthful
of the medicine, which he spat out again, pronouncing the sacramental *tsu* which accompanies the offerings made to the gods : he
subsequently went off, running and dancing and getting ready to
go forth and kill.   When each one had taken his share of the
medicine and it was all finished, the doctor said to them : "Now I

465

have given you all my strength ; go and slay." They crossed the river at night and having reached the left bank, at a point about ten kilometers from the Portuguese camp at Morakwene, they were made to observe the strictest silence for a long time. Then they felt that valour (burena) had taken possession of them!

Amongst the Ba-Nkuna the war-medicine is also administered under the form of *sprinkling*. This sprinkling may take place in time of peace, when danger threatens. The chief kills a black ox and the army, summoned to the capital, is sprinkled and eats the flesh of the ox. This will make the country ready for any eventuality. But the ceremony is much more serious when war is at hand. Then the "great medicine of the country," carefully kept in the calabashes of the Court magicians, is mixed with *psanyi* of slaughtered sheep and with white sand taken from the river. During the night, the mukhumbi is formed and all the men sit down, their heads bowed over their knees, their eyes closed, in perfect silence. Then one of the queens, an old woman who no longer has any sexual relations, enters the circle, absolutely naked. She dips a leafy branch into the magical infusion and marches all round, inside and outside, sprinkling all the warriors and muttering the following words : "Kill them, break their pots, kill their dogs, catch their chief, bring him here, bring so-and-so and so-and-so." The warriors tremble with emotion. They pray to their gods in a low tone : "Save me! Help me!" But none of them dares to raise his eyes! They know quite well that they would die!

It is extremely important that the officiating woman should be old and have had no sexual relations for a long time, or "the assagais would lose their strength ; the masculine weapons would become blind and the feminine weapons alone would see... The woman would have untied the knot of the assagai ; she would cross the way (tjemakanya) of the great medicine... She must be a quiet woman (a rula)". (Mankhelu).

Similar customs exist in *Maputju*, where the medicine is called "the medicine of hatred,"—that which dispels all natural feeling and makes a man capable of killing his fellow-man! I give the particulars of this curious medical treatment as I have them from one of the Natives of the country : there are no fewer than seven acts in this grand performance of "preparation for battle."

a) In the first place when the chief foresees that a campaign is imminent, he has water drawn, and all the necessary ingredients gathered together : then he goes into retirement for one month, during which he is busy preparing the medicine with the magician who knows all about the recipe.

b) At the end of this time the entire army is summoned to the capital. A bull is brought out before the assembled soldiers and the chief strikes it on the head with a stick : this infuriates the animal, which must be caught and thrown down by the men unarmed ; the chief then approaches and kills it with an axe. They dismember the carcase, cutting off the flesh in strips, which they cook in a large battered pot, stirring it with their assagais and pouring into it at the same time "the medicine of hatred."

c) On this day the army is mustered and formed in a circle. The Commander-in-Chief takes the meat, cuts it into small pieces and mixes with it certain human ingredients : a finger taken from a hostile petty chief killed in battle has been carefully preserved ; the dried up phalange is scraped and the bone-dust thus obtained is mixed with the medicine. This additional ingredient is to prevent any feeling of remorse, any prickings of conscience : "ku susa lipfalo," literally "to remove the diaphragm," the seat of the conscience, according to Ronga ideas. (See later on a more probable explanation of this rite.) The Commander-in-Chief takes the pieces of meat thus seasoned and throws them into the mouths of the soldiers, who must not touch them with their hands. The food must be received between the teeth ; any meat falling to the ground is picked up by the children.

d) On the following day, the whole army proceeds to a large lake (the lake of Shika, near the village of Nhlampfukazi) to be treated with another medicine, an emetic. This is placed on a skin in the middle of the lake : the skin is withdrawn, leaving the particles of the drug floating on the water ; each warrior must stoop down and swallow a mouthful of the emetic. He will vomit yesterday's meat : "fear will be thrown up and valour will remain" (ku hlantiwile butoya, ku sele burena).   The chief having mean-while taken up his position on a neighbouring hill, the several regiments rush towards him, surround him and beg to be sent as soon as possible to fight and to slay.

e) But, before this can be done, the chief returns to the capital, the army following him.   A double trial has still to be undergone. A large broom is made of small branches of trees soaked in fat from sheep's tails and is then set on fire.   The chief walks round carrying his flaming torch, passing it rapidly before the faces of the warriors formed in a circle.   Some of the helmets catch fire and the wearers are promptly ordered to fall out of the ranks.   The chief addresses them in angry tones : "Deliver up to me," he says, "the charms you are concealing!'Tis only I, the chief, who may possess enchanted drugs.   You certainly have some, as your plumes took fire...   Look at the other warriors ; the feathers on their heads are not burnt!"   This trial is probably a means of frightening suspected traitors or of expelling wizards (baloyi).

f) All shields are now "presented" all round the circle.   The chief bends back the point of an assagai and with it strikes each shield, but not with sufficient force to pierce it...   This "conse-cration" of the shields will doubtless make them a more secure protection against the enemy's weapons.

g) Lastly the series is closed by the "aspersion."   A mortar is produced in which some leaves are soaking ; these are stirred round in water and the chief sprinkles the whole army.   This is the final ceremony.   The chief remains at home : the warriors thus fortified and protected against all dangers start on their expedition.

This last act only is performed in the clans of Shirindja, Nwamba and Zihlahla.

H. ON THE WAR PATH. THE BATTLE. STRATEGY. PANICS. RETURN HOME.

The *mukhumbi* has been "built" for the last time.   Proclamations have all been issued.   Nothing remains but to start.

This *starting of the army* (ku thethwa) is also done according to prescribed rites. I once witnessed it, when the Nkuna army went to Sikororo's country on a kind of punitive expedition. The great ndjuna of the army, the Commander-in-Chief, Mankhelu, his stern face grimmer than ever, holding a hyena's tail in his hand, clad in a white shirt which was very little in keeping with the whole appearance of the mukhumbi, stepped inside the large circle and raised his tail... Then the *Dhlanazo*, the young bloods, ran towards him shouting : "Kwe-kwe-kwe!" Their cry is the same as that of the *Timbulwana* (lynx), their elders, who came next. Mankhelu pointed the tail in a certain direction and these two regiments started. The *Mafakubi* came in their turn, imitating the galop of the antelopes : "tshwi-tshwi-tshwi! gwu gwu... hwu, hwu!... eka-ka-ka-ka..." and finally shouting : "N'ta dya na man" — "with whom shall I eat it ?" — a strange sentence which may be, as previously mentioned, a reminiscence of a totemic period! (See page 366)... The *Matsyoni*, the seabirds, followed shouting "tswe-tswe-tswe ;" the *Mamphondo*, those of the horn, came shouting "tshuba-tshuba-tshuba" and imitating buffalos and rhinoceroses. The *Maphisi* started last, howling wildly like hyenas : "hum-hum-hum..."

If the field of battle is far away, if there is a long march to be made, special *marching songs* are sung on the road. The most impressive is the following : a soloist sings in a very high key :

Abafo ! — The enemy !

and the whole army answers in a rich and tuneful melody :

Enena-a-a! a-a ! — Here they are !

All the shields are held straight, ready to meet the foe. Here are two other marching songs :

Nangu moya wa tshisizwe !
We are the fire which burns the country !
Inkonyana ya ndlopfu inhlezio baen...
The calf of the elephant is exposed on the plain...

This means the chief who is in danger! Let us protect and deliver him.

As regards the *order of the march*, the battalions of the young men, stationed on either side of the entrance, go first ; they form the advanced guard, the post of greatest danger. The scouts, tinhlori (Dj.) tinhloli (Ro.), go in front ; each company has its leader to whom these scouts bring reports. It is the duty of the young men to surround the position to be carried and to make the assault. The two sides of the circle then follow, and lastly the chest of the army, forming the rear guard. The chief thus brings up the rear, protected by the battalions of veterans. But generally the chief does not go to battle ; he remains at home.

During the campaign, *the whole clan is subjected to many taboos.* Those who remain at home must *keep quiet* (rula). No noise must be heard in the villages. The women must not close the doors of the huts. It is taboo : their husbands might meet with "bitterness" (shibiti). They might lack strength to run away. Fire must be lit in the huts in the evening, in order that the warriors may "have light" where they are. It is taboo to omit this precaution. Work in the fields must be more or less suspended ; women may attend to it in the morning only, before the heat of the day, while the air is still fresh. "Then, if a warrior has stepped on a thorn, the thorn will be cool (titimeta) ; if he has knocked against a stump, the stump will be quiet and not hurt him. (Mboza.)" Old men who remain at home must keep watch, and if they see a messenger coming, they follow him to the chief. Should he bring bad news, they do not inform the women, as it is taboo to mourn over warriors killed in war before the return of the army. A fine is imposed upon those who contravene this law. It is taboo also to have sexual relations as long as the army is on the war-path. This would cause thorns to hurt the warriors and they would be defeated. (Mankhelu.)

According to Mankhelu, the mukhumbi may be again formed after arriving in the proximity of the hostile army. The battalions will be sent one after the other by the great ndjuna who will watch the progress of the fight. If he sees his men giving way, he "pours" (tshelela) new companies to help those who are fighting until they rush the position (gwabula) and put the enemy to flight. Then the pursuit begins. The dust flies up

470

to heaven! The vanquishers follow their enemies until they reach their villages. As a rule, *they kill every one,* women, children, old men and tired warriors who have been unable to run away. They take the oxen and burn the huts. However exceptions are made in some instances : Sigaole, the ally of the Whites, ordered his warriors to spare the lives of the people of Zihlahla, during the expedition of February 1895, and to take them prisoners instead. "If you find any inhabitants remaining in the villages" said he "go into them. Let some one draw a line on the ground around the village and forbid the soldiers to cross it and to massacre the people." Generally speaking, however, the only lives spared are those of the younger women and girls of whom they can hope to make some profit, either by taking them as wives or selling them to others for matrimonial purposes. These prisoners are called "heads" (tinhloko) (1). This is the only kind of slavery practised by our tribe. Such wives are not ill-treated, as a rule.

So far I have described the war-customs of the Natives when fighting with each other. Let me add some particulars taken from the Thonga-Portuguese war of 1894-1896 (App. X.) which throw some light on the Native modes of fighting against White people.

*

*   *

When opposed to White troops, the attack en masse would be too dangerous : regiments advancing in serried ranks would offer too good a target to the European artillery. From information I have gathered with reference to the battle of Makupe or Magule (Sept. 8 1895), it would appear that the Ba-Ronga advanced in skirmishing order, those provided with guns approaching very close to the lines of the Whites. During this fight, one of the most important of the whole campaign, the Portuguese Commanding Officer, M. F. d'Andrade, shewed great presence of mind : the Zihlahla and Nondwane

---

(1) Two women, members of our Church, were carried off in this way by some of the Zihlahla men (6th October 1894), and we had the greatest trouble in finding them. They were seized close to the town, while going to their food-stores and their captors had duly married them with the acquiescence of their chief.

471

warriors came into almost actual contact with the Portuguese square, whilst the Gaza regiments, which were in greatly superior force, remained at a distance and then retreated. They had been told by Gungunyana that they were not to kill White men, so their presence was a mere parade. The Ba-Ronga finding themselves thus deserted followed the same tactics! One of the warriors present on this occasion drew me a plan of the engagement on the floor of a hut! (See accompanying sketch).

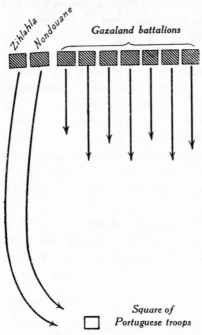

On the whole it must be admitted that the Natives of these parts seem greatly to prefer surprise attacks, sudden descents upon peaceful and unsuspecting folk, to any kind of regular pitched battle.

The Swazis used to arrive in the Delagoa plain very early in the morning, surround the villages and massacre indiscriminately all the inhabitants, in the years 1860-1870. The Ngonis of Gungunyana adopted the same method. The Matjolo warriors, whom the Portuguese sent against Zihlahla in February 1895, encamped in perfect silence within one hour's march of the spot where Nwamantibyane had taken refuge (Nhlalalene) and attacked his people when they least expected them. They indulged in the pleasure of killing numbers of women and children, whilst their male enemies fled into the palm marshes, shouting vociferously : "Make ready your rope to climb up to heaven... There will be no more rest on earth for you! Cook three meals : you may eat two but never a third." Empty threats! The greater part of the Native fights during this war consisted in ambuscades and treacherous slaughterings : lots of noise, plenty of bluster, but not much real bravery.

We shall arrive at the same estimate of Native valour if we consider *the great campaign* planned by Gungunyana in concert with Zihlahla and Mahazule, who had taken refuge in Gaza, during July-August 1895. Nine regiments, representing a large effective force, were to start from Manzimehlope, the country beyond the Nkomati River ; three of these were to ascend the left bank of the river, to cross it in the neighbourhood of Komati-Poort and to enter Swaziland, the Ngoni chief having made alliance with the Swazis. The other regiments were to cross the Nkomati to the West of the Sabie, and thence to go southward by Moveni. The remaining three, with whom were incorporated Zihlahla and Mahazule, were to ravage Shirindja, Ntimane and Nondwane, passing about one hour's march to the West of Lourenço Marques, exterminating the inhabitants of Matjolo (allies of the Whites), whose retreat to the town would be thus cut off... The nine regiments were to effect a junction at a place called Nkobotlwene, to the South of the Bay, where the forces of Gungunyana would fraternise with those of Maputju, with whom they were on good terms. For the space of seven months, tens of thousands of these warriors were to overrun the country and to annihilate all the tribes opposed to Gungunyana. The chief would not massacre the Whites, nor would he attack their town : he calculated on rendering them powerless by depriving them of the assistance of their Black allies, and expected them thus to sue for peace on honourable terms! Such, at least, was the plan of campaign which transpired after Gungunyana had been made prisoner, in the centre of his own country of Gaza, by a party of about forty White soldiers! The whole thing culminated in a single day's skirmish in the Ntimane country. The petty chiefs quarrelled amongst themselves ; only a few hardy warriors dared to cross the Nkomati and slaughtered some women at a short distance from the outpost of Chinabane. Finding themselves discovered, they at once recrossed the river and made off to the Northward.

The principal causes of the incapacity in military matters so noticeable amongst the Blacks during the war of 1894-1896, are doubtless the *internal jealousies* between the tribes and also, it must be said, the mysterious dread inspired by the White race, their artillery and their superior discipline.

The feeling of mistrust existing between Matjolo and Ñwamba, Nondwane, Zihlahla and Shirindja, also explains the terrible *panics* which occured during the military operations. On several occasions the Native forces were subject to panics which might have entailed the most serious results. As an instance I relate the following, which nearly led to the partial destruction of the Matjolo army. The Matjolo warriors, as also those of Ñwamba, had received orders from the Whites, at the end of January 1895, to attack Zihlahla and Mahazule. One of the young men of Matjolo, who was present during the operations, told me this story : "We were to have joined the men of Ñwamba at a village called Mukapan, but did not find them at the rendez-vous. As they had made common cause with Zihlahla at the beginning of the revolt, we had not much confidence in them. It looked as if they were in hiding and intended to attack us treacherously and kill us. At this time two panics occured. The first was at Hukwen, when a man dreamt that he was being killed, and cried out : "Yo! Uwe! There are people who are killing me!" It was pitch dark. Every one jumped to his feet. Some ran to hide in the forest, but others shouted : "The enemy are here!" Fighting began in the regiment of Geba, (composed of men of the same age as Sigaole, the chief), but no one was killed. A few individuals who kept their presence of mind restored order, but we came very near exterminating each other! The next night a Chopi of our troop had a fright, and cried out : "Why do you want to kill me, you men of Matjolo ? I will tell Sigaole's mother." He was promptly secured and forced to keep quiet for fear that he would rouse the Nondwane people, etc. A similar panic seized the troops of Mahazule, when they went to lay waste the country round Lourenço Marques (October 1894).

To avoid these panics, as far as possible, the Ba-Ronga arrange a *password* before starting on an expedition. I was able to learn two of these countersigns, after the war, by questioning some young men who had taken part in certain military operations. On one occasion the pass-word was as follows : "Be ge pi ?" These are Zulu words signifying : "What are you looking at ?" The requisite answer being : "Be ge pezulu"—"We are looking at the sky." In the famous attack made by the Zihlahla warriors on the town of Lourenço Marques, on 14th October 1894, the word was : "U landu bane ?"—"With whom have you a quarrel ?"—and the reply : "Ngi landa Mlungu!"—"I have a quarrel with the white man!"

Return from the battle. When a yimpi has been defeated in battle, but is not pursued by the enemy, it returns silently and disperses before reaching the capital, each warrior going back ashamed to his village. Mourning takes place in the villages of the deceased. But much lamenting is not allowed. It may be that the chief will prohibit any mourning if many have been killed, "because the whole country would mourn : — they have not been killed by the mat (likuku) at home, but by the assagai on the battle-field! They are men! If any one weeps he will have to pay £ 2." (Mboza.)

When the Maputju yimpis fought against Nondwane in 1876, in the battle which took place near Malangotiba, (3 km west of Rikatla), they were decimated and eventually repulsed. Their chief Musongi sent them back to fight again. They refused. Then he punished them in the following way : he condemned them to go and fetch water with pots, like women, but they had to go on their knees to the pool, saying : "It is the result of our cowardice" — (Ngi ndaba ya bugwala). Afterwards they had to extinguish a bush fire with their hands, and came home very much scorched and burnt.

When the yimpi is victorious, the return is marked by important songs called *hubu* (cl. dji-ma). The regiments follow each other, each singing his own *hubu*, and they at once build the mukhumbi when they reach the village of the chief. They dance, dance their doughty deeds. Suddenly silence is required ; the counsellors narrate to the chief how the fighting has proceeded and tell him the names of those who have killed enemies, those who have struck the first blow and their *bahlomuri*, viz., those who transfixed the leg and the arm. After which the heroes "gila" to their heart's content, together with the bahlomuri. They are proud! They are applauded! They are the great men of the day, the *tingwaza*, the saviours of the chief!

This leads me to consider the very curious customs connected with the slayers and the slain on the battle-field.

I. THE FATE OF THE SLAIN AND THE TREATMENT
OF THE SLAYERS.

I. *The fate of the slain.*

When a man has slain an enemy, he has covered himself with the most enviable glory : he has the right to perform the war-dance before the chief. He takes away all the garments from the dead body, which remains quite naked ; should the slain be a Pedi wearing the piece of skin called nsindo round his genitalia, the slayer takes it with him as a proof that he has killed a man. A second warrior passing the dying or dead enemy will transfix (hlomula) his arm. A third passing will pierce his leg. These two last have not done so meritorious a deed as the first : they have not slain but merely finished off (huhula) the enemy. They act as witnesses to the first man, who is the actual possessor of the corpse ; they acquire, however, an equal right to dance : they are the *bahlomuri* of the real slayer. Should a fourth man pass by and again stab the dead, he is credited with no glory at all.

Besides the stabbing in the arm and leg, the dead bodies of enemies are subjected to still further *mutilations* ; they are ripped open and eventually disembowelled, an operation designated by the Zulu word "qanza." This revolting custom seems to be carried out in a more complete way amongst the Ba-Pedi than amongst the Thongas. In the battle of Nov. 6 1901, when the Sikororo and Sekukuni forces were repulsed by Maaghe and Muhlaba at Shiluvane, and forty foes were killed (App. X), their corpses disappeared entirely, cut into pieces by the medicine men of the victorious clan ; magicians from all Zoutpansberg came and asked to buy parts of the slain in order to prepare their powerful charms. In fact, in their opinion, the flesh and blood of an enemy killed in battle is the most efficacious of all charms and makes a *first rate drug* called *murumelo*. This medicine is also used for other purposes : with it the seeds are smeared in order to ensure a good harvest. When the mealies are two feet high, the magician ties together leaves on stems at the four corners of the field, after having treated them with the drug ; the blacksmiths from the Iron Mountain of Zoutpansberg buy it and mix it with their mineral ore, in order to strengthen the iron which they melt in their furnaces (nonisa nsimbi). Without this help they would obtain but slag. The hunters inoculate themselves in the following way with the powder obtained from the tendons and the bones : they make incisions in the skin of their wrists and elbows, draw a little blood, mix it with the drug, cook both in a pot, expose their arrows and assagais to the smoke, and rub the incisions with the powder. They will then be able to aim straight (See Annotatio 15). The powder specially prepared from the tendons of slain enemies will be spread on the paths during future wars ; foes marching on it unknowingly will suddenly become unable to walk and will easily be killed.

The Zulus are said to have the same customs as the Pedis.

I cannot guarantee that all the Thonga clans observe all these customs. The Nkuna magicians, in olden times, before they were influenced by their Pedi neighbours, used to dissect the tendons of the back (riringa) of the slain enemy, which they smeared with his medulla and hung to the shields of the warriors... Enemies seeing these shields would "tjemeka nhlana" — "have their backs broken," a figurative expression which means to be terror stricken. A part of the body was also preserved and mixed with the war-medicine ; the idea which underlies this custom being evidently this : when you have eaten the flesh of your enemies, you have absorbed all their strength and they are unable to do you any further harm (1). We have seen that the "mbhulo," the "nyokwekulu," all the powerful "medicines of the country" carefully kept in each clan, contain a little human flesh. These drugs are used as protective war medicines ; most probably owing to the same principle.

II. *The treatment of the slayers.*

To have killed an enemy on the battle-field entails an immense glory for the slayers ; but that glory is fraught with great danger.

---

(1) This custom is the only remnant of anthropophagy remaining amongst the Thongas, and I wonder if this superstition is not the true explanation of the origin of cannibalism. Where cannibalism still prevails, as amongst the Fañ of the Congo, I am told that the bodies eaten are generally those of hostile clans, or occasionally that of a wife (who belongs to another clan according to the laws of exogamy). Is it not probable that, in the beginning, these feasts had a ritual and military value similar to that which we find in the administering of the war-medicine in South African tribes ? In the course of time, the Fañ acquired a taste for human flesh and ate it for their own pleasure. Dealing with anthropophagy, I must not forget that it occurred in several instances in South Africa after the devastation brought about by the Zulu expeditions of 1820-1830. In Zoutpansberg, in the mountains of Drakensberg, Natives reduced to starvation began to eat their fellow men. This also happened in the Bokhakha during the reign of Queen Male. (See Part IV.)

They have killed... So they are exposed to the mysterious and deadly influence of the *nuru* and must consequently undergo a medical treatment. What is the *nuru* ? *Nuru* is the spirit of the slain which tries to take its revenge on the slayer. It haunts him and may drive him into insanity : his eyes swell, protrude and become inflamed. He will go out of his mind, be attacked by giddiness (ndzululwan) and the thirst for blood may lead him to fall upon members of his own family and to stab them with his assagay. To prevent such misfortunes, a special medication is required : the slayers must *lurulula tiyimpi ta bu*, take away the nuru of their sanguinary expedition. (Lurulula comes from nuru, plur. miluru (1).

In what does this treatment consist ? The slayers must remain for some days at the capital. They are taboo. They put on old clothes, eat with special spoons because their hands are

(1) We met with the notion of *nuru* for the first time à propos of the rite of luma (p. 400) ; we shall find it again when dealing with hunting customs (Part IV). The nuru is to be feared not only in the case of slain enemies but in connexion with any human corpse. As a proof, I may quote the following curious story which Spoon told me and of the truth of which he was fully convinced. A traveller died under the great fig-tree of Libombo (near Rikatla). He had climbed on to the tree and fallen on his own stick, which he had planted in the ground. He was not buried, as no one knew him. So his corpse fell into decomposition on the spot; his skull became white. Later on a bush fire burnt all the grass and the skull was seen for years "saying mpha" (it was shining), the teeth "saying bva" (descriptive adverb, same meaning). One day the boys of Libombo went to pick wild figs from the tree and again saw the skull. Spoon was one of them. The fire had just passed by again. "We beat it with our sticks and amused ourselves by rolling it over like a ball. We did not know it was a human skull... When we got home we began to be seized by the drunkenness of nuru, the disease of those who have killed a man. During the night we were delirious (hanta-hanteka), our eyes swelled and were full of exudations (malanga), the four of us, Tsukela, Tlabin, Sibakuze and myself. Next morning my uncle went to the fig-tree and saw that we had killed a man there l The medicine-man who understands the treatment of nuru, Dudela, who had been a slayer in war, called us to his village. We stood in a line before him ; he poured a little of his powder into the hands of each one of us, took a little in his mouth, rubbed his forehead. Then he insulted us saying ; "You will die ! Who began beating that skull ?" Each of us denied having given the first blow. Then he said : "Take care ! Do not go there any more nor near that nkuhlu tree where another corpse has been burnt under the leaves l Go away."

When a man has murdered another in a scuffle, he can replace this nuru medicine by his own urine. He must drink a little of it and rub his forehead with it. The giddiness will pass away. If the murder has been committed from a distance, as with a gun, the nuru is not so much to be feared, as the enemy was far away. A little of the medicine will be sufficient to treat the murderer. Spoon is ignorant of the composition of the nuru drug.

478

"hot" and from special plates (mireko) and broken pots. They are forbidden to drink water. Their food must be cold. The chief kills oxen for them (yi ba lumisa hi tihomu) ; but if the meat were hot it would make them swell internally "because they are hot themselves, they are defiled (ba na nsila)." If they ate hot food, the defilement would enter into them. "They are black (ntima). This black must be removed" (Mankhelu). During all this time sexual relations are absolutely forbidden to them. They must not go home to their wives. In former times the Ba-Ronga used to tatoo them with special marks from one eyebrow to the other. Dreadful medicines were introduced into the incisions and there remained pimples "which gave them the appearance of a buffulo when it frowns" (1).

After some days a medicine-man comes to purify them (ku ba phutula), "to remove their black." There seem to be various means of doing it, according to Mankhelu. Seeds of all kinds are put into a broken pot and roasted, together with drugs and *psanyi* of a goat. The slayers inhale the smoke which emanates from the pot. They put their hands into the mixture and rub their limbs with it (ba tilula) especially the joints.

Viguet describes this last act thus :—Pieces of medicinal roots are put into the broken pot and roasted. They inhale the smoke. Then cow's milk is poured into the pot on the embers and, when it boils, they have to put their fingers into it, one hand after the other, and pass them across their lips emitting the sacramental : "tsu" (which proves that it is a sacrifice to the gods, a religious act). Afterwards they say : "Phee! phee!" — viz., phephela phansi, (Dj. tikela hansi), "Go down, sink." This means : "May you go deep into the earth, you, my enemy and not come back to torment me." The last part of the treatment consists in rubbing the biceps, the legs, and the whole body with this milk. The medicinal embers are carefully collected, and reduced to a powder ; this will be put into small bags of skin called *tintebe* which the slayer will wear round his neck. They contain

(1) Hence an expression which is still in common use. When a Ronga wants to defy some one he says to him : "You are a coward ! If you say you can tackle me come and kiss my forehead."

the medicine of the slayers of men. At bukanye time they can use it to *luma*, viz., to season the first calabash they drink (See page 400). For this purpose it is as good as the great mbhulo, "the medicine of the country," provided by the chief, and it will prevent them attacking their own people under the influence of drink. The *tintebe* will also be helpful in future battles. The insanity which threatens those who shed blood might begin early. So, on the battle-field itself, just after their deed, warriors are given a preventive dose of the medicine by those who have killed on previous occasions and who wear tintebe.

The period of seclusion having been concluded by the final purification, all the implements (mizilo) used by the slayers during these days, and their old garments, are tied together and hung by a string to a tree, at some distance from the capital, where they are left to rot (1).

· Having reached their homes, the slayers have still to complete the cure by chewing a piece of root called monungwane every morning and evening, and spitting it out in the direction of the rising or the setting sun with the same exclamation : "Phee! phee!" — "Go down, sink!" The piece of root is tied to the assagay (2).

The description of the rites performed for the treatment of the slayers applies especially to the Northern clans. But the following narrative of an old man named Makhani from the Rikatla region shows that similar customs were also in existence amongst the Ba-Ronga. This man had wounded an enemy in a battle ; the wound proved fatal and the

(1) I had the good luck to find those which were used for the purification of the slayers after the Mooudi fight during the Sikororo war and they are now in the Ethnographical Museum of Neuchâtel. They consist of half a dozen old calabashes, a pair of sandals, etc.

(2) Purification customs for the warriors are somewhat different amongst the Pedis. After the Mooudi battle, the slayers of Maaghe's yimpi had to undergo the following medicinal treatment : the heart of the slain having been torn out, the muscles of their faces sliced off, their limbs amputated, all these portions of human flesh mixed with drugs and ox-flesh were cooked in a pot, the assagais being used to stir the horrible broth. This was poured into a flat basket which it is taboo to touch ; some one drew it with a curved assagay as far as the middle of the square. Then the slayers, having been previously white-washed with clay, advanced on their knees, and, with vociferations or cries imitating vultures, caught a piece of meat in their teeth, not touching it with their hands. Their wives are said to participate in this meal, as being also contaminated by the defilement of their glorious husbands.

enemy died later on, after his return to his home. Makhani did not know this. One day he became suddenly delirious and rushed about all over the village trying to stab his own people. "Oho!" said those who saw him, "it is because the man he wounded has died!" They at once called the magician who possessed the nuru medicine, a man of the Mapsanganye clan, who came with his calabash. In this calabash there was a carved stick cut from a tree called shiralala, the extremity of which must always remain plunged in the medicine. The magician dipped this stick into a mixture made of honey and the drug, and passed it over the lips of Makhani, who seized it with his tongue, sucking it as the magician moved it from right to left, and licking his lips. A drop of the medicine was then put into each ear, on each upper eye-lid, and below the sternum. He was then cured and, taking a lighted torch, he threw it in the direction of the enemy's country with threatening words : "A ba fe, bafo, ba bola i. e. Let them die, the enemies, let them rot. I will kill still others!" Every day he had to go to the pool and wash his body, treating himself with the tintebe powder.

During the weeks following the battle heroes do not only wear the tintebe, besides these miluru amulets, they have the right to wear certain trophies. These are in the first place antelope or goat's horns pierced at the base ; they thread a string through the hole thus made and tie them round their necks (See illustrations, p. 33 and 453). They also make necklaces of small pieces of wood, notched in a peculiar manner and burnt in the fire ; a hole is made through these and they are strung together like beads and worn round the neck. Sometimes these necklaces are made so long that they are worn as a bandoleer. I recollect seeing the Matjolo warriors returning from their expedition of February 1895: they came to show themselves off to the Whites at Lourenço Marques, gloriously proud of having massacred defenceless women and children whom they had surprised in the early hours of the morning! People threw them pieces of silver which they converted into brandy! (1)

(1) The terrible malediction which rests on those who have killed an enemy is well illustrated by the following story which the Rev. C. Maphophe told me of an event that had taken place not long ago in the Shishongi country (Manyisa district). A man of the Ndzindzi family had killed a Ndjao during one of Gungunyana's expedi-

J. SOME REMARKS ABOUT WAR RITES.

The war rites of the Thongas, whatever may be their origin —
and they seem to be a mixture of old Thonga and new Zulu
customs, — form a very interesting and complete whole.

The most noticeable are the *national rites*. In war time, the very
existence of the clan is threatened, because the chief, the central and
vital cell of this organism, is in danger. Hence the readiness of all
the warriors to answer to the first call of the *shipalapala*, and to gather
round him, "building the circle," which protects him, the whole
clan forming a single village and binding itself by the striking ceremonies
of *guba* and by patriotic songs, to die for him. Notice that most of the
guba songs extol the chief. All these customs in which the individual
or collective courage is stimulated, the *guba* and the *gila*, are national
or social rites directed towards the salvation of the clan. They owe
their origin to the national idea.

But war also brings dangers to every warrior. Hence the *protective*
rites of sprinkling the mukhumbi with the war-medicine of the clan,
or of giving each man some of it to swallow. The rite is inspired by
the notion *similia similibus curantur*, the idea being that the warrior,
having eaten a small portion of the enemy, will become invulnerable to his blows.

But other rites, especially the war taboos, seem to owe their origin
to the *idea of passage*.

The *whole clan* enters upon a special phase as soon as war has been
decided upon by the chief, "who gives it" to his warriors. Hence the
taboos observed at home, many of which are exactly the same as those
of the circumcision school and of the period of mourning. We notice the
same contrast already so often mentioned : certain sexual prohibitions
are removed (e. g. a queen will enter quite naked into the mukhumbi!)

tions (before 1890). Three persons of that family died. The bones were consulted
and the diviner asked : "Have you not slain a Ndjao?" They answered: "Yes." —
"Then," said the bone-thrower "you will all die as this man has followed you." The
bones showed that, in order to avoid the destruction of their family, the Ndzindzis had
to offer a girl to the ghost of the slain, a living sacrifice. This girl would not be
allowed to marry, or even to be courted by boys. Should she have relations with a man
it would be necessary to replace her by another. Thus the angry ghost would be
propitiated.

On the other hand sexual relations, which are allowed in ordinary life, become taboo. This period of fighting seems really to be considered as a marginal period for the whole tribe.

It is so par excellence *for the warriors* and I think that many of the rites imposed upon them are to be explained in this way. As we saw, the period of margin is generally preceded by separation rites. (See page 74.) Some of these, which are very characteristic, are performed when the army starts : the leave-taking from the General with wild shouts, the custom of swallowing a piece of meat without touching it with the hands and taking an emetic afterwards, that of jumping over the ntjhopfa branch, the medicine of oblivion! etc. The triumphant return, the partaking of the meat of the oxen which have been taken, may be the aggregation ceremonies, viz., the acts by which the warriors return to their ordinary life.

Passage rites are still more distinct *in the case of the slayers* ; but their condition is worse, as it implies the idea of defilement following upon murder and is attended with the danger proceeding from the *nuru*. They are "hot" (an expression which also applies to the tabooed woman during her menses etc.); they are "black" (an epithet which also designates the grave-diggers, the bereaved mother, etc.). Hence a *seclusion* much more complete, a true period of margin with many alimentary and sexual (1) taboos. Possibly the incisions on the brow are an old kind of tatooing in connexion with this marginal period, similar to the inguinal incision of the widows (p. 201). The purification rites are of the same kind as those of the mourners, and particularly of the grave-diggers. The return to society, after their seclusion, is marked by rites of separation from the marginal period, which no doubt aim at getting rid of the defilement connected therewith. (Exposure of the *mizilo* outside the village in the bush.) Is it not striking to notice the correspondence between these rites in their peculiar sequence and those of the circumcision school, of mourning, of moving a village ?

See, as a conclusion to Part III, Practical Conclusions, No. VI : "The New era and the Future of the South African Tribe."

---

(1) The sexual taboos are so severe that, after the Mooudi battle, one of the slayers took great offence at a man who dared to touch his food, as the man was living in his home and had relations with his wife. The slayer was afraid that this contact might cause his own death or bring misfortune to his family.

APPENDIX I (See p. 31)

Characteristics of the six dialects of the Thonga language.

In the accompanying table I have compiled a list of characteristic words in the six main dialects of the Thonga language. The Ronga and Djonga lists have been made by myself, and represent those dialects as spoken in the Mpfumo and Nkuna clans. The population south of Delagoa Bay speaks a kind of sub-dialect of the Ronga, the Lwandle or Maputju. (Abbr. Map.). I owe to the Rev. L. Perrin the peculiar forms found in that district. The Rev. P. Loze of Lourenço Marques compiled for me the list of the Hlanganu equivalents, as they are met with in the Ñwamba clans. They are not very different from the Djonga. Probably the dialect of Hlanganu proper, in the Lebombo Hills, would show greater differences. The Rev. H. Guye, who resided in Khosen and in Shikhumbane (Lower Limpopo Valley), provided me with a Djonga-Khosa list, very similar to the Nkuna and with the characteristic forms of the Bila dialect (Station of Shikhumbane, 15 miles west of Chai-Chai), also of the Hlengwe as spoken in the Khambana District, on the eastern border of the Lower Limpopo (Kh.). The Hlengwe, being so extensively spoken, possesses many sub-dialects. The Rev. S. Malale, a Native minister, compiled the characteristic forms of the Tshauke (Tsh.) region and those of the Madzibi tribe (Madz.) dwelling in the hinterland of Inhambane. The American missionaries have already published many books in the Tswa sub-dialect spoken in the vicinity of Inhambane, so I have also been able to mention a few Tswa forms. Lastly I owe to the same Rev. S. Malale the Ñwalungu forms, those of Maluleke as well as those of the Ba-ka-Baloyi (Bal.) proper, and, in addition, those of the Hlabi (Hl.), which are very similar to the Djonga.

The orthography employed in these lists is that which the Swiss missionaries adopted for the Vocabulary and Grammar of the Thonga-Shangaan language. (Bridel, Lausanne 1908.) For our missionary books, we have always used the excellent and scientific system of Lepsius, with its two main principles : a letter must always have the same value, and a single sound must be represented by a single letter.

Appendix

Unhappily this system implies the use of special signs which are not found in the ordinary printing establishments, so we have had to adopt another conversational orthography for outside publications.

The *j* added to *t, d, r* and *sh* is not exactly the French *j*, but indicates a cerebralisation of the preceding sound. *Tj* is a *t* pronounced with the tip of the tongue bent somewhat backward, behind the palatal and towards the cerebral point. It is different from *tsh* which is *t + sh*, *sh* being the palatal *sh*, as in shore. *Dj* is not very different from the English *j* in just. *Rj* is a very much rolled *r*, tending towards the French *j* (as in jour) ; *shj* is a further modification of *r* where all guttural element has disappeared : a palatal *sh* cerebralised. These four sounds are not the pure *cerebral* sounds mentioned by Lepsius. I prefer describing them as *cerebralised*. However, in Malukele, *dj* sometimes becomes *dh*, as in the word mundhuku, and then it is pure cerebral. Besides the lateral sounds *hl, dl, tl*, very frequent in Thonga, there also occurs in Bila the Zulu *dhl*, which would perhaps be more correctly written *jl*.

Two peculiar sibilant sounds, *ps* and *bz*, (sw and zw in the Grammar) are accompanied by a special whistling noise. The v is not a true *v*, which is very rare in Thonga and is only met with in the combination *bv*, and in the Hlengwe ngovu, vuna, etc. It is a soft *b*, a fricative labial. A strong *b* is rare in all the dialects, except after *m* or before *y*. In the Maputju sub-dialect alone it is frequently used instead of the soft *b*. *N* is the nasal guttural *n* pronounced as *ng* in singing; it is the same sound as *ñ*.

The following comparison bears on three different subjects : the sounds, the grammatical forms and some characteristic words of the vocabulary. As regards sounds, notice especially the very interesting permutations of *r*, which find their explanation in the hypothesis of Meinhof on the Ur-Bantu. (Compare Meinhof, Grundrisse einer Lautlehre der Bantu Sprachen). This table will provide colonists with a shibboleth for the Thonga tribe, viz., with a means of ascertaining the origin of any Thonga with whom they may meet. They will be able to diagnose the clan to which he belongs. To understand it fully, it will be necessary to study the Ronga or Thonga grammars, to which I must refer the reader.

I. Phonetic permutations

	Ronga	Hlanganu	Djonga	Bila	Ñwalungu	Hlengwe
Stone	ribye (Map.) Djibye	ribye	ribye	ribye	ribye	ribye (Madz.) rige
Three	rjarju (Map.) Shjashju	raru	raru	raru	raru	raru
To till	djima	rima	rima	rima	rima	rima
Tongue	lidjimi	ririmi	ririmi	lirimi	lerimi lorimi	lerimi lorimi
Tongues	tindjimi	tirimi	tindjimi	tirimi	tindimi	tindimi (Madz.) tirimi
Shadow	ntjhuti	ndjuti ndruti	ndjuti	ndzuti	nduti	ntsuti ndzuti
Shadows	mintjhuti	mindjuti mindruti	miruti mindjuti	mindzuti	miruti minduti	mintsuti mindzuti miruti
Ant-hill	rjuka (Map.) Shjuka	ruka	tjhuka	ruka	tshuka	ruka
Mountain	nhavǎ	nhavǎ	ntjhavǎ	nthavǎ	ntshavǎ ntsavǎ	ntsavǎ
Part	ndjima (Map.) ndima	ndjima	ndjima	ndzima	ndima	ndzima
I	ndji (Map.) ndi	ndji ndri	ndji	ndzi	ndi	ndzi
To morrow	Mundjuku (Map.) munduku	mundruku	mundjuku		mundhuku mendhuku	mundzuku
To run	tjutjuma (Map.) tshutshuma	tjutjuma	tjutjuma	tsutsuma	tsutsuma	tsutsuma
Only	ntsena (Map.) mpsena	ntsena	ntsena (Hlabi) njena	ntse	ntsena	ntsena (Kh.) ntse
To learn	dondja (Map.) donda	dyondja	dyondja	dyondza	dyonda	gondza
To eat	da	dya	dya	dhla dhlambo		ga gambo
Sun	dambu	dyambu	dyambu	mbyana		gwana
Dog	mbyana	mbyana	mbyana	gwanye leli	byanyi lebyi	gwanyi legi ganyi legi
This grass	byanyi lebyi	byanhyi lebyi	byanyi lebyi		byosi lebyi	(Kh.) ...

Groupings (left brace labels): r, dj, tj, dy, by

	A	B	C	D	E	F
(w) To warm oneself	worja	ora	ora	wora	ora	wora
(hw) Moon	hweti	n̄hweti	nhweti	n̄hweti	n̄hweti	nhweti
(hl) To-day	namunhla	namuntlha	namuntlha (Hl.) nyamuntlha	nyamuntlha	nyamunlha	nyamuntlha
To-meet together	tlhangana	tlhangana	hlangana		hlangana tlhangana	tlhangana
(v̌) To speak	v̌ulav̌ula (Map.) bulabula	v̌ulav̌ula	v̌ulav̌ula	v̌ulav̌ula	v̌ulav̌ula	v̌ulav̌ula (Madz.) walawula
To place	v̌eka (Map.) beka	v̌eka	v̌eka	v̌eka		v̌eka
Belly	khurji (Map.) khudji	khuri	khwiri	khwiri	khwiri	(rumbu)
To have a good taste	nandjika (Map.) nandiha	nandjiha	nandjiha	nandjika	nandiha	nandziha
To have a bad smell	nuha		nunhwa	nunha		nunha
Tail	nkila	ntshila	ntshila	ntshila	ntshila (Bal.) ntsila	ntshila ntsila
To distribute food	khema	khema	phema (Hl.) khema	khema	phema	khema
To be short	goma	koma	koma	koma	koma	koma
Much	ngopfu	ngopfu	ngopfu	ngopfu	ngopfu	ngopfu (Tsh.) ngovu
To help	pfuna	pfuna	pfuna	pfuna	pfuna	pfuna (Tsh.) vuna
To dry up	phya	phya	phya	khwa		khwa

II. Grammatical forms

		A	B	C	D	E	F
cl. mu-v̌ă	man	mhunu	muhu	munhu	munhu	munhu	munhu
	men	v̌hanu	v̌ahu	v̌anhu	v̌anhu	v̌anhu	v̌anhu
	stranger	muyeni	ñeni	ñeni		ñweni, ñeni	
	handle	mphinyi (Map.) mphinyu	mbhinyi	mbinyi	mbenyi	mbhinyi	mphinyyi
cl. mu-mi	fig-trees	minkuwa	minkuwa	mikuwa	mikuwa	mikuwa	mikuwa

487

	Ronga	Hlanganu	Djonga	Bila	Ñwalungu	Hlengwe
this land	tiko ledji	tiko leri	tiko leri	tiko leli	tiko ledyi / (Bal.) leli	tiko legi
of mine (cl. dji-ma)	dja nga	ra nga	ra mee	la mina	dya mina / (Bal.) la mina	ga mina
of them	dja v̌u	ra v̌o	ra v̌oo	la v̌ona	dya v̌ona / (Bal.) la vona	ga v̌ona
that very one	djoledjo, djodjo	rolero, roro	rolero, rero	lolelo, lelo	dyoledyo, dyedyo / lolelo, lolo	golego / lolelo, lolo
night (cl. bu-ma)	v̌usiku	v̌usiku	v̌usiku	wusiku	v̌usiku	wusiku
limbs (cl. shi-psi)	psiro	psiro	psiro	psiro	psiro	psiro
goat	ambuti	ambuti	embuti			(Tsh.) bziro / ambuti
one man	mhunu muñwe	muñwe	uñwe	muñwe	wuñwe	
large trees	miṛi le'mikulu	le'yikulu	le'yikulu	le'yikulu	le yikulu	
high trees	ya ku leha	ya ku leha	yo leha	yo leha	yo leha / (Bal.) ya ku leha	
a big (or old) man	mhunu lwe'nkulu		lo'kulu (Hl.) lo'nkulu	lwe'nkulu	lo'nkulu	
three oxen	tihomu tiṛjarju	tiraru	tiraru / tinharu	tinharu	tinharu	tinharu
which day?	Siku djini?	rihi?	rihi?		rihi?	gihi?
the father alone	tatana pwsake (Map.) ha v̌upsakwe	e psakwe	yeshe	yeshe	yeshe	dadane yeshe / (Tsh.) yetshe
he has gone	a fambile	a	u	u	a	a / Tsh. u
I have taken him	ndji mu tekile	n'tekile	ñwe tekile	mu tekile	ñwe	mu
we have seen him	hi mu v̌onile	m'monile	m'monile	mu v̌onile	mu	mu
I love him	ndji mu ṛjandja		n'djandja	ndzi mu randza	ndi nwe randa	ndza mu randza
the trees are many	miṛi mi tele	yi tele	yange	yi	yi	yi
I have not gone	a ndji yanga	yanga	a ndji ya	yanga	yangi	yangi
I was going	afa ndji ya	a ndji ya / a ndji ta ya	ngi ndji ta ya	a ndzi ya	a ndi ya	a ndzi ya
I would go	anha ndji ta ya	amfa ndji te ya		ana ndzi ya	ingi ndi ta ya	a ndzi ta na ndzi ya
the man	lw'a fambaka	lwe a fambaka	l'a fambaka	lw'a fambaka	l'a fambaka	lw'a fambaka

488

English						
who will go	taka famba	nga ta famba	nga famba / nga ta famba	nga ta famba	nga famba / nga ta famba	(1 sh.) tambuleko / nga ta famba
who does not go	nga fambikiki / (Map.) fambikokoko	nga fambike	nga fambike	nga fambike	nga fambike	nga fambike / (Tsh.) nga fambiko
who has not gone	nga fambangakiki / (Map.) fambangakokoko		nga fambangike	nga fambangike	nga fambangike	nga fambangike / (Tsh.) nga fambangiko / (Tswa.) fambangikako
to be known	tibyiwa		tiviwa	tiviwa		tigwa
though	nambi	nambi	hambi	hambi	hambi	hambi / (Tswa.) hambu
whilst	kasi / (Map.) nkansi	kasi	kasi	kasi	kasi	kasi / (Tswa.) kanilezi
as	psang'epsi	psanga hepsi	tane he lepsi	ku kota	tane he / ku kota	ku kota

III. Vocabulary differences

English						
To make	yentsha	endla	endla	endla	endla / yendla	maha
To kill	dlaya	dlaya	dlaya	dhlaya	dlaya	dhlaya / (Tsh.) daya
To hear	yingela	twa	twa	twa	twa	
To be happy	tjhava	thava	tajka	tsaka	tsaka	tsaka
To look for	djyula	lava	la'a	lava	lava	lava
A thing	sha-ntshumu	sha-ntshumu	shilo	shilo	shilo	shilo
To care for	bekisa	vekisa	hlayisa	hlayisa	hlayisa	hlayisa
To trust	dumba	djyumba	tjemba	tsemba / themba	themba / (Bal.) psemba	themba / (Tsh.) gwandza
Sea	likhulu	lwandle	lwandle	lwandle	lwandle	lwandle / (Tswa) vimbi
Father!	tatana / (Map.) tati	tatana	tatana	tatana	tatani	tatani
Mother!	manana / (Map.) mami	manana	manana	mamani	mamani	mamani
Uterine nephew	mupsyana	muphyana	ntukulu	ntukulu	ntukulu	ntukulu / (Tsh.) nzukulu
Maternal uncle	malume	malume	kokwane	kokwane	kokwani	kokwani
Paternal aunt	rarana / (Map.) rari / fani	rarana	hahani	hahani	hahani	hahani
Bad	ku biha	ku biha	ku biha	ku biha		

APPENDIX II (See p. 40)

On Thonga names, nicknames and surnames.

As an illustration of the way in which the Thongas change their names, I give the story of those of Mboza and Elias.

Mboza was called at his birth "Mulamule," after his paternal uncle. The whole name was, in Zulu : "Mulamula nkwinzi izilwako," viz., "the man who calms the bull which fights." At about the age of sixteen, he changed it to Mahubula. At that time he was trying to collect divinatory bones in order to become a diviner. He had called one of these bones "Hubula," and after that his comrades began to apply the name to him. He was seized by the "folly of gods." (Part. VI). When he was cured of this pretended possession, the spirit which made itself known called itself Mboza. This was the name of a man of his village, his own nephew, who had gone to Johannesburg and had died there. When he became a Christian, and was baptised, Mboza kept his name. Most of the Natives like to take another name on that occasion, the name of a disciple or of a prophet. We are not very ready to comply with their wish, as we have already too many Daniels, Jonas and Petros, and Mboza probably yielded to this argument.

Elias was called "Shifenyo" on the day of his birth, after a man who happened to pass through the village. This visitor was a kind of beggar who used to follow people carrying food to the chief, hoping to get something to eat. The child was of a good family, but they gave him the name of this low and despised individual, a truly democratic act! When he was older, one of his friends said to him : "Your name does not suit you. Call yourself *Spoon*." He adopted the new appellation, and the women of his village used to make fun of him saying : "Come along, we will distribute the food with this spoon!" When baptised a Christian he became Elias, a somewhat onerous name, especially as our Elias is not as strong and perfect as a prophet ought to be... But Natives never shrink from assuming great names. They always feel themselves equal to them!

The names adopted at puberty by boys are very often European ones. There are scores of Jims, Sams, Bobs, etc. They also adopt as names European words or words of European origin, as : Spoon, Nglazi (glass) Komitshi (cup), Djass (jacket), Fulitshi (forage), Fifteen, etc.

490

APPENDIX

The really Native names very often begin with the prefix *mu* which is the personal singular prefix, (Musongi, Muzila, Mungutana, Mukentshe), or *Ñwa* conveying the idea of "son of" (Ñwamitwa, Ñwamashwele Ñwatjubula), or Nya used in the same sense, (Nyakubasa, Nyanise, Nyathi, probably of Zulu origin), or *Ma* which is also a personal prefix, (Manabe, Matende, Mathandana, Makhangala, Makasana, etc.). The prefix *Mi* means "daughter of," and is frequently met with (Misilana, Mintlohen, Mindinyana, etc.). As a rule it is employed only in names of women.

The prefix *Shi* which generally denotes things, objects, and has a neuter significance, is very often found in Ronga names. It is also a diminutive prefix, especially when the word ends in *ana*. So Shiribyana, a very common name, means a small stone (ribye) ; Shigidana, Shirombe, Shindjubi, etc. belong to the same class.

Some very curious names begin with the prefix *ba*, the pronoun of the third person plural. These are common amongst girls, generally of Chopi origin, who were slaves of the important Native women of Lourenço Marques and sold by them as concubines. For instance Bamuyeyisa means "they defy her," Bamusonda (Zulu), "they hate her," Batjhamahayena "they gossip about her," etc. In calling themselves by these names the girls express their bitterness.

But a great number of names have no prefix at all and often no meaning.

Nicknames are frequent amongst the Thongas and often entirely supplant the regular name. There was in Rikatla an old Mbekwa whom everyone called Nxoko... On inquiring into the origin of this curious name I was told the following story. One day Mbekwa was very happy and expressed his contentment by the exclamation ; "Nxoko" (x here denotes a peculiar click of the tongue against the cheek). This interjection was received with favour and he employed it henceforth to manifest his pleasure on other occasions. He even made a regular verb of it, saying : "I go to nxokela in such and such a place," viz. "to enjoy myself there." The word was so fascinating that he was named after it, and I should not be surprised if it were incorporated into the current language, which is enriched every day by new descriptive adverbs like nxoko. (See my Thonga Grammar, p. 84 and Vol. II.)

Nicknames are more especially applied to white people, as Natives fail to catch their true names. These are very cleverly chosen, being often a verbal description of the chief physical or mental characteristic of the white man. M. Torre do Valle has given a list of nicknames of the merchants and other inhabitants of Lourenço Marques in his *Diccionario Shironga-Portuguez*. It is well worth consulting, and the only thing wanting is a photograph of the white man and an explanation of the name ; it would be a splendid illustration of Native wit!

So far we have spoken only of *personal* names and nicknames. But, beside these, every man possesses his clan name, or surname, viz., the name of the first of his known ancestors. Grown up men prefer being addressed by this name, which is *shibongo*, viz. the name by which they are "glorified." This subject is treated in Part III (p. 360).

APPENDIX III (See p. 98)

Unnatural Vice in the Johannesburg Compounds.

In January 1915 one of my colleagues passing near one of the Johannesburg Compounds, saw a big company of Natives singing and walking in the direction of another Compound where a great dance was taking place. Amongst them there were a number of women. My colleague asked his Native evangelist how it was possible that so many women should be walking about in that part of the world, where the feminine element is very small. The man told him : "They are not women! They are *tinkhontshana*, boys who have placed on their chests the breasts of women carved in wood, and who are going to the dance in order to play the part of women. To-night when they return to their dormitories, their 'husbands' will have to give them 10/, and only on that condition will the tinkhontshana remove their breasts and comply with the desire of their husbands." I sent for this evangelist who knew everything about the inner life of the Compounds and asked him about it ; this is the information I received :

Unnatural vice (bukhontshana) has become a regular institution in the Compounds. The word *nkhontshana* seems to come from the Ngoni, a Zulu dialect spoken in the Limpopo plain. The nkhontshana is the boy used by another man to satisfy his lust, and the man is called his *nuna*, husband. When a gang of new workers arrives in a Compound, the Native induna, who has the supervision of the Compound, and the Native policemen, who have their rooms at the

APPENDIX

entrance of the yard, come and "humutsha" i. e. make proposals to the younger ones, not only to little boys (there are only a few of these) but also to boys up to the age of twenty and more. If these lads consent to become their bakhontshana, they will be treated with greater kindness than the others. Their husbands will give them 10/ to woo them (buta) and will choose for them easy occupations, as, for instance, sweeping the dormitories, whilst the others will have to go to the hard underground work. Those who have not been chosen on their arrival by the policemen will probably receive a similar proposal from their older companions in the mine, and these men will then help them in the difficult task of "be hole" i. e. digging their hole. But the "husband" will have not only to woo this peculiar kind of *nsati* (wife) ; he must also *lobola* her, and a feast sometimes takes place when as much as £ 25 is put on the ground, a goat is killed and a real contract made which binds the nkhontshana to his master for the whole time he remains in the Compounds. The elder brother of the boy will receive the money in this disgusting parody of the Bantu marriage.

Sometimes the husband pays his nkhontshana at the end of each month as much as £ 1.10 and this represents a big increase in the earnings of the boy.

What happens when the contract is broken ? The "husband" claims the money remitted by him. If the boy refuses to return it the matter may be brought before the Compound Manager, who generally dismisses the plaintiff, saying : "If the boy does not love you any more, let him go."

The cause of the evil is not difficult to detect : it is the segregation of the Native miners in these enormous conglomerations of males, far from home, far from their wives, a most abnormal condition of life for men who have always enjoyed the freedom of the African bush. When prostitutes were allowed to live near the Compounds, unnatural vice was not so common ; when they were driven out, bukhontshana at once increased enormously, and thus the disappearance of one evil brought a new one in its train. On the other hand, my informant asserted that Thongas (Matshanganas, as they are called in Johannesburg) had never much frequented the haunts of prostitution, from fear of venereal diseases. They prefered a nkhontshana ; the danger was not so great! As the word nkontshana comes from the Bilen country, the home of the Matshanganas, it might be thought that this vice was known and practised amongst Natives before it took on such extensive proportions in the Compounds. There is an old Thonga song which

493

says : "You, nkhontshana, get up, the cocks are crowing, be not
surprised by the rising sun." This song warns the girl who has gone
during the night to sleep in the lao, the boys' hut, that she had better
run away at once lest she should be found in a place where she ought
not to be. But it is a girl who is meant here and not a Johannesburg
nkhontshana! No! Greek heathenism knew this refinement of immorality and indulged in it, but Bantu heathenism, whatever may be its
corruption, never dreamed of it. Even to-day, though it is said to have
penetrated into some parts (as in the Maputju country), the Native
kraal feels a real abhorrence of it. I was told the following story.
A man, in Bilen, had married a woman ; he came to the Rand and took
his wife's brother as his nkhontshana. When he returned home, his
parents-in-law were very angry with him ; they gave him back the
lobolo money and took their daughter from him, saying : "You are a
hyena! You are a wizard! You might as well sin with your mother-
in-law!"... Unnatural vice was taught to the South African Bantus by
men of a foreign race ; it first invaded the prisons ; now it is raging in
these big Native miners' settlements, where it is deflouring the Bantu
youth. For if it does not immediately destroy their physical strength,
this perversion of one of the most essential functions of man corrupts
the sources of moral stamina and endangers the foundations of Bantu
social life.

Is there no remedy for this terrible evil ?

The worst aspect of the situation is that the immense majority of the
Natives themselves do not consider this sin as of any importance
at all. They speak of it with laughter. I was told that it is severely
prohibited by law and that any boy found guilty of bukhontshana is
condemned to twelve months' imprisonment. But it is extremely
difficult to bring the evidence necessary for conviction. The indunas
and Native policemen enter into a conspiration of silence, being themselves the first and greatest sinners in this respect. Happily the Mission
is fighting the evil as energetically as possible and the Compound
Managers help its agents to secure separate dormitories, where a certain
number of boys can find a refuge against contamination. A few
hundreds or thousands escape in this way, but what is that in comparison
with the tens of thousands who are exposed to this frightful temptation
in the Compounds fittingly spoken of, by a wise South African
statesman, as the University of crime ?

My informant, who was perfectly acquainted with the circumstances
of life in the Compounds, mentioned the following measures which he

thought might be useful in the repression of this vice. Prohibit the use of curtains enclosing two beds, this being an unmistakable sign that bukhontshana is practised behind them. Arrange the beds so that they do not touch each other. (I hear that some Mining Companies have spent and are still spending large sums of money to secure this end, but the actual sleeping accommodation ought to be entirely transformed if the Companies are determined effectively to check the evil.) Introduce a strict watch during the night. Put in electric light everywhere in order to illuminate the dormitories at any time when required. I do not know how far such measures would be effective. The only conclusion I would offer on this painful subject is this. As white civilisation is responsible for the introduction and the frightful development of this vice amongst the Natives, the Whites must not remain indifferent in the face of an iniquity which threatens the very life of the South African Tribe.

APPENDIX IV (See p. 221).

South African Bantu

I. Ancestors and Descendant

	Thonga-Ronga	Thonga-Djonga	Chopi	Zulu
Father	Tata. Roro	Tatana. Rara	Tate	Baba
Mother	Mamana. Ñhwa	Manana. Mana	Mame	Mame. Ma
Father's Father	Kokwana	Kokwana	Kokwana	Baba mkulu
Mother's Father	»	»	»	»
Father's Mother	»	»	»	»
Mother's Mother	»	»	»	»
Great Grandfather & Grandmother	Kokwana wa Tatana	»	»	Gogo
Son	Ñwana (wa ndjisanyana)	Ñwana (wa mufana)	Mwanana	Ndodana
Son's wife	Ñwingi	Ñwingi		Makoti. Malu kazane
Daughter	Ñwana (wa wanhonyana)	Ñwana (wa wanhwana)	Mwanana	Ndodakazi
Daughter's husband	Mukoñwana	Mukoñwana		Umkwenyane
Grandson, granddaughter	Ntukulu	Ntukulu	Mutukulu	Umzukulu
Grandson's son	Ntukulu wa shi kandjatjolo	Ntukulu shinguhe	Mutukulu wa shinguha	

II. Brothers and Sisters

	Thonga-Ronga	Thonga-Djonga	Chopi	Zulu
Elder Brother (of a boy) . . .	Nhondjwa. Hosi	Nhondjwa. Hosi	Nkoma	Umnewetu
» » (of a girl)	»	»	Ndi ya ngu. Tate	»
Younger Brother (of a boy) . . .	Ndjisana	Ndjisana	Nanda	Umfowetu
» » (of a girl) . . .	»	»	Ndi ya ngu	»
Elder Sister (of a boy)	Nhondjwa. Hosi	Nhondjwa. Hosi	Ndi ya ngu	Dadewetu
» » (of a girl)	»	»	Nkoma	»
Younger Sister (of a boy) . . .	Ndjisana	Ndjisana	Ndi ya ngu	»
» » (of a girl) . . .	»	»	Nanda	»
Elder Brother's Wife (for a boy) .	Namu	Namu	Ndombi	Makoti
» » » (for a girl) .	» Nhombe	»	»	»
Younger Brother's Wife (for a boy)	Ñwingi	Ñwingi	Ndombi	»
» » » (for a girl)	Namu. Nhombe			»
Elder Sister's Husband (for a boy)	Namu. Mukoñwana	Mukoñwana	Mukwasa	Umkwenyana
Younger Sister's Husband (for a boy)	Namu. Mukoñwana	Mukoñwana	Mukwasa	Umkwenyana
General name of Brothers and Sisters	Ba-Makwerju	Ba-Makweru	Ba-Ndi-ya-ngu	

Kinship System.

in the direct Line.

Xosa	Sutho (Basutoland)	Pedi-Khaha	Venda	Tonga (Inhambane)	Njao
u-Bawo	Ntate. Ra	Baba. Bô-pape	Khotsi	Nyehe. Baba	Baba
u-Ma	'Me (=Mme)	Mma. Bô-mmê	Mme	Mayime. Mayi	Mayi
u-Baw'omkulu	Ntate mohōlō	Kuku. Makgolo	Makhulu	Koko. Kokwe	Tshekulu
		Makgolo	»	»	»
u-Makulu	Nkhōnō. 'Me mohōlō	Makgolo	»	»	Mbiya
»	Nkhōnō 'Me mohōlō	Kuku	»	»	»
ɹ-Koko	Ntate mohōlō-hōlō	Makgoloko-toane	Makhulukuku	Koko wa baba	
ɹ-Nyana	Mora	Moroa	Mwana	Mwana	Mwana
ᴀ-Molokazana	Ngoetsi	Ngoeci	Mazwale	Ngadja mwana	Nyamwana
ɪ-Tombi	Morali	Moradi	Mwana	Mwana	Mwana
m-Kwenyana	Mokhoenyana	Mokgonyana	Muduhulu	Mwane	Mukwambo
m-Zukulwana	Setlōhōlō	Motlogolo	Muduhulu	Ntugulu	Muzukulu
	Setlōhōloana	Motlogolo-tlo-golwane		Ntugulu ginguha	Muzukulu shi-nguha

Their Wives and Husbands.

Xosa	Sutho (Basutoland)	Pedi-Khaha	Venda	Tonga (Inhambane)	Njao
m-Kuluwa	Mohōloane	Mogolo	Mukomana	Nkoma	Mukulu
m-Nakwetu (Buti)	Khaitseli	Kgaecadi	Khaladzi		
m-Ninawe	Moena	Morathó	Murathu	Nanda	Munukuna
m-Nakwetu (Buti)	Khaitseli	Kgaecadi	Khaladzi		
m-Dade (omkulu)	Khaitseli	Kgaecadi	Khaladzi	Ndi ya ngu	Mukulu
Dade wetu (Sisi)	Mohōloane	Mogolo	Mukomana		
Dade (om-cinci)	Khaitseli	Kgaecadi	Khaladzi		Munukuna
n-Sakwetu (Sisi)	Moena	Morathó	Murathu		
n-Kuluwakazi	Mohats'a mohō-loane	Mosadi oa mogolo	Mwane		Mayi
n-Kuluwakasi (Sisi)	Molamō	Mogadibo / Mmammuea	Mubuye		
n-Ninawekazi	Mohats'a ngoan'esu	Mosadi oa morathó	Musali wa murathu	Ngadja mwana	Nyamwana
ɪ-Ninawekazi (Sisi)	Molamō	Mogadibo / Mmammuea	Mubuye		
Sibari	Soar. Khaitseli	Mogoê	Mukwasha. Muduhulu	Mwane	Mukwambo
Sibari	Soar. Khaitseli	Mogoê	Mukwasha. Muduhulu	Mwane	Mukwambo
	Bana besu	Bo-ngoan'esu			

III. Children of

	Thonga-Ronga	Thonga-Djonga	Chopi	Zulu
Elder Brother's son (for a man) .	Ñwana	Ñwana	Mwana	Ndodana. Mtanami
» » (for a woman)	»	»	Tsandzana	Ndodana. Mtanami
Younger Brother's son (for a man).	»	»	Mwana	Ndodana. Mtanami
» » (for a woman)	»	»	Tsandzana	Ndodana. Mtanami
Sister's son (for a man)	Ntukulu. Mupsyana	Ntukulu	Mutukulu	Ndodana. Mtanami
» (for a woman) . . .	Ñwana	Ñwana	Mwana	Ndodana. Mtanami
Brother's daughter (for a man). .	Ñwana	Ñwana	Mwana	Ndodakazi. Mtanam
» » (for a woman) .	Ñwana. Nhlampsa	Ñwana. Nhlampsa	Tsandzana	Ndodakazi. Mtanam
Sister's daughter (for a man) . .	Ntukulu	Ntukulu	Mutukulu	Ndodakazi. Mtanam
» » (for a woman) .	Ñwana	Ñwana	Mwana	Ndodakazi. Mtanam

IV. Relatives on

	Thonga-Ronga	Thonga-Djonga	Chopi	Zulu
Father's Elder Brother	Tatana lwe' nkulu	Tatana lo' nkulu	Tata wa hombe	Baba mkulu
His wife	Mamana	Manana	Mame	Mame
Father's Younger Brother . . .	Tatane lwe' ntjongo	Tatana lo' ntjongo	Tata wa mudoto	Baba m'cane
His wife	Mamana	Manana	Mame	Mame m'cane
Father's Brother's Son. . . .	Makwerju	Makweru	Nkoma. Nanda.	Umfowetu
His wife (for a man)	Namu. Ñwingi	Namu. Ñwingi	Ndombi	Makoti
Father's Brother's Daughter . .	Makwerju	Makweru	Ndi ya ngu	Dadawetu
Her husband (for a boy) . . .	Mukoñwana	Mukoñwana	Mukwasa	Umkwenyana
» » (for a girl) . . .	Namu	Namu		Babekazi
Father's Sister.	Rarana. Rarakati	Hahana	Hahani	
Her Husband (for a boy) . . .	Namu	Mukoñwana	Mukwasa	Baba. Umkwnyane
» » (for a girl). . . .	Nkata. Nuna	Namu. Nuna	Ndombi	Baba
Father's Sister's Son (for a man).	Ntukulu. Shitale	Ntukulu	Mutukulu	Umzala
» » (for a woman)	Ñwana. Shitale	Ñwana	Mwana	»
Father's Sister's Daughter (for a man).	Ntukulu. Shitale	Ntukulu	Mutukulu	»
Father's Sister's Daughter (for a woman)	Ñwana, Shitale	Ñwana		»
The wife of Father's Sister's Son	Ntukulu	Ntukulu	Mutukulu	»
The Husband of Father's Sister's Daughter.	»	»	»	»

Brothers and Sisters.

Xosa	Sutho (Basutoland)	Pedi-Khaha	Venda	Tonga (Inhambane)	Njao
Nyana	Ngoana	Ngoana oa mo-golo	Mwana wa mu-komana	Mwana	Mwana
»	»	Ngoana oa mo-golo	Mwana wa kha-ladzi	»	»
»	»	Ngoana oa mo-rathó	Mwana wa mu-rathu	»	»
»	»	Ngoana oa mo-rathó	Mwana wa kha-ladzi	»	»
Nyana. um-Tshana	Mochana	Motlogolo	Muduhulu	Ntugulu	Muzukulu
Nyana. um-Tshana	»	»	Mwana	Nyahama	
Tombi	Morali		Mwana	Mwana	
»	»				
Tombi. um-Tshana	Mochana	Motlogolo	Muduhulu	Ntugulu	Muzukulu
Tombi. um-Tshana	Ngoana				

The Father's Side.

Xosa	Sutho (Basutoland)	Pedi-Khaha	Venda	Tonga (Inhambane)	Njao
Tata omkulu	Ntate mohōlō	Ramogolo	Khotsi muhulu	Baba kongolo	Baba mukulu
Ma-omkulu	Nkhōnō	Mamogolo	Mme muhulu	Mayi kongolo	Mayi
Tata-omcinci	Rangoane	Rangoanê	Khotsi munene	Baba dugwane	Baba muloko
Ma-omcinci	Rangoane. Mangoane	Mmanê	Mme munene	Mayi dugwane	Mayi
Kayise	Ngoan'esu	Ngoana ramo-golo	Mukomana	Ñwanduye	Hama
	Mohats'a ngoa-n'esu		Mmane	Namu	
Kayise	Khaitseli	Kgaecadi	Khaladzi	Gogadji	
Sibari	Soar. Khaitseli	Soar. Kgaecadi	Muduhulu	Mwane	
»				Nyahama	
Dadobawo	Rakhali	Rakgadi	Makhadzi	Hahani	Thethadji
Malume	Rakhali (oa monna)	Motlogolo	Mukwasha. Muduhulu	Mwane	Mukwambo
»				Namu	
n-Za	Motsoala	Motsoala	Muzwala	Ntugulu	
»	»	»	»	Nyahama	Muzukulu
»	Motsoala	»	Muzwala	Ntugulu	
»	»	»	»		
»	»	Mosadi oa motsoala	Muzwala	Ngandja mwana	Nyamwana
»	Motsoala	»	Mukwasha Muduhulu	Ntugulu	

V. *Relatives o*

	Thonga-Ronga	Thonga-Djonga	Chopi	Zulu
Mother's Brother	Malume	Malume. Ko-kwana	Kokwana	Malume
Mother's Brother's Wife (for a man)	Nsati	Kokwana	»	Mamekazi
» » (for a woman)	Malume	»	»	»
Mother's Brother's Son	Malume. Ntale	Kokwana	»	Umzala
His wife	Namu		»	»
Mother's Brother's Daughter . .	Mamana. Ntale	Manana	Mamanyana	»
Her Husband	Tatana	Tatana	Tate	»
Mother's Brother's Grandchildren	Bakokwana	Bakokwana	.	Ndodana. Ndakazi
Mother's Elder Sister	Mamana	Mamana	Mame	Mamekazi
Mother's Younger Sister	»	»	»	»
Mother's Sister's Husband . . .	Tatana	Tatana	Tate	Malume
Mother's Sister's Son (for a boy) .	Makwerju	Makwerju	Ndi ya ngu	Umzala
» » » (for a girl) .	»	»	»	
His Wife	Namu	Namu	Ndombi	Umzala. Kan
Mother's Sister's Daughter (for a boy)	Makwerju	Makweru	Ndi ya ngu	»
Mother's Sister's Daughter (for a girl)	»	»	»	»
Her Husband (for a boy) . .	Namu. Muko-ñwana	Mukoñwana	Mwane. Mu-kwasa	»
» » (for a girl) . . .	Mukoñwana	Namu. Nuna	Ndombi	»

VI. *Relatives o*

Wife	Nsati. Nkata	Nsati	Musikati	Umfazi
Wife's Father	Mukoñwana. Tatana	Mukoñwana. Tatana	Tate	Umkwe
Wife's Mother	Mukoñwana. Mamana	Mukoñwana. Mamana	Mame	Umkwekazi
Wife's Elder Brother	Mukoñwana	Mukoñwana	Musade	Umlamu. Siw
His Wife	Mukoñwana lwe'nkulu	Mukoñwana lo'nkulu	Nkokati	»
Wife's Younger Brother	Namu	Namu. Muko-ñwana	Musade. Ndombi	»
His Wife	Mukoñwana lwe'nkulu	Mukoñwana lwe'nkulu	Nkokati	»
Wife's Elder Sister	Mukoñwana. Mamana	Namu	Ndombi	»
Her Husband	Makwerju	Makweru wa shinauma	Nkoma	Umnakwetu

he Mother's Side.

Xosa	Sutho (Basutoland)	Pedi-Khaha	Venda	Tonga (Inhambane)	Ndjao
Malume	Malŏme	Malome	Malume	Koko	Tshekulu
Malume wesi-fazi	Malŏme. Nkhŏnŏ	Makgolo	Makhulu	»	Mbiya nkadji
Malume wesi-fazi	Malŏme. Nkhŏnŏ	»		»	
n Za	Motsoala	Motsoala	Muzwala	»	
»	Mosali oa mo-tsoala	Makgolo		»	
»	Motsoala	Motsoala	Muzwala	Ngadja mwana	Mayi
»	Monna oa mo-tsoala	Mogadjea oa motsoala	Mukwasha	Baba	
	Bana ba mo-tsoala	Bana ba ma-kgolo		Ba mwana mayi	
Makazi	Nkhŏnŏ. 'Me	Mmê-mogolo	Mme muhulu	Mayi kongolo	Mayi mukulu
»	Mangoane	Mmê ngoanê	Mmane	Mayi dugwane	Mayi muloko
Malume	Rangoane	Ramogolo. Rangoanê	Monna wa mme muhulu	Koko	
Kanina	Ngoan'esu	Mogolo. Morathó	Mukomana. Murathu	Wanduye	Hama
»	Khaitseli	Kgaecadi	Khaladzi		
»	Mosali oa ngoan'esu	Mogadjea oa mogolo		Namu. Mayana	
»	Khaitseli	Kgaecadi		Ntugulu	
»	Ngoan'esu	Mogolo. Morathó			
»	Monna oa khaitseli	Mogoê		Ntugulu	
»	Monna oa ngoan'esu	Mokgonyana		Nyahama	Hama

he Wife's Side.

Xosa	Sutho (Basutoland)	Pedi-Khaha	Venda	Tonga (Inhambane)	Ndjao
m-Fazi	Mosali	Mosadi	Musadzi	Mwangadji	Mukadji
Bawozala	Mohoe. Mo-khoenyana	Makgolo. Ra-tsoale	Makhulu	Baba. Sade	Mukwambo. Babe
Mazala. um-Kwekazi	Mohoehali	Mogoêgadi	Makhulu	Mayi	Mukwambo. Ba-Mbiya
m-Kwe. u-Si-bari	Soar. Khaitseli	Mogoê	Malume	Baba	Mukwambo
Sibari	Khaitseli	Makgolo	Makhulu	Mayi gogadji	Ba-Mbiya
m-Kwe. u-Si-bari	Soar. Khaitseli	Mogoê	Malume	Baba. Sade-nyana	Mukwambo
Sibari	Khaitseli	Makgolo	Makhulu	Mayi gogadji	Ba-Mbiya
m-Lanyakazi	Molamŏ	Makgolo. Mo-lamo	Mme muhulu	Mayi gogadji	Mwalamo. Mu-kadji muhulu
m-Nakwetu	Fube	Makgolo. Mo-lamo	Khotsi muhulu	Ndi ya ngu	Hama

VI. Relatives o

	Thonga-Ronga	Thonga-Djonga	Chopi	Zulu
Wife's Younger Sister	Namu. Nhombe	Namu	Ndombi	Umlamu
Her Husband	Makwerju	Makweru wa shinauma	Nanda	Umnakwetu
Wife's Brother's Son	Namu	Mukoñwana	Musade	Ndodane. M nami
His Wife	Mukoñwana lwe'nkulu	Mukoñwana	Nkokati	Makoti
Wife's Brother's Daughter . . .	Namu. Nsati	Namu. Nsati	Ndombi	Mtanami
Her Husband		Makweru	Ndi ya ngu	Umkwenyan
Wife's Sister's Son	Ñwana	Ñwana	Mwana	Mtanami
His Wife	Ñwingi	Ñwingi	Mwingi	Makoti
Wife's Sister's Daughter	Ñwana	Ñwana	Mwana	Mtanami
Her Husband	Ñwana	Ñwana	Mwana	Umkwenyan
Daughter of Wife's Brother's Son	Nsati. Namu	Nsati	Musikati	Umzukulu

VII. Relatives o

	Thonga-Ronga	Thonga-Djonga	Chopi	Zulu
Husband	Nuna. Nkata	Nuna	Mwamna	Ndoda. Umy
Husband's Father	Ñwingi	Ñwingi	Mwingi. Tate	Baba
Husband's Mother	Ñwingi	Ñwingi. Manana.	Mwingi. Mame	Mame
Husband's Elder Brother	Ñwingi	Ñwingi. Namu.	Ndombi	Umnewetu
His Wife	Makwerju	Makweru wa shinauma	Ndi ya ngu	Dadewetu
Husband's Younger Brother . .	Namu	Namu	Ndombi	Umnewetu
His Wife	Makwerju	Makweru wa shinauma	Mnanda	Dadewetu
Husband's Elder Sister	Mamana. Nhombe	Namu	Ndombi	Dadwetu
Her Husband	Mukoñwana lwe'nkulu	Mukoñwana lo'nkulu	Mukwasa	Umkwenyan
Husband's Younger Sister . . .	Namu. Nhombe	Namu	Ndombi	Dadewetu
Her Husband	Mukoñwana lwe'nkulu	Mukoñwana lo'nkulu	Mukwasa	Umkwenyan
Husband's Brother's Son	Ñwana	Ñwana	Mwana	Mtanami
His Wife	Ñwingi	Ñwingi	Mwana	Makoti
Husband's Brother's Daughter . .	Ñwana	Ñwana	Mwana	Mtanami
Her Husband	Ñwana	Mukoñwana		Umkwenyan
Husband's Sister's Son	Ntukulu. Nkata	Ntukulu. Nkata	Mutukulu	Mtanami
His Wife	Ntukulu	Ntukulu	»	Makoti
Husband's Sister's Daughter . .	Ntukulu	Ntukulu	»	Mtanami
Her Husband	»	»	»	Umkwenyan

The Wife's Side (continued).

Xosa	Sutho (Basutoland)	Pedi-Khaha	Venda	Tonga (Inhambane)	Njao
m-Lanyakazi	Molamō	Mogadjea	Murathu wa musadzi	Namu	Mwalamo. Mukadji muloko
m-Nakwetu	Fube	Mokgonyana	Khotsi munene	Ndi ya ngu	Hama
m-Tshana		Ngoana oa mogoê	Malume	Baba. Sade	Mwalamo
		Makgolo		Mayi gogadji	Ba-Mbiya
m-Tshanakazi			Muzwala wa mwana. Musadzi	Namu	Mukadji
				Ndi ya ngu	Hama
m-Tshana		Ngoana	Mwana	Mwana	Mwana
		Ngoeci		Ngadja mwana	Nyamwana
m-Tshanakazi		Ngoana		Ndoni	Mwana
		Mokgonyana		Mwane	Mukwambo
m-Ntana		Ngoana oa makgolo		Namu	

The Husband's Side.

Xosa	Sutho (Basutoland)	Pedi-Khaha	Venda	Tonga (Inhambane)	Njao
m-Yeni; in-Doda	Monna	Monna	Munna	Mwama	Mwamuna
-Bawozala	Matsalè (Ntate)	Matsoale. Rapsale	Mazwale	Babe	Baterala
-Mazala	Matsalè. 'Me	Matsoale. Ngoeci	Mazwale	Mayi	Mayi
m-Kuluwa	Mohōloane Ntate oa monna	Matsoale omonyane	Khotsi muhulu	Nyahəma	Mwalamo
m-Kuluwakazi	'Me		Muhadzinga	Mayi kongolo	
m-Ninawe	Moen'a monna	Morathó oa monna	Khotsi munene	Namu	Mwalamo
m-Ninawekazi	Ngoan'esu		Muhadzinga	Ngadjamwana	
-Dodakazi. Sisi	Molamō. 'Me	Mogadibo	Mubuye		Mwalamo
-Sibari	Soar	Mokgonyana	Mukwasha		»
-Dodakazi. Sisi	Molamō. Ma-'ngoane	Mogadibo			Mwalamo
-Sibari	Soar	Mokgonyana			
-Nyana	Ngoana	Ngoana		Nyahama	Mwana
-Tombi. u-Molokazane		Ngoeci		Ngadjamwana	»
-Tombi	Ngoana	Ngoana		Mwana	Mwana
m-Kwenyane		Mokgonyana		Mwane	Mukwambo
m-Ntana.		Motlogolo		Ntugulu	Muzukulu
m-Ntana. u-Molokazana		Mogadjea oa motlogolo		»	»
-Tombi		Motlogolo		»	»
m-Ntana				»	»

503

APPENDIX V (See p. 226)

As an example of *the absolute obedience due to the father*, I may quote the testimony of the Rev. Calvin Maphophe, one of the Native ministers of the Swiss Mission, now living in Lourenço Marques. It illustrates vividly the painful conflict which takes place in the heart of a Bantu boy when he is faced with the dilemma of either obeying a heathen father who forbids him to become a Christian, or going against the paternal will and joining the Church.

One day one of the little shepherds belonging to Maphophe's village in the Spelonken brought to his comrades an astonishing piece of news. He had gone to the missionary station and heard a white man say that there is a God in heaven and that this God created all things. His words were received with absolute incredulity by the company of boys herding the goats ; they answered : "It is an impossibility! Do we not know that the first man and woman came out of a reed ?" However young Matsivi (this was the name of Calvin Maphophe) and his brother Shihosi wished to set their minds at rest about the matter and they began to attend the service on Sundays. They were so struck by the message heard in the little church that they decided to learn more of this extraordinary teaching of the White people, and every Sunday they went to the Station. One of the men of the tribe informed their father that they were assiduous attendants at the Christian services. Maphophe called together all the men of his village and summoned the two boys before this tribunal. Pointing his finger at them he said : "These boys have dared to go to the White people and hear things which are dangerous to us. We do not wish them to become insane! Take it to heart both of you. It is over. Henceforth you must never go again to the village of the Whites. If you disobey, you will be beaten."

The two boys were terribly moved by their father's words. It is a recognised principle in the Bantu tribe that a child who wishes to do right must obey his father, and they were anxious to behave well... But the attraction they felt for the new teaching was too great. They solved the problem by running away from their home. This is not the place to tell the end of the story. It may be found in a little pamphlet "Le Pasteur Calvin Mapopé" published by the head-quarters of the Swiss Romande Mission (2, Chemin des Cèdres, Lausanne).

APPENDIX

APPENDIX VI (See p. 265)

*The story of Paulus K., illustrating the matlulana superstition and
the Thonga horror of polyandry.*

One of my pupils, who was already a married man of, perhaps, thirty-
two years of age, once came to me, very much distressed, to confess a
fault which seemed to weigh very heavy on his conscience. On a day
of feasting he had drunk too freely and had commited adultery with the
wife of his elder brother Guga. He fought with himself for years, not
daring to avow an action which seemed to him not merely ordinary
adultery but an incestuous act. He finally wrote to his brother :
"Though I know that we shall not be able to love each other any more
as before, though it pains me so much to separate from you, I will
confess! Please forgive me, as I intended to commit suicide on account
of my fault!"

The special gravity of the fault consisted in two circumstances :
1) She was his brother's wife and he was now unable to visit his
brother when ill, to take part in his burial, or to maintain friendly
relations with him. 2) Guga was his elder brother. This made the
case still worse.

The letter of Paulus to his fellow evangelists is touching : "I have
no right to stay in your assembly, because I have been overcome by
the Enemy and committed adultery with my elder brother's wife. I
have been long prevented (from confessing) by the Enemy's power.
Now I have wept before Jesus that He may help me to pierce the
abscess... Satan came and said to me : 'Will you not be ashamed to
confess such a thing before men ?' I nearly retreated. But at sunrise
I made haste to write to you, and now I feel peace and joy. It seems
to me that I am going to receive the Spirit of God."

APPENDIX VII (See p. 279)

*The story of Spoon Libombo, showing that, when the lobolo has not been paid
or has been returned, the children belong to the mother's and
not to the father's family.*

Spoon was the son of Shibaninge, a woman of the Libombo family,
and of Khobete of the Mazwaya family, who had lobola Shibaninge.

505

This man died during a war with the Portuguese, having been killed on Mbengelen island. The widow was "fambeliwa" (chosen) by Nsiki, Khobete's brother, who was to inherit her. But Nsiki did not really care for the widow. He did not prepare a *ntehe* for the baby nor provide the mother with ochre. Seeing this, Shibaninge went back to her relatives. When the time for the weaning of the little one arrived, a man named Mbobobo had irregular relations with the woman in order to "lumula" the child (See page 60). Mbobobo went so far as to take her to his home, upon which Nsiki claimed the lobolo paid by the Mazwayas and the Libombos gave it back to them. After that, Spoon lived in his mother's family and was called : "wa ka Libombo," "man of Libombo." But he had no real home (a nga na kwakwe). Being on the spot he was always chosen to help in the sacrifices : drinking the beer which remained in the pot after the libations to the gods in the gandelo, near the gate, stealing the offerings when the victims were killed in the sacred bush, etc. He was the "great ntukulu," because his mother belonged to the elder branch or first house of the family. So he took precedence of the other uterine nephews when they had to take part in the sacrifices.

APPENDIX VIII (See p. 281)

The story of Gidhlana Ngwetsa of Rikatla; a typical case illustrating the lobola, divorce, and leper customs of the Ba-Ronga.

Gidhlana was the sister of a man named Mubene. Both were the children of a fine old Ronga named Ngwetsa and one of his wives. Gidhlana was bought with lobola by a man named Khandlela (candle), son of Ñwamanghele, a man of the Manyisa clan settled near Rikatla. The marriage took place probably in 1893. The new pair did not live in peace. Gidhlana quarrelled with her husband. "Why ? Nobody knows! Are the affairs of the huts and the villages known to outsiders ?" She returned home to her father Ngwetsa. The husband waited a while. Then he followed her (landjela) and asked her to come back to the conjugal home. Her parents told her to obey. She went. But quarrelling soon recommenced. She fled a second time ; her husband and her parents-in-law did their best to induce her to go back. She refused. An uncle of hers took a stick and thrashed her, but nothing could persuade her. She stayed in her parents' village. In a neighbouring village dwelt a young man named Muzila, who was the chief of the Rikatla district (Page 381). He belonged to the Mazwaya clan, to the reigning family. He had two brothers, one of whom, called Gudu, was still a boy. This girl, Gidhlana, began to make friends with the boys of Muzila's village. Gudu sent a woman from the village of Ngwetsa to make proposals to Gidhlana (ku mu wopseta). This woman made proposals on behalf of Gudu (a wopsetela Gudu). The girl agreed. But, in the meantime, Gudu started for Johannesburg and Gidhlana was abducted by the other brother, who took her to the village of Muzila ; it was a case of marriage by theft (tlhuba) (See p. 119). Muzila was grieved at the conduct of these young men, and sent the girl to one of his counsellors to be watched over by him and, going to Ngwetsa, her father, he said : "We have stolen your pot. Look for it in our village, the village of Mazwaya's people." Ngwetsa was greatly puzzled. The first husband had not yet claimed his money back ; it was still in the hands of Ngwetsa and lo! the girl had already been taken by others! This was not right at all! They might have waited a little! All the men of Ngwetsa armed themselves and started as enemies (hi bulala) for the village of the thief. They killed a pig, entered the hut of the thief, took all his implements and made a heap of them on the square. The inhabitants all fled into the bush. But one of them came back with 10/. and said : "Have pity on us, please! We clasp your legs! (khoma milenge, viz., ask for forgiveness). You know ? To steal is a very old thing on earth!" "Yes, we know. The thief trusted his throat! (This is a proverb : he did not fear to swallow a large stone, thinking that his throat would be wide enough to let it pass!) He knew that he would have to pay this fine! All right! You are saved! Take the implements back into the hut."

The Ngwetsas took away with them the flesh of the pig, but they sent one joint to the thief, so that he might eat it with his new wife. In this way they gave their consent to the marriage. "They gave him his wife."

But very soon afterwards the first husband, Khandlela, came to Ngwetsa to claim the lobola money, as his wife had gone. Gudu had gone to Johannesburg, so nothing was to be found in that quarter. The discussion began. Ngwetsa said : "All right ; but 10/ of the lobola money must remain with us, for the fence of our village (lihlampfu)." This is generally done when a woman has been driven

away by her husband. Sometimes he must forego as much as
£ 1. or £ 2 of the lobolo, because he has not brought the woman
back in peace. He has spoilt the fence of the village by ill-treating a
girl coming from it. He must repair it with that money... Khandlela
refused, saying : "We have not driven her away! She went back of her
own accord ; you have even found a new husband for her!" What
could the Ngwetsas do ? They had just used the lobolo of Gidhlana
to buy a wife for Mubene, her brother. The money had already been
given to the Moyane clan from which a girl had been chosen by Mubene.
They consequently went to the Moyanes and asked them to return
the money. But the Moyanes said : "Your money has already
gone further. We have used it to buy a girl of Madjieta for our son.
We will go and fetch it." So two projected marriages were prevented ;
they would have been annulled, had they been already concluded! In
this way Khandlela found his money!

Later on Gudu came back from Johannesburg and took Gidhlana
as his wife. Hoping that he had earned some money, the Nwgetsas
went to him and said : "You have spoilt our flock (ntlhambi)" viz., the
oxen which we hoped to get by the sale of our daughter. "Now pay!"
Muzila said to them : "Look at Shaputa ; we trust in her!" Shaputa
was a little girl, the sister of Gudu. Muzila proposed to Ngwetsa's
people to consider her as theirs : "They would find money through
her." They consented to wait till she was of age. Some years elapsed.
Muzila moved to the Mabota country with Gudu. Gidhlana was
suddenly taken ill with leprosy and the disease made rapid progress.
She died. Muzila, the master of the village, informed Ngwetsa.
Ngwetsa did not come to the burial, neither did any member of the
family attend it. Was it not leprosy ? Is not the contagion terrible
for members of the family ?... Other people can bury a leper ;
his relatives never. However they allowed their fears to go too
far, for decency required that, in such a case, some relatives at least
should go and witness the burial, even though they might keep far away
from the grave. Their behaviour greatly grieved Muzila and entailed
unexpected consequences!

Shaputa grew to be a young woman and a suitor, of the Honwana
clan, came and bought her. The Ngwetsas heard of it and at once put in
their claim. Muzila informed Gudu, who was then staying near
Lourenço Marques. "He fell on his back from the shock!" (o gaa hi
le ntjhaku!) and refused to pay. Muzila said to Ngwetsa : "You
have forfeited your claim, as you did not attend the funeral. Moreover

the chief of our Mazwaya family, Magomanyama, says that no claim is accepted for a leper, for one drowned in the river, or for anyone who dies from smallpox or from the assagay."

Of course the Ngwetsas did not accept such an answer, but this is a typical Bantu affair (nandju), showing the many blessings of the lobola custom. The matter will have to be decided by the chief, or rather by the Portuguese Administrator, who must take a good deal of trouble, if he wishes to understand it rightly and to deliver an equitable judgment!

APPENDIX IX (See p. 530).

The story of Mboza and Muhambi and of the women inherited by them, illustrating the consequences of lobola and of its suppression.

Compare the genealogy of the Masuluke family (page 225).

Mboza had four brothers, three elder and a younger; Sam, the elder, had a son, Hlangabeza, who married by lobola a first wife and by abduction a second, Bukutje II. Fos, the second brother, married Bukutje I and had four children: three girls, Tshakaza, Estelle, Nhwaanin, and one boy, Muhambi. Sam and Fos both died, so Bukutje I was inherited by Mboza and her four children went to live in his village. In the meantime Mboza became a Christian, as also did Muhambi and the three girls. Wishing to lead a Christian life, he separated from Bukutje I, who, being still a heathen, committed herself with "an empty oil-tin" (p. 213), viz., a man of Inhambane who became her servant-husband. In 1904 a Christian young man, Moses, wooed the elder of the three girls and brought £ 20 to lobola her. This money was naturally due to Muhambi in order to allow him to lobola a wife for himself, and indeed Muhambi was betrothed to Ntshelebeti, daughter of Phulan Ngwetsa. This man was still a heathen and consequently wished his daughter to be paid for.

Having been told that it is not right for a Christian to accept lobolo money, Mboza and Muhambi, actuated by a most praiseworthy scruple, decided to return the money to Moses, and Muhambi started for Johannesburg in order to earn the lobolo due to Phulan. But this was not the end of this famous "bukosi!" The younger brother, Komatan, a consistent heathen, came to Mboza, very angry with him for his foolishness. "This is family property," said he, "and I do not consent to its being lost." So he claimed the £ 20, which was given to him, and out of which Mboza did not get a penny. Komatan himself did not intend to use it for his own benefit, as we shall see presently.

The following year, whilst Muhambi was still working in Johannesburg, Hlangabeza died. Muhambi was his heir, being his *makwabu*, first cousin on the paternal side. He was informed of his good luck, but answered that it was taboo for him (yila), as a Christian, to accept this inheritance. So Komatan took the first of Hlangabeza's wives, not as a wife, however, but because she had children and he wanted them to remain in the Masuluke family. The woman herself also took "an empty oil-tin," in the form of another Inhambane man. The second of Hlangabeza's wives, having been married by him by abduction, was not really the property of the Masulukes. But she had one child ; so Komatan took the lobolo money of Moses and remitted it to Denisa, this woman's father, and, in this way, he secured the property of both mother and child to the Masulukes. The woman, however, went to live with a Chopi in an irregular manner and had a second child by him. On January 29th, 1909, this woman of the Denisa family came to Muhambi. Her child had to be weaned, which is done by means of a rite in which the husband must take part. She had no true husband, so she vented all her anger before Mboza and Muhambi saying : "I have no husband, nobody to give me clothing, to pay my hut-tax, to repair my house. Have you indeed forsaken me?" — "Yes" answered Muhambi, "you cannot be my wife. I have married Ntshelebeti and, for us Christians, it is not allowable to take many wives." — "Then do not be surprised if I go and take another husband, and do not go and accuse me *shikanekiswen*, before the Portuguese Administrator, saying I have spoilt your property." — "We shall not *follow* you," said Muhambi, "you are free." — "But" added Mboza, "we are not sending you to commit sin! Go and think the matter over."

This was the end of the discussion. Mboza's answer is no answer at all. It only shows the great complexity and difficulty of the position. The whole story fitly illustrates how utterly bad the custom of lobola is, and what immense difficulties its suppression entails. Let me, however, remark that these difficulties would not have arisen had there not been a heathen relative (Komatan) to uphold the claim which the Christians had foregone. During the stage of transition many hard cases such as this must unfortunately occur!

APPENDIX

APPENDIX X

Short Account of two South African wars.

As regards war customs, I not only possess the information obtained from my ordinary sources, Mankhelu, Tobane, Mboza, Viguet, etc., but a certain amount of personal experience. I had indeed the good, or the bad luck, to witness two South African wars : the Ronga-Portuguese war of 1894-1896 and the Sikororo war in 1901. As many allusions are made to these wars in these pages, my readers may be interested in having a short account of them.

1) *The Ronga-Portuguese war*, of 1894-1896, was caused by the subchief Mubvesha, when he tried to make himself independent of his young suzerain, Mahazule, who had just succeeded his father Maphunga as legitimate heir of Nondwane (See page 410). Mubvesha succeeded in interesting the Portuguese Administrator in his cause, but the whole clan remained loyal to Mahazule, and, a dispute having arisen, on the 27th August 1894, at Hangwana (the seat of the Administrator), the Mazwaya army assembled and prepared to defend its chief. The Government then successively asked Ñwamantibyane, chief of Mpfumu, and Ngwanazi, chief of Maputju, for help against the rebels. Ñwamantibyane, after long hesitation, refused the call (See Appendix XI). The Maputju warriors came as far as the Tembe shore, but, when asked to cross the bay, they decamped. For some weeks the Native yimpis were the masters of the whole country, up to the boundary of the town of Lourenço Marques. But Portuguese troops soon arrived from Lisbon and re-took Hangwana, (10 miles from the town), in December. The Royal Commissioner, M. A. Ennes, with his aide de camp, General (then Captain) F. d'Andrade, having taken command of the campaign, a forward move was made. The Portuguese camped near Morakwen, on the Nkomati River, where a severe battle took place at daybreak on the 2nd February 1895. The yimpis of Mahazule and Ñwamantibyane attacked the Portuguese troops while it was still dark and nearly invaded their camp. But the white soldiers did not lose their heads ; they rapidly formed square and repulsed the enemy with great loss. At the same time Native allies of Matjolo and Mabota were driving the rebels from their retreats, so that they fled to the east of the Nkomati River into Gungunyana's territory : these Captain F. d'An-

drade followed into the Khosen country and defeated them on the 8th September 1895, at the battle of Magule (See page 471).

The Ngoni king, Gungunyana, had more or less encouraged the rebels to rise. When asked to give them up to the Portuguese he refused to do so. So the war had to be carried up to his stronghold of Mandlakazi. During many weeks the whole of Gungunyana's army, which was estimated at 25,000 to 30,000 men, camped near its king, ready to fight. But, for some unknown reason, the Portuguese army was delayed and the Thonga battalions, having nothing to eat, broke up. However, a strong bodyguard, the flower of the great king's troops, consisting principally of Ba-Ngoni, remained at the headquarters. When at last the Portuguese arrived in the neighbourhood of Mandlakazi, a sharp fight took place. The Ngoni warriors gallantly attacked the Portuguese square but were driven back with great loss, (305 killed, according to the official report). The royal kraal, Mandlakazi, was taken and destroyed and Gungunyana fled to Tshayimiti, the sacred wood where his ancestors were buried. Some weeks later, Captain Musinho d'Albuquerque, after a forced march, took him prisoner without any fighting, and brought him to Lourenço Marques, whence he was deported to Western Africa.

The Ba-Ngoni considered that they had been taken by surprise and not properly defeated ; so, in 1897, a serious revolt broke out, headed by Magigwane, the Commander-in-Chief of Gungunyana's yimpi. But it was soon successfully put down by the Portuguese forces, who divided up the country into a certain number of military zones, and the districts of Lourenço Marques and Inhambane have been perfectly quiet ever since.

2. *The Sikororo war* took place, in 1901, in the Shiluvane country, during the Anglo-Boer war, when the north of the Transvaal was, as it were, without white rulers. The successor of the famous Sekukuni, reigning in the Leydensburg district, Sekhukhukhu, tried to avail himself of the unsettled state of the country to realise an old political dream, viz., to become the paramount chief of the whole country. He interfered with the Maharimane clan, which inhabited the Drakensberg ranges, where the Oliphant crosses them before reaching the plain. This clan was divided into two : the legitimate heir was under the tutelage of a woman named Ñwanamohube, but his brother, Maphephe, wished to get rid of her, stating that she was exercising her authority against the interests of the country. Sekhukhukhu assured the queen-regent that he would help her if she joined him. He

entreated the Pedi chiefs dwelling on the northern side of the range, viz., Sikororo and Maaghe, to espouse his cause. Sikororo was a very strange old man who had retired into the mountains, far away from his villages, and a regent, named Rios, was carrying on the government in his stead. Rios agreed with Sekhukhukhu's proposals ; so did some of the subjects of Maaghe, the Masume clan. But Maaghe himself refused to do so and he was supported by Muhlaba, the Nkuna chief, who was an old ally of his.

The first encounter took place in the Maharimane valley, where Maphephe was defeated by the united yimpis of Sekhukhukhu and Ñwanamohube. He fled. In the meantime another foe, called by the Natives "Fighter-by-night," had opposed Sekhukhukhu in the Leydenburg district, invaded his territory, and defeated his troops. It seemed that this would put an end to the ambitious plans of the great Pedi chief... But such was not the case. Hearing of his enemy's defeat, Maphephe again took courage. Chased from his country, he sought a refuge with Maaghe, who was imprudent enough to welcome him and all his people in the Bokhaha valley. We witnessed the curious spectacle of a whole clan moving into our district of Shiluvane. The young chief was breathing vengeance. He soon began to make mischief, and organised a raid into Masume's territory. This put a match to the train. Rios avenged his friends by burning some villages of Muhlaba, and killing the pigs. A regular battle took place, on the 15th October 1901, between the armies of Maaghe and Muhlaba and those of Sikororo and Masume. The first had to retreat, but they suffered no loss, whilst they claimed to have killed 20 of the enemy. The situation was bad for them, as other chiefs threatened to join Sikororo and to deal summarily with them and their missionaries! I then went to ask for help at Leydsdorp, where the remainder of the Boer Commandoes were just passing, coming from Komati Poort on the way to Pietersburg. I had the good luck to meet there with a party of Hollanders, who at once volunteered to come and save women and children in danger! They stayed for two days at the Shiluvane station, where their presence caused a great sensation... But they had to look after their own affairs, and we were soon obliged to return to the same dangerous situation! On the 6th November 1901, the Sikororo yimpi, strengthened by the troops of Sekhukhukhu, Mabulanen, Masume etc., a regular confederation of yimpis, numbering 700 warriors (as it was estimated), invaded the peaceful Shiluvane valley at dawn, burning the huts, firing their rifles, and shouting wildly : "Moya! Moya!" (Wind! Wind! viz., projectiles of the enemy are but wind!) They went so far as to cross the Moudi rivulet, less than one mile from the Shiluvane Mission Station. The two allied chiefs were not on their guard and had very few men with them. However, they rushed to meet the invaders with such courage that these were surprised. Seeing the Christian Natives clad like Europeans, they believed the Hollanders were still there, and fled ignominiously, leaving some 40 of their warriors dead on the field of battle. These are the men whose flesh provided all the Zoutpansberg magicians with their powerful charms! Rios was killed, and it is said that his corpse was redeemed for the price of ten guineas by the old Sikororo. Others state that his skull was placed by Maaghe in the great drum of his capital. This defeat definitely broke the power of Sikororo, who made his submission, and was the last clash of arms worth mentioning in the war.

APPENDIX XI (See p. 463).

The position of Ñwamantibyane when the 1894 war broke out.

When the Portuguese asked Ñwamantibyane to help them against Mahazule, (August-September 1894), this young chief of twenty years of age at the most, assembled his army. An irresistible spirit of war was in the air. Held back by his counsellors, who were unwilling to fight against their rebellious compatriots, Ñwamantibyane hesitated to respond to the appeal of the Whites. He was seated, perplexed, in his camp, his demeanour morose and preoccupied, surrounded on the one hand by his "great ones," on the other by his young men who addressed him thus : "Give us, give us men to slaughter! Thou art nothing but a coward! Send us!" Those were tragic times!

He allowed a small contingent to go into the neighbourhood of Lourenço Marques, in order to reconnoitre (Nov. 6. 1894). This yimpi made several prisoners and stole the oxen of the Swiss Mission, which were grazing in the vicinity of the town. One of our young men, named Tandane, was taken prisoner by a man of Ñwamba. A passer-by, belonging to the Mabota clan, was also caught. All these captives were taken to the chief Ñwamantibyane, to whom the spoil belonged, his men having been the spoilers. The man who had captured the passer-by from Mabota begged the chief's permission to kill him, which was accorded ; this warrior, radiant with joy, immediately retired with his victim, slew him in cold blood and returned to dance before the chief. The Ñwamba man requested a like privilege. But Ñwamantibyane had other ends in view ; he wanted to make use of our young man to send a message to the Portuguese Governor, and so refused the permission asked. The man, a prey to an insatiable longing to shed blood, insisted. He was offered as compensation one, and even two, of the stolen oxen, but could not thus be satisfied. "I want my man," said he, "to kill him so that I can dance!" Ñwamantibyane had to employ force to silence him. Two oxen, twelve pounds sterling, counted as nothing to this black warrior compared with the fiendish delight he would derive from the *gila*!

As regards the conclusion of the story of Tandane, he came back with a letter from the chief asking why the Whites wanted to kill him, and begging for an interview. When the letter, written in Zulu by some of his boys, had been despatched, the young chief said : "Now I can breathe! When I eat something, it can pass through my throat!" The Portuguese Governor consented to the interview, but the letter sent back to Ñwamantibyane, in answer to his, was intercepted and so the war continued. See in the preceding Appendix how it spread to Gungunyana's country, and ended in the capture of this despot and the destruction of the Ngoni kingdom.

Phot. D. Lenoir.
Sham fight at Ndlebende's (Maputju).

LATIN NOTES

FOR MEDICAL MEN AND ETHNOGRAPHERS

———

Note 1 (p. 40).—The "shifado" with which every Thonga clothes the tip of the penis is an oval and hollow object. This covering is required for reasons that relate to modesty and cleanliness. If anyone has lost his shifado, it is a disgrace to him.

At one time among the Thonga, who received that custom from the Zulu people, the men used to wear what in their language is a "*mbayi,*" that is, a kind of tube from plaited leaves of the palm tree, which is called "milala."

The last "mbayi" were seen in the year 1895 or 1896 A.D., because they seemed to wear the shifado, made from the rind of a small gourd or from hard and hollowed and carefully polished wood, affixed to the tip of the genital organ, with less inconvenience.

Note 2 (p. 56). S.n.i. [Latin abbreviation], meaning: without having injected the semen. With regard to this, the sperm was to be spread outside by the husband (a nga mu weleri) ; this is coition when properly performed and, as it were, expiatory. Then the wife takes into her hands the pollutions of both (thyaka ra bona) and smears her navel with them.

Note 3 (p. 57). The father touches the bottom of the boy's body from the front and from behind with his penis.

Note 4 (p. 88). These are the formulae:

Shana khololwane ma ri tiba le'ri onhaka milebe?

Do you know the bird that injured the inner lips?

—I mbolo ya shuburu.

—It is the penis of an uncircumcised man.

LATIN NOTES

Banhwanyana ba ka Makwakwa ba kundja na ba hlanamile. N'yini?

The girls from the Makwakwa country copulate with open hands. What do these words mean?

—I mahlehlwa.

—Mahlehwa is semen.

(Hlehlwa is the seed of a creeper growing along the ground; this seed is of the same size as a two shilling piece and possesses, in its central part, two hooks standing up.)

Note 5 (p. 98, 182). The inner lips of the external genitals are designated by the word milebe (singular nebe), which the girls are accustomed to pull to such an extent that they may extend to five, ten or even fifteen centimeters. Sometimes they measure these lips with small sticks, boasting of their length among their female companions and even among their husbands. By these depraved customs, to be sure, the girls seek nothing other than the favor of a future husband, who, among the Ba-Pedi, may send his wife home and demand back his oxen, if he thinks that she has not extended her lips enough. The girls prepare a potful of food, which they close with a lid. In the evening the boys come to them and pay a fee to be admitted. They sit down on the floor of the house and watch the girls eating their dinner and putting their fingers into the pot. The girls whose *milebe* are four inches long use four fingers to eat; they are *bakulu*, i.e. adults, and the lovers rejoice. Or they may use only three, sometimes two. The young girls dine with hollow hands.

Note 6 (p. 154). If anyone has become weakened by advanced age or for any reason so impotent that he cannot emit sperm (a nga kumi mati), the rest of the men will discuss what is to be done. If it comes out at least a little, all ceremony is forbidden. And it is not lawful for those, who were to have joined themselves in the same rite, to perform the rite. That man will observe a fast for five days, very strictly, as the situation demands, and remedies suitable to the condition will be sought.

Note 7 (p. 154). A guilty husband and his wife will perform another rite for the sake of purifying themselves. The wife will wipe the genital organs of her husband and her own with a thoroughly polluted inner garment, which she will burn afterwards.

Both, approaching a fire, will warm the head and hands. Then the woman gathers the ashes, mixes them with fat and smears the limbs of her husband with this, after pulling his arms and legs with her fingers, this rite being called the "lula." Afterwards, for the two following

— 517 —

nights, they will copulate. If the husband has engaged in a practice of violation not with his wife but with some girl from another village, a diggers' hut will be given to him for him to come to perform the "lula" rite.

Note 8 (p. 155). If the parents of a woman live at a distance, her husband will be her traveling companion and will copulate with her the night before, in order to give new strength to the expiatory water.

Note 9 (p. 160). While he was performing "Khunye khunye"; by these words is meant copulation (khunyeta).

Note 10 (p. 160). The nobler the dead person was, the more obscene is the nature of the songs and customs of the marginal time. Viguetus relates: "When a leader or one of the chiefs is dead and the customary mourning has past, a private mourning, in connection with which oxen are sacrificed, is observed. Meat is tied to stakes fixed in the ground; then the people call a woman and she is told to take off her rear garment and not to have any garment except one in front, which, if she wishes, she may take off. Afterwards she will stretch apart to seize one of the pieces of meat with her teeth, so prominently that all the men may see her genitals, which generally is "taboo" (that is, unlawful)."

Note 11 (p. 161). Here the woman, with a little thinner color and with tall stature, adds: "Hi kundjana," that is, "Let us copulate."

Note 12 (p. 187). These are the very same words with which Makhelu describes the taboo (that is, unlawfulness) of a menstruating woman. A menstruating woman is a thing that above all is "yila." She is "yila," that is, unlawful, for six days. On the seventh day she *crosses a river* to bathe. On the eighth she is not yet allowed to copulate with her husband, because by chance some blood may adhere to her genitals without her knowledge. Rather "she becomes cold again." (By the word *phula* a menstruating woman is compared with a room remote from a fireplace.)

If a husband should copulate with his wife before that time, he would become sick, his genital organ would recede so much that he would not be able to urinate and in a short time he would die. Many have had such an end to their lives. The disease can be cured by the roots of the tree that is called *mayilana* or by a piece of a garment of the menstruating woman, which is to be drunk by the sick man after it has been reduced to a fine powder by a physician. The sick man will lose a great deal of blood and, when his genital organ comes out, he is safe.

Note 13 (p. 213). Since the purification ceremonies, in which genital matters have the principal roles, have been explained thus, let us inquire what those rites may signify.

Death is a thing that contaminates people above all else. It defiles everything that it touches, not only people themselves but also the things that belonged to the dead person.

Among people, the death of a relative affects the source of life above all, that is, the juices that create the life of its members. Hence both the vaginal juices of a woman and the spermatic juices of a man are to be taken away, but they are to be taken away in copulation under certain laws.

When a widow is cleansed, she is purified either by a stranger or by a new husband.

1) In order that the purification of a widow may be correct, copulation must be broken off and the man must be repelled before he emits semen; then the man will be contaminated but the woman cleansed. If a man has noticed a woman refraining in copulation, he will understand that she is a widow and wishes to kill him; then he calls his companions, who will seize the woman and restrain her by force while the man emits semen into her lap; then the woman will remain defiled; she will not have what she sought. On the other hand the man will be unharmed; he will not be contaminated.

2) When the purification is effected by a new husband, both enclose themselves in a house. A very great matter is in question; they shall not smoke tobacco. They drink medicines separately. Then they copulate as many times afterwards as the man is able to endure, ten times and oftener if he is able. But the man emits semen on the outside all those times; "bayisanyana ba fanela ku huma," i.e. "the children (the spermatozoa) must be removed," as one of those says who informed me about these things. Now the sources of life have been cleansed for the man, which it was necessary to do, since he himself also was impure by contamination. The woman also is pure, doubtlessly because of the good effect of the medicines which both drank before they copulated.

This interpretation explains the rite correctly when it is performed by defiled persons. But when it is performed by undefiled parents, as when there is question of "boha puri" (p. 56), then the matter must be explained differently. The father and the mother smear an infant's cotton diaper with genital juices, in order that their infant may be strengthened by vital juices and thus may be received into the life of the tribe.

These physiological conceptions, though they may be absolutely false from the scientific point of view, certainly proceed from deep intuitions regarding the mystery of life. I insist on the fact that they are not derived from religious ideas. It is a mistake to attempt to explain the whole life of the Bantus by their religion alone, as many writers are inclined to do. These sexual practices are not more religious than those prophylactic measures which we ourselves employ to preserve ourselves from tuberculosis or smallpox. They are dictated by a special notion of contagion which is admittedly false, scientifically speaking.

Note 14 (p. 285). After Doctor G. Liengmei, our physician, often cured men who sought medicine with which to procreate children, they confessed to him that they used to copulate each night with three or four wives. (From some monogamous persons we heard that the wife would be so exhausted that she used to go out to work at night in order to escape from her husband). When the physician urged them to abstain completely from cohabitation for five days, they never were able to agree to it. To be sure, they wanted to recover the power of regeneration without refraining from lust. Men even are said to use certain remedies when they are not yet ready for their desires, either in order to excite sexual passion or else in order that their wives may become pregnant. The cure is made double. First the testicles of a goat—(they say that this animal does not suffer exhaustion, mbuti a yi karali)—are cut out, mixed with many herbs, cooked and eaten by the man. Then he puts other collected herbs into beer. They say that the result is so great that a man who has only two wives should not use that remedy, since they may not suffice and he may commit a violation with wives of other men, which would be a misfortune for him.

Chaste men, as one may observe in the locality of Mpfumo, sleep in their own house and occasionally call to themselves a wife whom they desire. Many, however, imposing a rule on themselves, spend a month in turn at the house of each of their wives, so that discord may not arise among their wives.

Those who have several wives also use medicines to arouse lust. They think that one of these is especially effective. After a physician has cured himself, he withdraws into a mountainous place, in which female baboons are accustomed to emitting urine mixed with menstrual blood. This stays on the rocks and spreads a very foul odor. The physician takes this and cooks it and from it makes large pills that he sells to customers. They put these into beer.

They also present this remedy for curing serious wounds and offer it to children when they toss the head as baboons do.

Note 15 (p. 477). From the genital organ is made a powder, of which the effect is remarkable. When it is injected into the wrists of warriors, it confers such great skill on them that they do not throw any weapon in vain. Moreover, the weapons that are called assagaies are smeared with this powder.

PRACTICAL CONCLUSIONS

I. ON THE RITES OF INFANCY (P. 36-61).

The rule that a mother "must plough for her child three hoes" is excellent. It is undoubtedly a splendid preparation for future life to have been fed during three years on mother's milk. Will it be possible to maintain this law under the new conditions of civilized life which are being adopted more and more throughout the tribes ? Let us notice that this provision, though it was inspired partly in the interest of the child itself, is dictated mainly by a superstition concerning the lochia secretion, which is regarded as highly noxious and as keeping the mother in an unclean state for a long time. This superstition will not withstand the test of science and will pass away. On the other hand, polygamy was invented and flourishes partly on account of this law. A husband separated from the wife who is nursing a child wishes to have other women at his disposal. Polygamy is doomed to pass also. For both these reasons, it is to be feared that this healthy custom will not be maintained in the future. This is a pity, and we ought to do our best to encourage its continuance.

Many young married Natives leave their homes and go to Johannesburg to the mines for one or two years as soon as they see that their wife is pregnant. This is certainly on account of the above rule ; but this desertion of the conjugal home is hardly to be approved.

As regards the whole medical treatment characteristic of this period, which is considered more or less as a disease, it has no value at all. The big intestinal worm is, of course, merely a product of Native imagination. The children sometimes suffer from lombrics, but not more than white children. Convulsions are frequent as a result of malaria and dysentery, and neither the ever present *milombyana* nor the

521

bi-monthly *biyeketa* nor the powder of the reed can do anything to prevent them. The habit of always carrying water in the calabash and of never emptying it entirely is harmful. Dr Garin, our medical missionary, examined some of these milombyana calabashes with the microscope and found them full of bacteria of all kinds. It is a splendid *milieu de culture* for them. This milombyana custom is however hard to eradicate as the principle is deeply rooted in the Thonga mind : "The child grows by means of medicine" and even Christian converts respect it. They will relinquish it when a clearer notion of medical science has entered their heads — a time which is still remote, I fear!

From the missionary point of view, let us notice the analogy between the rite of the broken pot and Christian baptism as administered to children by most of the Churches. Natives readily accept a ceremony of benediction for the little ones, be it baptism proper or presentation with laying on of hands. But the heathen baptism is a baptism of smoke, and not of water — and is in relation to merely external dangers, while the Christian rite represents the purification of the soul from its sin and the new and pure life. Whatever may be the difference between the two customs, we find in the animistic rite a point of analogy which may help us to explain the spiritual sacrament and its deep significance.

II. ON CIRCUMCISION (See p. 94).

What judgment are we to pass on this custom to which some tribes still cling with great pertinacity ? The teaching of endurance and of hunting has certainly some value, but these rites as a whole have very little worth and are useless in the new economy of South Africa. The obcene language allowed during the Ngoma certainly tends to pervert the mind of the boys and constitutes an immoral preparation for sexual life.

Have we nothing to learn from the Ngoma ? More than two hundred thousand children of black South Africa are now attending our schools... more or less regularly. Hundreds of young men are boarding in our Normal Institutions. Do we always succeed in this great educational work ? Its results are not entirely satisfactory, because most of the children do not stay long enough in the school to be properly taught. As soon as they have acquired some knowledge of reading and writing, they leave and go to the towns to earn money.

PRACTICAL CONCLUSIONS

Whatever the teacher may say, they escape... I must confess that we do not control them as well as the Father of the Circumcision... The Ngoma shows us however that strict discipline is quite possible with Native boys and that we must deal with them without any touch of harshness, of course, but with a firm hand. When the inmates of our institutions complain that the sauce of their porridge is not savoury enough, we might remind them of the food their heathen comrades are eating in the Ngoma!

There is a striking resemblance between Bantu circumcision, Jewish circumcision and Christian baptism.

In Jewish circumcision, the same physical operation was performed, but it was performed on infants. It had undoubtedly also the meaning of a purification, a removal of pollution and an introduction into the holy nation. In the course of time, the idea was spiritualised and circumcision meant the removal of sin. But it had a strongly religious character : Jahvé marked his chosen people by their circumcision. This religious element is wanting in the Ngoma of the Thongas and the Suthos, where the national significance alone remains.

As regards baptism, the great difference between the heathen and the Christian rite is evidently this. Christian baptism is not only a religious but also a moral rite. In its normal form, which is the immersion of adult catechumens, it represents in a striking manner the washing away of sin and the admission to the Church of Christ ; it is a rite of passage ; separation from the old life of sin, marginal period of instruction, admission into a holy community...

The Ngoma has no such spiritual and moral idea attached to it, but it has been inspired by the same deep and true sense of the necessity in the evolution of man, of a progress consisting in the renunciation of a miserable past and the introduction into a higher life. This idea is one of those rays of light which we are happy to discover amidst the darkness of heathendom, one of those "points d'attache" to which we can link the truths of spiritual religion.

What ought to be the attitude of the Government and of Missions towards this custom ? As regards Governments, they could not immediately suppress the circumcision schools, though they have often been asked to do so, but it would seem that they might use their influence in checking them. As for the Mission, it has naturally fought against this school of heathenism, but not always with success ; boys, even Christian boys, are wonderfully attracted by it and many have left their

523

spelling-books for the formulæ of Manhengwane. Strange to say, it frequently happens that girls refuse to marry men who have not passed through this initiation! These facts, together with the legitimate wish to give African Christianity a true national character, have suggested to some missionaries the idea of establishing *Christian Circumcision Schools.* In a special meeting at the Conference of Le Zoute, September 1926, Canon Lucas of the Universities Mission told his colleagues the results of an experiment of this kind at his station of Masasi. The missionary himself took control of all proceedings. The boys began by entering the church, the elders representing the old men of the tribe. They were circumcised in the camp which had been previously blessed and the operation was performed by a qualified Native who had been trained by medical men. The parents of the boys were waiting outside the camp, dancing. When all the boys had been circumcised, they were told by the manager of the camp that this was done to incorporate them into the tribe, and the parents again engaged in a big dance. The men remained on the spot and proceeded to the erection of the buildings of the camp where the circumcised were kept for some weeks, and carefully treated till all of them were healed. During this period of seclusion, they received instead of the obscene formulæ, teaching bearing on seven subjects : truth, honour, purity, abstinence from drink, humility, love of one's neighbour and duties toward God. They had also to pass through various physical trials, and, at the end, they were exhorted to do penance for their past sins. Their hair was cut, and burnt together with their clothing and all the camp buildings. The parents were then summoned and danced the whole night, the men mysteriously bringing new clothing for the initiated. The boys then went to church, and, answering a question put by the missionary, they said : "I ask of God that I may be a righteous man." A special blessing was then given to them. An interesting fact is that the heathen population approved of this Christian Circumcision School and accepted it as an equivalent to the old. Some heathen parents even sent their sons to it! Seven hundred boys have already been received in it and Canon Lucas has gained an enormous influence over them! I only mention this attempt to "sublimate" the circumcision rites. Some missionaries are strongly opposed to this new departure, which they regard as a dangerous mixture of Christian ideas and heathen rites. Without expressing a definite opinion on the subject, I would insist on the point just mentioned : the real, genuine rite of passage of Christianity is baptism, and the African Church might perhaps be satisfied with it, as the Churches of all the Continents are. Is not the Church abandoning its true domain in taking circumcision under its patronage ? The operation is no doubt hygienic in most cases. Surgeons sometimes deem it necessary to prevent complications. It seems therefore more natural to leave circumcision to the province of medicine rather than to impose it as a collective rite on all Christian boys. I think that a deeper study of the question is necessary.

III. ON MARRIAGE CUSTOMS AND LOBOLA

(See p. 125 and 282).

What will be the fate of all these very picturesque marriage customs with the advent of civilisation ? Let us notice that amongst Christian converts, many of them have been abandoned as a matter of course, the bad habits of tjekela, the assault on the village, the preparation of beer, for instance. The part played by adult go-betweens is sometimes taken over by the elders of the Church, but often young people do not care for interference and conduct their own business.

Some other rites are preserved; the feast, of course, is amongst these, and we see boys ruining themselves in order to prepare a glorious wedding with splendid costumes and abundance of meat. On this point they are rather too conservative!

The religious ceremony has now become the Christian blessing which has taken the place of the heathen sacrifice to the ancestors; it is followed generally by a procession of the best men and the bridesmaids singing popular hymns, sometimes very solemnly worded, songs of repentance for instance, as they march to and fro in the nuptial village ; the women, even the men, of the two families hurling at each other's heads amenities of the same kind as in former times. This is a most peculiar mixture of the old and new elements and often filled us with wonder (See Zidji, p. 212). I think however that these rites are doomed to die out, because Christian marriage is no longer a collective act, but has been individualised together with the many other acts of social life. It remains a social act indeed, but an act accomplished by two individuals on their own responsibility and in mutual love. "Ceci tuera cela." This Christian or Western individualism will kill primitive collectivism and all its rites. However original and interesting the marriage ceremonies may be amongst the Bantus, I do not think they can be assimilated as such to the new ideal. Let that ideal inspire new customs in accordance with its own nature as well as with the gay and joyous character of the race!

As regards *Lobola*, when explaining the advantages and evil consequences of the custom in Native life, I have already shown that the latter greatly exceed the former. This shows the attitude that we ought to adopt towards it. But before coming to a conclusion on this point, let us go back to the first principles of sociology.

The White Governments and the religious bodies at work amongst the South African Natives are all Christian ; they belong to what is called Western Civilisation. Its conceptions with regard to the human individual are on a totally different level from those of the Native tribe. Since the Prophet of Nazareth pronounced these immortal words : "What would a man give for his soul," the era of individualism has set in. The infinite value of a human being has been discovered and this new principle has become predominant, not only in the religious, but also in the civil sphere. The proclamation during the French revolution of the "rights of man," which is looked upon as the greatest advance made by modern politics, is a direct result of this assertion of the value of the individual. While every century has to rediscover the formula conciliating the rights of the individual with the interests of collective Society, we all feel that this proclamation was one of the most precious conquests of humanity.

The lobola custom, invented by a society which is still in the collective, or half collective stage, is incompatible with the enlightened conceptions of Western civilisation, with its politics, its ideas of civil life, as well as its religion. It is inspired by a conception of the human being which belongs to another age. Here a wife belongs to her husband ; children belong to their father in a material sense, not in the moral sense which we can alone adopt, with our conception of the individual. A boy is nothing but a member of the clan, who must perpetuate its name and glory. A girl is nothing but the means of acquiring a wife for this boy, and so of increasing the clan. A wife is nothing but a piece of family property, bought by lobola, and is consequently inherited by other men when her husband dies. They are not moral human beings nor free human beings. The opposition between the collectivist and the Western conception is absolute and if we believe that we are in the right, it is the duty of both Colonial Governments and Christian Missions to try to amend this state of things in Native society.

PRACTICAL CONCLUSIONS

The obligation however is not the same for both. A *civil Government*, undertaking to rule a tribe brought into subjection by war or placed under the Protectorate of a European power, dealing with Natives who still retain their primitive way of living, cannot pretend to govern them immediately according to the laws of civilised nations. This would be an impossibility. Such a Colonial Government must respect Native laws and judge cases in accordance with them, otherwise it would not appear to the Natives as just ; and it is indispensable that, in their dealings with uncivilised people, White Authorities should always satisfy this sense of justice, which is so strong amongst Natives. However, I do not think that this consideration ought to be pushed too far.

Native Commissioners are quite right when they aim at a progressive change in the laws and customs of primitive collectivist people in the direction of more individual liberty, so that the principles of Native society may be amended, and founded on the same basis as ours, in course of time. The State has no power to produce this evolution, but is must be favourable to it, and consider with sympathy every effort that is made to elevate and purify the social and family system of the tribe. It has many means at its disposal to collaborate in this work, as we shall very soon see.

The *Christian Missions* can alone bring about this transformation, acting, as they do, on the hearts of the Natives, producing individual conviction in the conscience, opening a new horizon to the mind, creating amongst them a new society. For them the duty of fighting lobola is absolute, and I cannot understand how some missionaries think it may be tolerated in a Christian Church. The following reasons ought to be taken into consideration by them, in addition to those already mentioned :

1. The lobola, being a material method of concluding a marriage, tends to degrade the moral foundation of a true Christian union, mutual love in particular. We know by experience that individual *love* of a young man for a young girl, love as we conceive it, which was scarcely to be met with in the original collective Bantu society, is beginning to appear amongst the best of our converts. This will become the true and powerful bond which will more effactually strengthen conjugal union amongst them.

2. Lobola is intimately connected with polygamy, as the woman bought belongs to the husband's family and must be inherited by his younger brothers. If this man is already married, he is bound to become a polygamist. So is the only brother of many girls, who is

doomed by the custom to lobola for himself as many wives as the sisters he possesses.

So all Missions working amongst the Natives practising the lobola, ought to agree upon a determined campaign against it, with those moral weapons which spiritual bodies ought alone to use. And I would recommend *the following rules* to be universally adopted :

1. *Lobota* (p. 101) should be prohibited, viz., no Christian father should be allowed to ask for a lobolo when giving his daughter in marriage. He is converted ; he calls himself a Christian ; he cannot be permitted a practice which is the negation of the moral character of the human being.

2. In the case of *widows*, let it be well understood that, in Christian communities, they are free as soon as their husband is dead ; that they keep their children and that, when they go home with them, no money can be claimed by the heirs, whether the woman has been paid for or not.

3. As regards *children*, the *moral right* of possession of both father and mother in regard to them should be maintained to the exclusion of a special right arising from the lobola.

4. In the case of *a boy marrying the daughter of a heathen*, we cannot prevent him from paying a lobolo. The father is the master and, as we have no moral jurisdiction over him, we cannot oppose his claim. But, let it be well understood, that this payment will not give the new husband, who is a Christian, all the rights which accompany the lobolo under Native law. It would be wise to ask for a written stipulation from the husband in this case, as well as from the Christian father who gives his girl without lobolo. Let us be on our guard here! The lobolo being family property, if the father or the elder brothers, being Christians, do not claim it, another heathen relative will always appear on the scene and say : "If you do not want it, I claim it! The girl is *ours!*" I shall discuss this case later on.

5. When Christian girls, dependant upon a heathen father, wish to free themselves from the lobola, which appears to some of them as a degrading sale, they ought to be encouraged to save money in order to redeem themselves. We have seen many cases in which this proof of energy given by girls has been a blessing for them and for the Church. The same applies to a young widow who wishes to lead a pure life and to avoid becoming the wife of a polygamist heir.

If all missionaries agreed on these points, the practice of lobola would soon disappear. But *the aid of the State*, which I think is desirable and quite legitimate, if it keeps within the limits of its proper domain, could considerably hasten this evolution in Native society and the disappearance of this objectionable custom.

How can a Colonial Government collaborate in this transformation ?

1. *By an official registry department*, particularly a registry of marriages, by means of which the legitimacy of unions contracted before the Registrar will be established. This will meet one of the wants which the lobola custom met, in the uncivilised state of society ; the right of the father will not be contested, though lobolo has not been paid. These Native marriages might be registered in two categories, those accompanied by lobolo and those without it.

2. *By lowering* as much as possible *the sum required for lobolo*. This is within the province of the State. Everywhere the Native chief has fixed the amount, which has varied very greatly. I heard the Portuguese Administrator of Manyisa very rightly suggest the fighting of the custom by a reduction of the price. If, for instance, the lobola were to be fixed henceforth at £ 5, as money is now so easily found, this would in itself destroy the old heathen practice. The value of a wife would appear so much superior to this trifling sum that the whole transaction would seem ridiculous. Moreover any woman would be able to redeem herself from the servitude of the lobolo. But what happens in such cases is that the Natives, while consenting to ask only £ 5 before the Court of the Administrator, obtain a promise from the bridegroom that he will pay the remaining £ 10 or £ 15 secretly, and thus the attempt at reform is frustrated.

3. Native Commissioners could also do much in assisting girls and widows who make the courageous attempt to free themselves. It could very well be enacted as a law that any widow can free herself of the consequences of lobola by payment of £ 5, or less, and that she may keep her children. Such a provision would be only just, as a Civilised Government cannot allow a heathen to force a Christian woman to become the wife of a polygamist.

4. We would also ask the Authorities to recognise and proclaim the following principle. When the first legal claimant, the father or the elder brother, the "master of the lobolo," renounces his right to it, no other relative shall be allowed to claim it for himself. This is very important. Indeed as the lobolo is collective property, it frequently happens that a heathen relative comes forward and says : "I want it." Sometimes the Christian parents cannot, or will not, oppose his claim. It may even happen that a father has consented to give his daughter without lobolo and, when he dies, his heirs, who may be raw heathen,

will lodge their claim for the sum which the man had generously foregone. For this reason we should recommend that a statement be drawn up in each case of renunciation of lobola. This paper could always be shown to anybody trying to interfere with a lawful marriage celebrated without lobola. In the same way the heathen heirs of a Christian husband who had paid a lobolo to his father-in-law, would be unable to lay claim to the widow.

Amongst Christian Natives a middle course has sometimes been adopted. The bridegroom gives the father of the bride a present which is called *tjakisa*, i. e. to make joyful. It consists generally of a certain number of pounds sterling, inferior to the number required by the customary bride-price. By this means the suitor "soothes the heart" of his father-in-law, who would find it too hard to give his daughter for nothing. What are we to think of this expedient? Nobody can prevent one man from making a present to another. As long as it is clearly understood that this tjakisa is not a lobolo, and that it does not carry with it the evil consequences of the heathen lobolo, it may be accepted as a kind of transitory measure. But there are dangers in the adoption of this custom. As the idea of lobolo is always more or less present in the mind of all, you will find the father-in-law coming from time to time to ask for some more pounds, a fact which shows that his heart has not been sufficiently soothed .. and bad feeling is sure to arise and disturb the relationship, so much so that the worried husband will say : "I had better have paid a full lobolo at once!" I do not think we can absolutely prohibit the tjakisa, but I consider it as a "pis-aller" and greatly prefer to see the father of a Christian girl courageously renounce his claim to any special present. Such cases are happily frequent in the Native Congregations.

*

* *

The eradication of the lobola will take long, but it must take place if Native society is to pass beyond the level of collective social life, and to be raised to the status of a civilised community. There will be a transition period during which both Natives and their civilisers will have to show much patience, tact and ability ; many hard cases will arise. The story of Fos and Mboza, which I narrate in Appendix IX, illustrates these difficulties. But, whatever they may be, the reform is worth every effort and I will borrow my conclusion from a Native whom I once heard speak with splendid clearness and conviction on the subject. This man, an evangelist called Zebedea, brought an old Native to me, named Tumben, a Christian who was still very much attached to heathen customs. They discussed before me this question : Must Tumben claim a lobolo owed to him, in order to pay a lobolo which he owes to somebody else ? The old man thought he was entitled to make his claim. Zebedea asserted that he was not, and the evangelist was right. Christian spirituality required of Tumben that he should renounce the lobolo because he was a convert ; on the other hand he could not decline to pay his lobola debt to his creditor who was a heathen, and could not consequently accept the Christian point of view. The case was hard for the old man and the fight between his conscience and his interest was sad to witness. Zebedea found convincing arguments : "These lobola debts," he said, "are ropes which start from the neck of one and go to the neck of the other. Though your father dies, this rope still ties you, you are kept tied to your father's bones by this accursed rope! Others will get drawn into its coils and the strands become entangled round you! Cut it and be free!"

IV. ON POLYGAMY (See p. 289).

Practically, what must be the attitude of the Government and of Missions towards this custom ?

1. As regards civilised Governments, having still to reckon with Native law, they cannot at once prohibit all forms of polygamy.

But when they have established marriage registration, it would seem that they ought not to allow unions posterior to the first to be considered as legitimate. These marriages ought not to be registered, and if this distinction were strictly enforced, by and by Natives would become more aware of the illegitimate character of polygamic marriages. In the Transvaal, the Native Affairs Department at one time tried to fight directly against the custom in the following manner. As every man has to pay taxes according to the number of his wives, the tax for the first wife was fixed at £ 2, and he had to pay double that sum for each extra wife. But the provision was abandoned later on. Taxation however, has everywhere the effect of limiting polygamy. In Portuguese territory, Natives are taxed according to the number of huts they possess. As each wife lives in a separate house, polygamists are more heavily taxed than others.

Enactments such as these are, I suppose, all that a Government can do. It cannot suppress polygamy as long as the tribal system still holds good. But what law cannot effect, moral teaching can, and, in fact, the Christian Missions long ago began to fight against this evil.

2. All missionaries who have lived amongst the Bantus and know something of Native life, agree on one point. Polygamy is incompatible with the high moral ideal and the ideal of the family which Christianity brought into the world. Therefore they all work against it. They all also agree that a polygamist who wishes to become a Christian must by no means be prevented from doing so. He is to be accepted, as an inquirer and a candidate for baptism. But divergence of view begins on the question of receiving a polygamist into full church membership by baptism. Four different points of view may be distinguished on this question, corresponding to four different methods : the latitudinarian, the idealistic, the extreme and the midway.

The *latitudinarian view* taken by Bishop Colenso, for instance, is this : (I quote freely from *Ten weeks in Natal*, pages 139-140). "Enforcing separation on polygamist converts is quite unwarrantable. They have been married according to the practice of their land. We have no right to require them to cast off their wives and cause these poor creatures in the eyes of all their people to commit adultery! What is to become of their children ? And what is the use of our reading to them the Bible stories of Abraham, Israel and David with their many wives, etc. Let us admit polygamists of old standing to communion." The only difference which Bishop Colenso would admit between polygamists and monogamists, is that the former ought not to be admitted to offices in the church. The hope of those who hold this opinion is that, as polygamy is not to be allowed to young people, it will disappear of its own accord in the next generation. I am afraid, on this point, the reasoning may be wrong. Unhappily, Natives, in the present low state of their moral conscience, are quite cunning enough to delay their conversion until they are polygamists, in order to enjoy both carnal and spiritual blessings!

The *idealistic view* is taken by those who are satisfied with a promise on the part of the husband and his extra wives to have no further conjugal relations, and allow the separated spouses to remain in the husband's village, and the husband to care for them and their children. From an ideal point of view, the provision would be excellent and save much difficulty. But practically it is very dangerous, as we can hardly expect a Native husband to keep such a promise, made in order to obtain baptism. Sooner or later, it is to be feared that he will again make use of his rights ; will he thus be led to deceive his missionary, pretending to be monogamist, but leading the life of a polygamist. Experience shows that, unhappily, this fear is too well founded.

The *extreme point of view*. In some cases missionaries have required not only total separation, and a new and distant domicile for the separated wives, but that the husband should claim back all the lobola oxen, in order to break any tie still existing between him and them. This practice may be legitimate when we have reasons to doubt the good faith of the converted polygamist. But it ought not to be commended as a general rule, as it would make separation almost impossible. Would the parents of the separated wife be ready to give back the oxen, when the union is broken, not from any fault on the part of their daughter, but only for conscience sake on the part of the husband ? In this vexed question, we must put as few hindrances as possible in the way ; as regards the husband, he must be ready to lose the lobola money which he gave for the separated wives.

The midway course, which is followed by almost all the Missionary Societies, set forth in the regulations of the Berlin Society and in the report of the Anglican Conference of Bishops at Lambeth, is the following. Polygamists must not be admitted to baptism, but be accepted as candidates and kept under Christian instruction until such a time as they shall be in position to accept the law of Christ. (Resolution of the Lambeth Conference ; See Edinburgh World Missionary Conference Report of Com. II). Wives of polygamists, on the other hand, ought not to be denied baptism, if they deserve it, as it is not in their power to separate from the polygamic family.

This great principle being admitted, many questions of detail arise, for which I would recommend the following solutions :

1. Which wife should be retained ? Shall it be the first wife, or the Christian wife (supposing that the others are still heathen), or the wife who has the greatest number of children ? No fixed rule has been adopted by any Mission, so far as I know, and each case must be judged on its own merits and according to the higher principles of Christianity, the husband being exhorted to follow the course which is the most beneficial not to himself, but to the others.

2. The cast-off wives ought not to be rejected in any way. They ought to return to their parents, and their former husband ought to facilitate by all means their remarriage under the best possible conditions. I even think that he ought occasionally to provide them and their children with clothing, so that they should not feel abandoned.

As regards food, they are not to be pitied, as, amongst the Bantus, it is the wife who provides the food for the family!

3. The question of the children is the most difficult, and sometimes it is impossible to solve it quite satisfactorily. When they are still young, they naturally follow the mother. Fathers find it very hard to part with them. Why ? Doubtless on account of their natural love for them ; but, if you search deeper into their hearts, you will probably find other reasons. Perhaps unconsciously they still think, according to the old Bantu law, that children, especially girls, must bring a material advantage to their father. When they really adopt the spiritual Christian point of view that a father has more duties to perform towards his children than benefits to derive from them, the separation is no longer difficult.

4. Of course no Christian husband must be allowed to inherit a widow, nor to claim a lobola should this woman be married to another man.

"The change from polygamy to monogamy must involve great difficulties and even hardships," said the Bishops at Lambeth... "No trouble or cost or self-sacrifice ought to be spared to make any suffering which may be caused as light and easy to bear as possible..." However the question at stake is most important. The very fate of the Bantu Church, and of future society, depends on its solution, and a strict adherence to principle is necessary during this time of transition.

The result of the curious inquiry made amongst the Rikatla students on the subject confirms my conclusions. They were all convinced Christians and certainly did not leave the moral side of the question altogether out of account. Yet it was easy to see that polygamy was not to them something repellent and disgusting ; they failed to see the essential moral wrong of the custom. Not one of them mentioned the great moral principle of the equality of man and woman in the law of sexual purity. They did not seem to be shocked by the fact that the Bantu rule, whilst expecting from a wife perfect faithfulness to her husband, allows the latter to have as many wives as he can buy and to seduce as many girls as he chooses. In the background of the Bantu mind is deeply ingrained the idea that woman is owned, that man is her master and that marriage is a bargain. We cannot blame our converts if they do not at once reach a full understanding of these things. When I told them that marriage ought to be the union of two human beings bound together by mutual love, that consequently when a boy had given his whole heart to a girl, there remained no place for another, they seemed to be struck by the argument and accepted it readily, but the idea did not occur to them of itself.

This difficulty in grasping the immoral character of polygamy explains why such a great number of Christian Natives, even after having been monogamists for a time, so easily fall back into polygamy. I heard that in the Cameroons, when, owing to the war, the German missionaries had to leave the country, polygamy invaded the Native congregations wholesale, Native ministers themselves returning to it, and the French missionaries who came to the rescue of these Churches had a terrible battle to fight in order to restore monogamy. All this shows that a long education will be necessary before the Bantu mind is sufficiently transformed to be able to understand perfectly and then to accept freely and willingly the standards of Christian morality in this domain.

V. ON THE FATE OF THE THONGA VILLAGE (See p. 355).

What will be the fate of the little Bantu community, of the circular kraal of huts, well shut in behind its fence, under the shade of its symbolical tree, well "tied" under the absolute authority of the headman ? If we look at the new Native settlements, at the modern Native villages, built under the influence of civilisation and Christianity, we shall be struck at once by the fact that they are arranged in regular streets (1). This change is momentous and highly significative. The new Thonga village is no longer a well defined family. It has become an agglomeration of families belonging to different clans, attracted to a particular spot by the European town or by the Church and the school. The straight line, with its capacity of infinite prolongation, has taken the place of the circular, with its necessarily restricted length. Considering that new ideas are now invading the Bantu tribe from all sides, it is certain that the old circle will disappear more and more and that regular streets will be more generally adopted.

From the point of view of the picturesque, this is a great pity. For the ethnographer, the circle of huts, that curious Bantu commune with its striking laws, was ten times more interesting than the commonplace street

(1) In many Bantu tribes, those of Central Africa, even in the Ba-Chopi tribe, on the South-Eastern boundary of the Thonga country, the Natives already have straight streets. Is this plan original or not ? I suppose nobody can say. In the Thonga, Zulu and Sutho kraals, at any rate, the circular arrangement is a characteristic feature.

of square houses or galvanised iron sheds, which are a poor imitation of European dwellings. However, from the practical point of view, this change is unavoidable. It even undoubtedly stands for progress.

The *Native hut* is prettily shaped. I prefer the Thonga form, a circular wall on which a conical roof is placed, to the Zulu, a beehive resting on the ground, or even to the Kaffir, which combines the features of both, having also a circular wall but with a cupola roof. The conical

Phot. H. A. Junod.

Christian village of Shiluvane.

roof is a better protection against rain. But all these forms of dwelling have one great fault : they are not healthy. The rays of the sun cannot penetrate into the hut, and, though the top of the reeds is sometimes not plastered and allows a certain amount of ventilation, the air cannot circulate, because the hut has no window. Smoke must make its way through the thatch and it is very difficult indeed to obtain any current of air inside. If a new type of hut were to be adopted, with high walls, good-sized doors and windows, and a roof slightly overhanging the wall, these defects would be remedied. But civilised Natives have not tried to follow this plan. They have at once copied the European system, just as with their clothing! How often we have longed to see them adopt some peculiar costume appropriate to the climate and to their occupations! But when they cast off their belt of tails, it is to put on long trousers, and they all dream of a complete khakhi or serge suit ! So they will build square houses, and this certainly has its advantages ; the dwelling can be divided into many rooms and the different members of the family can all live under the same roof, which, from an educational point of view, is a good thing.

The *communism of food* is also a splendid feature and calculated to fill the most sanguine socialistic dreamer with joy! But this custom has been severely criticised from a hygienic point of view. The habit of all plunging their fingers into the same plate fosters tuberculosis and other contagious diseases ; but I do not think it is for this reason that the custom will die out. In the modern Native settlement many different families live together. They are not united by any ties of blood. Moreover they are sometimes so numerous that such communism would be practically impossible. The golden age has passed for ever!

With it has also passed away the merry lazy life of the half naked *munumzane*. The coming of civilisation has already deeply changed his mode of living, and the transformation will accentuate itself still further. I have heard Colonists cursing these black people, who believe that they can escape the law of work under which Europeans groan : "these niggers who think that they will be allowed to remain incorrigibly lazy fellows for all time !" I do not share this loudly expressed indignation. First the Native *doda* is by no means an idle man. He has his own occupations for the benefit of the kraal. Secondly, if his wants are few, and if he very soon reaches the happy state of a man who is not obliged to work, I see thousands of Europeans enjoying the life of a "rentier" as much as he does, and without any qualms of conscience. A South African trader who works hard to make his fortune, and hopes to leave the country as quickly as possible, in order to enjoy all the comforts of a European town, theatres, concerts and clubs, has not, after all, a much loftier ideal than the Native he curses... On the other hand, circumstances themselves enforce upon the Native that law of work and teach him that "dignity of labour" of which we so often hear. A civilised Native has increased his wants ten-fold. He requires the wherewithal to satisfy them. This is the only legitimate, the most powerful incentive to work. Fifty, sixty thousand Thongas, the elite of our tribe, are constantly streaming to Johannesburg, where they are considered the best mining boys. Many of them go there to earn lobola money. But they learn to spend money on other things, and those who are converts to Christianity become regular purchasers of clothing, of better food, of books. The high taxation to which they are subjected also forces them to work. As long as this does not exceed a reasonable limit, and as long as the State causes the Native community to benefit by the high taxes levied on it, it is justifiable although this way of enforcing labour is not so normally healthy as the creation of new wants (1). Another powerful influence which tends to make men work more and to relieve women from the toil of tilling the fields, is this. Wishing to make money by selling grain, the Natives are beginning to clear larger fields than before, and we note with pleasure that they have adopted the use of the plough instead of the hoe in a great many quarters. The consequence of this change is that the men now do

(1) Another means has been used to obtain the same result, i. e. compulsory labour (in Thonga *shibalu*). It is not at all my intention to treat this important but delicate subject here. The League of Nations created in 1924 a special Slavery Commission which has very ably and fully discussed the whole subject. These discussions have resulted in a Convention which was adopted by the Assembly of 1926 ; art. 5, which deals with forced labour, runs as follows :

The High Contracting Parties recognise that recourse to compulsory or forced labour may have grave consequences and undertake, each in respect of the territories placed under its sovereignty, jurisdiction, protection, suzerainty or tutelage, to take all necessary measures to prevent compulsory or forced labour from developing into conditions analogous to slavery.

It is agreed that :

(1) Subject to the transitional provisions laid down in paragraph (2) below, compuls ry or forced labour may only be exacted for public purposes.

(2) In territories in which compulsory or forced labour for other than public purposes still survives, the High Contracting Parties shall endeavour progressively and as soon as possible to put an end to the practice. So long as such forced or compulsory labour exists, this labour shall invariably be of an exceptional character, shall always receive adequate remuneration, and shall not involve the removal of the labourers from their usual place of residence.

(3) In all cases, the responsibility for any recourse to compulsory or forced labour shall rest with the competent central authorities of the territory concerned.

The League of Nations has thus established the general principles, and nearly thirty States have already signed the Convention ; amongst these we note with pleasure Great Britain and Portugal. Now the question has been transferred to the International Labour Office, which must deal with the application of the Convention. A special Committee of experts has been elected and it is hoped that it will fix general principles for Coloured Labour, which shall be submitted to the General Labour Conference in a not distant future.

I am glad to add that the Portuguese Government has recently issued a decree (N⁰ 12.533) which has been published in the *Bolletim official de Moçambique,* November 1926, and which contains the following article (Art. 5. § unico) : *Compulsory labour is only permitted when absolutely indispensable, for works of public interest and of undeniable urgency. This labour will be remunerated according to circumstances.*

the work of preparing the fields. As women have nothing to do with the cattle and as ploughing is done with oxen, men now perform this difficult labour, and so have to work hard. Is not this one splendid result of the spread of civilisation ? The fact cannot be denied that, as regards the mode of living and the distribution of work amongst men and women, a considerable change has already taken place and is being accentuated every day in the Thonga village. What will be the ultimate result of this ?

When discussing the Native problem, the most difficult of all South African problems, politicians, missionaries, civilised Natives and newspapers generally ask this question : "Is Native tribal life to be preserved or, on the contrary, destroyed ?" No clear, satisfactory, convincing reply has as yet been given. Tribal life is composed of two elements : communal life and national life, which ought to be considered separately. I deal here with the first of these elements only. The first remark I would venture to make is that it is somewhat presumptuous on our part to believe that we can exert any very great influence on the solution of this question. Whatever one may hope or fear, the evolution of the Bantu village, which began as soon as civilisation entered the land, will go on. It is not in the power of the Pope, of the Minister of Native Affairs, or of Superintendents of any large Missionary Societies, to prevent the transformation of the primitive patriarchal tribes, which is proceeding as a matter of necessity. Human society evolves continually, and the economic and social changes which have taken place in South Africa are so momentous that they will deeply affect and eventually completely transform the Bantu community. But (this is my second remark) what we can strive for is to control and guide this necessary evolution, and I should like to propose, to all those who can collaborate in the shaping of the future Bantu society, the two following suggestions :

1. Though the square house may supplant the round hut, though the hubo, the bandla and the absolute authority of the numzane may disappear, let us do our best to prevent the future Native village from being a servile imitation of our own European settlements. The more original the Natives remain, the more interesting and worthy to live they will be. The "place of jealousy" will disappear together with polygamy. But let us retain all that is pleasing and moral in the picturesque circle of huts : the respect for elders, the sense of family unity, the habit of mutual help, the readiness to share food with others. Cannot these virtues be retained in the Christian village, under the

direction of the missionary, or in the town location with its Council
of civilised Natives ? On the other hand, in the closed circle, there was
no place for strangers. Love and interest were restricted to members
of the family. In the new settlement we can hope to create a sense of
wider humanity, more in harmony with the traditions of modern life.

2. The evolution of Native society will certainly be accompanied
by much suffering and will not attain a satisfactory result, unless
much patience is displayed by both Whites and Blacks. Let the
conservative Natives and the dreamers of the past admit the necessity
for these changes. Let white men, who too often think that the black
population has been created in the sole interests of the European, allow
the transformation to come gradually and not unduly hasten it, in
their eagerness to make the Natives an asset to the country. I am
convinced that moral and religious teaching is of the utmost importance
in order to spread this spirit of wisdom, patience and good understanding amongst the South African tribes. I hope that in the future Bantu
village the demoralising public house will never be allowed to develop
the inordinate taste of the Natives for alcohol. But, in the meantime,
it is to be hoped that everywhere, amongst the buildings, square and
round, will be found the larger and more honoured edifices, the Church
and the School, in which worship takes place and teaching is provided.
The very existence of these races depends on these conditions.

VI. CONCLUSIONS ON THE THIRD PART.

The new era, and the future of the South African tribe.

The great philosopher Aristotle gave the following definition of
man : "Man is a political animal"—ξῶον πολιτικον, by which words
he rightly observed that man is not made to live alone, but in society.
This definition is applicable to the Bantu as well as to any other human
race ; the family is the first of these social aggregates ; the clan is the
second. The Bantus are essentially a political race and no one could
deny that they have invented a very interesting and practical political
system, a system which wonderfully combines two opposite principles :
the autocracy of the chief and the democratic spirit of the subject. The
Bantu citizens are truly citizens. They can sit on the hubo and give
their advice on all questions at stake, be they of a legislative, a political,
or a judicial character. This age-old participation in the discussion of

the affairs of the country has given them a sense of their importance, a gravity of speech and a dignity of manners which greatly impress a European visiting a typical Bantu village.

But this state of affairs is being modified very rapidly by the all-powerful civilisation which is invading South Africa from all sides like an irresistible tide. My description of the national life of the tribe, or clan, still applies to some parts of Thongaland ; but changes are coming so fast that soon it will have nothing more than an historic value. In some other parts of South Africa the old clan life has already totally disappeared.

If we have tried to foresee the future of the Bantu village, how much more serious is the question of the fate of the Bantu tribe ? I do not think I can pass it by without consideration, whatever may be the difficulties and the delicacy of what has been called the "Native problem."

In trying to find in what direction the present evolution of the South African tribes is tending, we must first consider what has been the influence of European civilisation on Native political life up to the present time. We are here dealing with past and well ascertained facts.

THE RESULT OF THE ENCOUNTER OF CIVILISATION AND BANTU TRIBAL LIFE UP TO THE PRESENT DAY.

a) Civilisation *has destroyed the military power* of the South African Bantus. Thirty years ago they could still fight against white people with some hope of success. Now their fighting power has been broken. They will always be able to kill a few white women, a few colonists settled amongst them, far away from the centres ; they might obtain some occasional victories against a badly conducted reconnoitring party : they cannot withstand a European Commando provided with Maxim quick-firing rifles and all the implements of modern warfare, even if they are ten times superior in numbers. The last Zulu rebellion gave a striking demonstration of this fact. The Zulu impi, with wonderful courage, rushed on the Whites with its assagais and its war songs. But six hundred of the Natives were shot dead by the mitrailleuses before they could approach near enough to throw an assagay! As long as the black race cannot fight with the white man on an equal footing as regards weapons, it cannot hope to regain its military power, whatever may be its valour or its patriotism. .

b) Having conquered the territory of South Africa, the White

541

Governments have everywhere placed Native Commissioners to watch over their coloured subjects. This has put *an end to the tribal wars.* Natives are no longer allowed to indulge in their old fighting customs. They may avail themselves of a war between Europeans to square up old accounts with each other, as happened during the Anglo-Boer war, but they are forbidden to follow the war-path any longer. In many parts of South Africa they have even been disarmed. This change, as a whole, is a favourable one. Native wars never brought blessing to the race. It tends however to destroy one of the springs of patriotism, and in this way it impoverishes the Native mind.

c) These Native Commissioners have placed a very effective check, not only upon the military tendencies of the tribe, but upon *the power of its chiefs.* The authority of the chief in the clan has certainly been diminished. In some instances he has been deposed, or banished in consequence of war, and the tribe has remained without a head and without force, as it were emasculated, and unable to guide itself. As Mankhelu said : "Our chief is the forest into which we retreat! Without him we are but women!" This was sadly noticeable in the case of the Zihlahla or Mpfumo clan, which was perhaps the most developed of all the Ronga kingdoms and which suffered most from the 1894-96 war. Its young chief Ñwamantibyane was caught and deported to some spot in Eastern Africa, and the clan was dismembered, a great number of men emigrating to the Transvaal ; the others remained dissatisfied but powerless in their old territory, and were incorporated with Matjolo or Mabota.

Even when the Native chief is maintained in his position by the Whites, his power is curtailed. As a judge, he is no longer allowed to inflict capital punishment. His tribunal only judges minor cases, and beside and beyond him, there is a further appeal, the Court of the White Commissioner, which is ready to consider every important case. Should the Native chief be unjust or selfish in his decisions, the subjects will go more and more to the White tribunal. It may be that their claims will not be so well understood as in their own *hubo,* but they will perhaps meet with fairer treatment. Shrewd and clever Native Commissioners thus succeed in attracting more applicants to their residences than the chief to his capital (1). This dual control leads to a progressive loosening of the tribal tie.

(1) This was the case for instance in Nondwane. The unjust and egoistical rule of Mubvesha compelled many of his subjects to go " shikanekiswen," viz., to the Portuguese Administrator of Morakven.

PRACTICAL CONCLUSIONS

d) Mission work, now so wide-spread all over the country, leads to the same result. It infuses a new moral and religious ideal into the minds of the people. The old customs, the sacred superstitions, many articles of the Native code, are rejected by the converts. They remain generally very submissive to the authority of their chief, pay their taxes, join the army, but, should the Authorities summon a "nyiwa," a gathering of the clan to smell out the witches, should statute labour be ordered for a Sunday, etc., their conscience does not allow them to obey. On the other hand Native converts, under their white missionary, generally form a Church, which sometimes becomes a kind of *imperium in imperio*, subject to its own laws. This is the necessary consequence of bad, or immoral, heathen customs (beer-drinking, lobola, polygamy) which the Christian ideal cannot tolerate. A deep gulf is thus created between Christians and heathens, and this also weakens the tribal life.

The causes which have brought about this change will probably increase in power in the course of time. The process of individualisation will go on ; so consequently will this process of destruction of the tribal tie, and we may confidently look forward to a moment when the clan will have lost its political cohesion and its members have become independent of any Native Authority.

e) Loss of the political sense. How are we to regard this possibility ? It may present certain advantages over the old state of things, but, to my mind, it entails a distinct and most regrettable loss for the Natives. The political sense, with the sense of responsibility, will have disappeared, and this sense is one of the most precious aids towards the building of character. Look at a gathering of old-fashioned indunas discussing a question affecting the welfare of the tribe under the guidance of their chief ; compare it with an assembly of half civilised Natives in a Town location, a low class tea-meeting, for instance, of men with no respect for any one, addicted to drink and immorality, having rejected the authority of White missionaries because they believe themselves to be so much better informed! There was in the first gathering a dignity, a sense of duty, which you will hardly find in the second...

It is no use for us white men to curse the degenerate Native or to weep over the disappearance of the old restraints. Let us rather confess that we are in a great measure responsible for these results. We have interfered with the Bantu clan by taking away its independence; we have deprived it of one of its character building features, political

543

responsibility. This must not be forgotten in the discussion of the Native problem. We have caused a loss, and it is our duty to try to restore to the Native mind that which we have unconsciously, perhaps without due consideration, taken from it.

We can never be contented with having obtained unpaid labourers to work our farms or paid miners to dig our gold. It is a question in which our dignity is involved that our interference in the affairs of the Natives should never result in a deterioration of their moral status.

I know that I am here approaching the most difficult, the most contested, the most delicate of all the questions connected with the Native problem, viz., the question of the political rights of the Natives, and I feel all my incompetence to deal with it. Should I be asked to suggest a solution of this vexed question, I would certainly refuse to do so. But I am here considering it not as a political theoriser but as an ethnographer, who has come to the conclusion that the present state of things has impaired the character of a race, and who is honestly searching for a remedy.

2. HOW CAN WE PRESERVE THE SENSE OF POLITICAL RESPONSIBILITY AMONGST SOUTH AFRICAN NATIVES ? (1)

Is this remedy the universal bestowal of the franchise on every male Native of twenty-one years of age, who is a British subject and has been six months resident in the country ?

a) The Native franchise. For many decades the Native population of Cape Colony has been offered the right of voting for members of Parliament. Any Native possessing a certain degree of education (able to write his own name), and a certain amount of property, or of revenue, can apply for the franchise. What has been the result of this generous policy ? Of the whole Native Cape population, only 8000 Bantus availed themselves of this opportunity. "They have exercised their privilege creditably and profitably," says the *Christian Express* of August 1908. They have fused into the two great political parties. No harm seems to have resulted for the country from the bestowal of this right

(1) These remarks were written in 1911 for the first edition, before the promulgation of the Natives Land Act, before the segregation proposals were made, and long before the proclamation of Gen. Hertzog's new Native policy. They are perhaps no longer quite up to date. I reproduce them, however, without amendation, as they contain general principles which seem to me of permanent value. Let me only express my gratitude for the fact that the idea of granting Native Councils to the South African Native tribes has made such wonderful progress.

on its black population. Distinct progress has even been made. Travelling through Cape Colony, after Natal and the Transvaal, I was struck by the difference in the manners and demeanour of the Natives and in the way in which they were treated. They look much more like citizens, actual citizens or virtual citizens, and the White men show them a consideration which they hardly meet with in other Colonies.

However the granting of the franchise is not a panacea for the evil which I am now considering. See how comparatively few Natives have availed themselves of it in the most advanced of the South African states! We know that statesmen from the other Colonies are very little disposed to follow the example of the Cape. Supposing however they should offer the franchise to coloured people all over the land, the great bulk of the Native population would be little helped by it. The qualifications required would probably be high and only a few would be able to avail themselves of the opportunity. Moreover the *uncivilised* men, who are still the great majority, could make no use of it. How could they form an opinion as regards the railway and mining questions, educational and economic problems which so greatly perplex our statesmen? How would they be able to decide between the attitude of progressives and conservatives and cast a reasoned and independent vote when electing members of Parliament? I could say the same of hundreds and thousands of *superficially educated* Natives. They know more or less how to read and write, but are absolutely unable to understand the tenth part of what is published in the "Star" or the "Argus," because their horizon is totally different from that of the white man, although they are perhaps not much inferior in intelligence to many European voters. To be able to write one's own name is not a sufficient qualification for taking part in the politics of the South African Union.

The black race is now in a period of transition, and nobody can foretell in what direction and how far it will evolve. It is possible that, after a hundred or two hundred years, the South African Bantus will have reached such a level of education as will enable them to exercise normally full political rights. For the present it seems to me that the franchise must remain the privilege of the few, of those thoroughly educated Zulus, Suthos and Thongas, who have reached the requisite moral and intellectual level. I think it would be a good and wise plan to offer it to them, subject to as high qualifications as may be deemed necessary : the franchise would be kept before them as an

THE LIFE OF A SOUTH AFRICAN TRIBE

ideal accessible to the best representatives of the race all through South Africa. Through them it would have an elevating effect on the whole Native population. But some other provision must be made for the masses who cannot yet rise to such a high level, and who must nevertheless cultivate political interests and discharge political duties *for the sake of their character.*

I think this provision ought to be twofold :—to strengthen the tribal system where it is still working satisfactorily, and to grant them a type of representation which would be able to protect Native interests in the South African Commonwealth.

b) Strengthening the tribal system. The great majority of South African Natives still live under the old tribal system, more or less amended by the dominating White Government. In the Protectorates, which contain 700,000 people, in Zululand, etc., it is still in full force. In other countries the chiefs have lost more of their power and the political activity of their subjects has diminished accordingly. Some dreamers would like tribalism to be absolutely abolished and the duality of control to disappear at once by the absorption of the Chief in the Native Commissioner. That would be a mistake. As long as he is not an enfranchised citizen of the State, let the uncivilised Native remain a responsible member of his clan. Therefore let us not hasten the death of clan life. If it must die, let it die a natural death... Individualism is growing every day. Moreover who knows if the Bantu tribe will not find a means of adapting itself to the new condition of things? It will be very interesting to watch the evolution of political life in the Protectorates, in Basutoland for instance, where the soil belongs to the Natives and is inalienable, where the dangerous contact with White people is reduced to a minimum, but where civilisation and Christianity are penetrating by leaps and bounds. Some chiefs have already been converted to Christianity, such as Khama in Bechuanaland, and many others in the various tribes ; amongst them, in the Thonga tribe, Muhlaba, chief of the Nkuna clan. They generally adopt civilised customs, build good houses, buy mules and carriages. Let us suppose a certain number of these to become thoroughly changed and to be followed by the bulk of their subjects under the guidance of thoughtful White missionaries : could not the Bantu clan then evolve into some new, original, and interesting political organism in which the evils of heathenism would have disappeared and a healthy national life would prevail? The Bantus are not republicans, but they are democrats. Why should not their tribal system get rid of its objectionable features,

546

preserving only those which are compatible with Christian morals and civilisation?

These are only questions which I put, and not definite opinions to which I would commit myself. At any rate, if the tribal system must and can be maintained for an unknown period, the Government ought to take some steps to ameliorate it, or at least to prevent its deterioration. It ought to pay special attention first of all to the character of the chiefs. They are after all Government servants, ruling to a certain

Phot. H.-A Junod.

Muhlaba's house (in the Thabina Location, N. E. Transvaal.)

extent over British or Portuguese subjects. Moral qualifications ought to be required of them as well as of any other civil or judicial employee. Their conduct ought to be the more carefully watched in that the new conditions under which they are placed are eminently dangerous to their morale. Under the old tribal law, their power was checked by the indunas ; they could even be deposed by a family council. Now the chief feels himself supported by the White Authorities and is tempted to take less care of the interests of his people. Many of them have become desperate drunkards. In some places they are allowed to obtain drink, which is absolutely refused to their subjects, and they sink deeply, morally speaking. This is a lamentable result indeed, and kills the political life of the clan more surely than would the disappearance of the chief. If the tribal system is to be preserved at all, a strong and careful supervision must be exercised over the chiefs, and care taken that the indunas, and the people, retain that share of authority which original tribalism entrusted to them.

c) Native representation. It will not be sufficient, however, to create a fence, as high and strong as possible, round the Bantu clan in order to keep it alive until the Native population is able to be enfranchised. Though South Africa is a country conquered and ruled by the White man, there are a great number of questions which equally concern both races. Natives pay taxes, high taxes, they contribute to the economic progress of the land, they provide the mines and agriculture with the indispensable manual labour. There are topics on which they ought to have a say and upon which the White Government ought not to decide without having heard their voice. In all legislation affecting them directly, or the use of the money levied on them, they ought to be consulted. They are not yet able to form a sound judgment on the politics of White South Africa, but they understand very well what concerns them, and so it would be but fair to give them the means of expressing their opinion. This truth has been recognised to a certain extent. The Transkei has its Native Council and Natal has recently established a similar organisation. Lord Selborne, in his admirable address delivered before the Congregation of the University of the Cape on 27th February 1909, strongly insisted on the necessity of creating such Councils in all the districts, and we are glad to see that this idea, which has been for a long time in the minds of many friends of the Natives, has been distinctly voiced by such a high authority.

These Councils ought to act, first, as Consultative bodies giving their advice each time that Parliament is proceeding to pass laws affecting the Natives. They might even be given permission to express their views, or if necessary their complaints, as regards the Native administration, and their wishes for the welfare of their folk. Such Councils would act as a safety valve. Natives, when dissatisfied, are often contented if they have the opportunity of giving vent to their grievance, whatever may be the result of their remontrances. But this provision would render a still greater service : it would develop the political sense of the tribal Natives, and educate them on questions of general interest which concern the whole of the coloured population, and not only their own petty clan. So they would be gradually prepared for a time when the duality of authority will have disappeared, and when they

548

will eventually become full citizens of the South African Commonwealth.

If we open the way to the franchise to the fully educated and civilised members of the race, if we wisely control the uncivilised masses still under tribal law, taking special care of the chiefs, educating their sons, fostering material, moral and intellectual progress amongst the clans, if we create everywhere Native Councils to afford them the opportunity of studying questions affecting the Native population, and of bringing Native opinion before Parliament, then we shall have done our best to restore that sense of political responsibility which we are now gradually destroying... We shall have done our duty in regard to the future of the South African Tribe.

What this future will be, no one can tell. It depends chiefly on the Natives themselves... Everyone knows that the Act of Union contains a clause which greatly hurt the feelings of the educated Bantus of South Africa. When news reached their shores that the Act had been ratified by the House of Commons, without amendment, the colour-bar included, they expressed their deep sorrow, thinking that their race had been unjustly treated... But one of their papers published the following comment : "The Natives, men, women, and children, must bend their energies to the advancement of themselves in all that civilisation and true Christianity means, so that their claim to equality of treatment for all civilised British subjects may be irresistible..." Let this manly advice be followed by the whole Native population and there is still hope for the South African Tribe, whatever modifications it may undergo during the coming generations.

TABLE OF CONTENTS

TABLE OF CONTENTS

SECOND PART

THE LIFE OF THE FAMILY AND OF THE VILLAGE.

TABLE OF CONTENTS

Table of Contents

A general Index will be found at the end of Vol. II.

LIST OF ILLUSTRATIONS

LIST OF ILLUSTRATIONS

DATE DUE

DEC 12 '72			
NO 08 '91			
APR 5 '95			
GAYLORD			PRINTED IN U.S.A.